Rick Steves' ®

W9-ALM-400

AMSTERDAM
BRUGES & BRUSSELS

Rick Steves & Gene Openshaw

LEGEND

- Pedestrian-Friendly Area
- Popular Shopping Area
- Self-Guided Jordaan Walk
- Landmark or Point of Interest
- Tourist Information Offices

0 ————— 250 meters
0 ————— 250 yards

LINDENGRACHT

HAARLEMMER WESTERDOKSTR.

NIEUWE WESTERDOKSTR.

LINDENSTRAAT

BOOMSTRAAT

WESTERSTRAAT

ANJELIERSSTR.

TUINSTR.

LINDENGRACHT

Brouwers

5

BROUWERSGRACHT

KATTENGAT

HEKELVELD

NIEUWENDIJK

Singel

LANGESTRAAT

Singel

OUDE NIEUWSTRAAT

VOORBURGWAL

STOCK
EXCHANGE

JORDAAN

EGELANTIERSSTRAAT

EGELANTIERSGRACHT

3

NIEUWE
LELIESTR.

LELIE-

BLOEMGRACHT

GRACHT

40

WESTERMARKT

SPUISTRAAT

NIEUWEZIJDS

VOORBURGWAL

NIEUWENDIJK

DAMRAK

BEURSSTR.

26

CENTER

32

Dam
Square

16

BLOEMGRACHT

BLOEMSTRAAT

RAADHUISSTRAAT

PALEISSTRAAT

DAMSTRAAT

ROZENGRACHT

ROZENSTRAAT

POST

REE HARTENSTRAAT

27

"NINE
LITTLE
STREETS"
SHOPS

OUDEZIJDS VOORBURGWAL

OUDEZIJDS ACHTERBURGWAL

LAURIERSTRAAT

LAURIERGRACHT

LAURIERSGRACHT

WOLVEN

KALVERSTRAAT

ROKIN

2

NES

MARNIXSTRAAT

ELANDSSTRAAT

20

ELANDSGRACHT

PRINSENGRACHT

BEREN

KEIZERSGRACHT

HERENGRACHT

SINGEL

4

6

Oude

Turfmarkt

N. DOELENSTR.

VOETBOOGSTR.

SPUI

LOOIERSGRACHT

LOOIERSGRACHT

RUN

HUIDEN

SPUI

MINT
TOWER

Munt-
plein

AMSTEL

STADHOUDERSKADE

LEIDSEGRACHT

LEIDSEGRACHT

LEIDSESTRAAT

KERKSTRAAT

KEIZERSGRACHT

HERENGRACHT

FLOWER
MARKET

14

Singel

REGULIERSDWARSSTR.

37

30

35

33

Leidseplein

22

LANGE
LEIDSEDWARSSTRAAT

KORTE

PRINSENGRACHT

NIEUWE SPIEGELSTRAAT

Singel

KEIZERSGRACHT

6

OVERTOOM

VONDELSTRAAT

Max
Euweplein

6

WETERINGSCHANS

TWEEDE WETERINGDWARSSTR.

POST

VIJZELSTRAAT

NOORDERSTRAAT

Vondel-
Park

ZANDPAD

VOSSIUSSTRAAT

SCHAPENBURGERPAD

PIETER CORNELISZ HOOFTSTR.

HOBBEMASTRAAT

STADHOUDERSKADE

LIJNBAANSGRACHT

NIEUW LOOIERSSTRAAT

F. SIMONSZSTRAAT

CONSTANTIJN HUYGENSSTR.

JAN LUIJKENSTRAAT

8

31

RIJKSMUSEUM

WETERINGSCHANS

DEN TEXSTRAAT

19

PAULUS POTTERSTRAAT

HONTHORSTSTR.

HOBBEMAKADE

NICOLAAS WITSENKADE

34

STEDELIJK
MUSEUM

38

Museum-
plein

Singelgracht

17

23

VAN GOGH
MUSEUM

To US Consulate & Concertgebouw

Amsterdam

Ferries to Amsterdam North

To A-10 Ring Road, Edam, Alkmaar & Hoorn

IJ River

CENTRAL STATION

Stationsplein

DE RUIJTERKADE

CRUISE SHIP DOCK

PIET HEIN KADE

CENTRAL LIBRARY (OPENBARE BIBLIOTHEEK AMSTERDAM)

OOSTERDOKSKADE

Dijksgracht

NEMO (SCIENCE MUSEUM)

Oosterdok

VOC SHIP AMSTERDAM

IJ TUNNEL

OOSTERDOK

PRINS HENDRIKKADE

BINNENKANT

OUDE WAAL

RAPENBURG

KATTENBURGSTR.

RED LIGHT DISTRICT

WAAG

Nieuwmarkt

ZEEDIJK

KROMME WAAL

Geldersekade

KONINGSSTRAAT

DIJKSTRAAT

SINT ANTONIESBREESTRAAT

KLOVENIERSBURGWAL

HOOGSTRAAT

ZANDSTR.

RAAMGRACHT

OUDESCHANS

NIEUWE UILENBURGERSTR

Uilenburgergracht

NIEUWEWEVAART

Nieuwevaart

HOOGTE

LAAGTE

ENTREPOTDOK

KADIJK

HOOGTE KADIJK

JODENHOUTTUINEN

JODENBREESTRAAT

Waterlooplein

VALKENBURGERSTRAAT

RAPENBURGERSTRAAT

NIEUWE HERENGRACHT

HERENGRACHT

Wertheim Park

HENRI POLAKLAAN

PLANTAGE KERKLAAN

PLANTAGE DOKLAN

Artis Zoo

PLANTAGE

PLANTAGE MIDDENLAAN

OPERA HOUSE

AMSTEL

Rembrandtplein

MUIDERSTRAAT

NIEUWE HERENGRACHT

PLANTAGE PARKLAAN

DRAWBRIDGE

HERMITAGE AMSTERDAM

NIEUWE KEIZERSGRACHT

PLANTAGE MUIDERGRACHT

HERENGRACHT

Nieuwe Keizersgracht

NIEUWE KEIZERSGRACHT

To Tropical Museum

SIGHTS

1. Amstelkring Museum
2. Amsterdam Museum
3. Anne Frank House
4. Begijnhof
5. Bike Rentals (3)
6. Canal-Boat Tours (4)
7. Central Library
8. Coster Diamonds & Mus.
9. Damrak Sex Museum
10. De Hortus Botanical Garden
11. Dutch Resistance Museum
12. Dutch Theater Memorial
13. Erotic Museum
14. Flower Market
15. Gassan Diamonds
16. Hash, Marijuana & Hemp Museum
17. Heineken Experience
18. Hermitage Amsterdam
19. House of Bols
20. Houseboat Museum
21. Jewish Hist. Museum
22. Leidseplein
23. Museumplein
24. NEMO (Science Museum)
25. Netherlands Maritime Museum
26. New Church
27. "Nine Little Streets" Shopping District
28. Old Church
29. Rembrandt's House
30. Rembrandtplein
31. Rijksmuseum
32. Royal Palace
33. Stadsschouwburg Theater
34. Stedelijk Museum
35. Tassen Museum
36. To Tropical Museum
37. Tuschinski Theater
38. Van Gogh Museum
39. Waterlooplein Flea Market
40. Westerkerk
41. Willet-Holthuysen Mus.

SIGHTS

Bruges

1 Almshouses (2)
2 Basilica of the Holy Blood
3 Begijnhof
4 Bell Tower
5 Bike Rentals (5)
6 Burg Square
7 Choco-Story: The Chocolate Mus.
8 Chocolate Shops (3)
9 Church of Our Lady
10 City Hall
11 Crowne Plaza Hotel (Ruins)
12 De Halve Maan Brewery
13 Fish Market
14 Friet Museum
15 Groeninge Mus.
16 Gruuthuse Mus.
17 To Jerusalem Church, Lace & Windmills
18 Markt (Market Square)
19 Memling Museum
20 Minnewater
21 Postcard Canal View
22 Renaissance Hall
23 't Zand Square

LEGEND

- Pedestrian-Friendly Area
- Self-Guided City Walk
- Landmark or Point of Interest
- Tourist Information Offices
- **P** Parking
- Viewpoint
- **B** Major Bus Stops

0 ——— 300 meters

0 ——— 300 yards

SIGHTS

1. To Atomium & Mini-Europe
2. Belgian Comic Strip Center
3. BELvue Museum
4. Bourse (Stock Exchange)
5. Brewery Museum
6. Church of St. Nicolas
7. City Museum
8. Costume & Lace Museum
9. European Parliament
10. Galeries Royales St. Hubert
11. Grand Place
12. Magritte Museum
13. Manneken-Pis Statue
14. Museum of Cocoa & Chocolate
15. Musical Instruments Museum
16. Notre-Dame du Sablon Church
17. Palace of Justice
18. Parc de Bruxelles

19. To Park of the Cinquantenaire
20. Place du Grand Sablon
21. Place du Petit Sablon
22. Place Poelaert (Viewpoint) & Elevator to Marolles District
23. To Royal Belgian Institute of Natural Sciences
24. To Royal Museum of Central Africa (in Tervuren)
25. Royal Museums of Fine Arts
26. Royal Palace
27. Rue des Bouchers
28. St. Michael's Cathedral
29. Tour d'Angle (Tower)
30. Town Hall

Transportation

31. Centraal/Central Train Station
32. To Midi/Zuid/South Train Station
33. To Nord/Noord/North Train Station
34. City Bus Tour Departure Points (3)

Rick Steves'

AMSTERDAM
BRUGES & BRUSSELS

Amsterdam's
Central Station

HARBOR
(IJ RIVER)

SINGEL

Damrak

SEX
Red Light
District

Pot

Anne Frank
House

Dam
Square

Waterlooplein

CANAL

Amsterdam
Museum

Canal Boats

AMSTEL

Rijksmuseum

Flower
Market

Beer
Heineken

AVALON
TRAVEL

CONTENTS

The Netherlands & Belgium

AIRPORT

50 MILES
100 KM

N

NORTH
SEA

ENGLAND

NETHERLANDS

DCH

GRONINGEN

HAARLEM   AMSTERDAM

THE HAGUE   SCHIPHOL   UTRECHT

DELFT   ARNHEM

ROTTERDAM   RHINE

EINDHOVEN

GERMANY

BRUGES

OSTENDE

DOVER

FLANDERS

ANTWERP   MAASTRICHT

GHENT   BRUSSELS   KÖLN

TO
LONDON   YPRES

BELGIUM   AACHEN

LIEGE   RHINE

LILLE   MONS   NAMUR

KOBLENZ

WALLONIE

FRANCE   BASTOGNE

LUX.   TRIER

LUXEMBOURG
CITY

TO PARIS

INTRODUCTION

Amsterdam, Bruges, and Brussels—the three greatest cities of the Low Countries—are a delight to experience. Rattling on your bike over the cobbles, savoring fresh pralines, lingering in flower-carpeted squares, you'll find a slow-down-and-smell-the-tulips world that enchants. Any time of year, you can enjoy the intimate charms of these cities.

Amsterdam is called "the Venice of the North," both for its canals and for its past position as an economic powerhouse. Bruges—once mighty, now mighty cute—comes with fancy beers in fancy glasses, lilting carillons, and lacy Gothic souvenirs of a long-gone greatness. Brussels—the de facto capital of Europe, with a low-rise Parisian ambience—exudes a *joie de vivre,* from its famous cuisine to its love of chocolate and comic strips.

Belgium and the Netherlands are called the Low Countries because nearly half their land is below sea level. Surrounded by mega-Europe, the Low Countries are easy to overlook. But travel here is a snap, the area is steeped in history, and all the charming icons of the region—whirring windmills, Dutch Masters, dike hikes, one-speed bikes, and ladies tossing bobbins to make fine lace—line up for you to enjoy. If ever an area were a travel cliché come true, it's the Low Countries.

This book covers the predictable biggies in and around Amsterdam, Bruges, and Brussels—and mixes in a healthy dose of Back Door intimacy. In Amsterdam you can see Vincent van Gogh's *Sunflowers*...and climb through Captain Vincent's tiny houseboat museum. You'll tour Brussels' ultramodern European Parliament and enjoy a Michelangelo statue in small-town Bruges. Beyond these three cities you'll discover the hidden charms of Haarlem, the funky, fashion-forward port of Antwerp, and the thriving urban scene of Ghent. And you'll meet intriguing people who will show you how to swallow pickled herring, paddle you in a canoe through the *polderland* to a stuck-in-the-mud (and stuck-in-the-past) village, and pop a taste of the latest chocolate into your mouth.

This book is selective, including only the top sights. The best is, of course, only my opinion. But after spending more than half of my adult life exploring and researching Europe, I've developed a sixth sense for what travelers enjoy.

About This Book

Rick Steves' Amsterdam, Bruges & Brussels is a personal tour guide in your pocket. Better yet, it's actually two tour guides in your pocket: The co-author of this book is Gene Openshaw. Since our first "Europe through the gutter" trip together as high-school buddies in the 1970s, Gene and I have been exploring the wonders of the Old World. An inquisitive historian and lover of European culture, Gene wrote most of this book's self-guided museum tours and neighborhood walks. Together, Gene and I keep this book up-to-date and accurate (though for simplicity, from this point "we" will shed our respective egos and become "I").

This book is organized by destination. Each recommended destination is a mini-vacation on its own, filled with exciting sights, strollable neighborhoods, homey and affordable places to stay, and memorable places to eat.

You'll find the following sections in this book:

Orientation includes specifics on public transportation, helpful hints, local tour options, tourist information, and easy-to-read maps designed to make the text clear and your arrival smooth. "Planning Your Time" sections suggest schedules for how to best use your limited time.

Sights describes the top attractions and includes their cost and hours.

Self-Guided Walks and **Tours** take you through interesting neighborhoods and must-see sights. In Amsterdam, these include the Rijksmuseum, Van Gogh Museum, Anne Frank House, a city walk, the Jordaan neighborhood, the Red Light District, and more. In nearby Haarlem, tour the Grote Kerk and the Frans Hals Museum. In Bruges you'll find a city walk and tours of the Groeninge and Memling museums, and in Brussels, take a Grand Place walk, an Upper Town walk, and a tour of the Royal Museums of Fine Arts and the Magritte Museum.

Sleeping describes my favorite hotels, from good-value deals to cushy splurges.

Eating serves up a range of options, from inexpensive pubs to fancier restaurants.

Smoking covers Amsterdam's best "coffeeshops," which openly sell marijuana.

Key to This Book

Updates

This book is updated every year, but things change. For the latest, visit www.ricksteves.com/update, and for a valuable list of reports and experiences—good and bad—from fellow travelers, check www.ricksteves.com/feedback.

Abbreviations and Times

I use the following symbols and abbreviations in this book:

Sights are rated:

▲▲▲	**Don't miss**
▲▲	**Try hard to see**
▲	**Worthwhile if you can make it**
No rating	**Worth knowing about**

When you see a ✪ in a sight listing, it means that the sight is covered in much more detail in one of the tour chapters.

Tourist information offices are abbreviated as **TI,** and bathrooms are **WC**s. To categorize accommodations, I use a **Sleep Code** (described on page 17).

Like the Netherlands and Belgium, this book uses the **24-hour clock** for schedules. It's the same through 12:00 noon, then keep going: 13:00, 14:00, and so on. For anything over 12, subtract 12 and add p.m. (14:00 is 2:00 p.m.).

When giving **opening times,** I include both peak season and off-season hours if they differ. So, if a museum is listed as "May-Oct daily 9:00-16:00," it should be open from 9 a.m. until 4 p.m. from the first day of May until the last day of October (but expect exceptions).

For **transit** or **tour departures,** I first list the frequency, then the duration. So a train connection listed as "2/hour, 1.5 hours" departs twice each hour, and the journey lasts an hour and a half.

Shopping gives you tips for shopping painlessly and enjoyably, without letting it overwhelm your vacation or ruin your budget.

Nightlife is your guide to evening fun, including music, comedy, movies, and other things to do after dark.

Chapters in the **Dutch Day Trips** section cover **Delft and The Hague, Near Arnhem,** and small towns and destinations (such as Dutch open-air folk museums) in the Netherlands. In addition to Bruges and Brussels, you'll find chapters on the major Belgian destinations of **Antwerp, Ghent,** and WWI sites at **Flanders Fields.**

Connections covers how to get to nearby destinations by train and bus, and includes information on getting to and from the airports.

The **History** chapter gives you a quick overview of Dutch and Belgian history and a timeline of major events.

INTRODUCTION

The **appendix** is a traveler's tool kit, with telephone tips, useful phone numbers, transportation information, recommended books and films, a festival list, climate chart, handy packing checklist, a hotel reservation form, and Dutch, Flemish, and French survival phrases.

Browse through this book and choose your favorite sights. Then have a great trip! Traveling like a temporary local and taking advantage of the information here, you'll enjoy the absolute most out of every mile, minute, and euro. I'm happy that you'll be visiting places I know and love, and meeting some of my favorite Europeans.

Planning

This section will help you get started on planning your trip—with advice on trip costs, when to go, and what you should know before you take off.

Travel Smart

Your trip to the Netherlands and Belgium is like a complex play—easier to follow and really appreciate on a second viewing. While no one does the same trip twice to gain that advantage, reading this book before your trip accomplishes much the same thing.

Design an itinerary that enables you to visit the various sights at the best possible times. Make note of festivals and the days when sights are closed. For example, nearly all museums in Bruges are closed on Mondays.

In the Low Countries, Sundays have the same pros and cons as they do for travelers in the US (special events, limited hours, banks and many shops closed, limited public transportation, no rush hours). Popular destinations are even more crowded on weekends. Rowdy evenings are rare on Sundays.

Mix intense and relaxed periods in your itinerary. To maximize rootedness, minimize one-night stands. It's worth a post-dinner drive or train ride to be settled into a town for two nights. B&Bs are more likely to give a better price to someone staying more than one night.

Every trip (and every traveler) needs at least a few slack days (for picnics, laundry, people-watching, and so on). Pace yourself. Assume you will return.

Reread this book as you travel, and visit local TIs. Upon arrival in a new town, lay the groundwork for a smooth departure; note the schedule for the train or bus you'll take when you depart. Drivers can study the best route to their next destination.

Get online at Internet cafés or your hotel, and buy a phone card or carry a mobile phone: You can get tourist information, research transportation connections, learn the latest on sights (spe-

Holidays and Weekends

Popular places are even busier on weekends...and can be inundated on three-day weekends. Plan ahead and reserve your accommodations and transportation well in advance.

The big holidays in the Netherlands are Easter weekend, Queen's Day (Koninginnedag, April 30), May 4 (Remembrance of the WWII Dead), May 5 (Liberation Day), Ascension, Pentecost, December 5 (St. Nicholas' Eve), Christmas (celebrated on Dec 25 and 26), and New Year's Day.

Belgium's major holidays include New Year's, Easter, Ascension, Pentecost, and Christmas, plus Labor Day (May 1), Belgian Independence Day (July 21), Assumption (Aug 15), All Saints' Day (Nov 1), and Armistice Day (Nov 11).

For a more complete list of festivals and holidays, see page 592 in the appendix.

cial events, English tour schedules, etc.), book tickets and tours, make reservations, reconfirm hotels, check weather, and keep in touch with loved ones.

Connect with the culture. Set up your own quest to find the best salted herring or canal boat ride. Be open to unexpected experiences. Slow down and enjoy the hospitality of the Dutch and Belgian people. Ask questions—most locals are eager to point you in their idea of the right direction. Keep a notepad in your pocket for organizing your thoughts. Wear your money belt, get used to the local currency, and learn how to estimate prices in dollars. Those who expect to travel smart, do.

Trip Costs

Five components make up your trip costs: airfare, surface transportation, room and board, sightseeing and entertainment, and shopping and miscellany.

Airfare: A basic, round-trip, US-to-Amsterdam flight costs $750-1,400, depending on where you fly from and when (cheaper in winter). You can often save time in Europe by flying into one city and out of another; if you're sticking to the Low Countries, you're never more than about three hours from Amsterdam's or Brussels' international airports.

Surface Transportation: If you're just touring Amsterdam, Bruges, Brussels, and nearby day-trip destinations, you're best off enjoying the region's excellent and affordable train system. Trains leave at least hourly between each of the cities. It costs about $55 for a ticket from Amsterdam to Brussels or to Bruges. If you plan to venture farther afield, you may want a rental car. Driving in the Low Countries is flat-out easy (figure $750 per person—based on two people sharing—for a three-week car rental, gas, and insurance). For more on public transportation, see the appendix.

Room and Board: You can thrive in the Low Countries on $120 a day per person for room and board (less for Bruges and Brussels, more for Amsterdam). That allows $20 for lunch, $30 for dinner, and $70 for lodging (based on two people splitting the cost of a $140 double room that includes breakfast). To live and sleep more elegantly, I'd propose a budget of $140 per day per person ($20 for lunch, $40 for dinner, and $80 each for a $160 hotel double with breakfast). Students and tightwads eat and sleep for as little as $60 a day ($30 per bed, $30 for meals and snacks).

Sightseeing and Entertainment: In big cities, figure $12-18 per major sight (Rijks, Memling, and Van Gogh museums); $3-5 for minor ones (climbing church towers or windmills); $10-18 for guided walks, boat tours, and bike rentals; and $30-60 for splurge experiences such as concerts, special art exhibits, big-bus tours, and guided canoe trips. An overall average of $20 a day works for most people. Don't skimp here. After all, this category is the driving force behind your trip—you came to sightsee, enjoy, and experience the Low Countries.

Shopping and Miscellany: Figure $1-2 per postcard, tea, or ice-cream cone, and $5 per beer. Shopping can vary in cost from nearly nothing to a small fortune. Good budget travelers find that this category has little to do with assembling a trip full of lifelong and wonderful memories.

Sightseeing Priorities

With affordable flights from the US, minimal culture shock, almost no language barrier, and a well-organized tourist trade, the Low Countries are a good place to start a European trip. Depending on the length of your trip, and taking geographic proximity into account, these are my recommended priorities:

2 days:	Amsterdam, Haarlem
4 days, add:	Bruges, more time in Amsterdam
5 days, add:	Brussels
6-7 days, add:	Antwerp and slow down
8-9 days, add:	Delft/The Hague and Ghent
10-14 days, add:	More time in Amsterdam, plus side-trips from Amsterdam (e.g., Edam/Waterland, Arnhem, the Historic Triangle, Alkmaar, and more)

When to Go

Although Bruges and Amsterdam can be plagued by crowds, the long days, lively festivals, and sunny weather make summer a great time to visit. It's rarely too hot for comfort. Brussels' fancy business-class hotels are also deeply discounted in the summer.

Peak Season: Amsterdam is surprisingly crowded—and hotel prices can be correspondingly high—in late March, April, and May, when the tulip fields are flowering in full glory. Seasonal conferences can also drive up prices in September in Amsterdam. July and August have typical summer crowds.

Shoulder Season: Late spring and fall are pleasant, with generally mild weather and lighter crowds (except during holiday weekends—see earlier sidebar).

Winter Season: Travel from late October through mid-March is cold and wet in this region, as coastal winds whip through these low, flat countries. It's fine for visiting Amsterdam, Bruges, Antwerp, and Brussels, but smaller towns and countryside sights feel dreary and lifeless. Some sights close for lunch, TIs keep shorter hours, and some tourist activities (like English-language windmill tours) vanish altogether.

Know Before You Go

Your trip is more likely to go smoothly if you plan ahead. Check this list of things to arrange while you're still at home.

You need a **passport,** but no visa or shots, to travel in the Netherlands and Belgium. You may be denied entry into certain European countries if your passport is due to expire within three to six months of your ticketed date of return. Get it renewed if you'll be cutting it close. It can take up to six weeks to get or renew a passport (for more on passports, see www.travel.state.gov).

Book your rooms in advance if you'll be traveling during peak season or around any major **holidays.**

Call your **debit- and credit-card companies** to let them know the countries you'll be visiting, to ask about fees, and more (see page 10).

Do your homework if you want to buy **travel insurance.** Compare the cost of the insurance to the likelihood of your using it and your potential loss if something goes wrong. For more information, see www.ricksteves.com/insurance.

If you're bringing an MP3 player, you can download free information from **Rick Steves Audio Europe,** featuring hours of travel interviews on the Low Countries and more (at www.ricksteves.com/audioeurope and iTunes; for details, see page 589).

The big three **museums** in Amsterdam—Rijks, Van Gogh, and Anne Frank—can come with long lines during high season. Consider buying tickets online from home (for details, see page 42). The Magritte Museum in Brussels requires you to reserve an entrance time, either online or at the ticket desk (see page 474).

If you're planning on **renting a car** in the Low Countries, you'll need your driver's license. It's recommended—but not required—that you also carry an International Driving Permit, available at your local AAA office ($15 plus two passport photos, www.aaa.com). Confirm pickup hours—many car-rental offices close Saturday afternoon and all day Sunday.

Check for **updates to this book** at www.ricksteves.com/update—if we're aware of anything important changing since this book went to press, we'll post it online.

Because **airline carry-on restrictions** are always changing, visit the Transportation Security Administration's website (www.tsa.gov/travelers) for an up-to-date list of what you can bring on the plane with you...and what you have to check.

Practicalities

Emergency and Medical Help: Dial 112 for police or medical emergencies in both the Netherlands and Belgium. Or ask at your hotel for help. They'll know the nearest medical and emergency services.

Lost or Stolen Passport: To replace a passport, you'll need to go in person to a US embassy (see page 582). And though not required, having a backup form of ID—ideally a photocopy of your passport and driver's license—speeds up a replacement. For more info, see www.ricksteves.com/help.

Borders: There are no border checks between the Low Countries, but when you change countries, you must still change telephone cards and postage stamps.

Time Zones: The Low Countries, like most of continental Europe, are generally six/nine hours ahead of the East/West Coasts of the US. The exceptions are the beginning and end of Daylight Saving Time: Europe "springs forward" the last Sunday in March (two weeks after most of North America) and "falls back" the last Sunday in October (one week before North America). For a handy online time converter, try www.timeanddate.com/worldclock.

Business Hours: Most stores throughout the Low Countries are open from about 9:00 until 18:00-20:00 on weekdays, but close early on Saturday (generally between 12:00 and 17:00, depending on whether you're in a town or a big city), and they are often closed on Sunday. In the Netherlands, the first Sunday of every month is "shopping Sunday" *(koopzondag)*, when many stores are open. In the Low Countries, many museums and sights are closed on Monday.

Watt's Up? Europe's electrical system is different from North America's in two ways: the shape of the plug (two round prongs) and the voltage of the current (220 volts instead of 110 volts). For your North American plug to work in Europe, you'll need an adapter, sold inexpensively at travel stores in the US and Canada.

As for the voltage, most newer electronics (including hair dryers, laptops, and battery chargers) convert it automatically—if you see a range of voltages printed on the item or its plug (such as "110-220"), it'll work in Europe. It's not worth trying to make older appliances work overseas; either go without or buy a cheap replacement in Europe.

Discounts: Discounts aren't listed in this book. However, many sights offer discounts for children under 18, seniors, groups of 10 or more, families, and students or teachers with proper identification cards (www.isic.org). Always ask. Some discounts are available only for EU citizens.

News: Americans keep in touch with the *International Herald Tribune* (published almost daily throughout Europe and online at www.iht.com). Another newsy site is http://news.bbc.co.uk. Every Tuesday, the European editions of *Time* and *Newsweek* hit the stands with articles of particular interest to travelers in Europe. Sports addicts can get their daily fix at www.espn.com or from *USA Today*. Many hotels have CNN or BBC News channels.

Money

This section offers you advice on how to pay for purchases on your trip (including getting cash from ATMs and paying with plastic), dealing with lost or stolen cards, VAT (sales tax), and tipping.

What to Bring
Bring both a credit card and a debit card. You'll use the debit card at cash machines (ATMs) to withdraw euros for most purchases, and the credit card to pay for larger items. Some travelers carry a third card as a backup, in case one gets demagnetized or eaten by a temperamental machine.

As an emergency backup, I'd also recommend carrying a few hundred dollars in hard cash (in easy-to-exchange $20 bills). Don't bother changing cash before you leave home—ATMs are easy to find and easy to use. Avoid using currency exchange booths (lousy rates and/or outrageous fees); if you have foreign currency to exchange, take it to a bank. And skip traveler's checks—they're a waste of time (long waits at slow banks) and a waste of money in fees.

Cash
Cash is just as desirable in the Low Countries as it is at home. Small businesses (hotels, restaurants, and shops) prefer that you pay your bills with cash. Some vendors will charge you extra for using a credit card, and some won't take credit cards at all.

Exchange Rate

I list prices in euros for the Netherlands and Belgium.

1 euro (€) = about $1.40

To convert prices in euros to dollars, add about 40 percent: €20 = about $28, €50 = about $70. Just like the dollar, the euro is broken into 100 cents. You'll find coins ranging from 5 cents to 2 euros, and bills from 5 euros to 50 euros. (To get the latest rates and print a cheat sheet, see www.oanda .com.)

So those €65 wooden clogs are about $100, and the €90 taxi ride through Brussels is...uh-oh.

Throughout Europe, ATMs offer the easiest and best way for travelers to get cash. To withdraw money from an ATM, you'll need a debit card (ideally with a Visa or MasterCard logo for maximum usability), plus a PIN code. Know your PIN code in numbers— there are no letters on European keypads. For security, it's best to shield the keypad when entering your PIN at the ATM.

When using an ATM, taking out large sums of money can reduce your per-transaction bank fees. If the machine refuses your request, don't take it personally; some cash machines limit the amount you can withdraw. Try again and select a smaller amount, or try a different machine.

If the ATM dispenses big bills, break them at a bank or larger store, since it's easier to pay for purchases at small businesses using smaller bills.

To keep your cash safe, use a money belt—a pouch with a strap that you buckle around your waist like a belt and wear under your clothes. Pickpockets target tourists. A money belt provides peace of mind, allowing you to carry lots of cash safely. Don't waste time every few days tracking down a cash machine—withdraw a week's worth of money, stuff it in your money belt, and travel!

Credit and Debit Cards

For purchases, Visa and MasterCard are more commonly accepted than American Express. You can use either a credit or a debit card for most transactions, but using a credit card offers a greater degree of fraud protection (since debit cards draw funds directly from your account).

Just like at home, credit or debit cards are accepted by larger hotels, restaurants, and shops. I typically use my credit card only in a few specific situations: to book hotel reservations by phone, to make major purchases (such as car rentals, plane tickets, and long hotel stays), and to pay for things near the end of my trip (to avoid another visit to the ATM).

Ask Your Credit- or Debit-Card Company: Before your trip, contact the company that issued your debit or credit cards.

• Confirm that your card will work overseas, and alert them that you'll be using it in Europe; otherwise, they may deny transactions if they perceive unusual spending patterns.

• Ask for the specifics on transaction **fees.** When you use your credit or debit card—either for purchases or ATM withdrawals—you'll often be charged additional "international transaction" fees of up to 3 percent (1 percent is normal) plus $5 per transaction. Some banks have agreements with European partners that reduce or eliminate the $5 transaction fee. If your fees are too high, consider getting a card just for your trip: Capital One (www.capitalone .com) and most credit unions have low-to-no international fees.

• If you plan to withdraw cash from ATMs, confirm your **daily withdrawal limit** (€300 is usually about the maximum). Some travelers prefer a high limit that allows them to take out more cash at each ATM stop, while others prefer to set a lower limit in case their card is stolen. Note that if you use a credit card for ATM transactions, it's technically a "cash advance" rather than a "withdrawal"—and subject to an additional cash-advance fee.

• Ask for your credit card's **PIN** in case you encounter Europe's chip-and-PIN system. For security reasons, most banks will only give out PINs by mail, so give yourself plenty of time to get the code if you don't already know it.

Chip and PIN: If your card is declined for a purchase in Europe, it may be because of chip and PIN, which requires cardholders to punch in a PIN instead of signing a receipt. Much of Europe—including the Netherlands, Belgium, Great Britain, Ireland, France, and Scandinavia—is adopting this system. Chip and PIN is used by some merchants and also at automated payment machines—such as those at train stations, parking garages, luggage lockers, and self-serve pumps at gas stations. If you're prompted to enter your PIN (but don't know it), ask if the cashier can print a receipt for you to sign instead, or just pay cash. If you're dealing with an automated machine that won't take your card, look for a cashier nearby who can make your card work.

Travelex is currently offering US travelers a chip-and-PIN card preloaded with euros (www.travelex.com). While handy, this service comes with exorbitant exchange rates; it's probably not worth it unless you are staying for several weeks in a country that's converted to chip-and-PIN cards, and you're willing to pay for the convenience. The easiest solution is to carry sufficient cash.

Dynamic Currency Conversion: If merchants offer to convert your purchase price into dollars (called dynamic currency

INTRODUCTION

conversion), refuse this "service." You'll pay even more in fees for the expensive convenience of seeing your charge in dollars.

Damage Control for Lost Cards

If you lose your credit or debit card, you can stop people from using it by reporting the loss immediately to the respective global customer-assistance centers. Call these 24-hour US numbers collect: Visa (410/581-9994), MasterCard (636/722-7111), and American Express (623/492-8427).

At a minimum, you'll need to know the name of the financial institution that issued you the card, along with the type of card (classic, platinum, or whatever). Providing the following information will allow for a quicker cancellation of your missing card: full card number, whether you are the primary or secondary cardholder, the cardholder's name exactly as printed on the card, billing address, home phone number, circumstances of the loss or theft, and identification verification (your birth date, your mother's maiden name, or your Social Security number—memorize this, don't carry a copy). If you are the secondary cardholder, you'll also need to provide the primary cardholder's identification-verification details. You can generally receive a temporary card within two or three business days in Europe.

If you promptly report your card lost or stolen, you typically won't be responsible for any unauthorized transactions on your account, although many banks charge a liability fee of $50.

Tipping

Tipping in the Low Countries isn't as automatic and generous as it is in the US, but for special service, tips are appreciated, if not expected. As in the US, the proper amount depends on your resources, tipping philosophy, and the circumstances, but some general guidelines apply.

Restaurants: Tipping is an issue only at restaurants that have table service. If you order your food at a counter, don't tip.

At Dutch and Belgian restaurants that have wait staff, service is included, although it's common to round up the bill after a good meal (usually 5-10 percent; so, for an €18.50 meal, pay €20).

Taxis: To tip the cabbie, round up. For a typical ride, round up about 5-10 percent (to pay a €4.50 fare, give €5; or for a €28 fare, give €30). If the cabbie hauls your bags and zips you to the airport to help you catch your flight, you might want to toss in a little more. But if you feel like you're being driven in circles or otherwise ripped off, skip the tip.

Special Services: Tour guides at public sites sometimes hold out their hands for tips after they give their spiel. If I've already paid for the tour, I don't tip extra unless the guide has really impressed me. At hotels, if you let porters carry your luggage, it's polite to give them a euro for each bag (another reason to pack light). I don't tip the maid, but if you do, you can leave a couple of euros at the end of your stay.

In general, if someone in the service industry does a super job for you, a small tip of a euro or two is appropriate, but not required.

When in doubt, ask. If you're not sure whether (or how much) to tip for a service, ask your hotelier or the tourist information office; they'll fill you in on how it's done on their turf.

Getting a VAT Refund

Wrapped into the purchase price of your souvenirs is a Value-Added Tax (VAT) of about 19 percent in the Netherlands and 21 percent in Belgium. If you make a purchase of more than a certain amount (€50 in the Netherlands, €125.01 in Belgium) at a store that participates in the VAT-refund scheme, you're entitled to get most of that tax back.

Getting your refund is usually straightforward and, if you buy a substantial amount of souvenirs, well worth the hassle. If you're lucky, the merchant will subtract the tax when you make your purchase. (This is more likely to occur if the store ships the goods to your home.) Otherwise, you'll need to:

Get the paperwork. Have the merchant completely fill out the necessary refund document, called a "Tax-Free Shopping Cheque." You'll have to present your passport at the store.

Get your stamp at the border or airport. Process your cheque(s) at your last stop in the EU (e.g., at the airport) with the customs agent who deals with VAT refunds. It's best to keep your purchases in your carry-on for viewing, but if they're too large or dangerous (such as knives) to carry on, track down the proper customs agent to inspect them before you check your bag. You're not supposed to use your purchased goods before you leave. If you show up at customs wearing Dutch wooden clogs and a Belgian lace wedding veil, officials might look the other way—or deny you a refund.

Collect your refund. You'll need to return your stamped document to the retailer or its representative. Many merchants work with services, such as Global Blue (www.global-blue.com) or Premier Tax Free (www.premiertaxfree.com), which have offices at major airports, ports, and border crossings. These services, which extract a 4 percent fee, can refund your money immediately in your currency of choice or credit your card (within two billing cycles). If the retailer handles VAT refunds directly, it's up to you to contact the merchant for your refund. You can also mail the documents from home, or quicker, from your point of departure (using a

INTRODUCTION

stamped, addressed envelope you've prepared or one that's been provided by the merchant). Then you'll have to wait—it can take months.

Customs for American Shoppers

You are allowed to take home $800 worth of items per person duty-free, once every 30 days. The next $1,000 is taxed at a flat 3 percent. After that, you pay the individual item's duty rate. You can also bring in duty-free a liter of alcohol (slightly more than a standard-size bottle of wine; you must be at least 21), 200 cigarettes, and up to 100 non-Cuban cigars.

As for food, you can take home vacuum-packed cheeses; dried herbs, spices, or mushrooms; and canned fruits or vegetables, including jams and vegetable spreads. Baked goods, candy, chocolate, oil, vinegar, mustard, and honey are OK. Fresh fruits or vegetables (even that banana from your airplane breakfast) are not permitted. Meats are generally not allowed. Just because a duty-free shop in an airport sells a food product doesn't mean it will automatically pass US Customs. Be prepared to lose your investment.

Note that you'll need to carefully pack any bottles of *jenever* and other liquid-containing items in your checked luggage, because of the three-ounce limit on liquids in carry-on baggage. To check customs rules and duty rates before you go, visit www.cbp.gov, and click on "Travel," then "Know Before You Go."

Sightseeing

Sightseeing can be hard work. Use these tips to make your visits to the Low Countries' finest sights meaningful, fun, efficient, and painless.

Plan Ahead

Set up an itinerary that allows you to fit in all your must-see sights. For a one-stop look at opening hours in Amsterdam, Bruges, and Brussels, see the "At a Glance" sidebars for these destinations. Most sights keep stable hours, but you can easily confirm the latest by checking with the local TI.

Don't put off visiting a must-see sight—you never know when a place will close because of a strike, budget cut, or restoration project. On holidays (see page 5), expect shorter hours or closures.

When possible, visit major sights first thing (when your energy is best), and save other activities for the afternoon. Hit the museum highlights first, then go back to other things if you have the stamina and time.

Going at the right time can also help you avoid crowds. This book offers tips on specific sights. Try visiting very early, at lunch, or very late. Evening visits (when possible) are usually peaceful, with fewer crowds.

Study up. To get the most out of the self-guided tours and sight descriptions in this book, reread them the night before your visit. The Rijksmuseum is much more entertaining if you've boned up on ruffs and Dutch Masters the night before.

At Sights

Here's what you can typically expect:

Some important sights have metal detectors or conduct bag searches that will slow your entry, while others may require you to check daypacks and coats. They'll be kept safely. If you have something you can't bear to part with, stash it in a pocket or purse. To avoid checking a small backpack, carry it under your arm like a purse as you enter. From a guard's point of view, a backpack is generally a problem, while a purse is not.

Flash photography is sometimes banned, but taking photos without a flash is usually OK. Look for signs or ask. Flashes damage oil paintings and distract others in the room. Even without a flash, a handheld camera will take a decent picture (or buy postcards or posters at the museum bookstore). If photos are permitted, video cameras are generally OK, too.

Museums may have special exhibits in addition to their permanent collection. Some exhibits are included in the entry price; others come at an extra cost (which you may have to pay even if you don't want to see the exhibit).

Many sights rent audioguides, which generally offer excellent recorded descriptions of the art. If you bring along your own pair of headphones and a Y-jack, two people can sometimes share one audioguide and save. Guided tours in English (widely ranging in quality) are most likely to occur during peak season.

Some sights run short films featuring their highlights and history. These are generally well worth your time. I make it standard operating procedure to ask when I arrive at a sight if there is a film.

Expect changes—artwork can be on tour, on loan, out sick, or shifted at the whim of the curator. To adapt, pick up any available free floor plans as you enter. Ask museum staff if you can't find a particular piece.

Most important sights have an on-site café or cafeteria (usually a good place to rest and have a snack or light meal). Museum WCs are free and generally clean.

Many places sell postcards that highlight their attractions. Before you leave, scan the postcards and thumb through the biggest guidebook (or skim its index) to be sure you haven't overlooked something that you'd like to see.

Most sights stop admitting people 30-60 minutes before closing time, and some rooms shut down early (often 45 minutes before the actual closing time). Guards usher people out, so don't save the best for last.

Every sight or museum offers more than what is covered in this book. Use the information in this book as an introduction—not the final word.

Sleeping

I favor accommodations (and restaurants) handy to your sightseeing activities. Rather than list hotels scattered throughout a city, I choose two or three favorite neighborhoods and recommend the best accommodations values in each, from $30 bunk beds to fancy-for-my-book $300 doubles.

I look for places that are friendly; clean; a good value; located in a central, safe, quiet neighborhood; English-speaking; and not mentioned in other guidebooks. I'm more impressed by a handy location and a fun-loving philosophy than flat-screen TVs and shoeshine machines. I also like local character and simple facilities that don't cater to American "needs." Obviously, a place meeting every criterion is rare, and all of my recommendations fall short of perfection—sometimes miserably. But I've listed the best values for each price category, given the above criteria. I've also thrown in a few hostels, private rooms, and other cheap options for budget travelers.

I've described my recommended accommodations using a Sleep Code (see sidebar). Prices listed are for one-night stays in peak season, but may go up during major holidays and festivals (see page 592), and generally include breakfast.

Given the economic downturn, hoteliers may be willing to make a deal. I'd suggest emailing several hotels to ask for their best price. Comparison-shop and make your choice. In general, prices can soften up if you do any of the following: offer to pay cash, stay at least three nights, or mention this book. You can also try asking for a cheaper room or a discount, or offer to skip breakfast.

As you look over the listings, you'll notice that some accommodations promise special prices to my readers who book direct (without using a room-finding service or hotel-booking website, which take a commission). To get these rates, mention this book when you reserve, then show the book upon arrival.

Before accepting a room, confirm your understanding of the

Sleep Code

(€1 = about $1.40)
To help you sort easily through these listings, I've divided the rooms into three categories based on the price for a standard double room with bath:

$$$ Higher Priced
$$ Moderately Priced
$ Lower Priced

I always rate hostels as $, whether or not they have double rooms, because they have the cheapest beds in town.

To give maximum information in a minimum of space, I use the following code to describe the accommodations. Prices listed are per room, not per person. Unless otherwise noted, English is spoken, breakfast is included, and credit cards are accepted. When a price range is given for a type of room (such as "Db-€80-120"), it means the price fluctuates with the season, size of room, or length of stay.

S = Single room (or price for one person in a double).
D = Double or twin. Double beds are usually big enough for nonromantic couples.
T = Triple (generally a double bed with a single, or three twin beds).
Q = Quad (usually two double beds).
b = Private bathroom with toilet and shower or tub.
s = Private shower or tub only (the toilet is down the hall).

According to this code, a couple staying at a "Db-€85" hotel would pay a total of €85 (about $120) for a double room with a private bathroom.

If I mention "Internet access" in a hotel description, there's a public terminal in the lobby for guests to use. If I list "Wi-Fi" or "cable Internet," you can access it in your room, but only if you have your own laptop.

complete price. The only tip my recommended hotels would like is a friendly, easygoing guest.

Types of Accommodations
Hotels
In this book, the price for a double room ranges from $70 (very simple, toilet and shower down the hall) to $300 (maximum plumbing and more), with most clustering at about $140. You'll pay more at Amsterdam hotels, less at Brussels hotels and Bruges B&Bs.

Most hotels have lots of doubles and a few singles, triples, and quads. And though groups sleep cheap, traveling alone can be expensive. Singles (except for the rare closet-type rooms that fit only a twin bed) are simply doubles used by one person, so they often cost nearly the same as a double.

A hearty breakfast with cereal, meats, local cheeses, fresh bread, yogurt, juice, and coffee or tea is standard in hotels.

For environmental reasons, towels are often replaced in hotels only when you leave them on the floor. (In cheaper places, they aren't replaced at all, so hang them up to dry and reuse.)

Hoteliers can be a great help and source of advice; they're experts on their cities. But remember, even at the best hotels, mechanical breakdowns occur: air-conditioning malfunctions, sinks leak, hot water turns cold, and toilets gurgle and smell. Report your concerns clearly and calmly (not angrily) at the front desk. For more complicated problems, don't expect instant results.

If you suspect night noise will be a problem, ask for a quiet room in the back or on an upper floor. To guard against theft in your room, keep valuables out of sight. Some rooms come with a safe, and other hotels have safes at the front desk. Use them if you're concerned.

Checkout can pose problems if surprise charges pop up on your bill. If you settle up your bill the night before you leave, you'll have time to discuss and address any points of contention.

Above all, keep a positive attitude. After all, you're on vacation. If your hotel is a disappointment, spend more time out enjoying the city you came to see.

Bed-and-Breakfasts

B&Bs offer double the cultural intimacy and—often—nicer rooms for a good deal less than most hotel rooms. Hosts usually speak English and are interesting conversationalists.

In the Low Countries, B&Bs are common in well-touristed areas outside the big cities. There are plenty to choose from in Haarlem, Antwerp, Ghent, and especially Bruges. Amsterdam also has B&Bs, though they tend to be more expensive and not as good a value as those in small towns (I've listed the better-value B&Bs in Amsterdam). Urban Brussels has only one recommended B&B. Local TIs have lists of B&Bs and can book a room for you, but you'll save money by booking direct with the B&Bs listed in this book.

Hostels

For about $30 a night, you can stay at a youth hostel. Travelers of any age are welcome, if they don't mind dorm-style accommodations or meeting other travelers. Most hostels offer kitchen facilities, Internet access, Wi-Fi, laundry (generally self-service), sometimes cheap meals, and other handy amenities. Hostels are also a tremendous source of local and budget travel information. Expect crowds in the summer, snoring, and lots of noisy youths. Family and private rooms are sometimes available on request, but it's mostly larger bunk-bed dorms (usually divided between boys and girls, but sometimes mixed).

There are two basic types of hostels: official and independent. **Official hostels** belong to the same parent organization (Hostelling International, or HI; also known as International Youth Hostel Federation, or IYHF). These hostels are required to adhere to various rules, making them predictable but sometimes institutional. At official hostels, you usually can't check in before 17:00 and must be out by 10:00, and there is often a 23:00 curfew. If you plan to spend at least six nights at official HI hostels, buy a membership card before you go ($28/year, www.hihostels.com); nonmembers pay an extra $5 per night to sleep at HI hostels.

The Low Countries also have plenty of **independent hostels,** where you'll find no midday lockout, no curfew, no membership requirement, co-ed dorms, simple double rooms, a more easy-going staff, and a rowdy atmosphere. Various organizations promote independent hostels, including www.hostelworld.com, www.hostelz.com, www.hostelseurope.com, and www.hostels.com.

Phoning

To call the Netherlands or Belgium, you'll need to know the country code: 31 for the Netherlands, and 32 for Belgium. To call the Netherlands from the US or Canada, dial 011-31-number in this book (drop the initial 0 from the hotel's number). If calling the Netherlands from another European country, dial 00-31-number in this book (without its initial 0). For Belgium, use "32" instead of "31." For more tips on calling, see page 576.

Making Reservations

Given the quality of the places I've found for this book, I'd recommend that you reserve your rooms in advance, particularly if you'll be traveling during peak season. Book several weeks ahead, or as soon as you've pinned down your itinerary. If traveling during major holidays and events, make reservations far in advance (see page 592). Just like at home, holidays that fall on a Monday, Thursday, or Friday can turn the weekend into a long holiday, so book ahead for the entire weekend.

Requesting a Reservation: To make a reservation, contact hotels directly by email, phone, or fax. Email is the clearest and most economical way to make a reservation. Or go straight to the hotel website: Many have secure online reservation forms and can instantly inform you of availability and any special deals. But be sure you use the hotel's official site and not a booking agency's site—otherwise you may pay higher rates than you should. Whether emailing, faxing, or calling, simple English is fine. Most hotels listed are accustomed to English-only speakers. If you're phoning from the US, be mindful of time zones (see page 8).

The hotelier wants to know these key pieces of information (also included in the sample request form in the appendix):

- number and type of rooms
- number of nights
- date of arrival
- date of departure
- any special needs (e.g., bathroom in the room or down the hall, twin beds vs. double bed, air-conditioning, quiet, view, ground floor, etc.)

When you request a room, use the European style for writing dates: day/month/year. For example, for a two-night stay in July, I would request: "1 double room for 2 nights, arrive 16/07/12, depart 18/07/12." Consider carefully how long you'll stay; don't just assume you can tack on extra days once you arrive. Mention any discounts offered—for Rick Steves readers or otherwise—when you make the reservation.

If you don't get a reply to your email or fax, it usually means the hotel is already fully booked (but you can try sending the message again, or call to follow up).

Confirming a Reservation: If the hotel's response includes its room availability and rates, it's not a confirmation. You must tell them that you want that room at the given rate. The hotelier may request your credit-card number for a one-night deposit to hold the room. While you can email your credit-card information (I do), it's safer to share that confidential info via phone call, fax, two successive emails, or secure online reservation form (if the hotel has one on its website).

Canceling a Reservation: If you must cancel your reservation, it's courteous to do so with as much advance notice as possible—at least three days. Simply make a quick phone call or send an email. Hotels and B&Bs lose money if they turn away customers while holding a room for someone who doesn't show up. Understandably, many places bill no-shows for one night.

Hotels in larger cities sometimes have strict cancellation policies. For example, you might lose a deposit if you cancel within two weeks of your reserved stay, or you might be billed for the entire visit if you leave early. Internet deals may require prepayment, with no refunds for cancellations. If concerned, ask about cancellation policies before you book.

If canceling by email, request confirmation that your cancellation was received to avoid being accidentally billed.

How Was Your Trip?

Were your travels fun, smooth, and meaningful? If you'd like to share your tips, concerns, and discoveries, please fill out the survey at www.ricksteves.com/feedback. I value your feedback. Thanks in advance—it helps a lot.

Reconfirm Your Reservation: Always call to reconfirm your room reservation a day or two in advance from the road. (Don't have a TI reconfirm rooms for you; they'll take a commission.) Smaller hotels and pensions appreciate knowing your estimated time of arrival. If arriving after 17:00, be sure to let your hotelier know.

On the small chance that a hotel loses track of your reservation, bring along a hard copy of their emailed or faxed confirmation.

Reserving Rooms as You Travel: It's possible to make reservations as you travel, calling hotels or B&Bs a few days to a week before your arrival. If everything's full, don't despair. Call a day or two in advance and fill in a cancellation. If you'd rather travel without any reservations at all, you'll have greater success snaring rooms if you arrive at your destination early in the day. If you anticipate crowds, call hotels at about 9:00 or 10:00 on the day you plan to arrive, when the hotel clerk knows who'll be checking out and just which rooms will be available.

Traveling as a Temporary Local

We travel all the way to Europe to enjoy differences—to become temporary locals. You'll experience frustrations. Certain truths that we find "God-given" or "self-evident," such as cold beer, ice in drinks, bottomless cups of coffee, hot showers, and bigger being better, are suddenly not so true. One of the benefits of travel is the eye-opening realization that there are logical, civil, and even better alternatives.

Europeans generally like Americans. But if there is a negative aspect to the image Europeans have of Americans, it's that we are big, loud, aggressive, impolite, rich, superficially friendly, and a bit naive.

My Dutch and Belgian friends place a high value on speaking quietly in restaurants and on trains. Listen while on the bus or in a restaurant—the place can be packed, but the decibel level is low. Try to adjust your volume accordingly to show respect for their culture.

While Europeans look bemusedly at some of our Yankee

excesses—and worriedly at others—they nearly always afford individual travelers all the warmth we deserve. Judging from all the happy feedback I receive from travelers who have used this book, it's safe to assume you'll enjoy a great, affordable vacation—with the finesse of an independent, experienced traveler.

Thanks, and have a *goede vakantie!*

Back Door Travel Philosophy
From *Rick Steves' Europe Through the Back Door*

Travel is intensified living—maximum thrills per minute and one of the last great sources of legal adventure. Travel is freedom. It's recess, and we need it.

Experiencing the real Europe requires catching it by surprise, going casual..."Through the Back Door."

Affording travel is a matter of priorities. (Make do with the old car.) You can travel—simply, safely, and comfortably—anywhere in Europe for $120 a day plus transportation costs (allow more in big cities). In many ways, spending more money only builds a thicker wall between you and what you came to see. Europe is a cultural carnival, and, time after time, you'll find that its best acts are free and the best seats are the cheap ones.

A tight budget forces you to travel close to the ground, meeting and communicating with the people, not relying on service with a purchased smile. Never sacrifice sleep, nutrition, safety, or cleanliness in the name of budget. Simply enjoy the local-style alternatives to expensive hotels and restaurants.

Connecting with people carbonates your experience. Extroverts have more fun. If your trip is low on magic moments, kick yourself and make things happen. If you don't enjoy a place, maybe you don't know enough about it. Seek the truth. Recognize tourist traps. Give a culture the benefit of your open mind. See things as different but not better or worse. Any culture has much to share.

Of course, travel, like the world, is a series of hills and valleys. Be fanatically positive and militantly optimistic. If something's not to your liking, change your liking.

Travel can make you a happier American as well as a citizen of the world. Our Earth is home to six and a half billion equally important people. It's humbling to travel and find that people don't have the "American Dream"—they have their own dreams. Europeans like us, but, with all due respect, they wouldn't trade passports.

Thoughtful travel engages us with the world. In tough economic times, it reminds us what is truly important. By broadening perspectives, travel teaches new ways to measure quality of life.

Globe-trotting destroys ethnocentricity, helping you understand and appreciate different cultures. Rather than fear the diversity on this planet, celebrate it. Among your prized souvenirs will be the strands of different cultures you choose to knit into your own character. The world is a cultural yarn shop, and Back Door travelers are weaving the ultimate tapestry. Join in!

THE
NETHERLANDS

THE NETHERLANDS

Holland: windmills, wooden shoes, cheese, tulips, and tranquility. In Holland's 17th-century Golden Age, Dutch traders sailed the seas to find exotic goods, creating a global economy. Tiny Holland was a world power—politically, economically, and culturally— with more great artists per square mile than any other country.

"Holland" is just a nickname for the Netherlands. North Holland and South Holland are the largest of the 12 provinces that make up the Netherlands. Today, the country is Europe's most densely populated and also one of its wealthiest and best organized. In 1944, the neighboring countries of Belgium, the Netherlands, and Luxembourg became the nucleus of a united Europe when they joined economically to form BeNeLux.

The average income in the Netherlands is higher than in the United States. Though only 8 percent of the labor force is made up of farmers, 70 percent of the land is cultivated—if you venture outside of Amsterdam, you'll travel through vast fields of barley, wheat, sugar beets, potatoes, and flowers.

The word *Netherlands* means "lowlands." The country occupies the low-lying delta near the mouth of three of Europe's large rivers, including the Rhine. In medieval times, inhabitants built a system of earthen dikes to protect their land from flooding caused by tides and storm surges. The fictional story of Hans Brinker— the little Dutch boy who saves the country by sticking his finger in a leaking dike—summed up the country's precarious situation. (Many Americans know this story from a popular 19th-century novel, but few Dutch people have ever heard of it.) In 1953, severe floods breached the old dikes, killing 1,800 and requiring a major overhaul of the system. Today's 350 miles of dikes and levees are high-tech, with electronic systems to monitor water levels. Dutch experts traveled to Louisiana after Hurricane Katrina to share

The Netherlands

their expertise with US officials after levee failure caused massive flooding.

Much of the Dutch landscape is reclaimed from the sea, rivers, and lakes. That's where Holland's famous windmills came in. After diking off large tracts of land below sea level, the Dutch used windmills to harness wind energy to lift the water up out of the enclosed area, divert it into canals, and drain the land. They cultivated hardy plants that removed salt from the soil, slowly turning marshy estuaries into fertile farmland. The windmills later served a second purpose for farmers by turning stone wheels to grind their grain.

Dutch reclamation projects are essentially finished (though a new province—Flevoland, near Amsterdam—has been drained, dried, and populated in the last 100 years—see the Schokland Museum chapter). But in this era of global warming and rising sea levels, the Dutch are developing plans to upgrade their dikes and bulk up their beaches to hold back the sea. They also continue to innovate, building floatable homes and greenhouses (which rise with the tides) and relocating dikes farther back from the rivers (to create wider floodplains). All this technological tinkering with

Netherlands Almanac

Official Name: Koninkrijk der Nederlanden (Kingdom of the Netherlands), or simply Nederland.

Population: 16.5 million people (1,023 people per square mile; 15 times the population density of the US). About 80 percent are Dutch; 5 percent hail from other EU countries; and the rest are mostly Indonesian, Turkish, Surinamese, and Moroccan. Less than a third are Catholic, 20 percent are Protestant, 6 percent are Muslim, and more than 40 percent have no religious affiliation.

Latitude and Longitude: 52°N and 5°E. The latitude is similar to Alberta, Canada.

Area: 16,000 square miles—about twice the size of New Jersey.

Geography: The Netherlands is located at the mouths of three major European rivers: the Rhine, the Waal, and the Meuse. It shares borders with Belgium, Germany, and the North Sea. The Dutch have been beating back the sea for centuries, forming *polders*—flat, low-lying reclaimed lands. The Netherlands has a mild marine climate.

Biggest Cities: Amsterdam is the largest city, with about 765,000 people, followed by Rotterdam (600,000) and The Hague (485,000).

Economy: The Netherlands is prosperous, with the planet's 22nd-largest economy ($659 billion), a per-capita GDP in the world's top 20 ($39,400), and one of Europe's lowest unemployment

nature prompted a popular local saying: "God made the Earth, but the Dutch made Holland."

Several Dutch icons came directly from the country's flat, reclaimed landscape: As mentioned, windmills and canals drained the land. Wooden shoes *(klompen)* allowed farmers to walk across soggy fields. (They're also easy to find should they come off in high water because they float.) Tulips and other flowers grew well in the sandy soil near dunes.

In the 1630s, Holland was gripped with "tulip mania" (see sidebar on page 30). Financial speculators invested wildly in exotic varieties, causing prices to skyrocket. You could buy a house with just three tulip bulbs. In February 1637, the bubble burst, investors were ruined, and the economic fallout helped contribute to the decline of the Dutch Golden Age.

The Netherlands' flat land makes it a biker's dream. The Dutch, who average four bikes per family, have put small bike roads (with their own traffic lights) beside nearly every major highway. You can rent bikes at most train stations and drop them off at most others. And you can take bikes on trains (outside of rush hour) for €6 per day. Dutch pedestrians know to look carefully for rates. Its port at Rotterdam is Europe's largest, and the country relies heavily on foreign trade. The nation's highly mechanized farms produce huge quantities of flowers, bulbs, and produce for export. The economy has also benefited from its many natural gas fields—including the huge Groningen field, one of the world's biggest. However, even this notably stable nation has suffered from the worldwide recession.

Government: The Netherlands is a parliamentary democracy, with its seat of government at The Hague, although the country's official capital is Amsterdam. The ceremonial head of state is Queen Beatrix, whose ascension to the throne on April 30, 1980 (also the birthday of her mother, Juliana), is celebrated each spring on Queen's Day. The Dutch parliament consists of two houses: the 150-member, directly elected Second Chamber (or Lower House); and the 75-member First Chamber (or Upper House), elected by provincial assemblies. The government is led by a prime minister.

Flag: The Netherlands' flag is composed of three horizontal bands of red (top), white, and blue.

The Dutch: They're among the world's tallest people—the average height for a man is 6'1" and for a woman, 5'6". The average age for both men and women is around 40 years old, and they'll live to be 79. They ride their bikes about 1.5 miles a day and smoke half as much marijuana as their American friends.

bikes before crossing the street—and so should you.

The Dutch can generally speak English, pride themselves on their frankness, and like to split the bill. Thriftiness, efficiency, and a dislike of wastefulness are longstanding Dutch traits. Traditionally, Dutch cities have been open-minded, loose, and liberal (to attract sailors in the days of Henry Hudson). And today, Amsterdam is a capital of alternative lifestyles—a city where nothing's illegal as long as nobody gets hurt. Coffee shops serve cannabis as well as cappuccinos, and prostitutes pose in government-licensed windows. The city is surprisingly diverse, housing many recent immigrants—a trend that, unfortunately, has resulted in tensions in recent years. The Netherlands in general and Amsterdam in particular are gay-friendly. Some of the biggest festivals and parades on the social calendar bring out the LGBT (lesbian, gay, bisexual, and transgender) crowd.

While freewheeling Amsterdam does have a quiet side (particularly in West Amsterdam, which contains the pleasant Jordaan neighborhood), travelers who prefer more small-town Dutch evenings can sleep in a small town nearby, such as Haarlem, and side-trip into the big city.

THE NETHERLANDS

Tulip Mania

When we think of the Netherlands, a few images spring to mind: windmills, wooden shoes, and, perhaps most vividly, tulips. A Dutch icon since the 17th century, the colorful flowers are actually native to central Asia ("tulip" comes from a Turkish word for "turban"). When the Holy Roman Emperor's ambassador to Constantinople first sent some bulbs westward in the mid-1500s, a few wound up in the hands of a Dutch botanist—and thus began one of the oddest chapters in the Netherlands' history.

The region's harsh conditions turned out to be ideal for the hardy bulbs, which also benefited from good timing: They

arrived in the Netherlands in the middle of the Dutch Golden Age, delighting a relatively affluent populace who were fond of beauty and able to pay for it. Within a generation the popularity of these then-exotic flowers—and for a few rare species in particular—grew from a trendy fad into an all-out frenzy. Prices shot skyward: Forty bulbs could fetch up to 100,000 florins (about $1.7 million in today's dollars); in the context of the times, an average laborer made around 150 florins a year. The most treasured variety was the Semper Augustus, with its distinctive red-and-white petals—just one bulb sold for 12 acres of land.

"Tulip mania" reached a fever pitch in late 1636, and for the next few months, frantic trading consumed the Dutch. Production of other goods declined as people dropped everything to get rich on the tulip exchange. Soon, instead of buying and selling actual bulbs, people began trading promisory vouchers—by that time, it wasn't really the flowers they were after, but the opportunity to resell them at a higher price. The number of potential buyers seemed endless...until it wasn't. In February of 1637, one of history's most famous speculative bubbles burst, leaving many tulip investors with empty contracts or bulbs worth only a tiny fraction of what they'd cost. But the demand for tulips never died out—a love of the flowers had been firmly planted in the Dutch psyche, and they continue to be an integral part of the culture as well as a major export.

To get a complete taste of the Netherlands, venture beyond Amsterdam and Haarlem. The efficient train system turns much of the country into a feasible day trip (or two). The quaint town of Delft (Vermeer's hometown, laced with canals) and its neighboring town, The Hague, make a rewarding day or two of sightseeing. Arnhem has the Arnhem Open-Air Folk Museum and the Kröller-Müller Museum of modern art nearby (in Hogue Veluwe National Park). The Historic Triangle offers a nostalgic loop trip on a steam train and boat. Keukenhof's flower garden is one of the world's best (open in spring only). Explore farther: there's Edam (an adorable village), Alkmaar (best on Friday for its cheese market), Aalsmeer (a bustling modern flower auction), Schokland (for a chance to walk on what was the bottom of the sea at this village/museum), open-air folk museums at Enkhuizen and Zaanse Schans, and more. Your top options are described in the Dutch Day Trips chapter.

Wherever you roam, you'll find the Netherlands to be something of an eye-opener. Behind its placid exterior, it's a complex mix of modern technology, honored traditions, quaint countryside, outrageous architecture, and no-nonsense, globally minded people.

Dutch Cuisine

Traditional Dutch food is basic and hearty, with lots of bread, soup, and fish. Dutch treats include cheese, pancakes *(pannenkoeken)*, and "syrup waffles" *(stroopwafels)*. Popular drinks are light, pilsner-type beer and gin *(jenever)*.

Treat your tongue to some new experiences in Holland: Try a pickled herring at an outdoor herring stand, linger over coffee in a "brown café," sip an old *jenever* with a new friend, and consume an Indonesian feast—a *rijsttafel*.

Lunch and dinner are served at typical American times (roughly 12:00-14:00 and 18:00-21:00). At restaurants, tipping is not necessary (15 percent service is usually included in the menu price), but a tip of about 5-10 percent is a nice reward for good service. In bars, rounding up to the next euro ("keep the change") is appropriate if you get table service, rather than ordering at the bar.

When ordering drinks in a café or bar, you can just pay as you go (especially if the bar is crowded), or wait until the end to settle up, as many locals do. If you get table service, take the cue from your waiter.

Cafés with outdoor tables generally do not charge more if you sit outside (unlike in France or Italy).

Waiters constantly say, *"Alstublieft"* (AHL-stoo-bleeft). It's a useful, catch-all polite word meaning, "please," "here's your order,"

THE NETHERLANDS

"enjoy," and "you're welcome." You can respond with a thank you by saying, *"Dank u wel"* (dahnk yoo vehl).

Dutch Specialties

Cheeses: Edam (covered with red wax) or Gouda (HHHOW-dah). Gouda can be young or old—*jong* is mellow; *oude* is salty, crumbly, and strong, sometimes seasoned with cumin or cloves.

French Fries: Commonly served with mayonnaise (ketchup and curry sauce are often available) on a paper tray or in a newspaper cone. Flemish *(Vlaamse) frites* are made from whole potatoes, not pulp.

Haring **(herring):** Pickled herring, often served with onions or pickles, sometimes with sour cream, on a thick, soft, white bun.

Hutspot: Hearty meat stew with mashed potatoes, onions, and carrots, especially popular on winter days.

Kroketten **(croquettes):** Log-shaped rolls of meats and vegetables (kind of like corn dogs) breaded and deep-fried, such as *bitterballen* (meatballs), *frikandellen* (sausages), or *vlammetjes* (spring rolls).

Pannenkoeken: Either sweet dessert pancakes or crêpe-like, savory dinner pancakes.

Typical Meals

Breakfast: Breakfasts are big by continental standards—bread, meat, cheese, and maybe an egg or omelet. Hotels generally put out a buffet spread, including juice and cereal.

Lunch: Simple sandwiches are called *broodjes* (most commonly made with cheese and/or ham). An open-face sandwich of ham and cheese topped with two fried eggs is an *uitsmijter* (OUTS-mi-ter). Soup is popular for lunch, including *erwtensoep*, a thick, hearty pea soup.

Snacks and Take-Out Food: Small stands sell french fries *(frites)* with mayonnaise, pickled herring, falafels (fried chickpea balls in pita bread), *shoarmas* (lamb tucked in pita bread), and *döner kebabs* (Turkish version of a *shoarma*). Delis have deep-fried croquettes *(kroketten)*.

Dinner: It's the biggest meal of the day, consisting of meat or seafood with boiled potatoes, cooked vegetables, and a salad. Hearty stews are served in winter. These days, many people eat more vegetarian fare.

Sweets: Try *poffertjes* (small, sugared puffy pancakes), *pannen-*

koeken (pancakes with fruit and cream), *stroopwafels* (syrup waffles), and *appelgebak* or *appeltaart* (apple pie).

Ethnic Foods

If you're not in the mood for meat and potatoes, sample some of Amsterdam's abundant ethnic offerings.

Indonesian *(Indisch):* The tastiest "Dutch" food is Indonesian, from the former colony. Find any Indisch restaurant and experience a *rijsttafel* (literally, "rice table"). With as many as 30 spicy dishes (ranging from small sides to entrée-sized plates) and a big bowl of rice (or noodles), a *rijsttafel* can be split and still fill two hungry tourists. Vegetarian versions are yours for the asking.

    Nasi rames is a cheaper, smaller version of a *rijsttafel*. Another popular dish is *bami goreng*—stir-fried noodles served with meat, vegetables, and *rijsttafel* items. *Nasi goreng* is like *bami*, but comes with fried rice. *Saté* is skewered meat, and *gado-gado* consists of steamed vegetables and hard-boiled eggs with peanut sauce. Among the most common sauces are peanut, red chili *(sambal)*, and dark soy.

Middle Eastern: Try a *shoarma* (roasted lamb with garlic in pita bread, served with bowls of different sauces), falafel, gyros, or a *döner kebab.*

Surinamese *(Surinaamse):* Surinamese cuisine is a mix of Caribbean and Indonesian influences, featuring *roti* (spiced chicken wrapped in a tortilla) and rice (white or fried) served with meats in sauces (curry and spices). Why Surinamese food in Amsterdam? In 1667, Holland traded New York City ("New Amsterdam") to Britain in exchange for the small country of Suriname (which borders Guyana on the northeast coast of South America). For the next three centuries, Suriname (renamed Dutch Guyana) was a Dutch colony, which is why it has indigenous Indians, Creoles, and Indonesian immigrants who all speak Dutch. When Suriname gained independence in 1975, 100,000 Surinamese immigrated to Amsterdam, sparking a rash of Surinamese fast-food outlets.

Types of Eateries

Any place labeled "restaurant" will serve full sit-down meals for lunch or dinner. But there are other places to fill the tank.

    An *eetcafé* is a simple restaurant serving basic soups, salads, sandwiches, as well as traditional meat-and-potatoes meals in a generally comfortable but no-nonsense setting.

    A *salon de thé* serves tea and coffee, but also croissants, pastries, and sandwiches for a light brunch, a lunch, or an afternoon snack.

    Cafés are all-purpose establishments, serving light meals at mealtimes and coffee, drinks, and snacks the rest of the day and night. *Bruin* cafés ("brown cafés") are named for their nicotine-stained walls—until smoking was banned indoors in 2008, they were filled with tobacco smoke. These places are usually a little more bar-like, with dimmer lighting and wood paneling.

A *proeflokaal* is a bar (with snacks) offering wine, spirits, or beer. A "coffeeshop" is the code word for an establishment where marijuana is sold and consumed, though most offer drinks and munchies, too (for details, see the Smoking chapter).

There's no shortage of stand-up, take-out places serving fast food, sandwiches, and all kinds of quick ethnic fare.

No matter what type of establishment you choose, expect it to be *gezellig*—a much-prized Dutch virtue, meaning an atmosphere of relaxed coziness.

Dutch Drinks

Beer: Order "a beer," and you'll get a *pils*, a light lager/pilsner-type beer in a 10-ounce glass with a thick head leveled off with a stick. (Typical brands are Heineken, Grolsch, Oranjeboom, and Amstel.) A common tap beer is Palm Speciale, an amber ale served in a stemmed, wide-mouth glass. Belgian beers are popular, always available in bottles and sometimes on tap (for more information, see page 333). *Witte* (white) beer is light-colored and summery, sometimes served with a lemon slice (it's like American Hefeweizen, but yeastier).

Jenever: Try this Dutch gin made from juniper berries. *Jong* (young) is sharper; *oude* (old) is mellow. Served chilled, *jenever* (yah-NAY-ver) is meant to be chugged with a *pils* chaser (this combination is called a *kopstoot*—head-butt). While cheese gets harder and sharper with age, *jenever* grows smooth and soft, so old *jenever* is best.

Liqueur: You'll find a variety of local fruit brandies and cognacs.

Wine: Dutch people drink a lot of fine wine, but it's almost all imported.

Coffee: The Dutch love their coffee, enjoying many of the same drinks (espresso, cappuccino) served in American or Italian coffee shops. Coffee usually comes with a small spice cookie. A *koffie verkeerd* (fer-KEERT, "coffee wrong") is an espresso with a lot of steamed milk.

Soft Drinks: You'll find the full array.

Orange Juice: Many cafés/bars have a juicer for making fresh-squeezed orange juice.

Water: The Dutch drink tap water with meals, but many prefer mineral water, still or sparkling (Spa brand is popular). At restaurants, you can get tap water free for the asking.

AMSTERDAM

ORIENTATION TO AMSTERDAM

Housed in Europe's most 17th-century city, Amsterdam is a progressive way of life. Physically, it's built upon millions of pilings. But more than that, it's built on good living, cozy cafés, great art, street-corner jazz, stately history, and a spirit of live and let live. It has 765,000 people and almost as many bikes. It also has more canals than Venice...and about as many tourists.

During the Dutch Golden Age, in the 1600s, Amsterdam was the world's richest city, an international sea-trading port, and the cradle of capitalism. Wealthy, democratic burghers built a planned city of canals lined with trees and townhouses topped with fancy gables. Immigrants, Jews, outcasts, and political rebels were drawn here by its tolerant atmosphere, while painters such as young Rembrandt captured that atmosphere on canvas.

The Dutch are unique. They are among the world's most handsome people—tall, healthy, and with good posture—and the most open, honest, and refreshingly blunt. They like to laugh. As connoisseurs of world culture, they appreciate Rembrandt paintings, Indonesian food, and the latest French film—but with an un-snooty, blue-jeans attitude.

Approach Amsterdam as an ethnologist observing a strange culture. Stroll through any neighborhood and see things that are commonplace here but rarely found elsewhere. Carillons chime quaintly in neighborhoods selling sex, as young professionals smoke pot with impunity next to old ladies in bonnets selling flowers. Observe the neighborhood's "social control," where an elderly man feels safe in his home knowing he's being watched by the prostitutes next door.

Be warned: Amsterdam, a bold experiment in freedom, may box your Puritan ears. Take it all in, then pause to watch the clouds blow past stately old gables—and see the Golden Age reflected in a quiet canal.

Amsterdam: A Verbal Map

Amsterdam's Central Train Station (Amsterdam Centraal), on the north edge of the city, is your starting point, with the TI, bike rental, and trams branching out to all points. Damrak is the main north-south axis, connecting Central Station with Dam Square (people-watching and hangout center) and its Royal Palace. From this main street, the city spreads out like a fan, with 90 islands, hundreds of bridges, and a series of concentric canals—named Herengracht (Gentleman's Canal), Keizersgracht (Emperor's Canal), and Prinsengracht (Prince's Canal)—that were laid out in the 17th century, Holland's Golden Age. Amsterdam's major sights are all within walking distance of Dam Square.

To the east of Damrak is the oldest part of the city (today's Red Light District), and to the west is the newer part, where you'll find the Anne Frank House and the peaceful Jordaan neighborhood. Museums and Leidseplein nightlife cluster at the southern edge of the city center.

Amsterdam by Neighborhood

Amsterdam can feel like a big, sprawling city, but its major sights cluster in convenient zones. Grouping your sightseeing, walks, dining, and shopping thoughtfully can save you time.

Central Amsterdam—the historic core—runs north-south from Central Station along Damrak, passing through two major city squares (Dam and Spui) and ending at the Mint Tower. The central spine of streets (Damrak, Kalverstraat, Rokin) has some of the city's main department, chain, and tourist stores. Flanking Damrak on the east is the city's oldest area (today's Red Light District) and the revitalized waterfront around the train station.

West Amsterdam lies west of Damrak—from Dam Square to the Anne Frank House. This pleasant area is famous for its four grand canals (Singel, Herengracht, Keizersgracht, and Prinsengracht) that circle the historic core. West Amsterdam has tree-lined canals fronted by old, gabled mansions, as well as many of my recommended accommodations and restaurants. Within West Amsterdam is the boutique shopping district known as the Nine Little Streets. Farther west is the quieter, cozier Jordaan neighborhood, which is good for a stroll, though it's mostly residential.

Southwest Amsterdam is defined by two main features: museums and a city park. The city's major art museums (Rijksmuseum, Van Gogh) and other sights cluster together on an expansive

AMSTERDAM ORIENTATION

Amsterdam by Neighborhood

square, Museumplein. The museums are just a short walk from Vondelpark, Amsterdam's version of a central park. The lively Leidseplein (a small square that's home to nightlife and restaurants) and the Spiegelkwartier (classy antique-shopping district) are nearby. While it's less central to stay in Southwest Amsterdam, I've recommended accommodations that are a quick, convenient walk to the area's tram lines.

Northeast Amsterdam has a children's science museum (NEMO) and nautical sights.

Southeast Amsterdam contains the former Jewish Quarter and the Jewish Historical Museum. Several sights can be found around the square known as Waterlooplein (Rembrandt's House and a flea market). Additional sights are gathered in a park-dotted

Amsterdam Landmarks

Dam (pronounced dahm)	Amsterdam's main square
Damrak (DAHM-rock)	main street between Central Station and Dam Square
Spui (spow, rhymes with cow)	both a street and square
Rokin (roh-KEEN)	street connecting Dam Square and Spui
Kalverstraat (KAL-ver-straht)	pedestrian street
Leidseplein (LIDE-zuh-pline)	lively square
Jordaan (yor-DAHN)	neighborhood in southwest Amsterdam
Museumplein (myoo-ZAY-um-pline)	square with Rijks and Van Gogh museums
gracht (khrockt, pronounced gutturally)	canal
straat (straht)	street
plein (pline)	public square
huis (house)	house
kerk (kerk)	church

area called the Plantage (Dutch Resistance Museum, a theater-turned-Holocaust-memorial, a zoo, and a botanical garden). Rembrandtplein, another nightlife center, is a five-minute walk away.

Planning Your Time

Amsterdam is worth a full day of sightseeing on even the busiest itinerary. And though the city has a couple of must-see museums, its best attraction is its own carefree ambience. The city's a joy on foot—and a breezier and faster delight by bike.

Amsterdam in One Day

9:00 Follow my self-guided Amsterdam City Walk, which takes you from the train station to the Rijksmuseum, with stops at the peaceful Begijnhof, the Amsterdam Museum, and the flower market. Break up the walk with a relaxing hour-long canal cruise (departs from Spui dock or from near Leidseplein).

14:00 Visit Amsterdam's two great art museums, located side by side: the Van Gogh Museum and the Rijksmuseum.

18:30 Tour the Anne Frank House. (Consider buying tickets online to skip long lines at sight.) Arrive earlier off-season, when it closes at 19:00.

Daily Reminder

The biggest Amsterdam sights—the Rijksmuseum, the Van Gogh Museum, and the Anne Frank House—are open daily year-round (the Anne Frank House until 22:00 July-Aug). The Westerkerk stays open late in summer (Mon-Sat until 20:00 July-Aug). The city's naughty sights, as you might expect, stay open late every day (the Hash, Marijuana, and Hemp Museum until 23:00, the Damrak Sex Museum until 23:30, and the Erotic Museum until 1:00 in the morning).

Sunday: These sights have limited, afternoon-only hours today—the Amstelkring Museum (13:00-17:00) and Old Church (13:00-17:00). The Westerkerk church and tower are closed, as is the Waterlooplein flea market.

Monday: The Houseboat Museum and Tropical Museum are closed today. From September through May, NEMO is closed today (but open in peak season). Many businesses are closed Monday morning.

Tuesday: The House of Bols is closed.

Wednesday: All recommended sights are open. The Hermitage Amsterdam is open until 20:00.

Thursday: All recommended sights are open.

Friday: The Van Gogh Museum and the House of Bols are open until 22:00.

Saturday: The Anne Frank House is open until 22:00 mid-March-mid-Sept, and until 21:00 in the off-season.

19:30   Wander the Jordaan neighborhood, enjoying dinner by a canal or on a cobbled, quiet street.

21:30   Stroll the Red Light District for some of Europe's most fascinating window-shopping.

Amsterdam in Two or More Days
Day 1

9:00   Follow my self-guided Amsterdam City Walk, leading from the train station to the Rijksmuseum, via the quiet Begijnhof, the Amsterdam Museum (make time to tour this), and the flower market.

12:00   Stop for lunch in the Spui neighborhood before completing the walk.

14:00   Visit Amsterdam's two outstanding art museums, located next to each other: the Van Gogh Museum and the Rijksmuseum.

18:00   Dinner.

20:00   Stroll the Red Light District for some memorable window-shopping.

Day 2

   10:00   Start your day with a one-hour canal boat tour (boats
            leave across from train station).
   11:00   Visit the sights of your choice around Rembrandtplein
            (Rembrandt's House, Waterlooplein flea market
            —closed Sun), Gassan Diamonds polishing demo,
            Dutch Resistance Museum), breaking for lunch at one
            of the recommended restaurants (Plancius or Café
            Koosje) near the Dutch Resistance Museum.
   14:30   Free time to shop and explore.
   17:00   Tour the Anne Frank House. (Consider booking
            tickets online to avoid long lines.)
   18:30   Take my self-guided Jordaan Walk.
   20:00   Dinner in the Jordaan neighborhood.

Day 3

Visit the nearby town of Haarlem (see Haarlem chapters) or Delft
(see the Delft and The Hague chapter).

Day 4

Side-trip by train to an open-air folk museum; choose among
Arnhem's, Enkhuizen's, or Zaandijk's (Zaanse Schans Museum).
Unless you're visiting far-flung Arnhem, you could also easily fit in
a short visit to nearby Edam.

Overview

(area code: 020)

Tourist Information

"VVV" (pronounced "fay fay fay") is Dutch for "TI," a tourist
information office. Amsterdam's tourist offices are crowded and
inefficient—avoid them if you can. You can save yourself a trip by
calling the TI at 020/201-8800 (Mon-Fri 8:00-18:00) or trying
0900-400-4040 (Mon-Fri 9:00-17:00). From the US dial 011-31-
20-551-2525.

   The main TI at Central Station is busy, but is convenient
when arriving by train (daily July-Aug 8:00-20:00, Sept-June 9:00-
18:00). An affiliated office is in the AUB/Last Minute Ticket Shop
on Leidseplein, tucked into the side of the giant Stadsschouwburg
Theater (Mon-Fri 10:00-19:30, Sat 10:00-18:00, Sun 12:00-18:00;
doesn't book hotel rooms). These TIs outside of Amsterdam are
helpful and less crowded: at Schiphol Airport (daily 7:00-22:00)
and in the town of Haarlem (see pages 253 and 216).

   Tickets: Although Amsterdam's main TI sells tickets to the

Anne Frank House (€1 extra per ticket, same-day tickets available) and the Rijks, Van Gogh, and Stedelijk museums (no fee at all TIs), it's quicker to get tickets in advance online (see below).

Maps and Brochures: Given the city's maze of streets and canals, I'd definitely get a good city map (€2.50 at Central Station TI, same map given away free at the TI in the AUB/Last Minute Ticket Shop—go figure). Also consider picking up any of the walking-tour brochures (€3 each, including tours covering city center, former Jewish Quarter, Jordaan, and funky De Pijp neighborhood). For entertainment, get a copy of *Time Out Amsterdam* (€3, €1.50 if bought with city map); for additional entertainment ideas, see the free papers listed later (under "Helpful Hints") and in the Entertainment in Amsterdam chapter.

Currency Exchange: At Central Station, **GWK Currency Exchange** offices have hotel reservation windows where clerks sell local and international phone cards and mobile-phone SIM cards, and answer basic tourist questions, with shorter lines than the TI (daily 8:00-22:00, near front of station in both the east and west corridors, tel. 020/627-2731).

Resources for Gay Travelers: A short walk from Central Station down Damrak is **GAYtic,** a TI specifically oriented to the needs of gay travelers. The office stocks maps, magazines, and brochures, and dispenses advice on nightlife as well as general tourist information (Mon-Sat 11:00-20:00, Sun 12:00-20:00, Spuistraat 44, tel. 020/330-1461, www.gaytic.nl, info@gaytic.nl). **Pink Point,** in a kiosk outside Westerkerk, next to the Homomonument, is less of a resource, but has advice about nightlife and sells gay-themed souvenirs (usually daily 10:00-18:00, 11:00-17:00 in winter, closed Tue-Wed Jan-Feb).

Advance Tickets and Sightseeing Cards

Advance Tickets for Major Sights: Avoid long ticket lines during high season (late March through October) by buying tickets online for the Anne Frank House, Rijksmuseum, Van Gogh Museum, and Stedelijk modern-art museum.

It's easy to buy tickets through each museum's website: www .annefrank.org (€0.50 surcharge per ticket, but worth it), www .rijksmuseum.nl, www.vangoghmuseum.com, and www.stedelijk .nl (no extra fee for Rijks, Van Gogh, or Stedelijk). Print out your ticket and bring it to the ticket-holder's line for a quick entry.

You can also buy tickets for these sights in advance at the TIs (main TI only for Anne Frank House), but their lines seem almost as long as the ones you're trying to avoid at the sights.

If You Don't Have Advance Tickets: Use a Museumkaart to get in quickly at covered sights (details in "Sightseeing Cards," next). If you don't have one, trim your wait in line by going to the

Anne Frank House the minute it opens, or late in the day; this works better in early spring and fall than in summer, when even after-dinner lines can be long. Visit the Van Gogh Museum on a Friday evening, when it's open until 22:00, with no lines and few crowds, even in peak season.

Sightseeing Cards: Two cards merit consideration for heavy-duty sightseers. If your trip includes any other Dutch city, you're more likely to save more money by purchasing the Museumkaart, which covers many sights throughout the Netherlands, than the overpriced I amsterdam Card, which is valid only in Amsterdam. (There's no reason to buy both.) Both cards allow you free entry to most of the sights in Amsterdam (including the Rijks and Van Gogh museums), but neither card covers the Heineken Brewery, Westerkerk tower, or any sights dealing with sex or marijuana. The Anne Frank House is covered by the Museumkaart but not the I amsterdam Card.

The **Museumkaart,** which costs just €45 and is valid for a year throughout the Netherlands, is a no-brainer for anyone visiting at least six museums (for example, an itinerary that includes these museums, for a total of €59.50: Rijksmuseum-€12.50, Van Gogh Museum-€14, Anne Frank House-€8.50, Amsterdam Museum-€10, Amstelkring Museum-€7, and the Dutch Resistance Museum-€7.50). The Museumkaart is sold at all participating museums, and, except at the Anne Frank House, you can use it to skip the ticket-buying line (though everyone has to go through security). If you plan to buy a Museumkaart, get it at a smaller, less-crowded museum (such as the Amsterdam Museum). You'll see ads for the **Holland Pass,** but it's not worth it—the Museumkaart is a much better deal.

The **I amsterdam Card,** which focuses on Amsterdam and includes most transportation, is not worth the cost unless you're planning on a day or two of absolutely nonstop sightseeing, and connecting it all by public transit. Along with many sights and discounts, this pass includes one free canal boat tour and unlimited use of trams, buses, and metro—but not trains (and except for the canal tour, all of these public-transit options are covered by a normal transit pass anyway—see "Getting Around Amsterdam," later). You have a set number of consecutive hours to use it (for example: Visit your first museum at 14:00 Mon with a 24-hour pass, and it's good until 13:59 on Tue). This pass doesn't allow you to skip lines at major sights, except at the Van Gogh Museum (€38/24 hours, €48/48 hours, or €58/72 hours; sold at major museums, TIs, and with shorter lines at the GVB transit office across from Central Station, next to TI; www.iamsterdamcard.com).

Arrival in Amsterdam
By Train: The portal connecting Amsterdam to the world is its aptly named Central Station (Amsterdam Centraal). Through

at least 2014, expect the station and the plaza in front of it to be a chaotic construction zone—the station is being completely reworked, and the locations of things described here may change before your visit.

Trains arrive on a level above the station. Go down the stairs or the escalator (at the "A" end of the platform). As you descend from the platforms, you'll find yourself in one of the corridors leading to the street exit for the city center (Centrum). Those wanting buses and river ferries should head in the opposite direction—to the north (Noord) exit.

The station is fully equipped for the traveler. You'll find GWK Travelex counters (described earlier) in both the east and west corridors, and international ticket offices near the exit of both corridors. Luggage lockers are in the east corridor, under the "B" end of the platforms (€5-7/24 hours, depending on size of bag, always open, can fill up on busy summer weekends). The station has plenty of shops and places to grab a bite to eat. On the train level, platform 2 is lined with eateries, including the tall, venerable, 1920s-style **First Class Grand Café**. Handy **Albert Heijn** supermarkets are easy to find at the ends of both the east and west corridors.

Exiting the station, you're in the heart of the city. Straight ahead, just past the canal, is Damrak street, leading to Dam Square. To your left are the TI and GVB public-transit offices. Farther to your left are bike rentals (**MacBike** is located in the station building, and **Star Bikes** is a five-minute walk past it, both listed on page 49). To the right of the station are the postcard-perfect neighborhoods of West Amsterdam; some of my recommended hotels are within walking distance (see map on page 180).

Just beyond the taxis are the platforms for the city's blue trams, which come along frequently, ready to take you anywhere your feet won't (buy ticket or pass from conductor). Trams #1, #2, and #5 (which run to nearly all my recommended hotels) leave from in front of the station's west (main) entrance. All trams leaving Central Station stop at Dam Square along their route. For more on the transit system, see page 47.

Arrival by Plane: For details on getting from Schiphol Airport into downtown Amsterdam, see page 213.

Helpful Hints

Theft Alert: Tourists are considered green and rich, and the city has more than its share of hungry thieves—especially on trams and at the many hostels. Wear your money belt.

Emergency Telephone Number: Throughout the Netherlands, dial 112.

Street Smarts: Beware of silent transportation—trams and bicycles—when walking around town. Don't walk on tram tracks or pink/maroon bicycle paths. Before you step off any sidewalk, do a double- or triple-check in both directions to make sure all's clear.

Sightseeing Strategies: To beat the lines at Amsterdam's most popular sights, plan ahead. You can bypass the main ticket-buyers' line at the Anne Frank House, and the Rijks, Van Gogh, and Stedelijk museums by buying online tickets before you go (see page 42 for details). Remember, Friday night is a great time to visit the Van Gogh Museum, which is open until 22:00 (far smaller crowds then).

Shop Hours: Most shops are open Tuesday through Saturday 10:00-18:00, and Sunday and Monday 12:00-18:00. Some shops stay open later (21:00) on Thursdays. Supermarkets are generally open Monday through Saturday 8:00-20:00 and are closed on Sundays.

Holidays: Every year, **Queen's Day** (Koninginnedag, April 30) and **Gay Pride** (Aug 5-7 in 2011, Aug 3-5 in 2012) bring crowds, fuller hotels, and inflated room prices.

Cash Only: Thrifty Dutch merchants hate paying the unusually high fees charged by credit-card companies here; expect to pay cash in unexpected places, including grocery stores, cafés, budget hotels, train-station machines and windows, and at some museums.

Internet Access: It's easy at cafés all over town, but the best place for serious surfing and email is the towering **Central Library,** which has hundreds of fast, free terminals (Openbare Bibliotheek Amsterdam, daily 10:00-22:00, free Wi-Fi, a 10-minute walk from train station, described on page 69). "Coffeeshops," which sell marijuana, usually also offer Internet access—letting you surf with a special bravado.

English Bookstores: For fiction and guidebooks—including mine—try the **American Book Center** at Spui 12, right on the square (Mon 11:00-20:00, Tue-Sat 10:00-20:00 except Thu until 21:00, Sun 11:00-18:30, tel. 020/535-2575, www.abc.nl). The huge and helpful **Selexyz Scheltema** is at Koningsplein 20 near the Leidsestraat (included in my Amsterdam City Walk; store open Mon 11:00-18:00, Tue-Sat 9:30-18:00 except Thu until 21:00, Sun 12:00-18:00; lots of English novels, guidebooks, and maps; tel. 020/523-1411). **Waterstone's Booksellers,** a UK chain, also sells British newspapers (near Spui at 152 Kalverstraat, Mon-Sat 10:00-18:30 except Mon until 18:00 and Thu until 21:00, Sun 11:00-18:00, tel. 020/638-3821).

Free Publications: Hefty, hip, and helpful *Amsterdam Magazine*

("Beyond Windmills, Wooden Shoes, and Weed") includes a city map, and is available all over the city. Boom Chicago's magazine, aimed at the hostelling crowd, is handed out on Leidseplein and available in some spots across town. You may find one or both of these in your hotel room: *Visitors Guide Amsterdam*, sort of a mini-yellow pages for tourists, with a fairly crummy map but good tips and (paid) listings; and *Rush on Amsterdam*, a glossy quarterly magazine that has current info on what's on at the city's museums, and even includes a pretty good map.

Entertainment: Pick up a copy of *Time Out Amsterdam* at either TI or the bookstores listed above (€3), check out this book's Entertainment in Amsterdam chapter, or call the **AUB/Last Minute Ticket Shop** (theater, classical music, and major rock shows, tickets sold only at shop, Leidseplein 26, tel. 0900-0191, calls costs €0.40/minute, www.amsterdamsuitburo.nl, www.lastminuteticketshop.nl).

Maps: The free tourist maps can be confusing, except for *Amsterdam Museums: Guide to 37 Museums* (includes tram info and stops, ask for it at the big museums, such as the Van Gogh). Several free magazines, listed above, include decent detachable maps. If you want a top-notch map, buy one (about €2.50). I like the *Carto Studio Centrumkaart Amsterdam*. Amsterdam Anything's virtual "Go Where the Locals Go" city map is worth checking out, especially if you have mobile Internet access (www.amsterdamanything.nl).

Pharmacy: The shop named **DA** (Dienstdoende Apotheek) has all the basics—shampoo and toothpaste—as well as a pharmacy counter hidden in the back (Mon-Sat 9:00-22:00, Sun 11:00-22:00, Leidsestraat 74-76 near where it meets Keizersgracht, tel. 020/627-5351).

Laundry: Try **Clean Brothers Wasserij** in the Jordaan (daily 8:00-20:00 for €7 self-service, €9 drop-off—ready in an hour—Mon-Fri 9:00-17:00, Sat 9:00-18:00, no drop-off Sun, Westerstraat 26, one block from Prinsengracht, tel. 020/627-9888) or **Powders** near Leidseplein (daily 7:00-22:00, €6.50 self-service, €10 drop-off available Mon-Wed and Fri 8:00-17:00, Sat-Sun 9:00-15:00, no drop-off Thu, Kerkstraat 56, one block south of Leidsestraat, mobile 06-2630-6057).

Best Views: Though the **Westerkerk** offers fine views from its tower (and is convenient if you're visiting the Anne Frank House), the best city views are from the **Central Library** (Openbare Bibliotheek Amsterdam; see page 69). The Oude Kerk tower and the rooftop terrace at the NEMO Science Museum also provide good views.

Getting Around Amsterdam

Amsterdam is big, and you'll find the trams handy. The longest walk a tourist would make is an hour from Central Station to the Rijksmuseum. When you're on foot, be extremely vigilant for silent but potentially painful bikes, trams, and crotch-high curb posts.

If you've got a car, park it—all you'll find are frustrating one-way streets, terrible parking, and meter maids with a passion for booting cars parked incorrectly. You'll pay €55 a day to park safely in a central garage, about €27 for a "day ticket" to park on the street (9:00-19:00), and about €3.50/hour in a parking lot. If you must bring a car to Amsterdam, it's best to leave it at one of the city's supervised park-and-ride lots (follow *P&R* signs from freeway, €6/24 hours, includes round-trip transit into city center for up to five people, 4-day maximum).

By Tram, Bus, and Metro

Amsterdam's public transit system includes trams, buses, and an underground metro; of these, trams are most useful for most tourists.

Tickets: The entire country's public transit network operates on a single ticket system called the OV-Chipkaart (for "Openbaar Vervoer"—public transit). For locals, it couldn't be easier. With a single pre-paid card, they can hop on any form of public transit in the country, scan their card, and the fare is immediately deducted. Cards can be reloaded automatically, straight from residents' bank accounts.

But travelers—who generally stay only a few days—must still rely on either single tickets or multiday passes. (While officially classified as "OV-Chipkaarten," these tickets and passes with electronic chips are nothing like the reloadable, valid-nationwide, plastic cards locals use.)

Within Amsterdam, a single transit ticket costs €2.60 and is good for one hour on the tram, bus, and metro, including transfers. Passes good for unlimited transportation are available for 24 hours (€7), 48 hours (€11.50), 72 hours (€15.50), and 96 hours (€19.50). (The I amsterdam sightseeing card, described on page 43, includes a transit pass.) Given how expensive single tickets are, consider buying a pass or renting a bike for your stay before you buy that first ticket.

The easiest way to buy a ticket or transit pass is to simply board a tram or bus and pay the conductor (no extra fee). Tickets and passes are also available at metro-station vending machines (there's one just outside Central Station), at GVB public-transit offices, and at TIs.

The helpful GVB public-transit information office in front of

Central Station can answer questions (next to TI, Mon-Fri 7:00-21:00, Sat-Sun 10:00-18:00). Its free, multilingual *Public Transport Amsterdam Tourist Guide* includes a transit map and explains ticket options and tram connections to all the sights. For more public transit information, visit www.gvb.nl.

Trams: Board the tram at any entrance not marked with a red/white "do not enter" sticker. If you need a ticket or pass, pay the

conductor (in a booth at the back); if there's no conductor, pay the driver in front. You must always "check in" as you board by scanning your ticket or pass at the pink-and-white scanner, and "check out" by scanning it again when you get off. The scanner will beep and flash a green light after a successful scan. Be careful not to accidentally scan your ticket or pass twice while boarding, or it becomes invalid. Checking in and out is very important, as controllers do pass through and fine violators. To open the door when you reach your stop, press a green button on one of the poles near an exit.

Trams #2 *(Nieuw Sloten)* and #5 *(A'veen Binnenhof)* travel the north-south axis, from Central Station to Dam Square to Leidseplein to Museumplein (Van Gogh and Rijks museums). Tram #1 (marked *Osdorp*) also runs to Leidseplein. At Central Station, these three trams depart from the west side of Stationsplein (with the station behind you, they're to your right).

Tram #14, which doesn't connect to Central Station, goes east-west (Westerkerk-Dam Square-Muntplein-Waterlooplein-Plantage). If you get lost in Amsterdam, don't sweat it—10 of the city's 17 trams take you back to Central Station.

Buses and Metro: Tickets and passes work on buses and the metro just as they do on the trams—scan your ticket or pass to "check in" as you enter and again to "check out" when you leave. The metro system is scant—used mostly for commuting to the suburbs—but it does connect Central Station with some sights east of Damrak (Nieuwmarkt-Waterlooplein-Weesperplein). The glacial speed of the metro-expansion project is a running joke among cynical Amsterdammers.

By Bike

Everyone—bank managers, students, pizza delivery boys, and police—uses this mode of transport. It's by far the smartest way to travel in a city where 40 percent of all traffic rolls on two wheels. You'll get around town by bike faster than you can by taxi. On my last visit, I rented a bike for five days, chained it up outside my

Bike Theft

Bike thieves are bold and brazen in Amsterdam. Bikes come with two locks and stern instructions to use both. The wimpy

ones go through the spokes, whereas the industrial-strength chains are meant to be wrapped around the actual body of the bike and through the front wheel, and connected to something stronger than any human. Do this diligently. Once, I used both locks, but my chain wasn't around the main bar of my bike's body. In the morning, I found only my front tire (still safely chained to the metal fence). If you're sloppy, it's an expensive mistake and one that any "included" theft insurance won't cover.

hotel at night, and enjoyed wonderful mobility. I highly encourage this for anyone who wants to get maximum fun per hour in Amsterdam. One-speed bikes, with *"brrringing"* bells, rent for about €10 per day (cheaper for longer periods) at any number of places—hotels can send you to the nearest spot.

Rental Shops: Star Bikes Rental has cheap rates, long hours, and inconspicuous black bikes. They're happy to arrange an after-hours drop-off if you give them your credit-card number and prepay (€5/4 hours, €7/day, €9/24 hours, €12/2 days, €17/3 days, daily 9:00-19:00, requires ID but no monetary deposit, 5-minute walk from east end of Central Station at De Ruyterkade 127, tel. 020/620-3215, www.starbikesrental.com).

MacBike, with 900 bikes and counting, is the bike-rental powerhouse—you'll see their bright-red bikes all over town (they do stick out a bit). It has a huge and efficient outlet at Central Station (€7/3 hours, €9.50/24 hours, €14/48 hours, €19/72 hours, more for 3 gears, 25 percent discount with I amsterdam Card, €50 deposit plus passport or credit-card imprint, no helmets, daily 9:00-17:45; at east end of station—on the left as you're leaving; tel. 020/620-0985, www.macbike.nl). They have two smaller satellite stations at Leidseplein (Weteringschans 2) and Waterlooplein (Nieuwe Uilenburgerstraat 116). Return your bike to the station where you rented it. MacBike sells several pamphlets outlining bike tours with a variety of themes in and around Amsterdam for €1-2.

Frederic Rent-a-Bike, a 10-minute walk from Central Station, has quality bikes and a helpful staff (€8/3 hours, €15/24 hours, €25/48 hours, €60/week, one-day rental €10 if returned by 17:30, 10 percent discount on multiday rental with this book, daily 9:00-17:30, no after-hours drop-off, Brouwersgracht 78, tel. 020/624-5509, www.frederic.nl).

Tips: No one wears a helmet. For safety, use arm signals, follow the bike-only traffic signals, stay in the obvious and omnipresent bike lanes, and yield to traffic on the right. Fear oncoming trams and tram tracks. Carefully cross tram tracks at a perpendicular angle to avoid catching your tire in the rut. Warning: Police ticket cyclists the same as they do drivers. Obey all traffic signals, and walk your bike through pedestrian zones. Fines for biking through pedestrian zones are reportedly €30-50. A handy bicycle routeplanner can be found at www.routecraft.com (select "bikeplanner," then click British flag at far right for English). For a "Do-It-Yourself Bike Tour of Amsterdam" and for bike tours, see page 53.

By Boat

While the city is great on foot, bike, or tram, you can also get around Amsterdam by boat. **Rederij Lovers** boats shuttle tourists on a variety of routes covering different combinations of the city's top sights. Their Museum Line, for example, cost €12.50, includes museum discounts, and stops near the Hermitage, Rijksmuseum/Van Gogh Museum, and Central Station (at least every 45 minutes, 4 stops, 1.5 hours). Sales booths in front of Central Station (and the boats) offer free brochures listing museum hours and admission prices. Most routes come with recorded narration and run daily 10:00-17:30 (tel. 020/530-1090, www.lovers.nl).

The similar **Canal Bus** is actually a boat, offering 14 stops on four different boat routes (€22/24-hour pass, departures daily 10:00-18:00, until 22:00 April-Oct, leaves near Central Station and Rederij Lovers dock, tel. 020/623-9886, www.canal.nl). They also run smaller tour boats with live commentary (see next page).

If you're simply looking for a floating, nonstop tour, the regular canal tour boats (without the stops) give more information, cover more ground, and cost less (see "Tours in Amsterdam," next page).

For do-it-yourself canal tours and lots of exercise, Canal Bus also rents "canal bikes" (a.k.a. paddleboats) at several locations: near the Anne Frank House, near the Rijksmuseum, near Leidseplein, and where Leidsestraat meets Keizersgracht (€8/hour per person, daily July-Aug 10:00-22:00, Sept-June 10:00-18:00).

By Taxi

For short rides, Amsterdam is a bad town for taxis. Given the good tram system and ease of biking, I use taxis less in Amsterdam than in just about any other city in Europe. The city's taxis have a high drop charge (€7.50) for the first two kilometers (e.g., from Central Station to the Mint Tower), after which it's €2.30 per kilometer (no extra fee for luggage; it's worth trying to bargain a lower rate, as competition among cabbies is fierce). You can wave them down, find a rare taxi stand, or call one (tel. 020/677-7777). You'll also see **bike taxis,** particularly near Dam Square and Leidseplein. Negotiate a rate for the trip before you board (no meter), and they'll wheel you wherever you want to go (€1/3 minutes, no surcharge for baggage or extra weight, sample fare from Leidseplein to Anne Frank House: about €6).

Tours in Amsterdam

By Boat

▲▲**Canal Boat Tours**—These long, low, tourist-laden boats leave continually from several docks around town for a relaxing, if unin-

spiring, one-hour introduction to the city (with recorded headphone commentary). Select a boat tour for convenience based on the starting point, or if a particular tour is free and included with the I amsterdam Card (which covers Blue Boat Company and Holland International boats). Tip: Boats leave only when full, so jump on a full boat to avoid waiting at the dock. Choose from one of these three companies:

Rondvaart Kooij is cheapest (€8.50, 3/hour in summer 10:00-22:00, 2/hour in winter 10:00-17:00, at corner of Spui and Rokin streets, about 10 minutes from Dam Square, tel. 020/623-3810, www.rederijkooij.nl).

Blue Boat Company's boats depart from near Leidseplein (€13; every half-hour April-Sept 10:00-18:00, also at 19:00; hourly Oct-March 10:00-17:00, 1.25 hours, Stadhouderskade 30, tel. 020/679-1370, www.blueboat.nl). Their 90-minute evening cruise has a live English-speaking guide (€15, nightly at 20:00, April-Sept also at 21:00 and 22:00, reservations required).

Holland International offers a standard one-hour trip and a variety of longer tours (€13, 1-hour "100 Highlights" tour with recorded commentary, 4/hour daily 9:00-22:00, 2/hour after 18:00; tel. 020/625-3035, www.hir.nl). Their €18, 90-minute "ultimate" tour with a live guide leaves twice daily (at 11:00 and 13:00).

No fishing allowed—but bring your camera. Some prefer to cruise at night, when the bridges are illuminated.

Hop-On, Hop-Off Canal Boats—Small, 12-person electric Canal Hopper boats leave every 20-30 minutes with live commentary on two different hop-on, hop-off routes (€22 day pass, €17 round-trip ticket, July-Aug daily 10:00-17:00, Sept-June Fri-Sun only, "yellow" west route runs 2/hour and stops near Anne Frank House and Rijksmuseum, less-frequent "orange" east route runs 3/hour and stops near Red Light District and Damrak, tel. 020/535-3303, www.canal.nl).

Wetlands Safari, Nature Canoe Tours near Amsterdam—If you want some exercise and a dose of the *polder* country and village life, consider this five-hour tour. Majel Tromp, a friendly villager who speaks great English, takes groups limited to 15 people. The program: Meet at the bus stops behind Central Station (leave the station from the west corridor and take the escalator up to the buses) at 9:30, catch a public bus, stop for coffee, take a 3.5-hour canoe trip (2-3 people per canoe) with several stops, tour a village by canoe, munch a rural canalside picnic lunch (included), then canoe and bus back into Amsterdam by 15:00 (€43, €3 discount with this book, May-mid-Sept Sun-Fri, reservations required, tel. 020/686-3445, mobile 06-5355-2669, www.wetlandssafari.nl, info@wetlandssafari.nl).

On Foot

Red Light District Tours—For a stroll through Amsterdam's most infamous neighborhood, consider my self-guided Red Light District Walk on page 99. But if you'd be more comfortable exploring with a group, a guided tour is a good way to go. **Randy Roy's Red Light Tours** consists of one expat American woman, Kimberley. She lived in the Red Light District for years and gives fun, casual, yet informative 90-minute walks through this fascinating and eye-popping neighborhood. And though the actual information is light, you'll walk through various porn and drug shops and have an expert to answer your questions. Call or email to reserve (€12.50 includes a drink in a colorful bar at the end, nightly at 20:00, Fri and Sat also at 22:00, no tours Dec-Feb, tours meet in front of Victoria Hotel—in front of Central Station, mobile 06-4185-3288, www.randyroysredlighttours.com, kimberley@randyroysredlighttours.com).

Free City Walk—**New Europe Tours** "employs" native, English-speaking students to give these irreverent and entertaining three-hour walks (using the same "free tour, ask for tips, sell their other tours" formula popular in so many great European cities). This long walk covers a lot of the city with an enthusiasm for the contemporary pot-and-prostitution scene (free, daily at 11:15 and 13:15,

just show up at the National Monument on Dam Square, www
.neweuropetours.eu).

Adam's Apple Tours—This walking tour offers a two-hour,
English-only look at the historic roots and development of
Amsterdam. You'll have a small group of generally 5-6 people and
a caring guide, starting off at Central Station and ending up at
Dam Square (€25; May-Sept daily at 10:00, 12:30, and 15:00 based
on demand; call 020/616-7867 to confirm times and book, www
.adamsapple.nl, Frank).

Private Guide—**Albert Walet** is a likeable, hardworking, and
knowledgeable local guide who enjoys personalizing tours for
Americans interested in knowing his city. "Ab" specializes in history and architecture, and exudes a passion for Amsterdam (€59/2
hours, €99/4 hours, up to 4 people, on foot or by bike, mobile
06-2069-7882, abwalet@yahoo.com). Ab also takes travelers to
nearby towns, including Haarlem, Leiden, and Delft.

By Bike

The **Yellow Bike Guided Tours** company offers city bike tours of
either two hours (€18.50, daily at 10:30) or three hours (€21.50,
daily at 13:30), which both include a 20-minute break. They also
offer a four-hour, 15-mile tour of the dikes and green pastures of
the countryside (€27.50, lunch extra, includes 45-minute break,
April-Oct daily at 19:30). All tours leave from Nieuwezijds Kolk
29, three blocks from Central Station (reservations smart, tel.
020/620-6940, www.yellowbike.nl). If you take one of their tours,
you can rent the bike for the rest of the day at a 50 percent discount
(€10/24 hours, ID and either €100 deposit or credit-card imprint
required). If you'd prefer a private guide, see Albert Walet, above.

Do-It-Yourself Bike Tour of Amsterdam—A day enjoying the
bridges, bike lanes, and sleepy, off-the-beaten-path canals on your
own one-speed is an essential Amsterdam experience. The real
joys of Europe's best-preserved 17th-century city are the countless intimate glimpses it offers: the laid-back locals sunning on

their porches under elegant gables,
rusted bikes that look as if they've
been lashed to the same lamppost
since the 1960s, wasted hedonists
planted on canalside benches, and
happy sailors permanently moored,
but still manning the deck.

For a good day trip, rent a
bike at or near Central Station (see
"By Bike" on page 48). Head west
down Haarlemmerstraat, working your wide-eyed way down the
Prinsengracht (drop into Café 't Papeneiland at Prinsengracht 2)

and detouring through the small, gentrified streets of the Jordaan neighborhood before popping out at Westerkerk under the tallest spire in the city.

Pedal south to the lush and peaceful Vondelpark, then cut back through the center of town (Leidseplein to the Mint Tower, along Rokin street to Dam Square). From there, cruise the Red Light District, following Oudezijds Voorburgwal past the Old Church (Oude Kerk) to Zeedijk street, and return to the train station.

Then, you can escape into the countryside by hopping on the free ferry behind Central Station (see below). In five minutes, Amsterdam will be gone, and you'll be rolling through your very own Dutch painting.

Taking Bikes Across the Harbor on a Free Ferry—Behind Central Station is a little commuter port where four ferries come and go constantly (free, bikes welcome, signs count down minutes until next departure), offering two quick little excursions. The middle two ferries run immediately across the harbor (3-minute ride). Bring your bike and ride two kilometers (1.25 miles) along the canal, through suburbs, and then into the *polderland* and villages.

Ferries leaving from the far-left "NDSM" wharf cruise 10 minutes across the North Sea Canal (2/hour, generally departing at :15 and :45). This gives a fun look at the fifth-biggest harbor in Europe (Rotterdam is number one); old wheat silos now renovated into upscale condos; and the shoreline of north Amsterdam, where the planned metro connection to the center is bringing growth, with lots of new apartments under construction. The ferry deposits you in an industrial wasteland (a vacant old warehouse just past the modern MTV headquarters building is filled with artist studios, wacky ventures, and a noisy skateboard hall). **IJ-Kantine** is a fine modern restaurant/café 30 yards from the ferry landing (daily from 9:00, tel. 020/633-7162).

By Public Minibus

For a quick, do-it-yourself public-bus tour along scenic Prinsengracht, catch Amsterdam's cute little Stop/Go minibus (€1, tickets valid one hour, buy from driver, transit passes valid, daily 9:00-17:30, 8 seats, can be muggy on hot days, www.gvb.nl).

It arcs along the city's longest canal, offering clever budget travelers a very cheap and fun 20-minute experience that's faster than a touristy canal tour. The scenic bus ride goes where normal big buses can't fit (along the bumpy and cobbled canalside lanes), giving you a delightful look at the workaday city. The high ride, comfortable seats, and big windows show you Amsterdam well.

The Stop/Go route follows the outside of the canal counterclockwise and returns clockwise along the inside. The buses have only four set stops (in front of the Central Library, at the river docks behind Central Station, at the main/west entrance of Central Station, and near the opera house/City Hall—Stopera—on Waterlooplein)—but you can just wave one down from anywhere on the route. Grab a seat in the back for the best view. If you see something fun, just jump out—there's another bus in 12 minutes. If the bus hits construction on Prinsengracht, it veers to the next street over, then heads back to the canal as soon as possible.

For this short tour, catch the bus at Central Station. From the station, the minibus passes characteristic cafés in the Jordaan district, countless houseboats, and the whole gamut of gables (under a parade of leaning, Golden Age buildings complete with all the hooks and pulleys). Rolling along the Prinsengracht, you'll see the long line at the Anne Frank House just before the towering Westerkerk. You'll pass within a block of the thriving Leidseplein and Rijksmuseum (look to the right at Spiegelgracht) before passing Rembrandtplein (with its fun 3-D *Night Watch* statues) and crossing the Amstel River to finish at the Waterlooplein flea market, near Rembrandt's House, Gassan Diamonds, and the metro station (subway trains run every 2 minutes, returning you to Central Station in 3 minutes).

From the bus, watch for these little bits of Amsterdam:

- green metal public urinals
- late 19th-century lamp poles
- bikes chained to anything unmovable (including the practical new "staple" design bike racks)
- *amsterdammertjes* ("little Amsterdammers," referring to the countless little dark-red bollards—bearing the city's emblem of three diagonal crosses—that protect walkers from passing traffic)
- underground recycling and garbage bins designed to keep workers from having to dump out bins into trucks (a law prohibits employees from lifting anything over 25 kilos—about 55 pounds)
- "*ja*" and "*nee*" stickers on mail slots, indicating whether residents accept junk mail and advertising (The cool people of the Jordaan are mostly "*nee nee*.")

SIGHTS IN AMSTERDAM

One of Amsterdam's delights is that it has perhaps more small specialty museums than any other city its size. From houseboats to sex, from marijuana to Old Masters, you can find a museum to suit your interests.

For tips on how to save time otherwise spent in the long ticket-buying lines of the big three museums—the Anne Frank House, Van Gogh Museum, and Rijksmuseum—see "Advance Tickets and Sightseeing Cards" on page 42. Admission prices are high: A sightseeing card such as the Museumkaart (or I amsterdam Card) can pay for itself quickly. Entry to most sights is free with a card (I've noted those that aren't covered).

Most museums require baggage check (usually free, often in coin-op lockers where you get your coin back).

The following sights are arranged by neighborhood for handy sightseeing. When you see a ✪ in a listing, it means the sight is covered in much more depth in one of my walks or self-guided tours. This is why Amsterdam's most important attractions get the least coverage in this chapter—we'll explore them later in the book.

Southwest Amsterdam

▲▲▲Rijksmuseum—Built to house the nation's great art, the Rijksmuseum (RIKES-moo-zay-oom) owns several thousand paintings, including an incomparable collection of Dutch Masters: Rembrandt, Vermeer, Hals, and Steen. The museum makes it easy for you to focus on the highlights, because that's all that is on display while most of the building undergoes several years of renovation (due to wrap up in early 2013). You'll be able to wander through a wonderful, concentrated dose of 17th-century Dutch masterpieces in the Philips Wing.

Amsterdam

¼ MILE
400 METERS

TO WATERLAND, ZAANSE SCHANS & ALKMAAR

HARBOR

TO NDSM PIER

'IJ RIVER

CENTRAL STATION

CITY LIBRARY

MARITIME MUSEUM (REOPENS LATE 2011)

VOC SHIP

OOSTERDOK

NEMO

TO HAARLEM

PRINS HENDRIKKADE

PRINS HENDRIKKADE

TO DUTCH RESISTANCE MUSEUM

PRINSEN · KEIZERS · HEREN · SINGEL

DAMRAK

Old Church

RED LIGHT DISTRICT

REMBRANDT HOUSE

MUIDER.

ANNE FRANK HOUSE

New Church

JODEN · BREEN

WATERLOO-PLEIN

HEMP MUSEUM

OPERA

HERMI-TAGE AMST.

JORDAAN

WESTER-KERK

RAADHUIS STR.

Royal PAL.

KALVER

HOOGSTR.

ROKIN

DAM

AMSTEL

HOUSE-BOAT MUSEUM

AMSTERDAM MUSEUM

WILL-HOL MUSEUM?

BEGIJNHOF

SPUI STRAAT

MUNT-PLEIN

TASSEN MUSEUM

UTRECHTSE STR.

"NINE LITTLE STREETS" SHOPS

LEIDSESTRAAT

SPIEGEL STR.

SINGEL GRACHT

LEIDSE

LEIDSE-PLEIN

KADE

STADHOUDERSKADE

HEINEKEN EXP.

~ MAJOR CANALS

⋯ OTHER WATER

B CANAL BOAT DEPARTURE POINT

← VIEW

VAN

VONDEL

House of Bols

BAERLESTR.

PAUL POTTER

RIJKS-MUSEUM

DE PIJP DISTRICT

MUSEUM-PLEIN

Van Gogh Museum

PARK

VONDEL PAVILION

STEDELIJK MUSEUM

DCH

Cost and Hours: €12.50, audioguide-€5, daily 9:00-18:00, last entry 30 minutes before closing, tram #2 or #5 from Central Station to Hobbemastraat. Info tel. 020/674-7047 or switchboard tel. 020/674-7000, www.rijksmuseum.nl. The Philips Wing entrance is near the corner of Hobbemastraat and Jan Luijkenstraat, on the south side of the Rijksmuseum—the part of the huge building nearest the Van Gogh Museum.

✪ See the Rijksmuseum Tour chapter.

▲▲▲**Van Gogh Museum**—Near the Rijksmuseum, this remark-able museum features works by the troubled Dutch artist whose art seemed to mirror his life.

Vincent, who killed himself in 1890 at age 37, is best known for sunny, Impressionist can-vases that vibrate and pulse with life. The museum's 200 paintings—a stroll through the artist's work and life—were owned by Theo, Vincent's younger, art-dealer brother. Highlights include *Sunflowers, The Bedroom, The Potato Eaters,* and many brooding self-portraits. The third floor shows works that influenced Vincent, from Monet and Pissarro to Gauguin, Cézanne, and Toulouse-Lautrec. While the museum's closed between October 2012 and March 2013, most of its high-lights will be on display at the nearby Hermitage Amsterdam (see page 74).

Cost and Hours: €14, more for special exhibits, worthwhile audioguide-€5, kids' audioguide-€2.50, daily 10:00-18:00, Fri until 22:00—with no crowds in evening, Paulus Potterstraat 7, tram #2 or #5 from Central Station to Van Baerlestraat Stop, tel. 020/570-5200, www.vangoghmuseum.nl.

✪ See the Van Gogh Museum Tour chapter.

▲▲**Stedelijk Museum**—After a long renovation project, the Stedelijk (STAYD-eh-lik) is expected to reopen in late 2011 in its spiffed-up building, which now flaunts an architecturally daring new entry facing Museumplein (near the Van Gogh Museum). The Netherlands' top modern-art museum, its fun, far-out, and

refreshing collection includes post-1945 experimental and conceptual art as well as works by Picasso, Chagall, Cézanne, Kandinsky, and Mondrian.

Cost and Hours: Likely €12, Tue-Sun 10:00-17:00, possibly Thu until 22:00, possibly open Mon, check website for reopening date and exact price and hours, café with outdoor seating, top-notch shop, Paulus Potterstraat 13/ Museumplein 10, tel. 020/573-2911, www.stedelijk.nl.

▲**Museumplein**—Bordered by the Rijks, Van Gogh, and Stedelijk museums, and the Concertgebouw (classical music hall), this park-like square is interesting even to art-haters. Amsterdam's best acoustics are found underneath the Rijksmuseum, where street musicians perform everything from chamber music to Mongolian throat singing. Mimes, human statues, and crafts booths dot the square. Skateboarders careen across a concrete tube, while locals enjoy a park bench or a coffee at the Cobra Café.

Nearby is **Coster Diamonds,** a handy place to see a diamond-cutting and polishing demo (free, frequent, and interesting

30-minute tours followed by sales pitch, popular for decades with tour groups, prices marked up to include tour guide kickbacks, daily 9:00-17:00, Paulus Potterstraat 2, tel. 020/305-5555, www.costerdiamonds.com). The end of the tour leads you straight into their Diamond Museum, which is worthwhile only for those who have a Museumkaart (which covers entry) or feel the need to see even more diamonds (€7.50, daily 10:00-17:00, tel. 020/305-5300, www.diamantmuseumamsterdam.nl). The tour at **Gassan Diamonds** is free and better (see page 73), but Coster is convenient to the Museumplein scene.

SIGHTS IN AMSTERDAM

House of Bols: Cocktail & Genever Experience—This leading Dutch distillery runs a pricey and polished little museum/marketing opportunity across the street from the Van Gogh Museum. The "experience" is a self-guided walk through what is essentially an ad for Bols—"four hundred years of working on the art of mixing and blending...a celebration of gin"—with some fun sniffing opportunities and a drink at a modern, mirrored-out cocktail bar for a finale. (It's essentially the gin-flavored version of the Heineken Experience, listed next.) The highlight is a chance to taste up to five different local gins with a talkative expert guiding you. Then have your barista mix up the cocktail of your dreams—based on what you learned during your sniffing.

Cost and Hours: €11.50, not covered by Museumkaart, Wed-Mon 12:00-18:45, Fri until 22:45, closed Tue, last entry 45 minutes before closing, must be 18, Paulus Potterstraat 14, tel. 020/570-8575, www.houseofbols.com. If you like the booze and hang out and talk, this can be a good deal (but do it after the Van Gogh Museum).

Heineken Experience—This famous old brewery welcomes visitors to a slick and entertaining beer-appreciation fest. It's a fun

Southwest Amsterdam

100 YARDS
100 METERS

TO MINT TOWER
& DAM SQUARE

LEIDSEPLEIN

VONDEL-
PARK

RIJKS-
MUSEUM

PHILIPS
WING

To
HEINEKEN
Experience

VONDEL
PAVILION

COSTER
DIAMONDS
+ MUSEUM

House of
BOLS

MUSEUM-
PLEIN

COBRA
CAFÉ

STEDELIJK
MUSEUM

VAN GOGH
MUSEUM

US
CONSULATE

DE PIJP
DISTRICT

CONCERT-
GEBOUW

B BOAT TOURS   --- PATH
🚊 TRAM 2+5 STOP   ◆ ENTRY POINT TO SIGHTS

trip, if you can ignore the fact that you're essentially paying for an hour of advertising (€15, includes two drinks, daily 11:00-19:00, last entry at 17:30; tram #16, #24, or #25 to Heinekenplein; an easy walk from Rijksmuseum, tel. 020/523-9222, www.heineken experience.com).

De Pijp District—This former working-class industrial and residential zone (behind the Heineken Experience, near the Rijksmuseum) is emerging as a colorful, vibrant district. Its spine is Albert Cuypstraat, a street taken over by a long, sprawling produce market packed with interesting people. The centerpiece is **Restaurant Bazar** (marked by a roof-capping golden angel), a church turned into a Middle Eastern food circus (see listing on page 196).

▲**Leidseplein**—Brimming with cafés, this people-watching mecca is an impromptu stage for street artists, accordionists, jugglers, and unicyclists. It's particularly bustling on sunny afternoons. The Boom Chicago theater fronts this square (see the Entertainment in Amsterdam chapter). Stroll nearby Lange Leidsedwarsstraat (one block north) for a taste-bud tour of ethnic eateries, from Greek to Indonesian.

▲▲**Vondelpark**—This huge, lively city park is popular with the Dutch—families with little kids, romantic couples, strolling seniors, and hippies sharing blankets and beers. It's a favored venue for free summer concerts. On a sunny afternoon, it's a hedonistic scene that seems to say, "Parents...relax."

Rembrandtplein and Tuschinski Theater—One of the city's premier nightlife spots is the leafy Rembrandtplein (the artist's statue stands here, along with a jaunty group of statues giving us *The Night Watch* in 3-D) and the adjoining Thorbeckeplein. Several late-night dance clubs keep the area lively into the wee hours. Utrechtsestraat is lined with upscale shops and restaurants. Nearby Reguliersdwarsstraat (a street one block south of Rembrandtplein) is a center for gay and lesbian nightclubs.

The **Tuschinski Theater,** a movie palace from the 1920s (a half-block from Rembrandtplein down Reguliersbreestraat),

glitters inside and out. Still a working theater, it's a delightful old place to see first-run movies. The exterior is an interesting hybrid of styles, forcing the round peg of Art Nouveau into the square hole of Art Deco. The stone-and-tile facade features stripped-down, functional Art Deco squares and rectangles, but is ornamented with Art Nouveau elements—Tiffany-style windows, garlands, curvy iron lamps, Egyptian pharaohs, and exotic gold lettering over the door. Inside (lobby is free), the sumptuous decor features red carpets, nymphs on the walls, and semi-abstract designs. Grab a seat in the lobby and watch the ceiling morph (Reguliersbreestraat 26-28).

Amsterdam at a Glance

▲▲▲**Rijksmuseum** Best collection anywhere of the Dutch Masters: Rembrandt, Hals, Vermeer, and Steen. **Hours:** Daily 9:00-18:00. See page 56.

▲▲▲**Van Gogh Museum** 200 paintings by the angst-ridden artist. **Hours:** Daily 10:00-18:00, Fri until 22:00. See page 58.

▲▲▲**Anne Frank House** Young Anne's hideaway during the Nazi occupation. **Hours:** March 15-Sept 14 daily 9:00-21:00, Sat and July-Aug until 22:00; Sept 15-March 14 daily 9:00-19:00, Sat until 21:00. See page 64.

▲▲**Vondelpark** City park and concert venue. **Hours:** Always open. See page 61.

▲▲**Amsterdam Museum** City's growth from fishing village to trading capital to today, including some Rembrandts and a playable carillon. **Hours:** Mon-Fri 10:00-17:00, Sat-Sun 11:00-17:00. See page 66.

▲▲**Dutch Resistance Museum** History of the Dutch struggle against the Nazis. **Hours:** Tue-Fri 10:00-17:00, Sat-Mon 11:00-17:00. See page 78.

▲▲**Amstelkring Museum** Catholic church hidden in the attic of a 17th-century merchant's house. **Hours:** Mon-Sat 10:00-17:00, Sun and holidays 13:00-17:00. See page 66.

▲▲**Stedelijk Museum** The Netherlands' top modern-art museum, due to reopen after renovation in late 2011. **Hours:** Tue-Sun 10:00-17:00, possibly Thu until 22:00, possibly open Mon. See page 58.

▲▲**Red Light District** Women of the world's oldest profession on the job. **Hours:** Best from noon into the evening; avoid late at night. See page 68.

▲**Museumplein** Square with art museums, street musicians, crafts, and nearby diamond demos. **Hours:** Always open. See page 59.

▲**Leidseplein** Lively square with cafés and street musicians. **Hours:** Always open, best on sunny afternoons. See page 61.

▲**Begijnhof** Quiet courtyard lined with picturesque houses. **Hours:** Daily 8:00-17:00. See page 66.

▲**Rembrandt's House** The master's reconstructed house, displaying his etchings. **Hours:** Daily 10:00-17:00. See page 72.

▲**Diamond Tours** Offered at shops throughout the city. **Hours:** Generally daily 9:00-17:00. See page 73.

▲**Willet-Holthuysen Museum** Elegant 17th-century house. **Hours:** Mon-Fri 10:00-17:00, Sat-Sun 11:00-17:00. See page 73.

▲**Hermitage Amsterdam** Russia's Tsarist treasures, on loan from St. Petersburg. **Hours:** Daily 10:00-17:00, Wed until 20:00. See page 74.

▲**Jewish Historical Museum** The Great Synagogue and exhibits on Judaism and culture. **Hours:** Daily 11:00-17:00. See page 75.

▲**Dutch Theater** Moving memorial in former Jewish detention center. **Hours:** Daily 11:00-16:00. See page 77.

▲**Tropical Museum** Re-creations of tropical-life scenes. **Hours:** Tue-Sun 10:00-17:00, closed Mon. See page 79.

▲**Hash, Marijuana, and Hemp Museum** All the dope, from history and science to memorabilia. **Hours:** Daily 10:00-23:00. See page 69.

Heineken Experience Mini-brewery and tasting bar. **Hours:** Daily 11:00-19:00. See page 59.

House of Bols: The Cocktail & Genever Experience Gin museum culminating in a cocktail bar. **Hours:** Wed-Mon 12:00-18:45, Fri until 22:45, closed Tue. See page 59.

Houseboat Museum (Woonbootmuseum)—In the 1930s, modern cargo ships came into widespread use—making small, sail-powered cargo boats obsolete. In danger of extinction, these little vessels found new life as houseboats lining the canals of Amsterdam. Today, 2,500 such boats—their cargo holds turned into classy, comfortable living rooms—are called home. For a peek into this *gezellig* (cozy) world, visit this tiny museum. Captain Vincent enjoys showing visitors around the houseboat, which feels lived-in because, until 1997, it was.

Cost and Hours: €3.50, not covered by Museumkaart; March-Oct Tue-Sun 11:00-17:00, closed Mon; Nov-Dec and Feb Fri-Sun 11:00-17:00, closed Mon-Thu; closed most of Jan; on Prinsengracht, opposite #296 facing Elandsgracht, tel. 020/427-0750, www.houseboatmuseum.nl.

West Amsterdam

▲▲▲**Anne Frank House**—A pilgrimage for many, this house offers a fascinating look at the hideaway of young Anne during the Nazi occupation of the Netherlands. Anne, her parents, an older sister, and four others spent a little more than two years in a "Secret Annex" behind her father's business. While in hiding, 13-year-old Anne kept a diary chronicling her extraordinary experience. Acting on a tip, the Nazis arrested the group in August of 1944 and sent them to concentration camps in Poland and Germany. Anne and her sister died of typhus in March of 1945, only weeks before their camp was liberated. Of the eight inhabitants of the Secret Annex, only Anne's father, Otto Frank, survived. He returned to Amsterdam and arranged for his daughter's diary to be published in 1947. It was followed by many translations, a play, and a movie.

Pick up the English pamphlet at the door. The thoughtfully designed exhibit offers thorough coverage of the Frank family, the diary, the stories of others who hid, and the Holocaust. It may be less crowded right when it opens or after 18:00.

Cost and Hours: €8.50, not covered by I amsterdam Card; March 15-Sept 14 daily 9:00-21:00, Sat and July-Aug until 22:00; Sept 15-March 14 daily 9:00-19:00, Sat until 21:00; last entry 30 minutes before closing, no baggage check, no large bags allowed inside, Prinsengracht 267, near Westerkerk, tel. 020/556-7100, www.annefrank.org.

✪ See the Anne Frank House Tour chapter.

Westerkerk—Located near the Anne Frank House, this land-mark church (free, generally open April-Sept Mon-Sat 11:00-15:00, closed Sun) has a barren interior, Rembrandt's body buried somewhere under the pews, and Amsterdam's tallest steeple.

The tower is open only for tours and offers a grand city view. The tour guide, who speaks English and Dutch, tells of the church and its carillon. Only six people are allowed at a time (it's first-come, first-served), so lines can be long (€6, 30-minute tour; departures on the half hour April-Sept Mon-Sat 10:00-18:00, July-Aug until 20:00, last tour leaves at 30 minutes before closing, closed Sun; Oct-March tourable only with a private tour—call 020/689-2565 or email anna@buscher-malocca.nl).

Central Amsterdam, near Dam Square

Royal Palace (Koninklijk Huis)—This palace was built as a lavish City Hall (1648-1655), when Holland was a proud new republic and Amsterdam was the richest city on the planet—awash in profit from trade. The building became a "Royal Palace" when Napoleon installed his brother Louis as king (1806). After Napoleon's fall, it continued as a royal residence for the Dutch royal family, the House of Orange. Today, it's one of four of Queen Beatrix's official residences. You can tour the interior and see several lavishly decorated rooms of chandeliers, paintings, statues, and furniture that reflect Amsterdam's former status as the center of global trade.

The huge, white central hall (Gallery or Citizens' Hall) is the palace's highlight—120 feet by 60 feet by 90 feet—and is lit by eight big chandeliers. At the far end, a statue of Atlas holds the globe of the world, and the ceiling painting shows Amsterdam triumphant amid the clouds of heaven. On the floor, inlaid maps show the known world circa 1750 (back when the West Coast of the US was still being explored). The hall is used today for hosting foreign dignitaries and for the royal family's wedding receptions.

The central hall leads directly to Room 1, where Louis Bonaparte's throne once sat in front of the fireplace. Room 2 has his era's Empire Style furniture (unornamented, high-polished wood, with Neoclassical motifs). Room 3 was then-Princess Beatrix's bedroom (1939-80).

Room 7, which overlooks Dam Square, is where the council of ex-mayors would meet every year to elect the four new burgomasters, who governed the city. The paintings over the fireplace, by Rembrandt's pupils, show righteous Romans whom Golden Age Amsterdammers modeled themselves after. Room 8 was the burgomasters' office, Room 11 is where the city council met, and Room 12 is still used as the guest bedroom for visiting dignitaries.

Cost and Hours: €7.50, daily 12:00-17:00 but often closed for official business—check calendar on website, tel. 020/620-4060, www.paleisamsterdam.nl.

✪ See page 85 of the Amsterdam City Walk chapter.

New Church (Nieuwe Kerk)—Barely newer than the "Old" Church (located in the Red Light District), this 15th-century sanctuary has an intentionally dull interior, after the decoration was removed by 16th-century iconoclastic Protestants seeking to unclutter their communion with God. This is where many Dutch royal weddings and all coronations take place. There's usually a steep entrance fee due to popular temporary exhibitions (€8; daily 10:00-17:00, Thu until 22:00, on Dam Square, info tel. 020/353-8168, tel. 020/638-6909, www.nieuwekerk.nl).

✪ See page 86 of the Amsterdam City Walk chapter.

▲Begijnhof—Stepping into this tiny, idyllic courtyard in the city center, you escape into the charm of old Amsterdam. (Please be considerate of the people who live around the courtyard, and don't photograph the residents or their homes.) Notice house #34, a 500-year-old wooden structure (rare, since repeated fires taught city fathers a trick called brick). Peek into the hidden Catholic church, dating from the time when post-Reformation Dutch Catholics couldn't worship in public. It's opposite the English Reformed church, where the Pilgrims worshipped while waiting for their voyage to the New World—marked by a plaque near the door.

Cost and Hours: Free, open to visitors Mon-Tue and Thu-Sat—see website for sporadic hours—and Sun for church service in English at 10:30, closed Wed, on Begijnensteeg lane, just off Kalverstraat between #130 and #132, pick up flier at office near entrance, www.ercadam.nl.

✪ See page 90 of the Amsterdam City Walk chapter.

▲▲Amsterdam Museum (Amsterdams Historisch Museum)—Follow the city's growth from fishing village to world trade center to hippie haven. Housed in a 500-year-old former orphanage, this creative museum features Rembrandt's paintings, good English descriptions, and a carillon loft. The loft comes with push-button recordings of the town bell tower's greatest hits and a self-serve carillon "keyboard" that lets you ring a few bells yourself. The museum's free pedestrian corridor—lined with old-time group portraits—is a powerful teaser. This museum is a fine place to buy the Museumkaart, and then use it to skip long lines at the Van Gogh Museum (for details, see page 43).

Cost and Hours: €10, good audioguide-€4.50, Mon-Fri 10:00-17:00, Sat-Sun 11:00-17:00, pleasant restaurant, next to Begijnhof, Kalverstraat 92, tel. 020/523-1822, www.ahm.nl.

✪ See the Amsterdam Museum Tour chapter.

Red Light District

▲▲Amstelkring Museum (Our Lord in the Attic/Museum Ons' Lieve Heer op Solder)—Although Amsterdam has long been known for its tolerant attitudes, 16th-century politics forced Dutch Catholics to worship discreetly. Near the train station in the Red Light District, you'll find a fascinating, hidden Catholic church filling the attic of three 17th-century merchants' houses.

Central Amsterdam

CENTRAL STATION

BIKE GARAGE

BIKE RENTAL

CITY LIBRARY

SHOPS

VVV

PRINS-HENDRIK-KADE

OOSTER-DOK

DAMRAK SEX MUSEUM

ST. NICHOLAS CHURCH

YELLOW BIKE TOURS

ZEEDIJK

PRINS-HENDRIKKADE

SPUISTRAAT

NIEUWEZIJDS VOORBURG.

DIJK

VOORBURG.

AMSTEL-KRING MUSEUM

TO NEMO & VOC SHIP

BEURS

STRAAT

OLD CHURCH

EROTIC MUSEUM

NEW CHURCH

DAMRAK

NIEUWEN-

WARMOES-

RED LIGHT DISTRICT

NIEUW-MARKT

SINT JANS

HEMP MUSEUM

OUDEZIJDS ACHTER-BURGWAL

ROYAL PALACE

DAM

DAM STRAAT

REMBRANDTS HOUSE

TO ANNE FRANK HOUSE & JORDAAN DISTRICT

KALVERSTRAAT

ROKIN

OUDEZIJDS VOOR-BURGWAL

WATER-LOO-PLEIN

SPUI

OPERA

HISTORY MUSEUM

STR.

SPUI

AMSTEL

BEGIJNHOF

SPUI

ROKIN

WILLET-HOLTHUYSEN MUSEUM

HEREN-

TUSCHINSKI THEATER

HUIDEN-STRAAT

MINT TOWER

MUNT-PLEIN

GRACHT

SINGEL

FLOWER MARKET

REMBRANDT-PLEIN

TASSEN MUSEUM

TO LEIDSEPLEIN & RIJKSMUSEUM

200 YDS.

200 METERS

DCH

M METRO   **B** OPSTAPPER BUS   **B** BOAT TOURS   ⬱ VIEW

T TRAMS: #1 (TO LEIDSEPLEIN), #2 & #5 (TO MUSEUMPLEIN)

SIGHTS IN AMSTERDAM

Don't miss the silver collection and other exhibits of daily life from 300 years ago (€7, Mon-Sat 10:00-17:00, Sun and holidays 13:00-17:00, no photos, Oudezijds Voorburgwal 40, tel. 020/624-6604, www.opsolder.nl).

○ See the Amstelkring Museum Tour chapter.

▲▲**Red Light District**—Europe's most popular ladies of the night tease and tempt here, as they have for centuries, in 400 display-case windows around Oudezijds Achterburgwal and Oudezijds Voorburgwal, surrounding the Old Church (Oude Kerk, described below). Drunks and druggies make the streets uncomfortable late at night after the gawking tour groups leave (about 22:30), but it's a fascinating walk earlier in the evening.

The neighborhood, one of Amsterdam's oldest, has hosted prostitutes since 1200. Prostitution is entirely legal here, and the prostitutes are generally entrepreneurs, renting space and running their own businesses, as well as filling out tax returns and even paying union dues. Popular prostitutes net about €500 a day (for what's called "S&F" in its abbreviated, printable form, costing €25-50 per customer).

○ See the Red Light District Walk chapter.

Sex Museums—Amsterdam has two sex museums: one in the Red Light District and another one a block in front of Central Station on Damrak street. While visiting one can be called sightseeing, visiting both is hard to explain. The one on Damrak is cheaper and more interesting. Here's a comparison:

The **Erotic Museum** in the Red Light District is five floors of uninspired paintings, videos, old photos, and sculpture (€7, not covered by Museumkaart, daily 11:00-1:00 in the morning, along the canal at Oudezijds Achterburgwal 54, tel. 020/624-7303; see page 109).

The **Damrak Sex Museum** tells the story of pornography from Roman times through 1960. Every sexual deviation is revealed in various displays. The museum includes early French pornographic photos; memorabilia from Europe, India, and Asia; a Marilyn Monroe tribute; and some S&M displays (€4, not covered by Museumkaart, daily 9:30-23:30, Damrak 18, a block in front of Central Station, tel. 020/622-8376).

Old Church (Oude Kerk)—This 14th-century landmark—the needle around which the Red Light District spins—has served as a reassuring welcome-home symbol to sailors, a refuge to the downtrodden, an ideological battlefield of the Counter-Reformation, and, today, a tourist sight with a dull interior (€5, more for temporary exhibits, Mon-Sat 11:00-17:00, Sun 13:00-17:00, tel. 020/625-8284, www.oudekerk.nl). It's 167 steps to the top of the church tower (€6, April-Sept Mon-Sat 13:00-17:00, closed Oct-March).

○ See page 103 of the Red Light District Walk chapter.

▲**Hash, Marijuana, and Hemp Museum**—This is a collection of dope facts, history, science, and memorabilia. Though small, it has a very memorable finale: the high-tech grow room, in which dozens of varieties of marijuana are grown in optimal hydroponic (among other) environments. Some plants stand five feet tall and shine under the intense grow lamps. The view is actually through glass walls into the neighboring **Sensi Seed Bank Grow Shop** (at #150), which sells carefully cultivated seeds and all the gear needed to grow them (€9, not covered by Museumkaart, daily 10:00-23:00, Oudezijds Achterburgwal 148, tel. 020/623-5961, www.hash museum.com).

The nearby **Cannabis College** is "dedicated to ending the global war against the cannabis plant through public education" (free, daily 11:00-19:00, Oudezijds Achterburgwal 124, tel. 020/423-4420, www.cannabiscollege.com). For more, ✪ see the Red Light District Walk chapter and the Smoking chapter.

Northeast Amsterdam
Central Library (Openbare Bibliotheek Amsterdam)—This huge, multistory glass building holds almost 1,400 seats—many with wraparound views of the city—and hundreds of free Internet terminals (and free Wi-Fi, which requires signing up at the desk). It's the classiest possible place to check email. This library, which opened in 2007, demonstrates the Dutch people's dedication to a freely educated populace (the right to information, they point out, is enshrined in the UN's Universal Declaration of Human Rights). This being Amsterdam, the library has almost twice as many bike racks as parking places. Everything's relaxed and inviting, from the fun kids' zone and international magazine and newspaper section on the ground floor to the cafeteria, with its dramatic view-terrace dining on the top (La Place, €10 meals, salad bar, daily 10:00-21:00). The library is a 10-minute walk from the east end of Central Station (daily 10:00-22:00, tel. 020/523-0900, www.oba.nl).

NEMO (National Center for Science and Technology)—This kid-friendly science museum is a city landmark. Its distinctive

copper-green building, jutting up from the water like a sinking ship, has prompted critics to nickname it the *Titanic*. Designed by Italian architect Renzo Piano (known for Paris' Pompidou Center and Berlin's Sony Center complex on Potsdamer Platz), the building's shape reflects its nautical surroundings as well as the curve of the underwater tunnel it straddles.

Several floors feature permanent and rotating exhibits that allow kids (and adults) to explore topics such as light, sound, and gravity, and play with bubbles, topple giant dominoes, and draw with lasers. The museum's motto: "It's forbidden NOT to touch!" Whirring, room-size pinball machines reputedly teach kids about physics. English explanations are available.

Up top is a restaurant with a great city view, as well as a sloping terrace that becomes a popular "beach" in summer, complete with lounge chairs, a sandbox, and a lively bar. On the bottom floor is an inexpensive cafeteria offering €3-5 sandwiches.

Cost and Hours: €13.50, July-Aug daily 10:00-17:00, Sept-June generally closed Mon, Oosterdok 2, above entrance to IJ tunnel. Tel. 0900-919-1100—€0.35/minute, www.e-nemo.nl. It's a 15-minute walk from Central Station or bus #22, #42, or #43 to the Kadijksplein stop. The roof terrace—open until 19:30 in the summer—is generally free.

VOC Ship *Amsterdam*—The good ship *Amsterdam* moors near the Netherlands Maritime Museum (described next), welcoming kids (and kids at heart) to join its crew.

The *Amsterdam* is a replica of a type of ship called an East Indiaman, which had its heyday during the 17th and 18th centuries, sailing for the Dutch East India Company (abbreviated VOC, for Vereenigde Oostindische Compagnie—you'll see it on insignias throughout the boat). Even though trade was the name of the game, with scurvy thieves in the waters, ships such as the *Amsterdam* had to be prepared to defend themselves. You'll see plenty of muskets, as well as cannons and gunpowder kegs.

Wander the decks, then duck your head and check out the captain's and surgeon's quarters, packed with items they would have used. Don't forget to climb down into the hold. The ship is a little light on good historical information (be sure to pick up the free flier, which explains terminology like the difference between the poop deck and the quarterdeck), but it's still a shipshape sight that entertains naval history buffs as well as *Pirates of the Caribbean* fans.

Cost and Hours: Now that the Netherlands Maritime Museum has reopened (see next listing), the ship is likely covered under the museum's entry ticket, with the same opening hours (and contact information).

Netherlands Maritime Museum (Nederlands Scheepvaartmuseum)—This huge collection of model ships, maps, and sea-battle paintings—newly reopened after years of major renovations—fills the 300-year-old Dutch Navy Arsenal. Given the Dutch seafaring heritage, I expected a more interesting museum; let's hope the renovations have perked up the place enough to justify its steep entry fee (€15, daily 9:00-17:00, English explanations, bus #22 or #42 to Kattenburgerplein 1, tel. 020/523-2222, www.scheepvaart museum.nl).

Southeast Amsterdam

To reach the following sights from the train station, take tram #9 or #14. All of these sights (except the Tropical Museum) are close to one another and can easily be connected into an interesting walk—or, better yet, a bike ride. Several of the sights in southeast Amsterdam cluster near the large square, Waterlooplein, dominated by the modern opera house.

For an orientation, survey the neighborhood from the lamp-lined Blauwbrug ("Blue Bridge")—a modest, modern version of Paris' Pont Alexandre III. The bridge crosses the Amstel River. From this point, the river is channeled to form the city's canals.

Scan clockwise. The big, curved modern facade belongs to the opera house, commonly called the "Stopera," as it's the combo City Hall *(stadhuis)* and opera. Behind the Stopera are these sights (not visible from here, but described next): the Waterlooplein flea market, Rembrandt's House, and Gassan Diamonds. To the right of the Stopera are the twin gray steeples of the Moses and Aaron Church, which sits roughly in the center of the former Jewish Quarter.

Several Jewish sights cluster to the right of the Moses and Aaron Church: the Jewish Historical Museum, the Portuguese Synagogue, and the dockworker statue (a Holocaust memorial). Just east of those is the De Hortus Botanical Garden.

The cute little drawbridge, while not famous, is certainly photogenic. (Its traditional counterbalance design is so effective that even a child can lift the bridge.) Beyond that is the gigantic Hermitage Amsterdam (it takes up an entire city block). Crossing the Amstel upstream is one of the city's romantic spots, the Magere Brug ("Skinny Bridge"). A block away is the city's best look at a Dutch Golden Age mansion, the Willet-Holthuysen Museum (a.k.a. Herengracht Canal Mansion).

Waterlooplein Flea Market—For more than a hundred years, the Jewish Quarter flea market has raged daily except Sunday (at the Waterlooplein metro station, behind Rembrandt's House). The long, narrow park is filled with stalls selling cheap clothes, hippie stuff, old records, tourist

Southeast Amsterdam

TO RED LIGHT DISTRICT

TO NEMO, VOC SHIP, MARITIME MUSEUM & IJ TUNNEL

REMBRANDT'S HOUSE

GASSAN DIAMONDS

UILENBURGERGRACHT

VALKENBURGERSTRAAT

ENTREPOTDOK

FLEA MARKET

WATERLOO-PLEIN

MOSES + AARON CHURCH

VALKENBURGERGRACHT

HERENGRACHT

WERT-HEIM PARK

RESISTANCE MUSEUM

❸

KERK-LAAN

OPERA

❶

M B

MR. VISSER-PLEIN

MUIDERSTRAAT

NIEUWE

PLANTAGE-MIDDEN

PLANTAGE

❹

ARTIS ZOO

JEWISH HISTORY MUSEUM

M

DOCK-WORKER STATUE

WEESPER-

HORTUS BOTANICAL GARDEN

DUTCH THEATER MEMORIAL

PLANTAGE LAAN

BLAUWBRUG

DRAW-BRIDGE

A.M.

TO REMBRANDT-PLEIN

HERMITAGE AMSTERDAM

STRAAT

NIEUWE KEIZERSGR.

TO TROPICAL MUSEUM & ❷

TO MAGERE (SKINNY) BRIDGE

DCH

200 YARDS

200 METERS

M METRO   B STOP/GO BUS

⬆ ENTRY POINT TO SIGHTS

❶ To Stayokay Stadsdoelen Hostel   ❸ Restaurant Plancius

❷ To Stayokay Zeeburg Hostel   ❹ Café Koosje

SIGHTS IN AMSTERDAM

knickknacks, and garage-sale junk.

▲**Rembrandt's House (Museum Het Rembrandt-huis)**—A middle-aged Rembrandt lived here from 1639 to 1658 after his

wife's death, as his popularity and wealth dwindled down to obscurity and bankruptcy. As you enter, ask when the next etching demonstration is scheduled and pick up the excellent included audioguide. Tour the place this way: Explore Rembrandt's reconstructed house (filled with exactly what his bankruptcy inventory of 1656 said he owned); imagine him at work in his reconstructed studio; marvel at his personal collection of exotic objects, many of which he included in paintings; attend the etching demonstration and ask the printer to explain the etching process (drawing in soft wax on a metal plate that's then dipped in acid, inked up, and printed); and then, for the finale, enjoy several rooms of original Rembrandt etchings. You're not likely to see a single painting, but the master's etchings are marvelous and well-described. I came away wanting to know more about the man and his art.

Cost and Hours: €9, includes audioguide, daily 10:00-17:00, etching demonstrations almost hourly, Jodenbreestraat 4, tel. 020/520-0400, www.rembrandthuis.nl.

▲**Diamonds**—Many shops in this "city of diamonds" offer tours. These tours come with two parts: a chance to see experts behind magnifying glasses polishing the facets of precious diamonds, followed by a visit to an intimate sales room to see (and perhaps buy) a mighty shiny yet very tiny souvenir.

The handy and professional **Gassan Diamonds** facility fills a huge warehouse one block from Rembrandt's House. A visit here plops you in the big-tour-group fray (notice how each tour group has a color-coded sticker so they know which guide gets the commission on what they buy). You'll get a sticker, join a free 15-minute tour to see a polisher at work, and hear a general explanation of the process. Then you'll have an opportunity to sit down and have color and clarity described and illustrated with diamonds ranging in value from $100 to $30,000. Before or after, you can have a free cup of coffee in the waiting room across the parking lot (daily 9:00-17:00, Nieuwe Uilenburgerstraat 173, tel. 020/622-5333, www.gassandiamonds .com, handy WC). Another company, **Coster,** also offers diamond demos. They're not as good as Gassan's, but convenient if you're near the Rijksmuseum (see page 59).

▲**Willet-Holthuysen Museum (a.k.a. Herengracht Canal Mansion)**—This 1687 townhouse is a must for devotees of

Hummel-topped sugar bowls and Louis XVI-style wainscoting. For others, it's a pleasant look inside a typical (rich) home with much of the original furniture and decor. Forget the history and just browse through a dozen rooms of beautiful saccharine objects from the 19th century.

Upon entering (through the servants' door under the grand entry), see photos of the owners during the house's heyday in the 1860s. The 15-minute video explains how the wealthy heiress Louise Holthuysen and the art-collecting bon vivant Abraham Willet got married and became joined at the hyphen, then set out to make their home the social hub of Amsterdam.

Picture the couple's servants in the kitchen—before electricity and running water—turning meat on the spit at the fireplace or filtering rainwater. Upstairs, where the Willet-Holthuysens entertained, wall paintings introduce you to Abraham's artistic tastes, showing scenes of happy French peasants and nobles frolicking in the countryside. Several rooms are decorated in the Louis XVI style, featuring chairs with straight, tapering legs (not the heavy, curving, animal-claw feet of earlier styles); blue, yellow, and purple-themed rooms; wainscoting ("wallpaper" covering only the lower part of walls); and mythological paintings on the ceiling.

The impressive gilded ballroom contains a painting showing the room in its prime—and how little it's changed. Imagine Abraham, Louise, and 22 guests retiring to the Dining Room, dining off the 275-piece Meissen porcelain set; chatting with friends in the Blue Room by the canal; or sipping tea in the Garden Room, gazing out at symmetrically curved hedges and classical statues. Up another flight is the bedroom, with a canopy bed and matching oak washstand and makeup table (and a chamber pot tucked under the bed). You can even browse the collection virtually using a computer terminal.

When the widow Louise died in 1895, she bequeathed the house to the city, along with its candelabras, snuff boxes, and puppy paintings.

Cost and Hours: €7, Mon-Fri 10:00-17:00, Sat-Sun 11:00-17:00; take tram #4, #9, or #14 to Rembrandtplein—it's a 2-minute walk southeast to Herengracht 605. Tel. 020/523-1870, www.willet holthuysen.nl. You can rent a €3 audioguide, or ask for a free blue notebook to learn more about the house's history.

Tassen Museum (Hendrikje Museum of Bags and Purses)—This hardworking little museum fills an elegant 1664 canal house with 500 years of bag and purse history—from before the invention of pockets through the 20th century. The collection, with lots of artifacts, is well-described in English and gives a fascinating insight into fashion through the ages that fans of handbags will love, and their partners might even enjoy. The creative and surreal bag styles of the 1920s and 1930s are particularly interesting (€7.50, daily 10:00-17:00, three floors—one houses temporary exhibits and two hold the permanent collection, start on top floor, behind Rembrandtplein at Herengracht 573, tel. 020/524-6452, www .tassenmuseum.nl).

▲Hermitage Amsterdam—The famous Hermitage Museum in St. Petersburg, Russia, loans art to Amsterdam for display in the Amstelhof, a 17th-century former nursing home that takes up a whole city block along the Amstel River.

Why is there Russian-owned art in Amsterdam? The Hermitage collection in St. Petersburg is so vast that they can only show about 5 percent of it at any one time. Therefore, the Hermitage is establishing satellite collections around the world. The one here in Amsterdam is the biggest, filling the large Amstelhof, a former retirement home. By law, the great Russian collection can only be out of the country for six months at a time, so the collection is always rotating. Curators in Amsterdam make a point to display art that complements—rather than just repeats—what the city's other museums show so well.

Cost and Hours: Generally €15, but price varies with exhibit; audioguide-€3, daily 10:00-17:00, Wed until 20:00; come later in the day to avoid crowds, mandatory free bag check, café, Nieuwe Herengracht 14, tram #4 to Rembrandtplein or #9 or #14 to Waterlooplein. Recorded info tel. 020/530-7488, www.hermitage.nl.

De Hortus Botanical Garden—This is a unique oasis of tranquility within the city (no mobile phones are allowed, because "our collection of plants is a precious community—treat it with respect"). One of the oldest botanical gardens in the world, it dates from 1638, when medicinal herbs were grown here. Today, among its 6,000 different kinds of plants—most of which were collected by the Dutch East India Company in the 17th and 18th centuries—you'll find medicinal herbs, cacti, several greenhouses (one with a fluttery butterfly house—a hit with kids), and a tropical palm house. Much of it is described in English: "A Dutch merchant snuck a coffee plant out of Ethiopia, which ended up in this garden in 1706. This first coffee plant in Europe was the literal granddaddy of the coffee cultures of Brazil—long the world's biggest coffee producer."

Cost and Hours: €7.50, not covered by Museumkaart; daily 10:00-17:00, Plantage Middenlaan 2A, tel. 020/625-9021, www .dehortus.nl. The inviting Orangery Café serves tapas.

▲Jewish Historical Museum (Joods Historisch Museum)—This interesting museum tells the story of the Netherlands' Jews through three centuries, serving as a good introduction to Judaism

and Jewish customs and religious traditions.

Originally opened in 1932, the museum was forced to close during the Nazi years. Recent renovations have brought it into the 21st century. Its current location comprises four historic former synagogues that have been joined by steel

Jews in Amsterdam

In 1940, one in ten Amsterdammers was Jewish, and most lived in the neighborhood behind Waterlooplein. Jewish traders had long been welcome in a city that cared more about business than religion. In the late 1500s, many Sephardic Jews from Spain and Portugal immigrated, fleeing persecution. (The philosopher Baruch Spinoza's ancestors were among them.) In the 1630s, Yiddish-speaking Eastern European Jews (Ashkenazi) poured in. By 1700, the Jewish Quarter was a bustling, exotic, multicultural world, with more people speaking Portuguese, German, and Yiddish than Dutch.

However, Jews were not first-class citizens. They needed the city's permission to settle here, and they couldn't hold public office (but then, neither could Catholics under Calvinist rule). Still, the Jewish Quarter was not a ghetto (enforced segregation), there were no special taxes, and cosmopolitan Amsterdam was well-acquainted with all types of beliefs and customs.

In 1796, Jews were given full citizenship. In exchange, they were required to learn the Dutch language and submit to the city's legal system...and the Jewish culture began assimilating into the Dutch.

In 1940, Nazi Germany occupied the Netherlands. On February 22, 1941, the Nazis began rounding up Jews and shipping them to extermination camps in Eastern Europe. By war's end, more than 100,000 of the country's 135,000 Jews had died.

Today, about 25,000 Jews live in Amsterdam, and the Jewish Quarter has blended with the modern city. For more information on Amsterdam's many Jewish sights, see www.jhm.nl.

and glass to make one modern complex.

The highlight is the Great Synagogue. Have a seat in the high-ceilinged synagogue, surrounded by religious objects, and picture it during its prime (1671-1943). The hall would be full for a service—men downstairs, women above in the gallery. On the east wall (the symbolic direction of Jerusalem) is the Ark, where they keep the scrolls of the Torah (the Jewish scriptures, comprising the first five books of Old Testament of the Bible). The rabbi and other men, wearing thigh-length prayer shawls, would approach the Ark and carry the Torah to the raised platform in the center of the room. After unwrapping it from its drapery and silver cap, a man would use a *yad* (ceremonial pointer) to follow along while singing the text aloud.

Video displays around the room explain Jewish customs, from birth (circumcision) to puberty (the bar/bat mitzvah, celebrating the entry into adulthood) to Passover celebrations to marriage—culminating in the groom stomping on a glass while everyone shouts "Mazel tov!"

The women's gallery upstairs displays Amsterdam's Jewish history from 1600 to 1900. From here, a skyway leads to the New Synagogue and the 20th century. The new, worthwhile exhibit on the "Jews of the Netherlands" uses personal artifacts and touchscreen computers to tell the devastating history of the Nazi occupation. By purposefully showing everyday objects such as chairs and clothes, the museum helps make an inconceivable period of time meaningful and real.

The museum has a modern, minimalist, kosher café, as well as temporary exhibition space, generally showing the work of Jewish artists.

Cost and Hours: €9, more for special exhibits, €12 comboticket covers Dutch Theater (next), daily 11:00-17:00, last entry 30 minutes before closing, free audioguide, displays all have English explanations, children's museum and kosher-style café on site, Jonas Daniel Meijerplein 2. Tel. 020/531-0310, www.jhm.nl.

▲**Dutch Theater (Hollandsche Schouwburg)**—Once a lively theater in the Jewish neighborhood, and today a moving memorial, this building was used as an assembly hall for local Jews destined for Nazi concentration camps.
On the wall, 6,700 family names pay tribute to the 104,000 Jews deported and killed by the Nazis. Some 70,000 victims spent time here, awaiting transfer to concentration camps. Upstairs is a small history exhibit with a model of the ghetto, plus photos and memorabilia (such as shoes and letters) of some victims, putting a human face on the staggering numbers. Monitors show actual footage of the Nazis rounding up Amsterdam's Jews. You can also see a few costumes from the days when the building was a theater. All in all, it offers relatively little to see but plenty to think about. Back in the ground floor courtyard, notice the hopeful messages that visiting school groups attach to the wooden tulips.

Cost and Hours: €12 combo-ticket with Jewish Historical Museum, daily 11:00-16:00, Plantage Middenlaan 24, tel. 020/531-0340, www.hollandscheschouwburg.nl.

▲▲Dutch Resistance Museum (Verzetsmuseum)—This is an impressive look at how the Dutch resisted their Nazi occupiers from 1940 to 1945. You'll see propaganda movie clips, study forged ID cards under a magnifying glass, and read about ingenious and courageous efforts—big and small— to hide local Jews from the Germans and undermine the Nazi regime.

Cost and Hours: €7.50 includes audioguide; Tue-Fri 10:00-17:00, Sat-Mon 11:00-17:00, English descriptions, no flash photos, mandatory and free bag check, tram #9 from station or #14 from Dam Square, Plantage Kerklaan 61. Tel. 020/620-2535, www.verzetsmuseum.org.

◐ Self-Guided Tour: The museum does a good job of presenting the Dutch people's struggle with a timeless moral dilemma: Is it better to collaborate with a wicked system to effect small-scale change—or to resist violently, even if your efforts are doomed to fail? You'll learn why some parts of Dutch society opted for the former, and others for the latter. While proudly describing acts of extraordinary courage, it doesn't shy away from the less heroic side of the story (for example, the fact that most of the population, though troubled by the persecution of their Jewish countrymen, only became actively anti-Nazi after gentile Dutch men were deported to forced-labor camps).

The first dozen displays set the stage, showing peaceful, upright Dutch people of the 1930s living oblivious to the rise of fascism. Then—bam—it's May of 1940 and the Germans invade the Netherlands, pummel Rotterdam, send Queen Wilhelmina into exile, and—in four short days of fighting—hammer home the message that resistance is futile. The Germans install local Dutch Nazis in power (the "NSB"), led by Anton Mussert.

Next, in the corner of the exhibition area, push a button to see photos of the event that first mobilized organized resistance. In February of 1941, Nazis start rounding up Jews from the neighborhood, killing nine protesters. Amsterdammers respond by shutting down the trams, schools, and businesses in a massive two-day strike. (This heroic gesture is honored today with a statue of a striking dockworker on the square called Jonas Daniel Meyerplein, where Jews were rounded up.) The next display makes it clear that this brave strike did little to save 100,000 Jews from extermination.

Turning the corner into the main room, you'll see numerous exhibits on Nazi rule (on topics including ID cards, propaganda, and the segregation of Jews) and the many forms of Dutch resistance: vandals turning Nazi V-for-Victory posters into W-for-Wilhelmina, preachers giving pointed sermons, schoolkids telling "Kraut jokes," printers distributing underground newspapers (such as *Het Parool,* which became a major daily paper), counterfeiters forging documents, and ordinary people hiding radios under floorboards and Jews inside closets. As the war progresses, the armed Dutch Resistance becomes bolder and more violent, killing German occupiers and Dutch collaborators. In September of 1944, the Allies liberate Antwerp, and the Netherlands starts celebrating...too soon. The Nazis dig in and punish the country by cutting off rations, plunging West Holland into the "Hunger Winter" of 1944 to 1945, during which 20,000 die. Finally, it's springtime. The Allies liberate the country, and at war's end, Nazi helmets are turned into Dutch bedpans.

Nearby: Two recommended eateries—Restaurant Plancius and Café Koosje—are on the same block as the museum (see listings on page 197), and Amsterdam's famous zoo is just across the street.

▲**Tropical Museum (Tropenmuseum)**—As close to the Third World as you'll get without lots of vaccinations, this imaginative museum offers wonderful re-creations of tropical life and explanations of Third World problems (largely created by Dutch colonialism and the slave trade). Ride the elevator to the top floor, and circle your way down through this immense collection, opened in 1926 to give the Dutch people a peek at their vast colonial holdings. Don't miss the display case where you can see and hear the world's most exotic musical instruments. The Ekeko cafeteria serves tropical food.

Cost and Hours: €9, Tue-Sun 10:00-17:00, closed Mon, tram #9 to Linnaeusstraat 2, tel. 020/568-8200, www.tropenmuseum.nl.

AMSTERDAM CITY WALK

From Central Station to the Rijksmuseum

Amsterdam today looks much as it did in its Golden Age, the 1600s. It's a retired sea captain of a city, still in love with life, with a broad outlook and a salty story to tell.

Take a Dutch sampler walk from one end of the old center to the other, tasting all that Amsterdam has to offer along the way. It's your best single stroll through Dutch clichés, hidden churches, surprising shops, thriving happy-hour hangouts, and eight centuries of history.

Orientation

Length of This Walk: Allow three hours.

Bike Rental: If you'd like to make this "walk" a much faster "roll," there's a handy bike-rental place in Central Station (MacBike, listed on page 49).

Alert: Beware of silent transport—trams and bikes. Walkers should stay off the tram tracks and bike paths, and yield to bell-ringing bikers.

WCs: You can find public toilets at fast-food places (generally €0.30) and near the entrance to the Amsterdam Museum.

Royal Palace: €7.50, daily 12:00-17:00 but often closed for official business, tel. 020/620-4060.

New Church: €8, daily 10:00-17:00, Thu until 22:00, on Dam Square. Info tel. 020/353-8168, tel. 020/638-6909.

Amsterdam Museum: €10, Mon-Fri 10:00-17:00, Sat-Sun 11:00-17:00, Kalverstraat 92, tel. 020/523-1822.

Begijnhof: Free, daily 8:00-17:00 for "tourist visits" (groups and guided tours). At other times, be quiet and stick to the area near the churches. Don't photograph homes or their residents, and remember that these are private dwellings (on

Begijnensteeg lane, just off Kalverstraat between #130 and #132). The English Reformed Church is sometimes open for tourists (free, Sun service in English at 10:30, closed Wed).

Rijksmuseum: €12.50, audioguide-€5, daily 9:00-18:00, last entry 30 minutes before closing, info tel. 020/674-7047, switchboard tel. 020/674-7000.

Van Gogh Museum: €14, audioguide-€5, kids' audioguide-€2.50, daily 10:00-18:00, Fri until 22:00, Paulus Potterstraat 7, tel. 020/570-5200.

Overview

This walk starts at the central-as-can-be Central Station. You'll walk about three miles, heading down Damrak to Dam Square, continuing south down Kalverstraat to the Mint Tower (Munt-toren), then wafting through the flower market (Bloemenmarkt), before continuing south to Leidseplein and jogging left to the Rijksmuseum. To return to Central Station, catch tram #2 or #5 from the southwest corner of the Rijksmuseum.

The Walk Begins

Central Station

Here, where today's train travelers enter the city, sailors of yore disembarked from seagoing ships to be met by street musicians,

pickpockets, hotel-runners, and ladies carrying red lanterns. When the station was built (on reclaimed land) at the former harbor mouth, Amsterdam lost some of its harbor feel, but it's still a bustling port of entry.

Central Station, with warm red brick and prickly spires, is the first of several Neo-Gothic buildings we'll see from the late 1800s, built during Amsterdam's economic revival. One of the towers has a clock dial; the other tower's dial is a weathervane. Watch the hand twitch as the wind gusts—N, Z, O, and W.

As you emerge from the train station, you'll immediately see a mess. The construction is for a new office and condo zone (left of station as you leave it) and subway line (in front of station). The new north-south metro line (to open in 2013) will complement the existing one. And though it sounds like a fine idea, the project has been riddled with delays.

Beyond the construction, the city spreads out before you in

a series of concentric canals. Ahead of you stretches the street called Damrak, which leads to Dam Square a half-mile away. To the left of Damrak is the city's old *(oude)* side; to the right is the new *(nieuwe)*.

The big church towering above the old side (at about 10 o'clock) is St. Nicholas Church, built in the 1880s, when Catholics—after about three centuries of oppression—were finally free to worship in public. The church marks the beginning of the Red Light District (for a tour of that neighborhood, ○ see the Red Light District Walk chapter). The city's biggest bike garage, a multistory wonder, is on your right in front of the Ibis Hotel. Parking your bike in the garage is free—courtesy of the government (they want to encourage biking).

• *We'll basically walk south from here to the Rijksmuseum. The art museum and the train station—designed by the same architect—stand like bookends holding the old town together. Follow the crowds south on Damrak, walking along the right side of the street.*

Damrak

Stroll past every Dutch cliché at the tourist shops: wooden shoes, plastic tulips, Heineken fridge magnets, windmill salt-shakers, and all things orange (hats and T-shirts). Listen to a hand-cranked barrel organ. Order french fries (called *Vlaamse frites*, or Flemish fries, since they were invented in the Low Countries), and dip them in mayonnaise, not ketchup. Eating international cuisine (Indonesian rijsttafel, Argentine steak, Middle Eastern *shoarma*—pronounced SHWAHR-mah) is going local in cosmopolitan Amsterdam. And you'll find the city's most notorious commodity displayed at the **Damrak Sex Museum** (see page 68).

This street was once a riverbed, where the Amstel River flowed north into the IJ (pronounced "eye") River behind today's train station. Both rivers then emptied into a vast inlet of the North Sea (the Zuiderzee), unique geography that turned Amsterdam into a major seaport. Today, the Amstel is channeled into canals,

Amsterdam City Walk—First Half

CENTRAL STATION **START**

B BOAT TOURS

To JORDAAN DISTRICT

OLD CHURCH

RED LIGHT DISTRICT

LELIESTR.

VOORBURGWAL

NIEUWENDIJK

DAMRAK

BEURS-PL.

GRAVEN.

RAADHUISSTRAAT

NIEUWEZIJDS

DAM SQUARE

De BIJENKORF DEPT. Store

VOORBURGWAL

PIJLS.

DAMSTR.

SPUISTRAAT

MKT.

KALVER-STRAAT

ROKIN

N.Z.

OUDEZIJDS

200 YARDS
200 METERS

AMSTERDAM MUSEUM

ST. LUCIEN.

BEGIJN-HOF

HET STEEG

SPUI

SPUI

ROKIN

MINT TOWER

N. DOELEN.

HEILIGE.

AMSTERDAM CITY WALK

HEREN

To LEIDSE-PLEIN

SINGEL

FLOWER MARKET

END (PART 1)

MUNT PL.

AMSTEL

REGULIERS.

VIJZEL.

DCH

❶ Damrak Sex Museum
❷ Stock Exchange
❸ Royal Palace
❹ New Church
❺ Magna Plaza (Shops)
❻ National Monument

❼ De Papegaai Hidden Catholic Church
❽ Amsterdam Museum, Courtyard & Civic Guard Gallery
❾ Begijnhof
❿ Spui Square
⓫ Rokin Street (Canal Cruises)
⓬ House of Hajenius
⓭ Kalvertoren Mall (Viewpoint)
⓮ V & D Dept. Store
⓯ Mint Tower & Muntplein
⓰ Tuschinski Theater
⓱ Rembrandtplein

its former mouth covered by Central Station, and the North Sea inlet has been diked off to make an inland lake. More than 100,000 ships a year reach the open waters by sailing west through the North Sea Canal, making Amsterdam Europe's fifth-busiest seaport.

Local landowners are concerned that the tunneling for the new subway line will cause their buildings to settle. The snoopy-looking white cameras mounted on various building corners (such as the Beurs) are monitoring buildings to check for settling.

• *The long brick building with the square clock tower, along the left side of Damrak, is the...*

Stock Exchange (Beurs)

Built with nine million bricks on about 5,000 tree trunks hammered into the marshy soil, the Beurs stands as a symbol of the city's long tradition as a trading town.

Back when "stock" meant whatever could be loaded and unloaded onto a boat, Amsterdammers gathered to trade. Soon, rather than trading goats, chickens, and kegs of beer, they were exchanging slips of paper and "futures" at one of the world's first stock exchanges. Traders needed moneychangers, who needed bankers, who made money by lending money...and Amsterdam of the 1600s became one of the world's first great capitalist cities, loaning money to free-spending kings, dukes, and bishops.

This impressive building, built in 1903 in a geometric, minimal, no-frills style, is one of the world's first "modern" (i.e., 20th-century-style) buildings, emphasizing function over looks. In 1984, the stock exchange moved next door (see the stock prices readout) to the Euronext complex—a joint, if overly optimistic, attempt by France, Belgium, and the Netherlands to compete with the power of Britain's stock exchange. The old Beurs building now hosts concerts and a museum for temporary exhibits.

Amsterdam still thrives as the center of Dutch business and is home to Heineken, Shell Oil, Philips Electronics, and Unilever. Amsterdammers have always had a reputation for putting business above ideological differences, staying neutral while trading with both sides.

• *Damrak opens into...*

Dam Square

The city got its start right here in about 1250, when fishermen in this marshy delta settled along the built-up banks of the Amstel River. They blocked the river with a *damme* and created a small village called "Amstel-damme." With access to the sea, the fishermen were soon trading with German riverboats traveling downstream and with seafaring boats from Stockholm, Hamburg, and London.

Dam Square was the center of it all.

The dam on the Amstel divided the *damrak* (meaning "outer

harbor"—for sea traffic) from the *rokin* ("inner harbor"—for river traffic). Land trade routes converged here as well, and a customs house stood in this spot. Today, the Damrak and Rokin (roh-KEEN) are major roads, and the city's palace and major department stores face the square, where mimes, jugglers, and human statues mingle with locals and tourists. This is the historic heart of the city. As the symbolic center of the Netherlands, it's where political demonstrations begin and end.

Circling the Square

Pan the square clockwise. The Royal Palace—the large domed building on the west side—is the former Town Hall. To its right stands the New Church (Nieuwe Kerk); it's located on the pedestrian-only shopping street called Nieuwendijk, which runs parallel to Damrak and stretches all the way to Central Station. Panning past Damrak, see the proud old De Bijenkorf ("The Beehive") department store (with a recommended café—see page 193). The Grand Hotel Krasnapolsky has a lovely circa-1900 Winter Garden. The white phallic obelisk is the National Monument. A few blocks behind the hotel is the edge of the Red Light District. To the right of the hotel stretches the street called the Nes, lined with some of Amsterdam's edgy live-theater venues. Rokin street is Damrak's counterpart, continuing past the square. Next comes touristy and overpriced Madame Tussauds and the entrance to the pedestrian-only shopping street, Kalverstraat (look for *Rabobank* sign).

You're at the historic heart and contemporary center of Amsterdam.

Royal Palace

The name is misleading, since Amsterdam is one of the cradles of modern democracy. For centuries, this was the Town Hall of a self-governing community that prided itself on its independence and thumbed its

nose at royalty. The current building, built in about 1650, is appropriately classical (like the democratic Greeks), with a triangular pediment featuring—fittingly for Amsterdam—denizens of the sea cavorting with Neptune (with his green copper trident).

After the city was conquered by the French, Napoleon imposed a monarchy on Holland, making his brother Louis the king of the Netherlands (1808). Louis used the City Hall as his "royal palace," giving the building its current name. When Napoleon was defeated, the victorious powers dictated that the Netherlands remain a monarchy, under a noble Dutch family called the House of Orange. If the current Queen Beatrix is in town, this is, technically, her residence. When Prince Willem-Alexander got married in 2002, the new couple shared a kiss on the balcony of the Royal Palace, delighting the crowd in Dam Square. The Royal Palace reopened to the public in 2009 after a lengthy renovation (for more on its interior, see page 65). Amsterdam is the nominal capital of the Netherlands, but all governing activity—and the Queen's actual permanent home—are in The Hague (a city 30 miles southwest).

• *A few paces away, to the right as you're facing the Royal Palace, is the...*

New Church (Nieuwe Kerk)

The "New" Church is 600 years old (newer than the 700-year-old "Old" Church in the Red Light District). The sundial above the entrance once served as the city's official timepiece.

The church's bare, spacious, well-lit interior (occupied by a new art exhibit every three months) looks quite different from the Baroque-encrusted churches found in the rest of Europe. In 1566, clear-eyed Protestant extremists throughout Holland marched into Catholic churches (like this once was), lopped off the heads of holy statues, stripped gold-leaf angels from the walls, urinated on Virgin Marys, and shattered stained-glass windows in a wave of anti-Catholic vandalism.

This iconoclasm (icon-breaking) of 1566 started an 80-year war against Spain and the Habsburgs, leading finally to Dutch independence in 1648. Catholic churches like this one were converted to the new dominant religion, Calvinist Protestantism (today's Dutch Reformed Church). From then on, Dutch churches downplayed the "graven images" and "idols" of ornate religious art.

From just inside the door, you can get a free look at the 1655 organ (far left end, often played for midday concerts); the stained-glass window (opposite entrance) showing Count William IV

City on a Sandbar

Amsterdam is built on millions of wooden pilings. The city was founded on unstable mud, which sits on stable sand. In the Middle Ages, buildings were made of wood, which rests lightly and easily on mud. But devastating fires repeatedly wiped out entire neighborhoods, so stone became the building material of choice. Stone is fire resistant, but was too heavy for a mud foundation, so for more support, pilings were driven 30 feet through the mud and into the sand. The Royal Palace sits upon 13,000 such pilings—still solid after 350 years. (The wood survives if kept wet and out of the air.) Since World War II, concrete, rather than wood, has been used for the pilings, with foundations driven 60 feet deep through the first layer of sand, through more mud, and into a second layer of sand. Today's biggest buildings have foundations that go down as much as 120 feet deep.

giving the city its "XXX" coat of arms; and the window (over entrance) showing the inauguration of Queen Wilhelmina. She eventually became the steadfast center of Dutch Resistance during World War II.

This church is where many of the Netherlands' monarchs are married and all are crowned. In 1980, Queen Beatrix—Wilhelmina's granddaughter—held her coronation in the New Church. When Beatrix dies or retires (her mother and grandmother both abdicated late in life), her son, Prince Willem-Alexander, will parade to the center of the church, sit in front of the golden choir screen, and—with TV lights glaring and cameras flashing—be crowned the next sovereign.

• *Looking between the Royal Palace and the New Church, you'll see the fanciful brick façade of the Magna Plaza shopping center.*

National Monument

The obelisk, which depicts a crucified Christ, men in chains, and howling dogs, was built in 1956 as a WWII memorial. Now it's considered a monument for peace.

The Nazis occupied Holland from 1940 to 1945. They deported 100,000 Amsterdam Jews, driving many—including young Anne Frank and her family—into hiding. Near the end of the war, the "Hunger Winter" of 1944-1945 killed thousands and forced many to survive on tulip bulbs. Today, Dutch people in their mid-70s—whose growth-spurt years coincided with the "Hunger Winter"—are easy to identify, because they are uniformly short.

• *From Dam Square, head south (at* Rabobank *sign) on...*

Kalverstraat

This pedestrian-only street is lined with many familiar franchise stores and record shops. (If you're on a bike, you must dismount and walk.) This has been a shop-ping street for centuries, and today it's notorious among locals as *the* place for cheesy, crass materialism. For smaller and more elegant stores, try the adjacent district called De Negen Straatjes ("The Nine Little Streets"), where 190 shops mingle by the canals (about four blocks west of Kalverstraat).

• *About 120 yards along (just before and across from the McDonald's), pop into...*

De Papegaai Hidden Catholic Church (Petrus en Paulus Kerk)

This Catholic church, though not exactly hidden (after all, you found it), keeps a low profile, even now that Catholicism has been legalized in Amsterdam. In the late 1500s, with Protestants fighting Catholics and the Dutch fighting Spanish invaders, Amsterdam tried to stay neutral, doing business with all parties. Finally, in 1578, Protestant extremists (following the teachings of Reformer John Calvin) took political control of the city. They expelled Catholic leaders and bishops, outlawed the religion, and allied Amsterdam with anti-Spanish forces in an action known to historians as the Alteration.

For the next two centuries, Amsterdam's Catholics were driven underground. Catholicism was illegal but tolerated, as long as it was practiced not in public, but in humble, unadvertised places like this. (The stuffed parrot—*papegaai*—hanging in the nave refers to the house formerly on this site, which had a carving of a parrot in its gable stone.)

Today, the church, which asks for a mere "15 minutes for God" *(een kwartier voor God)*, stands as a metaphor for how religion has long been a marginal part of highly commercial and secular Amsterdam (free, daily 10:00-16:00).

• *Farther along (about 75 yards) at #92, where Kalverstraat crosses Wijde Kapel Steeg, look to the right at an archway leading to the...*

Entrance and Courtyard of the Amsterdam Museum

On the arch is Amsterdam's coat of arms—a red shield with three Xs and a crown. The X-shaped crosses (which appear everywhere in town) symbolize heroism, determination, and mercy; they represent the crucifixion of St. Andrew, the patron saint of fishermen (and are not a reference to the city's sex trade). The crown dates to 1489, when Maximilian I (the Low Countries' first Habsburg ruler and later Holy Roman Emperor) paid off a big loan from city bankers and, as thanks for the cash, gave the city permission to use his prestigious trademark, the Habsburg crown, atop its shield. The

relief above the door (see photo), dated 1581, shows boys around a dove, asking for charity, reminding all who pass that this was an orphanage

Go inside. The pleasant café has a shaded courtyard with a pay toilet and old lockers for the orphans' uniforms.

• *The courtyard leads to another courtyard with the best city history museum in town, ✪ the Amsterdam Museum. Between the two courtyards (on the left) is a free, glassed-in passageway lined with paintings, called the...*

Civic Guard Gallery (Schuttersgalerij)

In these group portraits from Amsterdam's Golden Age (early 1600s), look into the eyes of the frank, dignified men (and some women) with ruffs and lace collars, who made Amsterdam the most prosperous city in Europe, sending trading ships to distant colonies and pocketing interest from loans. The weapons they carry are mostly symbolic, since these "Civic Guards," who once protected the town (fighting the Spanish), had become more like fraternal organizations of business bigwigs.

Many paintings look the same in this highly stylized genre. Military companies often sit in two rows. Someone holds the company flag. Rank is indicated by the weapons they hold: Captains wield pikes (axe-like weapons topped with spearhead-shaped tips); lieutenants hold partisans (pikes with sword-like tips); and privates wield hatchet-headed halberds or muskets. Later group portraits showed "captains" of industry going about their work, dressed in suits, along with the tools of their trade—ledger books, quill pens, and money.

Everyone looks straight out, and every face is lit perfectly. Each paid for his own portrait and wanted it right. It took masters like Rembrandt and Frans Hals to take the starch out of the collars and compose more natural scenes. Giant statues of Goliath and a knee-high David (from 1650) watch over the whole thing.

• *The gallery offers a shortcut to the Begijnhof, 75 yards farther south. But if the gallery is closed, backtrack to Kalverstraat, continue south, then turn right on Begijnensteeg. Either route leads to the entrance of the walled courtyard called the...*

Begijnhof

This quiet courtyard (pronounced gutturally: buh-HHHINE-hof), lined with houses around a church, has sheltered women since 1346. This was for centuries the home of Beguines—women who removed themselves from the world at large to dedicate their lives to God. It literally was a "woman's island"—a circle of houses facing a peaceful courtyard, surrounded by water. (To ensure a pleasant visit, see the "Begijnhof" listing in "Orientation" on page 80.)

The Beguines' ranks swelled during the Crusades, when so many men took off, never to return, leaving society with an abundance of single women. Later, women widowed by the hazards of overseas trade lived out their days as Beguines. Poor and rich women alike turned their backs on materialism and marriage to live here in Christian poverty. And though obedient to a mother superior, the members of the lay order of Beguines were not nuns. The Beguines were very popular in their communities for the unpretentious, simple, and Christ-like lives they led. They spent their days deep in prayer and busy with daily tasks—spinning wool, making lace, teaching, and caring for the sick and poor. In quiet seclusion, they inspired one another as well as their neighbors.

In 1578, when Catholicism was outlawed, the Dutch Reformed Church (and the city) took over many Catholic charities like this place. The last Beguine died in 1971, but this Begijnhof still provides subsidized housing to about 100 needy single women (mostly Catholic seniors and students). The Begijnhof is just one of about

75 *hofjes* (little housing projects surrounding courtyards) that dot Amsterdam.

Begin your visit at the statue of one of these charitable sisters. She faces the **wooden house** *(houten huys)* at #34, which dates from 1477 (the city's oldest). Originally, the whole city consisted of wooden houses like this one. To the left of the house is a display of carved gable stones that once adorned housefronts and served as street numbers (and still do at #19 and #26, the former mother superior's house).

The brick-faced **English Reformed Church** (Engelse Kerk, from 1420) was the Beguine church until 1607, when it became Anglican. The Pilgrims (strict Protestants), fleeing persecution in England, stopped here in tolerant Amsterdam and prayed in this church before the *Mayflower* carried them to religious freedom at Plymouth Rock in America. If the church is open (its hours are sporadic), step inside to see a stained-glass window of the Pilgrims praying before boarding the *Mayflower* (far end), an old pew they may have sat on (right wall), and a 1763 Bible (on the altar) with lot*ʃ*of old-*ʃ*tyle *ʃ*'s.

The "hidden" **Catholic Church** (notice the painted-out windows, second and third floors) faces the English **Reformed** Church. Amsterdam's oppressed 17th-century Catholics, who refused to worship as Protestants, must have eagerly awaited the day when, in the 19th century, they were legally allowed to say Mass. Step inside (through the low-profile doorway), pick up an English brochure near the entry, and tap softly on a "marble" column.

Today, Holland still has a religious divide, but not a bitter one. Roughly a third of the population is Catholic, a fifth is Protestant...and two-fifths list themselves as "unchurched."

• *Backtrack to busy Kalverstraat, turn right, and continue south. Pause at the intersection with Spuistraat, and look to the right.*

Spui and Rokin

A block to the right is the square called **Spui** (spow, rhymes with cow). Lined with cafés and bars, it's one of the city's more popular spots for nightlife and sunny afternoon people-watching.

A block to the left is the busy street called **Rokin.** A statue of Queen Wilhelmina (1880-1962) on the Rokin shows her riding daintily sidesaddle. Remember that in real life, she was the iron-willed inspiration for the Dutch Resistance against the Nazis.

Amsterdam City Walk—Second Half

B BOAT TOURS

MINT TOWER & MUNTPLEIN

SINGEL

REGULIERS

FLOWER MARKET

START (PART 2)

KEIZERS STRAAT

HERENGRACHT

PRINSEN GRACHT

LEIDSE GRACHT

KORTE

TARNIX STRAAT

LEIDSEPLEIN

LEIDSE KADE

LEIDSE DWARSSTRAAT

LIJNBAAN

METERING CHANS

SINGEL GRACHT

STAD HOUDERS KADE

VONDEL-PARK

HOBBEMA STR.

P.C. HOOFT STR.

JAN LUIJKEN

END

RIJKS-MUSEUM

To HEINEKEN EXPERIENCE & ALBERT CUYPSTR. MARKET

TO VAN GOGH MUSEUM

200 YARDS

200 METERS

DCH

18 Flower Market
19 Koningsplein
20 Selexyz Scheltema Bookstore
21 Metz & Co. (View)
22 Smartshop
23 The Delft Shop
24 Pipe Museum
25 Stadsschouwburg
26 TI & AUB/Last Minute Ticket Shop
27 Melkweg
28 Boom Chicago
29 "Restaurant Row"
30 Bulldog Café & Coffeeshop
31 Max Euweplein
32 Paradiso
33 Rijksmuseum
34 Trams #2 & #5

Canal cruises depart from the Rondvaart Kooij dock by the statue (yellow canal house, see "Canal Boat Tours" on page 51).

The **House of Hajenius,** at Rokin 92 (50 yards left of the canal dock, toward Central Station), is a temple of cigars, a "paradise for the connoisseur," showing "175 years of tradition and good taste." To enter this sumptuous Art Nouveau building with painted leather ceilings is to step back into 1910 (free, Tue-Sat 9:30-18:00, Sun 12:00-17:00, Mon 12:00-18:00). Don't be shy—the place is as much a free museum for visitors as it is a store for paying customers. The brown-capped canisters (under the wall of pipes, to the right) are for smelling fine pipe tobacco. Take a whiff. The personal humidifiers (read the explanation) allow locals (famous local names are on the cupboard doors) to call in an order and have their cigars waiting for them at just the right humidity. Look up at the humidifier pipes pumping moisture into the room. Upstairs in back is a small, free museum.

• *Head back toward the pedestrian street, Kalverstraat, and turn left when you get there. You'll pass various department stores with cafeterias.*

At the end of Kalverstraat, the **Kalvertoren** shopping complex offers a top-floor viewpoint and café (daily until 18:30, Thu until 21:00, find the slanting glass elevator located past the escalators). Across Kalverstraat, the **Vroom & Dreesman (V&D)** department store (at #200) is one of Holland's oldest chains. Inside, the recommended La Place is a sprawling self-service cafeteria—handy for a quick and healthy lunch.

• *Continue on Kalverstraat, which dead-ends at the...*

Mint Tower (Munttoren)

This tower, which marked the limit of the medieval walled city,

served as one of the original gates (the steeple was added later, in 1620). The city walls were girdled by a moat—the Singel canal. Until about 1500, the area beyond here was nothing but marshy fields and a few farms on reclaimed land.

From the busy intersection at Muntplein, look left (at about 10 o'clock) down Reguliersbreestraat. A long block east of here (where you see trees) is Rembrandtplein, another major center for nightlife (and site of the fun statue nicknamed "*The Night Watch* in 3-D"). Halfway down the block, the twin green domes mark the exotic **Tuschinski Theater,** where you can see current movies in a sumptuous Art Deco setting (see page 61). Take a seat in the lobby and stare at the ever-changing ceiling, imagining this place during the Roaring '20s.

• *Just past the Mint Tower, turn right and walk west along the south bank of the Singel, which is lined with the greenhouse shops of the...*

Flower Market (Bloemenmarkt)

This busy block of cut flowers, plants, bulbs, seeds, and garden supplies attests to Holland's reputation for growing flowers. Although tulips have long been associated with this country, they were originally imported from Turkey in the 1500s. The tulip is one of many beauties in the country's flower arsenal, and today, Holland is a major exporter of flowers. Certain seeds are certified and OK to bring back into the US (merchants have the details). For more on the history of tulips in Holland, see page 30.

• *The long Flower Market ends at the next bridge, where you'll see a square named...*

Koningsplein

Choke down a raw herring—the commodity that first put Amsterdam on the trading map—with locals who flock to this popular outdoor herring stand. (*Hollandse nieuwe* means the herring are in season.)

• *From Koningsplein, turn left, heading straight to Leidseplein. At first, the street southward is just labeled* Koningsplein *(Selexyz Scheltema, Amsterdam's leading bookstore, is at Koningsplein 20). Soon, Koningsplein becomes...*

Leidsestraat

Between here and Leidseplein, you'll cross several grand canals, following a street lined with fashion and tourist shops, and crowded

with shoppers, tourists, bicycles, and trams. Trams must wait their turn to share a single track as the street narrows.

The once grand, now frumpy, **Metz & Co.** department store (where Leidsestraat crosses Herengracht) offers a rare above-the-rooftops panoramic view of the city from its sixth-floor café.

Looking left down Herengracht, you'll see the **"Golden Curve"** of the canal, lined with grand, classical-style gables.

• *Past the posh stores, find the humble When Nature Calls Smartshop, located where Leidsestraat crosses Keizersgracht (at Keizersgracht 508, open daily until 22:00).*

When Nature Calls Smartshop

"Smartshops" like this one are clean, well-lighted, fully professional retail outlets that sell powerful drugs, many of which are illegal in America. Their "natural" drugs include harmless nutrition boosters (royal jelly), harmful but familiar tobacco, and herbal versions of popular dance-club drugs (herbal Ecstasy). The big item: marijuana seeds.

Prices are clearly marked, with brief descriptions of the drugs, their ingredients, and effects. The knowledgeable salespeople can give you more information on their "100 percent natural products that play with the human senses."

Still, my fellow Americans, *caveat emptor!* We've grown used to thinking, "If it's legal, it must be safe. If it's not, I'll sue." Though perfectly legal and aboveboard in the Netherlands, some of these substances can cause powerful, often unpleasant reactions.

• *Where Leidsestraat crosses Prinsengracht, just over the bridge on the right (at Prinsengracht 440), you'll find...*

The Delft Shop

The distinctive blue-and-white design characterizes glazed ceramics made in Delft (30 miles southwest of here and covered later; for info on the pottery, see the sidebar on page 267). Dutch traders learned the technique from the Chinese of the Ming dynasty, and many pieces have an Oriental look. The doodads with arms branching off a trunk are popular "flower pagodas," vases for displaying tulips.

• *Return to Leidsestraat, cross to the other side, and walk half a block until you reach Prinsengracht 488, home to the...*

Pipe Museum (Pijpenkabinet)

This small, quirky, classy museum holds 300 years of pipes in a 17th-century canal house. (It's almost worth the price just to see the inside of one of these elegant homes.) You enter through the street-level shop, Smokiana—which is almost a free museum in itself—selling new and antique pipes, various smoking curiosities, and scholarly books written by the shop's owner. If you want more, pay admission, and a docent accompanies you upstairs through a tour of smoking history. You begin with some pre-Columbian terra-cotta pipes (from the discoverers of tobacco, dating from 500 b.c.). You'll see plenty of intricate, finely decorated Baroque and Victorian paraphernalia. Ask questions—your guide is happy to explain why the opium pipes have their bowls in the center of the stem, or why some white clay pipes are a foot long (€5, Wed-Sat 12:00-18:00, closed Sun-Tue, tel. 020/421-1779, www.pijpen kabinet.nl).

• *Return once again to Leidsestraat, which empties into the square called...*

AMSTERDAM CITY WALK

Leidseplein

Filled with outdoor tables under trees; ringed with cafés, theaters, and nightclubs; bustling with tourists, diners, trams, mimes, and fire-eaters; and lit by sun- or lantern-light, Leidseplein is Amsterdam's liveliest square.

Do a 360-degree spin: Leidseplein's south side is bordered by the city's main serious theater, the **Stadsschouwburg**, which dates back to the 17th-century Golden Age (present building from 1890). Tucked inside the theater is the **AUB/Last Minute Ticket Shop,** which sells tickets to all the shows in town, including half-price, same-day tickets (after 12:00) to select shows (Leidseplein 26). To the right of the Stadsschouwburg, down a lane behind the big theater, stands the **Melkweg** ("Milky Way"), the once revolutionary, now institutional entertainment complex housing all things youth-oriented under one roof (Lijnbaansgracht 234a). Step into the lobby or check out posters plastered on the walls to find out who's playing tonight. On Leidseplein's west side, at #12, is the **Boom Chicago** nightclub theater, presenting English-language spoofs of politics, Amsterdam, and tourists (see the Entertainment in Amsterdam chapter). Pick up their free, informative intro-to-Amsterdam magazine at the door and see if any tickets are discounted and on the push list for tonight.

The neighborhood beyond Burger King is **"Restaurant Row,"** featuring countless Thai, Brazilian, Indian, Italian, Indonesian, and even a few Dutch eateries. Next, on the east end of Leidseplein, is the **Bulldog Café and Coffeeshop,** the flagship of several café/bar/coffeeshops in town with that name. (Notice the sign above the door: It once housed the police bureau.) A small green-and-white decal on the window indicates that it's a city-licensed "coffeeshop," where marijuana is sold and smoked legally.

• *From Leidseplein, turn left and head along the taxi stand down the broad, busy, tram-filled boulevard called Kleine-Gartman Plantsoen, which becomes Weteringschans. At the triangular garden, cross the street and pass under a row of tall, gray, Greek-style columns, entering...*

Canals

Amsterdam's canals tamed the flow of the Amstel River, creating pockets of dry land to build on. The city's 100 canals are about 10 feet deep, crossed by some 1,200 bridges, fringed with 100,000 Dutch elm and lime trees, and bedecked with 2,500 houseboats. A system of locks (back near the Central Station) controls the flow outward to (eventually) the North Sea and inward to the Amstel River. The locks are opened periodically to flush out the system.

Some of the boats in the canals look pretty funky by day, but Amsterdam is an unpretentious, anti-status city. When the sun goes down and the lights come on, people cruise the sparkling canals with an on-board hibachi and a bottle of wine, and even scows can become chick-magnets.

Max Euweplein

The Latin inscription above the colonnade—*Homo Sapiens non urinat in ventum*—means "People, don't pee into the wind." Passing between the columns, you soon reach a pleasant interior courtyard with cafés and a large chessboard with knee-high kings. (Max Euwe was a Dutch world chess champion; in 1957, he beat 14-year-old Bobby Fischer in 20 moves.) The square gives you access to the Casino, and just over the small bridge is the entrance to **Vondelpark.** Nearby are the Blue Boat Company's **canal boats,** offering one-hour tours (see "Canal Boat Tours" on page 51).

• *Return to Weteringschans street. Turn right and continue 75 yards east to a squat, red-brick building called...*

Paradiso

Back when rock-and-roll was a religion, this former church staged intimate concerts by big-name acts such as the Rolling Stones. In the late 1960s, when city fathers were trying hard to tolerate hordes of young pot smokers, this building was redecorated with psychedelic colors and opened up as the first place where marijuana could be smoked—not legally yet, but it was tolerated. Today, the club hosts live bands and DJs, and sells pot—legally (for current shows, see www.paradiso.nl).

• *Continue down Weteringschans to the first bridge, where you'll see the Rijksmuseum across the canal.*

The Rijksmuseum and Beyond

The best visual chronicle of the Dutch Golden Age is found in the Rijksmuseum's portraits and slice-of-life scenes.

For a tour of the Rembrandts, Vermeers, and others, ✪ see the Rijksmuseum Tour chapter.

On this walk, we've seen landmarks built during the city's late 19th-century revival: Central Station, the Stadsschouwburg, and now the Rijksmuseum. They're all similar, with red-brick and Gothic-style motifs (clock towers, steeples, prickly spires, and stained glass). Petrus Cuypers (1827-1921), who designed the train station and the Rijksmuseum, was extremely influential. Mainly a builder of Catholic churches, he made the Rijksmuseum, with its stained-glass windows, a temple to art. Most of the building is currently closed for renovation through 2013, with the highlights of the collection beautifully displayed in its Philips Wing (around back, on the right). Next to the Philips Wing, a small, free exhibit describes the exciting renovation project.

Behind the Rijksmuseum are the Museumplein (always entertaining) and the Van Gogh Museum (✪ see the tour chapter). The Heineken Experience (beer tour) is a half-mile east of the Rijksmuseum on Heinekenplein (see page 59), and the Albert Cuypstraat street market is a block south of the Heineken Experience.

To return to Central Station (or to nearly anyplace along this walk), catch tram #2 or #5 from the southwest corner of the Rijksmuseum. Or walk north on Nieuwe Spiegelstraat, which leads you (with a little detour) back to the Mint Tower.

AMSTERDAM CITY WALK

RED LIGHT DISTRICT WALK

Amsterdam's oldest neighborhood has hosted the world's oldest profession since 1200. The Red Light District lies between Damrak and Nieuwmarkt. Amsterdammers call it De Wallen, or "The Walls," after the old city walls that once stood here. On your walk, you'll see history, sleaze, and cheese—chickens in Chinatown windows, drunks in doorways, cruising packs of foreign twenty-somethings, cannabis in windows, and sex for sale.

The sex trade runs the gamut from sex shops selling porn and accessories to blue video arcades, from glitzy nightclub sex shows featuring strippers and sex acts to the real deal—prostitutes in bras, thongs, and high heels, standing in window displays, offering their bodies. Amsterdam keeps several thousand prostitutes employed—and it's all legal.

Amsterdam's current city government is trying to rein in the sex trade by limiting it to De Wallen. It's also hoping to splice other commerce into a district that for centuries has had variations on basically only one product. As many as half of the sex businesses may close over the next few years—not because of prudishness, but to limit the encroachment of organized crime. A major Red Light District landlord was essentially given the option either to lease many of his booths to the city or be zoned out of business. The city picked up the leases, and windows that once showcased "girls for rent" now showcase mannequins wearing the latest fashions—lit by lights that aren't red.

Not for Everyone: The Red Light District has something offensive for everyone. Whether it's in-your-face images of graphic sex, exploited immigrant women, whips and chains, passed-out drug addicts, the pungent smells of pot smoke and urine, or just the shameless commercialism of it all, it's not everyone's cup of tea.

And though I encourage people to expand their horizons—that's a great thing about travel—it's perfectly OK to say, "No, thank you."

Orientation

Length of This Walk: Allow two hours.

Photography: Consider leaving your camera in your bag. Absolutely avoid taking photos of ladies in windows—even with an inconspicuous camera phone—or a snarling bouncer may appear from out of nowhere to forcibly rip it from your hands. Taking even seemingly harmless pictures of ordinary people is frowned upon by privacy-loving locals. Photos of landmarks like the Old Church (Oude Kerk) and wide shots of distant red lights from the bridges are certainly OK, but remember that a camera is a prime target in this high-theft area.

When to Go: Mornings are quiet, but are also when you see more passed-out-drunk-in-a-doorway scenes. Afternoons bring out more prostitutes, and evenings (starting at about 20:00) are actually quite festive, with many tourists and out-of-towners. Avoid late nights (after about 22:30), when the tourists disappear.

Safety: Coming here is asking for trouble, but if you're on the ball and smart, it's perfectly safe. While there are plenty of police on horseback keeping things orderly, there are also plenty of rowdy drunks, drug-pushing lowlifes, con artists, and pickpockets (not to mention extremely persuasive women in windows). Assume any fight or commotion in the streets is a ploy to distract innocent victims who are about to lose their wallets. As always, wear your money belt and keep a low profile.

Tours: This walk is enough for most visitors, but if you want a more in-depth visit with a guide and a group, consider Randy Roy's Red Light Tours (described on page 52). The Prostitution Information Center offers tours only on Saturday at 17:00 (see page 105).

Old Church (Oude Kerk): €5, more for temporary exhibits, Mon-Sat 11:00-17:00, Sun 13:00-17:00, tel. 020/625-8284. You can climb the 167 steps to the top of the church tower (€6, April-Sept Mon-Sat 13:00-17:00, closed Oct-March).

Amstelkring Museum (Our Lord in the Attic): €7, Mon-Sat 10:00-17:00, Sun and holidays 13:00-17:00, no photos, Oudezijds Voorburgwal 40, tel. 020/624-6604.

Overview

The walk starts at the centrally located Dam Square. Two parallel streets with similar names—Oudezijds Voorburgwal and Oudezijds Achterburgwal—run north-south through the heart of De Wallen. You'll walk a big, long loop: north on Voorburgwal past the Old Church, hook around on Zeedijk street, and return on Achterburgwal, ending two blocks from Dam Square.

The Walk Begins

• *From Dam Square, head down Warmoesstraat (to the left as you face the big, fancy Grand Hotel Krasnapolsky). A long block ahead, you'll see a small shop on the right.*

Condomerie (Het Gulden Vlies)

This condom shop has a knack for entertainment. Inside is a small glass case displaying a condom museum. On the counter is a three-ring notebook displaying all of the inventory (Mon-Sat 11:00-18:00, closed Sun, Warmoesstraat 141, tel. 020/627-4174, www.condomerie.com).

• *From here, pass the two little street barricades with cute red lights around them and enter the traffic-free world of...*

De Wallen

Dildos, dirty playing cards, penis-headed lipsticks, S&M starter kits, kinky magazines, and blue videos—welcome to De Wallen.

While the Red Light District is notorious throughout the Netherlands, even small rural towns often have **sex shops** like these to satisfy their citizens' needs. Browsers are welcome inside the sex shops. Video arcades—giving access to dozens of porn films—charge by the minute.

According to legend, Quentin Tarantino holed up at the Winston Hotel for three months in 1993 to write *Pulp Fiction*. Farther down, you come to an intersection with the Old Church down the street on the right (you'll go to the church in a moment). Standing here, note the gay rainbow flags and the S&M flags (black and blue with a heart). Also notice the security cameras and modern lighting. Freedom reigns here, but everything is kept under a watchful eye by the two neighborhood police departments.

Throughout the Red Light District, you'll see Irish pubs, advertisements for football (soccer) games, and British, Scottish,

Red Light District Walk

❶ Condomerie

❷ Sex Shops, S&M Flags & Mr. B's

❸ Old Church

❹ Prostitutes in Narrow Alleyways

❺ Cheaper Prostitutes

❻ Prostitution Info Center & Room-Rental Office

❼ Princess Juliana Daycare

❽ Pill Bridge

❾ Amstelkring Museum

❿ Historic Building (1580)

⓫ View of Little Venice

⓬ Old Wooden House & Old Harbor View

⓭ Zeedijk Street & Locks

⓮ Buddhist Temple & Chinatown

⓯ The Waag & Nieuwmarkt

⓰ Banana Bar

⓱ Erotic Museum

⓲ Absolute Danny Shop

⓳ Theatre Casa Rosso

⓴ Cannabis College

㉑ Hash, Marijuana & Hemp Museum

㉒ Sensi Seed Bank Store

and Irish flags. The Red Light District is a very popular destination for Brits—who are just a cheap flight away from Amsterdam—and the money-savvy Dutch know their best customers.

At #97 is the Elements of Nature smartshop, a little grocery store of mind-bending natural ingredients.

At #89, Mr. B's Leather and Rubber Land, marked by the S&M flag, takes macho to painful and what seems like anatomically impossible extremes. Downstairs you'll find great deals on whips and masks.

• *Now, backtrack a few steps, and head down Wijde Kerksteeg to the church.*

Old Church (Oude Kerk)

Returning from a long sea voyage, sailors of yore would spy the steeple of the Old Church on the horizon and know they were

home. They thanked St. Nicholas—the patron of this church, seafarers, and Amsterdam—for their safe return.

Begun in about 1300 and dedicated to St. Nicholas, the gangly church was built in fits and starts during the next 300 years. Even when the rival New Church (Nieuwe Kerk) was built on Dam Square, Amsterdam's oldest church still had the tallest spire, the biggest organ, the most side-altars, and remained the neighborhood's center of activity, bustling inside and out with merchants and street markets.

The tower (290 feet high, with an octagonal steeple atop a bell tower), which still has original 14th-century components, was updated in the 18th century and served as a model for many other Dutch churches. The carillon's 47 bells chime mechanically or can be played by one of Amsterdam's three official carillonneurs.

The church is historic, but there's not much to see inside. Of the 2,500 gravestones in the floor, the most famous is opposite the entrance: "Saskia 19 Juni 1642," the grave of Rembrandt's wife. The church is spacious and stripped-down, due to iconoclastic vandals. In the 16th century, rioting anti-Spanish Protestants gutted the church, smashing windows and removing politically incorrect "graven images" (religious statues). One renowned girl threw her shoe at the Virgin statue. (Strict Calvinists at one point even removed the organ as a senseless luxury, until they found they couldn't stay on key singing hymns without it.) Atop the brass choir screen, an inscription *('t misbruyk in Godes...)* commemorates the iconoclasm: "The false practices introduced into God's church were undone here in 1578."

The church, permanently stripped of "pope-ish" decoration, was transformed from Catholic to Dutch Reformed, the name St. Nicholas' Church was dropped, and it became known by the nickname everyone called it anyway—the Old Church.

Around the Old Church

The church is surrounded by prostitution, yes, but there are other things as well—namely, everyday life. Attached to the Old Church like barnacles are small buildings, originally homes for priests, church offices, or rental units. The house to the right of the entrance (at #25), inhabited by an elderly woman, is very tiny—32 feet by 8 feet. Remember, someone lives here—be discreet. Near the church entrance, you'll find several curiosities: a statue of Belle, honoring "sex workers around the world"; a bronze breast in the pavement; and a green metal urinal that gets a lot of use.

• *From the urinal, go half a block south along the canal toward the Bulldog Café. Just before the coffeeshop, turn right at a narrow alleyway called Dollebegijnensteeg. Take a deep breath and squeeze into this tight opening.*

Prostitutes in Narrow Alleyways

You're right in the thick of high-density sleaze. Several narrow streets are lined with panty-and-bra-clad women in the windows winking at horny men, rapping on the window to attract attention, or looking disdainfully at sightseers. You may notice that different zones feature prostitutes from different lands—Asia, Africa, Eastern Europe. This is to cater to customer tastes, as regulars know what they want.

The area sure looks rough, but, aside from tricky pickpockets, these streets are actually very safe. The entire Red Light District is dotted with teeny-tiny video surveillance cameras, located above doorways and in narrow alleys. If prostitutes have or notice any trouble, they press a buzzer that swiftly unleashes a burly, angry bouncer or the police.

There are other pockets of prostitution around, but this is one of the most concentrated. Explore.

• *Return to the Old Church and start to circle the church clockwise. Around the back (on Oude Kerksplein), you'll see older, plumper (and cheaper) prostitutes.*

Although some women choose prostitution as a lucrative career, others are forced into it by circumstance—poverty, drug addiction, abusive men, and immigration scams. Since the fall of the Iron Curtain, many Eastern Europeans have flocked here for

Prostitution

Prostitution has been legal here since the 1980s. The women are often entrepreneurs, renting space and running their own

businesses. Women usually rent their space for eight-hour shifts. A good spot costs €100 for a half-day shift and €150 for an evening.

The rooms look tiny from the street ("Do they have to do it standing up?"), but most are just display windows, opening into a room behind or upstairs with a bed, a sink, and little else.

Prostitutes have to keep their premises hygienic, make sure their clients use condoms, and avoid minors. Most prostitutes opposed legalization, not wanting taxes and bureaucratic regulations.

Popular prostitutes charge €25-50 for a 20-minute visit and make about €500 a day. They fill out tax returns, and many belong to a loose union called the Red Thread. The law, not pimps, protects prostitutes. If a prostitute is diagnosed with HIV or AIDS, she gets a subsidized apartment to encourage her to quit the business. As shocking as this may seem to some, it's a good example of a pragmatic Dutch solution to a problem—getting the most dangerous prostitutes off the streets to combat the spread of AIDS.

the high wages. Russian and East European crime syndicates have muscled in. The line between victim and entrepreneur grows finer and less clear.

• *Around the back of the Old Church is the...*

Prostitution Information Center (PIC, at #3)

This center is only open on Saturdays, when it doles out information, books, condoms, T-shirts, and other off-beat souvenirs, and offers a €12.50 walking tour (Sat at 17:00). They have a map showing exactly where prostitution is legal and a small, frank booklet answering the most common questions tourists have about Amsterdam's Red Light District (free, open Sat 16:00-19:00 only, facing the Old Church at Enge Kerksteeg 3, tel. 020/420-7328, www.pic-amsterdam.com).

• *Next door is a...*

Room-Rental Office (Kamerverhuurbedrijf)

Women come here to rent window space and bedrooms to use for prostitution. Several of the available rooms are just next door. In return for their 8-, 12-, or 24-hour rental, they get security—the man at the desk keeps an eye on them on video surveillance. (See the monitors inside, and the small cameras and orange alarm lights above the doors.) The office also sells supplies (condoms by the case, lubricants, Coca-Cola).

This man does not arrange sex. The women who rent space from this business are self-employed. Customers negotiate directly with a woman at her door.

How does it work? A customer browses around. A prostitute catches his eye. If the prostitute is interested in his business (they are selective for their own safety), she winks him over. They talk at the door as she explains her price. Many are very aggressive at getting the man inside, where the temptation game revs up. A price is agreed and paid in advance.

Are there male prostitutes? Certainly, anything you might want is available somewhere in the Red Light District, but an experiment in the 1990s to put male prostitutes in windows didn't stand up. There are, however, "reconstructed women"—gorgeous transvestites who may (or may not) warn customers, to ward off any rude surprises. Blue lights (rather than red) mark where transvestites do business.

• *Continue circling clockwise around the church. Amid prostitutes in windows and just past the "sex-cinema," the orange brick building on the left is the...*

Princess Juliana Daycare

Life goes on, and locals need someplace to send their kids. This school was built in the 1970s, when the idea was to mix all dimensions of society together, absorbing the seedy into the decent. The location of this daycare center (for kids from newborn to four years old) would be a tough sell where I come from. (If you're having trouble finding this discreet building—which is sealed up tight—look for the black-and-white photo of the princess near a gunmetal-gray door.)

• *Turn left at the canal and continue north on Oudezijds Voorburgwal to the end of the canal. Along the way, you'll pass the...*

Pill Bridge and Little Venice

The first bridge you pass is nicknamed "Pill Bridge" for the retail items sold by the seedy guys who hang out here. Beyond that, on the left is the fascinating Amstelkring Museum, in the Our Lord in the Attic Church (at #40, one of the city's most visit-worthy museums—❂ see the Amstelkring Museum Tour chapter).

Near the next bridge (at #14) is a historic building from 1580 (built two years after Amsterdam's Protestants booted out their Spanish rulers, and two decades before the Dutch East India

Company formed, during a time of increasing overseas trade).

This part of the canal is called "Little Venice." Houses rise directly from the water here (no quays or streets). Like Venice, the city was built in a marshy delta area, on millions of pilings. And, like Venice, it grew rich on sea trade.

• *From here, passing a collection of fine gable stones embedded in the wall, continue straight up a small lane called Sint Olofssteeg to Zeedijk street. Turn left and walk along Zeedijk street to where it opens up to a viewpoint overlooking the marina, Damrak, and Central Station. On the corner, at Zeedijk 1, you'll find an...*

Old Wooden House and View of the Old Harbor

Picture the scene in the 1600s, when this café was a tavern, sitting right at what was then the water's edge. Boats sailed into the mouth of the harbor, located where Central Station sits today (on reclaimed land). Crews tied up in today's marina, arriving from, say, a two-year voyage to Bali, bringing home fabulous wealth. Sailors spilled onto Zeedijk street, were greeted by swinging ladies swinging red lanterns, stopped by St. Olaf's chapel to say a prayer of thanks, then anchored in this tavern for a good Dutch beer.

• *Backtrack up Zeedijk street, to the crest of a bridge, to see...*

The Zeedijk and the Locks

The street called Zeedijk runs along the top of the "sea dike" that historically protected sea-level Amsterdam from North Sea tides. Once a day, a city worker unlocks the green box (by the railing) and presses a button, the locks open, and the tides flush out the city's canals. If the gate is open, you might see water flowing in or out.

In the 1970s and 1980s, this street was unbelievably sleazy

(I live to tell)—a no-man's-land of junkies fighting amongst themselves. Today, it's increasingly trendy and upscale, fast becoming a vibrant neighborhood of urban diversity.

The street is a mix of ethnic restaurants (Thai and Portuguese) and bars, like the gay-oriented Queen's Head (at #20). The new building at #30, built in "MIIM" (1998), offers apartments for rent and sale to the neighborhood's new, upscale inhabitants.

The Café 't Mandje (at #63) was perhaps Europe's first gay bar. It opened in 1927, closed in 1985, and is now a working bar once again. It stands as a memorial to owner Bet van Beeren (1907-1967), "Queen of the Zeedijk." The original Zee-dyke, Bet cruised the street in leather on her motorcycle. The interior is crammed with photos and memorabilia. The neckties hanging from the ceiling recall Bet's tradition of scissoring off customer's ties.

• *Making a right before the Buurt Informatie Centrum, this walk heads onto Korte Stormsteeg street, back to the canalside red lights. But first, you may wish to venture a block or two farther south, where you'll find a temple and a prison.*

The Lotus Flower Chinese Buddhist Temple

You're in the midst of Amsterdam's Chinatown, featuring chickens in windows, Asian gift shops, and some of the city's best Chinese restaurants (such as Nam Kee at #113).

Enter the colorful, red-and-yellow, open-air temple by climbing the stairs and passing through one of three entry arches representing the Buddhist Threefold Path (clean living, meditation, and wisdom). Under the roof, on lotus flowers, sits a statue of Guan Yin, whose thousand hands are always busy helping Buddha.

Three nuns (who live in the convent) and Chinatown's faithful kneel before the goddess, burn incense, and offer her fruit and flowers. The walls hold terra-cotta panels bearing the names of donors (free, Tue-Sat 12:00-17:00, Sun 10:30-12:00, closed Mon, Zeedijk 106-118, www.ibps.nl).

The Waag and Nieuwmarkt

In 1488, this octagonal tower was the main gate of the city's eastern wall. Later, it became a weighing house *(Waag)*, then a prison. In the 1600s, the tower was an operating theater for med students, where Rembrandt sat, sketchpad in hand, to see a criminal's body dissected. The painting that resulted *(The Anatomy Lesson of Dr. Jan Deijman)* now hangs in the Amsterdam Museum.

Today, the Waag is a café, sitting in the middle of Nieuwmarkt Square (which sports a modern public urinal)—a scene that is somewhat seedy, but hip, bar-filled, and very local.

• *From the square, go back to Zeedijk street, head west a few steps down Korte Stormsteeg, then go left along the canal.*

Social Control

Holland has pioneered "social control," meaning that neighborhood security comes not from iron shutters, heavily armed cops, and gated communities, but from neighbors looking out for one another. Everyone knows everyone in this tight-knit neighborhood. If Magreet doesn't buy bread for two days, the baker asks around. Unlike in many big cities, there's no chance that anyone here could lie dead in his house unnoticed for weeks. Video surveillance cameras watch prostitutes, while prostitutes survey the streets, buzzing for help if they spot trouble. Watch the men who watch the women who watch out for their neighbors across the street who watch the flower shop on the corner—"social control."

Oudezijds Achterburgwal

This beautiful, tree-lined canal is the heart of Red Light District nightlife, playing host to most of the main nightclubs. The majority of the sights are along the right-hand side of the street.

Banana Bar (Bananenbar, at #37)

The facade of this nightclub is decorated with Art Nouveau eroticism that's classier than what's offered inside. For €45 you get admission for an hour, drinks included. Undressed ladies serve the drinks, perched atop the bar. Touching is not allowed, but you can order a banana, and the lady will serve it to you any way you like. For a full description, step into the lobby (open nightly until 2:00 in the morning, Oudezijds Achterburgwal 37, tel. 020/622-4670, www.bananenbar.nl).

• *At Molensteeg, cross the bridge to head to the right side of Oudezijds Achterburgwal. A few paces to the right from the bridge is the...*

Erotic Museum (at #54)

"Wot a rip-off!" said a drunk British lout to his mates as he emerged from the Erotic Museum. If it's graphic sex you seek, this is not the place. To put it bluntly, this museum is not very good.

What you will see, besides the self-pleasuring bicycle girl in the lobby, are erotic statuettes from Asian cultures and some mildly risqué John Lennon sketches of him and Yoko Ono (on the first floor); a collection of racy comic books, photos, and old French literature (on the second floor); reconstructions of what you see in today's Red Light District, including a prostitute's chambers, sex-shop window displays, and videos of nightclub sex shows (on the third floor); and finally, the S&M room, where you're greeted by a mannequin urinating on you (on the top floor). S-mannequins torment M-mannequins for their mutual pleasure, and there are photos of America's famous raunchy 1950s pinup girl, Bettie Page, in black hair, stockings, garters, and high heels (€7, daily 11:00-1:00 in the morning, Oudezijds Achterburgwal 54, tel. 020/624-7303). Note that Amsterdam has another, more entertaining sex museum—the Damrak Sex Museum (see page 68).

Absolute Danny (at #76)

This shop "for all your sensual clothing" sells leather and rubber outfits with dog collars suggesting bondage scenarios, in a full array of colors from red to black to...well, that's about it.

• *Continuing south on Oudezijds Achterburgwal, on the right (lined by pink elephants) you'll find the...*

Theatre Casa Rosso

This is the area's best-known nightclub for live sex shows. Unlike some sex shows that draw you in to rip you off with hidden charges, the Casa Rosso is a legitimate operation. Fixed-price tickets offer evening performances featuring strippers and live sex acts—some simulated, some real (€30, €45 includes drinks, nightly until 2:00 in the morning, Oudezijds Achterburgwal 106-108, tel. 020/627-8954, www.casarosso.nl).

• *Along the right side of the next block, you'll find three cannabis sights, starting with the...*

Cannabis College (at #124)

This free, public study center explains the positive industrial, medicinal, and recreational uses of cannabis. Books and newspaper clippings tell about practical hemp products, the medical uses of marijuana, and police prosecution/persecution of cannabis users. The pride and joy of the college is downstairs—the organic flowering cannabis garden, "where you can admire the plant in all her beauty." The garden (access by €3 donation) happens to fit the Dutch legal limit of three plants per person or five per household (free, daily 11:00-19:00, Oudezijds Achterburgwal 124, tel. 020/423-4420, www.cannabiscollege.com).

Hash, Marijuana, and Hemp Museum (at #148) and Gallery (at #130)

Two related establishments—a museum and a gallery of pot-related art—share the same ticket. The small museum is meatier: earnest, informative, and educational (if overpriced). If you patiently read the displays, you'll learn plenty about cannabis and its various uses throughout history.

The leafy, green cannabis plant was grown on large plantations by (among others) Dutch Golden Age merchants. They turned the fibrous stalks (hemp) into rope and canvas for ships, and used it to make clothing and lace.

Some cannabis plants—particularly mature females of the *sativa* and *indica* species—contain the psychoactive alkaloid tetrahydrocannabinol (THC) that makes you high. The buds, flowers, and leaves of the plant (marijuana) and the brown sap/resin/pitch that oozes out of the leaves (hashish, or hash) can be dried and smoked to produce effects ranging from euphoria to paranoia to the munchies.

Some peoples, from ancient Scythians and Hindus to modern Nepalis and Afghanis, have used cannabis as a sacred ritual drug. Modern Rastafarians, following a Bible-based religion centered in Jamaica, smoke cannabis, bob to reggae music, and praise God for creating "every herb" and calling them all "good" (Genesis 1:11-12).

The museum's highlight is the grow room, where you look through windows at real, live cannabis plants in various stages of growth, some as tall as my mom. Grown hydroponically (in water, no soil) under grow lights, at a certain stage they're "sexed" to weed out the boring males and "selected" to produce the most powerful strains (€9, daily 10:00-23:00, Oudezijds Achterburgwal 148, tel. 020/623-5961, www.hashmuseum.com).

Sensi Seed Bank Store

This shop is geared toward cannabis growers. They sell seeds, how-to books, and related knickknacks (free, daily 10:00-23:00, Oudezijds Achterburgwal 150, tel. 020/624-0386, www.sensi seeds.com).

• *Where Oudezijds Achterburgwal intersects Oude Doelen street, look to the right to see the Royal Palace on Dam Square, two blocks away.*

Congratulations

You've peeked at locals—from prostitutes to drug pushers to Buddhists to politically active heads with green thumbs—and survived. Now, go back to your hotel and take a shower.

JORDAAN WALK

This walk takes you from Dam Square—the Times Square of Amsterdam—to the Anne Frank House, and then deep into the characteristic Jordaan neighborhood. Cafés, boutiques, bookstores, and art galleries have gentrified the area. The walk is a cultural scavenger hunt, offering you a chance to experience the laid-back Dutch lifestyle and catch a few intimate details most busy tourists never appreciate. In the Jordaan (yor-DAHN) you'll see things that are commonplace in Amsterdam, but that you won't find in any other city in the world.

This is a short and easygoing walk—nice in the sleepy morning or en route to a Jordaan dinner in the evening. Bring your camera, as you'll enjoy some of Amsterdam's most charming canal scenes.

Orientation

Length of This Walk: Allow 90 minutes.

St. Andrew's Hof: Free, Mon-Sat 9:00-18:00, closed Sun, Egelantiersgracht 107.

Electric Ladyland: €5, Tue-Sat 13:00-18:00, closed Sun-Mon, Tweede Leliedwarsstraat 5-HS, tel. 020/420-3776.

Noordermarkt: This square at the end of Westerstraat is lively and colorful during the Monday-morning flea market.

Overview

The walk begins at Dam Square and ends at the center of the Jordaan by Egelantiers canal. From there it's just a short, scenic walk back to your starting point.

The Walk Begins

• *From Dam Square, leave the McDonald's, the mimes, and the tourists behind, and head to the place where real Amsterdammers live. Face the palace. Slip (to the right) between the palace and the New Church (Nieuwe Kerk), and you'll see the facade of the red brick...*

Magna Plaza Shopping Center

Built in 1899 on top of 4,560 pilings, this "modern"-looking building symbolized the city's economic revival after two centuries of decline. The revival was brought on by the opening of the North Sea Canal and increased industrialization, capped by a World's Fair in 1883. The shopping center, originally the main post office, now houses 40 stores. On the ground floor (on the left), the cheery cheese ladies (Diane and her mom, Coby) would love for you to try their Gouda—free and generous samples of three or four kinds, with explanations.

• *Exiting Magna Plaza, go left, walking 50 yards on busy Nieuwezijds Voorburgwal, then left again on tiny Molsteeg. From here, it's a straight shot west (though the street changes names along the way) past the Anne Frank House and into the Jordaan. On the corner is the...*

Mark Raven Gallery

Decades ago, I bought a Mark Raven T-shirt from a street vendor. Now this Amsterdam original has his own upscale shop, selling T-shirts and paintings featuring spindly lined, semi-abstract cityscapes. Raven works primarily with small etchings (as Rembrandt often did), which he transfers to a larger medium.

• *Head west down tiny Molsteeg. Like bike lanes all over town, the pink/maroon pavement alerts you that this stretch of street is actually a bike path—keep to the sides.*

Bicycles

At the intersection with Spuistraat, see the rows of bicycles parked along the street. Amsterdam's 765,000 residents own nearly that many bikes. The Netherlands' 16.5 million people own 16.5 million bikes, with many people owning two—a long-distance racing bike and a junky in-city bike, often deliberately kept in poor maintenance, so it's less enticing to the many bike thieves. Locals are diligent about locking their bikes twice: They lock the spokes and then use a heavy chain to attach the bike to something immovable.

JORDAAN WALK

Jordaan Walk

1 Magna Plaza Shopping Center
2 Mark Raven Gallery
3 Bicycles
4 Torensluis Bridge
5 Oude Leliestraat
6 Herengracht
7 Leliegracht
8 Keizersgracht
9 Westerkerk
10 Homomonument & Pink Point Info Center
11 Anne Frank House
12 Prinsengracht
13 Nieuwe Leliestraat
14 Center of the Jordaan
15 Main Shopping Street
16 St. Andrew's Hof
17 Electric Ladyland
18 Paradox Coffeeshop

The efficient Dutch appreciate a self-propelled machine that travels five times faster than walking, without pollution, noise, parking problems, or high fuel costs. On a *fiets* (bicycle), a speedy local can traverse the historic center in 10 minutes. As you explore, enjoy the quiet of a people-friendly town where bikes outnumber cars. Notice how 100 bikes might be parked along the road, yet they blend right in. Then imagine if each bike were a car. Notice also how biking seems to keep the populace fit and good-looking. People here say that Amsterdam's athletic clubs are more for networking than for working out.

• *After another block, the street opens onto a small square (understandably nicknamed "Big Head" square), with fine benches for picnics. It's actually a bridge, straddling the Singel canal, called the...*

Torensluis Bridge

With cafés and art galleries, this quiet neighborhood seems farther than just three blocks from busy Dam Square. The canal, which was originally the moat running around the medieval walled city, looks much as it might have during the Dutch Golden Age of the 1600s, when the city quickly became a major urban center. Pan 360 degrees and take in the variety of buildings.

The so-called **skinniest house in Amsterdam** is the red house at #166. In fact, it's just the entryway to a normal house that opens up farther back. Most Amsterdam buildings extend far back, with interiors looking quite different from what you might expect from the facade. Real estate has always been expensive on this canal, and owners were taxed by the amount of street frontage. A local saying at the time was, "Only the wealthy can live on the inside of a canal's curve" (where they would have maximum taxable frontage with a minimum of usable space).

The houses crowd together, shoulder to shoulder. Built on top of thousands of logs hammered vertically into the marshy soil, they've shifted with the tides over the years, some leaning to the sides. Many brick houses have iron rods strapped onto the sides, binding the bricks to an inner skeleton of wood. Most have big, tall windows to admit as much light as possible. Mingled among the old houses are a few modern buildings—the sleek, gray-metal, ugly ones are part of the university. And though these buildings try to match the humble, functional spirit of the older ones, they fail. It's the students they house who inject life into this neighborhood.

JORDAAN WALK

Two **characteristic bars** spill out onto the bridge. Van Zuylen is famous for its variety of beers, and the recommended Villa Zeezicht is popular for its sandwiches and apple pie. Both are great for their canal setting.

The "big head" statue of **Multatuli** (1820-1887) honors the "Dutch Rudyard Kipling," whose real name was Eduard Douwes Dekker. His autobiographical novel, *Max Havelaar* (1860),

follows a progressive bureaucrat's fight to improve the lives of Javanese natives slaving away on Dutch-owned plantations. He was the first author to criticize Dutch colonial practices—a very bold position back then.

Amsterdam's **canals** (roughly 50 miles of them) are about 10 feet deep. Back when the canals also functioned as sewers, they were flushed daily by opening the locks as the North Sea tides came in and out. You can glimpse the locks in the distance at the north end of the Singel canal—the white-flagpole thingies sprouting at 45-degree angles (beyond the dome) are part of the apparatus that opens and shuts the gates. The Dutch are credited with inventing locks in the 1300s. This single greatest invention in canal-building allows ships to pass from higher to lower water levels.

The green copper dome in the distance marks the Lutheran church. To the left of the church is the new city—reclaimed in the 1600s and destined to be the high-rent district. To the right is the old town.

• *Continue west on...*

Oude Leliestraat

Consumers will find plenty to consume on this block of shops and cafés that runs Amsterdam's gamut—Reypenaer's cheeses, Puccini's bonbons, Sukabumi's *rijsttafel*, Grey Area's marijuana, Foodism's vegetarian fare, Thirsty Dogg's traditional café fare, Cafeteria's lamb *shoarmas,* and more.

Grey Area bucks the trend of typical coffeeshops: whereas most cultivate a dark, exotic, opium-den atmosphere, this place is small, clean, and well-lit. The green-and-white decal in the window identifies it as #092 in the city's licensing program. This

JORDAAN WALK

Gables

Along the rooftops, Amsterdam's famous gables are false fronts to enhance roofs that are, generally, sharply pitched. Gables come in all shapes and sizes, and are sometimes decorated with animal and human heads, garlands, urns, scrolls, and curlicues. Despite the infinite variety, you can recognize several generic types.

A simple point gable just follows the triangular shape of a normal pitched roof. A bell gable—there's one two doors to the right of the skinny house—is shaped like (duh) a bell. Step gables, which are triangular in shape and lined with steps, are especially popular in Belgium. Spout gables have a rectangular protrusion at the peak. Neck gables rise up vertically from a pair of sloping "shoulders." Cornice gables make pointed roofs look classically horizontal. (There's probably even a clark gable, but frankly, I don't give a damn.)

esteemed coffeeshop was a recent winner of Amsterdam's Cannabis Cup, a high honor. (For more on this and other coffeeshops, see the Smoking chapter.)

• *The next canal is the...*

Herengracht

During the Dutch Golden Age boom in the 1600s, Amsterdam expanded, adding this canal named for the *Heren*, the wealthy city merchants who lined it with their mansions. Because the city was anti-royalty, there was no blue-blooded class; these *Heren* functioned as the town's aristocracy. Even today, the Herengracht is a high-rent district. (Notice that zoning here forbids houseboats.) The house that's kitty-corner across the bridge (Herengracht 150) fronts the canal, allowing visitors a cutaway of its entire depth—the long white side. Most Amsterdam buildings are much bigger than they appear from the front. On the roof, rods support the false-front gable (which originally supported a rich merchant's ego).

Parking is a problem in a city designed for boats, not cars. Parking signs (there's one along Herengracht, on the left) warn you to put money in the meter at the end of the block, or have your wheels shackled with "the boot," which stays on until you pay your fine. Parking in the center runs about €3.50 per hour in a parking lot or €27 for a "day ticket" to park on the street (daily 9:00-19:00, www.amsterdam.info/parking); parking fees and fines fund a substantial portion of the city's transportation budget.

• *Continue west, walking along the…*

Leliegracht

This is one of the city's prettiest small canals, lined with trees and crossed by a series of arched bridges (some of the city's 400). Notice that several of the buildings—furniture stores and bookstores—have staircases leading down below the street level to residences.

Many buildings have a beam jutting out from the top with a hook on the end. Attach a pulley to that, and you can lift up a sofa and send it through a big upper-story window—much easier than lugging it up a narrow staircase.

• *The next canal you cross is…*

Keizersgracht

The **Westerkerk** tower rises above the rooftops, capped with a golden crown and the Amsterdam coat of arms. The crown shape was a gift of the Habsburg Maximilian I, as thanks for a big loan. Rembrandt is buried under the floor of this "Western Church," which dates from 1631. Its carillons toll every 15 minutes, a sound that reminded Anne Frank—who hid out just down the street—that there was, indeed, an outside world.

About 100 yards south along the

Keizers canal, a triangular pink dock juts into the canal—the **Homomonument** (it's three small triangles within one large one). You may see flowers on the dock, remembering an AIDS victim. The pink-triangle design reclaims the Nazi concentration-camp symbol for gay men (lesbians had black triangles) and is a reminder of the persecution homosexuals still experience today.

Near the monument, on Westermarkt square, is a souvenir kiosk called Pink Point. Here the volunteer staff gives out information on gay and lesbian Amsterdam, especially nightlife (daily generally 10:00-18:00, shorter hours in winter, www.pinkpoint .org).

The green metal structure near the Homomonument is a public urinal (called a *urinoir*) that offers only minimal privacy. But for Dutch men, it's no problem.

The busy street just beyond the Homomonument is Raadhuisstraat, where there's a taxi stand, tram stops (for the handy east-west trams #13, #14, and #17), and a *friets* stand featuring art with the lowly fried potato worked into some famous paintings.
• *Continue west on Leliegracht.*

More on Leliegracht

Things that would seem odd anywhere else are commonplace in Amsterdam. The mail slots on several doors have stickers saying

Nee or *Ja* (no or yes), telling the postman what types of junk mail they'll accept or refuse. At #52, a handy bike ramp slants down the steps to a home below street level. And at #62, glance up to the first story to see a rearview mirror. Why go way down steep stairs to see who's at the door when you can just check the well-positioned mirror?
• *At the Prinsengracht, the* **Anne Frank House** *(❂ see the Anne Frank House Tour chapter) is 100 yards to the left, and the Westerkerk and its tower are another 50 yards beyond that.*

Prinsengracht

One of the most livable canals in town is lined with several of the city's estimated 2,500 houseboats. When small, sail-powered cargo ships became uneconomical with the advent of modern cargo boats in the 1930s, they found a new use—as houseboats lining the canals of Amsterdam, where land was so limited and pricey. Today, their cargo holds are fashioned into elegant, cozy living rooms. Moorage spots are prized and grandfathered in, making some of the junky old boats worth more than you'd think. Boaters can plug hoses and cables into outlets along the side of this canal to get water and electricity. (To learn more about houseboats, visit the charming Houseboat Museum, described on page 64.)

Notice the canal traffic. The official speed limit on canals is four miles per hour. At night, boats must have running lights on the top, the side, and the stern. Most boats are small and low, designed to glide under the city's bridges. The Prinsengracht bridge is average size, with less than seven feet of headroom (it varies with the water level); some bridges have less than six feet. Good maps indicate the critical height of the bridges.

Just across the bridge are several typical cafés. The relaxed Café de Prins serves food and drink both day and night. The old-timey De Twee Zwaantjes (a few doors to the right) occasionally features the mournful songs of the late local legend Johnny Jordaan. And the Café 't Smalle (not visible from here, a half-block to the right) has a deck where you can drink outside along a quiet canal (for details, see "Hungry?" on the next page).

• Once you cross the Prinsengracht, you enter the Jordaan neighborhood. Facing west (toward Café de Prins), cross the bridge and veer left down...

Nieuwe Leliestraat

Here the buildings are smaller, the ground-level apartments are remarkably open to the street, signs warn speeding drivers to *Let op!* (Watch out!) for the speed bumps *(drempels)*, and the mail slots sport more *Nees* than *Jas* (no junk mail, please). Welcome to the quiet Jordaan. Built in the 1600s as a working-class housing area, it's now home to artists and yuppies. Though many apartments have windows right on the street, the neighbors don't stare and the residents don't care. They even invite their friends for candlelit dinners right by the front window. The name *Jordaan* probably wasn't derived from the French *jardin*—but given the neighborhood's garden-like ambience, it seems like it should have been.

• At the first intersection, Eerste Leliedwarsstraat, turn right and go one block to the Egelantiers canal. The bridge over the canal is what I think of as...

The Center of the Jordaan

This place—with its bookstores, small cafés full of rickety tables, art galleries, and working artists' studios—captures the essence of the Jordaan.

Look down the quiet Egelantiers canal, lined with trees and old, narrow, gabled buildings and scattered with funky scows by day that become cruising Love Boats by night.

Look south at the Westerkerk, and you'll see a completely different view from the one that the tourists in line at the Anne

Frank House get. Framed by narrow streets, crossed with streetlamp wires, and looming over shoppers on bicycles, this is the church in its best light.

With your back to the church, look north down the street called Tweede (2E) Egelantiers Dwarsstraat, the laid-back neighborhood's main shopping and people street, lined with boutiques, galleries, antiques stores, hair salons, restaurants, and cafés. A few blocks down (but don't go there now), the street changes names a few times before it intersects Westerstraat, a wide, east-west boulevard with more everyday businesses. On Monday a street market fills the street all the way to Noordermarkt at Westerstraat's western end.

• *Just past the next bridge, going west along the Egelantiers canal, on the left at #107, is the entrance to...*

St. Andrew's Hof (Sint-Andrieshof)

Enter—quietly—through the black door marked *Sint-Andrieshof 107 t/m 145* (open Mon-Sat until 18:00, closed Sun, push hard on door) and encounter a slice of Vermeer—a tiny courtyard surrounded by a dozen or so residences. Take a seat on a bench and immerse yourself in this still world. This small-scale version of the Begijnhof is one of scores of *hofjes* (subsidized residences built around a courtyard) funded by churches, charities, and the city for low-income widows and pensioners.

Hungry?

Several recommended restaurants cluster in this area. Especially good are **Café Restaurant de Reiger** and **Café 't Smalle.** For descriptions of these and more Jordaan eateries, see page 194.

• *Your tour's over. It's a short walk back to Dam Square. But old hippies have two more stops: Heading back toward the center of town along the Egelantiers canal, make a right turn on Tweede (2E) Leliedwarsstraat, where you'll find...*

Hippie Highlights

A small shop with a flowery window display, **Electric Ladyland: The First Museum of Fluorescent Art,** hides an illuminated wonderland. It's the creation of Nick Padalino—one cool cat who really found his black-light niche in life. Downstairs, under Nick's shop, is a unique and tiny museum featuring fluorescent black-light art. Nick lovingly guides you, demonstrating fluorescence in minerals from all over the world and in everyday objects (stamps, candy, and so on). He seems to get a bigger kick out of it than even his customers. You can see the historic first fluorescent crayon from San Francisco in the 1950s. Wow. The label says, "Use with black light for church groups." Wow. (€5, Tue-Sat 13:00-18:00, closed Sun-Mon, Tweede Leliedwarsstraat 5-HS, tel. 020/420-3776, www.electric-lady-land.com).

A bit farther along, the **Paradox Coffeeshop** is the perfect coffeeshop for the nervous American who wants a mellow place to go local and friendly service to help out (light meals, fresh juice, easy music, daily 10:00-20:00, Eerste Bloemdwarsstraat 2, tel. 020/623-5639, see listing in the Smoking chapter).

RIJKSMUSEUM TOUR

At Amsterdam's Rijksmuseum ("Rijks" rhymes with "bikes"), Holland's Golden Age shines with the best collection anywhere of the Dutch Masters—from Vermeer's quiet domestic scenes, to Steen's raucous family meals, to Hals' snapshot portraits, to Rembrandt's moody brilliance.

The 17th century saw the Netherlands at the pinnacle of its

power. The Dutch had won their independence from Spain, trade and shipping boomed, wealth poured in, the people were understandably proud, and the arts flourished. This era was later dubbed the Dutch Golden Age. With no church bigwigs or royalty around to commission big canvases in the Protestant Dutch republic, artists had to find different patrons—and they discovered the upper-middle-class businessmen who fueled Holland's capitalist economy. Artists painted their portraits and decorated their homes with pretty still lifes and nonpreachy, slice-of-life art.

The main core of the Rijksmuseum is closed until 2013 for a massive renovation. Thankfully, the most famous masterpieces—nearly everything on the typical tourist's hit list—are on display in the wonderful and easy-on-the-feet Philips Wing (southwest corner of the museum, the part of the building nearest the Van Gogh Museum). This delightful exhibit offers one of the most exciting and enjoyable art experiences in Europe.

Orientation

Cost: €12.50.

Hours: Daily 9:00-18:00, closed only on Jan 1, last entry 30 minutes before closing.

Avoiding Crowds: The museum is most crowded from April to September (especially April to June), on weekends, and during morning hours. Avoid waits in the ticket-buying line by buying your ticket or pass in advance. No one can completely avoid the security line.

You can buy and print your ticket online at www.rijks museum.nl. The ticket is good any time (no entry time specified). Buying online has the added advantage of letting you enter through the "fast lane," scooting you to the front of the security line.

You can also buy tickets at the TI, Keytours (near the museum at Paulus Potterstraat 8, see map), at the AUB/Last Minute Ticket Shop on Leidseplein, and even at many hotels.

Getting There: The entrance to the Philips Wing is clearly marked near the corner of Jan Luijkenstraat and Hobbemastraat (may change with renovation). From Central Station, catch tram #2 or #5 (get out at Hobbemastraat, directly at the Philips Wing).

Information: The helpful information booth inside the museum has free maps and a good guidebook, *The Masterpieces* (€7.50). Info tel. 020/674-7047, switchboard tel. 020/674-7000, www .rijksmuseum.nl.

Audioguide Tour: The excellent €5 audioguide gives two tours—a "highlights" tour, and a more quirky and intimate tour narrated by a popular local artist.

Length of This Tour: Allow one hour.

Baggage Check: Leave your bag at the free checkrooms.

Cuisine Art: There are no eateries inside the museum. The closest place to eat is Cobra Café on Museumplein (15 percent discount with Rijksmuseum ticket, daily 10:00-18:00,

toward the Van Gogh Museum, tel. 020/470-0111).

Just a short walk away, you'll find several cafés on Nieuwe Spiegelstraat, and still more options near Leidseplein. Vondelpark has the delightful Café Vertigo (see page 196) and many picnic spots. Museumplein is perfect for a picnic.

Museumplein

NIEUW →
SPIEGEL STR.

↑ TO
MUNTPLEIN

S I N G E L -

G R A C H T

STADHOUDERSKADE

← TO
VONDELPARK &
LEIDSEPLEIN

JAN LUIJKENSTRAAT

HOBBEMAKADE

RIJKSMUSEUM
MAIN
BUILDING
UNDER
RENOVATION

TRAM
STOP
#2 +5

PHILIPS
WING

BIKE PATH

ENTER

HOBBEMASTRAAT

HOBBEMASTR.

COSTER
DIAMONDS

POTTERSTRAAT

MUSEUM
SHOP

COBRA
CAFÉ

VERMEERSTRAAT

KEYTOURS

POND

HOUSE
OF BOLS

PAULUS

HONTHORSTSTRAAT

ENTER

VAN GOGH
MUSEUM

NEW
WING
← ENTER

M U S E U M
P L E I N

STEDELIJK
MUSEUM

← ENTER

NOT TO SCALE:
PHILIPS WING
ENTRANCE TO
VAN GOGH MUSEUM
ENTRANCE IS
A 5 MIN. WALK

DCH

RIJKSMUSEUM

Photography: Not allowed.
Starring: Rembrandt van Rijn, Frans Hals, Johannes Vermeer, Jan Steen.

The Tour Begins

Dutch Art

Dutch art is meant to be enjoyed, not studied. It's straightforward, meat-and-potatoes art for the common man. The Dutch love the beauty of everyday things painted realistically and with exquisite detail. So set your cerebral cortex on "low" and let this art pass straight from the eyes to the heart, with minimal detours.

• *Enter the large Room 1, dominated by the large, colorful painting of a group of men eating, drinking, and staring at you,* Banquet in Celebration of the Treaty of Münster *(1648), by Bartholomeus van der Helst.*

Golden Age Treasures

Welcome to the Dutch Golden Age. Gaze into the eyes of the men who made Amsterdam the richest city on earth in the 1600s. Though shown in their military uniforms, these men were really captains of industry—shipbuilders, seamen, salesmen, spice-tasters, bankers, and venture capitalists—all part of the complex economic web that planned and financed overseas trade. Also in Room 1, find a ship's cannon and a big wooden model of a 74-gun Dutch man-of-war that escorted convoys of merchant ships loaded with wealth.

The five rooms on the ground floor display objects that bring Holland's Golden Age to life, including weapons, dolls' houses (*poppenhuizen*, Room 3), and precious objects (especially Delft-ware, inspired by Chinese porcelain, Room 5). Soak up the ambience to prepare for the paintings that the Golden Age generation produced and enjoyed.

• *Head upstairs and enter Room 6.*

Rijksmuseum—Philips Wing

Room 6
  AVERCAMP
    Winter Landscape with Ice Skaters

Room 7
  HALS
    The Merry Drinker
    Wedding Portrait of Isaac and Beatrix

  HEDA
    Still Life with Gilt Goblet

Room 8
  REMBRANDT
    Self-Portrait at an Early Age
    Jeremiah Lamenting
    Maria Trip
    "The Portrait of Saskia"
  ASSELYN
    The Threatened Swan

Room 9
  REMBRANDT
    "The Jewish Bride"

(Room 9 Continued)
    "De Staalmeesters"
    Self-Portrait as Apostle Paul

Room 10
  VERMEER
    The Kitchen Maid
    Woman Reading a Letter
    The Love Letter
    "The Little Street"

  STEEN
    The 'Burgher' of Delft

Room 11
  STEEN
    The Feast of St. Nicholas
    The Merry Family

Room 12
  REMBRANDT
    The Night Watch

RIJKSMUSEUM

New Genres

Rather than religious art, Dutch painters portrayed small-scale, down-home, happy subjects, such as portraits, landscapes, still lifes, and so-called "genre scenes" (snapshots of everyday life).

Hendrick Avercamp (1585-1634)— *Winter Landscape with Ice Skaters*

The village stream has frozen over, and the people all come out to play. (Even today, tiny Holland's speed-skating teams routinely beat those from much larger nations.) In the center, a guy falls flat on his face. A couple makes out in the hay-tower silo. There's a "bad moon on the rise" in the broken-down outhouse at left and another nearby. We see the scene from above (the horizon line is high), making it seem as if the fun goes on forever.

A song or a play is revealed to the audience at the writer's pace. But in a painting, we set the tempo, choosing where to look and how long to linger. Exercise your right to loiter. Avercamp, who was deaf and mute, presents a visual symphony of small scenes. Just skate among these Dutch people—rich, poor, lovers hand-in-hand, kids, and moms—and appreciate the silent beauty of this intimate look at old Holland.

• *Enter Room 7.*

Frans Hals (c. 1581-1666)—*The Merry Drinker* (1627)

You're greeted by a jovial man in a black hat, capturing the earthy, exuberant spirit of the Dutch Golden Age. Notice the details—the happy red face of the man offering us a glass of wine, the sparkle in his eyes, the lacy collar, the decorative belt buckle, and so on.

RIJKSMUSEUM

Now move in closer. All these meticulous details are accomplished with a few quick, thick, and messy brushstrokes. The beard is a tangle of brown worms, the belt buckle a yellow blur. His hand is a study in smudges. Even the expressive face is created with a few well-chosen patches of color. Unlike the still-life scenes, this canvas is meant to be viewed from a distance, where the colors and brushstrokes blend together.

Frans Hals was the premier Golden Age portrait painter. Merchants hired him the way we'd hire a wedding photographer. With a few quick strokes, Hals captured not only the features, but also the personality.

Rather than posing his subject, making him stand for hours saying "cheese," Hals tried to catch him at a candid moment. He often painted common people, fishermen, and barflies, such as this one. He had to work quickly to capture the serendipity of the moment. Hals used a stop-action technique, freezing the man in mid-gesture, where the rough brushwork creates a blur that suggests the man is still moving.

Two centuries later, the Impressionists learned from Hals' messy brushwork. In the Van Gogh Museum, you'll see how Van Gogh painted, say, a brown beard by using thick dabs of green, yellow, and red that blend at a distance to make brown.

Frans Hals—*Wedding Portrait of Isaac Abrahamsz Massa and Beatrix van der Laen* (1622)

This wedding portrait of a chubby, pleasant merchant and his bride sums up the story of the Dutch Golden Age. Because this overseas

trader was away from home for years at a time on business, Hals makes a special effort to point out his patron's commitment to marriage. Isaac pledges allegiance to his wife, putting his hand on his heart. Beatrix's wedding ring is prominently displayed dead center between them (on her right-hand forefinger, Protestant-style). The vine clinging to a tree is a symbol of man's support and woman's dependence. And in the distance at right, in the classical love garden, are other happy couples strolling arm-in-arm amid peacocks, a symbol of fertility.

In earlier times, marriage portraits put the man and wife in separate canvases, staring out grimly. Hals' jolly side-by-side couple reflects a societal shift from marriage as business partnership to an arrangement that's more friendly and intimate.

Hals didn't need symbolism to tell us that these two are prepared for their long-distance relationship—they seem relaxed together, but each looks at us directly, with a strong, individual identity. Good as gold, these are the type of people who propelled this soggy little country into its glorious Golden Age.

Various Still Lifes (c. 1630)

Savor the fruits of Holland's rich overseas trade—lemons from the south, pitchers from Germany, and spices from Asia, including

The Dutch Golden Age (1600s)

Who bought this art? Look around at the Rijksmuseum's many portraits, and you'll see ordinary middle-class people, merchants, and traders. Even in their Sunday best, you can tell that these are hardworking, businesslike, friendly, simple people (with a penchant for ruffled lace collars).

Dutch fishermen sold their surplus catch in distant areas of Europe, importing goods from these far lands. In time, fishermen became traders, and by 1600, Holland's merchant fleets ruled the waves with colonies as far away as India, Indonesia, and America (remember—New York was originally "Nieuw Amsterdam"). The Dutch slave trade—selling Africans to Americans—generated a lot of profit for luxuries such as the art you're viewing. Back home, these traders were financed by shrewd Amsterdam businessmen on the new frontiers of capitalism.

Look around again. Is there even one crucifixion? One saint? One Madonna? OK, maybe one. But this art is made for the people, not for the church. In most countries, Catholic bishops and rich kings supported the arts. But the Republic of the Netherlands, recently free of Spanish rule and Vatican domination, was independent, democratic, and largely Protestant, with no taste for saints and Madonnas.

Instead, Dutch burghers bought portraits of themselves and pretty, unpreachy, unpretentious works for their homes. Even poor people bought smaller canvases painted by "no-name" artists and designed to fit the budgets and lifestyles of this less-than-rich-and-famous crowd. We'll see examples of their four favorite subjects—still lifes (of food and mundane objects), landscapes, portraits (often of groups), and scenes from everyday life.

those most exotic of spices...salt and pepper. These carefully composed, photo-realistic still lifes reflect the same sense of pride the Dutch have for their homes, cultivating them like gardens until they're immaculate, decorative, and in perfect order.

Pick one, such as *Still Life with Gilt Goblet* (by Willem Claesz Heda, 1635). Get so close that the guard joins you. Linger over the little things: the pewterware, the seafood, the lemon peels, the rolls, and the glowing goblets that cast a warm reflection on the tablecloth. You'd swear you could see yourself reflected in the pewter vessels. At the very least, you can see the faint reflections of the food and even of

surrounding windows. The closer you get, the better it looks.
• *Enter Room 8.*

Rembrandt van Rijn (1606-1669)— Early Works

Rembrandt van Rijn is the greatest of all Dutch painters. Whereas most painters specialized in one field—portraits, landscapes, still lifes—Rembrandt excelled in them all.

Rembrandt—*Self-Portrait at an Early Age*

Here we see the young small-town boy about to launch himself into whatever life has to offer. Rembrandt was a precocious kid. His father, a miller, insisted that he become a lawyer. His mother hoped he'd be a preacher (look for a portrait of her reading the Bible, nearby). Rembrandt combined the secular and religious

worlds by becoming an artist, someone who can hint at the spiritual by showing us the beauty of the created world.

He moved to Amsterdam and entered the highly competitive art world. Amsterdam was a booming town and, like today, a hip and cosmopolitan city. Rembrandt portrays himself at age 22 as being divided—half in light, half hidden by hair and shadows— open-eyed, but wary of an uncertain future. As we'll see, Rembrandt's paintings are often light and dark, both in color and in subject, exploring the "darker" side of human experience.

Rembrandt—*Jeremiah Lamenting the Destruction of Jerusalem* (1630)

The Babylonians have sacked and burned Jerusalem, but Rembrandt leaves the pyrotechnics (in the murky background

at left) to Spielberg and the big screen. Instead, he tells the story of Israel's destruction in the face of the prophet who predicted the disaster. Jeremiah slumps in defeat, deep in thought, confused and despondent, trying to understand why this evil had to happen. Rembrandt turns his floodlight of truth on the prophet's deeply lined forehead.

Rembrandt wasn't satisfied to crank out portraits of fat merchants in frilly bibs, no matter what they paid him. He wanted to experiment, trying new techniques and more probing subjects. Many of his paintings weren't commissioned and were never even intended for sale. His subjects could be brooding and melancholy, a bit dark for the public's taste. His technique set him apart—you can recognize a Rembrandt canvas by his play of light and dark. Most of his paintings are a deep brown tone, with only a few bright spots glowing from the darkness. This allows Rembrandt to highlight the details he thinks are most important and to express moody emotions.

Light has a primal appeal to humans. (Dig deep into your DNA and remember the time when fire was not tamed. Light! In the middle of the night! This miracle separated us from our fellow animals.) Rembrandt strikes at that instinctive level.

Rembrandt—*Maria Trip* (1639)

This debutante daughter of a wealthy citizen is shy and reserved—maybe a bit awkward in her new dress and adult role, but still self-assured. When he chose to, Rembrandt could dash off a commissioned portrait like nobody's business. The details are immaculate—the lace and shiny satin, the pearls behind the veil, the subtle face and hands. Rembrandt gives us not just a person, but a personality.

Look at the red rings around her eyes, a detail a lesser painter would have airbrushed out. Rembrandt takes this feature, unique to her, and uses it as a setting for her luminous, jewel-like eyes. Without being prettified, she's beautiful.

Rembrandt—*A Young Woman* (a.k.a. *The Portrait of Saskia,* 1633)

It didn't take long for Amsterdam to recognize Rembrandt's great talent. Everyone wanted a portrait done by the young master, and

he became wealthy and famous. He fell in love with and married the rich, beautiful, and cultured Saskia. By all accounts, the two were enormously happy, entertaining friends, decorating their house with fine furniture, raising a family, and living the high life. In this wedding portrait, thought to be of Saskia, the bride's face literally glows. A dash of white paint puts a sparkle in her eye. Barely 30 years old, Rembrandt was the most successful painter in Holland. He had it all.

Rembrandt van Rijn
(1606-1669)

The son of a Leiden miller who owned a waterwheel on the Rhine ("van Rijn"), Rembrandt took Amsterdam by storm with his famous painting of *The Anatomy Lesson* (1632, currently in the Mauritshuis museum in The Hague). The commissions poured in for official portraits, and he was soon wealthy and married (1634) to Saskia van Uylenburgh. They moved to an expensive home in the Jewish Quarter (today's Rembrandt's House museum), and decorated it with their collection of art and exotic furniture. His portraits were dutifully detailed, but other paintings explored strong contrasts of light and dark, with dramatic composition.

In 1642, Saskia died, and Rembrandt's fortunes changed, as the public's taste shifted and commissions dried up. In 1649, he hired an 18-year-old model named Hendrickje Stoffels, and she soon moved in with him and gave birth to their illegitimate daughter. Holland's war with England (1652-1654) devastated the art market, and Rembrandt's free-spending ways forced him to declare bankruptcy (1656)—the ultimate humiliation in success-oriented Amsterdam. He moved to more humble lodgings on Rozengracht.

In his last years, his greatest works were his self-portraits, showing a tired, wrinkled man stoically enduring life's misfortunes. Rembrandt piled on layers of paint and glaze to capture increasingly subtle effects.

In 1668, his lone surviving son, Titus, died, and Rembrandt passed away the next year. His death effectively marked the end of the Dutch Golden Age.

Other "Rembrandts"

The Rijksmuseum displays real Rembrandts, paintings by others that look like his, portraits of Rembrandt by his students, and one or two "Rembrandts" that may not be his. A century ago, there were 1,000 so-called Rembrandt paintings in existence. Since then, a five-man panel of art scholars has declared most of those to be by someone else, winnowing the number of authentic Rembrandts to 300, with some 50 more that may one day be "audited" by the Internal Rembrandt Service. Most of the fakes are not out-and-out forgeries, but works by admirers of his distinctive style. So be careful the next time you plunk down $15 million for a "Rembrandt."

• *In Room 9, you'll find...*

Rembrandt's Later Works

Enjoying fame, wealth, and happiness, Rembrandt may have had it all, but not for long. His wife, Saskia, died. The commissions came more slowly. The money ran out. His mother died. One by one, his sons died. He had to auction off his paintings and furniture to pay debts. He moved out of his fine house to a cheaper place. His bitter losses added a new wisdom to his work.

Rembrandt—*Isaac and Rebecca* (a.k.a. *The Jewish Bride,* 1667)

The man gently draws the woman toward him. She's comfortable enough with him to sink into thought, and she reaches up

unconsciously to return the gentle touch. They're young but wizened. This uncommissioned portrait (known as *The Jewish Bride,* though the subject is unknown) is a truly human look at the relationship between two people in love. They form a protective pyramid of love amid a gloomy background. The touching hands form the center of this somewhat sad but peaceful work. Van Gogh said that "Rembrandt alone has that tenderness—the heartbroken tenderness."

Rembrandt was a master of oil painting. In his later years, he rendered details with a messier, more Impressionistic style. The red-brown-gold of the couple's clothes is a patchwork of oil laid on thick with a palette knife.

Rembrandt—*The Syndics of the Amsterdam Drapers' Guild* (De Staalmeesters, 1662)

Although commissions dwindled, Rembrandt could still paint an official group portrait better than anyone. In the painting made

famous by Dutch Masters cigars, he catches the Drapers Guild in a natural but dignified pose (dignified, at least, until the guy on the left sits on his friend's lap).

It's a business meeting, and they're all dressed in black with black hats—the standard power suit of the Dutch

Golden Age. They gather around a table examining the company's books. Suddenly, someone (us) walks in, and they look up. It's as natural as a snapshot, though X-rays show Rembrandt made many changes in posing them perfectly.

The figures are "framed" by the table beneath them and the top of the wood paneling above their heads, making a three-part composition that brings this band of colleagues together. Even in this simple portrait, we feel we can read the guild members' personalities in their faces. (If the table in the painting looks like it's sloping a bit unnaturally, lie on the floor to view it at Rembrandt's intended angle.)

Rembrandt—*Self-Portrait as the Apostle Paul* (1661)

Rembrandt's many self-portraits show us the evolution of a great

painter's style, as well as the progress of a genius's life. For Rembrandt, the two were intertwined.

Compare this later self-portrait (he's 55 but looks 70) with the youthful, curious Rembrandt of age 22 we saw earlier. With a lined forehead, a bulbous nose, and messy hair, he peers out from under several coats of glazing, holding old, wrinkled pages. His look is...skeptical? Weary? Resigned to life's misfortunes? Or amused? (He's looking at us, but not *just* at us—remember that a self-portrait is done staring into a mirror.)

This man has seen it all—success, love, money, fatherhood, loss, poverty, death. He took these experiences and wove them into his art. Rembrandt died poor and misunderstood, but he remained very much his own man to the end.

• *Enter Room 10.*

Johannes Vermeer (1632-1675)

Vermeer is the master of tranquility and stillness. He creates a clear and silent pool that is a world in itself. Most of his canvases show interiors of Dutch homes, where Dutch women engage in everyday activities, lit by a side window.

Vermeer's father, an art dealer, gave Johannes a passion for painting. Late in the artist's career, with Holland fighting draining wars against England, the demand for art and luxuries went sour in the Netherlands, forcing Vermeer to downsize—he sold his big home, packed up his wife and 14 children, and moved in with his mother-in-law. He died two years later, and his works fell into centuries of obscurity.

The Rijksmuseum has the best collection of Vermeers in the world—all four of them. (There are only some 30 in captivity.) But each is a small jewel worth lingering over.

Shhh...Dutch Art

You're sitting at home late one night, and it's perfectly calm. Not a sound, very peaceful. And then...the refrigerator motor turns off, and it's really quiet.

Dutch art is really quiet art. It silences our busy world, so that every sound, every motion is noticeable. You can hear cows tearing off grass 50 yards away. Dutch art is still. It slows our fast-lane world, so we notice the motion of birds. We notice how the cold night air makes the stars sharp. We notice that the undersides of leaves and cats are always a lighter shade than the tops. Dutch art stills the world so we can hear our own heartbeat and reflect upon that most noble muscle that, without thinking, gives us life.

To see how subtle Dutch art is, realize that one of the museum's most exciting, dramatic, emotional, and extravagant Dutch paintings is probably *The Threatened Swan* (in Room 8). It's quite a contrast to the rape scenes and visions of heaven of Italian Baroque paintings from the same time period.

Vermeer—*The Kitchen Maid* (c. 1658)

It's so quiet you can practically hear the milk pouring into the bowl.

Vermeer brings out the beauty in everyday things. The subject is ordinary—a kitchen maid—but you could look for hours at the tiny details and rich color tones. These are everyday objects, but they glow in a diffused light: the crunchy crust, the hanging basket, even the rusty nail in the wall with its tiny shadow. Vermeer

had a unique ability with surface texture, to show how things feel when you touch them.

The maid is alive with Vermeer's distinctive yellow and blue—the colors of many traditional Dutch homes—against a white backdrop. She is content, solid, and sturdy, performing this simple task as if it's the most important thing in the world. Her full arms are built with patches of reflected light. Vermeer squares off a little world in itself (framed by the table in the foreground, the wall in back, the window to the left, and the footstool at right), then fills this space with objects for our perusal.

Vermeer—*Woman Reading a Letter* (c. 1662-1663)

This painting likely will be away for renovation during your visit. If you do get to see it on display, notice how Vermeer's placid

scenes often have an air of mystery. The woman is reading a letter. From whom? A lover? A father on a two-year business trip to Indonesia? Not even taking time to sit down, she reads it intently, with parted lips and a bowed head. It must be important. (She looks pregnant, adding to the mystery, but that may just be the cut of her clothes.)

Again, Vermeer has framed a moment of everyday life. But within this small world are hints of a wider, wilder world—the

light coming from the left is obviously from a large window, giving us a whiff of the life going on outside. The map hangs prominently, reminding us of travel, and perhaps of where the letter is from.

Vermeer—*The Love Letter* (c. 1669-1670)

There's a similar theme here. The curtain parts, and we see through the doorway into a dollhouse world, then through the seascape on the back wall to the wide ocean. A woman is playing a lute when she's interrupted by a servant bringing a letter. The mysterious letter stops the music, intruding like a pebble dropped into the pool of Vermeer's quiet world. The floor tiles create a strong 3-D perspective that sucks us straight into the center of the painting—the woman's heart.

Vermeer—*View of Houses in Delft* (a.k.a. *The Little Street,* c. 1658)

Vermeer was born in the picturesque town of Delft, grew up near its Market Square, and set a number of his paintings there. This may be the view from his front door.

In *The Little Street,* the details actually aren't very detailed—the cobblestone street doesn't have a single individual stone in it. But Vermeer shows us the beautiful interplay of colored rectangles on the buildings. Our eye moves back and forth from shutter to gable to window... and then from front to back, as we notice the woman deep in the alleyway.

• *Enter Room 11.*

Jan Steen (1626-1679)

Not everyone could afford a masterpiece, but even poorer people wanted works of art for their own homes (like a landscape from Sears for over the sofa). Jan Steen (pronounced "yahn stain"), the Norman Rockwell of his day, painted humorous scenes from the lives of the lower classes. As a tavern owner, he observed society firsthand.

Jan Steen—*The Burgher of Delft and His Daughter* (1655)

This painting is the latest major acquisition of the Rijksmuseum and another star in its lineup. In August of 2004, they paid $15 million for it...and figured they got a great deal. While the rest of the Steen collection is in the next room (see later), the curators often display this one with Vermeer's works because it's pristine and peaceful—more like an exquisite Vermeer than a raucous Steen.

Steen's well-dressed burgher sits on his front porch, when a poor woman and child approach to beg, putting him squarely between the horns of a moral dilemma. On the one hand, we see his rich home, well-dressed daughter, and a vase of flowers—a symbol that his money came from morally suspect capitalism (the kind that produced the folly of 1637's "tulip mania," described on page 30). On the other hand, there are his poor fellow citizens and the church steeple, reminding him of his Christian duty. The man's daughter avoids the confrontation. Will the burgher set the right Christian example? This moral dilemma perplexed many nouveau-riche Dutch Calvinists of Steen's day.

This early painting by Steen demonstrates his mastery of several popular genres: portrait, still life (the flowers and fabrics), cityscape, and moral instruction.

Jan Steen—*The Feast of St. Nicholas*

It's Christmas time, and the kids have been given their gifts, including a little girl who got a doll. The mother says, "Let me see

Ruffs

I cannot tell you why men and women of the Dutch Golden Age found these ruffled, fanlike collars attractive, but they were the rage here and else-where in Europe. Ruffled collars and sleeves were first popular in Spain in the 1540s, but the style really took off with a marvelous discovery in 1565—starch. Within decades, Europe's wealthy merchant class was wearing nine-inch collars made from 18 yards of material.

The ruffs were detachable and made from a long, pleated strip of linen set into a neck (or wrist) band. You tied it in front with strings. Big ones required that you wear a wire frame underneath for support. There were various types—the "cartwheel" was the biggest, a "double ruff" had two layers of pleats, and a "cabbage" was somewhat asymmetrical.

Ruffs required elaborate maintenance. First, you washed and starched the linen. While the cloth was still wet, hot metal pokers were inserted into the folds to form the characteristic figure-eight pattern. The ruffs were stored in special round boxes to hold their shape.

By 1630, Holland had come to its senses, and the fad faded.

---

it," but the girl turns away playfully.

Everyone is happy except the boy, who's crying. His Christmas

present is only a branch in his shoe—like coal in your stocking, the gift for bad boys. His sister gloats and passes it around. The kids laugh at him. But wait—it turns out the family is just playing a trick. In the background, the grandmother beckons to him, saying, "Look, I have your real present in here." Out of the limelight, but smack in the middle, sits the father providing ballast to this family scene and clearly enjoying his children's pleasure.

Steen has frozen the moment, sliced off a piece, and laid it on a canvas. He's told a story with a past, a present, and a future. These are real people in a real scene.

Steen's fun art reminds us that museums aren't mausoleums.

Jan Steen—*The Merry Family* (1668)

This family—three generations living happily under one roof—is eating, drinking, and singing like there's no tomorrow. The bro-

ken eggshells and scattered cookware symbolize waste and extravagance. The neglected proverb tacked to the fireplace reminds us that children will follow in the footsteps of their parents. The father in this jolly scene is very drunk—ready to topple over—while in the foreground his mischievous daughter is feeding her brother wine straight from the flask. Mom and Grandma join the artist himself (playing the bagpipes) in a lively sing-along, but the child learning to smoke would rather follow Dad's lead.

Dutch Golden Age families were notoriously lenient with their kids. Even today, the Dutch describe a rowdy family as a "Jan Steen household."

• *Room 12 is dominated by...*

Rembrandt—*The Company of Frans Banning Cocq* (a.k.a. *The Night Watch*, 1642)

• *The best viewing spot is to the right of center—the angle Rembrandt had in mind when he designed it for its original location.*

This is Rembrandt's most famous—though not necessarily greatest—painting. Created in 1642, when he was 36, it was one

of his most important commissions: a group portrait of a company of Amsterdam's Civic Guards to hang in their meeting hall.

It's an action shot. With flags waving and drums beating, the guardsmen (who, by the 1640s, were really only an honorary militia of rich bigwigs) spill onto the street from under an arch in the back. It's

"all for one and one for all" as they rush to Amsterdam's rescue. The soldiers grab lances and load their muskets. In the center, the commander (in black, with a red sash) strides forward energetically with a hand gesture that seems to say, "What are we waiting for? Let's move out!" His lieutenant focuses on his every order.

Rembrandt caught the optimistic spirit of Holland in the

1600s. Its war of independence from Spain was heading to victory and the economy was booming. These guardsmen on the move epitomize the proud, independent, upwardly mobile Dutch.

Why is *The Night Watch* so famous? Compare it with other, less famous group portraits, where every face is visible and everyone is well-lit, flat, and flashbulb-perfect. These people paid good money to have their mugs preserved for posterity, and they wanted it right up front. Other group portraits may be colorful, dignified works by a master...but not quite masterpieces.

By contrast, Rembrandt rousted the Civic Guards off their fat duffs. By adding movement and depth to an otherwise static scene, he took posers and turned them into warriors. He turned a simple portrait into great art.

OK, some *Night Watch* scuttlebutt: First off, *"Night Watch"* is a misnomer. It's a daytime scene, but over the years, as the preserving varnish darkened and layers of dirt built up, the sun set on this painting, and it got its popular title. When the painting was moved to a smaller room, the sides were lopped off (and the pieces lost), putting the two main characters in the center and causing the work to become more static than intended. During World War II, the painting was rolled up and hidden for five years. In 1975, a madman attacked the painting, slicing the captain's legs, and in 1990, it was sprayed with acid (it was skillfully restored after both incidents).

The Night Watch, contrary to popular myth, was a smashing success in its day. However, there are elements in it that show why Rembrandt soon fell out of favor as a portrait painter. He seemed to spend as much time painting the dwarf and the mysterious glowing girl with a chicken (the very appropriate mascot of this "militia" of shopkeepers) as he did the faces of his employers.

Rembrandt's life darkened long before his *Night Watch* did. This work marks the peak of Rembrandt's popularity...and the beginning of his fall from grace. He continued to paint masterpieces. Free from the dictates of employers whose taste was in their mouths, he painted what he wanted, how he wanted it. Rembrandt goes beyond mere craftsmanship to probe into, and draw life from, the deepest wells of the human soul.

VAN GOGH MUSEUM TOUR

The Van Gogh Museum (we say "van GO," the Dutch say "van HHHOCK") is a cultural high even for those not into art. Located near the Rijksmuseum, the museum houses the 200 paintings owned by Vincent's younger brother, Theo. It's a user-friendly stroll through the work and life of one enigmatic man. If you like brightly colored landscapes in the Impressionist style, you'll like this museum. If you enjoy finding deeper meaning in works of art, you'll really love it. The mix of Van Gogh's creative genius, his tumultuous life, and the traveler's determination to connect to it makes this museum as much a walk with Vincent as with his art.

Orientation

Cost: €14, more for special exhibits, free for those under 18 and for those with one ear. Credit cards accepted if buying two or more tickets (€25 minimum).

Hours: Daily 10:00-18:00, Fri until 22:00, closed for renovations Oct 2012 through March 2013, when its highlights will be on display at the Hermitage Amsterdam (see page 74).

When to Go: Consider visiting on a Friday evening, when crowds are sparse and the atmosphere is cool, with musicians or a DJ and a wine bar in the lobby.

Avoiding Lines: Skip the 15-30-minute wait in the ticket-buying line by getting your ticket in advance. Your ticket is good any time (no entry time specified). You can buy tickets online at www.vangoghmuseum.nl, at the TI, or at Keytours (just up the street at Paulus Potterstraat 8, see map on page 60).

Getting There: It's the big, modern, gray-and-beige place a few blocks behind the Rijksmuseum at Paulus Potterstraat 7 (the entrance may change with renovation). From Central Station,

VAN GOGH MUSEUM

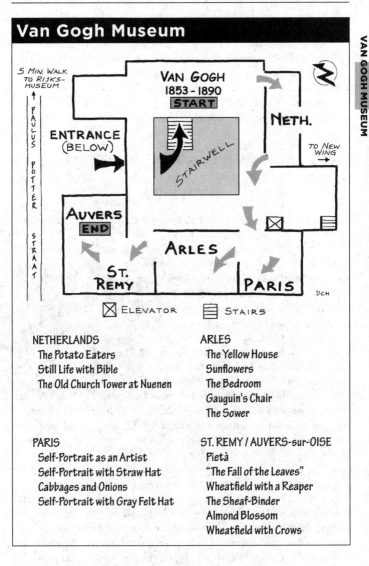

Van Gogh Museum

5 MIN. WALK TO RIJKS-MUSEUM

PAULUS POTTER STRAAT

VAN GOGH
1853 - 1890
START

NETH.

TO NEW WING

ENTRANCE
(BELOW)

STAIRWELL

AUVERS
END

ARLES

ST. REMY

PARIS

DCH

⊠ ELEVATOR   ▤ STAIRS

NETHERLANDS
The Potato Eaters
Still Life with Bible
The Old Church Tower at Nuenen

ARLES
The Yellow House
Sunflowers
The Bedroom
Gauguin's Chair
The Sower

PARIS
Self-Portrait as an Artist
Self-Portrait with Straw Hat
Cabbages and Onions
Self-Portrait with Gray Felt Hat

ST. REMY / AUVERS-sur-OISE
Pietà
"The Fall of the Leaves"
Wheatfield with a Reaper
The Sheaf-Binder
Almond Blossom
Wheatfield with Crows

catch tram #2 or #5 to Hobbemastraat.

Information: At the information desk, pick up a free floor plan (containing a brief history of the artist's brief life). The bookstore is understandably popular, with several good, basic "Vincent" guidebooks and lots of posters (with mailing tubes). A watchable 15-minute video with a basic introduction to Van Gogh plays continuously in the downstairs auditorium. Tel. 020/570-5200, www.vangoghmuseum.nl.

Audioguide Tour: The €5 audioguide includes 90 creatively

VAN GOGH MUSEUM

produced minutes of insightful commentaries about Van Gogh's paintings, along with related quotations from Vincent himself. The museum also rents a €2.50 audioguide geared toward kids.

Length of This Tour: Allow one hour.

Baggage Check: Free and mandatory.

Cuisine Art: The museum café (€10 plates, €6 salads, €4 sandwiches) is OK. The recommended Café Vertigo is nearby, in Vondelpark (see page 196).

Photography: No photos allowed.

Overview

The core of the museum and this entire tour is on the first floor, one flight up from the ground floor.

On the ground floor, you'll find the bookstore and café, along with paintings by artists who preceded and influenced Van Gogh's generation. The second floor has a study area and more paintings (including Van Gogh's smaller-scale works). The third floor shows works by his friends and colleagues, from smooth-surfaced Academy art, to Impressionists Claude Monet and Camille Pissarro, to fellow post-Impressionists Paul Gauguin, Paul Cézanne, and Henri de Toulouse-Lautrec. These are painters who influenced and were influenced by Van Gogh. The exhibition wing in the basement showcases temporary exhibitions.

The main collection of Van Gogh paintings on the first floor is arranged chronologically, taking you through the changes in Vincent van Gogh's life and styles. The paintings are divided into five periods of Vincent's life—the Netherlands, Paris, Arles, St. Rémy, and Auvers-sur-Oise—proceeding clockwise around the floor. (Although the busy curators frequently move the paintings around, they *usually* keep them within the same room, so look around; some may be upstairs.) Some background on Vincent's star-crossed life makes the museum even better, so I've included doses of biographical material for each painting.

The Tour Begins

• *Climb the stairs to the first floor. The first room—often displaying self-portraits—introduces you to the artist.*

Vincent van Gogh (1853-1890)

"I am a man of passions..."

—Vincent van Gogh

You could see Vincent van Gogh's canvases as a series of suicide notes—or as the record of a life full of beauty...perhaps too full of beauty. He attacked life with a passion, experiencing highs and lows more intensely than the average person. The beauty of the world overwhelmed him; its ugliness struck him as only another dimension of beauty. He tried to absorb all of life, good and bad, and channel it onto a canvas, and the frustration of this overwhelming task drove him to madness. If all this is a bit overstated—and I guess it is—it's an attempt to show the emotional impact that Van Gogh's works have had on many people, me included.

Vincent, a pastor's son from a small Dutch town, started working at age 16 as a clerk for an art dealership. But his two interests, art and religion, distracted him from his dreary work, and after several years, he was fired.

The next 10 years were a collage of dead ends as he traveled northern Europe pursuing one path after another. He launched into each project with incredible energy, then became disillusioned and moved on to something else: teacher at a boarding school, assistant preacher, bookstore apprentice, preacher again, theology student, English student, literature student, art student. He bounced around England, France, Belgium, and the Netherlands. He fell in love, but was rejected for someone more respectable. He quarreled with his family and was estranged. He lived with a prostitute and her daughter, offending the few friends he had. Finally, in his late 20s, worn out, flat broke, and in poor health, he returned to his family in Nuenen and made peace. He then started to paint.

• *For his stark early work, enter the next room.*

The Netherlands (1880-1885): Poverty and Religion

These dark, gray canvases show us the hard, plain existence of the people and town of Nuenen, in the rural southern Netherlands. We see simple buildings, bare or autumnal trees, and overcast skies—a world where it seems spring will never arrive. What warmth there is comes from the sturdy, gentle people themselves.

The style is crude—Van Gogh couldn't draw very well and would never become a great technician. The paint is laid on thick, as though painted with Nuenen mud. The main subject is almost always dead center, with little or no background, so there's a claustrophobic feeling. We are unable to see anything but the immediate surroundings.

The Potato Eaters (1885)

"Those that prefer to see the peasants in their Sunday-best may do as they like. I personally am convinced I get better results by painting them in their roughness.... If a peasant picture smells of bacon, smoke, potato steam—all right, that's healthy."

—Vincent van Gogh

In a dark, cramped room lit only by a dim lamp, poor workers help themselves to a steaming plate of potatoes. They've earned it. Vincent deliberately wanted the canvas to be potato-colored.

Vincent had dabbled as an artist during his wandering years, sketching things around him and taking a few art classes, but it wasn't until age 29 that he painted his first oil canvas. He soon threw himself into it with abandon.

He painted the poor working peasants. He worked as a lay minister among the poorest of the poor, peasants and miners. He joined them at work in the mines, taught their children, and even gave away his own few possessions to help them. The church authorities finally dismissed him for "excessive zeal," but he came away understanding the poor's harsh existence and the dignity with which they bore it.

Still Life with Bible (1885)

"I have a terrible need of—shall I say the word?—religion. Then I go out and paint the stars."

—Vincent van Gogh

The Bible and Emile Zola's *La Joie de Vivre*—these two books dominated Van Gogh's life. In his art he tried to fuse his religious upbringing with his love of the world's beauty. He lusted after life with a religious fervor. The burned-out candle tells us of the recent death of his father. The Bible is open to Isaiah 53: "He was despised and rejected of men, a man of sorrows...."

The Old Church Tower at Nuenen (1885)

The crows circle above the local cemetery of Nuenen. Soon after his father's death, Vincent—in poor health and depressed—moved briefly to Antwerp. He then decided to visit his brother Theo, an art dealer living in Paris, the art capital of the world. Theo's support—financial and emotional—allowed Vincent to spend the rest of his short life painting.

Vincent moved from rural, religious, poor Holland to Paris, the City of Light. Vincent van Gone.

• *Continue to...*

Paris (March 1886-Feb 1888): Impressionism

The sun begins to break through, lighting up everything he paints. His canvases are more colorful and the landscapes more spacious, with plenty of open sky, giving a feeling of exhilaration after the closed, dark world of Nuenen.

In the cafés and bars of Paris' bohemian Montmartre district, Vincent met the revolutionary Impressionists. He roomed with Theo and became friends with other struggling young painters, such as Paul Gauguin and Henri de Toulouse-Lautrec. His health improved, he became more sociable, had an affair with an older woman, and was generally happy.

He signed up to study under a well-known classical teacher but quit after only a few classes. He couldn't afford to hire models, so he roamed the streets, sketch pad in hand, and learned from his Impressionist friends.

The Impressionists emphasized getting out of the stuffy studio and setting up canvases outside on the street or in the countryside to paint the play of sunlight off the trees, buildings, and water.

As you see in this room, at first, Vincent copied from the Impressionist masters. He painted garden scenes like Claude Monet, café snapshots like Edgar Degas, "block prints" like the Japanese masters, and self-portraits...like nobody else.

Self-Portrait as an Artist (1888)

"I am now living with my brother Vincent, who is studying the art of painting with indefatigable zeal."

—Theo van Gogh to a friend

Here, the budding young artist proudly displays his new palette full of bright new colors, trying his hand at the Impressionist technique of building a scene using dabs of different-colored paint. A whole new world of art—and life—opened up to him in Paris.

Self-Portrait with Straw Hat (1887)

"You wouldn't recognize Vincent, he has changed so much....
The doctor says that he is now perfectly fit again. He is making
tremendous strides with his work.... He is also far livelier than
he used to be and is popular with people."

—Theo van Gogh to their mother
In Paris, Vincent learned the Impressionist painting technique. The shimmering effect comes from placing dabs of different colors side by side on the canvas. At a distance, the two colors blend in the eye of the viewer to become a third color. Here, Vincent uses separate strokes of blue, yellow, green, and red to create a brown beard—but a brown that throbs with excitement.

Still Lifes, such as Cabbages and Onions (1887)

Vincent quickly developed his own style: thicker paint; broad, swirling brushstrokes; and brighter, clashing colors that make even inanimate objects seem to pulsate with life. The many different colors are supposed to blend together, but you'd have to back up to Belgium before these colors resolve into focus.

Self-Portrait with Gray Felt Hat (1887-1888)

"He has painted one or two portraits which have turned out
well, but he insists on working for nothing. It is a pity that he
shows no desire to earn some money because he could easily do
so here. But you can't change people."

—Theo van Gogh to their mother
Despite his new sociability, Vincent never quite fit in with his Impressionist friends. As he developed into a good painter, he became anxious to strike out on his own. Also, he thought the social life of the big city was distracting him from serious work. In this painting, his face screams out from a swirling background of molecular activity. He wanted peace and quiet, a place where he could throw

himself into his work completely. He headed for the sunny south of France.

• *Travel to the next room to reach...*

Arles (Feb 1888-May 1889): Sunlight, Beauty, and Madness

Winter was just turning to spring when Vincent arrived in Arles, near the French Riviera. After the dreary Paris winter, the colors of springtime overwhelmed him. The blossoming trees inspired him to paint canvas after canvas, drenched in sunlight.

The Yellow House (a.k.a. *The Street*, 1888)

"It is my intention...to go temporarily to the South, where there is even more color, even more sun."

—Vincent van Gogh

Vincent rented this house with the green shutters. (He ate at the pink café next door.) Look at that blue sky! He painted in a

frenzy, working feverishly to try and take it all in. For the next nine months, he produced an explosion of canvases, working very quickly when the mood possessed him. His unique style evolved beyond the Impressionists'—thicker paint, stronger outlines, brighter colors (often applied right from the paint tube), and swirling brushwork that

makes inanimate objects pulse and vibrate with life.

Sunflowers (1889)

"The worse I get along with people, the more I learn to have faith in Nature and concentrate on her."

—Vincent van Gogh

Vincent saw sunflowers as his signature subject, and he painted a half-dozen versions of them, each a study in intense yellow. If he signed the work (look on the vase), it means he was proud of it.

Even a simple work like these sunflowers bursts with life. Different people see different things in *Sunflowers*. Is it a happy painting, or is it a melancholy one? Take your own emotional temperature and see.

The Bedroom (1888)

"I am a man of passions, capable of and subject to doing more or less foolish things—which I happen to regret, more or less, afterwards."

—Vincent van Gogh

Vincent was alone, a Dutchman in Provence. And that had its downside. Vincent swung from flurries of ecstatic activity to bouts of great loneliness. Like anyone traveling alone, he experienced those high highs and low lows. This narrow, trapezoid-shaped, single-room apartment (less than 200 square feet) must have seemed like a prison cell at times. (Psychologists have pointed out that most everything in this painting comes in pairs—two chairs, two paintings, a double bed squeezed down to a single—indicating his desire for a mate. Hmm.)

He invited his friend Paul Gauguin to join him, envisioning a sort of artists' colony in Arles. He spent months preparing a room upstairs for Gauguin's arrival.

Gauguin's Chair (1888)

"Empty chairs—there are many of them, there will be even more, and sooner or later, there will be nothing but empty chairs."

—Vincent van Gogh

Gauguin arrived. At first, they got along great, painting and carousing. But then things went sour. They clashed over art, life, and personalities. On Christmas Eve 1888, Vincent went ballistic. Enraged during an alcohol-fueled argument, he pulled out a knife and waved it in Gauguin's face. Gauguin took the hint and quickly left town. Vincent was horrified at himself. In a fit of remorse and madness, he mutilated his own ear and presented it to a prostitute.

The Sower (1888)

A dark, silhouetted figure sows seeds in the burning sun. It's late in the day. The heat from the sun, the source of all life, radiates out in thick swirls of paint. The sower must be a hopeful man, because the field looks slanted and barren. Someday, he thinks, the seeds he's planting will grow into something great, like the tree that slashes diagonally across the scene—tough and craggy, but with small, optimistic blossoms.

In his younger years, Vincent had worked in Belgium sowing the Christian gospel in a harsh environment (see Mark 4:1-9). Now in Arles, ignited by the sun, he cast his artistic seeds to the wind, hoping.

• *Continue into the next room. Note that paintings featured in the rest of this tour are shifted around a lot. They'll probably be displayed...but likely in a different order.*

St. Rémy (May 1889-1890): The Mental Hospital

The people of Arles realized they had a madman on their hands. A doctor diagnosed "acute mania with hallucinations," and the local vicar talked Vincent into admitting himself to a mental hospital. Vincent wrote to Theo: "Temporarily I wish to remain shut up, as much for my own peace of mind as for other people's."

In the mental hospital, Vincent continued to paint whenever he was well enough. He often couldn't go out, so he copied from books, making his own distinctive versions of works by Rembrandt, Delacroix, Millet, and others.

We see a change from bright, happy landscapes to more introspective subjects. The colors are less bright and more surreal, the brushwork even more furious. The strong outlines of figures are twisted and tortured.

Pietà, after Delacroix (1889)

It's evening after a thunderstorm. Jesus has been crucified, and the corpse lies at the mouth of a tomb. Mary, whipped by the cold wind, holds her empty arms out in despair and confusion. She is the tender mother who receives us all in death, as though saying, "My child, you've been away so long—rest in my arms." Christ has a Vincent-esque red beard.

At first, the peace and quiet of the asylum did Vincent good, and his health improved. Occasionally, he was allowed outside to paint the gardens and landscapes. Meanwhile, the paintings he had sent to Theo began to attract attention in Paris for the first time. A woman in Brussels bought one of his canvases—the only painting he ever sold during his lifetime. In 1987, one of his *Sunflowers* sold for $40 million. Three years later a portrait of Vincent's doctor went for more than $80 million.

The Garden of Saint Paul's Hospital (a.k.a. *The Fall of the Leaves*, 1889)

> "...*a traveler going to a destination that does not exist....*"
>
> —Vincent van Gogh

The stark brown trees are blown by the wind. A solitary figure (Vincent?) winds along a narrow, snaky path as the wind blows leaves on him. The colors are surreal—blue, green, and red tree trunks with heavy black outlines. A road runs away from us, heading nowhere.

Wheatfield with a Reaper (1889)

> "*I have been working hard and fast in the last few days. This is how I try to express how desperately fast things pass in modern life.*"
>
> —Vincent van Gogh

The harvest is here. The time is short. There's much work to be done. A lone reaper works uphill, scything through a swirling wheat field, cutting slender paths of calm.

The Sheaf-Binder, after Millet (1889)

> "*I want to paint men and women with that something of the eternal which the halo used to symbolize....*"
>
> —Vincent van Gogh

Vincent's compassion for honest laborers remained constant following his work with Belgian miners. These sturdy folk, with their curving bodies, wrestle as one with their curving wheat. The world Vincent sees is charged from within by spiritual fires, twisting and turning matter into energy, and vice versa.

The fits of madness returned. During these spells, he lost all sense of his own actions. He couldn't paint, the one thing he felt driven to do. He wrote to Theo, "My surroundings here begin to weigh on me more than I can say—I need air. I feel overwhelmed by boredom and grief."

Auvers-sur-Oise (May–July 1890): Flying Away

> *"The bird looks through the bars at the overcast sky where a thunderstorm is gathering, and inwardly he rebels against his fate. 'I am caged, I am caged, and you tell me I have everything I need!' Oh! I beg you, give me liberty, that I may be a bird like other birds.' A certain idle man resembles this idle bird...."*
>
> —Vincent van Gogh

Almond Blossom (1890)

Vincent moved north to Auvers, a small town near Paris where he could stay at a hotel under a doctor friend's supervision. On the way

there, he visited Theo. Theo's wife had just had a baby, whom they named Vincent. Brother Vincent showed up with this painting under his arm as a birthday gift. Theo's wife later recalled, "I had expected a sick man, but here was a sturdy, broad-shouldered man with a healthy color, a smile on his face, and a very resolute appearance."

In his new surroundings, he continued painting, averaging a canvas a day, but was interrupted by spells that swung from boredom to madness. His letters to Theo were generally optimistic, but he worried that he'd soon succumb completely to insanity and never paint again. The final landscapes are walls of bright, thick paint.

Wheatfield with Crows (1890)

> *"This new attack...came on me in the fields, on a windy day, when I was busy painting."*
>
> —Vincent van Gogh

On July 27, 1890, Vincent left his hotel, walked out to a nearby field, and put a bullet through his chest.

This is the last painting Vincent finished. We can try to search the wreckage of his life for the black box explaining what hap-

pened, but there's not much there. His life was sad and tragic, but the record he left is one not of sadness, but of beauty—intense beauty.

The windblown wheat field is a nest of restless energy.

Scenes like this must have overwhelmed Vincent with their incredible beauty—too much, too fast, with no release. The sky is stormy and dark blue, almost nighttime, barely lit by two suns boiling through the deep ocean of blue. The road starts nowhere, leads nowhere, disappearing into the burning wheat field. Above all of this swirling beauty fly the crows, the dark ghosts that had hovered over his life since the cemetery in Nuenen.

ANNE FRANK HOUSE TOUR

ANNE FRANK
TAGEBUCH

On May 10, 1940, Germany's Luftwaffe began bombing Schiphol Airport, preparing to invade the Netherlands. The Dutch army fought back, and the Nazis responded by leveling Rotterdam. Within a week, the Netherlands surrendered, Queen Wilhelmina fled to Britain, and Nazi soldiers goose-stepped past the Westerkerk and into Dam Square, where they draped huge swastikas on the Royal Palace. A five-year occupation began. The Netherlands had been neutral in World War I, and Amsterdam—progressive and modern, but a bit naive—was in for a rude awakening.

The Anne Frank House immerses you, in a very immediate way, in the struggles and pains of the war years. Walk through rooms where, for two years, eight Amsterdam Jews hid from Nazi persecution. Though they were eventually discovered, and seven of the eight died in concentration camps, their story has an uplifting twist—the diary of Anne Frank, which bolsters the human spirit, affirming that it cannot be crushed.

Orientation

Cost: €8.50, covered by Museumkaart but not I amsterdam Card.

Hours: March 15-Sept 14 daily 9:00-21:00, Sat and July-Aug until 22:00; Sept 15-March 14 daily 9:00-19:00, Sat until 21:00; last entry 30 minutes before closing. Unlike many of Amsterdam's museums, the Anne Frank House is open on most holidays, although it does close for Yom Kippur (Oct 8 in 2011, Sept 26 in 2012).

Avoiding Lines: You can skip the long ticket-buying line (which is especially long in the daytime during summer) by reserving an entry time and buying a ticket at the main TI or online at www.annefrank.org (€0.50/ticket fee). You must present a print-out of your ticket; if you don't have access to a printer, try emailing your confirmation to your hotel and asking them to print it—or bring your confirmation number to the museum and explain the situation. With your ticket in hand, you can skip the line and ring the buzzer at the low-profile door marked *Entrance: Reservations Only*. Without an advance ticket, try arriving when the museum opens (at 9:00) or after 18:00, when the crowd tends to thin out.

Getting There: It's at Prinsengracht 267, near Westerkerk and about a 20-minute walk from Central Station. You can also take tram #13, #14, or #17—or bus #170 or #172—to the Westermarkt stop, about a block south of the museum's entrance.

Information: The museum has excellent information in English, including a pamphlet at the door and good descriptions with quotes from the diary throughout. Use this chapter as background, and then let the displays and videos tell you more. Tel. 020/556-7100, www.annefrank.org. Note that the house has many steep, narrow stairways.

Length of This Tour: Allow one hour.

Baggage Check: The museum has a strict no-big-bags policy—but doesn't offer you a place to check them.

Cuisine Art: The museum café serves simple fare and has good views (daily 9:30-18:00).

The Tour Begins

We'll walk through the rooms where Anne Frank's family and

four other Jews hid for 25 months. The front half of the building, facing the canal, remained the offices and warehouses of an operating business. The back half, where the Franks and others lived, was the Secret Annex, its entrance concealed by a bookcase.

• *After the ticket desk, enter the ground-floor exhibit. After viewing the important five-minute video, go upstairs to the offices/warehouses of the front half of the building.*

First Floor: Offices

From these offices, Otto Frank ran a successful business called Opekta, selling spices and pectin for making jelly. When the Nazis gained power in Germany in 1933, Otto moved his family from Frankfurt to tolerant Amsterdam, hoping for a better life.

Photos and displays show Otto with some of his colleagues. During the Nazi occupation, while the Frank family hid in the back of the building, these brave people kept Otto's business running, secretly bringing supplies to the Franks. Miep Gies, Otto's secretary (see her in the video), brought food every few days, while bookkeeper Victor Kugler cheered up Anne with the latest movie magazines.

• *Go upstairs to the...*

Second Floor: Warehouse

Two models show the two floors where Anne, her family, and four others lived. Dollhouse furniture helps you envision life in the now-bare living quarters. In the first model, find the swinging bookcase that hid the secret entrance leading to Anne's parents' room (with wood stove). Anne's room is next to it, with a blue bed, a brown sofa, a table/chair/bookcase ensemble, and photos on the wall. On the upper floor (the next model) was the living area and the rooms where another family—the Van Pels—stayed. All told, eight people lived in a tiny apartment smaller than 1,000 square feet.

At first the Nazi overlords were tolerant of, and even friendly with, the vanquished Dutch. But soon they imposed restrictions that affected one in ten Amsterdammers—that is, Jews. Jews had to wear yellow-star patches and register with the police. They were banned from movie theaters and trams, and even forbidden to ride bikes.

In February of 1941, the Nazis started rounding up Jews, shipping them by train to "work camps," which, in reality, were transit stations on the way to death camps in the east. Outraged, the people of Amsterdam called a general strike that shut down the city for two days...but the Nazis responded with even harsher laws.

In July of 1942, Anne's sister Margot got her **call-up notice** for a "work-force project." Otto handed over the keys to the business to his Aryan colleagues, sent a final postcard to relatives, gave the family cat to a neighbor, spread rumors that they were fleeing to Switzerland, and prepared his family to "dive under" (*onderduik*, as it was called) into hiding.

Photos of *The People in Hiding* put faces on the eight people—all Jewish—who eventually inhabited the Secret Annex. First was the Frank family—Otto and Edith and their daughters, 13-year-old Anne and 16-year-old Margot. A week later, they were joined

Life in the Annex

By day, it's enforced silence, so no one can hear them in the offices. They whisper, tiptoe, and step around squeaky places in the floor. The windows are blacked out, so they can't even look outside. They read or study, and Anne writes in her diary.

At night and on weekends, when the offices close, one or two might sneak downstairs to listen to Winston Churchill's BBC broadcasts on the office radio. Everyone's spirits rise and sink with news of Allied victories and setbacks.

Anne's diaries make clear the tensions, petty quarrels, and domestic politics of eight people living under intense pressure. Mr. Van Pels annoys Anne, but he gets along well with Margot. Anne never gets used to Mr. Pfeffer, who is literally invading her space. And, most of all, pubescent Anne is often striking sparks with her mom. (Anne's angriest comments about her mother were deleted from early editions of the published diary.)

Despite their hardships, the group feels guilty: They have shelter, while so many other Jews are being rounded up and sent off.

As the war progresses, they endure long nights when the house shakes from Allied air raids, and Anne cuddles up in her dad's bed.

Boredom tinged with fear—this existentialist hell is captured so well in Anne's journal.

by the Van Pels (called the "Van Daans" in the *Diary*), with their teenage son, Peter. A few months later, Fritz Pfeffer (called "Mr. Dussel" in the *Diary*) was invited in.

• *It's now time to enter the hiding place. At the back of the second floor warehouse is the clever hidden passageway into the Secret Annex.*

Secret Annex

The Bookcase Entrance

On a rainy Monday morning, July 6, 1942, the Frank family—wearing extra clothes to avoid carrying suspicious suitcases—breathed their last fresh air, took a long look at the Prinsengracht canal, and disappeared into the back part of the building, where they spent the next two years. Victor Kugler concealed the entrance to the annex with this swinging bookcase, stacked with business files.

Though not exactly a secret (since it's hard to hide an entire building), the annex was just one of thousands of back-houses *(achterhuis)*, a common feature in Amsterdam, and the Nazis had no reason to suspect anything on the premises of the legitimate Opekta business.

• *Pass through the bookcase entrance into...*

Otto, Edith, and Margot's Room

The family carried on life as usual. Otto read Dickens' **Sketches by Boz**, Edith read from a **prayer book** in their native German, and the children continued their studies, with Margot taking **Latin lessons** by correspondence course. They avidly followed the course of the war by radio broadcasts and news from their helpers. As the tides of war slowly turned and it appeared they might one day be saved from the Nazis, Otto tracked the Allied advance on a **map** of Normandy.

The room is very small, even without the furniture. Imagine yourself and two fellow tourists confined here for two years...

Pencil lines on the wall track Margot's and Anne's heights, marking the point at which these growing lives were cut short.

Anne Frank's Room

Pan the room clockwise to see some of the young girl's idols in photos and clippings she pasted there herself: American actor Robert Stack, the future Queen Elizabeth II as a child, matinee idol Rudy Vallee, figure-skating actress Sonja Henie, and, on the other wall, actress Greta Garbo, actor Ray Milland, Renaissance man Leonardo da Vinci, and actress Ginger Rogers.

Out the window (which had to be blacked out) is the back courtyard, which had a chestnut tree and a few buildings. (In 2010, the tree, which Anne had greatly enjoyed, toppled in a storm.) These things, along with the Westerkerk bell chiming every 15 minutes, represented the borders of Anne's "outside world."

Imagine Anne sitting here at a small desk, writing in her diary.

In November of 1942, the Franks invited a Jewish neighbor to join them, and Anne was forced to share the tiny room. Fritz Pfeffer (known in the *Diary* as "Mr. Dussel") was a middle-aged dentist with whom Anne didn't get along. Pfeffer wrote a farewell letter to his non-Jewish fiancée, who continued to live nearby and receive news of him from Miep Gies without knowing his where-abouts.

The Bathroom

The eight inhabitants shared this bathroom. During the day, they didn't dare flush the toilet.

• *Ascend the steep staircase—silently—to the...*

Common Living Room

This was also the kitchen and dining room. Otto Frank was well off, and early on, the annex was well-stocked with food. Miep Gies would dutifully take their shopping list, buy food for her "family" of eight, and secretly lug it up to them. Buying such large quantities in a coupon-rationed economy was highly suspect, but she knew a sympathetic grocer (a block away on Leliegracht) who was part of a ring of Amsterdammers risking their lives to help the Jews.

The **menu** for a special dinner lists soup, roast beef, salad, potatoes, rice, dessert, and coffee. Later, as war and German restrictions plunged Holland into poverty and famine, they survived on canned foods and dried kidney beans.

At night, the living room became sleeping quarters for Hermann and Auguste van Pels.

Peter van Pels' Room

On Peter's 16th birthday, he got a Monopoly-like board game called "The Broker" as a present.

Initially, Anne was cool toward Peter, but after two years together, a courtship developed, and their flirtation culminated in a kiss.

The staircase (no visitor access) leads up to where they stored their food. Anne loved to steal away here for a bit of privacy. At night they'd open a hatch to let in fresh air.

One hot August day, Otto was in this room helping Peter learn English, when they looked up to see a man with a gun. The hiding was over.

• *From here we leave the Secret Annex, returning to the Opekta storeroom and offices in the front house. As you work your way downstairs, you'll see a number of exhibits on the aftermath of this story.*

The Aftermath

Front House: The Arrest, Deportation, and Auschwitz Exhibits

They went quietly. On August 4, 1944, a German policeman accompanied by three Dutch Nazis pulled up in a car, politely entered the Opekta office, and went straight to the bookcase entrance. No one knows who tipped them off. The police gave the surprised hiders time to pack. They demanded their valuables and stuffed them into Anne's briefcase...after dumping her diaries onto the floor.

Taken in a van to Gestapo headquarters, the eight were processed in an efficient, bureaucratic manner, then placed on a train to Westerbork, a concentration camp northeast of the city (see their 3-inch-by-5-inch **registration cards**).

From there they were locked in a car on a normal passenger train and sent to Auschwitz, a Nazi extermination camp in Poland (see the **transport list,** which includes "Anneliese Frank"). On the platform at Auschwitz, they were "forcibly separated from each other" (as Otto later reported) and sent to different camps. Anne and Margot were sent to Bergen-Belsen.

Don't miss the **video** of one of Anne's former neighbors who, by chance, ended up at Bergen-Belsen with Anne. In English she describes their reunion as they talked through a barbed-wire fence shortly before Anne died. She says of Anne, "She didn't have any more tears."

Anne and Margot both died of typhus in March of 1945, only weeks before the camp was liberated. Five of the other original eight were either gassed or died of disease. Only Otto survived.

The Franks' story symbolizes Holland's Jews. The seven who died were among 100,000 Dutch Jews killed during the war years. (Before the war, 135,000 Jews lived in the Netherlands.) Of Anne's school class of 87 Jews, only 20 survived.

• *The next room is devoted to Anne's father.*

The Otto Frank Room

Listen to a 1967 video of Anne's father talking about how the diaries were discovered in the annex. The case holds a rotating display: You may find notebooks that Otto kept during the hiding period, or letters he wrote after the war as he tried to get Anne's diaries published.

• *Downstairs you come to...*

The Diaries

See Anne's three diaries, which were published after the war. Anne received the first diary (with a red-plaid binding) as a birth-

day present when she turned 13, shortly before the family went into hiding. She wrote her diary in the form of a letter to an imaginary friend named Kitty. The other two diaries were written in school-exercise books. Also on display are a book of Anne's short stories, a notebook she kept of favorite quotes, and some loose-leaf pages on which she rewrote and revised parts of her diary.

Often on display (either here or elsewhere) are video interviews with survivors. Miep Gies—who passed away in 2010 at the age of 100— describes how she found Anne's diaries in the Secret Annex following the arrest, and gave them to Otto after the war. Another video shows Otto's reaction.

Though the annex's furniture was ransacked during the arrest, the rooms remained virtually untouched, and we see them today much as they were.

Otto decided to have the diaries published, and in 1947, *De Achterhuis (The Back-House)* appeared in Dutch, soon followed by many translations, a play, and a movie. While she was alive, Anne herself had recognized the uniqueness of her situation and had been in the process of revising her diaries, preparing them to one day be published.

• *Continue downstairs to the ground-floor exhibits.*

The Moral

In the back, a small section tells the story of Otto's struggles to save the house from demolition and turn it into a museum.

Otto wanted the Anne Frank House to be, in his words, "more than a museum." In the larger room an interactive exhibit, called "Free2Choose," helps fulfill his wish. Brief and very well-done video segments present real-life situations in which human-rights values—democracy, equality, tolerance, multiculturalism, religious freedom, and free speech—have come into conflict with one another. At the end of each segment, you can vote your opinion on the dilemma, then see how others have responded. You may be surprised. The point? To keep visitors from leaving the museum with pat feelings of easy moral clarity.

The Anne Frank Foundation is obviously concerned that we learn from Europe's Nazi nightmare. The thinking that made the Holocaust possible still survives. Even today, some groups promote the notion that the Holocaust never occurred and contend that stories like Anne Frank's are only a hoax. It was Otto Frank's dream that visitors come away from the Anne Frank House with an indelible impression—and a better ability to apply these lessons to our contemporary challenges.

AMSTELKRING MUSEUM TOUR

Our Lord in the Attic—
A Hidden Catholic Church

For two centuries (1578-1795), Catholicism in Amsterdam was illegal but tolerated (like pot in the 1970s). When hard-line Protestants took power in 1578, Catholic churches were vandalized and shut down, priests and monks were rounded up and kicked out of town, and Catholic kids were razzed on their way to school. The city's Catholics were forbidden to worship openly, so they gathered secretly to say Mass in homes and offices. In 1663, a wealthy merchant built Our Lord in the Attic (Museum Ons' Lieve Heer op Solder), one of a handful of places in Amsterdam that served as a secret parish church until Catholics were once again allowed to worship in public. This unique church—embedded within a townhouse in the middle of the Red Light District—comes with a little bonus: a rare glimpse inside a historic Amsterdam home straight out of a Vermeer painting.

Orientation

Cost: €7.
Hours: Mon-Sat 10:00-17:00, Sun and holidays 13:00-17:00.
Getting There: It's at Oudezijds Voorburgwal 40, a seven-minute walk from either Central Station or Dam Square.
Information: Tel. 020/624-6604, www.opsolder.nl. Note that the museum has several steep, narrow staircases.
Photography: No photos allowed.
Length of This Tour: Allow one hour.

The Tour Begins

Exterior

Behind the attic windows of this narrow townhouse sits a 150-

seat, three-story church the size of a four-lane bowling alley. Beneath it is the home of the wealthy businessman who built the church. This 17th-century townhouse, like many in the city, also has a back house *(achterhuis)* that was rented out to another family. On this tour we'll visit the front house, then the church, then the back house. Before entering, notice the emergency-exit door in the alley. This was once the hidden church's main entrance.

• *Step inside. Buy your ticket and climb the stairs to the first floor, where we begin touring the front house. The first stop is a room with a big fireplace, the...*

Parlor

By humble Dutch standards, this is an enormous, highly ornate room. Here, in the largest room of the house, the family received guests and hosted parties. The decor is the Dutch version of classical, where everything comes in symmetrical pairs—corkscrew columns flank the fireplace, the coffered ceiling mirrors the patterned black-and-white marble floor, and a fake exit door balances the real entrance door.

Over the fireplace is the coat of arms of Jan Hartman (1619-1668), a rich Catholic businessman who built this house for his family and the church for his fellow Catholics in the neighborhood. The family symbol, the crouching hart (deer), became the nickname of the church—*Het Hert.*

The painting over the fireplace *(The Presentation in the Temple)* has hung here since Hartman's time and shows his taste for Italian, Catholic, Baroque-style beauty. On the wall opposite the windows, the family portrait is right out of the Dutch Golden Age, showing a rich Catholic businessman and his family of four...but it's not Hartman.

• *Now ascend the small spiral staircase that leads to a room facing the canal, called the...*

Canal Room

Unlike the rather formal parlor, this was where the family hung out, staring out the windows or warming themselves at the stove. The furnishings are typical of a wealthy merchant's home at the time. The wood stove and the textiles on the walls are re-creations but look like the originals. In the Dutch custom (still occasionally seen today), the family covered tables with exotic Turkish rugs imported by traders of the Dutch East India Company. The Delftware vase would have been filled with tulips, back then still an exotic and expensive transplant from the East. The tall ceramic doodad is a multi-armed tulip vase. Its pagoda shape reminds us that Delftware's designs and techniques originated in China.

Despite the family's wealth, space was tight. In the 1600s, entire families would often sleep together in small bed cabinets. They sat up to sleep, because they believed that if they lay down, the blood would pool in their heads and kill them.

The black ebony knickknack cabinet is painted with a scene right out of the 1600s Red Light District. On the right door, the Prodigal Son spends his inheritance, making merry with bare-breasted, scarlet-clothed courtesans—high-rent prostitutes who could also entertain educated, cello-loving clients. On the left door, the Prodigal Son has spent it all. He can't pay his bill, and is kicked out of a cheap tavern—still half-dressed—by a pair of short-changed prostitutes.

• *As you climb the staircase up to the church, you can look through a window into the small...*

Chaplain's Room

Originally the maid's room, this humble bedroom is now furnished to look as it did in the 1800s, when the church chaplain lived here. See the tiny bed cabinet decorated with a small skull—a reminder of mortality—and a pipe on the table. Next to the room is the font used by worshippers to wet their fingers and cross themselves upon entering the church.

• *Continue up to the church.*

Our Lord in the Attic Church—Nave and Altar

The church is long and narrow, with an altar at one end, an organ

at the other, and two balconies overhead to maximize the seating in this relatively small space. Compared with Amsterdam's whitewashed Protestant churches, this Catholic church has touches of elaborate Baroque decor, with statues of saints, garlands, and baby angels. The balconies are suspended from the ceiling and held in place by metal rods.

Anti-Catholic = Anti-Spanish

The anti-Catholic laws were imposed by Protestants, partly as retribution for the Catholics' own oppressive rule, partly from a desire to reform what was seen as a corrupted religion...but mostly for political reasons.

By a quirk of royal marriage, Holland was ruled from afar by Spain, Europe's most militantly Catholic country, home of the Inquisition, the Jesuits, and the pope's own Counter-Reformation army. In 1578, Amsterdam's hard-line Protestants staged the "Alteration"—a coup kicking out their Spanish oppressors and allying the city with the Prince of Orange's rebels.

Catholics in the city—probably a majority of the population—were considered guilty by association. They were potential enemies, suspected as puppets of the pope, spies for Spanish kings, or subverters of the social order. In addition, Catholics were considered immoral worshippers of false idols, bowing down to graven images of saints and the Virgin Mary.

Catholic churches were seized and looted, and prominent Catholics were dragged to Dam Square by a lynch mob, before being freed, unharmed, outside the city gates. Laws were passed prohibiting open Catholic worship. For two centuries, Protestant extremists gave Catholics a taste of their own repressive medicine. However, Amsterdam's long tradition of tolerance meant that Catholics were not actually arrested or prosecuted under these laws. Still, many families over many generations were torn apart by the religious and political strife of the Reformation.

This attic church certainly is hidden, but everyone knew it was here. In tolerant (and largely Catholic) Amsterdam, it was rare for Catholics to actually be arrested or punished (after the Protestants' initial anger of 1578), but they were socially unacceptable. Hartman was a respected businessman who used his wealth and influence to convince the city fathers to look the other way as the church

was built. Imagine the jubilation when the church opened its doors in 1663, and Catholics could finally gather together and worship in this fine space without feeling like two-bit criminals.

The **altar** is flanked by classical columns and topped with an arch featuring a stucco God the Father, a dove of the Holy Spirit, and trumpeting angels.

The **base of the left column**—made of wood painted to look like marble—is hollow. Inside is a fold-out wooden pulpit that could be pulled out for the priest to preach from—as explained with photos on the wall opposite.

The **altarpiece painting** (Jacob de Wit's *Baptism of Jesus*) is one of four (three survive) that could be rotated with the feast days. Step into the room behind the altar to see the two spares. In a glass case on the back side of the altar, squint at the ship-in-a-bottle miniature home devotionals.

• *Behind the altar is a room called the...*

Lady Chapel

A 400-year-old altar dedicated to Our Lady—the Virgin Mary, the mother of Christ—contains more of the images that so offended

and outraged hard-line Protestants. See her statue with baby Jesus and find her symbols, the rose and crown, in the blue damask altar cloth.

Catholics have traditionally honored Mary, addressing prayers to her or to other saints, asking them to intercede with God on their behalf. To Calvinist extremists, this was like bowing down to a false goddess. They considered statues of the Virgin to be among the "graven images" forbidden by the Ten Commandments (Exodus 20:4).

The **collection box** (*voor St. Pieter,* on the wall by the staircase down) was for donations sent to fund that most Catholic of monuments, the pope's own church, the Basilica of St. Peter in Rome—to Calvinists, the center of corruption, the "whore of Babylon."

• *Later, we'll head down the stairs here, but first climb the stairs to the first balcony above the church.*

Lower Balcony

The window to the left of the altar (as you face it) looks south across ramshackle rooftops (note the complex townhouse-with-back-house design of so many Amsterdam buildings) to the steeple of the Old Church (Oude Kerk). The Old Church was the main Catholic church until 1578, when it was rededicated as Dutch Reformed (Protestant), the new official religion of the Netherlands. For the next hundred years, Catholics had no large venue to gather in until Our Lord in the Attic opened in 1663.

The 1749 **organ** is small, but more than adequate. These days, music-lovers flock here on special evenings for a *Vondelkonzert* (wandering concert). They listen to a few tunes here, have a drink,

AMSTELKRING MUSEUM

Calvinism

Holland's Protestant movement followed the stern reformer John Calvin more than the beer-drinking German Martin Luther. Calvin's French followers, called Huguenots, fled religious persecution in the 1500s, finding refuge in tolerant Amsterdam. When Catholic Spain began persecuting them in Holland, they entered politics and fought back.

Calvin wanted to reform the Catholic faith by condemning corruption, simplifying rituals, and returning the faith to its biblical roots. Like other Protestants, Calvinists emphasized that only God's grace—and not our good works—can get us to heaven.

He went so far as to say that God predestined some for heaven, some for hell. Later, some overly pious Calvinists even claimed to be able to pick out the lucky winners from the unlucky, sinful losers. Today, the Dutch Reformed Church, as well as some other Reformed and Presbyterian churches, carry on Calvin's brand of Christianity.

then move on to hear more music at, say, the Old Church or the Royal Palace.

Next to the organ, the painting *Evangelist Matthew with an Angel* (*De Evangelist Mattheus*, c. 1625, by Jan Lievens) features the wrinkled forehead and high-contrast shadings used by Lievens' more famous colleague, Rembrandt.

• *Stairs next to the organ lead you to the...*

Upper Balcony

Looking down from this angle, the small church really looks small. It can accommodate 150 seated worshippers. From here the tapering roofline creates the "attic" feel that gives the church its nickname.

• *At the back of the upper balcony is the...*

Canalside Room—Religious Art

This kind of religious hardware is standard in Catholic church services—elaborate silver-and-gold monstrances (ornamental holders in which the Communion wafer is displayed), chalices (for the Communion wine), ciboria (chalices with lids for holding consecrated wafers), pyxes (for storing unconsecrated wafers), candlesticks, and incense burners. "Holy earth boxes" were used for Catholics denied burial in consecrated ground. Instead, they put a little consecrated dirt in the box and placed it in the coffin.

While you admire these beautiful pieces, remember that it was this kind of luxury, ostentation, and Catholic mumbo-jumbo that drove thrifty Calvinists nuts.

Looking out the window, you can see that you're literally in the attic. Straight across the canal is a house with an ornate gable featuring dolphins. This street was once the city's best address.

• *Back down on the lower balcony, circle around to the window just to the right of the altar for a...*

Northern View

Look north across modern junk on rooftops to the impressive dome and twin steeples of St. Nicholas Church, near Central Station. This is the third Amsterdam church to be dedicated to the patron saint of seafarers and of the city. The first was the Old Church (until 1578), then Our Lord in the Attic (1663). Finally, after the last anti-Catholic laws were repealed (1821), St. Nicholas was built as a symbol of the faith's revival.

When St. Nicholas Church was dedicated in 1887, Our Lord in the Attic closed up shop. The next year, wealthy Catholics saved it from the wrecking ball, turning it into one of Amsterdam's first museums.

• *Head back downstairs, passing through the room behind the altar with the Lady Chapel, and taking the stairs (past the offering box) down to the...*

Confessional

The confessional dates from 1740. The priest sat in the left half, while parishioners knelt in the right to confess their sins through a grilled window. Catholic priests have church authority to forgive sins, whereas Protestants take their troubles directly to God.

The sociologist Max Weber theorized that frequently forgiven Catholics more easily accept the status quo, whereas guilt-ridden Protestants are driven to prove their worth by making money. Hence, northern Protestant countries—like the Netherlands—became capitalist powerhouses, while southern Catholic countries remained feudal and backward. Hmm.

• *Go down another flight and turn right, into the...*

Jaap Leeuwenberg Room (Room 10)

We've now left the church premises and moved to the back-house rooms that were rented out to other families. This room's colors are seen in countless old homes—white walls, ochre-yellow beamed ceiling, oxblood-red landing, and black floor tiles. The simple colors, lit here by a light shaft, make small rooms seem bright and spacious.

• Some very steep stairs lead down to the...

17th-Century Kitchen

This reconstructed room was inhabited as-is until 1952. Blue-tiled walls show playful scenes of kids and animals. Step into the small pantry, then open a door to see the toilet.

• Climb the rope back up the stairs and turn left to find exhibits on Amsterdam's other Catholic churches and the "Miracle of Amsterdam." Then descend a different set of stairs into the...

19th-Century Kitchen

This just looks so Dutch, with blue tiles, yellow walls, and Vermeer-esque lighting from a skylight. The portrait opposite the fireplace depicts the last resident of this house on her First Communion day. When she died, in 1953, her house became part of this museum.

Think of how her age overlaps our age...of all the change since she was born. Consider the contrast of this serene space with the wild world that awaits just outside the door of this hidden church. And plunge back into today's Amsterdam.

AMSTERDAM MUSEUM TOUR

Dozens of rooms (with great English explanations) take you creatively through Amsterdam's story—from fishing village, to sea-trading superpower, to hippie haven, to city of immigrants. Simply follow the *Grand Tour* signs, and you'll see every room on your hike through 1,000 years of Amsterdam history. I've highlighted a few stops worth checking out.

Orientation

Cost: €10.
Hours: Mon-Fri 10:00-17:00, Sat-Sun 11:00-17:00.
Getting There: It's on Kalverstraat 92, next to the Begijnhof, in downtown Amsterdam.
Information: Plenty of English descriptions are posted throughout the museum. Tel. 020/523-1822, www.ahm.nl.
Audioguide Tour: The well-done audioguide costs €4.50.
Length of This Tour: Allow one hour.
Cuisine Art: The classy Mokum Museum Café has a pleasant courtyard (€9 plates, €6-9 salads and sandwiches).

The Tour Begins

Ground Floor Entrance Hall: Growth of the City

Take time to watch the interesting video displays in the first room. "The Growth of Amsterdam" (at the far end of the room) takes you through the city's rise. Watch the population go from zero to 750,000 in 1,000 years. Witness the birth of the city—the damming of the Amstel, which created Dam Square, the commercial zone where the Damrak's sea harbor met the Rokin's river port. Then follow the subsequent canalization as the city fills in its fortified center and continues to expand outward in rings.

• *Exit at the far end of the room and go up the first set of stairs. Enter the room with the sign above that says* Start/Rondgang 1350-2000 Grand Tour.

Rooms 2-7: From a City of Monasteries to a Trading Power

Rooms 2-3 display items from when Amsterdam was a Catholic city rich with monasteries and local craftsmen. Rooms 4 and 5 cover the time when Holland was becoming a great sea-trading power. Room 6 shows the growth of Dam Square, with models of the Royal Palace/Town Hall and the tower of the New Church (Nieuwe Kerk).

• *Climb the stairs.*

Rooms 8-9: Amsterdam's Harbor and Medieval Justice

Look for the interesting model (in the stairwell) showing how ships got in and out of the city's shallow harbor. Ingenious 150-foot wooden pontoons, pumped full of air, were attached to the sides of ships to float them high over sandbars. The next room (Room 9, with the tough-sounding title "Social Care, Stern Discipline") displays instruments of medieval-style justice and paintings of great faces, from the big shots to the orphans who used to inhabit this building. This room provides a handy opportunity to study the paintings hanging in the atrium outside this wing, called the Shooting Gallery. There are several 17th-century group portraits of shooting club members, including fine English descriptions.

• *In Room 10, find a staircase up to the carillon.*

Carillon Lessons

Invented by Dutch bellmakers in the 1400s and perfected in the 1600s, this musical instrument is a Flemish specialty. The carillon player (called a "carillonneur"), seated at his keyboard up in the tower, presses keys with his fists and feet, jerking wires that swing clappers against tuned bells. The bells range in size from 20-pound high notes to 8-ton low notes, struck by 100-pound clappers. These days, some carillons have electric actions to make the carillonneur's job easier, plus player-piano mechanisms to automate the playing.

Mozart, Vivaldi, Handel, and Bach—all of whom lived during the carillon's heyday—wrote Baroque music that sounds beautiful on bells.

Sit down and pound your fists on the keys. Hitting the red-marked keys, play a chromatic scale (successive keys) as fast as you can. Hit 'em hard. Try to pound out "Louie Louie" (Hint: The notes are "C," "F," and "G"). Then push the buttons on the walls to hear recordings of actual Amsterdam carillons in action—and imagine the fists flying.

• *Cross the skybridge (over the Civic Guard's Gallery) into Room 11, where you'll find...*

Rembrandt's
The Anatomy Lesson of Dr. Jan Deijman

His famous *Anatomy Lesson of Dr. Tulp* (1632) put young Rembrandt on Amsterdam's artistic map two decades earlier. Now, in 1656,

Rembrandt returned to the dissection room for another anatomy lesson—this time from Dr. Jan Deijman.

A fire in 1732 damaged this group portrait, incinerating the surrounding spectators and leaving us with just the stars of the scene—Dr. Deijman and the corpse. The body of this recently hanged thief ("Black Jack" Fonteijn) was donated to the surgery theater in the Waag (today's Red Light District), where Dr. D. held a dissecting demonstration for med students and the paying public. Rembrandt attended, sketch pad in hand.

The corpse's feet are right in our face (similar to Mantegna's famous *Dead Christ*), a masterpiece of foreshortening. We stare into the gaping hole of his disemboweled stomach. The doctor (his head was burned off in the fire) does the work, opening the head and exposing the brain, while the assistant looks on calmly, hand on hip.

• *Enjoy the rest of the paintings here. Return to Room 10, pass directly through it, and continue through Rooms 12-16 until you reach Room 17. Hop on the bike—that's what it's for—and take a ride through Amsterdam in the 1920s. The next few rooms, "Modern City," give you a sense of life in the 20th century.*

Amsterdam's Story

Visualize the physical layout of this man-made city: built on trees, protected by dikes, and laced with canals in the marshy delta at the mouth of the Amstel River. Location, location, location. Boats could arrive here from Germany by riverboat down the Rhine, from England across the Channel and down the IJ River, and from Denmark by entering the Zuiderzee inlet of the North Sea. No wonder that St. Nicholas, protector of water travelers, was the city's patron saint.

As early as 1300, Amsterdam was already an international trade center of German beer, locally caught herring, cloth, bacon, salt, and wine. Having dammed and canalized the Amstel and diked out the sea tides, the Dutch drained land, sunk pilings, and built a city from scratch. When the region's leading bishop granted the town a charter (1300), Amsterdammers could then set up law courts, judge their own matters, and be essentially autonomous. The town thrived.

By 1500, Amsterdam was a walled city of 12,000, with the Singel canal serving as the moat. Midcentury, the city had a growth spurt when its trading rival Antwerp fell to Spanish troops, and a flood of fellow Flemish headed north, fleeing chaos and religious persecution.

In 1602, hardy Dutch sailors (and Englishman Henry Hudson) tried their hand at trade with the Far East. When they returned, they brought with them valuable spices, jewels, luxury goods... and the Golden Age.

The Dutch East India Company (abbreviated as "VOC" in Dutch), a state-subsidized import/export business, combined nautical skills with capitalist investing. With 500 or so 150-foot ships cruising in and out of Amsterdam's harbor, it was the first great multinational corporation. Amsterdam's Golden Age (c. 1600-1650) rode the wave of hard work and good fortune. Over the next two centuries, the VOC would send a half-million Dutch people on business trips to Asia, broadening their horizons. (If you're interested in the history of the Dutch East India Company, walk the planks of the VOC Ship *Amsterdam*, a re-created trading ship docked near the Netherlands Maritime Museum; see the listing on page 70.)

Rooms 17-21: 20th-Century Sociology

Rooms 18 and 19 show you how the population jumped in contemporary Amsterdam, causing a shortage of housing. Many residents are crammed into small apartments, either in historic buildings or in developments of city-built housing. Many Indonesians, Surinamese, and Muslims have immigrated here in recent years (see page 564). Tracing the evolution of housing in Amsterdam in the 20th century, you study typical apartments from aerial views and dollhouses. The big blue board of doorbells represents the

This city of the Golden Age was perhaps the wealthiest on earth, thriving as the "warehouse of the world." Goods came from everywhere. The VOC's specialties were spices (pepper and cinnamon), coffee and tea, Chinese porcelain (Delftware's Eastern inspiration), and silk. Meanwhile, the Dutch West India Company concentrated on the New World, trading African slaves for South American sugar. With its wealth, Amsterdam built in grand style, erecting the gabled townhouses we see today. The city expanded west and south, adding new neighborhoods.

But by 1650, Amsterdam's overseas trade was being eclipsed by new superpowers—England and France. Inconclusive wars with Louis XIV and England drained the economy, destroyed the trading fleet and demoralized the people. Throughout the 1700s, Amsterdam was a city of backwater bankers rather than international traders, although it remained the cultural center of Holland. In early 1795, Napoleon's French troops occupied the country, and the economy was dismal.

A revival in the 1800s was spurred by technological achievements. The Dutch built a canal reconnecting Amsterdam directly with the North Sea (1824-1876), railroads laced the small country, and the city expanded southward by draining new land. The Rijksmuseum, Central Station, and Magna Plaza were built as proud monuments to the economic upswing.

The 1930s Depression hit hard, followed by five years of occupation under the Nazis, aided by pro-Nazi Dutch. The city's large Jewish population was decimated by Nazi deportations and extermination (falling from about 80,000 Jews in 1940 to just 16,000 in 1945).

With postwar prosperity, 1960s Amsterdam again became a world cultural capital as the center for Europe's hippies, who came here to smoke marijuana. Grassroots campaigns by young, artistic, politically active people promoted free sex and free bikes.

Today, Amsterdam is a city of 765,000 people jammed into small apartments (often with the same floor plan as their neighbors'). Since the 1970s, many immigrants have become locals. One in 10 Amsterdammers is Surinamese, and one in 10 prays toward Mecca.

residents who live in a suburban apartment complex (in a district called Fleerde, which has probably never seen a tourist). Hit the red buzzers to meet the residents and tour their homes.

• *Continue through a few more rooms, then head upstairs to the second floor.*

Rooms 22-24: World War II to the Hippie Age

Amid sobering displays of the Nazi occupation of Amsterdam, don't miss the color footage of Liberation Day in 1945 (on the video monitor in the stairwell). In the 1960s, hippies from around the world were drawn to freewheeling Amsterdam. A socialist group called the Provos provoked the Establishment by publishing an outrageous magazine (the first issue contained a page of smokable paper made from marijuana), staging pro-pot events, and promoting innovative (but ultimately unsuccessful) campaigns to

provide free white bicycles and white electric-powered cars to city commuters. You can trace the evolution of Amsterdam's "no war on drugs" and even listen to a Ted Koppel interview with former New York mayor Ed Koch and his Dutch counterparts on the pros and cons of legalizing marijuana.

In Room 24, you enter a reconstruction of the famous Café 't Mandje, a gay bar on Zeedijk street, as it looked in 1967. See a photo of owner Bet van Beeren and her motorcycle in the window, then step inside to see her hanging collection of neckties, which she cut off delighted customers with a butcher knife. (For more about this bar, see page 108.)

• Go down the stairs and, as you leave the museum, find the room opposite the ticket desk (between the WC and the exit door).

Former Orphanage and Regents' Chamber

The first small room tells of the former orphanage located here. Originally a cloister, it became an orphanage in 1570 and took in kids until the 1960s.

Finally, you enter a stately Regents' Room (for the orphanage's board of directors), where you'll see grand, ego-elevating paintings honoring big shots. Many of the Dutch Masters' paintings you'll see in the Netherlands' museums were commissioned to decorate rooms like this.

SLEEPING IN AMSTERDAM

Greeting a new day by descending steep stairs and stepping into a leafy canalside scene—graceful bridges, historic gables, and bikes clattering on cobbles—is a fun part of experiencing Amsterdam. But Amsterdam is a tough city for budget accommodations, and any hotel room under €140 (or B&B room under €100) will have rough edges. Still, you can sleep well and safely in a great location for €100 per double.

I've grouped my hotel listings into three neighborhoods, each of which has its own character. Staying in **Central Amsterdam** is ideal for people who like shopping, tourist sights, and easy access to public transportation (including Central Station). On the downside, the area has traffic noise, concrete, and urban grittiness, and the hotels can lack character.

West Amsterdam (which includes the Jordaan) has Old World ambience, with quiet canals, old gabled buildings, and candle-lit restaurants. It's also just minutes on foot to Dam Square. Many of my hotels are charming, friendly gabled mansions. The downside here is that you'll pay more.

Southwest Amsterdam has two main areas for accommodations: near Leidseplein (more central) and near Vondelpark (farther away). The streets near the bustling Leidseplein have restaurants, tourist buzz, nightlife, canalside charm, B&B coziness, and walkable (or easy tram) access to the center of town. Farther afield is the quieter semi-suburban neighborhood around Vondelpark and Museumplein, close to the Rijks and Van Gogh museums. You'll find good hotel values and ready access to Vondelpark and the art museums, but you're a half-hour walk (or 10-minute tram ride) to Dam Square.

Some national holidays merit your making reservations far in advance (see "Holidays and Weekends" on page 5). Amsterdam is

---

Sleep Code

(€1 = about $1.40, country code: 31, area code: 020)
S = Single, **D** = Double/Twin, **T** = Triple, **Q** = Quad, **b** = bathroom,
s = shower only. Nearly everyone speaks English. Credit cards
are accepted, and prices include breakfast and tax unless
otherwise noted.

   To help you easily sort through these listings, I've divided
the rooms into three categories, based on the price for a
standard double room with bath:

   $$$ Higher Priced—Most rooms €140 or more.
   $$ Moderately Priced—Most rooms between €80-140.
   $ Lower Priced—Most rooms €80 or less.

   Prices can change without notice; verify the hotel's
current rates online or by email. For other updates, see www
.ricksteves.com/update.

---

jammed during tulip season (late March-mid-May), conventions, festivals, and on summer weekends. During peak season, some hoteliers will not take weekend bookings for people staying fewer than two or three nights.

   Around just about every corner in downtown Amsterdam, you'll see construction: cranes for big transportation projects and small crews of bricklayers repairing the wobbly, cobbled streets that line the canals. Canalside rooms can come with great views—and early-morning construction-crew noise. If you're a light sleeper, ask the hotelier for a quiet room in the back. Smoking is illegal in hotel rooms throughout the Netherlands. Parking in Amsterdam is even worse than driving—if you must park a car, ask your hotelier for advice.

   If you'd rather trade big-city action for small-town coziness, consider sleeping in Haarlem, 20 minutes away by train (see Haarlem chapters).

West Amsterdam

Stately Canalside Hotels
These hotels, a half-mile apart, both face historic canals. They come with lovely lobbies (some more ornate than others) and rooms that can feel like they're from another century. This area oozes elegance and class, and it is fairly quiet at night.

   $$$ The Toren is a chandeliered, historic mansion with a pleasant, canalside setting and a peaceful garden out back for guests. Run by Eric and Petra Toren, this smartly renovated, super-romantic hotel is classy yet friendly, with 38 rooms in a great location on a quiet street two blocks northeast of the Anne Frank House. The capable staff is a great source of local advice. The gilt-frame, velvet-curtained rooms are an opulent splurge (tiny Sb-€115, Db-€200, deluxe Db-€250, third person-€40, prices bump way up during conferences and decrease in winter, rates do not include 5 percent tax, breakfast buffet-€12, air-con, elevator, Internet access and Wi-Fi, Keizersgracht 164, tel. 020/622-6033, fax 020/626-9705, www.thetoren.nl, info@thetoren.nl). To get the best prices, check their website for their "daily rate," and in the "remarks" field, ask for the 10 percent Rick Steves cash discount.

$$$ Hotel Ambassade, lacing together 59 rooms in a maze of connected houses, is elegant and fresh, sitting aristocratically on Herengracht. The staff is top-notch, and the public areas (including a library and a breakfast room) are palatial, with antique furnishings and modern art (Sb-€195, Db-€195-245, spacious "deluxe" Db with canal view-€295, Db suite-€345, Tb-€245-295, extra bed-€40, ask for Rick Steves discount when booking, see website for specials, rates do not include 5 percent tax, breakfast-€17, air-con, elevator, free Internet access and Wi-Fi, Herengracht 341, for location see map on page 180, tel. 020/555-0222, www.ambassade-hotel.nl, info@ambassade-hotel.nl, Roos—pronounced "Rose").

Simpler Canalside Hotels

These places have basic rooms—some downright spare, none plush—and most do without an elevator or other extras. Each of them, however, offers a decent night's sleep in a lovely area of town.

$$ Hotel Brouwer is a woody and homey old-time place. It's situated in a tranquil yet central location on the Singel canal and rents eight rooms with canal views, old furniture, and soulful throw rugs (Sb-€60, Db-€95, Tb-€120, rates don't include 5 percent tax, cash only, small elevator, free Wi-Fi and Internet access, located between Central Station and Dam Square, near Lijnbaanssteeg at Singel 83, tel. 020/624-6358, www.hotelbrouwer.nl, akita@hotelbrouwer.nl).

$$ Hotel Hoksbergen is a welcoming, well-run canalside place in a peaceful location where helpful, hands-on owners Tony and Bert rent 14 rooms (Db-€98, Tb-€143, five Qb apartments-€165-198, fans, free Wi-Fi, Singel 301, tel. 020/626-6043, www.hotelhoksbergen.com, info@hotelhoksbergen.nl).

$$ Hotel Hegra is cozy and affordable, with 11 tight rooms filling a 17th-century merchant's house overlooking the canal (S-€50, D-€79, Ds-€89-€109, Db-€105-€119, Ts-€115-€125, Tb-€130, some rooms with canal view, pay Internet access, free Wi-Fi, bike rental, just north of Wolvenstraat at Herengracht

Hotels & Restaurants in West Amsterdam

1 The Toren
2 Hotel Ambassade
3 Hotel Brouwer
4 Hotel Hoksbergen
5 Hotel Hegra
6 Hotel Chic & Basic Amsterdam
7 Hotel Van Onna
8 Wiechmann Hotel
9 Boogaard's B&B
10 Maes B&B
11 Heren B&B
12 Herengracht 21 B&B
13 Sunhead of 1617 B&B
14 Truelove Guesthouse Reception
15 Frederic Rent-a-Bike & Guestrooms
16 Hotel Pax & Sara's Pancake House
17 Hotel Aspen
18 To The Shelter Jordan
19 Restaurant de Luwte
20 De Bolhoed Restaurant
21 Café Restaurant de Reiger
22 Café 't Smalle
23 Thai Fusion
24 Toscana Italian Restaurant
25 Winkel Café
26 Restaurant 't Stuivertje
27 Ristorante Toscanini
28 Villa Zeesicht
29 Café 't Papeneiland
30 Stubbe's Haring (Fish Stand)
31 Albert Heijn Grocery (3)
32 Paradox Coffeeshop
33 The Grey Area Coffeeshop
34 Siberië Coffeeshop
35 La Tertulia Coffeeshop
36 Launderette
37 GAYtic (LGBT Tourist Info)

SLEEPING IN AMSTERDAM

269, tel. 020/623-7877, www.hotelhegra.nl, info@hotelhegra.nl, Robert).

$$ Hotel Chic & Basic Amsterdam has a boutique-hotel feel, even though it's part of a Spanish chain. With its mod utilitarian design and younger clientele, it provides a break from all the lace curtains. Located in a quiet neighborhood near Central Station, it offers 25 minimalist rooms and public areas that are bathed in space-age white. Rooms with canal views are pricier and breezier (Sb-€95-130, Db-€120-155, €20 more on holiday weekends, less in winter, cheaper prices are for less sleek "vintage" rooms without canal views, free coffee, continental breakfast, fans on request, tangled floor plan connecting three canalside buildings, free Internet access and Wi-Fi, Herengracht 13, tel. 020/522-2345, www.chicandbasic.com, amsterdam@chicandbasic.com, manager Bernardo Campo).

$$ Hotel Van Onna has 41 simple, industrial-strength rooms, some with canal views. The price is right, and the leafy location makes you want to crack out your easel. The popular top-floor attic rooms are cozy hideaways (Sb-€45-65, Db-€80-100, Tb-€125-135, Qb-€170-190, price depends on season, cash only, cot-like beds are sufficient, no phones or TVs, free Internet access and Wi-Fi, in the Jordaan at Bloemgracht 104, tel. 020/626-5801, www.hotelvanonna.nl, info@hotelvanonna.nl, Leon and Tsibo).

$$ Wiechmann Hotel's 37 rooms are sparsely furnished with just the dark-wood essentials, but they're spacious, and the *gezellig* public areas are chock-full of Old World charm (Sb-€65-105, Db-€125-165, Tb-€205, Qb-€230, Db suite-€260, prices lower in winter, check online for best price, 15 percent cheaper for 3 or more nights if booking through their website, some canal views, back rooms are quiet, free Internet access and Wi-Fi, nicely located at Prinsengracht 328-332, tel. 020/626-3321, www.hotelwiechmann.nl, info@hotelwiechmann.nl, John and Taz the welcome dog).

B&Bs and Private-Room Rentals

B&Bs offer a chance to feel like a local during your visit. The first and third listings here are in a peaceful residential neighborhood that's a short walk from Central Station; the second and fourth are in slightly busier areas. The last two listings are services that manage and rent many apartments and rooms in West Amsterdam.

$$ Boogaard's B&B is a delightful pad on a narrow lane right out of Mister Rogers' neighborhood. The B&B, which has four comfortable rooms and an inviting public living room, is run by Peter, an American expat opera singer. Peter, who clearly enjoys hosting Americans in his home, serves his fresh-baked goodies at breakfast and treats you royally. As his place is popular with my readers, it's smart to book well in advance (Db-€120, 2-night minimum; furnished family apartment with kitchen-€240 for 4 people, 3-night minimum; prices don't include 5 percent tax, air-con, DVD library, free laundry, free Wi-Fi, loaner cell phones and laptops, Langestraat 34, tel. 064/358-6835, www.boogaardsbnb .com, info@boogaardsbnb.com).

$$ Maes B&B (pronounced "mahss") is a dynamite value, renting tastefully cozy rooms for much less than you'd pay at a hotel. Instead of a reception desk, you get antique-filled rooms, the use of a full kitchen, and a warm welcome from Ken and Vlad. They also run **Heren B&B,** a crisply modern space around the corner from Maes, with large rooms—one with a canal view (both locations: Sb-€95, Db-€105, bigger Db-€115-125, extra bed-€30, suites and full apartments also available, free Internet access and Wi-Fi, if street noise bothers you ask for room in back, Herenstraat 26, tel. 020/427-5165, www.bedandbreakfastamsterdam.com, maes info@xs4all.nl).

$$ Herengracht 21 B&B has two stylish, intimate rooms in a canal house filled with art and run by lovely Loes Olden (2-floor Db-€125, canal-view Db-€135, air-con, free Wi-Fi, Herengracht 21, tel. 020/625-6305, mobile 06-2812-0962, www.herengracht21 .nl, loes@herengracht21.nl).

$$ Sunhead of 1617 B&B justifiably calls itself a "bed and delicious breakfast," but you're just as likely to remember the thoughtfully decorated, flower-filled rooms and the personality of owner Carlos (rear Db-€119, front Db-€129, Db apartment-€169, Tb apartment-€210, more on holidays, free Wi-Fi, mobile 06-2865-3572, Herengracht 152, www.sunhead.com, carlos@sunhead.com).

$$ With **Truelove Guesthouse,** a room-rental service, you'll feel like you're staying at your Dutch friends' house while they're out of town. Sean and Paul—whose tiny antique store on Prinsenstraat doubles as the reception desk for their rental service—have 15 rooms and apartments in houses sprinkled throughout the northern end of the Jordaan neighborhood. The apartments are stylish and come with kitchens and pull-out beds (Db-€90-105, Db apartment-€100-120, Qb apartments-€140-220, prices soft in off-season and midweek, 10 percent more with credit card, 2-night minimum on weekends, no breakfast, pick up keys in store at Prinsenstraat 4, store tel. 020/320-2500, mobile 06-2480-5672, fax 084-711-4950, www.cosyandwarm-amsterdam.com, trueloveantiek@zonnet.nl).

$ Frederic Rent-a-Bike & Guestrooms, with a bike-rental shop as the reception, is a collection of private rooms on a gorgeous canal just outside the Jordaan, a five-minute walk from Central Station. Frederic has amassed about 100 beds, ranging from dumpy €70 doubles behind the bike-rental shop, to spacious and elegant apartments (from €46/person; these places require a 2-night minimum, occasionally more). Some places are ideal for families and groups of up to six. He also rents houseboat apartments. All are displayed on his website (phone bookings preferred, book with credit card but pay with cash, no breakfast, Brouwersgracht 78, tel. 020/624-5509, www.frederic.nl, info@frederic.nl, Frederic and Marjolijn). His excellent bike shop is open daily 9:00-17:30 (€15/24 hours).

Southwest Amsterdam

Charming B&Bs near Leidseplein

The area around Amsterdam's rip-roaring nightlife center (Leidseplein) is colorful, comfortable, and convenient. These canalside mom-and-pop places are within a five-minute walk of rowdy Leidseplein, but generally are in quiet and typically Dutch settings. Within walking distance of the major museums, and steps off the tram line, this neighborhood offers a perfect mix of charm and location.

$$ Hotel de Leydsche Hof is a hidden gem located on a canal. Its two large rooms are a symphony in white, overlooking a tree-filled backyard. Frits and Loes give their big, elegant, old building a stylish air. Breakfast is served in the grand canal-front room (Db-€120, cash only, 2-night minimum, free Internet access and Wi-Fi, Leidsegracht 14, tel. 020/638-2327, mobile 06-5125-8588, www.freewebs.com/leydschehof, loespiller@planet.nl).

$$ Wildervanck B&B, run by Helene and Sjoerd Wildervanck, offers two tasteful rooms in an elegant 17th-century canal house (big Db on first floor-€135, Db with twin beds on ground floor-€120, extra bed-€30, 2-night minimum, breakfast in their pleasant dining room, free Wi-Fi, family has three girls, Keizersgracht 498, on Keizersgracht canal just west of Leidsestraat, tel. 020/623-3846, www.wildervanck.com, info@wildervanck.com).

$$ Hotel Keizershof is wonderfully Dutch, with six bright, airy rooms—some with canal views—in a 17th-century canal house with a lush garden and a fine living room. A very steep spiral staircase leads to rooms named after old-time Hollywood stars. The enthusiastic hospitality of Mrs. de Vries and her daughter, Hanneke, give this place a friendly, almost small-town charm (S-€70, D-€90, Ds-€100, Db-€115, 2-night minimum, reserve with credit card but pay with cash, free Internet access and Wi-Fi; tram #16, #24, or #25 from Central Station, Keizersgracht 618, where Keizers canal crosses Nieuwe Spiegelstraat; tel. 020/622-2855, www.hotelkeizershof.nl, info@hotelkeizershof.nl).

Near Vondelpark and Museumplein

These options cluster around Vondelpark in a safe neighborhood. Though they don't have a hint of Old Dutch or romantic canalside

Hotels & Restaurants in Southwest Amsterdam

SLEEPING IN AMSTERDAM

�456 TRAM 2+5 STOP
📧 BOAT TOURS
--- PATH

↑ ENTRY POINT TO SIGHTS

1 Hotel de Leydsche Hof
2 Wildervanck B&B
3 To Hotel Keizershof
4 Hotel Piet Hein
5 Hotel Fita
6 To Hotel Filosoof & Tulips B&B
7 Hotel Alexander
8 Hotel Hestia
9 Hotel Parkzicht
10 Stayokay Vondelpark Hostel
11 To Restaurant Bazar
12 Café Vertigo
13 Cobra Café
14 The Bulldog Coffeeshop
15 Launderette

flavor, they're reasonable values and only a short walk from the action. Unless noted, the places below have elevators. Many are in a pleasant nook between rollicking Leidseplein and the park, and most are a 5- to 15-minute walk to the Rijks and Van Gogh museums. They are easily connected with Central Station by trams #1, #2, and/or #5.

$$$ Hotel Piet Hein offers 81 stylishly sleek yet comfortable rooms as well as a swanky lounge, good breakfast, and a pleasant garden, all on a quiet street (Sb-€115, Db-€175, extra-posh Db-€200-250, Tb-€205, extra bed-€30, specials on website, air-con in some rooms, free Wi-Fi and Internet access, Vossiusstraat 51-53, tel. 020/662-7205, www.hotelpiethein.nl, info@hotelpiethein.nl).

$$$ Hotel Fita has 15 bright rooms in a great location—100 yards from the Van Gogh Museum, an even shorter hop from the tram stop, and on a corner with no car traffic. The decor may not be the latest, but all the amenities are there—including espresso machines in every room—and the welcome is very warm (Sb-€105, two small ground-floor Db-€135, Db-€145-165 depending on size, Tb-€205, free laundry service, free Wi-Fi and Internet access in lobby, Jan Luijkenstraat 37, tel. 020/679-0976, fax 020/664-3969, www.fita.nl, info@fita.nl, joking and colorful owner Hans).

$$ Hotel Filosoof greets you with Aristotle and Plato in the foyer and classical music in its generous lobby. Its 38 rooms, some across the street from reception, are decorated with themes; the Egyptian room has a frieze of hieroglyphics. Philosophers' sayings hang on the walls, and thoughtful travelers wander down the halls or sit in the garden, rooted in deep discussion. The rooms are small, but the hotel is endearing (Db-€110-130 weeknights, €130-150 Fri-Sat, bigger "deluxe" rooms-€20 extra, suites-€60 extra, prices depend on season and don't include tax; no breakfast, free Internet access and Wi-Fi, 3-minute walk from tram line #1, get off at Jan Pieter Heijestraat, Anna van Den Vondelstraat 6, tel. 020/683-3013, fax 020/685-3750, www.hotelfilosoof.nl, reservations@hotel filosoof.nl).

$$ Hotel Alexander is a modern, newly renovated 32-room hotel on a quiet street. Some of the rooms overlook the garden patio out back (Db-€135, prices soft in winter—call or check their website for best deal, Internet access, pay Wi-Fi, tel. 020/589-4020, fax 020/589-4025, Vondelstraat 44-46, www.hotelalexander .nl, info@hotelalexander.nl).

$$ Tulips B&B, with a bunch of cozy rooms—some on a canal—is run by a friendly Englishwoman, Karen, and her Dutch husband, Paul. Rooms are clean, white, and bright, with red carpeting, plants, and flowers (D-€85, Db-€120, suite-€150, extra bed-€30, discounts for longer stays, cash only, prefer 3-night stays on weekends, includes milk-and-cereal breakfast, no shoes, no elevator but not a lot of stairs, free Wi-Fi, south end of Vondelpark at Sloterkade 65, 7-minute walk from trams #1 and #2, directions sent when you book, tel. 020/679-2753, rooms@bedandbreakfast amsterdam.net, www.bedandbreakfastamsterdam.net).

$$ Hotel Hestia, on a safe street, is efficient and family-run, with 18 clean, airy, and generally spacious rooms (Sb-€83-93, very small Db-€101-107, standard Db-€128-148, Tb-€158-176, Qb-€188-206, Quint/b-€218-236, can be less in winter—check website for best price, Roemer Visscherstraat 7, tel. 020/618-0801, fax 020/685-1382, www.hotel-hestia.nl, info@hotel-hestia.nl, Arnaud).

$$ Hotel Parkzicht, an old-fashioned, no-frills, dark-wood place with extremely steep stairs, rents 13 big, plain, and somewhat frayed rooms on a street bordering Vondelpark (S-€49, Sb-€59, Db-€79-92, Tb-€140, closed Nov-March, no elevator, free Wi-Fi, some noise from neighboring youth hostel, Roemer Visscherstraat 33, tel. 020/618-1954, fax 020/618-0897, www.parkzicht.nl, hotel @parkzicht.nl).

Central Amsterdam

Basic Hotels in the City Center

You won't get a warm welcome at either of the two following hotels. But if you're looking for a no-nonsense room that's convenient to plenty of tram lines, these hotels fit the bill.

$$$ Hotel Ibis Amsterdam Centre, located next door to the Central Station, is a modern, efficient, 187-room place. It offers a central location, comfort, and good value, without a hint of charm (Db-€140-160 Nov-Aug, Db-€200 Sept-Oct, breakfast-€15, check website for deals, book long in advance—especially for Sept-Oct, air-con, pay Internet access; facing Central Station, go left toward the multistory bicycle garage to Stationsplein 49; tel. 020/522-2899, fax 020/522-2889, www.ibishotel.com, h1556@accor.com). When business is slow, usually in mid-summer, they occasionally rent rooms to same-day drop-ins for around €100.

$$ Hotel Résidence Le Coin offers 42 larger-than-average rooms complete with small kitchenettes. Located near the Mint Tower, this hotel is a two-minute walk to the Flower Market and a five-minute walk to Rembrandtplein (Sb-€119, small Db-€139, bigger Db-€154, Qb-€230, extra bed-€37, breakfast-€12, pay Wi-Fi, by the University at Nieuwe Doelenstraat 5, tel. 020/524-6800, fax 020/524-6801, www.lecoin.nl, hotel@lecoin.nl).

Budget Hotels Between Dam Square and the Anne Frank House: Inexpensive, well-worn hotels line the convenient but noisy and unromantic main drag, Raadhuisstraat. Expect a long, steep, and depressing stairway, with noisy rooms in the front and

SLEEPING IN AMSTERDAM

Hotels & Restaurants in Central Amsterdam

200 YARDS
200 METERS
B BOAT TOURS

CENTRAL STATION

STATIONSPLEIN

To JORDAAN DISTRICT

OLD CHURCH
RED LIGHT DISTRICT

ST. NIC.

BEURS PL.

DE BIJENKORF DEPT. STORE

DAM

AMSTERDAM MUSEUM

ST. LUCIEN

BEGIJN HOF

HET STEEG

SPUI

MINT TOWER

KALVER TOREN MALL

FLOWER MARKET

To LEIDSEPLEIN

MUNT PL.

DCH

5 Kantjil To Go
6 Café 't Gasthuys
7 De Jaren Café
8 Pannenkoekenhuis Upstairs
9 La Place (V&D Dept. Store)
10 Atrium Univ. Cafeteria
11 Brasserie Rest. de Roode Leeuw
12 Dam Café (De Bijenkorf Dept. Store)
13 Albert Heijn Groceries (4)
14 The Dampkring Coffeeshop

1 To Hotel Ambassade
2 Hotel Ibis Amsterdam Centre
3 Hotel Résidence Le Coin
4 Restaurant Kantjil en de Tijger

quieter rooms in the back. Though neither of the places below serves breakfast, they're both steps from a recommended pancake house. For locations, see the map on pages 180-181.

$ Hotel Pax has 11 large, plain, but airy rooms with Ikea furniture—a lot like a European dorm room (S-€35-45, D-€65, Db-€80, T-€85, Tb-€100, prices drop dramatically in winter, no breakfast, six rooms share two showers and two toilets, Raadhuisstraat 37, tel. 020/624-9735, hotelpax@tiscali.nl, run by go-getters Philip and Pieter).

$ Hotel Aspen, a few doors away and a great value for a budget hotel, has eight tidy, stark, and well-maintained rooms (S-€40, tiny D-€55-65, Db-€75-80, Tb-€95, Qb-€110, prices same 365 days a year, no breakfast, free Wi-Fi and Internet access, Raadhuisstraat 31, tel. 020/626-6714, fax 020/620-0866, www.hotelaspen.nl, info@hotelaspen.nl, run by kindhearted Rudy and Esam).

Hostels

Amsterdam has a world of good, cheap hostels located throughout the city. Most are designed for the party crowd, but here are a few quieter options. They all offer dorm beds; Stayokay Vondelpark also has some basic doubles.

In the Jordaan: **$ The Shelter Jordan** is a scruffy, friendly, Christian-run, 100-bed place in a great neighborhood. Although most of Amsterdam's hostels are pretty wild, this place is drug- and alcohol-free, with boys on one floor and girls on another. These are Amsterdam's best budget beds (bunks in 12-20-bed dorms-€23.50, €28 Fri-Sat and around holidays, same bunks in shoulder season-€20.50, less in off-season; bunks in 6-8-bed dorms-€1.50 extra; bunks in 4-5-bed rooms-€4 extra; includes sheets and breakfast, Internet access in lobby, near Anne Frank House at Bloemstraat 179, tel. 020/624-4717, www.shelter.nl, jordan@shelter.nl). The Shelter serves hot meals; runs a snack bar in its big, relaxing lounge; offers lockers; and leads nightly Bible studies.

In the Red Light District: **$ The Shelter City** is Shelter Jordan's sister—similar, but definitely not preaching to the local choir. And though its 180 beds are buried in the heart of the red lights, it feels very well-run and perfectly safe (same prices as Shelter Jordan, bunks in Qb-€6 extra, D-€49 for spouses or single-sex; same amenities, rules, and Bible study; Barndesteeg 21, see map on page 102, tel. 020/625-3230, fax 020/623-2282, www.shelter.nl, city @shelter.nl).

In Vondelpark: **$ Stayokay Vondelpark (IYHF),** with 530 beds in 130 rooms, is one of Amsterdam's top hostels for the under-25 set (€20-37/bed in 4- to 20-bed dorms, D-€60-95—most with bunk beds, higher prices are for March-Oct, members save €2.50, price depends on demand—cheapest when booked in advance, family rooms, lots of school groups, lockers, laundry, pay Internet access and Wi-Fi, bike rental, right on Vondelpark at Zandpad 5, tel. 020/589-8996, fax 020/589-8955, www.stayokay.com, vondel park@stayokay.com). Though Stayokay Vondelpark and Stayokay Stadsdoelen (listed next) are generally booked long in advance, occasionally a few beds open up each day at 11:00.

Near Waterlooplein: **$ Stayokay Stadsdoelen (IYHF)**, smaller and simpler than its Vondelpark sister (listed above), has only large dorms and no private bathrooms, but is free of large school groups (€17-32/bed with sheets and breakfast in 10-bed dorms, members save €2.50, price depends on demand—cheapest when booked in advance, lockers, pay Internet access, bike rental, Kloveniersburgwal 97, see map on page 72, tel. 020/624-6832, fax 020/639-1035, www.stayokay.com, stadsdoelen@stayokay .com).

Farthest East: **$ Stayokay Zeeburg (IYHF)** is a 500-bed hostel with all the modern services. While it's pretty far from the center, by tram or bike you're just 15 minutes from Damrak street (€20-30/bed in 6- to 14-bed dorms, price depends on demand—cheapest when booked in advance, pay Internet access and Wi-Fi, lockers, games, restaurant, bike rental, tram #14 to Timorplein 21, tel. 020/551-3190, fax 020/623-4986, www.stayokay.com, zeeburg@stayokay.com).

SLEEPING IN AMSTERDAM

EATING IN AMSTERDAM

Of Amsterdam's thousand-plus restaurants, no one knows which are best. I'd pick an area and wander. The rowdy food ghetto thrives around Leidseplein; if you don't mind eating in a touristy area, wander along Leidsedwarsstraat, Restaurant Row. The area around Spui canal and that end of Spuistraat also is trendy and not as noisy. For fewer crowds and more charm, find something in the Jordaan district. Most hoteliers keep a reliable eating list for their neighborhood and know which places keep their travelers happy. We've listed some handy places to consider.

To dine cheaply yet memorably alongside the big spenders, grab a meal to go, then find a bench on a lively neighborhood square or along a canal. Sandwiches *(broodjes)* of delicious cheese on fresh bread are cheap at snack bars, delis, and *broodjes* restaurants. Ethnic restaurants serve cheap, splittable carryout meals. Ethnic fast-food stands abound, offering a variety of meats wrapped in pita bread. Easy to buy at grocery stores, yogurt in the Netherlands (and throughout northern Europe) is delicious and often drinkable right out of its plastic container.

In Central Amsterdam

For the locations of these eateries, see the "Hotels and Restaurants in Central Amsterdam" map on page 188.

On and near Spui

Restaurant Kantjil en de Tijger is a thriving place with a plain and noisy ambience, full of happy eaters who know a good value. The food is purely Indonesian; the waiters are happy to explain your many enticing options. Their three *rijsttafels* (traditional "rice tables" with about a dozen small courses) range from €20 to €30 per person. Though they are designed for two people, three people can make a meal by getting a *rijsttafel* for two and ordering a soup or light dish for the third person. A good budget alternative to the full-blown *rijsttafel* is a *nasi rames*—10 small dishes on one big plate for €13 (daily 12:00-23:00, early-bird €10 dinner daily 16:30-18:45, reservations smart, mostly indoor with a little outdoor seating, Spuistraat 291, tel. 020/620-0994).

Kantjil to Go, run by Restaurant Kantjil, is a tiny take-out bar serving up inexpensive but delicious Indonesian fare (€5 for 300 grams, €6.50 for 600 grams, vegetarian specials, daily 12:00-21:00, Thu-Sat until 22:00, storefront at Nieuwezijds Voorburgwal 342, around the back of the sit-down restaurant listed above, tel. 020/620-3074). Split a large box (they'll happily give you an empty extra box for your dining pleasure), grab a bench on the charming Spui Square around the corner, and you've got perhaps the cheapest hot meal in town.

Near the Mint Tower

Café 't Gasthuys, one of Amsterdam's many brown cafés (so called for their smoke-stained walls), has a busy dumbwaiter cranking out light lunches, sandwiches, and reasonably priced, if uncreative, dinners. It offers a long bar, a lovely secluded back room, peaceful canalside seating, and sometimes slow service (€5-9 lunch plates, €11-15 dinner plates, daily 12:00-16:30 & 17:30-21:30, Thu-Sat until 22:00; Grimburgwal 7—from the Rondvaart Kooij boat dock, head down Langebrugsteeg, and it's one block down on the left; tel. 020/624-8230).

De Jaren Café ("The Years Café") is a chic yet inviting place—clearly a favorite with locals. Upstairs is the minimalist restaurant with a top-notch salad bar and a canal-view deck (serving €14-20 dinners after 17:30, including fish, meat, and veggie dishes, and salad bar, or €12 for salad bar only). Downstairs is a modern Amsterdam café, great for light lunches (soups, salads, and sandwiches served all day and evening) or just coffee over a newspaper. On a sunny day, the café's canalside patio is a fine spot to nurse a drink; this is also a nice place to go just for a drink in the evening and enjoy the spacious Art Deco setting (daily 10:00-24:00, Nieuwe Doelenstraat 20-22, a long block up from Muntplein, tel. 020/625-5771).

Pannenkoekenhuis Upstairs is a tiny, characteristic perch up some extremely steep stairs, where Arno Jakobs cooks and serves delicious €7 pancakes to four tables throughout the afternoon (Fri-Sat 12:00-18:00, Sun 12:00-17:00, closed Mon-Thu, Grimburgwal 2, tel. 020/626-5603).

La Place, on the ground floor of the V&D department store, has an abundant, colorful array of fresh, appealing food served cafeteria-style. A multistory eatery that seats 300, it has a small outdoor terrace upstairs. Explore before you make your choice. This bustling spot has a lively market feel, with everything from made-on-the-spot beef stir-fry, to fresh juice, to veggie soups (€3 pizza and €4 sandwiches, Sun-Mon 11:00-20:00, Tue-Sat 10:00-20:00, Thu until 21:00, at the end of Kalverstraat near Mint Tower, tel. 020/622-0171). For fast and healthy take-out food (sandwiches, yogurt, fruit cups, and more), try the bakery on the department store's ground floor. (They run another branch, which has the city's ultimate view terrace, on the top floor of the **Central Library**—Openbare Bibliotheek Amsterdam—near Central Station.)

Atrium University Cafeteria, a three-minute walk from Mint Tower, feeds travelers and students from Amsterdam University for great prices, but only on weekdays (€6 meals, Mon-Fri 11:00-15:00 & 17:00-19:30, closed Sat-Sun; from Spui, walk west down Landebrug Steeg past canalside Café 't Gasthuys three blocks to Oudezijds Achterburgwal 237, go through arched doorway on the right; tel. 020/525-3999).

Between Central Station and Dam Square

Brasserie Restaurant de Roode Leeuw (*roode leeuw* means "red lion") offers a peaceful, calm respite from the crush of Damrak. During the day, the whole restaurant shares the same menu, but after 18:00, it's split roughly in half, with finer service, cloth tablecloths, and higher prices in back, and a more casual setup (and better people-watching on Damrak street) up front. Either way, you'll get a menu filled with traditional Dutch food, good service, and the company of plenty of tourists. Call ahead to reserve a window seat (restaurant: €15-20 entrées, €30 three-course fixed-price meal with traditional Dutch choices; brasserie: €10-15 entrées; daily 12:00-22:00, Damrak 93-94, tel. 020/555-0666).

Dam Café, on the first floor of the De Bijenkorf department store on Dam Square, has a small lineup of inexpensive salads, sandwiches, and desserts. Enjoying views of busy Damrak, comfortable seating, and an upscale café vibe, you'll feel miles above the chaotic streets below (€8-11 salads, Mon 11:00-18:00, Tue-Fri 10:30-18:00, Thu until 21:00, Sat 9:30-18:00, Sun 12:00-18:00, Dam 1, tel. 088-245-9080). For a much wider range of dishes but no Dam views, head up to **Kitchen,** the store's swanky fifth-floor self-service restaurant (similar prices and hours as café).

Munching Cheap

Traditional fish stands sell €3 herring sandwiches and other salty treats, usually from easy photo menus. **Stubbe's Haring,** where the Stubbe family has been selling herring for 100 years, is handy and well-established, a few blocks from Central Station (Tue-Fri 10:00-18:00, Sat 10:00-17:00, closed Sun-Mon, at the locks where Singel canal boat arrives at the train station, see map on pages 180-181). Grab a sandwich and have a picnic canalside.

Supermarkets: You'll see **Albert Heijn** grocery stores (daily 8:00-22:00) all over town. Four helpful, central locations are Dam Square (Nieuwezijds Voorburgwal 226), Mint Tower (Koningsplein 4), Leidsestraat (at Konigsplein, on the corner of Leidsestraat and Singel), and Central Station (far end of passage under the tracks).

In West Amsterdam

Near the Anne Frank House and in the Jordaan District

Nearly all of these places are within a few scenic blocks of the Anne Frank House, providing handy lunches and atmospheric dinners in Amsterdam's most charming neighborhood. For locations, see the map on pages 180-181.

Restaurant de Luwte is romantic, located on a picturesque street overlooking a canal. It has lots of candles, a muted but fresh modern interior, spacious seating, a few cool outdoor canalside tables, and French Mediterranean cuisine (€20 entrées, €30 three-course fixed-price meal, big dinner salads for €18, daily 18:00-22:00, Leliegracht 26-28, tel. 020/625-8548, manager Maarten). Ask about their specials.

De Bolhoed has serious vegetarian and vegan food in a colorful setting that Buddha would dig, with a clientele that appears to dig Buddha (big splittable portions, €15 dinners, light lunches, daily 12:00-22:00, dinner starts at 17:00, Prinsengracht 60, tel. 020/626-1803).

Café Restaurant de Reiger must offer the best cooking of any *eetcafé* in the Jordaan. Famous for its fresh ingredients and delightful bistro ambience, it's part of the classic Jordaan scene. In addition to an English menu, ask for a translation of the €17.50-20 daily specials on the chalkboard. They're proud of their fresh fish and French-Dutch cuisine. The café, which is crowded late and on weekends, takes no reservations, but you're welcome to have a drink (€3 house wine and fun little bar munchies menu) at the bar while you wait (Tue-Sun 17:00-24:00, closed Mon, veggie options, Nieuwe Leliestraat 34, tel. 020/624-7426).

Café 't Smalle is extremely charming, with three zones where you can enjoy a light lunch or a drink: canalside, inside around the bar, and up some steep stairs in a quaint little back room. The café is open daily until midnight, and simple meals (salads, soup, and fresh sandwiches) are served 11:00-17:30 (plenty of fine €2-3 Belgian beers on tap and interesting wines by the glass, at Egelantiersgracht 12 where it hits Prinsengracht, tel. 020/623-9617).

Thai Fusion, despite the name, serves straight-up top-quality Thai food in a sleekly modern, black-and-white room wedged neatly in the middle of the Nine Little Streets action (€15-20 main courses, €25-30 two-course meals, Mon-Fri 16:30-22:30, Sat-Sun 12:00-22:30, good veggie options, Berenstraat 8, tel. 020/320-8332).

Toscana Italian Restaurant is the Jordaan's favorite place for good, inexpensive Italian cuisine, including pizza, in a woody, Dutch-beer-hall setting (€6-8 pizza and pastas, €16 main courses, daily 16:00-23:30, fast service, Haarlemmerstraat 130, tel. 020/622-0353).

Winkel, the North Jordaan's cornerside hangout, serves appetizing French-Dutch meals at its plentiful outside tables and easygoing interior. It really gets hopping on Monday mornings, when the Noordermarkt flea market is underway, but Amsterdammers come from across town all week for the *appeltaart* (€11-14 dinner plates, €5 snacks served after 16:00, daily 8:00-24:00 except Sun from 10:00, Noordermarkt 43, tel. 020/623-0223).

Sara's Pancake House is a basic pancake diner where extremely hardworking Sara cranks out sweet and savory €8-10 flapjacks made from fresh, organic ingredients (daily until 22:30, later on weekends, breakfast served until noon, Raadhuisstraat 45, tel. 020/320-0662).

Restaurant 't Stuivertje is a small, family-run neighborhood eatery tucked away in the Jordaan, serving French-inspired Dutch cuisine in an elegantly cozy but unpretentious atmosphere (€15-25 main courses, dinner salads, Wed-Sun 17:30-22:00, closed Mon-Tue, Hazenstraat 58 near Elandsgracht, tel. 020/623-1349).

Ristorante Toscanini is an up-market Italian place that's always packed. It's so popular that the staff can be a bit arrogant, but the lively, spacious ambience and great Italian cuisine more than make up for that—if you can get a seat. Reservations are essentially required (the staff recommends two weeks notice for Fri and Sat). Otherwise your best bet is to arrive when they open at 18:00 (€14 first courses, €20 main courses, Mon-Sat 18:00-22:30, closed Sun, deep in the Jordaan at Lindengracht 75, tel. 020/623-2813).

Villa Zeesicht has all the romantic feel of a classic European café. The cozy interior is crammed with tiny tables topped by tall candlesticks, and wicker chairs outside gather under a wisteria-covered awning. The menu is uninventive—come here instead for the famous *appeltaart* and for the great people-watching on Torensluis bridge (€11-16 plates, daily 9:00-21:30, Torensteeg 7, tel. 020/626-7433).

Drinks Only: Café 't Papeneiland is a classic brown café with Delft tiles, an evocative old stove, and a stay-awhile perch overlooking a canal with welcoming benches. It's been the neighborhood hangout since the 17th century (drinks but no food, overlooking northwest end of Prinsengracht at #2, tel. 020/624-1989). It feels a little exclusive; patrons who come here to drink and chat aren't eager to see it overrun by tourists. The café's name means "Papists' Island," since this was once a refuge for Catholics; there used to be an escape tunnel here for priests on the run.

In Southwest Amsterdam

Near Leidseplein

Stroll through the colorful cancan of eateries on Leidsedwarsstraat, Restaurant Row, just off Leidseplein, and choose your favorite. Nearby, the busy Leidsestraat offers plenty of starving-student options (between the Prinsengracht and the Herengracht) offering fast and fun food for around €5 a meal.

Beyond the Rijksmuseum

Restaurant Bazar offers one of the most memorable and fun budget eating experiences in town. Converted from a church, it has spacious seating and mod belly-dance music, and is filled with young locals enjoying good, cheap Middle Eastern and North African cuisine. Reservations are a good idea if you plan to eat after 20:00 (fill up with the €8.50 daily plate, delicious €13 couscous, or €16 three-course meal of the day; daily 11:00-23:00, until 24:00 on weekends, Albert Cuypstraat 182, tel. 020/675-0544). Restaurant Bazar marks the center of the thriving Albert Cuyp market, which is wrapped up by about 17:00, though the restaurant is open late.

In Vondelpark

Café Vertigo offers a fun selection of excellent soups, salads, and sandwiches. It's a surprisingly large complex of outdoor tables; an indoor pub; and an elegant, candlelit back-room restaurant beneath the grand, Italian Renaissance Vondel Pavilion. The service can be slow, but if you grab an outdoor table, you can watch the world spin by (daily 10:00-24:00 except off-season weekdays from 11:00, Vondelpark 3, tel. 020/612-3021).

In Southeast Amsterdam

Near the Dutch Resistance Museum

For locations of the following eateries, see the map on page 72.

Restaurant Plancius, adjacent to the Dutch Resistance Museum, is a handy, modern spot for lunch. Its good indoor and outdoor seating make it popular with the museum staff and broadcasters from the nearby local TV studios (creative breakfasts, hearty fresh sandwiches, light €5-9 lunches and €16-19 dinners, daily 10:00-22:00, Plantage Kerklaan 61a, tel. 020/330-9469).

Café Koosje, located halfway between the Dutch Resistance Museum and the Dutch Theater, is a corner lunchtime pub/bar ringed with outdoor seating. Inside, casual wooden tables and benches huddle under chandeliers, and the hip, young waitstaff serve beer and salads big enough for two (€5 sandwiches, €11 salads, food served daily 9:00-22:00, Plantage Middenlaan 37, on the corner of Plantage Kerklaan, tel. 020/320-0817).

SMOKING

Tobacco

A quarter of Dutch people smoke tobacco. Holland has a long tradition as a smoking culture, being among the first to import the tobacco plant from the New World. (For a history of smoking, visit the Pipe Museum—see page 95.)

Tobacco shops, such as the House of Hajenius (see page 92), glorify the habit, yet the Dutch people are among the healthiest in the world. Tanned, trim, firm, 60-something Dutch people sip their beer, take a drag, and ask me why Americans murder themselves with Big Macs.

Still, their version of the Surgeon General has finally woken up to the drug's many potential health risks. Warning stickers bigger than America's are required on cigarette packs, and some of them are almost comically blunt, such as: "Smoking will make you impotent...and then you die." (The warnings have prompted gag stickers like, "Life can kill you.")

Since 2008, a Dutch law has outlawed smoking tobacco almost everywhere indoors: on trains and in hotel rooms, restaurants, cafés, and bars.

Marijuana (a.k.a. Cannabis)

Amsterdam, Europe's counterculture mecca, thinks the concept of a "victimless crime" is a contradiction in terms. Drive under the influence of anything and you're toast. Heroin and cocaine are strictly illegal in the Netherlands, and the police stringently enforce laws prohibiting their sale and use. But, while hard drugs are definitely out, marijuana causes about as much excitement as a bottle of beer. When tourists call an ambulance after smoking too much pot, medics just say, "Drink something sweet and walk it off."

Throughout the Netherlands, you'll see "coffeeshops"—cafés selling marijuana, with display cases showing various joints or baggies for sale. The minimum age for purchase is 18, and coffeeshops can sell up to five grams of marijuana per person per day. However, the newly conservative Dutch government is floating a proposal to ban tourists from buying marijuana—only Dutch citizens with a *wietpas* (weed pass) would be able to buy a joint. It's unclear whether the proposal will be formally put into law, but be aware that the high times may be a changin'.

The Dutch buy marijuana by asking, "Can I see the cannabis menu?" Because it's illegal to advertise marijuana, the buyer has to take the initiative and request a menu. In some places there's actually a button you must push and hold down to see an illuminated menu, the contents of which look like the inventory of a drug bust.

The Netherlands' indoor-smoking ban pertains to tobacco smoke, not pot smoke. But the Dutch, like the rest of Europe, mix their marijuana with tobacco. It might seem strange to an American, but these days, if a coffeeshop is busted, it's for tobacco. Coffeeshops with a few outdoor seats have a huge advantage, as their customers can light up outside. Shops without the outdoor option are in for an extra challenge, as many local smokers would rather get their weed to go than smoke it without tobacco at their neighborhood coffeeshop. As a substitute for tobacco, shops have started mixing a kind of herb tea into joints. Prerolled joints are now sold three ways: pure, with the nontobacco "hamburger helper" herb mix, or with tobacco. If you like your joint tobacco-free anyway, pure marijuana joints are much easier to find than they used to be.

Shops sell marijuana and hashish both in prerolled joints and in little baggies. Some places sell individual joints (€2-5). Others sell only small packs of three or four joints. Baggies of marijuana usually cost €10-15. Some shops charge per gram. The better pot, though costlier, is actually a better value, as it takes less to get high—and it's a better high. Shops have loaner bongs and inhalers, and they dispense cigarette papers like toothpicks. As long as you're a paying customer (e.g., you buy a cup of coffee), you can pop into any coffeeshop and light up, even if you didn't buy your pot there.

Don't ever buy pot on the street in Amsterdam, and don't smoke marijuana openly while walking down the street.

Well-established coffeeshops are considered much safer, and coffeeshop owners have an interest in keeping their trade safe and healthy. They warn Americans—unused to the strength of the local stuff—to try a lighter leaf. In fact, they are generally very patient in explaining the varieties available.

The Dutch sell several forms of the cannabis plant—they smoke more hashish (the sap of the cannabis plant) than the leaf of the plant (which they call "marijuana" or "grass"). While each shop has different brands, it's all derived from two types of marijuana plant: *Cannabis indica* and *Cannabis sativa. Indica* gets you a "stoned, heavy, mellow, couch-weed" high. *Sativa* is light, fun, "uplifting," and more psychedelic. *Sativa* makes you giggle.

Most of the pot you'll see is locally grown. Technological advances have made it easier to cultivate exotic yet local strains. Coffeeshops know it's much safer to deal with Dutch-grown plants than to import marijuana from a foreign land (international trafficking gives rise to a whole different level of legal complexity than just growing your own). Most shops get their inventory from the pot equivalent of local home- or micro-brewers. Shops with better "boutique suppliers" get the reputation for having better-quality weed (and regularly win the annual Cannabis Cup).

Each shop is allowed to keep an inventory of up to 500 grams (about a pound) in stock—the tax authorities don't want to see more than this on the books at the end of each accounting cycle, and a shop can lose its license if it exceeds this amount. However, the wholesale dimension of the business is the famous "gray area" in the law: A shop can sell a ton of pot with no legal problems, as long as it maintains that tiny stock of 500 grams and just refills it as needed. The reason the inventory level is kept so low: Authorities want shops to stay small and not become bases for exportation. Providing pot to neighboring countries would bring more international pressure on the Netherlands to crack down on its coffeeshop culture.

Another legal trend is that licenses are not being renewed in some neighborhoods, as the city seeks to maintain a wide smattering of shops, avoiding too big a concentration in any one area. A national law that went into effect in 2011 would close all coffeeshops near schools, including the landmark Bulldog Café on Leidseplein. But Amsterdam's mayor has vowed to look for a way to keep its central coffeeshops open. Stay tuned.

So what am I? Pro-marijuana? Let's put it this way: I agree with the Dutch people, who remind me that a society either has to allow alternative lifestyles...or build more prisons. More than 850,000 Americans are arrested for marijuana use in one year alone. (Only the US and Russia lock up more than 1 percent of their citizens.)

The Dutch are not necessarily pro-marijuana, but they do believe that a prohibition on marijuana would cause more problems than it solves. Statistics support the Dutch belief that their system works. They have fewer hard drug problems than other countries. And they believe America's policy is based on fear, misinformation, and electoral politics, rather than rationality. The Dutch have found that their drug policy does not result in more pot smoking. (Statistically, compared to the Dutch, twice as many Americans have smoked pot.)

If you'd like to learn more about marijuana (and don't feel like Googling "Rick Steves marijuana"), drop by Amsterdam's Cannabis College or the Hash, Marijuana, and Hemp Museum. To see where cannabis growers buy their seeds, stop by the Sensi Seed Bank Store. These three places are located on Oudezijds Achterburgwal street (see pages 109-111). Back home, if you'd like to support an outfit dedicated to taking the crime out of pot, read up on the National Organization for the Reform of Marijuana Laws (www.norml.org).

Coffeeshops

Most of downtown Amsterdam's coffeeshops feel grungy and foreboding to American travelers who aren't part of the youth-hostel crowd. The neighborhood places (and those in small towns around the countryside) are much more inviting to people without piercings, tattoos, and favorite techno artists. I've listed a few places with a more pub-like ambience for Americans wanting to go local, but within reason. For locations, see the maps in the Sleeping in Amsterdam chapter.

Paradox is the most *gezellig* (cozy) coffeeshop I found—a mellow, graceful place. The managers, Ludo and Wiljan, and their

staff are patient with descriptions and happy to walk you through all your options. This is a rare coffeeshop that serves light meals. The juice is fresh, the music is easy, and the neighborhood is charming (single tobacco-free joints-€3, loaner bongs, games, daily 10:00-20:00, two blocks from Anne Frank House at Eerste

Bloemdwarsstraat 2, tel. 020/623-5639, www.paradoxcoffeeshop .com).

The Grey Area coffeeshop—a hole-in-the-wall spot with three tiny tables—is a cool, welcoming, and smoky place appreciated among local aficionados as a perennial winner of Amsterdam's Cannabis Cup awards. Judging by the autographed photos on the wall, many famous Americans have dropped in (say hi to Willie Nelson). You're welcome to just nurse a bottomless cup of coffee (daily 12:00-20:00, they close relatively early out of consideration for their neighbors, between Dam Square and Anne Frank House at Oude Leliestraat 2, tel. 020/420-4301, www.greyarea.nl). The Grey Area is run by two friendly Americans, Adam and Jon. They are helpful and even have a vaporizer if you want to "smoke" without smoking.

Siberië Coffeeshop is a short walk from Central Station, but feels cozy, with a friendly canalside ambience. Clean, big, and bright, this place has the vibe of a mellow Starbucks (daily 11:00-23:00, Fri-Sat until 24:00, free Wi-Fi for customers, helpful staff, English menu, Brouwersgracht 11, tel. 020/623-5909, www .siberie.nl).

La Tertulia is a sweet little mother-and-daughter-run place with pastel decor and a cheery terrarium atmosphere (Tue-Sat 11:00-19:00, closed Sun-Mon, sandwiches, brownies, games, Prinsengracht 312, www.coffeeshopamsterdam.com).

The Bulldog is the high-profile, leading touristy chain of coffeeshops. These establishments are young but welcoming, with reliable selections. They're pretty comfortable for green tourists wanting to just hang out for a while. The flagship branch, in a former police station right on Leidseplein, is very handy, offering alcohol upstairs, pot downstairs, and fun outdoor seating where you can watch the world skateboard by. There's a chance it may close because it's considered too near a school, but it will likely stay open (daily 10:00-1:00 in the morning, Fri-Sat until 3:00, Leidseplein 17, tel. 020/625-6278, www.bulldog.nl). They opened their first café (on the canal near the Old Church in the Red Light District) in 1975.

The Dampkring is a rough-and-ready constant party. It's a high-profile, busy place, filled with a young clientele and loud music, but the owners still take the time to explain what they offer. Scenes from the movie *Ocean's Twelve* were filmed here (daily 10:00-1:00 in the morning, close to Spui at Handboogstraat 29, tel. 020/638-0705, www.damp kring.nl).

Smartshops

These business establishments (one is listed on page 94) sell "natural" legal drugs. Many are harmless nutritional supplements, but they also sell stimulants similar to Ecstasy and strange drug cocktails rolled into joints. It's all perfectly legal, but if you've never taken drugs recreationally, don't start here.

SHOPPING IN AMSTERDAM

Amsterdam brings out the browser even in those who were not born to shop. Ten general markets, open six days a week (generally 9:30-17:00, closed Sun), keep folks who brake for garage sales pulling U-turns. Markets include Waterlooplein (the flea market), the huge Albert Cuyp street market, and various flower markets (such as the Singel canal Flower Market near Mint Tower).

For information on shopping, pick up the TI's *Shopping in Amsterdam* brochure. To find out how to get a VAT (Value-Added Tax) refund on your purchases, see page 13.

Most shops in the center are open 10:00-18:00 (Thu until 21:00); the businesslike Dutch know no siesta, but many shopkeepers take Sunday and Monday mornings off. Supermarkets are generally open Monday-Saturday 8:00-20:00, although most Albert Heijn grocery stores are open until 22:00 and on Sunday.

Department Stores

When you need to buy something but don't know where to go, two chain stores—Hema and Vroom & Dreesmann (V&D)—are handy for everything from inexpensive clothes and notebooks to food and cosmetics. **Hema** is at Kalverstraat 212, in the Kalvertoren mall (Mon 11:00-18:30, Tue-Sat 9:30-18:30 except Thu until 21:00, Sun 12:00-18:30). **Vroom & Dreesmann,** with its great La Place cafeteria, is at Kalverstraat 203 (Mon 11:30-19:30, Tue-Thu 10:30-19:30 except Thu until 21:00, Fri-Sat 10:00-20:00, Sun 11:00-19:00; cafeteria on ground floor—see page 192).

The **De Bijenkorf** department store is old-time fancy and central on Dam Square; its little café on the first floor up is perfect for people-watching out over the square (see page 193). **Metz & Co.** is decent but getting dowdy; its sixth-floor café also has good views (located where Leidsestraat intersects Herengracht).

Amsterdam's Top Shopping Zones

Jordaan—The Jordaan, with its main drag Westerstraat, is a veritable wonderland of funky, artsy shops. Once a working-class district, this colorful, old neighborhood is now upscale. On Mondays you'll find the busy Noordermarkt market at the end of Westerstraat and spilling onto the neighboring street, Lindengracht.

Leidsestraat—This bustling shopping street has trendy, elegant shops, along with the Metz & Co. department store.

The Nine Little Streets—De Negen Straatjes is home to 190 diverse shops mixing festive, creative, nostalgic, practical, and artistic items. Trendy cafés dot the area. The cross streets make a tic-tac-toe with a couple of canals and bicycle-friendly canalside streets just west of Kalverstraat. Look for the zone where Hartenstraat, Wolvenstraat, and Huidenstraat cross the Keizersgracht and Herengracht canals (see the color map at the beginning of this book). Walking west from the Amsterdam Museum puts you right in the thick of things.

Kalverstraat-Heiligeweg-Spui—This is the busiest shopping corridor in town. Kalverstraat, a pedestrian street, is a human traffic jam of low-end shoppers. It feels soulless, but if you explore the fringes, there are some interesting places.

Spiegelkwartier—Located between the Rijksmuseum and the city center, this is *the* place for art and antiques. You'll find 70 dealers offering 17th-century furniture, old Delftware, Oriental art, clocks, jewelry, and Art Nouveau doodads. Wander down Spiegelgracht and Nieuwe Spiegelstraat.

Prinsheerlijk—Along Herenstraat and Prinsenstraat, you'll find high-end fashion, interior design, and gift shops. If you're looking for jewelry, accessories, trendy clothing, and fancy delicatessens, this may be an expensive but rewarding stroll.

Magna Plaza Shopping Center—Formerly the main post office, this grand 19th-century building has been transformed into a stylish mall with 40 boutiques. You'll find fashion, luxury goods, and gift shops galore. It's just behind the Royal Palace a block off Dam Square (see page 113).

P. C. Hooftstraat—The city's most expensive shopping street is between Museumplein and Vondelpark.

Albert Cuyp Market—Amsterdam's biggest open-air market, stretching for several blocks along Albert Cuypstraat, bustles daily (roughly 9:00-17:00) except Sunday. You'll find fish, exotic vegetables, bolts of fabric, pantyhose, bargain clothes, native Dutch and ethnic food stands (especially *stroopwafels* and Surinamese *rotis*), and great people-watching. It's located a 10-minute walk east of Museumplein and a block south of the Heineken Experience (tram #16 or #24).

Popular Souvenirs

Amsterdam has lots of one-of-a-kind specialty stores. Poke around and see what you can find. If you want to bring home edibles and drinkables, see page 14 for restrictions.

Wooden Shoes—Once crucial for navigating soggy Amsterdam, these are now simply something to clomp around in.

Delftware—Ceramic plates, vases, and tiles decorated with a fake Chinese blue-and-white design popularized in the 1600s. Only a few licensed places sell the real stuff (expensive) and antiques (very expensive). You can find fireplace tiles (cheap) at most gift shops.

Diamonds—Cut or uncut, expensive or really expensive. Diamond dealers offer free cutting and polishing demos at their shops. Gassan Diamonds, near Rembrandt's House, is best (page 73); Coster is on Potterstraat, behind the Rijksmuseum (page 59).

Jenever—Dutch gin (made from juniper berries) is sold in traditional stone bottles.

Marijuana Pipes—These need to be clean and unused, because even a little residue can get you busted at US Customs. Note that, these days, American laws are written in a way that—technically—even importing an unused pipe could get you arrested.

Chocolate—Belgian or Dutch Verkade or Droste cocoa are sold in tins.

Flower Seeds and Bulbs—Look for ones that are packed with a seal that promises they are US Customs-friendly.

Posters and Art Postcards—There's a good selection at the Van Gogh Museum bookshop (also sells protective mailing tubes).

Old Maps—They capture the Dutch Golden Age.

Old Books—You can find treasures in musty bookstores.

ENTERTAINMENT IN AMSTERDAM

Many Amsterdam hotels serve breakfast until 11:00 because so many people—visitors and locals—live for nighttime in this city.

On summer evenings, people flock to the main squares for drinks at outdoor tables. Leidseplein is the liveliest square, surrounded by theaters, restaurants, and nightclubs. The slightly quieter Rembrandtplein (with adjoining Thorbeckeplein and nearby Reguliersdwarsstraat) is the center of gay clubs and nightlife. Spui features a full city block of bars. And Nieuwmarkt, on the east edge of the Red Light District, is a bit rough, but is probably the most local.

The Red Light District (particularly Oudezijds Achterburgwal) is less sleazy in the early evening, and almost carnival-like as the neon lights come on and the streets fill with tour groups. But it starts to feel scuzzy after about 22:30 (❸ see the Red Light District Walk chapter).

Information

Pick up one of these free papers for listings of festivals and performances of theater, film, dance, cabaret, and live rock, pop, jazz, and classical music. The hip monthly *Amsterdam Magazine* is made for tourists, but savvy enough to appeal to locals; its "upcoming" section has a solid listing of entertainment options (available all over, includes good map). The irreverent *Boom!* has the basics on the youth and nightlife scene, and is packed with practical tips and countercultural insights (includes €5 discount on Boom Chicago comedy theater act described on next page; available at TIs and many bars). *Unfold Amsterdam* is a biweekly fold-out with tips on current art-scene events (available at bookstores). *Uitkrant* is in Dutch, but it's just a calendar of events, and anyone can figure out the name of the event and its date, time, and location (available at TIs, bars, and bookstores).

Newsstands sell *Time Out Amsterdam*, Dutch papers (Thursday editions generally list events), and the *International Herald Tribune* (has special Netherlands insert).

Box Office: The **AUB/Last Minute Ticket Shop** at Stadsschouwburg Theater is the best one-stop-shopping box office for theater, classical music, and major rock shows. The Last Minute window sells half-price, same-day tickets to certain shows (Mon-Sat 10:00-19:30, Sun 12:00-18:00, Leidseplein 26, tel. 0900-0191—€0.40/minute, www.lastminuteticketshop.nl).

Music

You'll find classical music at the Concertgebouw (free 12:30 lunch concerts on Wed; arrive at 12:00 for best first-come, first-serve seating; at far south end of Museumplein, tel. 0900-671-8345, www.concertgebouw.nl) and at the former Beurs (on Damrak). For opera and dance, try the opera house in the Stopera building (Waterlooplein 22, tel. 020/625-5455). In the summer, Vondelpark hosts open-air concerts.

Two rock music (and hip-hop) clubs near Leidseplein are **Melkweg** (Lijnbaansgracht 234a, tel. 020/531-8181, www.melk weg.nl) and **Paradiso** (Weteringschans 6, tel. 020/626-4521, www .paradiso.nl; see page 97). They present big-name acts that you might recognize if you're younger than I am.

Jazz has a long tradition at the **Bimhuis** nightclub, east of the Red Light District (Oude Schans 73-77, tel. 020/788-2188, www .bimhuis.nl).

The nearby town of Haarlem offers free pipe-organ concerts on Tuesday evenings in summer at its 15th-century church, the **Grote Kerk** (at 20:15 mid-May-mid-Oct, additional concerts Thu at 15:00 July-Aug, see page 222).

Comedy

Boom Chicago, an R-rated comedy improv act, was started 15 years ago by a group of Americans on a graduation tour. They have been entertaining tourists and locals ever since. The two-hour English-only show is a series of rude, clever, and high-energy improvisational skits offering a raucous look at Dutch culture and local tourism (€20 weekdays, generally €24 Fri-Sat; Sun-Fri shows at 20:15, sometimes also Fri at 23:30, Sat at 19:30 and discounted show at 22:30; confirm times when you buy your ticket, ticket office open daily from 13:00 until 15 minutes after curtain time, no Mon shows Jan-March, tel. 020/423-0101, www.boomchicago.nl). It all happens at the 300-seat Leidseplein Theater at Leidseplein 12; enter through the skinny Boom Bar (optional meal and drink service).

They do *Best of Boom* (a collection of their greatest hits over the years) as well as new shows for locals and return customers. When sales are slow, ticket-sellers on the street out front offer steeply discounted tickets, with a drink included. Drop by that afternoon and see what's up.

Theater
Amsterdam is one of the world centers for experimental live theater (much of it in English). Many theaters cluster around the street called the Nes, which stretches south from Dam Square.

Movies
It's not unusual for movies at many cinemas to be sold out—consider buying tickets during the day. Catch modern movies in the 1920s setting of the classic **Tuschinski Theater** (between Muntplein and Rembrandtplein, described on page 61).

Museums
Several museums stay open late. The **Anne Frank House** always stays open until at least 19:00 year-round; it's open daily until 22:00 in July and August and closes late on Saturdays year-round (22:00 peak-season, 21:00 off-season). The **Hermitage Amsterdam** stays open until 20:00 on Wednesdays. The **Van Gogh Museum** is open on Fridays until 22:00 and sometimes has music and a wine bar in the lobby.

The **Hash, Marijuana, and Hemp Museum** is open daily until 23:00. And the **sex museums** always stay open late (Damrak Sex Museum until 23:30, Erotic Museum until 1:00 in the morning).

Skating After Dark
Amsterdammers get their skating fix every Friday night in summer and early fall in Vondelpark. Huge groups don inline skates and meet at the round bench near the Vondel Pavilion (around 20:15, www.fridaynightskate.com). Anyone can join in. You can rent skates at the shop at the far end of the park (Vondeltuin Rental, daily 11:00-20:00 in good weather; first hour-€5, then €2.50/hour; price includes helmet, wrist guards, and knee guards; at southeastern edge of park, mobile 0627-565-576, www.vondeltuin.nl).

AMSTERDAM CONNECTIONS

The Netherlands is so small, level, and well-covered by trains and buses that transportation is a snap. Buses take you where trains don't go, and bicycles take you where buses don't go. Bus stations and bike-rental shops cluster around train stations. The easy-to-navigate airport is well-connected to Amsterdam and other destinations by bus and train.

By Train

Amsterdam is the country's hub, but all major cities are linked by speedy trains that come and go every 15 minutes or so. For information on tickets, deals, and railpasses, see page 583. Dutch rail schedules are online at www.ns.nl (domestic trains) and www.nsinternationaaal.nl (international trains).

Amsterdam Central Station (and Alternatives)

Amsterdam's Central Station is being renovated—a messy construction project that's expected to last through 2014 (see "Arrival in Amsterdam" on page 43 for more details on the station). The station's train-information center can require a long wait. Save lots of time by getting train tickets and information at a small-town station (such as Haarlem), the airport upon arrival (wonderful service), or a travel agency. You can buy tickets ahead of time for the next day.

If you have a railpass, it's quicker to validate it when you arrive at Schiphol Airport than in Amsterdam's Central Station, where ticket-counter lines are long; you can stretch your railpass by buying an inexpensive ticket from the airport into Amsterdam and using your first "flexi" day for a longer trip.

From Amsterdam Central Station by Train to Domestic

Destinations: Schiphol Airport (4-6/hour, 15 minutes, €3.70, have coins handy to buy from a machine to avoid lines), **Haarlem** (6/hour, 20 minutes, €3.70 one-way, €7.10 same-day round-trip; see page 225 for a train-window tour of the countryside), **Keukenhof** (catch train to Leiden—4/hour, 35 minutes; then bus #54, called Keukenhof Express, to garden—4/hour, 30 minutes), **Aalsmeer** (take bus instead; see next page), **Zandvoort** (2/hour, 30 minutes), **Delft** (2/hour direct, 1 hour, more with transfer in Leiden or The Hague), **The Hague/Den Haag** (2/hour, 50 minutes, more with change in Leiden), **Rotterdam** (6/hour, 60-70 minutes; pricier fast trains 2-3/hour, 40 minutes), **Arnhem** (4/hour, 1 hour, half with transfer in Utrecht), **Kröller-Müller Museum/Hoge Veluwe National Park** (get off at Ede-Wageningen—4/hour, 1 hour, half with transfer in Utrecht; from Ede-Wageningen, take bus to Otterlo near park entrance—1-2/hour, 15 minutes), **Utrecht** (4/hour, 30 minutes), **Edam/Volendam/Marken** (take bus; see below), **Hoorn** (start of Historic Triangle; 2/hour, 35 minutes; more with change in Zaandam, 45 minutes), **Enkhuizen/Zuiderzee Museum** (2/hour, 1 hour), **Alkmaar** (4/hour, 40 minutes), **Zaanse Schans Open-Air Museum** (get off at Koog-Zaandijk; train direction: Uitgeest; 4/hour, 15 minutes).

By Train to International Destinations: Bruges/Brugge (hourly, 3.25-3.75 hours, transfer at Antwerp Central or Brussels Midi; transfer can be tight—be alert and check with conductor), **Brussels** (Intercity trains hourly, 2.75 hours), **Ostend** (for ferries to UK; hourly, 4 hours, 3 changes), **London** (6/day, 4.75-5.5 hours, with transfer to Eurostar Chunnel train in Brussels; Eurostar discounted with railpass, www.eurostar.com), **Copenhagen** (2/day, 11.25 hours, multiple transfers; one direct night train), **Frankfurt** (every 2 hours, 4 hours direct), **Munich** (roughly hourly, 7.5-8.75 hours, 1-2 transfers; night train possible via Hamburg, 15.5 hours), **Bern** (5/day, 8-9 hours, fastest trains change once in Frankfurt), **Paris** (nearly hourly, 3.25 hours direct on fast Thalys train or 5 hours with change to Thalys train in Brussels, www.thalys.com). When booking Thalys trains, even railpass-holders need to buy a seat reservation (generally €26-33 in second class or €41-54 in first class—the first-class reservation generally gets you a meal). If your railpass covers only France but not BeNeLux, the reservation will cost more. (Railpasses without France are not accepted on Thalys trains.) Save money by taking a bus to Paris—described on the next page.

By Bus

The biggest companies serving towns near Amsterdam include Arriva (www.arriva.nl) and Connexxion (www.connexxion.nl).

From Amsterdam by Bus to: Edam/Volendam (Arriva

bus #112, #116, #110, or #118; 2/hour, 30-45 minutes), **Marken** (Arriva bus #111, 2/hour, 40 minutes), **Aalsmeer Flower Auction** (Connexxion bus #172, 4/hour, 1 hour). Buses depart from just north of Amsterdam's Central Station (exit station through the back of the west passageway, and head up the escalator).

To Paris by Bus: If you don't have a railpass, the cheapest way to get to Paris is by Eurolines bus (about 6/day, 8 hours, €46 one-way, €86 round-trip; price depends on demand—nonrefundable, advance-purchase one-way tickets as cheap as €17 and round-trip as cheap as €28, check online for deals, Julianaplein 5, Amstel Station, five stops by metro from Central Station, tel. 020/560-8788, www.eurolines.com).

By Plane

Amsterdam's Schiphol Airport

Schiphol (SKIP-pol) Airport is located about 10 miles southwest of Amsterdam's city center. Like most of Holland, it is user-friendly and below sea level. With an appealing array of shops, eateries, and other time-killing opportunities, Schiphol is a fine place to arrive, depart, or change planes. A truly international airport, Schiphol has done away with Dutch—signs are in English only.

Information: Schiphol flight information can give you flight times and your airline's Amsterdam phone number for flight reconfirmation (tel. 0900-0141, from other countries dial +31-20-794-0800, www.schiphol.nl). To reach the airlines directly, call: KLM and Northwest—tel. 020/474-7747; Delta—tel. 020/201-3536; United—tel. 020/201-3708; US Airways—tel. 020/201-3550; Continental—tel. 020/346-9381; Martinair—tel. 020/601-1767; SAS—toll tel. 0900-7466-3727; Lufthansa—toll tel. 0900-123-4777; British Airways—tel. 020/346-9559; and easyJet—toll tel. 0900-265-8022.

Orientation: Schiphol has four terminals. Terminal 1 is for flights to most European countries (not including the UK); Terminals 2 and 3 are for flights to the UK, US, and other non-European countries; and the new, smaller Terminal 4 (attached to Terminal 3) is for low-cost carriers. Inside the airport, the terminal waiting areas are called Lounges; an inviting shopping and eating zone called Holland Boulevard runs between Lounges 2 and 3.

Arrival at Schiphol: Baggage-claim areas for all terminals empty into the same arrival zone, called Schiphol Plaza—with ATMs, shops, eateries, a busy **TI** (near Terminal 2), a train station, and bus stops for getting into the city. You can validate your Eurailpass and hit the rails immediately, or, to stretch your railpass, buy an inexpensive ticket into Amsterdam today and start the pass later.

Airport Services: The ABN/AMRO **banks** offer fair exchange rates (in both arrivals and lounge areas). The **GWK Travelex** currency-exchange office is located in Arrivals 3 and sells SIM cards for mobile phones. **Jill and James,** in Schiphol Plaza, near Terminal 4, is a useful all-purpose service counter that sells SIM cards, has an ATM, and ships packages. The **Orbitel** mobile shop just outside Terminal 2 sells only one brand of SIM cards.

You can surf the **Internet** (for a price) and make phone calls at the Communication Centres (one on the top level of Lounge 2, another on the ground floor of Lounge 1; both are behind customs and not available once you've left the security checkpoint). Convenient luggage **lockers** are at various points around the airport—allowing you to leave your bag here on a lengthy layover (both short- and long-term lockers; biggest bank of lockers near the train station at Schiphol Plaza).

Airport Train Ticket Counter: To get train information, buy a ticket, or validate your railpass, take advantage of the fantastic "Train Tickets and Services" counter (Schiphol Plaza ground level, just past Burger King). They have an easy info desk, almost no lines (much quicker than the ticket desk at the Amsterdam train station downtown), and issue tickets for a fee (€0.50 for domestic tickets, €3.50 for tickets to Belgium, Luxembourg, and nearby German cities; up to €10 for other international tickets).

Time-Killing Tips: If you have extra time at Schiphol, check out the Rijksmuseum Amsterdam Schiphol, a little art gallery and museum store on Holland Boulevard, the lively shopping/eating zone between Lounges 2 and 3. The Rijksmuseum loans a dozen or so of its minor masterpieces from the Dutch Golden Age to this unique airport museum, including actual Dutch Masters by Rembrandt, Vermeer, and others (free, daily 5:15-21:30).

To escape the airport crowds, follow signs for the Panorama Terrace to the third floor of Terminal 2, where you'll find a quieter, full-of-locals cafeteria, a kids' play area, and a view terrace where you can watch planes come and go while you nurse a coffee. If you plan to visit the terrace on arrival, stop there before you pass through customs.

From Schiphol Airport to Amsterdam: Direct **trains** to Amsterdam's Central Station run frequently (4-6/hour, 15 minutes, €3.70). The Connexxion **shuttle bus** takes you to your hotel neighborhood; there are three different routes, so ask the attendant which one works best for your hotel (2/hour, 20 minutes, €15 one-way, €24.50 round-trip, one route stops at Westerkerk near Anne Frank House and many recommended hotels, other routes may cost a couple euros more, departs from lane A7 in front of airport, reserve at least 2 hours ahead for shuttles to airport, tel. 088-339-4741, www.airporthotelshuttle.nl). Allow about €40 for a **taxi** to downtown Amsterdam. **Bus #197** is handiest for those staying in the Leidseplein district (€4, buy ticket from driver, departs from lane B9 in front of airport).

From Schiphol Airport to Haarlem: The big red #300 **bus** is direct, stopping at Haarlem's train station and near the Grote Markt/Market Square (4-10/hour, 40 minutes, €4—buy ticket from driver, departs from lane B6 in front of airport). The **train** is slightly cheaper and just as quick, but you'll have to transfer at the Amsterdam-Sloterdijk station (6/hour, 30-40 minutes, €5.40). Figure about €45 to Haarlem by **taxi.**

From Schiphol Airport by Train to: Delft (6/hour, 45 minutes, transfer in The Hague, Rotterdam, or Leiden; less frequent direct trains take 20 minutes longer), **The Hague/Den Haag** (2/hour, 35 minutes, more with change in Leiden), **Rotterdam** (3/hour, 45 minutes; more by pricier fast trains, 25 minutes), **Bruges/Brugge** (hourly, 3.5 hours, change in Antwerp and/or Ghent), **Brussels** (hourly, 2.5 hours).

From Schiphol Airport by Bus to: Keukenhof (bus #58, 4/hour, 40 minutes), **Aalsmeer** (Connexxion bus #198, 4/hour, 18 minutes).

HAARLEM

HAARLEM ORIENTATION AND SIGHTS

Cute and cozy, yet authentic and handy to the airport, Haarlem is a good home base, giving you small-town warmth overnight, with easy access (20 minutes by train) to wild-and-crazy Amsterdam during the day.

Bustling Haarlem gave America's Harlem its name back when New York was New Amsterdam, a Dutch colony. For centuries Haarlem has been a market town, buzzing with shoppers heading home with fresh bouquets, nowadays by bike.

Enjoy the market on Monday (clothing) or Saturday (general), when the town's atmospheric main square bustles like a Brueghel painting, with cheese, fish, flowers, and families. Make yourself at home; buy some flowers to brighten your hotel room.

Overview

(area code: 023)

Tourist Information

Haarlem's TI (VVV), in the town center, is friendlier, more helpful, and less crowded than Amsterdam's, so ask your Amsterdam questions here (Mon-Fri 9:30-17:30, Sat 10:00-17:00, closed most Sun but may be open 12:00-16:00, across from V&D department store at Verwulft 11, toll tel. 0900-616-1600—€0.50/minute, www.haarlem.nl, info@vvvhaarlem.nl).

The TI offers a good selection of maps and sightseeing- and walking-tour brochures, and sells discounted tickets (€1-2 off) for the Frans Hals Museum and the Teylers Museum.

The little yellow computer terminal on the curb outside the west entrance of the train station prints out free maps any time.

(It's fun...just dial the street and hit "print." Drivers will also find these terminals stationed at roads coming into town.)

Arrival in Haarlem

By Train: Lockers are available at the station on platform 3a (€3.65/day, no coins—use a credit card or buy a "Chipknip" prepaid debit card at a ticket window). Two parallel streets flank the train station (Kruisweg and Jansweg). Head up either street, and you'll reach the town square and church within 10 minutes. If you need help, ask a local person to point you toward Grote Markt (Market Square). If you're arriving by train from Amsterdam, see the end of this chapter for a description of sights you'll see out the train window along the way.

By Bus: Buses from Schiphol Airport stop both in the center (Centrum/Verwulft stop, a short walk from Grote Markt) and at the train station. For more on bus connections from the airport, see page 214.

By Car: Parking is expensive on the streets (€2.50/hour). It's cheaper (€1/30 minutes; €2.50 overnight—19:00-8:00) in these central garages: at the train station, at the southern end of Gedempte Oude Gracht (the main thoroughfare), near the recommended Die Raeckse Hotel, and near the Frans Hals Museum. The most central garage, near the Teylers Museum, is pricier (€1.50 every 40 minutes—essentially, €2.75/hour).

By Plane: For details on getting from Schiphol Airport to Haarlem, see page 214.

HAARLEM ORIENTATION

Helpful Hints

Blue Monday and Early Closures: Most sights are closed on Monday, except the church. Two sights close early the rest of the week: **Corrie Ten Boom House** (15:30) and **De Adriaan windmill** (16:00).

Internet Access: Try **Hotel Amadeus** (overlooking Grote Markt, €1/30 minutes), **High Times Coffeeshop** (free if you buy some pot, Lange Veerstraat 47—see sidebar on page 252), or **Suny Teletechniques** (€2/hour, daily 10:00-24:00, near train station at Lange Herenstraat 4, tel. 023/551-0037).

Post Office: There isn't one. To buy stamps, head to a newsstand with the orange *TNT* logo; if you need to send a package, ask your hotelier for help.

Laundry: My Beautiful Launderette is handy and fairly central (€6 self-service wash and dry, daily 8:30-20:30, €9 full service available Mon-Fri 9:00-17:00, near V&D department store at Boter Markt 20).

Bike Rental: You can rent bikes from **Pieters Fietsverhuur** at the train station (fixed-gear bike-€6.50/day, more for 3-speed bike, €50 deposit and passport number required, Mon-Sat 6:00-24:00, Sun 8:00-24:00, Stationsplein 7, tel. 023/531-7066). They have only 50 bikes to rent and often run out by midmorning—especially when the weather's good. **Rent a Bike Haarlem** charges more, but is friendly and efficient, and carries plenty of new, good-quality bikes. If you're renting for less than a full day, negotiate a cheaper price (fixed-gear bike-€10/day, 3-speed bike-€13.50/day, mountain bikes available, after-hours drop-off possible, ID but no money required for deposit; April-Sept daily 9:00-18:00; Oct-March Tue-Fri 10:00-17:30, Thu until 18:00, Sat 10:00-17:00, closed Sun-Mon; near station at Lange Herenstraat 36, tel. 023/542-1195, www.rentabikehaarlem.nl).

Taxi: The drop charge of €7.50 gets you a little over a mile.

Local Guide: Consider hiring **Walter Schelfhout,** a bearded repository of Haarlem's historical fun facts. If you're into beer lore, Walter's your guy (€75/2 hours, also leads a beer walk, tel. 023/535-5715, mobile 06-1258-9299, schelfhout@dutch .nl).

Best View: At **La Place** (top-floor cafeteria of the V&D department store—see page 251), you get wrap-around views of the city as you sip your €2 self-serve tea.

Best Ice Cream: Gelateria Bartoli (on the south side of the Grote Kerk) is the local favorite (daily April-Sept 12:00-22:00, March and Oct-Dec 12:00-17:30 in good weather, closed Jan-Feb).

Sights in Haarlem

▲▲Grote Markt (Market Square)

Haarlem's Grote Markt, where 10 streets converge, is the town's delightful centerpiece... as it has been for 700 years. To enjoy a coffee or beer here, simmering in Dutch good living, is a quintessential European experience. Observe. Sit and gaze at the church, appreciating essentially the same scene that Dutch artists captured centuries ago in oil paintings

Haarlem

TO OVERVEEN & ZANDVOORT

STATEN BOLWERK

TRAIN STATION

TO AMST.

STN. PLEIN

BUS STN.

KENAU PARK

PARK LAAN

100 YARDS
100 METERS

TO WINDMILL

RED LIGHT DISTRICT

CORRIE TEN BOOM HOUSE

GROTE MARKT

GROTE KERK

ⒷBUS #300

TOWN HALL

MEAT MKT.

CANAL CRUISES

BOTER MARKT

TEYLERS MUSEUM

V+D DEPT. STORE

TO AMST.

HISTORY MUSEUM HAARLEM

FRANS HALS MUSEUM

GASTHUISVEST

DCH

that now hang in museums.

Just a few years ago, trolleys ran through the square, and cars were parked everywhere. But today it's a pedestrian zone, with market stalls filling the square on Mondays and Saturdays, and café tables dominating on other days.

This is a fun place to build a picnic with Haarlem finger foods and enjoy great seating on the square. Look for pickled herring (take-away stand on the square), local cheese (Gouda and Edam—tasty shop a block away on Barteljorisstraat), french fries with mayonnaise (recommended old-time fries place behind the church on Warmoesstraat), and, in the summer, *stroopwafels* (waffles with built-in syrup) and *poffertjes* (little sugar doughnuts, cooked on the spot).

As you enjoy a snack, take this simple spin tour of the square.
• *Overseeing the square is the...*

L. J. Coster Statue: Forty years before Gutenberg invented movable type, this man carved the letter *A* out of wood, dropped it into some wet sand, and saw the imprint it left. He got the idea of making movable type out of wood (and later, he may have tried using lead). For Haarlemmers, that was good enough, and they credit their man, Coster, with inventing modern printing. In the statue, Coster (c. 1370-1440) holds up a block of movable type and points to himself, saying, "I made this." How much Coster did is uncertain, but Gutenberg trumped him by building a printing press, casting type in metal, and pounding out the Bible.

• *Coster is facing the...*

Town Hall: Whereas most of medieval Europe was ruled by kings, dukes, and barons, Haarlem has been largely self-governing since 1425. This building—built from a royal hunting lodge in the mid-1200s, then rebuilt after a 1351 fire—has served as Haarlem's Town Hall since about 1400. The facade dates from 1630.

The town drunk used to hang out on the bench in front of the Town Hall, where he'd expose himself to newlyweds coming down the stairs. Rather than arresting the man, the townspeople simply moved the bench (a typical Dutch solution to the problem).
• *Next to the church is the...*

Meat Market (Vleeshal), 1603: The fine Flemish Renaissance building nearest the cathedral is the old meat hall, built by the rich butchers' and leatherworkers' guilds. The meat market was on the ground floor, the leather was upstairs, and the cellar was filled with ice to preserve the meat. It's decorated with carved bits of early advertising—sheep and cows for sale. Today, rather than

Haarlem of the Golden Age

Parts of Haarlem still look like they did four centuries ago, when the city was a bustling commercial center rivaling Amsterdam. It's easy to imagine local merchants and their wives dressed in black with ruff collars, promenading on Grote Markt.

Back then, the town was a port on the large Haarlemmer Lake, with the North Sea only about five miles away. As well as being the tulip capital of the country, Haarlem was a manufacturing center, producing wool, silk, lace, damask cloth, furniture, smoking pipes (along with cheap, locally grown tobacco), and mass quantities of beer. Haarlemmers were notorious consumers of beer—it was a popular breakfast drink, and the average person drank six pints a day.

In 1585, the city got an influx of wealthy merchants when Spanish troops invaded the culturally rich city of Antwerp, driving Protestants and Jews north. Even when hard-line, moralistic Calvinists dominated Haarlem's politics, the city remained culturally and religiously diverse.

In the 1700s, Haarlem's economy declined, along with that of the rest of the Netherlands. In the succeeding centuries, industry—printing, textiles, ship building—once again made the city an economic force.

meat, the hall shows off temporary art exhibits in the Museum De Hallen (€5, Tue-Sat 11:00-17:00, Sun 12:00-17:00, closed Mon, tel. 023/511-5775, www.dehallen.com) and bits of the town's past in the Archaeology Museum (free, Wed-Sun 13:00-17:00, closed Mon-Tue, in the cellar of the Museum De Hallen, tel. 023/542-0888).

More Sights in Haarlem

▲Church (Grote Kerk)—This 15th-century Gothic church (now Protestant) is worth a look, if only to see Holland's greatest pipe organ (from 1738, 100 feet high). Its more than 5,000 pipes impressed both Handel and Mozart. Note how the organ, which fills the west end, seems to steal the show from the altar. Quirky highlights of the church include a replica of Foucault's pendulum, the "Dog-Whipper's Chapel," and a 400-year-old can-nonball.

To enter, find the small *Entrée* sign behind the Coster statue on Grote Markt.

Cost and Hours: €2.50, not covered by Museumkaart, Mon-Sat 10:00-17:00, closed Sun to tourists, tel. 023/553-2040, www .bavo.nl.

Concerts: Consider attending (even part of) a **concert** to hear the Oz-like pipe organ (regular free concerts Tue at 20:15 mid-May-mid-Oct, additional concerts Thu at 15:00 July-Aug; bring a sweater—the church isn't heated).

For a self-guided tour, see the ✪ Grote Kerk Tour chapter.

▲▲Frans Hals Museum—Haarlem is the hometown of Frans Hals, the foremost Dutch portrait painter of the 17th-century Golden Age. This refreshing museum, once an almshouse for old men back in 1610, displays many of Hals' greatest paintings, crafted in his nearly Impressionistic style. You'll see group portraits and paintings of old-time Haarlem (€7.50, often €10 with special exhibits, Tue-Sat 11:00-17:00, Sun 12:00-17:00, closed Mon, Groot Heiligland 62, tel. 023/511-5775, www.franshalsmuseum.nl).

For a self-guided tour, see the ✪ Frans Hals Museum Tour chapter.

History Museum Haarlem—This small museum, across the street from the Frans Hals Museum, offers a glimpse of old Haarlem. Request the English version of the 10-minute video, low-key Haarlem's version of a sound-and-light show. Study the large-scale model of Haarlem in 1822 (when its fortifications were still intact), and wander the three rooms without English descriptions (overpriced at €4, Tue-Sat 12:00-17:00, Sun 13:00-17:00, closed Mon, Groot Heiligland 47, tel. 023/542-2427, www.historisch museumhaarlem.nl). The adjacent architecture center (free) may be of interest to architects.

▲Corrie ten Boom House—Haarlem was home to Corrie ten Boom, popularized by her inspirational book (and the movie that followed), *The Hiding Place*. Both tell about the Ten Boom family's experience protecting Jews from the Nazis. Corrie ten Boom gives the other half of the Anne Frank story—the point of view of those who risked their lives to hide Dutch Jews during the Nazi occupation (1940-1945).

The clock shop was the Ten Boom family business. The elderly father and his two daughters—Corrie and Betsy, both in their 50s—lived above the store and in the brick building attached in back (along Schoutensteeg alley). Corrie's bedroom was on the top floor at the back. This room was tiny to start with, but then the family built a second, secret room (less than a yard deep) at the very back—"the hiding place," where they could hide six Jews at a time. Devoutly religious, the family had a long tradition of tolerance, having hosted prayer meetings here in their home for both Jews and Christians for generations.

The Gestapo, tipped off that the family was harboring Jews, burst into the Ten Boom house. Finding a suspicious number of ration coupons, the Nazis arrested the family, but failed to find the six Jews (who later escaped) in the hiding place. Corrie's father and sister died while in prison, but Corrie survived the Ravensbrück concentration camp to tell her story in her memoir.

The Ten Boom House is open only for English tours—check the sign on the door for the next start time. The gentle and loving one-hour tours come with a little evangelizing that some may find objectionable.

Cost and Hours: Free, but donations accepted; April-Oct Tue-Sat first tour at 10:00, last tour at 15:30; Nov-March Tue-Sat first tour at 11:00, last tour around 14:30; closed Sun-Mon; 50 yards north of Grote Markt at Barteljorisstraat 19; the clock-shop people get all wound up if you go inside—wait in the little side street at the door, where tour times are posted; tel. 023/531-0823, www.corrietenboom.com.

▲**Teylers Museum**—Famous as the oldest museum in Holland, Teylers is a time-warp experience, filled with all sorts of fun curios for science buffs: fossils, minerals, primitive electronic gadgetry, and examples of 18th- and 19th-century technology (it also has two lovely painting galleries and hosts good temporary exhibits). The science-oriented sections of this place feel like a museum of a museum. They're serious about authenticity here: The presentation is perfectly preserved, right down to the original labels. Since there was no electricity in the olden days, you'll find little electric lighting...if it's dark outside, it's dark inside. The museum's benefactor, Pieter Teyler van der Hulst, was a very wealthy merchant who willed his estate, worth the equivalent of €80 million today, to a foundation whose mission was to "create and maintain a museum to stimulate art and science." The museum opened in 1784, six years after Teyler's death (his last euro was spent in 1983—now it's a national museum). Add your name to the guest book, which goes back to before Napoleon's visit here. The freshly renovated oval room—a temple of science and learning—is the core of the museum; in the art salons paintings are hung in the old style. An excellent (and, I'd say, essential) audioguide is included.

Cost and Hours: Overpriced at €9, Tue-Sat 10:00-17:00, Sun 12:00-17:00, closed Mon, Spaarne 16, tel. 023/516-0960, www.teylersmuseum.eu. The museum's modern café has good prices and faces a delightful garden.

The Haarlemmermeer

The land between Haarlem and Amsterdam—where trains speed through, cattle graze, and 747s touch down—was once a lake the size of Washington, D.C., called the Haarlemmermeer.

In the 1500s, a series of high tides and storms caused the IJ River to breach its banks, flooding this sub-sea-level area and turning a bunch of shallow lakes into a single one nearly 15 feet deep, covering 70 square miles. By the 1800s, floods were licking at the borders of Haarlem and Amsterdam, and the residents needed to act. First, they dug a ring canal to channel away water (and preserve the lake's shipping business). Then, using steam engines, they pumped the lake dry, turning marshy soil into fertile ground. The Amsterdam-Haarlem train line that soon crossed the former lakebed was the country's first.

▲**De Adriaan Windmill**—Haarlem's old-time windmill, located just a 10-minute walk from the station and Teylers Museum, welcomes visitors with a short video, a little museum, and fine town views (€3, not covered by Museumkaart; March-Oct Wed-Fri 13:00-16:00, Sat-Sun 10:00-16:00, closed Mon-Tue; same hours in winter except only open Fri-Sun, Papentorenvest 1, tel. 023/545-0259, www.molenadriaan.nl).

Canal Cruise—Making a scenic 50-minute loop through and around Haarlem with a live guide who speaks Dutch and sometimes English, **Post Verkade Cruise**'s little trips are more relaxing than informative (€9.50; April-Oct daily departures at the top of the hour 12:00-16:00; also evening cruises, across canal from Teylers Museum at Spaarne 11a, tel. 023/535-7723, www.post verkadecruises.nl). For a similar experience in an open boat, find **Haarlem Canal Tours**, nearby on Korte Spaarne (€12.50, leaves every 1.5 hours daily 10:00-19:00, may not run in bad weather and off-season, www.haarlemcanaltours.com).

▲**Red Light District**—Wander through a little Red Light District that's as precious as a Barbie doll—and legal since the 1980s (2 blocks northeast of Grote Markt, off Lange Begijnestraat, no senior or student discounts). Don't miss the mall on Begijnesteeg marked by the red neon sign reading 't Steegje ("free"). Just beyond that, the nearby 't Poortje ("office park") costs €6 to enter. Jog to the right to pop into the much more inviting "Red Lantern" (window-shopping welcome, at Korte Begijnestraat 27). As you wander through this area, remember that the people here don't condone prostitution any more than your own community back home probably does; they just find it practical not to criminalize it and drive it underground, but instead to regulate it and keep the practice as safe as possible.

Amsterdam to Haarlem Train Tour

Since you'll probably take the train from Amsterdam to Haarlem, here's an out-the-window tour to keep you entertained while you travel. Departing from Amsterdam, grab a seat on the right (with your back to Amsterdam, top deck if possible). Everything is on the right unless I say it's on the left.

You're riding the oldest train line in Holland. Leaving Amsterdam, you'll see the cranes and ships of its harbor—sizable, but nothing like Europe's biggest in nearby Rotterdam.

On your left, a few minutes out of Amsterdam, you should be able to see an old **windmill** (you can visit a similar one in Haarlem). In front of it, the little garden plots and cottages are escapes for big-city people who probably don't even have a balcony.

Coming into the **Sloterdijk Station** (where trains connect for Amsterdam's Schiphol Airport), you'll see huge office buildings, such as Dutch Telecom KPN. These sprouted after the station made commuting easy. On the horizon, sleek and modern windmills whirl.

Passing through a forest and by some houseboats, you enter a *polder*—an area of reclaimed land. This is part of an ecologically sound farm zone, run without chemicals. Cows, pigs, and chickens run free—they're not raised in cages. The train tracks are on a dike, which provides a raised foundation less susceptible to flooding, so the transportation system generally keeps running, even in bad weather. Looking out at another dike in the distance (visible on clear days), consider that you're actually in the most densely populated country in Europe.

On the right, just after the Ikea building, find a big beige-and-white building. This is the **mint,** where currency is printed (top security, no advertising). This has long been a family business—see the name: Joh. Enschedé.

As the train slows down, you're passing through the Netherlands' biggest train-car-maintenance facility, and entering Haarlem. Look left. The domed building is a **prison,** built in 1901 and still in use. The **De Adriaan windmill** that you see was rebuilt in 2002, after the original burnt down in 1932 (the windmill is open for afternoon visits—see previous page).

When you cross the Spaarne River, you'll see the great **church spire** of the Grote Kerk towering over Haarlem, as it has since medieval times, back when a fortified wall circled the town. Notice the white version of the same spire capping the smaller church (between the prison and the big church): This was the original sandstone steeple that stood atop the big church. However, structural problems forced its move to another church, and a new spire was built for the big church.

Exit the train into one of Holland's oldest stations, adorned with Art Nouveau decor from 1908. Welcome to Haarlem.

GROTE KERK TOUR

Haarlem's impressive Grote Kerk (Great Church), one of the best-known landmarks in the Netherlands, is visible from miles around, rising above the flat plain that surrounds it. From the Grote Markt (Market Square), you see the church at a three-quarters angle, emphasizing both its length (240 feet) and its height (260 feet).

Orientation

Cost: €2.50, not covered by Museumkaart.

Hours: Mon-Sat 10:00-17:00, closed Sun to tourists, Sun service at 10:00 (May-Oct). The church also holds a daily 15-minute prayer service at 12:45 (May-Oct) and an evensong service on Sunday at 19:00 (May-Sept). Occasionally, the church is closed for a wedding or a funeral; if you see a closed sign when it's supposed to be open, return in a couple of hours.

Getting There: The church is on the main square, a 10-minute walk south of the train station.

Information: The leaflet at the ticket desk offers basic information in English. Tours are offered on Saturdays, by request (€4). Tel. 023/553-2040, www.bavo.nl.

WC: Nice WCs are inside, just after the ticket desk.

Music: Consider attending even just part of a concert to hear Holland's greatest pipe organ. Free concerts generally are offered throughout the summer (Tue at 20:15 mid-May-mid-Oct, additional concerts Thu at 15:00 July-Aug; concerts last about one hour). In even years, an organ competition is held here in July, bringing nearly nightly performances at 20:15. If you're coming for a concert, bring a sweater—the thick stone walls keep the church cool, even during summer. Entrance to the evening concerts is through the south

transept, around the back of the church.
Length of This Tour: Allow one hour.

Overview

After a fire destroyed the old church (1328), the Grote Kerk was built over a 150-year period (c. 1390-1540) in the late Gothic style of red-and-gray brick, topped with a slate-covered wood roof and a stacked tower bearing a golden crown and a rooster weathervane.

Originally Catholic, the church was named after St. Bavo, a local noble who frequented seventh-century Red Light Districts during his youth. After his conversion, he moved out of his castle and into a hollow tree, where he spent his days fasting and praying. In the late 1500s, the St. Bavo Church became Protestant (Dutch Reformed) along with much of the country. From then on, the anti-saint Protestants simply called it the Great Church.

The Tour Begins

• *Before entering, take a few minutes to walk around this incredible building.*

Exterior

Notice the rough buttress anchors, which were never needed. Money ran out, and the planned stone ceiling (which would have required these buttresses) was replaced by a lighter wooden one. Some windows are bricked up because the organ fills the wall.

The original stone tower crowned the church from 1522 until 1530, when the church began sink-ing under its weight. The tower was removed and replaced by the lighter, lead-covered-wood version you see today. (The frugal Dutch recycled the old tower, using it to cap the Bakenesser church, a short walk away.)

Because the tower was used as a lookout by Napoleon, it was classified as part of the town's defense. As a result, the tower (but not the rest of the church) became city property, and, since Haarlem's citizens own it, they must help pay to maintain it.

The base of the church is encrusted, barnacle-like, with shops—selling jewelry, souvenirs, haircuts, and artwork in the col-onnaded former fish market—harkening back to medieval times, when religion and commerce were more intertwined. The little shops around the cathedral have long been church-owned, rented

Grote Kerk

ALTAR

CHOIR

PULPIT→

ENTER
(TICKETS,
SHOP
+ WC
INSIDE)

**GROTE
MARKT**

ORGAN

1. Center of Church Viewpoint
2. Poor Peasant Bending
3. Grave of Frans Hals
4. "Pillar Biter"
5. Three Little Ships
6. Memorial to Hydraulic Engineers
7. Brewers' Chapel & Café
8. Giant & Dwarf Marks
9. Old Map of "Harlemum"
10. Church Rosters
11. Pelican Lectern
12. Mary's Chapel
13. Foucault's Pendulum
14. Dog-Whipper's Chapel
15. Model of the Church
16. Cannonball
17. Evening Concert Entrance

GROTE KERK

out to bring in a little cash.

During the day, a machine plays music on the bells of the Grote Kerk's carillon (live carillonneurs play occasionally). If you're in Haarlem at night, you'll hear the carillon chiming a simple "de dong dong, de dong dong" ("Don't worry, be hap-py") at 21:00. In days gone by, this used to warn citizens that the city gates would soon close for the night.

• *Enter the church on the Grote Markt side, near the north transept (look for the small* Entrée *sign). Walk to the center of the church and take it all in.*

Interior

Simple white walls, a black floor, a brown ceiling, and a mahogany-colored organ make this spacious church feel vast, light, and airy. Considering it was built over a span of 150 years, its architecture is surprisingly homogenous. Originally, much of the interior was painted in bright patterns, similar to the carpet-like frescoes on some columns near the center of the church. But in 1566, Protestant extremists stripped the church of its graven images and ornate Catholic trappings, leaving it relatively stark, with minimal decoration. They whitewashed everything. The frescoes you see today were restored when the whitewash was removed in the 1980s.

Look up to see the fan-vaulted cedar ceiling from 1530. Look down to see tombstones paving the floor. And look midway up the walls to catch squatting characters supporting the pilasters. The three-story organ fills the west wall.

• *We'll circle the church, but first stand at the candle-lined, fence-like brass barrier and look into an enclosed area of wooden benches ("stalls") and the altar, known as the...*

Choir

After the church's foundation was laid, the choir was built first and used for worship for more than a century while the rest of the building was completed.

Today, the brass-and-wood barrier keeps tourists from entering the most sacred area, just as peasants were kept out in medieval times. While the commoners had to stand during services, local big shots got to perch their heinies on the little ledges (called misericords, carved in 1512) of the **wooden stalls** that line the choir; the eighth stall along the left-hand side shows a poor peasant bending over to bear a rich guy's bum on his back. The stalls are also decorated with the coats of arms of noble families, whose second sons traditionally became priests.

The choir's floor holds a simple slab marked with a lantern—the **grave of Frans Hals** (*graf van Frans Hals*), Haarlem's own master artist of the Golden Age. When he was a child,

Hals' family moved to Haarlem, and he lived and worked here all his life, worshipping in the Grote Kerk. A friend of mayors and

preachers, he chronicled middle-class citizens and tavern life, producing hundreds of masterpieces...and 10 kids.

At both ends of the brass barrier, look for the endearing knee-level carvings of the "pillar biter." The message of these carvings, aimed at those who were "more Catholic than even the pope," was this: Don't go overboard on devotion.

More than a thousand wealthy people are buried under the church's pavement stones. Only those with piles of money to give to the church could be buried in a way that gave them an advantage in the salvation derby. But even though the dead bodies were embalmed, they stunk. Imagine being a peasant sitting here, trying to think about God...and thinking only of the stench of well-fed bodies rotting below. Here is where the phrase "stinking rich" was born.

• *To your right (as you face the choir), suspended between columns, are...*

Three Little Ships

Sailing under the red-white-and-blue Dutch flag and the flag of a rearing lion, ships like these helped make Holland the world's number-one sea-trading nation in the 1600s.

The biggest model ship of the three is a frigate. These fast, heavily armed, three-masted, fully rigged ships rode shotgun for merchant vessels, protecting them from pirates in their two-year journey to the Far East and back. This one has a flat-bottomed hull, which was necessary to ply Amsterdam's shallow harbor. It could fire a 21-gun salute from each side, and extra cannons on the poop deck and forecastle made it more powerful

than the average frigate. The keel has an iron saw, a Dutch military specialty for slicing through the chains that commonly blocked harbors (see the chain between two towers near the bow).

• *At the next column down, just to the right, is the...*

Memorial to Hydraulic Engineers

The marble relief shows Neptune in his water chariot. In low-lying Holland of the 1800s, when flooding could mean life or death, hydraulic engineers were heroes, specifically the two commemorated here.

• Behind the columns, set into the wall of the church, is the...

Brewers' Chapel (Brouwerskapel)

This chapel, with its humble café, marks the long and short of the city's 750-year history—literally. On the chapel's central pillar, black lines on the column show the height of Haarlem's short-est citizen, thigh-high (33 inches) Simon Paap, who supposedly died in a dwarf-tossing incident, and—wow!—8-foot-8-inch-tall Daniel Cajanus.

• On the wall to the left of the café hangs an...

Old Map of "Harlemum"

The map shows the walled city in 1688, with ramparts and a moat. Surrounding panels showcase Haarlem's 750-year history. The

lower-left panel shows the 1572-1573 Siege of Haarlem, as brave Haarlem women join their menfolk in battle—bombs exploding around them—to fight off invading Spanish troops.

The lower-right panel shows knights kneeling before a king in the 12th century, while in the dis-tance, ships sail right along the city walls. Up until the 1840s, when it

was drained and reclaimed, there was a large lake (the Haarlem-mermeer) standing between Haarlem and Amsterdam. The Grote Kerk, when viewed by distant travelers, seemed to float like a stately ship on the lake, as seen in the landscape along the bottom of the map.

• From here, circle the church counterclockwise, heading around the altar. Just after rounding the bend, on the wall, you'll see the first of the church's many lists of prominent church members, dating back to 1577, when the church became Protestant. The first roster, from 1770, has mesmerizingly ornate calligraphy. Opposite this list, inside the choir, is the...

Pelican Lectern

According to medieval lore, pelicans are so attentive to their chicks that mothers, when necessary, feed their young with their own blood. Because of this myth, the pelican became a symbol of Christ's self-sacrifice. This lectern from 1499 has a brass bird that looks just like other symbolic pelicans—shown stabbing itself with its own beak—except for one important difference: It looks like an eagle. Apparently, its creator had never come across an actual pelican.

• Just past the end of the choir is...

Mary's Chapel (Maria Kapel)

Inside the iron cage on the chapel's back wall is an old wood-and-iron chest that served as a safe for the church's cash and precious documents—such as those papers granting the power to sell forgiveness. See the board of keys for the many doors in this huge complex. Notice also the sarcophagi. Once filled with the "stinking rich," boxes like this were buried five deep below the church floor. Such high-density burying maximized the revenue generated by selling burial spots.

Foucault's Pendulum

In the north transept, a ball on a wire hangs from the ceiling (see the brass sphere in the far-right corner). When set in motion (by a church tour guide, mostly on Saturdays), it swings across a dial on the floor, re-creating physicist Léon Foucault's pendulum experiment in Paris in 1851. If it's swinging, stand here patiently and watch the earth rotate on its axis.

As the pendulum swings steadily back and forth, the earth rotates counterclockwise underneath it, making the pendulum appear to rotate clockwise around the dial. The earth rotates once every 24 hours, of course, but at Haarlem's latitude of 52 degrees, it makes the pendulum (appear to) sweep 360 degrees every 30 hours, 27 minutes (to knock over the bowling pin). Stand here for five minutes, and you'll see the earth move one degree.

As the world turns, find several small relief statues (in a niche on the right-hand wall) with beheaded bodies and defaced faces—victims of the 1566 Iconoclastic Fury, when angry Protestant extremists vandalized Dutch Catholic churches (as this once was).

• *Ten yards farther on, the shallow niche is the...*

Dog-Whipper's Chapel

In a sculpted relief (top of column at left end of chapel, above eye level), an angry man whips an angry dog while striding over another angry dog's head. Back when churches served as rainy-day marketplaces, this man's responsibility was to keep Haarlem's dogs out of the church.

The Organ

Even when silent, this organ impresses. Finished in 1738 by Amsterdam's Christian Muller, it features a mahogany-colored casing with tin pipes and gold trim, studded with statues of musicians and an eight-piece combo of angels. Lions on the top hold Haarlem's coat of arms—a sword, surrounded by stars, over a banner reading *Vicit Vim Virtus* ("Virtue Conquers Violence"). There are larger pipe organs in the world, but this is one of the best.

With three keyboards, a forest of pedals, and 65 stops (the knobs on either side of the keyboards), this magnificent organ produces an awesome majesty of sound. Picture 10-year-old Mozart at the controls of this 5,000-pipe sound machine. In 1766, he played Haarlem at the tail end of his triumphant, three-year whirlwind tour of Europe. He'd just returned from London, where he met J. C. Bach, the youngest son of Johann Sebastian Bach (1685-1750), the grandfather of organ music. Mozart had recently written several pieces inspired by Bach, and he may have tried them out here.

"Hal-le-lu-jah!" That famous four-note riff may have echoed around the church when Handel played here in 1740, the year before his famous oratorio, *Messiah*, debuted. The 20th-century organist/humanitarian Albert Schweitzer also performed here.

The organist sits unseen amid the pipes, behind the section that juts out at the bottom. While the bellows generate pressurized air, the organist presses a key, which opens a valve, admitting forced air through a pipe and out its narrow opening, producing a tone. An eight-foot-long pipe plays middle C. A four-foot-long pipe plays C exactly one octave up. A 20-foot pipe rumbles the rafters. With 5,068 pipes ranging from more than 20 feet tall to just a few inches, this organ can cover eight octaves (a piano plays seven), and each key can play a variety of sounds. By pulling one of the stops (such as "flute" or "trumpet"), the organist can channel the air into certain sets of pipes tuned to play together to mimic other instruments. For maximum power, you "pull out all the stops."

• *Cross in front of the organ to find the glass box holding a...*

Model of the Church

A hundred times smaller than the church itself, this model still took a thousand work-hours to build. See if you can spot the matchsticks, washers, screens, glue, wire, and paper clips used to make it.

• *Just beyond the model, to the left of the chapel with the green metal gate and above eye level, is...*

A Cannonball in the Wall

Duck! Placed here in 1573, this cannonball commemorates the city's finest hour: the Siege of Haarlem.

In the winter of 1572-1573, Holland rebelled against its Spanish oppressors. Haarlem proclaimed its alliance with William of Orange (and thus, independence from Spain). In response, the angry Spanish governor—camped in Amsterdam—laid siege to Haarlem. The winter was cold, food ran low, and the city was bombarded by Spanish cannons. Inside huddled 4,000 cold, hungry Calvinists. At one point, the city's women even joined the men on the barricades, brandishing kitchen knives.

But Spain had blockaded the Haarlem Lake (the Haarlemmermeer), and by June 12, 1573, Haarlem had to surrender. The Spanish rounded up 1,500 men (three-quarters of Haarlem's able-bodied male population) and executed them to send a message to the rest of the country. Still, Haarlem's brave seven-month stand against overwhelming odds became a kind of Dutch Alamo, inspiring their countrymen to fight on.

Following Haarlem's brave lead, other Dutch towns rebelled, including Amsterdam (see page 562). Though Holland and Spain would skirmish for another five decades, the battles soon moved southward, and Spanish troops would never again seriously penetrate the country's borders.

• *Back in the middle of the nave, returning to where you began, you'll pass the impressive wooden...*

Pulpit

Elaborately carved from oak in 1679, the pulpit is topped with a tower-shaped roof. Brass handrails snake down the staircase—serpents fleeing the word of God. In this simply decorated Protestant church, the pulpit is perhaps the most ornate element, directing worshippers' eyes to the speaker. During the Reformation, Protestants changed the worship service. As teaching became more important than ritual, the pulpit was given a higher profile.

• *This ends our tour—complete with pillar biters, dwarves and giants, a towering wall of organ pipes, and hanging ships. Who said, "When you've seen one Gothic church, you've seen them all"?*

FRANS HALS MUSEUM TOUR

Frans Hals (c. 1582-1666) is Haarlem's most famous son. He was a bold humanist who painted everyday people in their warts-and-all glory, a forerunner of Impressionist brushwork, a master of composition, and an articulate visual spokesman for his generation—the generation of Holland's Golden Age.

Stand eye-to-eye with life-size, lifelike portraits of Haarlem's citizens—brewers, preachers, workers, bureaucrats, and housewives. Take a close look at the people who built the Dutch Golden Age, and then watched it start to fade.

Orientation

Cost: €7.50 (often €10 when entry includes a special exhibit).

Hours: Tue-Sat 11:00-17:00, Sun 12:00-17:00, closed Mon.

Getting There: The museum is at Groot Heiligland 62, a delightful five-minute stroll from the main square.

Renovation: The museum is undergoing a renovation that may affect the placement of some pieces or your route through the museum. The famous *Civic Guard* painting by Frans Hals will remain on display in Room 14.

Information: Frans Hals' masterpieces never leave Room 14 (and nearby rooms), but the other paintings can rotate—ask a guard if you can't locate them easily. The entire museum is thoughtfully described in English. Tel. 023/511-5775, www.franshalsmuseum.nl.

If you'll be visiting six or more museums in the Netherlands, consider buying the €45 Museumkaart pass here. It covers your entry to both the Frans Hals and Teylers museums in Haarlem, and lets you skip the ticket-buying line at bigger sights, such as the Van Gogh Museum in Amsterdam

Frans Hals Museum—Room 14

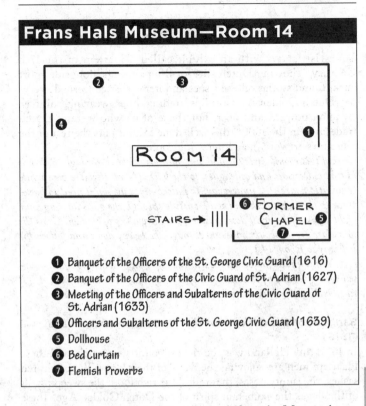

● Banquet of the Officers of the St. George Civic Guard (1616)

● Banquet of the Officers of the Civic Guard of St. Adrian (1627)

● Meeting of the Officers and Subalterns of the Civic Guard of St. Adrian (1633)

● Officers and Subalterns of the St. George Civic Guard (1639)

● Dollhouse

● Bed Curtain

● Flemish Proverbs

(for more on sightseeing passes, including the Museumkaart, see page 43).

Length of This Tour: Allow one hour.

Cuisine Art: The Frans Hals Lunchcafé serves sandwiches and other simple food (daily 12:00-16:30, only drinks and dessert served after 15:30).

Overview

Frans Hals' paintings are just one part of the collection. The

museum fancies itself as *the* museum of the Dutch Golden Age, offering you the rare opportunity of enjoying 17th-century art in a 17th-century building. Well-described exhibits unfold as the rectangular museum wraps around a peaceful central courtyard. The building's layout makes sense when you realize it was built as subsidized housing for poor old men (in 1610).

The Tour Begins

Your visit starts with an exhibit called "Haarlem in the 17th Century," showing Dutch slice-of-life paintings alongside short background stories on the issues and items that concerned everyday Dutch Golden Agers: tulips, trading, linen-weaving, militias, "women power," and beer. For those of us who weren't Dutch tradesmen in the 1600s, this well-done exhibit puts the rest of the museum's artwork in an interesting context.

• *From this room, circle the museum counterclockwise, through the art of Hals' predecessors and colleagues, to the back. (Note: If you're here while renovations are still underway, to follow my tour you'll need to backtrack to the ticket desk and walk outside through the glass door on your right—just after ticket desk; push button on wall to open door. Cross the courtyard, re-enter the museum through the heavy door, and follow the hallway to Room 14.)*

You'll know you've arrived in the right place when you find yourself well-guarded by canvases full of companies of men in uniform. We'll start with the men in the bright red sashes.

Banquet of the Officers of the St. George Civic Guard (1616)

In 1616, tiny Holland was the richest country on earth, and these Haarlem men are enjoying the fruits of their labor. The bright red sashes, the jaunty poses, the smiles, the rich food, the sweeping tilt of the flags...the exuberant spirit of the Dutch Golden Age. These weekend warriors have finished their ceremonial parade through town and hung their weapons on the wall, and now they sit down for a relaxed, post-show party.

The man in the middle (next to the flag-bearer, facing us) is about to carve the chicken, when the meal is interrupted. It's us, arriving late through the back door, and heads turn to greet us. Rosy-cheeked Nicolaes Woutersz van der Meer (see his portrait on page 243), hand on hip, turns around with a friendly look, while the man to the right, the colonel in charge, waves us in. Frans Hals knew these men well as friends and colleagues, since he himself was a lifelong member of this Civic Guard company.

This band of brothers is united by common gestures—two men have hands on hips, three turn their palms up, two plant their hands downward, three clutch wine glasses. But mostly, they're joined by the uniform sashes. The red sashes slant both left and

Frans Hals
(c. 1582-1666)

At age 10, Frans Hals, the son of a weaver, moved with his family to Haarlem. He would spend the rest of his life there, rarely traveling even to nearby Amsterdam.

His early years are known to us only through his paintings of taverns and drunks, musicians and actors, crafted in a free and colorful style (like the Rijksmuseum's *The Merry Drinker* on page 128). In 1610, he married and joined Haarlem's St. Luke's Guild of painters. In 1612, he was admitted to the prestigious St. George Civic Guard. In 1617, widowed Hals married again, producing (altogether) ten children, five of whom took up painting.

Hals' group portrait of the St. George Civic Guard (1616) put him on the map as Haarlem's premier portrait painter. For the next five decades, he abandoned the lighthearted slice-of-life scenes of his youth and dedicated himself to chronicling Haarlem's prosperous, middle-class world of businessmen and professionals—people he knew personally, as well as professionally.

Despite his success, Hals had trouble with money. In 1654, he had to sell his belongings to pay debts, and he fought poverty for the rest of his life. Commissions became scarce, as the public now preferred more elegant, flattering portraits. His final works (1650-1666) are dark and somber, with increasingly rough and simple brushwork.

In 1664, the city granted him a pension for his years of service. When he died two years later, his work quickly passed out of fashion, dismissed as mere portraiture. In the 1800s, the Impressionists rediscovered him, and today he's recognized for his innovations, craftsmanship, and unique style.

right, perfectly forming opposing diagonals.

With this painting, Frans Hals broke the mold of stuffy group portraits. He relegates the traditional symbolic weapons to the shelf (upper right) and breaks up the traditional chorus line of soldiers by placing the men naturally around a table. Van der Meer sticks his elbow in our faces (another Hals trademark) to define a distinct foreground, while the flag-bearer stakes out the middle ground, and a window at the back opens up to a distant, airy background.

Then Hals sets the scene in motion. A guy on the left leans over to tell a joke to his friend. The dashing young flag-bearer in the middle turns back to listen to the bald-headed man. An ensign (standing, right side) enters and doffs his cap to Captain Van der Meer. And then we barge in, interrupting the banquet, but welcomed as one of the boys.

Banquet of the Officers of the Civic Guard of St. Adrian (1627)

The men are bunched into two symmetrical groups, left and right, with a window in the back. The figures form a Y, with a tilted flag marking the right diagonal (echoed by several tilted ruffs), and a slanting row of heads forming the left diagonal (echoed by several slanting sashes). The diagonals meet at the back of the table, marking the center of the composition, where the two groups of men exchange food, drink, and meaningful eye contact.

Meeting of the Officers and Subalterns of the Civic Guard of St. Adrian (1633)

Six years later, Hals painted many of these same men gathered around an outdoor table. The horizontal row of faces is punctuated by three men standing sideways, elbows out. Again, the men are united by sashes that slant in (generally) the same direction and by repeated gestures—hands on hips, hands on hearts, and so on.

Officers and Subalterns of the St. George Civic Guard (1639)

When 57-year-old Frans Hals painted this, his last Civic Guard portrait, he included himself among his St. George buddies. (Find Frans in the upper left, second from left, under the faint gray—number 19.)

As he got older, Hals refined and simplified his group-portrait style, using quieter colors, the classic two horizontal rows of soldiers, and the traditional symbolic weapons.

A decade after this was painted, Holland officially ended its war with Spain (Treaty of Munster, 1648), the Civic Guards lost their military purpose, businessmen preferred portraits showing themselves as elegant gentlemen rather than crusty soldiers, and the tradition of Civic Guard group portraits quickly died.

FRANS HALS MUSEUM

Civic Guard Portraits

The fathers of the men pictured in this room fought, suffered imprisonment, and died in the great Siege of Haarlem (1572-1573), which helped turn the tide against Spanish oppression. But their sons were bankers, merchants, traders, and sailors, boldly conquering Europe on the new frontier of capitalism. The Civic Guards became less of a militia, and more a social club for upwardly mobile men. Their feasts—huge eating and drinking binges, punctuated by endless toasts, poems, skits, readings, dirty limericks, and ceremonial courses—could last for days on end.

Standard Civic Guard portraits (like many of those in the Rijksmuseum in Amsterdam) always showed the soldiers in the same way—two neat rows of men, with everyone looking straight out, holding medieval weapons that tell us their ranks. It took master artists like Hals and Rembrandt to turn these boring visual documents into art.

• *Backtrack and, just after the WCs, look on your left for the five steps leading up to the...*

Former Chapel

Take a look inside. You'll find a **fancy dollhouse** *(poppenhuis),* the hobby of the lady of the house (her portrait is on the left). Handmade by the finest local craftsmen, this delicately crafted dollhouse offers a glimpse of wealthy 18th-century living.

The exquisite **bed curtain,** brought back from New England, decorated the bed of a wealthy Dutch family who lived in colonial America. It's embroidered with bulb flowers known during the 17th century—and well-described in English.

On the wall is ***Flemish Proverbs*** *(Vlaamse Spreekwoorden),* a fun painting that shows 72 charming Flemish scenes representing different folk sayings. (It's a copy of a 17th-century work by Pieter Brueghel the Younger.) Pick up the chart to identify these clever bits of everyday wisdom. True to form, this piece of Flemish art isn't preachy religious art or political propaganda; rather, it shares

the simple, decent morals of these hardworking people.

• *Continue counterclockwise around the museum, pausing to enjoy the exquisite still lifes in Room 16. These lush paintings give us a sense of how good life is, and how important it is to embrace it before it all rots and falls away.*

Frans Hals' Style

- Hals' forte is portraits. Of his 240 paintings, 195 are individual or group portraits, mostly of Haarlem's citizens.
- His paintings are life-size and realistic, capturing everyday people—even downright ugly people—without airbrushing out their blemishes or character flaws.
- Hals uses rough, Impressionistic brushwork, where a few thick, simple strokes blend at a distance to create details. He works quickly, often making the rough sketch the final, oil version.
- His stop-action technique captures the sitter in midmotion. Aided by his rough brushwork, this creates a blur that suggests the person is still moving.
- Hals adds 3-D depth to otherwise horizontal, widescreen canvases. (Men with their elbows sticking out sometimes serve to define the foreground.)
- His canvases are unified by people wearing matching colors, using similar poses and gestures, and gathered in symmetrical groups.
- His paintings have a relaxed, light-hearted, even comical atmosphere. In group portraits, the subjects interact with one another. Individual portraits meet your eyes as if meeting an old friend.
- His works show nothing religious—no Madonnas, Crucifixions, angels, or Bible scenes. If anything, he imbues everyday objects with heavenly beauty and grants ordinary people the status of saints.

When you reach the hallway that is Room 17, look for the...

Portrait of Jacobus Zaffius (1611)

Arr–r–r–r–rh! This fierce, intense, rough-hewn man is not a pirate, but a priest, the rogue leader of an outlawed religion in Haarlem—Catholicism. In the 1600s, Haarlem was a Protestant town in the midst of a war against Catholic Spain, and local Catholics were guilty by association. But Zaffius refused to be silenced. He turns to glare and snarl at the Protestant town fathers. He was so personally imposing that the city tolerated his outspokenness.

The face jumps out from a background of neutral gray-brown-black. His features are alive—head turning, mouth twisting, face wrinkling up, beard bristling. Hals captures him in action, using a slow shutter speed. The rough brushstrokes of the fur coat and beard suggest the blur of motion of

this agitated individual. This is Frans Hals' first known portrait, painted when he—a late starter in the art world—was nearly 30.
• *Make a left into Room 18 to see the...*

Portraits of Nicolaes Woutersz van der Meer and his wife, Cornelia Claesdr Vooght (1631)

Hals knew Nicolaes van der Meer, a fellow Civic Guard lodge member, personally. Van der Meer was a brewer, an important

post in a city where average beer consumption was six pints a day per person (man, woman, and child). He was also the mayor, so his pose is official and dignified, larger than life-size. But the face is pure Dutch Golden Age—red-cheeked and healthy, confident and intelligent, his even gaze tinged with wisdom. This mayor kept a steady hand on the tiller of Haarlem's ship of state.

The face is the focus of this otherwise messy painting. The ruffled collar is a tangle of simple, figure-eight swirls of white paint; the brocaded coat is a patchwork of white lines; and the lace cuffs are a few broad outlines. But out of the rough brushwork and somber background, Van der Meer's crystal-clear eyes meet ours. The finely etched crow's-feet around his eyes suggest that Hals had seen this imposing man break into a warm smile. Hey, I'd vote for him as my mayor.

The companion painting shows Van der Meer's companion, his wife, **Cornelia.** Husband-and-wife portraits were hung

together—notice that they share the same background, and the two figures turn in toward each other. Still, both people are looking out at us, not clinging to each other, suggesting mature partners more than lovey-dovey newlyweds. Married couples in Golden Age Holland divvied up the work—men ran the business, women ran the home—and prided themselves on their mutual independence. (Even today,

in progressive Holland, fewer women join the workforce than in many other industrial nations.) Cornelia's body is as imposing as her husband's, with big, manly hands and a practical, slightly suspicious look. The intricate work in her ruff collar tells us that Hals certainly could sweat the details when it suited his purpose.

Regents of the St. Elisabeth Hospital of Haarlem (1641)

These aren't the Dutch Masters cigar boys, though it looks like Rembrandt's famous (and later) *De Staalmeesters* (described in the Amsterdam Rijksmuseum Tour chapter). It's a board meeting, where five men in black hats and black suits with lace collars and cuffs—the Dutch Golden Age power suit—sit around a table in a brown room.

Pretty boring stuff, but Hals was hired to paint their portraits, and he does his best. Behind the suits, he captures five distinct

men (this photo shows three of them). The man on the far left is pondering the universe or raising a belch. The man on the right (facing us) looks like the classic Dutch Golden Age poster boy, with moustache, goatee, ruddy cheeks, and long hair. The middle guy is nearly clean-shaven. Hals links these unique faces with one of his trademark techniques—

similar poses and gestures. The burping man and the goateed man are a mirror image of the same pose—leaning on the table, hand on chest. Several have cupped hands; several have hands laid flat, or on their chests, or on the table. And the one guy keeps working on that burp.

• *Continue to Room 19. On the wall straight ahead are the...*

Regents of the Old Men's Almshouse (1664)

These men look tired. So was Holland. So was Hals. At 82, Hals, despite years of success, was poor and dependent on the charity of the city, which granted him a small pension.

He was hired to paint the board of directors of the Old Men's Almshouse, located here in the building that now houses the Frans Hals Museum. Though Hals himself never lived in the almshouse, he fully understood what it was to be penniless and have to rely on money doled out by men like these.

The portrait is unflattering, drained of color. Somber men dressed in black peer out of a shadowy room. These men were trying to administer a dwindling budget to house and feed an aging population. Holland's Golden Age was losing its luster.

The style is nearly Impressionistic—collars, cuffs, and gloves rendered with a few messy brushstrokes of paint. Hands and faces are a patchwork of light and dark splotches. Despite the sketchiness, each face captures the man's essence.

Historians speculate that this unflattering portrait was Hals' revenge on tightwad benefactors, but the fact is that the regents were satisfied with their portrait. By the way, the man just to the right of center isn't drunk, but suffering from facial paralysis. To the end, Hals respected unvarnished reality.

• *Directly behind you, find the...*

Regentesses of the Old Men's Almshouse (1664)

These women ran the women's wing of the almshouse, located across the street. Except for a little rouge on the women's pale

faces, this canvas is almost a study in gray and black, as Hals pared his palette down to the bare essentials. The faces are subtle variations on old age. Only the woman on the right resolutely returns our gaze.

The man who painted this was old, poor, out of fashion, in failing health, perhaps bitter, and dying. In contrast with the lively group scenes of Hals' youth, these individuals stand forever isolated. They don't look at one another, each lost in her own thoughts, perhaps contemplating mortality (or stifling belches). Their only link to one another is the tenuous, slanting line formed by their hands, leading to the servant who enters the room with a mysterious message.

Could that message be...death? Or just that this tour is over?

HAARLEM SLEEPING, EATING, NIGHTLIFE & CONNECTIONS

Jet-lagged travelers arriving in the Netherlands should consider Haarlem a convenient home base: There's fast-and-easy access to Amsterdam or Schiphol Airport, and other side-trips are a quick train trip away. This chapter describes Haarlem's best places to sleep, eat, and relax at night, along with transportation connections.

Sleeping in Haarlem

The helpful Haarlem TI can nearly always find you a €27.50 bed in a private home (but for a €5.50-per-person fee, plus a cut of your host's money; two-night minimum, €30-35 for single room). Avoid this if you can; it's cheaper to reserve by calling direct. Nearly every Dutch person you'll encounter speaks English.

Haarlem is most crowded on Easter weekend (April 22-24 in 2011, April 6-8 in 2012), in April (particularly the flower parade—April 16 in 2011—and Queen's Day, on April 30), May, July, and August (especially during Haarlem's jazz festival on the third weekend of Aug). Also see "Holidays and Weekends" on page 5.

The prices listed here include breakfast (unless otherwise noted) and usually include the €2-per-person-per-day tourist tax. To avoid excessive street noises, forgo views for a room in the back. Hotels and the TI have a useful parking brochure.

In the Center
Hotels and B&Bs
$$$ Hotel Lion D'Or is a classy 34-room business hotel with all the professional comforts, pleasingly posh decor, and a handy but less-than-quaint location (Db-€150, Fri-Sat Db-€125, extra bed-€15, check website for special deals, 8 percent Rick Steves discount

Sleep Code

(€1 = about $1.40, country code: 31, area code: 023)
S = Single, **D** = Double/Twin, **T** = Triple, **Q** = Quad, **b** = bathroom,
s = shower only. Nearly everyone speaks English. Credit cards
are accepted and breakfast is included unless otherwise
noted.

To help you easily sort through these listings, I've divided
the rooms into three categories, based on the price for a
standard double room with bath:

$$$ Higher Priced—Most rooms €85 or more.
$$ Moderately Priced—Most rooms between €60-85.
$ Lower Priced—Most rooms €60 or less.

Prices can change without notice; verify the hotel's
current rates online or by email. For other updates, see www
.ricksteves.com/update.

with 2-night stay if you book direct, air-con, elevator, pay Internet access and Wi-Fi, across the street from train station at Kruisweg 34, tel. 023/532-1750, fax 023/532-9543, www.hotelliondor.nl, reservations@hotelliondor.nl, friendly Dirk Pauw).

$$$ Stempels Hotel, modern yet elegant, is located in a renovated 250-year-old building. With bare floors, comfy high-quality beds, and minimalist touches in its 17 rooms, what it lacks in warmth it makes up for in style and value. Double-paned windows help keep down the noise—it's just a block east of Grote Markt—with a bustling brasserie and bar downstairs (standard Sb-€90, standard Db-€105-110, pricier rooms and suites available, breakfast-€12, in-room computers with free Internet access and Wi-Fi, Klokhuisplein 9, tel. 023/512-3910, www.stempelsin haarlem.nl, info@stempelsinhaarlem.nl).

$$$ Hotel Amadeus, on Grote Markt, has 15 small, bright, and basic rooms, some with views of the square. This charming hotel, ideally located above an early 20th-century dinner café, is relatively quiet, especially if you take a room in the back. Its lush old lounge/breakfast room on the second floor overlooks the square, and Mike and Inez take good care of their guests (Sb-€60, Db-€85, Tb-€110, check website for special deals, 5 percent Rick Steves discount off full price with 2-night stay and cash, pay Internet access and Wi-Fi, Grote Markt 10—from square it's a steep climb to lounge and then an elevator, tel. 023/532-4530, fax 023/532-2328, www.amadeus-hotel.com, info@amadeus-hotel .com). The Hotel Amadeus' breakfast room overlooking the main square is a great place to watch the town greet a new day—and one of my favorite Haarlem moments.

$$$ Ambassador City Centre Hotel, with 29 comfortable rooms in a big, plain hotel, is located just behind the Grote Kerk. If you're willing to trade some street noise for amazing church views, ask for a room in the front (Db-€100, often less off-season, breakfast buffet-€14, free Internet access and Wi-Fi, Oude Groenmarkt 20, tel. 023/512-5300, www.acc-hotel.nl, info@acc-hotel.nl). They also run **Hotel Joops,** with 32 rooms, a block away (rooms are €10 cheaper; studios and apartments with kitchenettes for 2-4 people-€120-150 depending on season and number of people).

$$ Central **Hotel Malts** rents 12 bright, simple, and fresh rooms for a good price. The rooms in front are big, but not recommended for light sleepers (small D-€69, small Db-€79, standard Db-€85, big Db-€95, check website for best prices, no elevator, free Wi-Fi, Zijlstraat 56, tel. 023/551-2385, www.maltshotel.nl, info@maltshotel.nl, Marco).

Rooms in Restaurants

These places are all run as sidelines by restaurants, and you'll know it by the style of service and rooms. Lobbies are in the restaurant, and there are no public spaces. Still, they are handy and—for Haarlem—inexpensive.

$$ Hotel Carillon overlooks the town square and comes with a little traffic and bell-tower chimes. With run-down public spaces and st-e-e-e-p stairs, it's an old-school, over-the-restaurant place. The rooms themselves, however, are freshly updated and pleasant. The front rooms come with more street noise and great town-square views (tiny loft S-€40, Db-€80-90, Tb-€102, Qb-€110, 5 percent Rick Steves discount if you ask when you reserve and show book on arrival, no elevator, free Wi-Fi, Grote Markt 27, tel. 023/531-0591, fax 023/531-4909, www.hotelcarillon.com, info@hotelcarillon.com, owners Kelly Kuo, Andres Haas, and June).

$$ Die Raeckse Hotel, family-run and friendly, is not as central as the others and has less character and more traffic noise—but its 21 rooms are decent and comfortable. Quiet rooms in back cost more than the noisy rooms on the street—but they're worth it (Sb-€55, smaller Db-€80-85, big Db-€85-90, Tb-€120, Qb-€130-145, €5/night discount for 2-night stay, ask for Rick Steves discount with this book Nov-March, free but time-limited Internet access, free Wi-Fi, Raaks Straat 1, tel. 023/532-6629, fax 023/531-7937, www.die-raeckse.nl, dieraeckse@zonnet.nl).

Near Haarlem

$$$ Hotel Haarlem Zuid, with 300 modern rooms, is sterile but a good value for drivers. It sits in an industrial zone a 20-minute walk from the center, on the road to the airport (Db-€88-110,

SLEEPING IN HAARLEM

Haarlem Hotels & Restaurants

TO OVERVEEN & ZANDVOORT & **9**

STATEN BOLWERK

TRAIN STATION **18**

TO AMST.

KENAU PARK

PARK

STN. PLEIN

1

BUS STN.

SUNY INTERNET

100 YARDS

100 METERS

PARK LAAN

18

TO WINDMILL

RED LIGHT DISTRICT

14

CORRIE TEN BOOM HOUSE

7

5

6

GROTE MARKT ENTER

GROTE KERK

2

19

TOWN HALL

3

12

10

4

20

B

13

11

16

17

LAUNDE-RETTE

BOTER MARKT

15

CANAL CRUISES

B

B

TEYLERS MUSEUM

V+D DEPT. STORE

21

HISTORY MUSEUM HAARLEM

TO AMST. & **8**

FRANS HALS MUSEUM

GASTHUIS VEST

KORTE HOUTSTRAAT

D.C.H.

B BUS #300

1 Hotel Lion D'Or
2 Stempels Hotel
3 Hotel Amadeus
4 Ambassador City Centre Hotel
5 Hotel Malts
6 Hotel Carillon
7 Die Raeckse Hotel
8 To Hotel Haarlem Zuid
9 To Stayokay Haarlem Hostel
10 Jacobus Pieck Eetlokaal & Friethuis de Vlaminck
11 De Lachende Javaan Rest.

12 La Plume Restaurant
13 Pizzeria-Rist. Venezia
14 Vlam in de Pan & 't Theehuis Coffeeshop
15 Spaarne 66 Restaurant Bar
16 Lambermon's Brasserie & Restaurant
17 La Place Cafeteria
18 Albert Heijn Supermarkets (2)
19 DekaMarkt Supermarket
20 High Times Coffeehouse
21 Vijfhoek (Five Corners)

breakfast-€13, elevator, free parking, laundry service, fitness center-€5, reasonable hotel restaurant, Toekanweg 2, tel. 023/536-7500, fax 023/536-7980, www.hotelhaarlemzuid.nl, haarlemzuid @valk.com). Bus #300 conveniently connects the hotel with the train station, Grote Markt, and the airport (every 10 minutes, stop: Europaweg).

$ **Stayokay Haarlem Hostel,** completely renovated and with all the youth-hostel comforts, charges €25-30 for beds in four- and six-bed dorms. They also rent simple €60-80 doubles (€2.50 less for members, includes sheets and breakfast, save by booking on their website, pay Internet access and Wi-Fi, laundry service, reception open 8:00-20:30 but late arrivals okay, Jan Gijzenpad 3, two miles from Haarlem station—take bus #2 from station, or a 10-minute walk from Santpoort Zuid train station, tel. 023/537-3793, www .stayokay.com/haarlem, haarlem@stayokay.com).

Eating in Haarlem

Restaurants

Jacobus Pieck Eetlokaal is popular with locals for its fine-value "global cuisine," good salads, and unpretentious flair. Sit in the peaceful garden courtyard, at a sidewalk table, or in the romantically cozy interior. The Oriental Peak Salad is a perennial favorite, and the dish of the day (*dagschotel,* €12.50) always sells out (great €7 sandwiches at lunch, Mon 11:00-16:00 only, Tue-Sat 10:00-22:00, closed Sun, cash only, Warmoesstraat 18, behind church, tel. 023/532-6144).

De Lachende Javaan ("The Laughing Javanese") is a long-established Indonesian place serving a memorable *rijsttafel* (€20-24, Tue-Sun 17:00-22:00, closed Mon, Frankestraat 27, tel. 023/532-8792).

La Plume Restaurant steakhouse is noisy, with a happy, local, and carnivorous crowd enjoying the candlelit scene (€15-20 meals, daily 17:30-23:00, Fri-Sat until 24:00, *satay* and ribs are favorites, Lange Veerstraat 1, tel. 023/531-3202). The relaxing outdoor seating faces the church and a lively pedestrian street.

Pizzeria-Ristorante Venezia, run for 25 years by the same Italian family from Bari, is *the* place to go for pizza or pasta (€8-10 choices, daily 13:00-23:00, facing V&D department store at Verwulft 7, tel. 023/531-7753). You'll feel like you're in Rome at a good indoor table, or sit outdoors for good people-watching.

At **Vlam in de Pan,** a dynamo named Femke serves vegetarian delights: soup, salad, veggie sushi, quiches, and other fresh, mostly organic foods. Enjoy the small, funky dining area, or get your food to take away (€10-15 plates, Tue-Fri 16:00-21:00, closed Sat-Mon, Smedestraat 13, tel. 023/551-1738).

Lange Veerstraat Restaurant Row: If you don't know what you want to eat, stroll the delightful Lange Veerstraat behind the church and survey a fun range of restaurants (from cheap falafels to Cuban, and much more).

On the Spaarne River Canal: Haarlem seems to turn its back on its river with most of the eating energy a couple of blocks away. To enjoy a meal with a nice canal view, consider the **Spaarne 66 Restaurant Bar.** The Lemmers girls (a mom and her daughters) run this cozy eatery, with a woody, old-time interior and fine outdoor canalside seating (light €7 lunches, €20 Mediterranean/Dutch dinner plates, €30 three-course fixed-price meal, Wed-Mon 11:00-24:00, closed Tue, Spaarne 66, tel. 023/551-3800).

Dressy Splurge: At **Lambermon's,** expert chef Michèl Lambermon serves chichi pan-European cuisine in a suave, modern, corner restaurant. The brasserie on the ground floor offers €25 two-course lunches and €35 three-course dinners (€23-28 main courses, Mon-Sat 12:00-15:00 & 18:00-22:00, Sun 14:00-22:00; pricier restaurant upstairs open Wed-Sat 18:00-22:00 only, closed Sun-Tue; Korte Veerstraat 1, tel. 023/542-7804).

Budget Options

La Place is a snazzy chain cafeteria that dishes up fresh, healthy budget food with Haarlem's best view. Sit on the top floor or the roof garden of the V&D department store (Mon 11:00-18:00, Tue-Sat 9:30-18:00, Thu until 21:00, closed Sun except for first Sun of month 12:00-17:00, Grote Houtstraat 70, on corner of Gedempte Oude Gracht, tel. 023/515-8700).

Friethuis de Vlaminck is your best bet for a cone of old-fashioned, fresh Flemish-style fries (€2, daily 11:00-18:30, Warmoesstraat 3, behind church, tel. 023/532-1084). Winnie offers a dazzling array of sauces. With his help, you can be adventurous.

Supermarkets: **Albert Heijn** has two convenient locations. One is in the train station (Mon-Fri 6:30-21:00, Sat 7:00-21:00, Sun 8:00-21:00, cash only), the other is at Kruisstraat 10 (Mon-Sat 8:00-20:00, closed Sun, cash only). The **DekaMarkt** is a few blocks east of Grote Markt (Mon-Sat 8:00-20:00, Thu-Fri until 21:00, Sun 16:00-21:00, Gedempte Oude Gracht 54, between V&D department store and post office).

Nightlife in Haarlem

Haarlem's evening scene is great. Consider four basic zones: Grote Markt in the shadow of the Grote Kerk; Lange Veerstraat; Boter Grote Markt; and Vijfhoek (Five Corners).

Grote Markt is lined with trendy bars that seem made for nursing a drink—**Café Studio** is generally the hot spot for a drink

Marijuana in Haarlem

Haarlem is a laid-back place for observing the Dutch approach to recreational marijuana. The town is dotted with about a dozen coffeeshops, where pot is sold and smoked by relaxed, noncriminal types. These easygoing coffeeshops are more welcoming than they may feel—bartenders understand that Yankee travelers might feel a bit out of their element and are happy to answer questions.

If you don't like the smell of pot, avoid places sporting wildly painted walls; plants in the windows; or Rastafarian yellow, red, and green colors. The following two shops are inviting and particularly friendly to American visitors:

The tiny **'t Theehuis,** which feels like a hippie teahouse, was Haarlem's first coffeeshop (c. 1984). Along with a global selection of pot, it has 50 different varieties of tea on the menu and a friendly staff. Martijn, who offers weekly menus, is happy to roll you the €3 joint of your choice (daily 13:00-22:00, a block off Grote Markt at Smedestraat 25).

High Times, with a living-room ambience and loaner bongs, offers smokers 12 varieties of joints in racks behind the bar (neatly pre-packed in trademarked "Joint Packs," €3-4.50, Mon-Fri 8:00-23:00, Sat from 9:00, Sun from 11:00, free Internet access for customers, Lange Veerstraat 47). Across the street, at Crackers Pub, you can see what too much alcohol does to people.

here (at Grote Markt 25); I'd also duck into the dark interior of **In Den Uiver** (near the Grote Kerk entry at Riviervischmarkt 13, live jazz Thu and Sun). Lange Veerstraat (behind the Grote Kerk) is colorful and bordered with lively spots. Boter Grote Markt is more convivial and local, as it's less central and away from the tourists. Vijfhoek, named for the five lanes that converge here, is incredibly charming, although it has only one pub (with plenty of drinks, bar snacks, a relaxed crowd, and good indoor or outdoor seating). Also worth exploring is the area from this cutest corner in town to the New Church (Nieuwe Kerk), a couple blocks away. If you want a more high-powered scene, Amsterdam is just 20 minutes away by train.

Haarlem Connections

For general tips about public transportation in the Netherlands—including types of trains, reading timetables, and how and where to buy tickets—see the appendix. If you take the train from Amsterdam to Haarlem, see page 225 for a train-window tour of the countryside.

From Haarlem by Train to: Zandvoort (2/hour, 11 minutes), **Amsterdam** (6/hour, 20 minutes, €3.70 one-way, €7.10 same-day round-trip), **The Hague/Den Haag** (6/hour, 40 minutes, some transfer in Leiden), **Delft** (2/hour, 40 minutes), **Rotterdam** (4/hour, 55 minutes, half require change in Leiden), **Hoorn** (2/hour, 1 hour, more with change in Amsterdam Sloterdijk), **Alkmaar** (2/hour, 35 minutes), **Brussels** (hourly, 2.75 hours, transfer in Rotterdam), **Bruges/Brugge** (hourly, 3.5 hours, 2-3 changes—avoid Thalys connections if traveling with a railpass).

From Haarlem by Bus to Aalsmeer: Connexxion **buses #140** and **#175** connect Haarlem to bus #172, which goes to the flower auction in Aalsmeer (4/hour, 1 hour, see "Getting There" on page 259).

To Schiphol Airport: Your best option is the **bus** (4-10/hour, 40 minutes, €4—buy ticket from driver, bus #300). To catch the bus from the middle of Haarlem, head to the Centrum/Verwulft stop, near the V&D department store. To catch it from the train station, look for the stop marked "Zuidtangent." (Construction of a new underground bike-parking lot near the train station may temporarily move this bus stop a block or two from the station, most likely to the tree-lined street called Parklaan). You can also get there by **train** (6/hour, 30-40 minutes, transfer at Amsterdam-Sloterdijk station, €5.40 one-way) or **taxi** (about €45).

DUTCH DAY TRIPS

Any Dutch native will tell you: To really experience everyday life in the Netherlands, get out of Amsterdam. In a country as tiny as Holland, day-tripping is easy to do. Within a half-hour of leaving Central Station, you can be deep in the Dutch countryside—lush, green, and filled with tulips, red-brick houses, quaint canals, and black-and-white cows. It's a refreshing break from urban Amsterdam. Match your interest with the village's specialty: flower auctions, open-air folk museums, fresh cheese, Delft Blue porcelain, or modern art. Take some time to learn a few basic Dutch phrases for the sake of politeness (see the appendix), but don't obsess—even outside of Amsterdam, just about everyone speaks English.

If you're based in Amsterdam, note that Haarlem (covered in the preceding chapters) makes a great day trip in itself. This chapter introduces many other easy day trips from Amsterdam (or from Haarlem).

For those interested in Dutch culture, I describe three open-air museums in this book: Arnhem, Zuiderzee in Enkhuizen, and Zaanse Schans. Doing more than one is overkill for most visitors—read my descriptions and choose one. Arnhem's is the best, but the farthest from Amsterdam. Enkhuizen's Zuiderzee is also good and can be conveniently combined with the Historic Triangle route. Zaanse Schans is the least appealing and most entrepreneurial, but the closest to Amsterdam. All of these are covered in more detail in the next seven chapters.

Planning Your Time

If you only have a day or two to venture outside of Amsterdam or Haarlem, use this list to help you decide where to go. I've listed the destinations in the chapter order they appear in this book.

Keukenhof, Aalsmeer, and Zandvoort

Any of these is an easy half-day side-trip from Haarlem or
Amsterdam, but note that Keukenhof's gardens are open only
in spring (see dates below), Aalsmeer's auction operates only on
weekday mornings (closed Sat-Sun), and Zandvoort's beach is best
in summer.

▲▲▲**Keukenhof** This can't-miss garden show, in the town of
Lisse, is open for only two months every spring (March 24-May
20 in 2011, likely similar dates in 2012).

▲▲**FloraHolland Aalsmeer Flower Auction** Close to the airport, this vast auction warehouse shows you the business side of
the Netherlands' beautiful flower scene (open weekday mornings
year-round).

Zandvoort This lively beach resort town, practically a suburb of
Haarlem, is handy for a quick getaway.

Delft and The Hague

Allow a full day to visit the adjacent towns of Delft and The
Hague—though either destination makes a fun day trip on its

own. Delft is also a fine place to spend the night. (Delft's morning markets are on Thu and Sat; The Hague's Peace Palace is closed Sat-Sun, and its minor museums are closed Mon.)

▲▲**Delft** This lovely hometown of the painter Vermeer and the Delftware factory is a delightful place to relax by a canal. For more activity, zip into The Hague, just next door.

▲▲**The Hague** This big-city seat of Dutch government offers good museums, including the excellent Mauritshuis art gallery.

Museums near Arnhem

Allow an extremely long day to visit the open-air and modern-art museums (but not on Mon, when art museum is closed); you'll need to leave Amsterdam by 8:00. If you stay overnight near the art museum (in Otterlo), you'll have more time to fit in the train museum on your return to Amsterdam.

▲▲**Arnhem Open-Air Folk Museum** Holland's original, biggest, and best open-air folk museum, Arnhem sprinkles traditional buildings from around Holland across a delightful park, and populates them with chatty docents to give you a flavor of old-time lifestyles.

▲▲**Kröller-Müller Museum** This excellent modern-art museum has dozens of Van Goghs and a sculpture garden. It's located on the outskirts of the city of Arnhem, within the vast Hoge Veluwe National Park, which has free loaner bikes you can ride to the museum.

▲**Spoorwegmuseum** Holland's biggest and best train museum is located in the crossroads town of Utrecht.

Schokland Museum

Easiest by car, it takes about a half-day to visit this far-flung sight.

▲**Schokland** A former island left high and dry when the surrounding sea was drained, this village is now a museum in the middle of reclaimed farmland.

Edam, Volendam, and Marken

Figure on a day (leaving Amsterdam by 10:00) to visit these picturesque villages, in the region aptly called Waterland. If you have only a half-day, choose Edam. (Edam's museum is closed Mon and its market is held Wed morning.)

▲▲**Edam** In this quiet town, you can mellow out like a hunk of aging cheese. There are no real sights, but its tiny main square and peaceful canals may win you over.

Volendam A transit hub for the Waterland region, this workaday town has a fine seafront promenade and a boat across to Marken.

Marken Once an island, and now connected by a causeway to the mainland, this time-warp fishing village preserves traditional buildings and lifestyles.

The Historic Triangle

Allow a full day for this excursion. Leave Amsterdam for Hoorn by 9:38 (confirm time at station) if you want to have enough time to visit the Zuiderzee Museum before it closes. The Triangle trip is usually offered daily in peak season (not always on Mondays) and less frequently off-season; see the Historic Triangle chapter for details.

▲▲**The Historic Triangle** Take this enjoyable trip by catching a steam train in the town of Hoorn to the town of Medemblik, and then sailing on a 1920s-era boat to Enkhuizen to visit the Zuiderzee open-air folk museum.

▲**Enkhuizen Zuiderzee Museum** With an emphasis on seaside lifestyles, this well-presented open-air folk museum is the grand finale of a Historic Triangle day, or can be visited directly from Amsterdam.

Alkmaar and Zaanse Schans Open-Air Museum

Allow a half-day for Alkmaar—ideally Friday morning for the town's cheese market, held in spring and summer. Allow a full day to add the open-air museum. Both are described in the Alkmaar and Zaanse Schans Open-Air Museum chapter.

▲**Alkmaar** This likeable town is especially fun to visit, and easily worth ▲▲ during its Friday-morning cheese market (early April-early Sept only, 10:00-12:30).

Zaanse Schans Open-Air Museum Packed with windmills (and greedy shops), this sight is just a quick 15-minute train ride (plus a 15-minute walk) from central Amsterdam.

Transportation Tips

Train: If you're day-tripping, ask about "day return" tickets (same-day round-trip), which are cheaper than two one-way tickets. Before you board at Amsterdam's Central Station, check the yellow train-schedule boards or ask at the information counter to confirm the details of your trip (such as times, necessary transfers, delays, and the name of the station you'll be using—for example, to get to Zaanse Schans, you'll get off at the Koog-Zaandijk station). When riding a train to any big town, note that "CS" always stands for "Central Station"—usually the one you want (unless I note otherwise). You'll find train information online at www.ns.nl.

Driving: Although the roads are excellent, densely populated Holland can be a time-consuming place for drivers. Traffic congestion is notoriously bad, especially around rush hour near Amsterdam, Rotterdam, The Hague, Utrecht, and other big cities. Everything in this book is covered by the excellent, detailed ANWB Wegenkaart *Nederland midden* map (1:200,000, sold at bookstores).

KEUKENHOF, AALSMEER, & ZANDVOORT

Of all the Amsterdam day trips, these three side-trips near Haarlem require the least brainpower: two flower experiences (a garden show and a flower auction) and a beach retreat.

▲▲▲Keukenhof

This is the greatest bulb-flower garden on earth, open for only two months in spring. Each spring, seven million flowers, enjoying the sandy soil of the Dutch dunes and *polderland*, conspire to thrill even the most horticulturally challenged. This 80-acre park is packed with tour groups daily; for the least crowds and the best light, go late in the day. Keukenhof is located at the northern tip of the town of Lisse, at the centre of the "Dune and Bulb Region."

Cost and Hours: €14.50, not covered by Museumkaart, open March 24-May 20 in 2011, likely similar dates in 2012, daily 8:00-19:30, last entry at 18:00, tel. 0252/465-555, www.keukenhof.nl.

Combo-Ticket: €21 combo-ticket covers park entry and round-trip bus transport from Leiden, Schiphol Airport, or The Hague (available on Keukenhof website, GWK Travelex office in Leiden's station, Schiphol Airport's TI, and Connexxion bus counter at The Hague's Central Station).

Getting There: Whether you're starting from Amsterdam or Haarlem, catch one of the frequent trains to Leiden (4/hour, 35 minutes), then take bus #54 (Keukenhof Express) straight to the garden (4/hour, allow 1.25 hours total from Amsterdam, 1 hour total from Haarlem).

From Schiphol Airport, catch bus #58 (4/hour, 40 minutes). From The Hague's Central Station, take bus #89 (Mon-Fri only, 2/hour, 50 minutes).

Drivers will find Lisse well-marked from the A-6 expressway south of Amsterdam.

▲▲FloraHolland Aalsmeer Flower Auction (Bloemenveiling)

Get a bird's-eye view of the huge Dutch flower industry in this cavernous building where the world's flower prices are set. You'll wander on elevated walkways (through what's claimed to be the

biggest commercial building on earth) over literally trainloads of freshly cut flowers. About half of all the flowers exported from Holland are auctioned off here, in four huge auditoriums. The flowers are shipped here overnight (for maximum freshness), auctioned at the crack of dawn, and distributed as quickly as possible. For the best floral variety and auction action, the earlier, the better (best before 9:30, and the auction closes down by 11:00).

Standing above all those blooms, take a deep, fragrant breath and hold it in. As you wander, keep an eye out for tulip-shaped "listening posts," and press the English button for on-the-spot information. Peering into the auction halls, you'll see that clocks are projected on two big screens. This is a "Dutch auction," meaning that the price starts high and then ticks down, until buyers push the button at the price they're willing to pay. Think about the high stakes and the need for decisiveness...there's no time to think things over as the auctioneer calls, "Going once, going twice..."

Most of the flowers are purchased by wholesalers and exporters. You'll see the busy beehive of the distribution process as workers scurry to load carts of flowers onto little tractors to zip to awaiting buyers. Up along the ceiling, look for the suspended orange trams. This "Aalsmeer Shuttle" zips loads of flowers over the workers' heads to the distribution center across the street, far more quickly and efficiently than trucks.

You'll wind up at the even more elaborate Rose Market, where 450 buyers keep their eyes peeled on three different auction clocks as they jostle to buy the auction's most popular item. As you circle back to the entrance, you'll see the company's testing lab, where they actually create and test new varieties of flowers.

Cost and Hours: €5, Mon-Fri 7:00-11:00, closed Sat-Sun, gift shop, cafeteria, tel. 0297/392-185, www.floraholland.com.

Getting There: By bus, you can reach the flower auction from Amsterdam (Connexxion bus #172 from Central Station, 4/hour, 1 hour, get off at "BVFH Hoofdingang" stop) or from Haarlem (take bus #140 to the town of Aalsmeer, or #175 to Amstelveen, at either place transfer to bus #172, 4/hour, 1 hour). Aalsmeer, which is close to the airport, makes a handy last fling for drivers before dropping off your car at the airport and catching a late-morning weekday flight out (bus #198 also runs between the auction and the airport; 4/hour, 20 minutes). From the A-6 expressway south of Amsterdam, drivers take the Aalsmeer exit (#3) and follow signs for *Aalsmeer*, then *Bloemenveiling*. Once you reach the complex, carefully follow the *P Tourist* signs to park on top of the garage, then take the elevator downstairs and follow *Tourist* signs to the visitors center.

Zandvoort

For a quick and easy look at the windy coastline in a shell-lover's Shangri-la, visit the beach burg of Zandvoort. This pretty, mani-cured resort has plenty of cafés, ice-cream parlors, *Vlaamse frites* stands, restaurants, and boutiques. Just beyond the town is the vast and sandy beach, lined with cafés and rentable chairs. Above it all is a pedestrian promenade and a line of high-rise hotels. South of the main beach, sunbathers work on all-over tans. Come to Zandvoort if the weather's hot and you want a taste of the sea and sun, if you want to see how Dutch and German holiday-makers have fun, or if you just want an excuse for a long bike ride from Haarlem.

Tourist Information: The helpful TI is on Bakkerstraat (Mon-Fri 9:00-17:00, Sat 10:00-17:00, Sun 11:00-16:00, tel. 023/571-7947, www.vvvzandvoort.nl).

Getting There: It's easy to reach by train (2/hour, 30 min-utes from Amsterdam, 11 minutes from Haarlem). For a breezy 45-minute bike ride west of Haarlem, follow road signs for *Bloemendaal*, then *Zandvoort*.

DELFT &
THE HAGUE

These adjoining cities, both conveniently situated just an hour southwest of Amsterdam, are as different as night and day. Sleepy Delft is the charming cultural capital, with soothing canals, an inviting square, royal tombs squirreled away under an exclamation-point church tower, and ties to Vermeer. The citified Eurocrat center of The Hague offers sightseers a few busy but rewarding hours of urban museum-hopping, including the chance to meet a famous girl with a pearl earring.

The two cities are linked by a simple tram or train ride. Together, they form a handy yin and yang of enjoyable experiences.

Planning Your Time

It's easy to day-trip to Delft and The Hague from Amsterdam or Haarlem—but if you spend the night anywhere in the Netherlands

outside the capital, make it Delft.

Whether side-tripping or home-basing, for a busy day of contrasts, visit both Delft and The Hague. In the morning, take in The Hague's sights (the Mauritshuis museum is tops). Then continue to Delft to visit its churches, Vermeer Center, and Royal Dutch Delftware Manufactory (closes at 17:00)...or to simply mellow out by a canal.

DELFT

Delft

Peaceful as a Vermeer painting and as lovely as its porcelain, Delft has a special soul. Enjoy this typically Dutch, "I could live here" town best by simply wandering around, watching people, munching local syrup waffles, or daydreaming on the canal bridges. If you're eager for some sightseeing, visit a pair of churches, learn more about favorite son Vermeer, or tour the famous porcelain factory.

Think of Delft as an alternative to Haarlem: a low-key, mid-sized city with fast and easy connections to a big metropolis (The Hague). And, laced with tranquil and picturesque canals, Delft might even win the cuteness contest.

Orientation to Delft

(area code: 015)

Delft feels much smaller than its population of 95,000. (Because they're squeezed between the two giant cities of Rotterdam and The Hague, locals describe Delft as a "small town.") Almost everything of interest (except the porcelain factory) clusters within the former walls of the canal-lined Old Town, across the street from the train station. The vast Markt (Market Square), with the tall and skinny spire of the New Church, marks the center of the Old Town. A couple of blocks to the southeast is the lively, restaurant-lined Beestenmarkt. You could walk from one end of the Old Town to the other in about 15 minutes.

Tourist Information

This TI is a tourist's dream. Pick up the good free brochure, which includes a map, or you can just get the map separately (April-Sept Sun-Mon 10:00-16:00, Tue-Fri 9:00-18:00, Sat 10:00-17:00; Oct-March Mon 11:00-16:00, Tue-Sat 10:00-16:00, Sun 11:00-15:00; free Internet access, free baggage storage for day-trippers, 2-minute walk north of Markt to Hippolytusbuurt 4, tel. 015/215-4051, www.delft.nl). If you want to visit the Royal Dutch Delftware Manufactory, pick up the half-off discount coupon (may also be available at your hotel).

Walking Tours: The TI sells a brochure describing a pleasant self-guided walking tour (€3.50); skip the €1 "Vermeer Walk" pamphlet. In the summer (Easter-Sept), the TI offers a €10

Delft

DELFT

TRAM #1 STOPS TO THE HAGUE

DCH

❶ Hotel Bridges House
❷ Hotel Leeuwenbrug
❸ Hotel de Emauspoort
❹ Hotel de Koophandel
❺ Het Konings Huys Hotel

❻ Kleyweg's Stads Koffyhuis
❼ De V Pub
❽ Vlaanderer
❾ Daily Wok

two-hour walking tour of town that includes a canal-boat trip (Sun-Fri at 11:30, Sat at 12:30, also in Oct on weekends only).

Arrival in Delft

By Train: Delft's train station likely will be a mess during your visit, as the station and trains are being moved underground. While construction is underway, the station has no lockers, but you can leave bags for free at the TI.

From the train station, it's about a 10-minute walk to the Markt at the center of the Old Town: Exit straight ahead, walk

DELFT

across the canal, then continue into town, following signs for *Centrum*.

By Car: Drivers take the Delft exit #9 off the A-13 expressway. Parking garages are scattered around the city (€12/24 hours, higher per-hour rates for shorter time periods).

Sights in Delft

In the Old Town

▲**Churches**—Delft has two grand churches that hold tombs of prominent local residents. They're both covered by the same €3.50 ticket (not covered by Museumkaart) and are open the same hours (April-Oct Mon-Sat 9:00-18:00; Nov-Jan Mon-Fri 11:00-16:00, Sat 10:00-17:00; Feb-March Mon-Sat 10:00-17:00; closed to tourists Sun year-round, tel. 015/212-3025, www.nieuwekerk-delft.nl).

The giant, Gothic **New Church** (Nieuwe Kerk) boldly presides over the town from its prominent position overlooking the

Markt. Inside are buried the beloved Dutch ruler William I ("The Silent") of Orange (1533-1584) and the Dutch royalty that succeeded him. It was William who rallied the Dutch to begin their revolt against the Spanish Habsburg rulers. William's ornate tomb—a canopied monument to his greatness—dominates the choir area. It features two representations of William: one of white marble, reclining peacefully; and a strong, armored king in bronze, sitting royally. The sweet dog at his feet symbolizes loyalty. Above the pooch, the angel of Fame blows a trumpet (notice that this whole bronze statue is supported by just one slim foot).

At the corners of his monument are female statues representing Liberty, Justice, Religion, and Fortitude. Unfortunately, all these fine virtues could not save William from being gunned down by an assassin's bullet (just up the street, right here in Delft).

William I was the founder of the dynasty that still (in name) rules the Netherlands. His most famous descendant is one of the few not buried here. William III of Orange (1650-1702), as grandson of the English king, was called upon by the English Parliament to bring peace and order after the turmoil of England's

Johannes Vermeer
(1632-1675)

The great Dutch Golden Age painter Johannes Vermeer was born in Delft, grew up near the Markt, and set a number of his paintings here. His father, an art dealer, gave Johannes a passion for painting. Late in the artist's career, with Holland fighting draining wars against England, the demand for art and luxuries went sour in the Netherlands, forcing Vermeer to downsize—he sold his big home, packed up his wife and 14 children, and moved in with his mother-in-law. He died two years later.

Vermeer painted some 37 surviving works (though experts debate whether all of them were actually his). Although Vermeer painted landscapes and scenes from mythology and the Bible, he specialized in depicting the everyday actions of regular people. And though his scenes are usually still and peaceful, he artfully conveys deep tension, and suggests a complicated story with subtle body language (the subject glances at something out of view) or the inclusion of a small item (a letter that seems pregnant with significance). Vermeer also was a master of light, capturing it with an artistry that would make the Impressionists jealous two centuries later.

After centuries of relative obscurity—we still know very little about him—Vermeer and his paintings are now appreciated. Delft owns none of his works (you'll have to visit Amsterdam's Rijksmuseum, with four masterpieces, or The Hague's Mauritshuis museum). However, the town's Vermeer Center pays tribute to this great artist and his talent.

Civil War. William III was crowned King of England and ruled alongside his wife, Mary. The two gave their name to a fledgling college in the American Colonies (and William III lies buried in London).

Most of William I's descendants of the House of Orange are also buried in this church. A few paces in front of William (near the transept), a large stone slab marks the entrance to the sprawling underground labyrinth that holds crates of Oranges. (The crypt is strictly off-limits for anyone unrelated.) Besides ruling Holland, the Orange family had owned the independent principality of Orange in the south of France since medieval times. The Royal Family's official color was—what else?—orange, which is why today's Dutch wear orange to soccer matches and consider it their national color (despite having a flag that's red, white, and blue).

If you want to work off your *pannenkoeken*, you can climb the New Church's **tower** (€3.50, three levels and 376 steps in a very narrow staircase, last entry one hour before church closes, may close in bad weather, watch your head). This is a particularly dizzying tower climb, one of Europe's most dramatic. On a clear day you can see the towers of The Hague and, in the other direction, Rotterdam.

A few blocks away, listing over a canal as if it's about to tip in, is the **Old Church** (Oude Kerk). Although smaller and less impressive (inside and out) than the New Church, this church feels more lived-in. Light filters through stained-glass windows, falling on the tombs of two local boys done good: Johannes Vermeer and Anton van Leuwenhoek (who invented the microscope, then used it to discover bacteria). Vermeer usually wins the "most flowers" award. Aside from these talented bones, the church is as dead as its residents.

▲**Vermeer Center (Vermeercentrum)**—Although it doesn't have any Vermeer originals, this intelligent exhibit does a good job of tracing the career and unique creative mind of Delft's favorite resident. Everything is well-described in English. Begin in the basement, where a short movie orients you to Vermeer and his ties to Delft. Then view copies of all 37 known Vermeer paintings, arranged chronologically and accompanied by brief and interesting commentary. Upstairs, a mock-up of "Vermeer's studio" thoughtfully analyzes and explains some of Vermeer's techniques (€7, not covered by Museumkaart, daily 10:00-17:00, a block from the Markt—through the gap where Vermeer's house used to be—at Voldersgracht 21, tel. 015/213-8588, www.vermeerdelft.nl). The café is good for a drink or snack, and the shop is the perfect place to buy some sou-vermeers.

Markets—Multiple all-day markets are held on Thursdays (general market on the Markt, flower market on Hippolytusbuurt Square) and on Saturdays (general on Brabantse Turfmarkt and Burgwal, flea market at Hippolytusbuurt Square in summer, and sometimes an art market at Heilige Geestkerkhof).

Royal Dutch Delftware Manufactory (Koninklijke Porceleyne Fles)

The Delft Blue earthenware made at this factory is famous worldwide, making this the biggest tourist attraction in town. The

Dutch East India Company, partly headquartered in Delft, imported many exotic goods, including Chinese porcelain. The Chinese designs became trendy and were copied by many of the local potters. Three centuries later, their descendants are still going strong, and you can see them at work in this factory—the only one left of an original 32.

Delft Blue Manufacturing Process

Delft Blue earthenware is made from a soupy mix of clay and water. To make plates, the glop is rotated on a spinning disk

until it looks like a traditional Dutch pancake. This "pancake" is then placed in a plate mold, where a design is pressed into it.

To make vases, pitchers, cups, and figurines, the liquid clay is poured into hollow plaster molds. These porous molds work like a sponge, sucking the water out of the clay to leave a layer of dry clay along the mold walls. Once the interior walls have reached the correct thickness, all excess clay within is poured off and recycled.

After the clay object is removed from the mold, it's fired in the kiln for 24 hours. The pottery removed from the kiln is called "biscuit." Next, painters trace traditional decorations with sable-hair pencils onto the biscuit pottery; these are then painted with a black paint containing cobalt oxide. The biscuit immediately soaks up the paint, making it a very unforgiving medium for mistakes.

The objects are dipped into an opaque white glaze and then fired a second time. A chemical reaction transforms the black paint into the famous Delft Blue, and the white glaze melts into a translucent, glass-like outer layer.

While it's basically a small museum exhibit attached to a giant shop—and, for some, doesn't merit the trip—for those who enjoy porcelain, this is worthwhile.

You can rent a €2 audioguide, but it's not essential, as English descriptions are posted throughout. First you'll watch the five-minute video (ask for English as you enter), then follow the small tile arrows through the collection. Along with tableware and vases, you'll also see gorgeous pictures made from tiles (including a giant replica of Rembrandt's *The Night Watch*) and outdoor architectural elements (such as chimneys). After the museum, you'll walk through part of the factory, past racks upon racks of unfired pieces. Take some time to watch artisans at work—and feel free to stop and chat with them.

Cost and Hours: €8, €4 with coupon available at TI and many hotels, not covered by Museumkaart, daily 9:00-17:00 except closed Sun Nov-March, Rotterdamsweg 196, tel. 015/251-2030, www.royaldelft.com.

Getting There: It's about a 15-minute walk south of the Old Town, on Rotterdamsweg (just off map on page 263). To get from the train station to the factory, catch bus #40 or #121 (€1.60, 2/ hour, 5 minutes, direction: Julianalaan or Jaffalaan, get off at Rotterdamsweg). Or you can take a bike-taxi (€3.50/person one-way, ask TI to call one for you), a canal boat (€6, April-Oct hourly 11:00-17:00, no boats off-season, 45-minute round-trip, guide on board, catch along Oude Delft canal; also rents paddle boats for €12.50/hour; tel. 015-212-6385, www.rondvaart.nl), or a Royal Delft Line bus (€3.50 one-way, €7 day ticket, 2/hour, late April-mid-Sept only, Tue-Sat 11:30-17:00, Sun 13:00-17:00, no bus Mon, leaves from station and city center).

Near Delft: Rotterdam

The Hague isn't the only big Dutch city near Delft. About the same distance in the opposite direction is the Netherlands' (and Europe's) largest port, Rotterdam—which bounced back after being bombed flat in World War II. And though it lacks the charm of Delft and the great museums of The Hague, it might be worth a visit if you're curious to round out your Dutch urban experience. See its towering Euromast, take a harbor tour, and stroll its great pedestrian zone (**TI** tel. 010-271-0120, www.vvv.rotterdam.nl).

Sleeping in Delft

Delft's accommodations aren't cheap, but the ones listed here are well-run and offer good value for the money.

$$$ Hotel Bridges House, with 11 rooms around the corner from the Markt, is wood-beamed elegant and was once the home of painter Jan Steen. Energetic Jan-Willem van der Blom works hard to bring class and charm to this lovely canalside splurge (Sb-€129-164, Db-€153-198, higher prices are for very roomy junior suites, prices can be lower in winter, extra bed-€20, free Internet access and Wi-Fi, air-con, Oude Delft 74, tel. 015/212-4036, fax 015/213-3600, www.bridges-house.com, info@bridges-house .com).

$$ Hotel Leeuwenbrug, a former warehouse and now a business-class hotel, has 36 clean rooms (some with canal views), Old World atmosphere, and a helpful staff (very small Sb-€55, standard Sb-€83-102, deluxe Sb-€125, standard Db-€98-112, deluxe Db-€135, may be cheaper July-Aug—check their website for best rates, elevator, free Internet access and Wi-Fi, Koornmarkt 16, tel. 015/214-7741, fax 015/215-9759, www.leeuwenbrug.nl, sales @leeuwenbrug.nl, Mr. Wubben).

$$ Hotel de Emauspoort, picture-perfect and family-run, is relaxed, friendly, and wrapped around the family's 1922 bakery. It's ideally located one block from the Markt. The 26 rooms, decorated with pleasantly old-fashioned wooden furniture and named for

Sleep Code

(€1 = about $1.40, country code: 31, area code: 015)
S = Single, **D** = Double/Twin, **T** = Triple, **Q** = Quad, **b** = bathroom,
s = shower only. Unless otherwise noted, credit cards are
accepted, breakfast is included, and hoteliers speak English.

To help you easily sort through these listings, I've divided
the rooms into three categories, based on the price for a
standard double room with bath:

$$$ **Higher Priced**—Most rooms €120 or more.
$$ **Moderately Priced**—Most rooms between €70-120.
$ **Lower Priced**—Most rooms €70 or less.

Prices can change without notice; verify the hotel's
current rates online or by email. For other updates, see www
.ricksteves.com/update.

sea heroes and Delft artists (most you've never heard of), overlook
a canal or peek into the courtyard. Romantics can stay in one of
their two "Gypsy caravans": "Pipo de Clown" or "Mammaloe"
(Sb-€88, Db-€99, stunning "Vermeer Room" Db-€150, Tb-€138,
Qb-€175, free Internet access, pay Wi-Fi, behind church/Markt
at Vrouwenregt 9-11, tel. 015/219-0219, fax 015/214-8251, www
.emauspoort.nl, info@emauspoort.nl, Jeroen).

$$ Hotel de Koophandel has 25 painting-over-the-bed
rooms right on the charming, lively, tree-and-restaurant-lined
Beestenmarkt square (Sb-€94, Db-€114, extra bed-€30, 3 ground-
floor rooms, reception closed 23:00-7:00, Beestenmarkt 30, tel.
015/214-2302, fax 015/212-0674, www.hoteldekoophandel.nl, info
@hoteldekoophandel.nl).

$$ Het Konings Huys is a hotel/restaurant right on the
Markt, renting seven basic, lightly renovated rooms. Its price and
location make it sensible for travelers on a budget who don't mind
the lack of service, some noise at night in rooms facing the square,
and en-suite bathrooms shoehorned into a corner (S-€52, Sb-€68,
D-€59, Db-€81, Tb-€99, breakfast-€8, Markt 38-40, tel. 015/212-
5115, fax 015/213-6069, www.hetkoningshuys.eu).

Eating in Delft

As Delft is a university town, lively, affordable eateries abound.
Most places have outdoor seating, sometimes on an inviting square
or on a little barge floating in the canal out front.

Kleyweg's Stads Koffyhuis is a local institution that's won
prizes for its sandwiches (see the trophies above the counter). This

is a great spot for an affordable bite, either in the country-cozy interior or out on a canal barge (€5-8 sandwiches, €6-10 pancakes, big €12 salads, Mon-Fri 9:00-20:00—until 19:00 Oct-March, Sat 9:00-18:00, closed Sun, just down the canal from the Old Church at Oude Delft 133, tel. 015/212-4625).

De V is a lively pub with a pleasantly cozy ambience and a local following loyal to its straightforward and well-priced food. Sit in the crowded area near the bar, or elbow your way up top to the glassed-in patio (€8 daily specials, €10-15 main dishes, daily 16:00-24:00, food served 18:00-22:00, just past the TI and Old Church along the canal at Voorstraat 9, tel. 015/214-0916).

Around Beestenmarkt (Beast Market): Named for the livestock that was once sold here, this square feels more local and appealing than the more prominent Markt (described below). Do a spin around the square to scope out the food and seating (indoor or outdoor) you like best. I ate well at **Vlaanderer,** serving good, trendy, pricey, well-presented food. You can sit out on the square; in the dimly lit, old-fashioned dining room; or in the partly glassed-in patio out back (€19-22 main dishes, €39 fixed-price meals, daily 12:00-24:00, Beestenmarkt 16, tel. 015/213-3311).

Around the Markt (Market Square): Delft's giant Markt, under the looming tower of the New Church, is a scenic spot for a meal. Most of the places around here are interchangeable, but tucked behind the Town Hall (across the square from the church) are some good options that also have outdoor seating.

Asian: For a break from flapjacks, try **Daily Wok,** a mod Thai eatery serving up affordable but good food just a few steps off the Markt (€4-7 meals, Mon-Sat 12:30-21:00, Sun 15:00-22:00, Oude Langendijk 230, tel. 015/213-7222).

Delft Connections

From Delft to The Hague

It's easy and cheap to travel between these neighboring towns, either by train or tram.

Tram #1 leaves from in front of the Delft train station and clatters through residential neighborhoods to The Hague. This connection is frequent, comes with nice urban scenery, and delivers you right into the center of The Hague's tourist zone (€3.20, about 6/hour, 4/hour on weekends, direction: Scheveningen Noorderstrand, get off after about 30 minutes at The Hague's Centrum stop for TI, parliament area, and most sights). You can continue on this tram directly to the Peace Palace (Vredespaleis stop, about 5 minutes beyond Centrum stop) or go all the way to the beach at Scheveningen (Kurhaus stop, about 15 minutes beyond Centrum stop).

Regular **trains** depart from Delft's station for The Hague (€2.30, €4.10 round-trip, 4/hour, 15 minutes). Get off at The Hague's Central Station (CS), not the Hollands Spoor station (HS). The train is cheaper and appears to be faster than the tram, but from The Hague's Central Station it's still a 15-minute walk or a 5-minute tram ride to reach the tourist zone (for details, see "Arrival in The Hague," on next page).

By Train from Delft

From Delft, trains go to **Amsterdam**'s Central Station (4/hour, 1 hour; 2/hour direct, others transfer in Leiden or The Hague), **Haarlem** (2/hour direct, 40 minutes), and **Arnhem** (2-4/hour, 1.75 hours, transfer in The Hague or Rotterdam, then Utrecht). To reach **Bruges** (hourly, 3 hours), you'll need to change in Ghent, Antwerp, and Rotterdam.

The Hague (Den Haag)

The Dutch constitution may identify Amsterdam as the official "capital," but The Hague has been the Netherlands' seat of government since 1588. Or, as locals say, the money is made in Rotterdam, divided in The Hague, and spent in Amsterdam.

The Hague is the home of several fine museums—including the excellent Mauritshuis art gallery—and international organizations such as the International Court of Justice (at the tourable Peace Palace, where nations try to settle their disputes without bloodshed) and the UN International Criminal Tribunal for the Former Yugoslavia (not tourable). Urban but still manageable— if not exactly charming—The Hague is ideal for a few engaging hours of sightseeing.

Orientation to the Hague

(area code: 070)
Though it has nearly a half-million residents (the Netherlands' third-largest city), The Hague feels manageable for a sightseer. On a quick visit, begin at the Centrum tram stop, between the TI and the Parliament complex; most worthwhile museums are near here.

The Hague

TO PANORAMA MESDAG,
PEACE PALACE,
MADURODAM
GEMEENTEMUSEUM
& SCHEVENINGEN

400 METERS
¼ MILE

ESCHER IN THE PALACE

HIST. MUSEUM

NOORD-EINDE PALACE

PRISON TOWER MUSEUM

MAURITSHUIS ROYAL PICTURE GALLERY

CENTRAL TRAIN STATION

BINNENHOF PARLIAMENT COMPLEX

GROTE KERK

CITY HALL

SPUI PL.

TO HOLLANDS SPOOR STATION

DCH

I list no hotels for The Hague because Delft—so close it's practically a neighborhood of this city—is a much more appealing place to hang your hat.

Tourist Information

The TI is in City Hall (Stadhuis), two stops after the Station HS stop on tram #1. Pick up the free map; the better €2 map isn't worth it, but the free information guide—while heavy on glossy promotion—is worth having for a longer visit (Mon 12:00-18:00, Tue-Fri 9:30-18:00, Sat 9:30-17:00, Sun 11:00-17:00, tel. 070/361-8860, www.denhaag.com).

Arrival in The Hague

The major sights in The Hague are well-signed—just look for the black-and-gold directional arrows.

By Tram: If coming on tram #1 from Delft, get off at the Centrum stop.

By Train: The Hague has two train stations: Central Station ("Den Haag CS," or just "Centraal Station") and Hollands Spoor ("Den Haag HS," used by more international trains). Central

Station is closer to the tourist area.

To get from Central Station to the TI, follow Rijnstraat (which parallels the tram tracks that pass the station, to your left as you leave the station), walking back under the train tracks to where Rijnstraat ends. Turn right through the imposing glass building, and follow Turfmarkt for five minutes to the City Hall (Stadhuis), near the corner of Turfmarkt and Spui. To get from the station to the main sights, exit toward the sign for *Uitgang Centrum* (to the left with your back to the tracks, near the Burger King). Here you can catch tram #16 (direction: Wateringen) and take it two stops to the Centrum stop. Or, for a 15-minute walk, turn right and walk past the big bike-parking lot, then turn left, cross the tram tracks, and head up Bezuidenhoutseweg. After the road changes names a few times, it leads you to Hofweg; the Binnenhof Parliament complex will be on your right.

From the Hollands Spoor station, you can reach the TI by backtracking along the tram tracks on Spui to find Spuiplein, home of the TI and City Hall (Stadhuis). To reach the main sights, walk out in front of the station and take tram #1 (direction: Scheveningen Noorderstrand) to the Centrum stop.

Sights in The Hague

In The Hague's City Center

All of these attractions are within a 10-minute walk of the TI (most are even closer).

Binnenhof Parliament Complex—The castle-like Binnenhof complex, overlooking a giant pond right in the center of The

Hague, is the seat of Dutch political power. The prime minister's office is here, and it's also the meeting place of the two-house parliament, or Staten-Generaal. Most of the power resides in the directly elected Second Chamber (a.k.a. House of Representatives), whereas the mostly figurehead First Chamber (a.k.a. Senate, but actually more like the UK's House of Lords) meets once weekly to harrumph their approval.

It's surprisingly easy to dip into the low-key Parliament complex (just saunter through the brick gateway across the street from the TI). In the inner courtyard—surrounded by orange-and-white-striped awnings—you'll find a golden fountain depicting the Netherlands' current Queen Beatrix, a reminder that the respectful Dutch parliamentarians govern with her symbolic approval. Dominating the middle of the complex is the historic Knights'

Hall (Ridderzaal), where the two houses meet jointly on special occasions. Tours of the complex are sometimes possible (ask at the office downstairs around the right side of the Knights' Hall, call 070/364-6144, or check www.binnenhofbezoek.nl).

▲▲**Mauritshuis Royal Picture Gallery**—The Hague's top art gallery features an easy-to-appreciate collection of Dutch Golden Age art, including top-notch pieces by Vermeer (his famous *Girl with a Pearl Earring* lives here), Rembrandt, Rubens, and many others. The beautifully restored 17th-century palace is an ideal setting for this exquisite art. While calling it a "mini-Rijksmuseum" might be a stretch, and the ticket price is steep, the Mauritshuis is well worth a visit.

Cost and Hours: €10.50, includes great English audioguide, €1.50 more for special exhibits; April-Sept Mon-Sat 10:00-17:00, Sun 11:00-17:00; Oct-March same hours except closed Mon; café, no photos, free and mandatory bag check, next door to the Binnenhof Parliament complex at Korte Vijverberg 8, tel. 070/302-3456, www.mauritshuis.nl.

Getting There: From the TI, it's on the far side of the parliament; cut straight through the Binnenhof courtyard and look left when you pop out on the other side.

❍ **Self-Guided Tour:** This tour covers the basics; if you have more time, take advantage of the excellent, included audioguide. The collection, displayed on two floors, is constantly moved around—pick up a floor plan as you enter to find the current location of these pieces.

Vermeer, *Girl with a Pearl Earring* (c. 1665): Sometimes called "the Dutch *Mona Lisa*" for its enigmatic qualities, this canvas became a sensation in recent years as the subject of a popular book and film. This is a "tronie" (TROH-nee)—the painter's goal is not to depict a particular person, but to capture a mood or character. In fact, we don't even know who this mysterious girl is. Wearing a blue turban and with a gigantic pearl dangling from her earlobe, she glances over her shoulder and catches the viewer's gaze...expectantly, maybe even seductively. Vermeer's straightforward scene subtly implies a much more complicated story than we'll ever know. The artist was also a master of color and at suggesting shape with light—look closely and you'll see that the famous pearl is essentially formed by two simple brushstrokes. For more on Vermeer, see page 265.

Vermeer, *View of Delft* (c. 1660-1661): If this were a photograph, it'd be a bad one...you'd want to wait for the clouds to pass to snap another one with the entire scene bathed in light. But Vermeer, an expert at capturing light effects on canvas, uses the cloudy/sunny contrast to his advantage, illuminating the foreground and the distant, inner part of town instead of the more predictable middle ground. This makes your eye probe deep into the canvas, subconsciously immersing you in Vermeer's world.

Rembrandt, *The Anatomy Lesson of Dr. Nicolaes Tulp* (1632): Notice Rembrandt's uniquely engaging version of a (typically dull) group portrait—inquisitive faces lean in, hanging on the doctor's every word. The cadaver resembles a notorious criminal of the day. For more on Rembrandt, see page 133.

Rembrandt, *Portrait of an Elderly Man* (1667): Painted when Rembrandt was 61, this portrait is typical of his style: The clothes are painted lightly, but the face is caked on. Look closely at his ruddy cheeks, built up by layer after layer of paint, carefully slathered on by the master.

Peter Paul Rubens, *Old Woman and a Boy with Candles* (c. 1616-1617): In this touching scene, the elderly woman passes her light to the boy—encouraging him to enjoy life in a way that she perhaps hasn't. Her serene smile suggests her hope that he won't have the same regrets she does.

Frans Hals, *Laughing Boy* (c. 1625): This loveable painting depicts an exuberant scamp grinning widely despite his decaying teeth and rat's-nest hair. Like *Girl with a Pearl Earring*, this is a "tronie," or character study, rather than a portrait of an important person. For more on Frans Hals, see page 239.

Jan Steen, *Girl Eating Oysters* (c. 1658-1660): This seemingly innocent scene—a still life combined with a portrait, on the smallest canvas Steen ever painted—is loaded with 17th-century sexual innuendo. Oysters were considered a powerful aphrodisiac, and behind the subject, peeking through the curtains, we can see a bed. Her impish grin seals the deal that she's got more than shellfish on her mind.

And Lots More: These paintings are just the beginning. Look around to find works by Jan Brueghel the Elder (a painting of the Garden of Eden, done jointly with Rubens), Hans Holbein, Anthony van Dyck, Hans Memling, and many other famous painters. The gallery also hosts good temporary exhibits.

Prison Tower Museum (Gevangenpoort)—This torture museum, in a 13th-century gatehouse that once protected a castle on the site of today's parliament, shows you the medieval mind at its worst. You'll tour the sight with a required 30-minute tour (usually in Dutch, but you can use a free English guidebook). You'll get the full story on crime and punishment here from 1420 to 1823 (€7.50, Tue-Fri 10:00-17:00, Sat-Sun 12:00-17:00, closed Mon, tours depart :45 after the hour, also at :15 after the hour during busy times, last tour leaves at 15:45, across from parliament at Buitenhof 33, tel. 070/346-0861, www.gevangenpoort.nl).

Panorama Mesdag—For a look at the 19th century's attempt at virtual reality, stand in the center of this 360-degree painting of nearby Scheveningen in the 1880s, with a 3-D, sandy-beach foreground. As you experience this nostalgic attraction, ponder that this sort of "art immersion" experience was once mind-blowingly cutting-edge (€6.50, Mon-Sat 10:00-17:00, Sun 12:00-17:00, a few blocks east of the parliament area at Zeestraat 65, tel. 070/364-4544, www.panorama-mesdag.com).

Escher in the Palace (Escher in Het Paleis)—Compared with The Hague's other museums, this place is just a trifle...but an entertaining one. (Think of it as "art museum lite.") Celebrating Dutch optical illusionist M. C. Escher (1898-1972), the exhibit displays replicas of many of his works and traces his artistic evolution—from the Mediterranean landscapes of his beloved Italy, to shapes that melt into one another, to mind-bending experiments in angles and perspective. Hands-on displays on the top floor let you step right into an Escher engraving. The entry price is worth it, given the museum's extras: fun temporary exhibits, far-out chandeliers by Dutch artist Hans van Bentem, and the chance to stroll the former winter palace of Queen Emma, who lived here for three decades—it remained a royal residence until 1991. I'm guessing the skull-and-crossbones chandelier wasn't around then (€7.50, not covered by Museumkaart, Tue-Sun 11:00-17:00, closed Mon, last entry 30 minutes before closing, mandatory bag check-€1 deposit, Lange Voorhout 74, tel. 070/427-7730, www.escherinhetpaleis.nl).

Other Museums—Top options include the **Historical Museum of The Hague** (Haagshistorischmuseum), with pieces from the Rijksmuseum's collection on Dutch history (€5, Tue-Fri 10:00-17:00, Sat-Sun 12:00-17:00, closed Mon, across the pond from parliament at Korte Vijverberg 7, tel. 070/364-6940, www.haagshistorischmuseum.nl); and the **Gemeentemuseum**, displaying modern and contemporary art, including a large collection by Dutchman Piet Mondrian (€10, Tue-Sun 11:00-17:00, closed Mon, no photos, farther out at Stadhouderslaan 41, tram #17 or bus #24 from Central Station, tel. 070/338-1111, www.gemeentemuseum.nl).

Outside The Hague's City Center

The following sights lie north of the main tourist zone. And though worthwhile for the thorough sightseer, they're more difficult to reach than the previous sights.

▲**Peace Palace (Vredespaleis)**—The palace houses the International Court of Justice and the Permanent Court of Arbitration. These two Peace Palace courts attempt to reach amicable settlements for international disagreements, such as border disputes. While the judicial process is interesting, the building itself is the big draw. A gift from American industrialist Andrew Carnegie, it's filled with opulent deco-

rations donated by grateful nations who found diplomatic peace here, from exquisite Japanese tapestries, to a Hungarian Zsolnay-tile fountain, to French inlay floors. On the required tour, you'll see the judicial chambers and the grandly decorated halls, and learn how modern nations attempt to resolve their disputes here instead of on the battlefield. Don't confuse this place with the International Criminal Tribunal for the Former Yugoslavia, which is not open to the public.

Cost and Hours: €5; required guided tours Mon-Fri at 10:00, 11:00, 14:00, and 15:00, plus 16:00 May-Sept; closed Sat-Sun, when court is in session, or if there's an event at the palace; you must reserve in advance and bring your passport (required to enter), tel. 070/302-4137, www.vredespaleis.nl.

Getting There: Take tram #1 directly from Delft, or tram #10 or bus #24 from The Hague's Central Station, and get off at the Vredespaleis stop (right in front of the palace).

Scheveningen—This "Dutch Coney Island," with its broad sandy beach, is at its liveliest on sunny summer afternoons (but

is dead when the weather cools). Its biggest appeal is watching urbanites from The Hague and Delft enjoy a day at the seashore. Dominating the scene is the long double-decker pleasure pier, with shops down below, a boardwalk up top, and a bungee-jumping pavilion at the far end. A café-

lined promenade stretches along the sand. Take northbound tram #1 from Delft or from Hofweg/Spui (the street in front of the Binnenhof and The Hague's TI), or take tram #9 from The Hague's Central Station. Get out at Kurhaus (one stop before the end of the line) and follow signs for *Boulevard/Strand* and *Pier*.

By the way, if you can't pronounce this tongue-twisting name (roughly SKHHHEH-veh-ning-eh), you're not alone. In World War II, Dutch soldiers would quiz suspicious visitors on how to pronounce this name as a test to determine who was Dutch-born and ferret out potential German spies.

Madurodam—The mini-Holland amusement park, with miniature city buildings that make you feel like Godzilla, is fun for kids (adults-€14.50, kids 3-11-€10.50, not covered by Museumkaart, daily April-June 9:00-20:00, July-Aug 9:00-23:00, Sept-March 9:00-18:00, last entry one hour before closing, George Maduroplein 1, tram #8 and #9 or bus #22 from Central Station, tel. 070/416-2400, www.madurodam.nl).

The Hague Connections

The Hague's Central Station (CS) is handier for sightseers; the Hollands Spoor station (HS) is used mostly by international trains.

From The Hague's Central Station by Train to: Delft (4/hour, 15 minutes), **Amsterdam** (2/hour, 50 minutes, more with change in Leiden), **Haarlem** (6/hour, 40 minutes, some transfer in Leiden), **Arnhem** (4/hour, 1.5 hours, transfer in Utrecht), **Bruges** (hourly, 3 hours, change in Antwerp).

From The Hague's Central Station by Bus to: Keukenhof (bus #89, Mon-Fri only, 2/hour, 50 minutes).

By Tram to Delft: Take tram #1 from any stop (€3.20, about 6/hour, 4/hour on weekends, direction: Delft Tanthof, about 30 minutes). If you're headed to the Markt in Delft, get off at the Prinsenhof stop (a little north of the Markt) or at Binnenwatersloot (the next stop south). The tram also stops at the train station.

MUSEUMS NEAR ARNHEM

Arnhem Open-Air Folk Museum
• Kröller-Müller Museum
• Spoorwegmuseum

While the city of Arnhem itself is nothing special, it's close to a pair of fun and worthwhile side-trips: the Arnhem Open-Air Folk Museum and the exceptional Kröller-Müller Museum. Of all the Netherlands' open-air folk museums, Arnhem's—set just within the city limits—feels the most authentic. Its classically Dutch buildings sprawl across rolling hills, with rich details around every corner. Nearby, the Kröller-Müller Museum, located in the middle of Hoge Veluwe National Park, displays a world-class collection of modern art (including roomfuls of Van Goghs—they own 87 of them). It's also a delight to pedal through the park on free white bikes.

Rail enthusiasts can make a pilgrimage to the Spoorwegmuseum in Utrecht, an easy stop (and a common transfer point) on the train route, located roughly midway between Amsterdam and Arnhem.

Planning Your Time

Arnhem, an hour southeast of Amsterdam by train, is doable as a side-trip from Amsterdam. Unfortunately, the two main sights—the folk museum and the art museum—are far from each other and far from Arnhem's Central Station—so you'll need to allow extra time to catch the bus to either one. Both are superb and worth the time and effort, but if you want to see both, you should either spend the night in the town of Otterlo (recommended) or be prepared for a long day of somewhat-rushed sightseeing. Note that the Kröller-Müller Museum is closed on Monday.

By Car: Drivers with short attention spans can visit both the open-air folk museum and Kröller-Müller Museum within a day... and might have time left to park the car and go for a pedal through the national park. Figure just over an hour's drive from Amsterdam to Arnhem, then about a 20-minute ride into the national park,

MUSEUMS NEAR ARNHEM

Arnhem Transportation

3 MILES
5 KM

TO APELDOORN

ST. HUBERTUS LODGE

OTTERLO CENTRUM

N-304

A-50

022

OTTERLO ROTONDE

VISITORS CENTER

KRÖLLER-MÜLLER MUSEUM

BUS #108

N-304

BUS #106

N-310

DCH

BUS #105

N-224

21

OPEN-AIR FOLK MUSEUM

A-12

25

20

26

24

SCHAARS-BERGEN

BUS #3,13

A-348

EDE-WAGENINGEN TRAIN STN.

A-50

ARNHEM TRAIN + BUS STN.

27

TO UTRECHT + AMSTERDAM

A-325

TO GERMANY

+++ RAIL
24 —o— FREEWAY W/ EXIT #S
— OTHER ROADS
--- BUS ROUTES

HOGE VELUWE NATIONAL PARK
♦ PARK ENTRANCES

then an hour back to Amsterdam.

By Public Transportation: It's possible to get to both the Arnhem Open-Air Folk Museum and the Kröller-Müller Museum in one very long but fulfilling day of sightseeing—but it's only worthwhile if you get an early start. Because no bus connects the open-air folk museum and the Kröller-Müller Museum, you'll have to return to Arnhem's bus station between sights—limiting the amount of time you'll have at each place.

To do everything in one day, I'd catch an early train (around 8:00) from Amsterdam Central Station to Arnhem (4/hour, 1 hour, half transfer in Utrecht), then take a short walk to the bus station and hop a bus (2/hour, 15 minutes) for the Arnhem Open-Air Folk Museum. Plan to arrive when it opens at 10:00. To make this schedule work, you need to leave the folk museum by 13:00, which gives you enough time to bus back to the Arnhem station and catch another bus to Otterlo (2/hour), near Hoge Veluwe National Park. Once in Otterlo, you can take yet another bus directly to the Kröller-Müller Museum (in the middle of the national park), or walk 15 minutes to the entrance of the park and borrow a bike to ride there (for all the details on Otterlo, see page 291). In the national park, do the museum first (closes at 17:00), then the visitors center (closes at 18:00 in summer), then wind down your day by biking around the park. Plan on a long day and a late return to Amsterdam (bus or walk back into Otterlo, catch bus #108 to Ede-Wageningen—departs from Otterlo Rotonde near the edge of town at the top of each hour until 23:00, then take the train back to Amsterdam).

If you're spending the night in Otterlo, you can get a later start from Amsterdam, linger at the open-air folk museum (having left your things in a locker at Arnhem station), relax that evening in Otterlo, and tour the art museum and national park at a leisurely pace the next morning.

For specifics on the connections between these sights, and the towns they're near, see each listing.

By Bike: Pedal enthusiasts may want to rent some wheels in Arnhem to get to the open-air folk museum; it's a strenuous 20-minute uphill ride to the museum, then a breezy, easy 10-minute glide back into town (ask for directions at bike shop, listed under "Arrival in Arnhem," below).

Orientation to Arnhem

(area code: 026)
Arnhem is a dreary urban city of about 140,000 people. Tourists view Arnhem as a transit hub useful only for reaching the open-air folk museum on its outskirts and the nearby Kröller-Müller Museum and national park. A few hotels line up across from the train station, but I'd rather sleep in charming little Otterlo, near the park entrance (see "Sleeping in Otterlo" on page 292). Arnhem's old town—nowhere near as charming as similar towns in the Netherlands—is just across the busy ring road from the train and bus stations. Restaurants with outdoor seating cluster around the square called Korenmarkt and, a few steps deeper into the old town, around Jaansplaats.

Tourist Information
Arnhem's TI is across the street from the bus station (Mon-Fri 9:30-17:30, Sat 9:30-17:00, closed Sun, Stationsplein 13, tel. 0900-112-2344—€0.45/minute, www.vvvarnhem.nl). The TI provides a free city map and sells a detailed €10 regional map that includes the national park and Kröller-Müller Museum (the national park's visitors center sells a cheaper map).

Arrival in Arnhem
Arnhem's **train station** is surrounded by a sea of construction and urban blight, as they're in the midst of a multiyear project to build

a super-modern station complex. Expect changes to the following information.

The station has **WCs** (€0.40) and **lockers** (€3.65/24 hours, takes credit cards only). You'll also find a Rijwiel **bike-rental shop** (€7.50/day for 3-speed bike—you'll need all 3 speeds—plus €50 refundable deposit, open daily very long hours). While the temporary station is in place, exit the station to the left and look for stairs up to the bike shop; by 2012, the shop likely will be in front of the station.

The **bus station** is to the right as you exit the train station, along the busy street. Along the way is the convenient Connexxion bus-information office—ideal for confirming bus schedules (closed for lunch on weekends, location subject to change). The station is actually a giant garage with lettered bus bays. Check the sign near the entry to the bus area to find the departure bay for your bus. For the Arnhem Open-Air Folk Museum (Openluchtmuseum), take bus #3 (in July-Aug, #13 works as well); for Otterlo (near the Kröller-Müller Museum and national park), take bus #105.

Arnhem Open-Air Folk Museum (Openluchtmuseum)

Arnhem has the Netherlands' first, biggest, and best folk museum, rated ▲▲. You'll enjoy a huge park of windmills, old farmhouses and other buildings (relocated from throughout the Netherlands), traditional crafts in action, and a pleasant education-by-immersion in Dutch culture. It's great for families.

Orientation

Cost and Hours: €14.50, April-Oct daily 10:00-17:00, Dec-mid-Jan daily 11:00-19:00; €4 in Nov and mid-Jan-March, when the buildings are closed but the grounds are open shorter hours.

Getting There: To reach the open-air folk museum from the Arnhem bus station, take one of two **buses** (check the board for the departure bay): In July and August (and on some holidays), handy bus #13 zips you directly to the town's zoo, then to the museum entrance (3-4/hour, €1.10). At other times, take bus #3 (make sure it's marked *Alteveer*, as some #3 buses go elsewhere; about 2/hour, 20 minutes, €1.10). Bus #3 drops you a five-minute walk from the museum entrance: Cross the street, head right, then left down the tree-lined avenue to the roundabout, then turn right (following signs for *Openluchtmuseum*). From the Arnhem train station, you can also **walk** or ride a **bike** (uphill most of the way, figure 30 minutes by foot or 20 minutes by bike). A **taxi** from the station costs about €17.

By **car** from Amsterdam, take A-2 south to Utrecht, then A-12 east to Arnhem. Just before Arnhem, take the Arnhem Nord exit (#26) and follow *Openluchtmuseum* signs to the museum (€4.50 parking, buy parking ticket when you buy entrance ticket). If driving from Haarlem, skirt Amsterdam to the south on A-9, take A-2 south to Utrecht, and then follow the previous instructions (via A-12).

Information: Tel. 026/357-6111, www.openluchtmuseum.nl.

Getting Around: A free, old-fashioned tram does a lazy counterclockwise circle around the museum grounds, making six stops (well-marked on park maps).

Self-Guided Tour

You could spend the whole day exploring this wonderful open-air museum. But to hit a few highlights, follow this tour. Because the layout of the grounds can be confusing, pick up the good free map at the entry—I've used the numbers on that map to help you navigate this tour. Don't hesitate to dip into any buildings that intrigue you, even if they're not on this tour—most have brief English explanations outside, and some have English-speaking docents inside. (Ask them questions...that's their job.) Especially with kids, it would be a shame to do this place in a rush—there's so much to experience.

• *Start in the...*

Entrance Pavilion: Consider buying the in-depth English guidebook, and ask about special events and activities, especially for kids. Downstairs are exhibits on traditional Dutch costumes and replicas of various storefronts. You'll also find Arnhem's effort to keep up with the Disneys: the high-tech **"HollandRama"** multimedia experience (inside the big copper blob you saw out front; runs about hourly—schedule posted by stairs). You'll sit on a giant platform that rotates inside a spherical theater to gradually reveal various Dutch dioramas: windmills, a snowy countryside, house and store interiors, and so on. Although the narration is in Dutch, the 20-minute presentation is an enjoyable rest.

• *To hit the park, exit straight out of the entrance pavilion and walk up the path. You're likely to see animals in the pasture on your right—if so, take a closer look: they're rare Dutch breeds, not the high-yield animals used in modern farms. No longer cost-effective, these special animals are raised by the museum as part of its mission to preserve a piece of Dutch folk life.*

After a few buildings on the left, step inside the one-story...

"Cheese-Cover" Farmhouse (#4.1, just before the pond): The cows lived on one side of this house from 1745, and the people on the other (notice the claustrophobic cupboard-beds). Along the cow stalls, see the patterns the farmwife would make with fresh sand and seashells each summer to show off family status.

• *Nearby, cross the...*

Yellow Drawbridge (#4.2): Dating from 1358, this takes you to perhaps the most scenic part of the park: a pond surrounded by windmills and cabins (inspired by the Waterland area around Marken—described in the Edam, Volendam, and Marken chapter). Pause on the bridge to look toward the sawmill. You might see kids playing with a small rope-pulled ferryboat.

Continue across the drawbridge into the little **village.** Along the way are some tempting shops where you can pick up an edible souvenir, including a well-stocked general store, a bakery, and a fragrant candy store.

Village Square (#4.13): you can play here with toys from the 1800s. See if you can make the "flying Dutchman" fly, or try to ride an original "high-wheeled velocipede" without falling off. On the square is a restaurant specializing in *poffertjes* (puffy mini-pancakes dusted with powdered sugar), with indoor and outdoor seating.

• *Behind the* poffertje *shop, cross the little bridge toward the windmills, pass the boat workshop, and enter the...*

Fisherman's Cottage (#4.11): The black-tarred exterior hides a bright and colorful interior. Notice the rope-controlled smoke hatch, rather than a chimney. Wooden cottages like these were nicknamed "smokehouses." In front of the cottage is the boatyard, where vessels could be pulled out of the water to scrape off the barnacles.

• *Backtrack through the village square, then continue on to the...*

Laundry (#5.1, on the right): Inside, an industrial-strength agitator furiously pounds stubborn stains to smithereens. (There was no "delicate cycle" back then.) On nice days, the clean sheets are spread out on the lawn to dry.

• *For an optional detour (best for train buffs), hook around through the little cottages across the street, then turn right to reach the...*

Train Depot (#6.1): Inside, you can actually walk underneath a train to check out its undercarriage. The adjacent **goods shed** (#6.8) holds a virtual-reality postal carriage.

• *Head back past the laundry, then go beyond the cafeteria to reach the small, yellow windmill. Here, turn left and walk up the path, watching for the low-profile brown building through the trees on your right, near the bridge.*

Paper Mill (#5.4): At this building, dating from around 1850, you'll learn that farmers often made paper in their spare time to help make ends meet. Inside, you might see a demonstration of linen rags being turned into pulp, and then into paper. Peek upstairs at the finished paper hanging to dry.

• *Leaving the mill, walk straight ahead on the brick path, passing various buildings on your right-hand side until you reach the...*

Herb Garden (#11.1): This tranquil, hedge-lined garden is worth exploring. The map at the entry explains the various parts of the garden, each growing herbs for different purposes: dyes, food, medicine, and so on. Listen for the squeals of lively children from the playground behind the garden.

• *Continue past the garden and cross the tram tracks to the...*

Freia Steam-Dairy Factory (at #7.1, with the big smoke-stack): Named after Freia, the Norse goddess of agriculture, this was the Netherlands' first privately owned cheese and butter factory. Borrow the English explanations at the entry, sample some free cheese, and try to follow the huge belt of the steam engine as it whirls through the factory.

• *Leaving the factory, loop around to the right—past the little black-and-green windmill—then turn right again, down the path just before the brick-and-thatch forest hut. On the right, look for the...*

Peat Hut (#7.6): Humble little huts like these were used by day laborers and covered with the same turf that those laborers were paid so poorly to gather.

• *Continue to a big, thatched-roof...*

Farmhouse (#8.1): Step into the vast and rough 1700s interior, listen to recorded animal noises, and scope out the layout: grain stored up above, cows along the main room, and at the far end, a (no doubt smelly) residential zone for people.

• *Cross the tram tracks in front of the farmhouse to reach the tiny...*

Schoolhouse (#8.2): Aside from its brick construction (most were made of clay), this is typical of village schoolhouses from around 1730. Only kids from 6 to 12 years old, mostly boys, attended school, with an emphasis on reading and writing, with summers off to help on the farm. Imagine the schoolhouse back then, fragrant with smoke from the peat fire. Notice the slates used to follow along with lessons (stored in the wooden "lockers" on the walls). An underperforming student would have to wear the donkey picture around his neck.

Just beyond the schoolhouse is the **Pancake House** (#9.1; good for a snack or meal—see "Eating at the Arnhem Open-Air Museum," below), with an adjacent playground.

• *Cross the tram tracks to peek into the...*

Church (#10.1): In the typical Dutch style, the church has an austere white interior, a central pulpit, and wooden pews.

• *Then continue along the tracks through the village, past the **Brabant Café** (#12.3), to the modern, working **brewery** (#12.4, on the left), where you can duck inside for a free sample.*

Just beyond, on the left, look for the...

Four Laborers' Houses (#12.5): These houses offer a fascinating glimpse into the lifestyles of four generations of workers: from 1870, 1910, 1954, and 1970. See how home fashion and amenities progressed from the rustic 1870s to the garish 1970s.

• *Continuing through the village, the **hospital** on the left (#12.9), from 1955, really does smell like a hospital. Next, the long **collection center** (#13.8) shows off a mind-numbing array of Dutch bric-a-brac, with futuristic exhibits about recycling and conservation. Just beyond it is a formal hedge garden. Finally, cross the tram tracks and walk to the big, white...*

Platform Windmill (#15.6): Hike up the steep steps of the park's centerpiece for an aerial view over the museums.

• *Our tour is over. Head back to the entrance, or continue exploring to your heart's content.*

Eating at the Arnhem Open-Air Museum

The open-air museum has several good budget restaurants and covered picnic areas. The **café** in the entrance pavilion is inexpensive but has limited choices (€4-5 sandwiches)—it's more enjoyable to eat inside the park. The rustic **Pancake House** (Pannekoeken Huis, a.k.a. "Restaurant de Hanekamp") serves hearty and sweet splittable Dutch flapjacks (€6-9 pancakes, soups, salads, and sandwiches). **Brabant Café**, in the "village" of Budel, resembles an old-fashioned farmhouse café and offers desserts and snacks. The **De Kasteelboerderij Café-Restaurant** at the Oud-Beijerland Manor is a giant place that can feed 300 visitors at once (traditional €8 *dagmenu*—plate of the day; open daily July-Aug, otherwise Sun only).

Arnhem Connections

From Arnhem by Train to: Amsterdam (4/hour, 1 hour, half with transfer in Utrecht), **The Hague** (4/hour, 1.5 hours, transfer in Utrecht; then another 15 minutes to **Delft**).

Kröller-Müller Museum

The Kröller-Müller Museum of top-notch modern art, rated ▲▲, is located within Hoge Veluwe National Park, the Netherlands' largest at 13,000 acres. While the south end of the park is just outside Arnhem, the museum is buried deep in the forest close to the opposite end of the park, near the town of Otterlo. Because the museum is situated within the national park, you must buy a ticket for both the museum and the park.

This memorable museum shows off the collection of Helene Kröller-Müller (1869-1939), who was a wealthy fan of avant-garde art, and includes an outstanding collection of Van Goghs. The modern museum seamlessly blends artistic beauty and its own peaceful park setting. Stroll through the delightfully landscaped sculpture garden, and spend some time with virtually all the top artists of the late 19th and early 20th centuries.

Orientation

Cost and Hours: €16 combo-ticket includes national park entry, not covered by Museumkaart, open Tue-Sun 10:00-17:00, sculpture garden closes at 16:30, closed Mon, Houtkampweg 6, tel. 031/859-1241, www.kmm.nl.

Getting There: Public-transportation connections to the Kröller-Müller Museum and Hoge Veluwe National Park are complicated, potentially involving several changes. (Even the park's employees don't bother trying to commute by bus.) Give yourself plenty of time, and try to confirm bus schedules when planning your day. These instructions get you to the northwest entrance of the park, near Otterlo, just over a mile from the Kröller-Müller Museum.

From Amsterdam: First, take the train to Ede-Wageningen (4/hour, 1 hour, half with a transfer in Utrecht). Exit the Ede-Wageningen station toward signs marked *Centrum* to find the bus stops, where you can catch bus #108 to Otterlo (bus marked *Apeldoorn*, runs hourly about :40 past the hour, or 2/hour on weekday mornings before 11:00, 15 minutes). Hop off the bus at Otterlo Rotonde (a roundabout on the edge of town). From here, walk five minutes into the town center, and then hang a left to the park entrance (about 20 minutes total), where you can buy your park ticket (€8) at the northwest entrance and hop on a free white bike to ride to the Kröller-Müller Museum or the park's visitors center.

If you'd rather take a bus (instead of walk) from Otterlo Rotonde to the park, take bus #106 (1-2/hour, bus marked *Hoenderloo,* check posted schedule for the next bus). Your ticket includes both the bus ride and entrance to the park (€8, buy from driver). Ask the driver to let you off at the Kröller-Müller Museum; turn right at the giant blue trowel and follow the road for a few minutes past the parking lot with all the white bikes; the museum entrance is on the left.

If the schedules don't line up well, you can also get from Amsterdam to the park via Arnhem (see below).

From Arnhem Central Station: Arnhem is a one-hour train ride from Amsterdam. From Arnhem Central Station, the Kröller-Müller Museum is 12 miles away. There's no direct bus to the museum, so you'll go via the town of Otterlo: Go next door to Arnhem's bus station (see "Arrival in Arnhem" on page 281), take bus #105, and get off at Otterlo Centrum (1-2/hour, 20 minutes). Once in Otterlo, you can take bus #106 or walk to the park (both options described under "Arrival in Otterlo" on page 291). You can hire a taxi from Arnhem's station, but it's expensive (about €45).

By Car: From Amsterdam, take A-1 southeast, then exit on N-310 to Otterlo. From Arnhem, take A-12 north, then pick up N-310 to Otterlo. Parking inside the park costs €6, or you can pay €2 to park at the entrance and bike or walk in.

Getting Around Hoge Veluwe National Park: Once at Hoge Veluwe, you have various options for connecting the attractions. My favorite plan: Bus from Otterlo directly to the Kröller-Müller Museum, pick up a free white bike to pedal to the park's visitors center, then bike back to the museum (or, with more time, bike around the park).

By Bike: The park has 1,700 white bikes—an endearing remnant of Holland's hippie past—that you're free to use to make your explorations more fun. The one-speed bikes, with no hand brakes (just pedal brakes), are good enough to get around on, but not good enough to get stolen. Just pick one up (or drop one off) wherever you see a bike rack, including at park entrances or at any attraction. While riding through the vast green woods, make a point of getting off your bike to climb an inland sand dune.

By Bus: Bus #106 does a convenient circuit around the park, connecting the "Otterlo Rotonde" stop (at the edge of town), the "Otterlo Centrum" stop (in the town center), the Otterlo entrance to the park, a stop 200 yards from the Kröller-Müller Museum, and the park's visitors center. Unfortunately, its frequency isn't ideal (hourly on weekdays, 2/hour on weekends until 18:00; last bus at 20:00 May-Aug, earlier in off-season). But it can be a handy way to connect the dots if you're tired or in a hurry. Tickets to enter the park, bought on board the bus, cover your bus ride (€8).

The Museum Collection

A stern-looking statue of Monsieur Jacques (the museum's mascot) greets you on the entry path. Once inside, pick up the informative guide-booklet and drop your bag at the mandatory bag check. Computers near the entry let you tailor a self-guided tour to your interests. Each work is labeled (but not described) in English, and there is no audioguide.

There are two parts to the museum: the outside sculpture garden and the interior art collection.

The **sculpture garden** shows off more than a hundred sculptures, displayed on 60 rolling

acres of lawn. You can appreciate works by Auguste Rodin, Barbara Hepworth, Claes Oldenburg, Christo, and others—or just enjoy this excuse for a walk in a pretty park with something fun to look at. Look for Jean Dubuffet's beloved *Garden of Enamel*, a giant, psychedelic, black-and-white roller rink you can climb around on. Since the garden closes at 16:30, head here first if you're arriving later in the day.

Inside, the permanent **art collection** is like a Who's Who of modern art. The works are displayed chronologically and grouped by movement, in keeping with Helene Kröller-Müller's wishes to foster understanding and appreciation of new art styles. You'll go from the hazy landscapes of the Impressionists (Monet, Manet, Renoir), to the intricate compositions of the Pointillists (Seurat, Pissarro), to the bold innovations of the Post-Impressionists (Gauguin, Van Gogh), to the slinky scenes of Art Nouveau (Toulouse-Lautrec), to the shattered-glass canvases of the Cubists (Picasso, Braque, and Gris), and, finally, to the colorful grids of Dutchman Piet Mondrian.

The museum's highlight is its Vincent van Gogh collection, the second-largest in the world (after Amsterdam's Van Gogh

Museum; Kröller-Müller usually displays about 50 of their 87 Vincent canvases). Look for some famous pieces, including various self-portraits, some *Sunflowers*, and *Café de Nuit*, the famous scene of an al fresco café on a floodlit Arles square. Notice how thickly the paint is caked on to create the almost-3-D lamp, the work's focal point.

Eating at the Kröller-Müller Museum: Consider the self-service restaurant Monsieur Jacques (€5 soups and sandwiches, €11 salads, Tue-Sun 10:00-16:30, closed Mon).

After visiting the museum, grab a free white bike for the three-quarter-mile pedal to the national park's visitors center, described below.

Sights in Hoge Veluwe National Park

Hoge Veluwe National Park

The Netherlands' biggest national park, rated ▲▲, is a delight to explore. On a quick visit, a short pedal and a visit to the Kröller-Müller Museum are enough; with more time, also swing by the visitors center and bike to your heart's content. The hunting lodge within the park, the former residence of the Kröller-Müller family (described on next page), makes a fun destination. If you head deeper into the park, you'll find a surprising diversity of terrain, from inland sand dunes to lakes to peat bogs to moorland. Get advice, maps, and brochures at the park entrances or at the visitors center.

Cost and Hours: Entry to the park costs €8; a €16 combo-ticket includes the Kröller-Müller Museum, not covered by Museumkaart. The park is open daily June-July 8:00-22:00, May and Aug 8:00-21:00, April 8:00-20:00, Sept 9:00-20:00, Oct 9:00-19:00, Nov-March 9:00-18:00, last entry one hour before closing (tel. 055/378-8100, www.hogeveluwe.nl).

Visitors Center (Bezoekerscentrum)—This is a good place to get your bearings in the park, with a helpful information desk, a nature exhibit, WCs, a playground, a restaurant, and a hub for free loaner bikes (daily April-Oct 9:30-18:00, Nov-March 9:30-17:00). Browse the collection of brochures and maps, including the good €2.50 map of the park, and the €1 self-guided bike tour, with commentary on the main stops.

The **nature exhibit** features interactive, kid-oriented exhibits, well-explained in English. It's divided into two parts: An above-ground section focuses on the parks' various landscapes and the animals that live above ground; then you'll go through a tunnel to reach the second section, called the "Museonder," which shows life underground (animals, fossils, the water table), with conservation-themed displays. Ask for an English showing of the nature films when you enter (a favorite is the 20-minute movie about park deer).

Eating at the Visitors Center: The good **Restaurant de Koperen Kop** serves up surprisingly tasty self-service cafeteria food, with indoor or outdoor seating (€8-12 plates, daily April-Oct 9:30-18:00, Nov-March 9:30-17:00).

St. Hubertus Lodge—This dramatic hunting lodge, at the north end of the park, is another popular excuse for a bike ride. Once the countryside residence of the modern art-collecting Kröller-Müller family, it's perched on the edge of a lake with a tower looming overhead. Designed to resemble the antlers of a stag, this structure evokes the story of St. Hubert, who supposedly discovered a crucifix miraculously dangling between a deer's antlers (sporadic tours, in Dutch only). The 45-minute walk around the adjacent lake is dotted with sculptures. Combining this lodge, the Kröller-Müller Museum, and the visitors center makes for a fun 6.5-mile biking loop.

Otterlo

The tiny village of Otterlo is located just outside the northwest entrance to the park, which is the closest one to the Kröller-Müller Museum. Though not exciting, it's a good place to spend the night near the park (see "Sleeping in Otterlo," next page). The town has tandem-bike tourists zipping through on their way to the park, cafés, and a meager **TI** (100 yards south of the town center, open Mon-Thu 8:00-18:00, Fri 8:00-20:00, Sat 8:00-17:00, closed Sun; ATM in lobby, Dorpsstraat 9, tel. 0318/614-444).

Arrival in Otterlo: There are two different bus stops in Otterlo. "Otterlo Rotonde" is at a roundabout on the busy road that skirts the edge of town; from here it's about a five-minute walk into the town center. "Otterlo Centrum" is right in the middle of town (described below). Buses #105 (from Arnhem) and #106 (into the park itself) stop at both the Rotonde and Centrum stops; bus #108 (from Ede-Wageningen and trains to Amsterdam) stops only at the Rotonde stop.

From **Otterlo Centrum,** follow the directional signs: The TI is along the main road, and the park is down the major intersecting road. From here it's about a 15-minute walk to the park entrance (or a very fast ride on bus #106).

Sleep Code

(€1 = about $1.40, country code: 31, area code: 0318)
S = Single, **D** = Double/Twin, **T** = Triple, **Q** = Quad, **b** = bathroom, **s** = shower only. Unless otherwise noted, credit cards are accepted, breakfast is included, and hoteliers speak English.
  To help you easily sort through these listings, I've divided the rooms into two categories, based on the price for a standard double room with bath:

  $$ Higher Priced—Most rooms €125 or more.
  $ Lower Priced—Most rooms less than €125.

  Prices can change without notice; verify the hotel's current rates online or by email. For other updates, see www.ricksteves.com/update.

Sleeping in Otterlo

Consider spending the night in Otterlo if you'd like to have a relaxing time at the museum, the national park, and nearby Arnhem. Both of these accommodations are on the road between Otterlo Centrum and the northwest entrance to the park; Sterrenberg is closer to the park, and Kruller is closer to the town center.

$$ Boutique Hotel Sterrenberg, located 400 yards from the park entrance, is a Dutch designer's take on a traditional hunting lodge. With woodsy touches and modern flair in its 33 rooms, it's a pleasant splurge (Sb-€100-150, Db-€130-190, price depends on season and room size, pricier "luxury" rooms, great Sunday-night deals include dinner, elevator, free Internet access, pay Wi-Fi, restaurant with terrace, swimming pool, sauna, 6 rentable bikes for guests—€7/day—or use free white bikes within nearby park gates, about a quarter-mile to park entrance and 1.5 miles to Kröller-Müller Museum, Houtkampweg 1, tel. 0318/591-228, fax 0318/591-693, www.sterrenberg.nl, info@sterrenberg.nl).

$ Hotel Kruller has 17 stylishly simple rooms over a busy restaurant (small Sb-€59, mid-size Sb-€79, small Db-€79, mid-size Db-€99, large Db-€119, cheaper for 2 or more nights, free Internet access and Wi-Fi, Dorpsstraat 19, tel. 0318/591-231, fax 0318/592-034, www.kruller.nl, info@kruller.nl).

Utrecht

The bustling student city of Utrecht lies smack-dab between

Arnhem to the east, The Hague (and Delft and Rotterdam) to the west, and Amsterdam to the north (4 trains/hour, 30 minutes). You might change trains here; if so, and if you have time to kill, consider poking around the central zone, which is charming compared to Utrecht's grossly commercial train station. Utrecht has plenty to keep you busy for an hour or a day (the station's lockers are near the elevator to track 7, €3.65/24 hours).

Spoorwegmuseum (Railway Museum)—The most interesting sight in town is Holland's biggest and best display of all things locomotive. It's full of vintage

engines and cars (including the Dutch royal family's official train), model railways, a ride for kids, and a Disneyesque recreation of an Industrial Age mining village. Even the most train-blasé will want to spend at least two hours here (pricey at €14.50, Tue-Sun 10:00-17:00, closed Mon, at east edge of town in old-fashioned Maliebaanstation, tel. 030/230-6206, www.spoorwegmuseum.nl).

Getting There: The easiest way to get to the museum is by a special "Maliebaan" train that leaves hourly from Utrecht's Central Station (departs at about :45 after the hour, last train at 15:45, 15 minutes, €2). It's a pleasant 15-minute walk from the train station to the museum (well-signed all the way). If you'd prefer the bus, hop the GVU bus #3 from Central Station (direction: Fockema Andrealaan, get off at Maliebaan stop).

Museum Speelklok (Musical Clock Museum)—This fun museum is worthwhile only if you take the 50-minute included tour, which shows you musical clocks, calliopes, and street organs in all their clicking, clanking, and tooting glory (€9 includes tour, Tue-Sun 10:00-17:00, closed Mon, tours depart on the hour, last tour at 16:00, well-signed 10-minute walk from station, located on busy shopping street in city center at Steenweg 6, tel. 030/231-2789, www.museumspeelklok.nl).

Domtoren (Cathedral Tower)—Utrecht's exact center is unmistakably marked by this impressive tower. At 368 feet, it's

Holland's highest tower—so big that city buses can drive through the arch at its base. It was once the west entrance of the city's cathedral, before most of the High Gothic church was destroyed in a storm in 1674. The tower is even more remarkable considering that it's also the central spire of an even bigger (imaginary) cathedral. To help cement Utrecht's standing as a seat of Church power, four churches were built at the endpoints of an invisible city-sized cross—symbolically making Utrecht one gigantic mega-cathedral (tower climbable only with €8 guided tour; April-Sept daily 11:00-16:00, Oct-March daily 12:00-16:00; tour leaves from nearby TI at Domplein 9/10, no elevator). At the tower's base is a lively cluster of cafés.

SCHOKLAND
MUSEUM

About a fifth of the Netherlands is reclaimed land—much of it a short drive northeast of Amsterdam. To appreciate the Dutch quest to show the sea who's boss (and what the sea did to deserve it), visit the museum at Schokland.

Once a long, skinny island with a few scant villages, Schokland was gradually enveloped by the sea, until the king condemned and

evacuated it in 1859. But after the sea around it was tamed and drained, Schokland was turned into a museum of Dutch traditions...and engineering prowess.

Today Schokland is a long way to go for a little museum, and it only makes sense by car, but the area offers a fascinating drive for engineers or anyone else who wants to understand how the Dutch have confidently grabbed the reins from Mother Nature.

Orientation

Cost and Hours: €3.50; April-Oct Tue-Sun 11:00-17:00, closed Mon except July-Aug Mon 11:00-17:00; Nov-March Fri-Sun 11:00-17:00, closed Mon-Thu; Middelbuurt 3, tel. 0527/251-396, www.schokland.nl.

Getting There: It's about an hour's **drive** north of Amsterdam (assuming there's no traffic), but the trip offers travelers an insightful glimpse at Dutch land reclamation. From Amsterdam's ring freeway, follow signs for *Almere*—first southeast on A-1, then northeast on A-6. You'll drive the

Taming the Zuiderzee

The Dutch have always had a love/hate relationship with the tempestuous Zuiderzee ("South Sea"). While it provided the Dutch with a convenient source of fish and trade—and an outlet to the Atlantic—the unpredictable bay also made life challenging. Over the centuries, entire towns were gradually eroded off the map.

But in 1918, the Dutch fought back and began to ingeniously tame the sea and "reclaim" their land with the Zuiderzee Works: First they built a sturdy dike (the Afsluitdijk) across the mouth of the sea to turn a dangerous, raging ocean into a mild puddle (the IJsselmeer); then they began to partition pieces of the sea floor, dike them off, and drain the water. The salty new seabed soil was treated organically and eventually became fertile farmland.

The best place to see the result of this process is in Flevoland, the Netherlands' newest state and home to Schokland. Some of the residents are older than the land they live on, which was reclaimed in the 1960s. An area that was once a merciless sea is now dotted with tranquil towns. The roads, commercial centers, and neighborhoods—made affordable to the masses—are all carefully planned and as tidy as can be.

length of the very flat reclaimed island of Flevoland (past the towns of Almere and Lelystad), and pass a striking line of power-generating windmills spinning like gigantic pinwheels as you cross out of Flevoland and into Noordoostpolder—the reclaimed "Northeast Polder" that includes Schokland. Take the Urk exit (#13), turn right, and follow blue signs for *Schokland*.

By **public transportation,** it's possible but not worth the effort (train from Amsterdam to Lelystad, bus to Emmeloord, then bus to Ens, then a two-mile walk to Schokland).

Self-Guided Tour

After buying your ticket, you'll watch a 15-minute **film** (press button to start in English) about the history of the town, its loss to the sea, and its reclamation.

Then tour the exposition called **Schokland: An Island in Time,** which explains how Schokland was reclaimed as part of what would become the Northeast Polder, beginning in 1936. After being enclosed by a sturdy dike, a year-long project drained this area of water in 1942 (while the Netherlands was occupied by the Nazis). Various Allied bombers were shot down and crashed into this area (including one whose mangled propeller is displayed just outside the museum), joining the dozens of ship-wrecks that already littered the seafloor.

A model shows the full territory of the Northeast Polder, which is carefully planned in concentric circles around the central town of Emmeloord (with Schokland and another former island, Urk, creating a pair of oddball bulges in the otherwise tidy pattern).

The exhibit explains that this isn't the first time this area has been dry land. From prehistoric times through the Middle Ages, much of what is today the Northeast Polder was farmed (many old tools have been discovered). In 1100, medieval engineers even attempted a primitive (and ultimately unsuccessful) effort to reclaim the land. Other remains from former residents include bones from mammoths and other prehistoric mammals, and a primitive 2,450-year-old canoe.

Then you'll head into the **Schokkerhuisje** to learn about the people who lived here (called *Schokkers*) until they were evacuated in 1859. Up to 650 people at a time lived on Schokland, residing in settlements on hills called *terpen* while they farmed the often-flooded land below. Like the rest of the Netherlands, this little island was divided in half by religion: part Catholic, part Protestant. This museum holds artifacts from the former town of Middelbuurt. You'll see traditional *Schokker* costumes (abandoned when they left the island) and a map of the entire island.

Back outside, go into the former **town church,** with a ceiling like the hull of a ship, a pulpit like a crow's nest, and a model ship hanging from the ceiling—appropriate for the seafaring residents of a once nearly submerged island.

Finally, follow the path (below the church) to walk around the base of the former island—now surrounded by **farm fields.** When farmers first tilled their newly reclaimed soil a half-century ago, they uncovered more than just muck and mollusks. You'll see a pair of rusty anchors and a giant buoy that used to bob in the harbor—now lying on its side and still tethered to the ground. Examine the stone dike and black wooden seawall built by residents in a futile attempt to stay above water. The post with the blue strip helped residents keep an eye on the ever-rising water level.

Nearby: If you're intrigued by all of this, you can walk a six-mile path (with posted information) that covers the entire length of the former island (get a map from the museum). Or, for a quick look, drive to the forlorn old **lighthouse,** improbably perched overlooking a vast field of grazing cows—without a coastline in

sight. In fact, the lighthouse marks
the far tip of what was Schokland
Island—and, because it was situated along a major trade route, this
lighthouse was once extremely
important. Today, this white
elephant is an evocative symbol
of Holland's complex relationship
with the sea. To get there by car,

leave the museum parking lot and turn left onto the main road,
then take the first right (marked *Oude Haven Schokland*) and follow
the road through the woods for about three minutes. When you
reach the next big road, turn right, then look for the lighthouse on
the left (with parking nearby).

EDAM, VOLENDAM, & MARKEN

The aptly named region of Waterland (VAH-ter-land), just north of Amsterdam on the west shore of the IJsselmeer, is laced with canals and sprinkled with picturesque red-brick villages. Three in particular—the homey cheesemaking village of Edam, the workaday waterfront town of Volendam, and the trapped-in-a-time-warp hamlet of Marken—offer visitors an enticing peek at rural Holland.

If choosing just one Waterland town, make it Edam—and consider spending the night. Because of its charm and its proximity to Amsterdam, this region is popular. But if you'd like to get a taste of traditional Dutch living, it's worth joining the crowds.

Planning Your Time

The most efficient way to see this area is as a one-day loop trip by public transportation from Amsterdam (or Haarlem); to have enough time for the whole loop, get started by 10:00. Begin with a bus from Amsterdam to Edam. Then, after enjoying Edam, continue by bus to Volendam for a stroll and to catch the boat across to Marken. Leave Edam by around 14:00 in order to have sufficient time in Volendam (you'll want at least an hour there), and to be able to reach Marken before its museum and shops close at 17:00. Poke around salty Marken before taking the bus back to Amsterdam.

All of the bus rides in this loop are covered by the €7.50 "Waterland Ticket" from the Arriva bus company (not covered by Amsterdam transit passes). The Volendam-Marken boat costs extra and doesn't take cars; drivers must leave their cars in Volendam while they take the round-trip boat ride to Marken.

Edam

This adorable cheesemaking village is sweet but not saccharine, and is just 30 minutes by bus from Amsterdam. It's mostly the

terrain of day-trippers, who can mob the place on summer weekends. For the ultimate in cuteness and peace, make your home in tiny Edam (ay-DAHM) and stay overnight.

Although Edam is known today for cheese, it was once an industrious shipyard and port. But having a canal to the sea caused such severe flooding in town—cracking walls and spilling into homes—that one frustrated resident even built a floating cellar (which you can visit in what's now Edam's oldest house). To stop the flooding, the harbor was closed off with locked gates (you'll see the gates at Dam Square next to the TI). Eventually the harbor silted up, forcing the decline of the shipbuilding trade.

Edam's Wednesday market is held year-round, but it's best in July and early August, when the focus is on cheese. You, along with piles of other tourists, can meet the cheese traders and local farmers.

Orientation to Edam

(area code: 0299)

Edam is a very small town—you can see it all in a lazy 20-minute stroll. It's so nice, though, that you may be tempted to stay longer. Dam Square, with the City Hall and its TI, is right along the big canal called Spui (rhymes with "cow"); the town's lone museum is just over the big bridge.

Tourist Information

The TI, often staffed by volunteers, is in City Hall on Dam Square. Pick up the €0.50 *Edam Holland* brochure and consider the €2.50 *A Stroll Through Edam* brochure outlining a self-guided walking tour (mid-March-Oct Mon-Sat 10:00-17:00, closed Sun except July-Aug open Sun 12:00-16:30; Nov-mid-March Mon-Sat 10:00-15:00, closed Sun; WC and ATM just outside, tel. 0299/315-125, www.vvv-edam.nl).

Arrival in Edam

The bus "station"—really just a parking lot for buses—is a five-minute walk from Dam Square and the TI. At the canal by the bus lot, turn right and walk along the water (on Schepenmakersdijk). Cross the next bridge (a white bridge just wide enough for two people), and head straight up the street toward the gray-and-gold bell tower. Hook right around the church, pass one bridge, and you'll wind up across the canal from Dam Square.

Helpful Hints

Cheese Market: In July and early August, farmers bring their cheese by boat and horse to the center of town on Wednesday mornings (10:30-12:30), where it's weighed and traded by Edamers in traditional garb.

Internet Access: You can get online at the library (daily 9:00-17:00, from Dam Square follow Hoogstraat south as it crosses three bridges and changes names—the library is at William Pontstraat 27).

Services: Free WCs are located behind City Hall near the canal.

Bike Rental: Tiny Edam has two bike shops full of friendly folks. **Ronald Schot** is near the cheese market, between Dam Square and the Grote Kerk (€7/half-day, €8.50/day, €14/24 hours, Tue-Fri 8:30-18:00, Sat 8:30-16:00, closed Sun-Mon except by appointment, sells regional maps with bike routes, Grote Kerkstraat 7/9, tel. 0299/372-155, www.ronaldschot .nl) and **Ton Tweewielers** is between Dam Square and the bus station (€8/day, tandem-€17.50/day, April-Oct daily 8:00-18:00, closed Nov-March, free maps, Schepenmakersdijk 6, tel. 0299/371-922, www.tontweewielers.nl, Friet).

Sights in Edam

▲**Edam's Museum: Edam's Oldest House**—The 400-year-old historical home across the bridge from Dam Square provides a fun peek at what all these old canal houses once looked like inside. This house is particularly interesting for its floating cellar, designed to accommodate changes in water level without destabilizing the house. The downstairs is well-described by the English explanations provided at the ticket desk. Go upstairs to see an exhibit on Edam's history (Dutch only, but with plenty of self-explanatory pictures, including one particularly good diagram showing how windmills lift water). The top floor has an exhibit on the locally produced Fris art pottery. For more exhibits about Edam's history, go back across the bridge to the museum in City Hall (covered by the same ticket).

Cost and Hours: €3, Easter-Oct Tue-Sat 10:00-16:30, Sun 13:00-16:30, closed Mon and Nov-Easter, Dam Square 8, tel. 0299/372-644, www.edamsmuseum.nl.

▲**Take a Stroll**—The best thing to do in Edam is to just wander its storybook lanes and canals. Consider taking the short walking tour outlined in the TI's booklet *A Stroll Through Edam*.

Grote Kerk—Perched on the edge of town, the Grote Kerk (Big Church) feels surprisingly huge for tiny Edam. Its vast interior is covered by a ceiling constructed just like a stone vault—but built of wood, because heavier stone would have made the building sink into the wet ground. The wooden catwalks are original. Near the pulpit, find the "cabinet organ"—many 19th-century Dutch homes had one of these, cleverly disguised to evade a tax on organs. Pick up the church's €2 booklet for more on the church's interior, including some good background on the stained-glass windows. If you haven't landed in Edam on cheese-market day, look for the TV tucked in the side wall, which plays a loop video of scenes around town, including the cheese market.

Cost and Hours: Free, daily 13:30-17:00. The church's tower is open for climbing, but only when enough people show up to make it worth the attendant's time (€2).

Getting There: From Dam Square, walk over the bridge, turn left, then head right down Prinsenstraat to Nieuwenhuizenplein, the traditional cheese-market square. Find the "cheese weigh house" on the left—the one with the cheese frieze—and peek inside if it's open. Continue through the square to the canal, which leads to the church.

Sleeping in Edam

These two hotels are both distinctive, classy, and expensive (where there's a range, the price depends on room size and amenities). For cheaper rooms in private homes, check www.vvv-edam.nl or ask at the TI.

$$ L'Auberge Damhotel, centrally located on a canal across the street from City Hall, has 11 nicely renovated rooms with snazzy bathrooms and over-the-top plush decor—each one a bit different. Rooms at the front have canal views (Db-€125-165, Tb-€185, Qb-€195, air-con, free Wi-Fi, Keizersgracht 1, tel. 0299/371-766, fax 0299/374-031, www.dam hotel.nl, info@damhotel.nl).

$ Hotel de Fortuna is an eccentric canalside place with flowers and the sounds of ducks and other birds. It offers steep stairs and 23 low-ceilinged

Sleep Code

(€1 = about $1.40, country code: 31, area code: 0299)
S = Single, **D** = Double/Twin, **T** = Triple, **Q** = Quad, **b** = bathroom,
s = shower only. Unless otherwise noted, credit cards are
accepted, breakfast is included, and hoteliers speak English.

To help you easily sort through these listings, I've divided
the rooms into two categories, based on the price for a
standard double room with bath:

$$ Higher Priced—Most rooms €125 or more.
$ Lower Priced—Most rooms less than €125.

Prices can change without notice; verify the hotel's
current rates online or by email. For other updates, see www
.ricksteves.com/update.

rooms in a cozy collection of five ancient buildings in the old cen-
ter of Edam. It's been run by the Dekker family for more than
30 years (Sb-€85-95, Db-€98-115, luxury Db-€140, free Wi-Fi,
Spuistraat 3, tel. 0299/371-671, fax 0299/371-469, www.fortuna
-edam.nl, fortuna@fortuna-edam.nl).

Eating in Edam

Edam's lanes are lined with tourist-friendly restaurants (all of these
are within a block of Dam Square). Considering how close it is to
Amsterdam, I'd come here for a romantic dinner in the country-
side, then head back to my lodgings in the big city.

Hotel de Fortuna and **L'Auberge Damhotel,** listed earlier,
each have a fine restaurant with classy, high-priced food (reserva-
tions smart on weekends). Hotel de Fortuna has more rustic charm,
with a romantic dining room and seating in a gorgeous garden
alongside a picturesque canal (€20-25 main dishes, three-course
"Fortuna *menu*" for €32.50, pricier fixed-price meals also available,
daily 12:00-15:00 & 18:00-21:30). Damhotel's outdoor seating is

right on Dam Square, in the shadow
of the Town Hall, and their inte-
rior feels dressy (€7-13 sandwiches
at lunchtime, €20-30 main dishes,
€35-45 fixed-price meals, daily 8:00-
24:00).

De Prinsenbar and Eetcafé
is a good bet for a light lunch or a
midday snack. Their €5.50 *Portie
gemengde Hollandse Kaas* is a sampler

of regional cheeses with bread—a nibbler plate that goes well with a little Belgian *beerje* (€3.50 soups, €3.50-5 salads, €4 pancakes, €6-10 pub grub meals, April-Sept daily 12:00-24:00, Oct-March Mon-Fri 16:00-24:00, Sat-Sun 10:30-24:00, food served all day June-Aug but only Sat-Sun 12:00-16:00 in off-season, Prinsenstraat 8, tel. 0299/372-911).

Picnickers can stock up on gourmet groceries or pick up a sandwich at **Foodlovers** (Mon-Fri 8:30-18:00, Sat 8:30-17:00, Sun 9:30-17:00, next door to cheese shop overlooking Spui canal across from Dam Square, tel. 0299/373-069). Ask them to heat up a handmade pizza for you.

Edam Connections

Arriva runs frequent buses between **Edam** and **Amsterdam.** From Amsterdam, buses leave from the bus platforms behind Central Station (from the station's west corridor, exit the station and take escalators up to the bus stops). Bus #112 is the most direct option (2/hour Mon-Fri, 30-minute trip, no buses after 18:30 or on weekends). You can also take bus #116 (2/hour Mon-Sat, similar duration, no buses after 18:45), bus #110 (2/hour daily, slower and with more stops, runs until 24:00), or bus #118 (2/hour daily, much slower and lots of stops, runs until 24:00). For bus schedules, see www.9292ov.nl.

By Bus to Volendam on the "Waterland Loop": Buses #110 and #118 zip you from Edam to Volendam in about 12 minutes (4/hour daily). Hop off at the Zeestraat stop (other buses also go to Volendam, but not to this handy town-center stop).

Volendam

Less cute and more functional than the other two Waterland towns, Volendam enjoys some workaday charm of its own—including a lively dike-top walkway stretching along a shimmering bay, and a fun town museum.

Tourist Information: Stop by the TI to pick up a free Volendam/Marken map (mid-March-Oct Mon-Sat 10:00-17:00, Sun 11:00-16:00 except closed Sun in Oct; Nov-mid-March Mon-Sat 10:00-15:00, closed Sun; tel. 0299/363-747, www.vvv-volendam.nl).

VOLENDAM

Arrival in Volendam: If arriving by bus from Edam, get off at the Zeestraat stop. The museum and TI are within a block, in the modern part of town. To reach the boat to Marken, walk straight from the bus stop toward the water, then turn left and walk along the dike.

Sight: The **Volendams Museum,** the town's lone sight, is located in the same building as the TI. Its hokey but endearing little collection oozes local pride. You'll wander through displays of traditional costumes, replica house and shop interiors, scenes from village life, and nostalgic old grainy black-and-white movies that are worth watching even if you don't speak Dutch. The corner display showing Waterland life during World War II is worth a look, but the museum's highlight is the Cigarband House, where a local artist glued 11 million cigarbands to big boards to create giant images—from Dutch windmills to Venice to a sour-looking Statue of Liberty (€3, borrow English descriptions at entry, mid-March-Oct daily 10:00-17:00, closed Nov-mid-March, Zeestraat 41, tel. 0299/369-258, www.volendamsmuseum.nl).

To reach the waterfront from the museum, walk two blocks down Zeestraat to Europaplein, head left, cross the dark-green bridge, turn right, then zigzag back across the next bridge and follow the brick steps up to the harbor.

Along the Waterfront: Volendam's inviting **promenade** has a lively boardwalk appeal and is lined with souvenir shops, indoor/outdoor eateries, and Dutch clichés—a good place to spend time waiting for your boat. The walls inside **Hotel Spaander** (eight houses down from the northern end of the harbor, on the right) are decorated with paintings by starving artists who slept or ate there. Don't miss the maze of sleepy residential courtyards below sea level just behind the promenade, with an adorable dollhouse charm and fewer crowds.

"Marken Express": This boat connects Volendam with Marken (€5 one-way, €7.50 round-trip, bike-€1 extra each way, mid-March-Oct daily about 11:00-17:30, departs every 30-45 minutes, in March and Oct sails only if there's enough passengers, by appointment only Nov-mid-March, 30-minute crossing, leaves from northern corner of harbor, no outside food allowed on board, tel. 0299/363-331, www.marken-express.nl).

VOLENDAM

Marken

Famous as one of the Netherlands' most traditional fishing communities, Marken is a time-passed hamlet in a bottle—once virtually abandoned, now revived but kept alive solely as a tourist attraction. This island town once had a harbor for whaling and herring fishing, but when the Zuiderzee began to silt up in the late 17th century, it became more and more difficult to eke out a living here,

and many people from Marken fled to easier conditions on the mainland. When the Zuiderzee was diked off in 1932 to become a giant freshwater lake (the IJsselmeer), it forced saltwater fishermen to adapt or to find a new calling (which most did). Marken became a virtual ghost town. But in 1957, a long causeway was constructed from the mainland to the hamlet, which allowed easy access for visitors—who today come in droves to walk its tiny lanes.

Arrival in Marken: From the boat dock at the little harbor, follow signs to the museum in the town center. Marken has no TI; the nearest one is in Volendam.

Sights: The village of Marken has two districts: Havenbuurt, near the harbor; and Kerkbuurt, near the church. Arriving by boat, you'll first wander through the colorful Havenbuurt, then head for the charming Kerkbuurt to get a taste of Marken's old-time charm. As you walk, notice the unique local architecture, adapted to survive the challenging local conditions: Because the tides could be so temperamental, houses here tend to cluster on little hills called *werven,* or are built on pilings to keep them high and dry. Traditional Marken homes, while dull and black-tarred outside, are painted a cheerful yellow and blue inside.

The town's main attraction is the modest **Marker Museum,** celebrating the 16th-century costumes (still worn for special events) and traditional lifestyles of the people of Marken. As you enter, ask for an English showing of the good eight-minute movie (€2.50, April-Oct Mon-Sat 10:00-17:00, Sun 12:00-16:00, closed Nov-March, tel. 0299/601-904, www.markermuseum.nl).

Just outside town, on the way to the parking lot and the bus stop, you'll pass Marken's raised **cemetery,** where graves are marked with numbers rather than names. With more time, you can walk (about 40 minutes) out to the **lighthouse,** dubbed Paard van Marken ("Horse of Marken"), picturesquely situated at the far end of the island, at the tip of a sandy spit.

MARKEN

Marken Connections: Bus #111 connects Marken with Amsterdam's Central Station (2/hour, 40 minutes, leaves at :29 and :59 past the hour until 17:00, then at :06 and :36 until midnight). In Marken, catch the bus along the main road that skirts the town, a little past the south end of the harbor and just past the big parking lot. For info on the boat to Volendam, see "Marken Express," page 305.

MARKEN

THE HISTORIC TRIANGLE

Hoorn • Medemblik
• Enkhuizen Zuiderzee Museum

The Historic Triangle (De Historische Driehoek) is a manageable and enjoyable one-day journey through the Dutch countryside north of Amsterdam. You'll start in the small town of Hoorn (an easy train trip from Amsterdam or Haarlem), catch a toot-toot steam train to the town of Medemblik, and then sail on a 1920s-era boat to Enkhuizen, home of an excellent open-air folk museum (see page 313). Particularly good for families—and a fantasyland for trainspotters—the Historic Triangle trip is a charming way to pass a day. Dutch grandmothers feed snacks to towheaded toddlers, gusts of steam billow gracefully behind the engine, and cows nod sleepily in the fields. When you reach Enkhuizen, a collection of engaging time-warp villages at the Zuiderzee Museum caps it all off.

Orientation

Cost: Allow about €50 per adult for the entire trip, including the open-air museum in Enkhuizen. If you have a Museumkaart, you're in luck: it covers the museum, the steam train, and the boat trip (but not the Amsterdam-Hoorn and Enkhuizen-Amsterdam sections—about €17, covered by railpass).

Without a Museumkaart, a variety of **combo-tickets** will save you a couple of euros. You can buy these only at the station in Hoorn; buy the regular train tickets at the station in Amsterdam.

If you're not doing the museum in Enkhuizen, get the €19.70 ticket covering just the steam train and the boat (buy your Amsterdam-Hoorn and Enkhuizen-Amsterdam train tickets separately—or use a railpass). If you're doing the whole thing, get the €32.30 combo-ticket, which also covers museum entry and the train from Enkhuizen back to Hoorn (though not all the way back to Amsterdam). This combo-ticket combines perfectly with a €14.10 day return ticket between Amsterdam and Hoorn—making your total cost €46.40.

Without any discounts, here's how the price breaks down per leg (2011 prices): Train from Amsterdam to Hoorn-€7.30; steam train to Medemblik-€11.25; boat to Enkhuizen-€9.30; museum entry-€14; train from Enkhuizen back to Amsterdam-€9.80 (Enkhuizen to Hoorn is €3.60). If you're in a hurry and just want to see the museum, skip the steam train and boat, and go directly by train from Amsterdam to Enkhuizen (€19.10 day return ticket, 1 hour).

Schedule: The Historic Triangle trip is offered most of the year, with the frequency determined by the season. Trains leave Hoorn at 11:00 every Sat and Sun from the last weekend of March until mid-November. From mid-April to the end of October, trains also leave Hoorn at 11:00 Tue-Fri. During peak times (first week of May, late July-mid Aug, and third week of Oct), trains leave Hoorn twice daily at 11:00 and 13:30. The trip doesn't run mid-Nov-late March. Because holidays or special events can affect the schedule, it's smart to confirm train departure times (tel. 0229/214-862, www.museumstoomtram.nl, info@museum stoomtram.nl). Reservations are not necessary or even possible, except for big groups (if they run out of room, they just add more cars to the train).

Note that on summer days when there are two (or more) departures, you must take the 11:00 steam train from Hoorn if you want to arrive in Enkhuizen in time to see the open-air museum. The museum closes at 17:00, and you can likely get back to Amsterdam about 18:30.

At peak times, when trains leave twice a day, the extra departures open up more options beyond the basic route I've described here. For example, you could hop off the steam train in Twisk, get on a shuttle bus (included in either combo-ticket) to Medemblik's steam engine museum, then continue on the bus directly to the boat. Or you could just do the boat and steam train both ways (skipping the open-air museum). For more on these options, ask at the station in Hoorn or contact the folks at the Museumstoomtram.

Historic Triangle Tour

Train from Amsterdam to Hoorn

To do the basic trip in time to see the open-air museum in Enkhuizen, catch the 11:00 steam train in Hoorn. To make this

connection, leave Amster-
dam's Central Station on the
9:38 train to Hoorn (2/hour,
35 minutes). Once in Hoorn,
you'll have about 45 minutes
to buy your tickets and poke
around the interesting old
station (opens at 10:00) before
boarding the steam train.
(Take the 9:08 train from

Amsterdam if you want more time to peruse the Hoorn station
exhibits; late risers can leave Amsterdam at 10:08, which gives you
a tight 18 minutes in Hoorn to make a beeline for the steam train.)

▲Hoorn Station

While pleasant, the town of Hoorn itself has little to offer (**TI** is a
2-minute walk from the train station—across the park and on the
corner, open Mon 13:00-18:00, Tue-Fri 9:30-17:30, Thu also 19:00-
21:00, until 17:00 Sept-April, Sat 9:30-17:00, closed Sun, Veemarkt
4, tel. 0229/218-343, www.vvvhoorn.nl).

Arriving at Hoorn's modern train station, exit the train and
find the modern pedestrian overpass (following *stoomtram* signs)
that runs up and over the tracks, leading to the small, old-timey
station. (Both old and new trains share the same train tracks, but
on opposite sides.) Buy your combo-ticket here for the steam train,
boat, and open-air museum. Then poke around to kill time while
you wait for the steam train's departure.

The station has a genteel little waiting room where you can
buy coffee or snacks (also available on the train). Outside you can
climb the stairs to the cute signal house *(seinhuis)*, where the conductor pulls a long line of levers to change tracks (see the complex

diagram posted overhead). As he demonstrates pulling the levers, watch the signals
flip at the far end of the tracks to notify
the trains.

Then head alongside those tracks and
into the workshop *(werkplaats)*, where a
crew of devoted engineers keeps all those
proud, old steam trains in working order.
You can actually climb the steep steplad-
ders into some of the gorgeously reconstructed locomotives, and imagine pulling
levers, turning valves, and shoveling coal
to keep the "iron horse" moving.

Before long...all abooooard!

▲▲"Museum Steam Train" (Museumstoom-tram) from Hoorn to Medemblik

From Hoorn it's a relaxing 1.5-hour steam-train ride to Medemblik (1.25 hours in peak season). The trains are the kind that ran

through Holland from 1879 through 1966; the train you'll be riding has a chassis from the 1920s, but the cars are furnished circa 1950s. It's a time-warp back to when train trips really had style, with wooden-bench seats, leather belts to keep windows secured in place, and nattily uniformed conductors.

After you choose a seat inside the train, you can get up and walk around. The best views (farthest from the soot, noise, and vibrations of the engine) are standing on the train balcony at the very back of the train. You'll feel like a whistle-stop presidential candidate as the train plods through the Dutch countryside.

The train makes three stops: ten minutes in Wognum-Nibbixwoud, and about three minutes each in Twisk and Opperdoes. All three have dollhouse-cute stations, recently reno-

vated and decorated to evoke times past. Notice the little potbellied stoves between rooms and the old travel posters on the walls. At Wognum, peek into the old-fashioned outhouses. Stops are also a good chance to walk around and peer inside the locomotive, where you can see engineers constantly adjusting valves and levers, and opening the little door to shovel in more coal from the pile at their feet.

The costumed conductor occasionally walks through the cars, giving instructions in Dutch (if you're curious, ask him to repeat what he said in English when he passes). The train periodically stops so a conductor can hop out, scurry out in front of the engine, and flag traffic to a stop the old-fashioned way.

Enjoy the purely Dutch countryside on this serene, old-fashioned joyride. Count sheep. Moo at cows. Watch horses playfully run alongside the train. Look for ducks in the canals and pheasants in the fields. Go ahead, order the *poffertjes* (puffy mini-pancakes, €3.30). If you see Dutch kids waving to the train from their backyards, wave back. The modern white windmills in the distance jolt you back into the 21st century, just in time to arrive at...

Medemblik

You'll have about an hour in this pleasant one-street town before boarding the boat (confirm the boat's exact departure time before leaving the train station). Exit the station and bear left, then right, to walk up the main drag—a pretty market street lined with cafés, bakeries, shops, and postcard stands. Because time is short here, you'll have to pick and choose: If you're hungry, you could grab a quick sandwich or a coffee and a snack at an outdoor café, but you likely won't have time for a full meal. (Basic food is available on the upcoming boat ride.)

Or, if you feel like sightseeing, head to the first block of the main street (on the right), where you'll find a cute, if overpriced, **bakery museum.** Displayed on two floors of an old bakery, the exhibit shows off baking bric-a-brac and covers everything from Christmas spice cookies and sugar sculptures to chocolate and marzipan. The live demonstrations are the highlight—depending on the day, you might see a baker making cookies, candies, or ice cream in an old-fashioned machine (€5; July-Aug daily 11:00-17:00; mid-Feb-June and Sept-Dec Tue-Sun 12:00-17:00, closed Mon; closed Jan-mid-Feb, Nieuwstraat 8, tel. 0227/545-014, www.deoudebakkerij.nl).

Two other Medemblik sights—a steam-engine museum and a castle museum—are too far from the station to visit in the one hour between the steam train and boat. But if you have more time, the **TI**—at the end of the main street on the right—has information on both, as well as a €3 self-guided tour brochure for the town (July-Aug Mon-Sat 10:00-12:00 & 13:00-17:00, May-June and Sept Mon-Sat 11:00-16:00, April and late Oct Mon-Sat 11:00-15:00 except only open 10:00-12:00 in mid-April; closed Sun, in early Oct, and Nov-March; Kaasmarkt 1, tel. 0227/542-852).

Shortcut Back to Hoorn: If you want to skip the boat trip and open-air museum at Enkhuizen, and instead return to Hoorn, you can ride back on the steam train, or catch the bus (bus #139, 2/hour in afternoon, otherwise 1/hour, 25 minutes, €2, buy ticket from driver; slower milk-run bus #415 runs hourly Mon-Sat only, 1 hour). Note that there's usually no direct overland connection from Medemblik to Enkhuizen—if you miss the boat, you'll have to take the bus back to Hoorn, then the train or bus from there to Enkhuizen.

Boat from Medemblik to Enkhuizen

Catch the *MS Friesland* to Enkhuizen just over the dike from the Medemblik station (you'll see the boat moored there as your train pulls in). It's a 75-minute putter along the coast to the Zuiderzee Museum in Enkhuizen. You can grab a bite in the boat's surprisingly comfortable dining room (€2-2.50 sandwiches and meatloaflike "hamburgers," no food served toward end of ride). If you've brought a picnic, grab a wicker chair and enjoy the peaceful, windswept deck. Kids can safely run around on the open spaces of the top deck, or play wooden board games in the lounge. In good weather, you'll pass small pleasure craft—little sailboats and windsurfers—close enough to shake hands.

▲Enkhuizen Zuiderzee Museum

The boat from Medemblik drops you right at the rear entrance of this wonderful open-air folk museum. The museum's original

buildings were collected from around the Zuiderzee (ZOW-der-zay, "South Sea"), which was diked off in 1932 to become a lake called the IJsselmeer. With the ensuing transition from saltwater to freshwater, and the later reclamation and repurposing of land, the traditional culture on display at this museum became virtually extinct; this museum was created to preserve that culture. You'll meet people who do a convincing job of role-playing no-nonsense 1905 villagers. You're welcome to take their picture, but they won't smile—no one said "Have a nice day" back then. On weekends, children enjoy trying out old-time games, playing at the dress-up chest, and making sailing ships out of old wooden shoes (small fee for some activities).

Cost and Hours: €15, kids 4-12-€8.50, free for kids under 4, family ticket-€35, April-Oct daily 10:00-17:00; also open Nov-March daily 10:00-17:00, but the buildings are closed, making it a pricey ticket to see just the indoor museum and deserted grounds; tel. 0228/351-111, www.zuiderzeemuseum.nl.

Getting There: If you don't want to do the whole Historic Triangle trip, you can just take the train to the museum from Amsterdam (or Haarlem). Trains make the one-hour trip between Amsterdam and Enkhuizen every half-hour. From the Enkhuizen station, take the shuttle boat or walk 20 minutes to the museum (see "Back to Amsterdam," later). Drivers pay €5 to park here.

➔ Self-Guided Tour: The Zuiderzee Museum is a delight to explore, with something for all the senses—smell the wood fires and tanning vats, savor a bite of aged cheese, watch a windmill turn, hold a lump of coal, and catch the sound of wooden clogs on

THE HISTORIC TRIANGLE

a brick road. This tour is a start, but don't be afraid to poke into houses (even if they seem to be populated) and backyards.

A museum attendant greets you at the **dock** where the boats arrive. Show your Historic Triangle ticket, or (if you don't have one) buy a museum ticket. From here, head to the left of the museum buildings (a nature preserve lies off to the right). Follow signs for *Informatiecentrum* into the row of brick houses, where you can pick up a map at the information center.

The museum is organized into units. Use the map to visit these in counterclockwise order. Throughout the open-air museum, notice that every building has a little plaque with a brief English description and a map showing the building's original location in the Zuiderzee region. The first section, the **fishing village,** includes many fun-to-explore homes. On some days, dressed-up locals populate the ramshackle village street from Urk—once a remote island across the Zuiderzee, now a strange little lump on a vast, flat *polder.*

Head to the ***polder*** area, near the windmill. Windmills harness the power of the wind to turn Archimedes' screws, which, by rotating in a tube, pump water up over a dike and into the sea—continuing to drain reclaimed *polder* land. Nearby vats are used to cure fishing nets and a smoke-house where you can buy a tasty snack of smoked herring or eel.

Next, circle around to the **urban canal** zone (near the pavilion), lined with shops—such as a bakery, a gift shop, and a cheese shop where 15,000 clumps of Gouda could be aged (the vacuum-packed samples make another fun snack). Don't miss the pharmacy (marked *Apotheke "De Groote Gaper,"* under the queen with her mouth hanging open). Past the

counter where the pharmacist weighs out little bottles of camphor, you'll find a room full of open-mouthed giant heads. Traditionally, Dutch pharmacies were marked by a head with a gaping mouth (opening wide to say "aaaah" for the doctor, or for taking a pill). Many of these original heads are dark-skinned—medicine, like people from the east or south of Europe, was considered mysterious and magical. A nearby theater shows a dramatic film that includes some grainy black-and-white footage of traditional

Zuiderzee life (with English subtitles). As you curl around along the little canal, you'll find other trades represented, such as a barber and a cooper (barrel-maker).

Afterward, head into the **church district,** surrounding a reconstructed church dating from the 15th century. Because local builders were more familiar with boats than buildings, standing inside this church feels like being under an overturned boat (a common feeling in many Dutch village churches). Around the church are more shops, including the blacksmith. Don't miss the schoolhouse, with two period classrooms: one from 1905 and another from 1930. Just across the canal from the church area is a big self-service restaurant, with indoor and outdoor seating (€3 sandwiches, €5-10 meals).

Finally, walk toward the cute, enclosed **harbor,** filled with Zuiderzee watercraft from ages past (just beyond it is a modern harbor, filled with pleasure boats). The little cluster of houses just beyond the harbor (where you may be able to catch a rope-making demonstration) is based on the island village of Marken (for info on visiting the real Marken, see the previous chapter).

As you leave the park through the main entrance, you can visit the **indoor museum** if you have time to spare (same ticket and hours): Exit to the left and walk two blocks, watching for the museum on your right. This space shows off temporary exhibits (only some of which relate to the Zuiderzee), as well as an impressive hall filled with nine old Zuiderzee boats. Notice that many of them have big, flat fins on the sides. Because the Zuiderzee could be very shallow, these boats didn't have a keel; the fins could be extended down into the water to provide more stability.

Back to Amsterdam

From the indoor museum, it's a scenic 15-minute walk, mostly along the water, through the bricks-and-canals town to the Enkhuizen train station: Exit the indoor museum to the right, follow the wall, and cross three bridges (watching for *Station* directional signs). Or go back to the dock at the Zuiderzee Museum and catch a shuttle boat to the station (free with museum ticket, 4/hour, 10 minutes, last boat from museum at 17:30).

ALKMAAR & ZAANSE SCHANS OPEN-AIR MUSEUM

Two handy day trips line up north of Amsterdam: Alkmaar is a famous cheesemaking town with a charming square and a bustling cheese market; Zaanse Schans, while the least interesting of Holland's open-air museums, is also its most convenient—offering a taste of traditional life a stone's throw from the capital. Consider combining the two destinations for a full day of sightseeing, ideally on a Friday in spring or summer, when Alkmaar's festive cheese market enlivens the town.

Alkmaar

Alkmaar is Holland's cheese capital (and, perhaps, the unofficial capital of high cholesterol). In addition to being an all-around delightful city, Alkmaar has a rich history and a zesty cheese-loving spirit. And though it's enjoyable to visit any time, don't miss this town during its bustling Friday-morning cheese market (early April-early Sept).

Orientation to Alkmaar

(area code: 072)

Once a stoutly walled city, Alkmaar (pop. 95,000) now has a tidy Old Town laced by canals. The main square, Waagplein, is named for Alkmaar's cheese-weighing. The mighty Weigh House, containing the TI and Cheese Museum, is at one end of the square, and the Beer Museum is at the other. (Think of it as "Holland's Wisconsin.") From this area, the main pedestrian drag, Langestraat, leads visitors to the Grote Kerk and Stedelijk Museum.

Tourist Information

Alkmaar's TI, in the old Weigh House, sells a €2.50 town walking tour brochure (April-Oct Mon-Sat 10:00-17:00, Fri opens at 9:00; Nov-March Mon 13:00-17:00, Tue-Sat 10:00-17:00; closed Sun year-round, Waagplein 2, tel. 072/511-4284, www.vvvalkmaar.nl).

Arrival in Alkmaar

From the train station, it's a 15-minute walk to the town center. The route is well-marked (just follow signs for *Centrum*): Exit the station to the right and veer left with the arterial down Stationsweg, then turn left (onto Scharlo) when the street dead-ends. Soon you'll cross a canal and see the big church (Grote Kerk), with the modern Stedelijk Museum to the left. From the church, walk straight up the main pedestrian street (Langestraat). When you reach the next canal, turn left and walk one more block to the main square and TI.

Sights in Alkmaar

▲▲**Cheese Market (Kaasmarkt)**—Tellingly, Alkmaar's biggest building isn't the church or the town hall, but the richly decorated **Weigh House** (Waaggebouw), used since the 16th century for weighing cheese. (It was converted from an old chapel.) The right to weigh, sell, and tax cheese is what put Alkmaar on the map in the Middle Ages, and it's still what the town is celebrated for today.

Think about the udder importance of cheese to this culture—wheying the fact that it has long kept the Dutch economy moo-ving. If you travel through the Dutch countryside, you'll pass endless fields filled with cows, which are more reliable than crops in this marshy landscape. Because cheese offers similar nutritional value to milk, but lasts much longer without refrigeration, it was a staple on long sea voyages—and Holland was the first country to export it. Today the Netherlands remains the world's biggest cheese exporter.

There's no better time to sample a sliver of this proud wedge of Dutch culture than during Alkmaar's **cheese market,** which takes place on Fridays in the spring and summer (early April-early Sept, 10:00-12:30). Early in the morning, cheesemakers line up their giant orange wheels in neat rows on the square. Prospective buyers (mostly wholesalers) examine and sample the cheeses and make their selections. Then the cheese is sold off with much fanfare, as an emcee narrates the action (in Dutch and English). To close the deal, costumed cheese carriers run the giant wheels back and forth to the Weigh House just as they have for centuries: They load a wheel onto a "cheese-barrow"—kind of a wooden stretcher—then sling each end over their shoulders on ropes and run it to and fro. The cheese carriers' guild has four "fraternities" of seven carriers each: red, yellow, blue, and green (with color-coded hats, cheese-barrows, and scales). Each fraternity is headed by a "cheese father," who enforces the strict rules and levies fines on carriers who show up late or drink beer before carrying cheese (which is strictly forbidden).

On cheese-market days, the town erupts in a carnival atmosphere, becoming one big street fair with festive entertainers and vendors selling souvenirs, snacks...and, of course, cheese. It can get crowded—especially midmorning—but the Cheese Museum (below) is surprisingly empty, and its windows allow great unobstructed views of the action below.

▲**Cheese Museum (Het Hollands Kaas Museum)**—This is probably the Netherlands' best cheese museum...and in this country, that's saying something. With displays on two floors above the TI in the Weigh House, the museum explains both traditional and modern methods of cheesemaking. You'll learn that as the economy evolved, cheesemaking went from being the work of farmers' wives to factory workers. You'll find old equipment (much of it still used for today's cheese market), such as big scales, wagons, cheese-barrows, and (upstairs) old presses for squeezing the last bit of whey out of the cheese molds. Ask for an English showing of the 15-minute movie that traces the history and traditions of Alkmaar cheesemaking. (You'll find out what a "cheesehead" really is, and the technical difference between Gouda and Edam cheeses.) Other, smaller screens around the museum show informative movies—press the flag for English subtitles (€3; April-Oct Mon-Sat 10:00-16:00, Fri from 9:00 during cheese market, closed

Sun; closed Nov-March except open Sat 10:00-16:00; enter TI at Waagplein 2 and walk up the stairs to the museum, tel. 072/515-5516, www.cheesemuseum.com).

Beer Museum (Nationaal Biermuseum De Boom)—This hokey old museum, in a former brewery, shows off an endearing collection about beer production across the centuries—from the days of barrels to the earliest bottling plants. The 1700s-era replica bar has sand on the floor, from a time when men were men and didn't have to aim into a spittoon. While interesting, the museum's explanations are scant (pick up the English descriptions as you enter). If you're not a beer-lover or a backyard brewer, I'd skip it (€3.50, Mon-Sat 13:00-16:00, Fri from 10:00 during cheese market, closed Sun, across Waagplein from the Weigh House at Houttil 1, tel. 072/511-3801, www.biermuseum.nl).

Grote Kerk—Alkmaar's "Great Church" is similar to others in Holland (such as Haarlem's and Delft's). Visit if you want to see a typically austere Dutch interior (€2.50, April-early Sept Tue-Sat 10:00-17:00, Sun 12:00-17:00, closed Mon; off-season open only for concerts and special events). The church hosts frequent concerts (for schedules, call 072/514-0707 or see www.grotekerk-alkmaar.nl).

Stedelijk Museum Alkmaar—The Stedelijk, which has its primary collection in Amsterdam, also runs this worthwhile branch in little Alkmaar. The museum has two parts: a permanent collection about the history of Alkmaar and a space for temporary exhibits. The 15-minute movie in the town history section is excellent, enlivened by props and sound effects (ask to see it in English). But the rest of the history exhibit—with stiff group portraits, other paintings, and artifacts from the town's illustrious past—is only in Dutch and difficult for nonlocals to appreciate. Visit here only if the temporary exhibit intrigues you (€6, Tue-Sun 10:00-17:00, closed Mon, Canadaplein 1, tel. 072/548-9789, www.stedelijk museumalkmaar.nl).

Alkmaar Connections

Alkmaar is connected by frequent fast trains to **Amsterdam** (4/hour, 40 minutes). However, these trains do not stop at the Zaanse Schans museum (see next page). To visit the **Zaanse Schans** museum on your way back to Amsterdam, take a train from Alkmaar to Uitgeest (2/hour), where you can transfer to a slower regional train (typically just across the platform) to Koog-Zaandijk (sometimes abbreviated as "Koog Z"; trip takes 40 minutes total). On busy days, the info desk in the tunnel of the Alkmaar train station hands out schedules for this connection.

Zaanse Schans Open-Air Museum

This re-created 17th-century town puts Dutch culture—from cheesemaking to wooden-shoe carving—on a Lazy Susan. Located on the Zaan River in the town of Zaandijk, the museum is devoted to the traditional lifestyles along the Zaan—once lined with hundreds of windmills, used for every imaginable purpose, and today heavily industrialized (including a giant corporate chocolate factory you'll pass on the way). In the 1960s, houses from around the region were transplanted here to preserve traditional culture. Most of the exhibits are run by quirky locals who've found their niche in life, and do it with gusto.

Zaanse Schans (ZAHN-ze skhahns), a hodgepodge of loosely related attractions in a pretty park with old houses, feels less like a museum than Arnhem's or Enkhuizen's open-air museums. And, since each attraction charges a separate entry fee (and those that are free are either selling or promoting something), it also feels more crassly commercial...you'll be nickel-and-dimed for your cultural education. But it's undeniably handy, just 15 minutes by train (plus a 15-minute walk) from downtown Amsterdam. Two of the attractions here—the Dutch Clock Museum and the tourable, working windmills—are unique and genuinely interesting. Because it's the easiest one-stop look at the Netherlands' traditional culture, Zaanse Schans can be flooded at midday by busloads of tour groups. To avoid the hordes, come early or late.

Orientation

Cost and Hours: Entry is free, but it costs a euro or two to visit each historical presentation. If you'll be visiting the main Zaans Museum and at least one windmill, you'll save a little money with the €9.50 **Zaanse Schans Card** (also gives you discounts at some shops and cafés). The grounds are open all the time because people actually live here. During the spring and summer (April-Sept), most of the building interiors are open daily 9:00-17:00 (though many are closed Mon, and individual opening and closing times can vary by up to an hour, as noted below in each listing). After about 16:30, things get really quiet. In the off-season (Oct-March), only some of the buildings are open (roughly 9:00-17:00 on Sat-Sun, shorter hours or closed entirely Mon-Fri; specific month-to-month hours listed at www.zaanseschans-museum.nl).

Getting There: From Amsterdam, catch a slow **train** going toward Uitgeest (4/hour, €2.80 one-way, €5.30 day return), ride for about 15 minutes, then hop out at Koog-Zaandijk (or "Koog Z"). Reaching Koog-Zaandijk from Alkmaar requires a change in Uitgeest (see "Alkmaar Connections," earlier).

Once at the Koog-Zaandijk station, it's about a 15-minute walk to the museum (well-marked, just follow the signs... and the other tourists). Go through the underpass and exit straight ahead, watching on your left for a TI machine where you can pull the crank to get a map. Then continue straight until the road forks. (If this area seems surprisingly sweet-smelling for an industrial district, thank the nearby chocolate factory.) From the fork, follow *Zaanse Schans* signs. Turn left, then right across the river, which puts you at the "back entrance" to the park, near the Clock Museum (signs to *Ned. Uurwerkmuseum*).

If **driving** from Amsterdam, take A-8 (direction: Zaanstad/Purmerend), turn off at *Purmerend A-7*, then follow signs to *Zaanse Schans* (parking-€7).

Information and Services: The visitors center, located in the Zaans Museum building, has a good, free map of the grounds. Ask if any events are scheduled for that day (daily 9:00-17:00, lockers, free WCs in museum, otherwise €0.50 in park, tel. 075/681-0000, www.zaanseschans-museum.nl).

Self-Guided Tour

I've arranged these sights in order from the train station. Drivers should park at the Zaans Museum and then visit these in reverse order, or walk five minutes to the Dutch Clock Museum and begin there.

▲**Dutch Clock Museum (Museum van het Nederlandse Uurwerk)**—More interesting than it sounds, this collection is brought to life by its curator, clock enthusiast Pier van Leeuwen. If he's not too busy, Pier can show you around and will lovingly describe his favorite pieces. (Or pick up the free brochure and explore seven centuries' worth of timepieces on your own.) Upstairs is a big, bulky, crank-wound turret clock from around 1520. Back then, the length of an "hour" wasn't fixed—there were simply 12 of them between sunrise and sunset, so the clock's weights could be adjusted to modify the length of an hour at different times of year. Also up here are the museum's prized possessions: two of the world's four surviving, original 17th-century pendulum clocks, which allowed for more precision in timekeeping. Downstairs, appreciate the fine craftsmanship of the Zaans clocks (one clock is wound by being pushed up on a rack, rather than pulling a chain) and Amsterdam clocks (€6; April-Oct Tue-Sun 10:00-17:00, closed Mon; Nov-Dec Sat-Sun only 12:00-16:30, closed Mon-Fri; Jan-March open Sun only 11:00-17:00, closed Mon-Sat; tel. 075/617-9769, www.mnuurwerk.nl).

• *Next door is the...*

Albert Heijn Grocery "Museum" (Museumwinkel)—Little more than a thinly veiled advertisement for the Dutch supermarket chain, this replica grocery store from the 1880s re-creates the first shop run by Albert Heijn. The scant exhibits lead you to a room promoting Heijn coffee (free, get English description sheet; Easter-Oct Tue-Sun 11:00-13:00 & 13:30-16:00, closed Mon; Nov-Easter Sat-Sun only 12:00-16:00, closed Mon-Fri; tel. 075/616-9619).

• *A few doors up the street is the recommended De Hoop op d'Swarte Walvis restaurant. Just beyond is the dock for the...*

Boat Cruise (Rederij de Schans Rondvaarten)—This 45-minute boat tour floats visitors through the park and adjacent town (€6; departs on the hour April-June Tue-Sat 12:00-15:00, Sun 11:00-16:00, closed Mon; July-Aug daily 11:00-16:00; Sept Tue-Sun 12:00-15:00, closed Mon; closed Oct-March; tel. 065/329-4467, www.rederijdeschans.nl).

• *From here, enjoy a lovely view of the windmills. But before you go on to visit them, poke into the little village area across from the boat landing. First you'll pass an adorable curiosity shop that's a pack-rat's heaven. Then you'll encounter the...*

Bakery Museum (Bakkerijmuseum)—This fragrant and very modest "museum" displays old bakery equipment (including cookie molds) and sells what it bakes. Borrow the English descriptions to navigate the slapdash exhibit (€1 to enter museum, various treats available—most around €2.50, March-Oct Tue-Sun 10:00-17:00; Nov-April Sat-Sun only 11:00-17:00, closed Tue-Fri; closed Mon year-round, tel. 075/617-3522).

• *Now head for the...*

▲**Windmills (Molens)**—The very industrious Zaan region is typified by these hardworking windmills, which you'll see everywhere. Mills are built with sturdy oak timber frames to withstand the constant tension of movement. To catch the desired amount of wind, millers—like expert sailors—know just how much to unfurl the sails. When the direction of the wind shifts, the miller turns the cap of the building, which weighs several tons, to face the breeze.

You can tour several of Zaanse Schans' old-fashioned windmills, each one used for a different purpose (€3 per mill, hours vary, tel. 075/621-5148, www.zaansemolen.nl). **De Gekroonde Poelenburg** is a sawmill, where stout logs are turned into building lumber (open sporadically). **De Kat** ("The Cat") grinds dyes. Watch its gigantic millstones rolling over the colored dust again and again, as wooden chutes keep it on its path. Climb the steep steps (practically a ladder) for a closer look at the wooden gears and the fine views out over the museum grounds (April-June and Sept-Oct Tue-Sun 9:00-17:00, closed Mon; July-Aug daily 9:00-17:00;

Nov-March Sat-Sun only 9:30-16:30, closed Mon-Fri). **De Zoeker** ("The Seeker") crushes oil from seeds and nuts, a drop at a time—up to an incredible 100 quarts per day (March-Oct Sun-Fri 9:30-16:30 except closed Sun in March, closed Nov-Feb and Sat year-round). Other mills may also be open for your visit. If deciding which mill to visit, choose one that's spinning—you'll see more action inside. And though these structures appear graceful, and even whimsical from the outside, on a windy day you can really experience the awesome power of the mills by getting up close to their grinding gears.

• *After exploring the windmills, cross the little canal to the big...*

De Catharina Hoeve Cheese Farm (Kaasmakerij)—Essentially a giant cheese shop, this is worthwhile only if you catch one of their presentations. A movie shows how cheese is made, and periodically a costumed Dutch maiden explains the process in person (about five quarts of milk are used to make about a pound of cheese) and dispenses samples...followed by a confident sales pitch (free entry, daily April-Oct 9:00-18:00, Nov-March 9:00-17:00, tel. 075/621-5820, www.henriwillig.com).

• *Walk past the mini-windmill to a shopping zone, which includes the...*

Wooden Shoe Workshop (Klompenmakerij)—More engaging than the park's other free attractions, this shoe store features a well-presented display of clogs from different regions of the Netherlands. You'll see how clogs were adapted for various purposes, including wooden clogs with boot-like leather to the knee, frilly decorative bridal clogs, high-heel clogs, roller-skate clogs, and spiky clogs for ice fishing. Watch the videos, and try to catch the live demonstration that sends wood chips flying as a machine carves a shoe. Your visit ends—where else?—in the vast clog shop (free entry, daily April-Oct 9:00-18:00, Nov-March 9:00-17:00, tel. 075/617-7121, www.woodenshoeworkshop.nl).

• *Nearby is the recommended De Kraai restaurant, and just across the big parking lot is the final attraction, the...*

▲**Zaans Museum and Verkade Pavilion**—This museum, with a modern structure that evokes both the hull of a ship and the curved body of a whale, is the focal point of the complex. In addition to housing the visitors center, it has a fresh, modern multimedia presentation that explains Holland's industrial past and present with the help of a good, included audioguide. The exhibit, with some English descriptions, is thematically divided into four parts: life, work, wind, and water.

The other half of the building is given over to Verkade, a beloved Dutch brand of cookie (translations here use the British "biscuit"). The pavilion is essentially a very slick version of several other "museums" around the park—thinly disguised branding opportunities for major Dutch companies. Nonetheless, this re-created cookie factory is a fun treat, thanks to the free samples, well-written explanations, and clever computer-based games. Don't miss your chance to make like Lucy and Ethel and try to see how many virtual cookies you can pack off a speeding conveyor belt and into a box—my score: 1,253 (€7.50, daily 10:00-17:00, tel. 075/681-0000, www.zaanseschans-museum.nl).

Eating at the Zaanse Schans Open-Air Museum

Pannenkoeken Restaurant de Kraai, located in the open-air museum, is a self-service eatery offering traditional sweet and savory pancakes (€8-10 pancakes; Feb-Oct daily 9:00-18:00; Nov-Dec daily 10:00-17:00; Jan Sat-Sun only 10:00-17:00, closed Mon-Fri; on slow days may close earlier, indoor and outdoor seating).

De Hoop op d'Swarte Walvis ("The Hope of the Black Whale") is the park's splurge, with a white-tablecloth interior, outdoor seating, and an ambitiously priced menu (€6-7 sandwiches, €30-35 main dishes at dinner, daily 11:00-22:00 except closed Sun in Feb, dinner served 18:00-21:30, tel. 075/616-5629).

BELGIUM

BELGIUM

Belgium falls through the cracks. It's nestled between Germany, France, and Netherlands, and it's famous for waffles, sprouts, and a statue of a little boy peeing. No wonder many travelers don't even consider a stop here. But visitors find that Belgium is one of Europe's best-kept secrets. There are tourists—but not as many as the country's charms merit. After all, Belgium produces some of Europe's best beer, creamiest chocolates, most beloved comic strips, and tastiest french fries. From funky urban neighborhoods to tranquil *begijnhofs*, from old-fashioned lace to cutting-age Euro-fashions, from cows mooing in a pastoral countryside to gentrified Hanseatic cityscapes bristling with spires...Belgium delights.

Ten and a half million Belgians are packed into a country only a little bigger than Maryland. With nearly 900 people per square mile, it's the second most densely populated country in Europe (after the Netherlands). This population concentration, coupled with a well-lit rail and road system, causes Belgium to shine at night when viewed from space—a phenomenon NASA astronauts call the "Belgian Window."

Belgium is divided—linguistically, culturally, and politically—between Wallonia in the south, where they speak French, and Flanders in the north, where they speak Flemish—an old sailors' dialect that's even more guttural than textbook Dutch (insert your own "phlegmish" pun here). There's also a small minority of German-speakers, in a far-eastern region that once belonged to Germany. Even though about 60 percent of the population speaks Flemish, French-speakers have politically dominated the nation for most of its history—a source of much resentment for the Flemish. Talk to locals to learn how deep the cultural rift is (for starters, read the sidebar on page 328).

Though mostly French-speaking, Belgium's capital, Brussels,

is officially bilingual. Because of Brussels' international importance as the capital of the European Union, more than 25 percent of its residents are foreigners.

It's here in Belgium that Europe comes together: where Romance languages meet Germanic languages; Catholics meet Protestants; and the BeNeLux union was established 40 years ago, planting the seed that today is sprouting into the unification of Europe. Belgium flies the flag of Europe more vigorously than any other place on the Continent.

That could be, in part, because history hasn't been very kind to little Belgium—surrounded, as it is, by much bigger and more powerful nations: France, Germany, the Netherlands, and Britain, each of which has at one time or another found Belgium a barrier on its march to empire. After putting up with tyrants from Charlemagne to the Austrian Habsburgs to Napoleon, Belgium paid the costliest price in both World Wars—most notably at Flanders Fields near Ypres (Ieper) in World War I, and at the Battle of the Bulge near Bastogne in World War II. But its crossroads location has also made Belgium stronger: Belgians are savvy businesspeople, excellent linguists, and talented chefs who've learned how to blend together delicious culinary influences from various cultures.

Belgians have a directness that some find refreshing (and

BELGIUM

The Battle for Belgium: Flemish vs. French

Although little, peace-loving Belgium—whose capital, Brussels, is also the capital of the European Union—seems like a warm and cozy place, its society is split right down the middle by a surprisingly contentious linguistic divide with roots dating back to the nation's inception: the Flemish people of Flanders versus the French-speakers of Wallonia.

In 1830, Belgium's Francophone (French-speaking) aristocracy led the drive for independence from the Netherlands. They said, "Belgium will be French, or will not be." And so it was: Linguistic and cultural oppression ruled the day, as the Flemish language was suppressed as unworthy of higher thinking. Even in Flanders, where Flemish people are the majority, most power has traditionally been in the hands of the Francophone bourgeoisie. Education at prestigious universities, for example, was only in French.

The Flemish often feel they'd have been better off had Belgium remained part of the Netherlands...which would have respected their native tongue in their homeland. That's why most Flemish people are not particularly nationalistic about their language—rather than being blinded by Flemish pride, they readily acknowledge that Flemish and Dutch are essentially the same.

Today's Flemish baby boomers remember feeling picked on by their Francophone classmates. To travelers, it almost seems as if Flanders and Wallonia are different countries. For example,

others term brusque), and revel in their sardonic sense of humor. They're not particularly romantic or melodramatic, and—with the wry glimmer in their eye—it can be hard to tell whether they're putting you on. This ties in with their appreciation for a good comic strip. The "ninth art" of comics is deeply respected in Belgium. Some of the world's most beloved comic characters—including the Smurfs and Tintin—were created by Belgians. If you ask a twentysomething Belgian what career they're pursuing, and he or she says "comic books," nobody snickers.

From an accommodations point of view, the Flemish forte is its variety of cozy, funky, affordable B&Bs well-run by gregarious entrepreneurs and typically located up a flight or two of steep, narrow stairs. I've listed my favorite B&Bs in each town (except in Brussels, where they're rare).

Bruges and Brussels are the best two first bites of Belgium. Bruges is a wonderfully preserved medieval gem that expertly nurtures its tourist industry, bringing the town a prosperity it hasn't enjoyed for 500 years, when—as one of the largest cities in the world—it helped lead northern Europe out of the Middle Ages.

each region has its own "national" tourist office, which effectively ignores the other half of the country.

In 1970, Belgium began a gradual process of decentralizing its government (loosely following the Swiss cantonal model), and giving more administrative autonomy to its three regions: Flemish-speaking Flanders, French-speaking Wallonia, and the bilingual city-state of Brussels. Incremental reforms over the last 40 years have separated the Flemish and the Francophones more and more. Each group can now more closely pursue its own agenda, but the flipside is that the country is not as effortlessly bilingual as before. A generation ago, virtually every Belgian spoke both Flemish and French. Today, Flemish students can choose whether to take French or English as a second language... and many choose English. On my last visit to Brussels, I saw a sign in a shop window saying, "Bilingual staff wanted." What used to be commonplace is becoming a rarity.

Despite all the reforms, the longstanding Flemish-Francophone rivalry has flared up again in the last couple of years. Of Belgium's many political parties, the Nieuw-Vlaamse Alliantie (N-VA), which advocates for the secession of Flanders from Belgium altogether, won the highest percentage of the vote in 2010 elections (both in Flanders and in Belgium over-all). It's conceivable that a day may come in the not-too-distant future when a unified "Belgium" no longer exists on the map of Europe.

Brussels is simply one of Europe's great cities. With the finest town square in the country (if not the Continent), a chocolate shop on every corner, a French taste for class and cuisine, and a smatter-ing of intriguing museums, it's equally ideal for a quick stopover as it is for a multiday visit.

With more time, two other Belgian cities are worth visiting. Historic, Old World Ghent—with a proud history as an impor-tant trading and university town—is well-preserved and pictur-esque, packed with charming little museums. And big, bustling Antwerp—with a port that rivals Rotterdam as Europe's largest—has recently enjoyed a dramatic renaissance. It's gone from being a dirty, dangerous, and depressing city to a trendy, newly spiffed-up mecca with fun boutiques, lively neighborhoods, fine muse-ums, and a youthful vibe. To round out your Belgian experience, spend a few hours in the Flemish countryside around the town of Ypres—both for the pastoral scenery, and to visit World War I's Flanders Fields.

While not "undiscovered" (especially popular Bruges), Belgium is certainly underrated. Those who squeeze in a day or two

Belgium Almanac

Official Name: Royaume de Belgique/Koninkrijk België, or simply Belgique in French and België in Flemish.

Population: Of its 10.5 million people, 58 percent are Flemish, 31 percent are Walloon, and 11 percent are "mixed or other." About three-quarters are Catholic, and the rest are Protestant or other.

Latitude and Longitude: 50°N and 4°E. The latitude is similar to Alberta, Canada.

Area: With only 12,000 square miles, it's slightly smaller than the state of Maryland and one of the smallest countries in Europe.

Geography: Belgium's flat coastal plains in the northwest and central rolling hills make it easy to invade (just ask Napoleon or Hitler). There are some rugged mountains in the southeast Ardennes Forest. The climate is temperate.

Biggest Cities: The capital city of Brussels has about 1.8 million people, followed by Antwerp's 950,000.

Economy: With few natural resources, Belgium imports most of its raw materials and exports a large volume of manufactured goods, making its economy unusually dependent on world markets. It can be a sweet business—Belgium is the world's number-one exporter of chocolate. It's prosperous, with a Gross Domestic Product of $383 billion and a GDP per capita of $36,800. As the "crossroads" of Europe, Brussels is the headquarters of NATO and the capital of the European Union.

Government: A parliamentary democracy, Belgium's official head of state is King Albert II. Regional tensions dominate politics: Flemish-speaking, entrepreneurial Flanders wants more autonomy, while the French-speaking "rust belt" of Wallonia is reluctant to give it. The division has made it increasingly difficult for the Belgian Parliament to form a stable coalition government. One prime minister recently said that Belgians are united only by the king, a love of beer, and the national soccer team. Voting is compulsory. More than 90 percent of registered voters participated in the last general election (compared with approximately 62 percent in the US).

Flag: Belgium's flag is composed of three vertical bands of black, yellow, and red.

The Average Belgian: The average Belgian is 42 years old—five years older than the average American—and will live to be 79. He or she is also likely to be divorced—Belgium has the highest divorce rate in Europe, with 60 for every 100 marriages. Beer is the national beverage: on average, Belgians drink 26 gallons a year, just behind the Austrians and just ahead of the Brits.

BELGIUM

for Belgium wish they had more time. Like sampling a flavorful praline in a chocolate shop, that first enticing taste just leaves you wanting more. Go ahead, it's OK...buy a whole box of Belgium.

Belgian Cuisine

Belgians brag that they eat as much as the Germans and as well as the French. They are among the world's leading carnivores and beer consumers. Belgium is where France meets northern Europe, and you'll find a good mix of both Flemish and French influences here. The Flemish were ruled by the French and absorbed some of the fancy cuisine and etiquette of their overlords. (The Dutch, on the other hand, were ruled by the Spanish for 80 years and picked up nothing.) And yet, once Belgian, always Belgian: Instead of cooking with wine, Belgians have perfected the art of cooking with their own unique beers, imbuing the cuisine with a hoppy sweetness.

Belgians eat lunch when we do, but they eat dinner later (if you dine earlier than 19:30 at a restaurant, you'll eat alone or with other tourists). Tax and service are always included in your bill (though a 5-10 percent tip is appreciated). You can't get free tap water; Belgian restaurateurs are emphatic about that. Tap water comes with a smile in the Netherlands, France, and Germany, but that's not the case in Belgium, where you'll either pay for water, enjoy the beer, or go thirsty.

Belgian Specialties

Although this book's coverage focuses on the Flemish part of the country, people speak French first in Brussels—so both languages are given below (Flemish/French); if I've listed only one word, it's used nationwide. While the French influence is evident every-where, it's ratcheted up around Brussels.

Traditional Dishes

Stoofvlees/Carbonnade: Rich beef stew flavored with onions, beer, and mustard. It's often quite sweet (sweetened with brown sugar or gingerbread). It's similar to the French beef bourgui-gnon, but made with beer instead of red wine.

(Gentse) Waterzooi: Creamy soup made with chicken, eel, or fish; originated in Ghent.

Konijn met pruimen/lapin à la flamande: Marinated rabbit braised in onions and prunes.

Filet américain: Beware—for some reason, steak tartare (raw) is called "American."

Biersoep/soupe à la bière: Beer soup—though remember that beer can be included in just about any dish.

BELGIUM

...à la flamande: Anything cooked in the Flemish style, which generally means with beer.

Seafood

Mosselen/moules: Mussels are served everywhere, either cooked plain *(natuur/nature),* with white wine *(witte wijn/vin blanc),* with shallots or onions *(marinière),* or in a tomato sauce *(provençale).* You get a big-enough-for-two bucket and a pile of fries. Go local by using one empty shell to tweeze out the rest of the *mosselen.* When the mollusks are in season, from about mid-July through April, you'll get the big Dutch mussels (most are from the coastal area called Zeeland, just north of Belgium). Locals take a break from mussels in May and June, when only the puny Danish kind are available.

Noordzee garnalen/crevettes: Little gray shrimp, generally served in one of two ways: inside a carved-out tomato or in croquettes (minced and stuffed in breaded, deep-fried rolls).

Paling in het groen/anguilles au vert: Eel in green herb sauce. Although a classic dish, this is less common these days, as good-quality eel is in short supply.

Caricoles: Sea snails. Very local, seasonal, and (like eel) hard to find, these are usually sold hot by street vendors.

Vegetables and Side Dishes

Rode kol/chou rouge à la flamande: Red cabbage with onions and prunes.

Asperges: White asparagus, available only for a short time in spring, and usually served in cream sauce.

Witloof/chicoree or *chicon:* Endive, the classic Belgian vegetable, usually served as a side dish. This coarse, bitter green is eaten both raw and cooked.

Spruitjes/choux de Bruxelles: Brussels sprouts (in cream sauce).

Stoemp: Mashed potatoes and vegetables, most common in Brussels.

Snacks

Friets/frites: Belgian-style fries taste so good because they're deep-fried twice—once to cook, and once to brown. The natives eat them with mayonnaise or other flavored sauces, but not ketchup. The Dutch call them *Vlaamse frites*—"Flemish fries"—but the Flemish just call them *friets.* Look for a *frituur* (fry shop) or a *frietkot* (fry wagon).

Cheeses: While the French might use wine or alcohol to rub the rind of their cheese to infuse it with flavor, the Belgians use (surprise, surprise) beer. There are 350 types of Belgian cheeses. From Flanders, look for Vieux Brugge ("Old Bruges") and

BELGIUM

Chimay (named for the beer they use on it); from Wallonia, Remoudou and Djotte de Nivelles are good.

Croque monsieur: Grilled ham-and-cheese sandwich.

Tartine de fromage blanc: Open-face cream-cheese sandwich, often enjoyed with a cherry Kriek beer and found mostly in traditional Brussels bars.

Desserts and Sweets

Chocolates: The two basic types of Belgian chocolates are **pralines** (what we generally think of as "chocolates"—a hard chocolate shell with various fillings) and **truffles** (a softer, crumblier shell, often spherical, and also filled).

Wafels/Gaufres: Belgians recognize two general types of waffles: **Liège-style** (dense, very sweet—with a sugary crust, and heated up) and **Brussels-style** (lighter and fluffier, dusted with powdered sugar and sometimes topped with marmalade). And though Americans think of "Belgian" waffles for breakfast, Belgians generally have them (or pancakes, *pannenkoeken*) as a late-afternoon snack (around 16:00)—though the delicious Liège-style waffles are sold 'round the clock to tourists as an extremely tempting treat. You'll see little windows, shops, and trucks selling these *wafels,* either plain (for Belgians and purists) or topped with fruit, jam, chocolate sauce, ice cream, or whipped cream (for tourists). You'll find the Brussels-style waffles mostly in teahouses, and only in the afternoon (14:00-18:00).

Speculoos: Spicy gingerbread biscuits served with coffee.

Dame blanche: Chocolate sundae.

Pistolets: Round croissants.

Chocolade mousse: Just what it sounds like.

Belgian Beers

Belgium has about 120 different varieties of beer and 580 different brands, more than any other country—the locals take their beers as seriously as the French do their wines. Even small café menus include six to eight varieties. Connoisseurs and novices alike can be confused by the many choices, and casual drinkers probably won't like every kind offered, since some varieties don't even taste like beer. Belgian beer is generally yeastier and higher in alcohol content than beers in other countries.

In Belgium, certain beers are paired with certain dishes. To bring out their flavor, different beers are served at cold, cool, or room temperature, and each has its own distinctive glass. Whether wide-mouthed, tall, or fluted, with or without a stem, the glass is meant to highlight the beer's qualities. A memorable Belgian beer experience is drinking a Kwak beer in its traditional tall glass. The glass, which widens at the base, stands in a wooden holder—you pick the whole apparatus up—frame and glass—and drink. As you near the end, the beer in the wide bottom comes out at you quickly, with a "Kwak! Kwak! Kwak!" Critics say this gimmick distracts drinkers from the fact that Kwak beer is mediocre at best.

To get a draft beer in Bruges, where Flemish is the dominant language, ask for *een pintje* (ayn pinch-ya; a pint); in Brussels, where French prevails, request *une bière* (oon bee-yair). Don't insist on beer from the tap. The only way to offer so many excellent beers fresh is to serve them bottled, and the best varieties generally are available only by the bottle. "Cheers" is *proost* or *gezondheid* in Flemish, and *santé* (sahn-tay) in French. The colorful cardboard coasters make nice, free souvenirs.

Here's a breakdown of types of beer, with some common brand names you'll find either on tap or in bottles. (Some beers require a second fermentation in the bottle, so they're only available in bottles.) This list is just a start, and you'll find many beers that don't fall into these neat categories. For encyclopedic information on Belgian beers, visit www.belgianstyle.com.

Ales (Blonde/Red/Amber/Brown): Ales are easily recognized by their color. Try a blonde or golden ale (Leffe Blonde, Duvel), a rare and bitter sour red (Rodenbach), an amber (Palm, De Koninck), or a brown (Leffe Bruin).

Lagers: These are light, sparkling, Budweiser-type beers. Popular brands include Jupiler, Stella Artois, and Maes.

Lambics: Perhaps the most unusual and least beer-like, *lambics* are stored for years in wooden casks, fermenting from wild yeasts that occur naturally in the air. Tasting more like a dry and bitter farmhouse cider, pure *lambic* is often blended with fruits to counter the sour flavor. Some brand names include Cantillon, Lindemans, and Mort-Subite ("Sudden Death").

Fruit *lambics* include those made with cherries *(kriek)*, raspberries *(frambozen)*, peaches *(pêche)*, or blackcurrants *(cassis)*. The result for each is a tart but sweet beer, similar to a dry pink champagne. People who don't usually enjoy beer tend to like these fruit-flavored varieties.

White (Witte): Based on wheat instead of hops, these are milky-yellow summertime beers. White beer, similar to a Hefeweizen, is often flavored with spices such as orange peel or coriander.

BELGIUM

Trappist Beers: For centuries, between their vespers and matins, Trappist monks have been brewing heavily fermented, malty beers. Three typical Trappist beers (from the Westmalle monastery) are Trippel, with a blonde color, served cold with a frothy head; Dubbel, which is dark, sweet, and served cool; and Single, made especially by the monks for the monks, and considered a fair trade for a life of celibacy. Other Trappist monasteries include Rochefort, Chimay, and Orval. Try the Trappist Blauwe Chimay—extremely smooth, milkshake-like, and complex.

Strong Beers: The potent brands include Duvel (meaning "devil," because of its high octane, camouflaged by a pale color), Verboten Vrucht ("forbidden fruit," with Adam and Eve on the label), and the not-for-the-fainthearted brands of Judas, Satan, and Lucifer. Gouden Carolus is good, and Delerium Tremens speaks for itself.

Mass-Produced Beers: Connoisseurs say you should avoid the mass-produced labels (Leffe, Stella, and Hoegaarden—all owned by InBev, which owns Budweiser in America) when you can enjoy a Belgian microbrew (like Chimay) instead.

BRUGES
Brugge

ORIENTATION TO BRUGES

With pointy gilded architecture, stay-a-while cafés, vivid time-tunnel art, and dreamy canals dotted with swans, Bruges is a heavyweight sightseeing destination, as well as a joy. Where else can you ride a bike along a canal, munch mussels and wash them down with the world's best beer, savor heavenly chocolate, and see Flemish Primitives and a Michelangelo, all within 300 yards of a bell tower that jingles every 15 minutes? And do it all without worrying about a language barrier?

The town is Brugge (BROO-ghah) in Flemish, and Bruges (broozh) in French and English. Its name comes from the Viking word for wharf. Right from the start, Bruges was a trading center. In the 11th century, the city grew wealthy on the cloth trade.

By the 14th century, Bruges' population was 35,000, as large as London's. As the middleman in the sea trade between northern and southern Europe, it was one of the biggest cities in the world and an economic powerhouse. In addition, Bruges had become the most important cloth market in northern Europe.

In the 15th century, while England and France were slugging it out in the Hundred Years' War, Bruges was the favored residence of the powerful Dukes of Burgundy—and at peace. Commerce and the arts boomed. The artists Jan van Eyck and Hans Memling had studios here.

But by the 16th century, the harbor had silted up and the economy had collapsed. The Burgundian court left, Belgium became a minor Habsburg possession, and Bruges' Golden Age abruptly ended. For generations, Bruges was known as a mysterious and dead city. In the 19th century, a new port, Zeebrugge, brought renewed vitality to the area. And in the 20th century, tourists discovered the town.

Today, Bruges prospers because of tourism: It's a uniquely

well-preserved Gothic city and a handy gateway to Europe. It's no secret, but even with the crowds, it's the kind of place where you don't mind being a tourist.

Bruges' ultimate sight is the town itself, and the best way to enjoy it is to get lost on the back streets, away from the lace shops and ice-cream stands.

Planning Your Time

Bruges needs at least two nights and a full, well-organized day. Even nonshoppers enjoy browsing here, and the Belgian love of life makes a hectic itinerary seem a little senseless. With one day—other than a Monday, when the three museums are closed—the speedy visitor could do the Bruges blitz described below (also included in my Bruges City Walk):

  9:30   Climb the bell tower on the Markt (Market Square).

10:00   Tour the sights on Burg Square.

11:30   Tour the Groeninge Museum (reopened June of 2011).

13:00   Eat lunch and buy chocolates.

14:00   Take a short canal cruise.

14:30   Visit the Church of Our Lady and see Michelangelo's *Madonna and Child*.

15:00   Tour the Memling Museum.

16:00   Catch the De Halve Maan Brewery tour (note that their last tour runs at 15:00 in winter on weekdays).

17:00   Relax in the Begijnhof courtyard.

18:00   Ride a bike around the quiet back streets of town or take a horse-and-buggy tour.

20:00   Lose the tourists and find dinner.

If this schedule seems insane, skip the bell tower and the brewery—or stay another day.

Bruges Overview

The tourist's Bruges—and you'll be sharing it—is less than one square mile, contained within a canal (the former moat). Nearly everything of interest and importance is within a convenient cobbled swath between the train station and the Markt (Market Square; a 20-minute walk). Many of my quiet, charming, recommended accommodations lie just beyond the Markt.

Tourist Information

The main tourist office, called **In&Uit** ("In and Out"), is in the big, red concert hall on the square called 't Zand (daily 10:00-18:00, take a number from the touch-screen machines and wait, 't Zand 34, tel. 050-444-646, www.brugge.be). The other TI is at the train

Bruges Museum Tips

Admission prices are steep, but they include great audioguides—so plan on spending some time and really getting into it. For information on all the museums, call 050-448-711 or visit www.brugge.be.

Museum Passes: The 't Zand TI and city museums sell a **museum combo-ticket** (any five museums for €15, valid for 3 days). Because the Groeninge and Memling museums cost €8 each, art lovers will save money with this pass.

The **Brugge City Card** is a more extensive pass covering entry to 22 museums, including all the major sights (€34/48 hours, €39/72 hours, sold at TIs and many hotels). If you'll be doing some serious sightseeing, this card can save you money. Its long list of bonuses and discounts includes a free canal boat ride (March-Nov), a visitors' guide, and discounts on bike rental, parking, and some performances.

Blue Monday: In Bruges, nearly all museums are open Tuesday through Sunday year-round from 9:30 to 17:00 and are closed on Monday. If you're in Bruges on a Monday, the following attractions are open: bell-tower climb on the Markt, Begijnhof, De Halve Maan Brewery Tour, Basilica of the Holy Blood, City Hall's Gothic Room, and chocolate shops and museum. You can also join a boat, bus, or walking tour, or rent a bike and pedal into the countryside.

station (Mon-Fri 10:00-17:00, Sat-Sun 10:00-14:00).

The TIs sell the €2.50 *Love Bruges Visitors' Guide,* which comes with a map (costs €0.50 if bought separately), a few well-described self-guided walking tours, and listings of all the sights and services (free with Brugge City Card). You can also pick up a free monthly English-language program called *events@brugge* and a free, fun map/guide "made by locals for young travelers." The TIs have information on train schedules and tours (see "Tours in Bruges," later). Many hotels give out free maps with more detail than the map the TIs sell.

Arrival in Bruges

By Train: Coming in by train, you'll see the bell tower that marks the main square (Markt, the center of town). Upon arrival, stop by the train station TI to pick up the *Love Bruges Visitors' Guide* (with map). The station has ATMs and lockers (€3-4).

The best way to get to the town center is by **bus.** Buses #1-9, #11-17, and #25 go to the Markt (all marked *Centrum*). Simply hop on, pay €1.60 (€1.20 if you buy in advance at Lijnwinkel shop just outside the train station), and you're there in four minutes (get off at third stop—either Markt or Wollestraat). Buses #4 and #14 continue to the northeast part of town (to the windmills and recommended accommodations on and near Carmersstraat, stop: Gouden Handstraat). If you arrive after 20:30, when the daytime bus routes end, you can still take the bus, but the "evening line" buses run much less frequently (buses marked *Avondlijn Centrum, Avondlijn Noord*—#91, *Avondlijn Oost*—#92, and *Avondlijn Zuid*—#93 all go to the Markt).

The **taxi** fare from the train station to most hotels is about €8.

It's a 20-minute **walk** from the station to the center—no fun with your luggage. If you want to walk to the Markt, cross the busy street and canal in front of the station, head up Oostmeers, and turn right on Zwidzandstraat. You can rent a **bike** at the station for the duration of your stay, but other bike-rental shops are closer to the center (see "Helpful Hints," below).

By Car: Park in front of the train station in the handy two-story garage for just €2.50 for 24 hours. The parking fee includes a round-trip bus ticket into town and back for everyone in your car. There are pricier underground parking garages at the square called 't Zand and around town (€9/day, all of them well-marked). Paid parking on the street in Bruges is limited to four hours. Driving in town is very complicated because of the one-way system. The best plan for drivers: Park at the train station, visit the TI at the station, and rent a bike or catch a bus into town.

Helpful Hints

Market Days: Bruges hosts markets on Wednesday morning (on the Markt) and Saturday morning ('t Zand). On good-weather Saturdays, Sundays, and public holidays, a flea market hops along Dijver in front of the Groeninge Museum. The Fish Market sells souvenirs and seafood Tuesday through Saturday mornings until 13:00.

Shopping: Shops are generally open from 10:00 to 18:00. Grocery stores usually are closed on Sunday. The main shopping street, Steenstraat, stretches from the Markt to 't Zand Square. The **Hema** department store is at Steenstraat 73 (Mon-Sat 9:00-18:00, closed Sun).

Internet Access: Punjeb Internet Shop, just a block off the Markt, is the most central of the city's many "telephone shops" offering Internet access (€1.50/30 minutes, €2.50/hour, daily 9:00-20:00, Philipstockstraat 4). **Bean Around the World** is a cozy coffeehouse with imported Yankee snacks and free

Wi-Fi for customers (€1/15 minutes on their computers, Thu-Mon 10:00-19:00, Wed 11:30-19:00, closed Tue, Genthof 5, tel. 050-703-572, run by American expat Olene).

Post Office: It's on the Markt near the bell tower (Mon-Fri 9:00-18:00, Sat 9:30-15:00, closed Sun, tel. 050-331-411).

Laundry: Bruges has three self-service launderettes, each a five-minute walk from the center; ask your hotelier for the nearest one.

Bike Rental: Bruges Bike Rental is central and cheap, with friendly service and long hours (€3.50/hour, €5/2 hours, €7/4 hours, €10/day, show this book to get student rate—€8/day, no deposit required—just ID, daily 10:00-22:00, free city maps and child seats, behind the far-out iron facade at Niklaas Desparsstraat 17, tel. 050-616-108, Bilal). **Fietsen Popelier Bike Rental** is also good (€4/hour, €8/4 hours, €12/day, 24-hour day is OK if your hotel has a safe place to store bike, no deposit required, daily 10:00-19:00, sometimes open later in summer, free Damme map, Mariastraat 26, tel. 050-343-262). **Koffieboontje Bike Rental** is just under the bell tower on the Markt (€4/hour, €9/day, €20/day for tandem, these prices for Rick Steves readers, daily 9:00-22:00, free city maps and child seats, Hallestraat 4, tel. 050-338-027).

Other rental places include the less-central **De Ketting** (cheap at €6/day, Mon-Fri 9:00-12:15 & 13:30-18:30 except Mon opens at 10:00, Sat 9:30-12:15, closed Sun, Gentpoortstraat 23, tel. 050-344-196, www.deketting.be) and **Fietspunt Brugge** at the train station (€9.50/day, €6.50/half-day after 14:00, €13 deposit, Mon-Fri 7:00-19:30, closed Sat-Sun, just outside the station and to the left as you exit, tel. 050-302-329).

Best Town View: The bell tower overlooking the Markt rewards those who climb it with the ultimate town view.

Getting Around Bruges

Most of the city is easily walkable, but you may want to take the bus or taxi between the train station and the city center at the Markt (especially if you have heavy luggage).

By Bus: A bus ticket is good for an hour (€1.20 if you buy in advance at Lijnwinkel shop just outside the train station, or €1.60 on the bus). And though you can buy various day passes, there's really no need to buy one for your visit. Nearly all city buses go directly from the train station to the Markt and fan out from there;

they then return to the Markt and go back to the train station. Note that buses returning to the train station from the Markt also leave from the library bus stop, a block off the square on nearby Kuiperstraat (every 5 minutes). Your key: Use buses that say either *Station* or *Centrum*.

By Taxi: You'll find taxi stands at the station and on the Markt (€8/first 2 km; to get a cab in the center, call 050-334-444 or 050-333-881).

Tours in Bruges

Bruges by Boat—The most relaxing and scenic (though not informative) way to see this city of canals is by boat, with the cap-

tain narrating. The city carefully controls this standard tourist activity, so the many companies all offer essentially the same thing: a 30-minute route (roughly 4/hour, daily 10:00-17:00), a price of €7 (cash only), and narration in three or four languages. Qualitative differences are because of individual guides, not companies. Always let them know you speak English to ensure you'll understand the spiel. Two companies give the group-rate discount to individuals with this book: Boten Stael (just over the canal from Memling Museum at Katelijnestraat 4, tel. 050-332-771) and Gruuthuse (Nieuwstraat 11, opposite Groeninge Museum, tel. 050-333-393).

Bruges by Bike—**QuasiMundo Bike Tours** leads daily five-mile English-language bike tours around the city (€25, €3 discount with this book, 2.5 hours, departs March-Oct at 10:00, in Nov only with good weather, no tours Dec-Feb). For more details and contact info, see their listing under "Near Bruges," later.

City Minibus Tour—City Tour Bruges gives a rolling overview of the town in an 18-seat, two-skylight minibus with dial-a-language headsets and video support (€14.50, 50 minutes, pay driver). The tour leaves hourly from the Markt (10:00-20:00 in summer, until 19:00 in spring, until 18:00 in fall, less in winter, tel. 050-355-024, www.citytour.be). The narration, though clear, is slow-moving and a bit boring. But the tour is a lazy way to cruise past virtually every sight in Bruges.

Walking Tour—Local guides walk small groups through the core of town (€9, 2 hours, daily July-Aug, Sat-Sun only mid-April-June and Sept-Oct, depart from TI on 't Zand Square at 14:30—just drop in a few minutes early and buy tickets at the TI desk). Though earnest, the tours are heavy on history and given in two languages,

Bruges

SEE HOTEL & RESTAURANT DETAIL MAPS

Sights & Services
1. In&Uit Tourist Info (in Concert Hall)
2. De Halve Maan Brewery Tour
3. Dumon Chocolate
4. The Chocolate Line
5. Confiserie De Clerck
6. Choco-Story: The Chocolate Museum
7. Friet Museum
8. Internet Café
9. Bike Rentals (5)
10. City Minibus Tours

Accommodations & Restaurants
11. Hotel Egmond
12. Hotel 't Keizershof
13. To Waterside B&B
14. To B&B AM/PM
15. Snuffel Backpacker Hostel
16. Bistro de Bekoring

P PARKING
B BOAT TOURS
Ⓑ BUS
≗ VIEW

1/4 MILE
400 METERS

so they may be less than peppy. Still, to propel you beyond the pretty gables and canal swans of Bruges, they're good medicine. In the off-season, "winter walks" leave from the same TI four evenings a week (€9, Nov-Feb Sat-Mon and Wed at 17:00).

Local Guide—A private two-hour guided tour costs €50 (reserve at least one week in advance through TI, tel. 050-448-686). Or contact Christian Scharlé and Daniëlle Janssens, who give two-hour walks for €70, three-hour guided drives for €150, and full-day tours of Bruges and Brussels for €200 (Christian's mobile 0475-659-507, Daniëlle's mobile 0476-493-203, www.tourmanagement belgium.be, tmb@skynet.be).

Horse-and-Buggy Tour—The buggies around town can take you on a clip-clop tour (€36, 35 minutes; price is per carriage, not per person; buggies gather in Minnewater, near entrance to Begijnhof). When divided among four or five people, this can be a good value.

Near Bruges

Popular tour destinations from Bruges are Flanders Fields (famous WWI sites about 40 miles to the southwest; see that chapter for more information) and the picturesque town of Damme (4 easy-to-bike miles to the northeast).

Quasimodo Countryside Tours—This company offers those with extra time two entertaining, all-day, English-only bus tours through the rarely visited Flemish countryside. The "Flanders Fields" tour concentrates on WWI battlefields, trenches, memorials, and poppy-splattered fields (Tue-Sun at 9:15, no tours Mon or in Jan, 8 hours, visit to In Flanders Fields Museum not included). The other tour, "Triple Treat," focuses on Flanders' medieval past and rich culture, with tastes of chocolate, waffles, and beer (departs Mon, Wed, and Fri at 9:15, 8 hours). Be ready for lots of walking.

Tours cost €60, or €50 if you're under 26 (cash preferred, €10 discount on second tour if you've taken the other, includes sandwich lunch, 9- or 30-seat bus depending on demand, non-smoking, reservations required—call 050-370-470, www.quasimodo.be). After making a few big-hotel pickups, the buses leave town from the Park Hotel on 't Zand Square (arrange for pickup when you reserve).

Flanders Fields Battlefield Daytours by Nathan—Nathan (or his right-hand man, Karl) leads small groups on minibus day trips to the WWI sights between here and Ypres (Ieper). While pricier than Quasimodo's tour (listed above), Nathan's are more intimate: eight travelers on a minibus rather than a big busload (allowing your guide to tailor the tours to passengers' interests and nationalities); pickup from any hotel or B&B (because the small bus is allowed in the town center); and an included restaurant lunch instead of a picnic. Nathan's tours also include free time at the excellent museums in Ypres and Passchendaele (€65, €3 discount when booked direct using this book, price includes admissions, cash only, departs Tue-Sun around 8:45 from your hotel or B&B, 8.5 hours, call 050-346-060 or toll-free 0800-99133 to reserve, www.visitbruges.org, info@visitbruges.org). In the evening, Nathan offers a shorter **Last Post Evening Tour,** with a stop at Tyne Cot Cemetery en route to the moving 20:00 bugle call at the Menin Gate in Ypres (€40, no discounts, departs Tue-Sun around 18:15 from your B&B/hotel, returns to Bruges around 21:15).

Bike Tours—QuasiMundo Bike Tours, which runs bike tours around Bruges (listed earlier), also offers a daily "Border by Bike"

tour through the nearby countryside to Damme (€25, €3 discount with this book, March-Oct, departs at 13:00, 15 miles, 4 hours, tel. 050-330-775, www.quasimundo.com). Both their city and border tours include bike rental, a light raincoat (if necessary), water, and a drink in a local café. Meet at the metal "car wash" fountain on Burg Square 10 minutes before departure. If you already have a bike, you're welcome to join either tour for €15. Jos, who leads most departures, is a high-energy and entertaining guide.

Charming Mieke of **Pink Bear Bike Tours** takes small groups

on an easy and delightful 3.5-hour guided pedal along a canal to the historic town of Damme and back, finishing with a brief tour of Bruges. English tours go daily through peak season and nearly daily the rest of the year (€22, €2 discount with this book, €15 if you already have a bike, meet at 10:25 under bell tower on the Markt, tel. 050-616-686, mobile 0476-744-525, www.pinkbear.freeservers.com).

For a do-it-yourself bike tour, see page 355. For bike rental shops in Bruges, see page 342.

SIGHTS IN BRUGES

These sights are listed in walking order, from the Markt (Market Square), to Burg Square, to the cluster of museums around the Church of Our Lady, to the Begijnhof (10-minute walk from beginning to end, without stops). For a self-guided walk and more information on the major sights, see the Bruges City Walk chapter.

▲**Markt (Market Square)**—Ringed by a bank, the post office, lots of restaurant terraces, great old gabled buildings, and the iconic bell tower, this square is the modern heart of the city (most city buses run from near here to the train station—it's a block down Kuiperstraat at the library bus stop). Under the bell tower are two great Belgian-style french-fry stands, a quadrilingual Braille description of the old town, and a metal model of the tower. In Bruges' heyday as a trading center, a canal came right up to this square. Geldmuntstraat, just off the square, is a delightful street with many fun and practical shops and eateries.

▲▲**Bell Tower (Belfort)**—Most of this bell tower has presided over the Markt since 1300, serenading passersby with carillon music. The octagonal lantern was added in 1486, making it 290 feet high—that's 366 steps. The view is worth the climb and probably even the €8 (daily 9:30-17:00, 16:15 last-entry time strictly enforced—best to show up before 16:00, €0.30 WC in courtyard).

▲▲**Burg Square**—This opulent square is Bruges' civic center, the historic birthplace of Bruges, and the site of the ninth-century castle of the first count of Flanders. Today, it's an atmospheric place to take in an outdoor concert while surrounded by six centuries of architecture.

▲**Basilica of the Holy Blood**—Originally the Chapel of Saint Basil, this church is famous for its relic of the blood of Christ, which, according to tradition, was brought to Bruges in 1150 after the Second Crusade. The lower chapel is dark and solid—a fine example of Romanesque style. The upper chapel (separate entrance, climb the stairs) is decorated Gothic. An interesting treasury museum is next to the upper chapel (treasury-€1.50; April-mid-Oct daily 9:30-12:00 & 14:00-18:00; mid-Oct-March Thu-Tue 10:00-12:00 & 14:00-16:00, Wed 10:00-11:45 only; Burg Square, tel. 050-336-792, www.holyblood.com).

▲**City Hall**—This complex houses several interesting sights. Your €2 ticket includes an audioguide; access to a room full of old town maps and paintings; the grand, beautifully restored **Gothic Room** from 1400, starring a painted and carved wooden ceiling adorned with hanging arches (daily 9:30-17:00, last entry 30 minutes before closing, Burg 12); and the less impressive **Renaissance Hall** (Brugse Vrije), basically just one ornate room with a Renaissance chimney (same hours, separate entrance—in corner of square at Burg 11a).

▲▲▲**Groeninge Museum**—This recently renovated museum, which reopened in June of 2011, houses a world-class collection of mostly Flemish art, from Memling to Magritte. While there's plenty of worthwhile modern art, the highlights are the vivid and pristine Flemish Primitives. ("Primitive" here means "before the Renaissance.") Flemish art is shaped by its love of detail, its merchant patrons' egos, and the power of the Church. Lose yourself in the halls of Groeninge: Gaze across 15th-century canals, into the eyes of reassuring Marys, and through town squares littered with leotards, lace, and lopped-off heads (€8, more for special exhibits, Tue-Sun 9:30-17:00, closed Mon, Dijver 12, tel. 050-448-743, www.brugge.be).

✪ See the Groeninge Museum Tour chapter.

Gruuthuse Museum—Once a wealthy brewer's home, this 15th-century mansion is a sprawling smattering of everything from medieval bedpans to a guillotine. As it's undergoing an extensive restoration, the museum is only partially open until October of 2011; after that it closes completely until the end of 2012 (if open: €6, includes entry to apse in Church of Our Lady, Tue-Sun 9:30-17:00, closed Mon, Dijver 17, Bruges museums tel. 050-448-711, www.brugge.be).

▲▲**Church of Our Lady (Onze-Lieve-Vrouwekerk)**—The church stands as a memorial to the power and wealth of Bruges in its heyday. A delicate *Madonna and Child* by Michelangelo is near the apse (to the right if you're facing the altar). It's said to be the only

Bruges at a Glance

▲▲▲**Groeninge Museum** Top-notch collection of mainly Flemish art. **Hours:** Tue-Sun 9:30-17:00, closed Mon. See page 349.

▲▲**Bell Tower** Overlooking the Markt, with 366 steps to a worthwhile view and a carillon close-up. **Hours:** Daily 9:30-17:00. See page 348.

▲▲**Burg Square** Historic square with sights and impressive architecture. **Hours:** Always open. See page 348.

▲▲**Memling Museum/St. John's Hospital** Art by the greatest of the Flemish Primitives. **Hours:** Tue-Sun 9:30-17:00, closed Mon. See page 350.

▲▲**Church of Our Lady** Tombs and church art, including Michelangelo's *Madonna and Child.* **Hours:** Church open Mon-Fri 9:30-17:00, Sat 9:30-16:45, Sun 13:30-17:00 only; museum and apse closed Mon. See page 349.

▲▲**Begijnhof** Benedictine nuns' peaceful courtyard and Beguine's House museum. **Hours:** Courtyard open daily 6:30-18:30, museum open Mon-Sat 10:00-17:00, Sun 14:30-17:00, shorter hours off-season. See page 351.

▲▲**De Halve Maan Brewery Tour** Fun tour that includes beer. **Hours:** April-Oct daily on the hour 11:00-16:00, Sat until 17:00; Nov-March Mon-Fri at 11:00 and 15:00 only, Sat-Sun on the hour 11:00-16:00. See page 352.

Michelangelo statue to leave Italy in his lifetime (thanks to the wealth generated by Bruges' cloth trade). If you like tombs and church art, pay to wander through the apse (Michelangelo viewing is free, art-filled apse-€2, covered by Gruuthuse admission; church open Mon-Fri 9:30-17:00, Sat 9:30-16:45, Sun 13:30-17:00; museum and apse closed Mon, last entry 30 minutes before closing, Mariastraat, www.brugge.be).

▲▲**Memling Museum/St. John's Hospital (Sint Janshospitaal)**—The former monastery/hospital complex has a fine museum in what was once the monks' church. It contains six much-loved paintings by the greatest of the Flemish Primitives, Hans Memling. His *Mystical Wedding of St. Catherine* triptych is a highlight, as is the miniature, gilded-oak shrine to St. Ursula (€8,

▲▲Biking Exploring the countryside and pedaling to nearby Damme. **Hours:** Rental shops generally open daily 9:00-19:00. See page 354.

▲Markt Main square that is the modern heart of the city, with carillon bell tower (described on opposite page). **Hours:** Always open. See page 348.

▲Basilica of the Holy Blood Romanesque and Gothic church housing a relic of the blood of Christ. **Hours:** April-mid-Oct daily 9:30-12:00 & 14:00-18:00; mid-Oct-March Thu-Tue 10:00-12:00 & 14:00-16:00, Wed 10:00-11:45 only. See page 348.

▲City Hall Beautifully restored Gothic Room from 1400, plus the Renaissance Hall. **Hours:** Daily 9:30-17:00. See page 349.

▲Chocolate Shops Bruges' specialty, sold at Dumon, The Chocolate Line, Confiserie De Clerck, and on and on. **Hours:** Shops generally open 10:00-18:00. See page 352.

Gruuthuse Museum 15th-century mansion displaying an eclectic collection that includes furniture, tapestries, and lots more. **Hours:** Tue-Sun 9:30-17:00, closed Mon, partly open until October of 2011, then closed entirely through end of 2012. See page 349.

Choco-Story: The Chocolate Museum The whole delicious story of Belgium's favorite treat. **Hours:** Daily 10:00-17:00. See page 353.

includes fine audioguide, Tue-Sun 9:30-17:00, closed Mon, last entry 30 minutes before closing, across the street from the Church of Our Lady, Mariastraat 38, Bruges museums tel. 050-448-713, www.brugge.be).

✪ See the Memling Museum Tour chapter.

▲▲Begijnhof—Inhabited by Benedictine nuns, the Begijnhof courtyard (daily 6:30-18:30) almost makes you want to don a habit and fold your hands as you walk under its wispy trees and whisper past its frugal little homes. For a good slice of Begijnhof life, walk through the simple Beguine's House museum (€2, Mon-Sat 10:00-17:00, Sun 14:30-17:00, shorter hours off-season,

English explanations, museum is left of entry gate).

Minnewater—Just south of the Begijnhof is Minnewater, an idyllic world of flower boxes, canals, and swans.

Almshouses—As you walk from the Begijnhof back to the town center, you might detour along Nieuwe Gentweg to visit one of about 20 almshouses in the city. At #8, go through the door marked *Godshuis de Meulenaere 1613* into the peaceful courtyard (free). This was a medieval form of housing for the poor. The rich would pay for someone's tiny room here in return for lots of prayers.

Bruges Experiences: Beer, Chocolate, Windmills, and Biking

▲▲De Halve Maan Brewery Tour—Belgians are Europe's beer connoisseurs, and this handy tour is a great way to pay your respects.

The brewery makes the only beers brewed in Bruges: Brugse Zot ("Fool from Bruges") and Straffe Hendrik ("Strong Henry"). The happy gang at this working-family brewery gives entertaining and informative 45-minute tours in three languages. Avoid crowds by visiting at 11:00 (€6 includes a beer, lots of very steep steps, great rooftop panorama; tours run April-Oct daily on the hour 11:00-16:00, Sat until 17:00; Nov-March Mon-Fri 11:00 and 15:00 only, Sat-Sun on the hour 11:00-16:00; Walplein 26, tel. 050-444-223, www.halvemaan.be).

During your tour, you'll learn that "the components of the beer are vitally necessary and contribute to a well-balanced life pattern. Nerves, muscles, visual sentience, and healthy skin are stimulated by these in a positive manner. For longevity and lifelong equilibrium, drink Brugse Zot in moderation!"

Their bistro, where you'll drink your included beer, serves quick, hearty lunch plates. You can eat indoors with the smell of hops, or outdoors with the smell of hops. This is a good place to wait for your tour or to linger afterward. For more on Belgian beer, see page 333.

▲Chocolate Shops—Bruggians are connoisseurs of fine chocolate. You'll be tempted by chocolate-filled display windows all over town. While Godiva is the best big-factory/high-price/high-quality brand, there are plenty of smaller family-run places in Bruges that offer exquisite handmade chocolates. All three of the following chocolatiers are proud of their creative varieties, generous with their samples, and welcome you to assemble a 100-gram assortment of five or six chocolates.

Dumon: Perhaps Bruges' smoothest, creamiest chocolates are at Dumon (€2.20/100 grams). Madame Dumon and her children (Stefaan, Natale, and Christophe) make their top-notch choco-

late daily and sell it fresh just off the Markt (Thu-Tue 10:00-18:00 except closes Sun at 17:00, occasionally open Wed, old chocolate molds on display in basement, Eiermarkt 6, tel. 050-346-282; two other Dumon shops around town offer the same chocolate, but not the same experience). The Dumons don't provide English labels because they believe it's best to describe their chocolates in person—and they do it with an evangelical fervor. Try a small mix-and-match box to sample a few out-of-this-world flavors, and come back for more of your favorites.

The Chocolate Line: Locals and tourists alike flock to The Chocolate Line (pricey at €5/100 grams) to taste the *gastronomique* varieties concocted by Dominique Person—the mad scientist of chocolate. His unique creations mix chocolate with various, mostly savory, flavors. Even those that sound gross can be surprisingly good (be adventurous). Options include Havana cigar (marinated in rum, cognac, and Cuban tobacco leaves—so, therefore, technically illegal in the US), lemongrass, lavender, ginger (shaped like a Buddha), saffron curry, spicy chili, Moroccan mint, Pop Rocks/cola chocolate, wine vinegar, fried onions, bay leaf, sake, lime/vodka/passion fruit, wasabi, and tomatoes/olives/basil. The kitchen—busy whipping up 80 varieties—is on display in the back. Enjoy the window display, refreshed monthly (daily 9:30-18:00 except Sun-Mon opens at 10:30, between Church of Our Lady and the Markt at Simon Stevinplein 19, tel. 050-341-090).

Confiserie De Clerck: Third-generation chocolate maker Jan sells his handmade chocolates for just €1.20/100 grams, making this one of the best deals in town. Some locals claim his chocolate's just as good as at pricier places—taste it and decide for yourself. The time-warp candy shop itself is so delightfully old-school, you'll want to visit no matter what (Mon-Wed and Fri-Sat 10:00-19:00, closed Sun and Thu, Academiestraat 19, tel. 050-345-338).

Choco-Story: The Chocolate Museum—This museum is rated ▲ for chocoholics. The Chocolate Fairy leads you through 2,600 years of chocolate history—explaining why, in the ancient Mexican world of the Mayas and the Aztecs, chocolate was considered the drink of the gods, and cocoa beans were used as a means of payment. With lots of artifacts well-described in English, the museum fills you in on the production of truffles, bonbons, hollow figures, and solid bars of chocolate. Then you'll view a delicious little video (8 minutes long, repeating continuously, alternating Flemish, French, and then English; peek into the theater to check the schedule. If you have time before the next English showing, visit the exhibits in the top room). Your finale is in the "demonstration room," where—after a 10-minute cooking demo—you get a taste (€7, €11 combo-ticket includes nearby Friet Museum, daily 10:00-17:00; where Wijnzakstraat meets Sint Jansstraat at Sint Jansplein, 3-minute walk from the Markt; tel. 050-612-237, www.choco-story.be). The Chocolate Museum is adjacent to (and offers a combo-ticket with) a lamp museum that's very skippable, unless you're a hard-core lamp enthusiast (in that case, boy, are you in luck).

Friet Museum—It's the only place in the world that enthusiastically tells the story of french fries, which, of course, aren't even French—they're Belgian (not worth €6, €11 combo-ticket includes Chocolate Museum, daily 10:00-17:00, Vlamingstraat 33, tel. 050-340-150, www.frietmuseum.be).

Windmills and Lace by the Moat—A 15-minute walk from the center to the northeast end of town (faster by bike) brings you to four windmills strung along a pleasant grassy setting on the "big moat" canal. The St. Janshuys **windmill** is open to visitors (€2; May-Aug Tue-Sun 9:30-12:30 & 13:30-17:00, closed Mon, last entry at 16:30; Sept same hours but open Sat-Sun only; closed Oct-April; go to the end of Carmersstraat and hang a right).

The **Folklore Museum,** in the same neighborhood, is cute but

forgettable (€2, Tue-Sun 9:30-17:00, last entry at 16:30, closed Mon, Balstraat 43, tel. 050-448-764). To find it, ask for the Jerusalem Church. On the same street is a lace shop with a good reputation, **'t Apostelientje** (Tue 13:00-17:00, Wed-Sat 9:30-12:15 & 13:15-17:00, Sun 10:00-13:00, closed Mon, Balstraat 11, tel. 050-337-860, mobile 0495-562-420).

▲▲Biking—The Flemish word for bike is *fiets* (pronounced "feets"). And though Bruges' sights are close enough for easy walking, the town is a treat for bikers, and a bike quickly gets you into dreamy back lanes without a hint of tourism. Take a peaceful evening ride through the town's nooks and crannies and around the outer canal. Consider keeping a bike for the duration of your stay—it's the way the locals get around. Along the canal that circles the town is a park with a delightful bike lane. Rental shops have maps and ideas (see "Bike Rental" on page 342 for more info).

☞ **Self-Guided Bike Ride to Damme:** For the best short bike trip out of Bruges, rent a bike and pedal four miles each way to the nearby town of Damme. You'll enjoy a whiff of the countryside and see a work-ing windmill while riding along a canal to a charming (if well-discovered) small market town. Allow about two hours for the leisurely round-trip bike ride and a brief stop in Damme. The Belgium/Netherlands border is a 40-minute pedal (along the same canal) beyond Damme.

• *Head east from Bruges' Markt through Burg Square and out to the canal. (You could stop to see the Jerusalem Church and a lace shop—described earlier—on the way.) At the canal, circle to the left, riding along the former town wall and passing four windmills (one is open for viewing, described earlier). After the last windmill, named Dampoort, turn right across the second of two bridges (at the locks), then continue straight along the north/left bank of the Damme Canal (via Noorweegse Kaai/Damse Vaart-West).*

The Damme Canal (Damse Vaart): From Dampoort you'll pedal straight and level along the canal directly to Damme. There's

no opportunity to cross the canal until you reach the town. The farmland to your left is a *polder*—a salt marsh that flooded each spring, until it was reclaimed by industrious local farmers. The Damme Canal, also called the Napoleon Canal, was built in 1811 by Napoleon (actually by his Spanish prisoners) in a failed attempt to reinvigo-rate the city as a port. Today locals fish this canal for eels and wait for the next winter freeze. Old-timers have fond memories of skat-ing to Holland on this canal—but nowadays it's a rare event (ask locals about the winter of 2008-2009).

Schelle Windmill (Schellemolen): Just before arriving in Damme, you'll come upon a working windmill that dates from 1867. More clever than the windmills in Bruges, this one is designed so just the wood cap turns to face the wind—rather than the entire building. If it's open, climb up through the creaking, spinning, wind-powered gears to the top floor (free, April-Sept Sat-Sun 9:30-12:30 & 13:00-18:00, closed Mon-Fri and Oct-March).

In its day (13th-15th centuries), Bruges was one of the top five European ports...and little Damme was important, as well. Today all you see is land—the once-bustling former harbors silted up, causing the sea to retreat. Pause atop the bridge just beyond the windmill, with the windmill on your right and the spire of Bruges' Church of Our Lady poking up in the distance. It's easy to imagine how, at Napoleon's instructions, the canal was designed to mimic a grand Parisian boulevard—leading to the towering church back in Bruges.

• *From here, the canal continues straight to Holland. (If tempted...you're a third of the way to the border.) Instead, cross the bridge and follow Kerkstraat, which cuts through the center of town, to Damme's main square and City Hall.*

Damme: Once a thriving medieval port, and then a moated garrison town, Damme is now a tourist center—a tiny version of

Bruges. It has a smaller-but-similar City Hall, a St. John's Hospital, and a big brick Church of Our Lady. You can tell by its 15th-century City Hall that, 500 years ago, Damme was rolling in herring money. Rather than being built with Belgian bricks (like other buildings around here), the City Hall was made of French limestone. Originally the ground floor was a market and fish warehouse, with government offices upstairs.

• *Continue on Kerkstraat as it leads two blocks farther to the Church of Our Lady. Along the way, you could side-trip to the left, down Pottenbakkersstraat, which takes you to a quaint little square called Haringmarkt (named for the Herring Market that made Damme rich in the 15th century). The trees you see from here mark the lines of the town's long-gone 17th-century ramparts.*

Returning to Kerkstraat, continue on to the big church.

The Church of Our Lady: This church, which rose and fell with the fortunes of Damme, dates from the 13th century. Inside are two Virgin Marys: To the right of the altar is a 1630 wooden statue of Mary, and to the left is Our Lady of the Fishermen (c. 1650, in a glass case). Over the nave stands Belgium's oldest wooden statue, St. Andrew, with his X-shaped cross.

Outside, behind the 13th-century church tower, is a three-faced, modern fiberglass sculpture by the Belgian artist Charles Delporte. Called *View of Light*, it evokes three lights: morning (grace), midday (kindness), and evening (gentleness). If you like his work, there's more at his nearby gallery.

• *To return to Bruges, continue past the church on Kerkstraat. Just before crossing the next bridge, follow a scenic dirt lane to the right that leads you back to the Damme Canal (and Damse Vaart-Zuid). Take this road back to Bruges. If you want a change of pace from the canal, about half-way back turn off to the left (at the white bridge and brick house), then immediately turn right on Polderstraat and follow the smaller canal back to the outskirts of Bruges.*

BRUGES CITY WALK

This walk, which takes you from the Markt (Market Square) to the Burg to the cluster of museums around the Church of Our Lady (the Groeninge, Gruuthuse, and Memling), shows you the best of Bruges in a day.

Orientation

Length of This Walk: Allow two hours for the walk, plus time for Bruges' two big museums (Groeninge and Memling—see chapters covering these museums).

Museum Passes: If you're planning to visit all the sights listed on this walk, save money by buying one of the city's sightseeing passes (explained on page 340).

Bell Tower (Belfort): €8, daily 9:30-17:00, 16:15 last entry strictly enforced, on the Markt.

Basilica of the Holy Blood: Treasury-€1.50; April-mid-Oct daily 9:30-12:00 & 14:00-18:00; mid-Oct-March Thu-Tue 10:00-12:00 & 14:00-16:00, Wed 10:00-11:45 only; Burg Square, tel. 050-336-792.

City Hall's Gothic Room: €2, includes audioguide and entry to Renaissance Hall, daily 9:30-17:00, last entry 30 minutes before closing, Burg 12.

Renaissance Hall (Brugse Vrije): €2, includes audioguide and admission to City Hall's Gothic Room, daily 9:30-17:00, last entry 30 minutes before closing, entrance in corner of square at Burg 11a.

Groeninge Museum: €8, more for special exhibits, Tue-Sun 9:30-17:00, closed Mon, Dijver 12, tel. 050-448-743.

Church of Our Lady: Free peek at Michelangelo sculpture, €2 for art-filled apse, included in Gruuthuse admission; church open

Bruges City Walk

START

MARKT

BURG

Groeninge Museum

Church of Our Lady

Memling Museum

Begijn-Hof

Minnewater

END

N

View

To 't Zand

To Train Station

1/4 MILE

400 METERS

BRUGES CITY WALK

1 Market Square
2 Bell Tower
3 Burg Square
4 Basilica of the Holy Blood
5 City Hall
6 Renaissance Hall
7 Ruins in Crowne Plaza Hotel
8 Blinde-Ezelstraat
9 Fish Market

10 Huidevettersplein
11 Postcard Canal View
12 Gruuthuse Museum
13 Groeninge Museum
14 Church of Our Lady
15 Memling Museum
16 De Halve Maan Brewery
17 Begijnhof
18 Minnewater

Mon-Fri 9:30-17:00, Sat 9:30-16:45, Sun 13:30-17:00 only; museum and apse closed Mon, last entry 30 minutes before closing, Mariastraat.

Gruuthuse Museum: Partially open until Oct 2011, then closed through 2012; €6 when open, includes entry to apse of Church of Our Lady, Tue-Sun 9:30-17:00, closed Mon; Dijver 17, Bruges museums tel. 050-448-711.

Memling Museum: €8, includes good audioguide, Tue-Sun 9:30-17:00, closed Mon, last entry 30 minutes before closing, Mariastraat 38, Bruges museums tel. 050-448-713.

De Halve Maan Brewery Tour: €6 tour includes a beer; April-Oct daily on the hour 11:00-16:00, Sat until 17:00; 11:00 is least crowded; Nov-March Mon-Fri at 11:00 and 15:00 only, Sat-Sun on the hour 11:00-16:00; Walplein 26, tel. 050-444-223.

Begijnhof: Courtyard free, daily 6:30-18:30; Beguine's House museum costs €2, open Mon-Sat 10:00-17:00, Sun 14:30-17:00, shorter hours off-season.

The Walk Begins

Markt (Market Square)

Ringed by the post office, lots of restaurant terraces, great old gabled buildings, and the bell tower, this is the modern heart of the city. And, in Bruges' heyday as a trading city, this was also the center. The "typical" old buildings here were rebuilt in the 19th century in an exaggerated Neo-Gothic style (Bruges is often called "more Gothic than Gothic"). This pre-Martin Luther style was a political statement for this Catholic town.

A canal came right up to this square. Imagine boats moored where the post office stands today. In the 1300s, farmers shipped their cotton, wool, flax, and hemp to the port at Bruges. Before loading it onto outgoing boats, the industrious locals would spin, weave, and dye it into a finished product.

By 1400, the economy was shifting away from textiles and toward more refined goods, such as high-fashion items, tapestry, chairs, jewelry, and paper—a new invention (replacing parchment) made in Flanders with cotton that was shredded, soaked, and pressed.

The square is adorned with **flags,** including the red-white-and-blue lion flag of Bruges, the black-yellow-and-red flag of Belgium, and the blue-with-circle-of-yellow-stars flag of the

European Union.

The **statue** depicts two friends, Jan Breidel and Pieter de Coninc, clutching sword and shield and looking toward France as they lead a popular uprising against the French king in 1302. The rebels identified potential French spies by demanding they repeat two words—*schild en vriend* (shield and friend)—that only Flemish locals (or foreigners with phlegm) could pronounce. They won Flanders its freedom. Cleverly using hooks to pull knights from their horses, they scored the medieval world's first victory of foot soldiers over cavalry, and of common people over nobility. The French knights, thinking that fighting these Flemish peasants would be a cakewalk, had worn their dress uniforms. The peasants had a field day afterward scavenging all the golden spurs from the fallen soldiers after the Battle of the Golden Spurs (1302).

Geldmuntstraat, a block west of the square, has fun shops and eateries. Steenstraat is the main shopping street and is packed with people. Want a coffee? Stop by the Café-Brasserie Craenenburg on the Markt. Originally the house where Maximilian of Austria was imprisoned in 1488, it's been a café since 1905 (daily 7:30-23:00, Markt 16).

Bell Tower (Belfort)

Most of this bell tower has stood over the Markt since 1300. The octagonal lantern was added in 1486, making it 290 feet high. The tower combines medieval crenellations, pointed Gothic arches, round Roman arches, flamboyant spires, and even a few small flying buttresses (two-thirds of the way up).

Try some Belgian-style fries from either stand at the bottom of the tower. Look for the small metal model of the tower and the Braille description of the old town. Enter the courtyard. Opposite the base of the bell tower, find the posted schedule of free carillon concerts

(normally June-mid-Sept Mon, Wed, and Sat at 21:00; mid-Sept-May Wed, Sat, and Sun at 11:00 plus Sat at 21:00; sit on benches in courtyard—a great experience). There's also a WC in the courtyard (€0.30).

Climb the tower (at €8, the price is steeper than its 366 steps). Just before you reach the top, peek into the carillon room. The 47 bells can be played mechanically with the giant barrel and movable tabs (as they are on each quarter hour), or with a manual keyboard (as they are during concerts). The carillonneur uses his fists and feet, rather than fingers. Be there on the quarter hour, when things ring. It's *wonderbaar* at the top of the hour.

Atop the tower, survey Bruges. On the horizon, you can see the towns along the North Sea coast.

• *Leaving the bell tower, turn right (east) onto Breidelstraat, and thread yourself through the lace and waffles to Burg Square.*

Burg Square

This opulent square is Bruges' historical birthplace, political center, and religious heart. Today it's the scene of outdoor concerts and local festivals.

Pan the square to see six centuries of architecture. Starting with the view of the bell tower above the gables, sweep counter-clockwise 360 degrees. You'll go from Romanesque (the interior of the fancy, gray-brick **Basilica of the Holy Blood** in the corner), to the pointed Gothic arches and prickly steeples of the white sandstone **City Hall**, to the well-proportioned Renaissance windows of the **Old Recorder's**

House (next door, under the gilded statues), to the elaborate 17th-century Baroque of the **Provost's House** (past the park behind you). The park at the back of the square is the site of a cathedral that was demolished during the French Revolutionary period. Today, the foundation is open to the public in the **Crowne Plaza Hotel** basement (we'll visit it in a few minutes). The modern, Japanese-designed fountain plays with motifs of lace and water, but locals simply call it "the car wash."

• *Complete your spin and walk to the small, fancy, gray-and-gold building in the corner of Burg Square.*

Basilica of the Holy Blood

The gleaming gold knights and ladies on the church's gray facade remind us that this double-decker church was built (c. 1150) by a brave Crusader to house the drops of Christ's blood he'd brought back from Jerusalem.

Lower Chapel: Enter the lower chapel through the door labeled *Basiliek*. The stark and dim decor reeks of the medieval piety that drove crusading Christian Europeans to persecute Muslims. With heavy columns and round arches, the style is pure

The Legend of the Holy Blood

Several drops of Christ's blood, washed from his lifeless body by Joseph of Arimathea, were preserved in a rock-crystal vial in Jerusalem. In 1150, the patriarch of Jerusalem gave the blood to a Flemish soldier, Derrick of Alsace, as thanks for rescuing his city from the Muslims during the Second Crusade. Derrick (also called Dedric or Thierry) returned home and donated it to the city. The old, dried blood suddenly turned to liquid, a miracle repeated every Friday for the next two centuries, and verified by thousands of pilgrims from around Europe who flocked here to adore it. The blood dried up for good in 1325.

Every year on Ascension Day (June 2 in 2011, May 17 in 2012), Bruges' bankers, housewives, and waffle vendors put on old-time costumes for the parading of the vial through the city. Crusader knights re-enact the bringing of the relic, Joseph of Arimathea washes Christ's body, and ladies in medieval costume with hair tied up in horn-like hairnets come out to wave flags. Most of the remaining Bruges citizens just take the day off.

Romanesque. The annex along the right aisle displays somber statues of Christ being tortured and entombed, plus a 12th-century relief panel over a doorway showing St. Basil (a fourth-century scholarly monk) being baptized by a double-jointed priest, and a man-size dove of the Holy Spirit.

• *Go back outside and up the staircase to reach the...*

Upper Chapel: After being gutted by Napoleon's secular-humanist crusaders in 1797, the upper chapel's original Romanesque decor was redone in a Neo-Gothic style. The nave is colorful, with a curved wooden ceiling, painted walls, and stained-glass windows of the dukes who ruled Flanders, along with their duchesses.

The painting at the main altar tells how the Holy Blood got here. Derrick of Alsace, having helped defend Jerusalem *(Hierosolyma)* and Bethlehem *(Bethlema)* from Muslim incursions in the Second Crusade, kneels (left) before the grateful Christian patriarch of Jerusalem, who rewards him with the relic. Derrick returns home (right) and kneels before Bruges' bishop to give him the vial of blood.

The relic itself—some red stuff preserved inside a clear, six-inch tube of rock crystal—is kept in the adjoining room (through the three arches). It's in the tall, silver tabernacle on the altar. (Each Friday—and increasingly on other days, too—the tabernacle's doors will be open, so you can actually see the vial of blood.) On holy days, the relic is shifted across the room and displayed on the throne under the canopy.

Treasury (next to Upper Chapel): For €1.50, you can see the impressive gold-and-silver, gem-studded, hexagonal reliquary (c.

1600, left wall) that the vial of blood is paraded around in on feast days. The vial is placed in the "casket" at the bottom of the four-foot-tall structure. On the wall, flanking the shrine, are paintings of kneeling residents who, for centuries, have tended the shrine and organized the pageantry as part of the 31-member Brotherhood of the Holy Blood. Elsewhere in the room are the Brothers' ceremonial necklaces, clothes, chalices, and so on.

In the display case by the entrance, find the lead box that protected the vial of blood from Protestant extremists (1578) and French Revolutionaries (1797) bent on destroying what, to them, was a glaring symbol of Catholic mumbo-jumbo. The broken rock-crystal tube with gold caps on either end is a replica of the vial, giving you an idea of what the actual relic looks like. Opposite the reliquary are the original cartoons (from 1541) that provided the designs for the basilica's stained glass.

• *Go back out into the square.*

City Hall (Stadhuis)

Built in about 1400, when Bruges was a thriving bastion of capitalism with a population of 35,000, this building served as a model for town halls elsewhere, including Brussels. The white sandstone facade is studded with statues of knights, nobles, and saints with prickly Gothic steeples over their heads. A colorful double band of cities' coats of arms includes those of

Bruges (Brugghe) and Dunkirk (Dunquerke). Back then, Bruges' jurisdiction included many towns in present-day France. The building is still the City Hall, and it's not unusual to see couples arriving here to get married.

Entrance Hall: The ground-level lobby leads you to a picture gallery (free, closed Mon) with scenes from Belgium's history, from the Spanish king to the arrival of Napoleon, shown meeting the mayor here at the City Hall in 1803.

• *You can pay to climb the stairs for a look at the...*

Gothic Room: Some of modern democracy's roots lie in this

ornate room, where, for centuries, the city council met to discuss the town's affairs (€2 entry includes audioguide—which explains both the upstairs and the ground floor—and entrance to the adjacent Renaissance Hall). In 1464, one of Europe's first parliaments, the Estates General of the Low Countries, convened here. The fireplace at the far end bears a proclamation from 1305, which says, "All the artisans, laborers...and citizens of Bruges are free—all of them" (provided they pay their taxes).

The elaborately carved and painted wooden ceiling (a Neo-Gothic reconstruction from the 19th century) features tracery in gold, red, and black. Five dangling arches ("pendentives") hang down the center, now adorned with modern floodlights. Notice the New Testament themes carved into the circular medallions that decorate the points where the arches meet.

The **wall murals** are late 19th-century Romantic paintings depicting episodes in the city's history. Start with the biggest painting along the left wall, and work clockwise, following the numbers found on the walls:

1. Hip, hip, hooray! Everyone cheers, flags wave, trumpets blare, and dogs bark, as Bruges' knights, dressed in gold with black Flemish lions, return triumphant after driving out French oppressors and winning Flanders' independence. The Battle of the Golden Spurs (1302) is remembered every July 11.

2. Bruges' high-water mark came perhaps at this elaborate ceremony, when Philip the Good of Burgundy (seated, in black) assembled his court here in Bruges and solemnly founded the knightly Order of the Golden Fleece (1429).

3. The Crusader knight, Derrick of Alsace, returns from the Holy Land and kneels at the entrance of St. Basil's Chapel to present the relic of Christ's Holy Blood (c. 1150).

4. A nun carries a basket of bread in this scene from St. John's Hospital.

5. A town leader stands at the podium and hands a sealed document to a German businessman, renewing the Hanseatic League's business license. Membership in this club of trading cities was a key to Bruges' prosperity.

6. As peasants cheer, a messenger of the local duke proclaims the town's right to self-government (1190).

7. The mayor visits a Bruges painting studio to shake the hand of Jan van Eyck, the great Flemish Primitive painter (1433). Jan's wife, Margareta, is there, too. In the 1400s, Bruges rivaled Florence and Venice as Europe's cultural capital. See the town in the distance, out Van Eyck's window.

8. Skip it.

9. City fathers grab a ceremonial trowel from a pillow to lay the fancy cornerstone of the City Hall (1376). Bruges' familiar towers stand in the background.

10. Skip it.

11. It's a typical market day at the Halls (the courtyard behind the bell tower). Arabs mingle with Germans in fur-lined coats and beards in a market where they sell everything from armor to lemons.

12. A bishop blesses a new canal (1404) as ships sail right by the city. This was Bruges in its heyday, before the silting of the harbor. At the far right, the two bearded men with moustaches are the brothers who painted these murals.

In the adjoining room, old paintings and maps show how little the city has changed through the centuries. A map (on the left wall) shows in exquisite detail the city as it looked in 1562. (The map is oriented with south on top.) Find the bell tower, the Church of Our Lady, and Burg Square, which back then was bounded on the north by a cathedral. Notice the canal (on the west) leading from the North Sea right to the Markt. A moat encircled the city with its gates, unfinished wall, and 28 windmills (four of which survive today). The mills pumped water to the town's fountains, made paper, ground grain, and functioned as the motor of the Middle Ages. Most locals own a copy of this map that shows how their neighborhood looked 400 years ago.

• *Back on the square, leaving the City Hall, turn right and go to the corner.*

Renaissance Hall (Brugse Vrije)

Present your Gothic Room ticket to enter this elaborately decorated room with its grand Renaissance chimney carved from oak

by Bruges' Renaissance man, Lancelot Blondeel, in 1531. If you're into heraldry, the symbolism makes this room worth a five-minute stop. If you're not, you'll wonder where the rest of the museum is.

The centerpiece of the incredible carving is the Holy Roman Emperor Charles V. The hometown duke, on the far left, is related to Charles V. By making the connection to the Holy Roman Emperor clear, this carved family tree of Bruges' nobility helped substantiate their power. Notice the well-guarded family jewels. And check out the expressive little cherubs.

• *Leaving the building, walk straight ahead and hook around the cream-colored building to your right.*

Ruins in the Crowne Plaza Hotel

One of the old town's newest buildings (1992) sits atop the ruins of the town's oldest structures. In about A.D. 900, when Viking ships regularly docked here to rape and pillage, Baldwin Iron Arm built a fort *(castrum)* to protect his Flemish people. In 950, the fort was converted into St. Donatian's Church, which became one of the city's largest.

Ask politely at the hotel's reception desk to see the archaeological site—ruins of the fort and the church—in the basement. If there's no conference in progress, they'll let you walk down the stairs and have a peek.

In the basement of the modern hotel are conference rooms lined with old stone walls and display cases of objects found in the ruins of earlier structures. On the immediate left hangs a photo of a document announcing the *Vente de Materiaux* (sale of material). When Napoleon destroyed the church in the early 1800s, its bricks were auctioned off. A local builder bought them at auction, and now the pieces of the old cathedral are embedded in other buildings throughout Bruges.

See oak pilings, carved to a point, once driven into this former peat bog to support the fort and shore up its moat. Paintings show the immensity of the church that replaced it. The curved stone walls you walk among are from the foundations of the ambulatory around the church altar.

Excavators found a town water hole—a bonanza for archaeologists—turning up the refuse of a thousand years of habitation:

pottery, animal skulls, rosary beads, dice, coins, keys, thimbles, pipes, spoons, and Delftware.

Don't miss the 14th-century painted sarcophagi—painted quickly for burial, with the crucifixion on the west end and the Virgin and Child on the east.

• *Back on Burg Square, walk south under the Goldfinger family (through the small archway) down the alleyway called...*

Blinde-Ezelstraat

Midway down on the left side (knee level, past the doorway), see an original iron hinge from the city's south gate, back when the city was ringed by a moat and closed nightly at 22:00. On the right wall, at eye level, a black patch shows you just how grimy the city had become before a 1960s cleaning. Despite the cleaning and a few fanciful reconstructions, the city today looks much as it did in centuries past.

The name "Blinde-Ezelstraat" means "Blind Donkey Street." In medieval times, the donkeys, carrying fish from the North Sea on their backs, were stopped here so that their owners could put blinders on them. Otherwise, the donkeys wouldn't cross the water between the old city and the fish market.

• *Cross the bridge over what was the 13th-century city moat. On your left are the arcades of the...*

Fish Market (Vismarkt)

The North Sea is just 12 miles away, and the fresh catch is sold here (Tue-Sat 6:00-13:00, closed Sun-Mon). Once a thriving market, today it's mostly souvenirs...and the big catch is the tourists.

• *Take an immediate right (west), entering a courtyard called...*

Huidevettersplein

This tiny, picturesque, restaurant-filled square was originally the headquarters of the town's skinners and tanners. On the facade of the Hotel Duc de Bourgogne, four old relief panels above the windows show scenes from the leather trade—once a leading Bruges industry. First, tan the hide in a bath of acid; then, with tongs, pull it out to dry; then beat it to make it soft; and, finally, scrape and clean it to make it ready for sale.

• *Continue a few steps to Rozenhoedkaai street, where you can look back to your right and get a great...*

Postcard Canal View

The bell tower reflected in a quiet canal lined with old houses—this view is the essence of Bruges. Seeing buildings rising straight from the water makes you understand why this was the Venice of the North. Can you see the bell tower's tilt? It leans about four feet. The tilt has been carefully monitored since 1740, but no change has been detected.

To your left (west) down the Dijver canal (past a flea market on weekends) looms the huge spire of the Church of Our Lady, the tallest brick spire in the Low Countries (quite possibly behind scaffolding during your visit). Between you and the church are the Europa College (a post-graduate institution for training future "Eurocrats" about the laws, economics, and politics of the European Union) and two fine museums.

• *Continue walking with the canal and the bell tower on your right. About 100 yards ahead, on the left, is the copper-colored sign that points the way to the Groeninge Museum, our next stop. If you'd like to head there now, skip ahead.*

But if you're here before October of 2011, you might want to consider a quick detour to the Gruuthuse Museum, a medieval mansion with a small exhibit. To reach it, continue past the copper sign and over the canal. Just after the gray-and-white Arentshuis, on your left, is a brick archway leading to the...

Gruuthuse Museum

This 15th-century mansion of a wealthy Bruges merchant displays period furniture, tapestries, coins, and musical instruments. Extensive renovation will have this museum in a state of disarray until it closes in October of 2011 (the earliest it'll reopen will be at the end of 2012).

If you get in, use the leaflets in each room to browse through a collection of secular objects that are both functional and beautiful. Here are some highlights:

On the left, in the first room (or **Great Hall**), the big fireplace, oak table, and tapestries attest to the wealth of Louis Gruuthuse, who got rich providing a special herb used to spice up beer.

Tapestries like the ones you see here were a famous Flemish export product, made in local factories out of raw wool imported from England and silk brought from the Orient (via Italy). Both beautiful and useful (as insulation), they adorned many homes and palaces throughout Europe.

The Gruuthuse mansion abuts the Church of Our Lady and has a convenient little **chapel** (upstairs via the far corner of Room 16) with a window overlooking the interior of the huge church. In their private box seats above the choir, the family could attend services without leaving home. From the balcony, you can look down on two reclining gold statues in the church, marking the tombs of Charles the Bold and his daughter, Mary of Burgundy (the grandmother of powerful Charles V).

• *Leaving the Gruuthuse, head right from the archway and backtrack until you find the sign for the...*

Groeninge Museum

This sumptuous collection of paintings, which reopened in June of 2011 after a renovation, takes you from 1400 to 1945. The highlights are its Flemish Primitives, with all their glorious detail.

If you decide to visit, ✪ see the Groeninge Museum Tour chapter.

• *Leaving the Groeninge, take your first left, into a courtyard. You'll see the prickly church steeple ahead. Head up and over the picture-perfect 19th-century pedestrian bridge. From the bridge, look to the right and up at the corner of the Gruuthuse mansion, where there's a teeny-tiny window, a toll-keeper's lookout. The bridge gives you a close-up look at Our Lady's big buttresses and round apse.*

From the bridge, veer left along the hedge-lined path, and find the church entry on the right.

Church of Our Lady

This church stands as a memorial to the power and wealth of Bruges in its heyday.

A delicate *Madonna and Child* by **Michelangelo** (1504) is near the apse (to the right as you enter), somewhat overwhelmed by the ornate Baroque niche it sits in. It's said to be the only

Michelangelo statue to leave Italy in his lifetime, bought in Tuscany by a wealthy Bruges businessman, who's buried beneath it.

As Michelangelo chipped away at the masterpiece of his youth, *David*, he took breaks by carving this one in 1504. Mary, slightly smaller than life-size, sits while young Jesus stands in front of her. Their expressions are mirror images—serene, but a bit melancholy, with downcast eyes, as though pondering the young child's dangerous future. Though they're lost in thought, their hands instinctively link, tenderly. The white Carrara marble is highly polished, something Michelangelo only did when he was certain he'd gotten it right.

If you like tombs and church art, pay €2 to wander through the apse (also covered by Gruuthuse Museum ticket, if museum is open). The highlight is the reclining statues marking the tombs of the last local rulers of Bruges: Mary of Burgundy, and her father, Charles the Bold. The dog and lion at their feet are symbols of fidelity and courage.

In 1482, when 25-year-old Mary of Burgundy tumbled from a horse and died, she left behind a toddler son and a husband who was heir to the Holy Roman Empire. Beside her lies her father, Charles the Bold, who also died prematurely, in war. Their twin deaths meant Bruges belonged to Austria, and would soon be swallowed up by the empire and ruled from afar by Habsburgs—who didn't understand or care about its problems. Trade routes shifted, and goods soon flowed through Antwerp, then Amsterdam, as Bruges' North Sea port silted up. After these developments, Bruges began four centuries of economic decline. The city was eventually mothballed. It was later discovered by modern-day tourists to be remarkably well-pickled, which explains its current affluence.

The wooden balcony to the left of the painted altarpiece is part of the Gruuthuse mansion next door, providing the noble family with prime seats for Mass.

Along the outside of the choir, to the left as you face the balcony, notice the row of dramatic wooden statues. (Contrast these with the meek pre-Renaissance figures in the apse's medieval stained glass.)

Excavations in 1979 turned up fascinating grave paintings on the tombs below and near the altar. Dating from the 13th century, these show Mary represented as Queen of Heaven (on a throne, carrying a crown and scepter) and Mother of God (with the baby Jesus on her lap). Since Mary is in charge of advocating with Jesus for your salvation, she's a good person to have painted on the wall of your tomb. Tombs also show lots of angels—generally patron saints of the dead person—swinging thuribles (incense burners).

The church's tower is likely to be hidden behind scaffolding during your visit, but if you're here after its structural retrofit is complete, you may be able to climb it (ask at apse entry desk).

Before leaving the church, take a moment to behold the Baroque wooden pulpit, with a roof that seems to float in mid-air.

• *Just across Mariastraat from the church entrance is the entry to the St. John's Hospital's Visitors Center, labeled* Site Oud Sint-Jan *(with a €0.50 public WC). About 20 yards farther south on Mariastraat, and to the left, is the entrance to the museum that now fills that hospital's church, the...*

Memling Museum

This medieval hospital contains some much-loved paintings by the greatest of the Flemish Primitives, Hans Memling. His *Mystical Wedding of St. Catherine* triptych deserves a close look. Catherine and her "mystical groom," the baby Jesus, are flanked by a headless John the Baptist and a pensive John the Evangelist. The chairs are there so you can study it. If you know the Book of Revelation, you'll understand St. John's wild, intricate vision. The St. Ursula Shrine, an ornate little mini-church in the same room, is filled with impressive detail.

 ✪ See the Memling Museum Tour chapter.

• *Continue south (with the museum behind you, turn right) about 150 yards on Mariastraat. Turn right on Walstraat (a small black-and-white sign points the way to Minnewater and the Begijnhof). It leads you into the pleasant square called Walplein, where you'll find the...*

De Halve Maan Brewery

If you like beer, take a tour here (Walplein 26). See page 352.
• *Leaving the brewery, head right, make your first right, and just past the horse-head fountain, where the horse-and-buggy horses stop to drink, turn right and head over the pedestrian bridge. From here, the lacy cuteness of Bruges crescendos as you approach the...*

Begijnhof

*Begijnhof*s (pronounced gutturally: buh-HHHINE-hof) were built to house women of the lay order, called Beguines, who spent

their lives in piety and service without having to take the same vows a nun would. Primarily because of military fatalities, there were more women than men in the medieval Low Countries. The order of Beguines offered women (often single or widowed) a dignified place to live and work. When the order died out, many *begijnhof*s were taken over by towns for subsidized housing. Today, single religious women live in the small homes. Benedictine nuns live in a building nearby. Tour the simple museum to get a sense of Beguine life.

In the church, the rope that dangles from the ceiling is yanked by a nun to announce a sung vespers service.

• *Exiting on the other side of the brick church, hook left toward a lake.*

Minnewater

Just south of the Begijnhof is Minnewater ("Water of Love"), a peaceful, lake-filled park with canals and swans. This was once far from quaint—it was a busy harbor where small boats shuttled cargo from the big, ocean-going ships into town. From this point, the cargo was transferred again to flat-bottomed boats that went through the town's canals to their respective warehouses and to the Markt.

When locals see these swans, they recall the 15th-century mayor—famous for his long neck—who collaborated with the Austrians. The townsfolk beheaded him as a traitor. The Austrians warned them that similarly long-necked swans would inhabit the place to forever remind them of this murder. And they do.

• *You're a five-minute walk from the train station (where you can catch a bus to the Markt) or a 15-minute walk from the Markt—take your pick.*

GROENINGE MUSEUM TOUR

In the 1400s, Bruges was northern Europe's richest, most cosmopolitan, and most cultured city. New ideas, fads, and painting techniques were imported and exported with each shipload. Beautiful paintings were soon an affordable luxury, like fancy clothes or furniture. Internationally known artists set up studios in Bruges, producing portraits and altarpieces for wealthy merchants from all over Europe.

Understandably, the Groeninge Museum has one of the world's best collections of the art produced in the city and surrounding area. This early Flemish art is less appreciated and understood today than the Italian Renaissance art produced a century later. But by selecting 11 masterpieces, you'll get an introduction to this subtle, technically advanced, and beautiful style. Hey, if you can master the museum's name (HHHROON-ih-guh), you can certainly handle the art.

Orientation

Cost and Hours: €8, more for special exhibits, Tue-Sun 9:30-17:00, closed Mon.

Reorganization: The museum reopened in June of 2011 after extensive renovation. The artwork described in this tour may have moved; ask a museum staff member for help if you can't find something.

Information: €4 audioguide for special exhibits, tel. 050-448-743, www.brugge.be.

Getting There: The museum is at Dijver 12, near the Gruuthuse Museum and Church of Our Lady. One big copper sign and several small *museum* signs mark the nearby area, leading you to the Groeninge's blue front door.

Length of This Tour: Allow one hour.

Overview

Pick up a map as you enter and be prepared for changes from the tour outlined below. Use this chapter as background to the huge collection's highlights, then browse, seeking out the works you'd like to learn more about.

The Tour Begins

• In Room 1, look for...

Gerard David (c. 1455-1523)—
Judgment of Cambyses (1498)

That's gotta hurt.

A man is stretched across a table and skinned alive in a very businesslike manner. The crowd hardly notices, and a dog just

scratches himself. According to legend, the man was a judge arrested for corruption (left panel) and flayed (right panel), then his skin was draped (right panel background) over the new judge's throne.

Gerard David, Memling's successor as the city's leading artist, painted this for the City Hall. City councilors could ponder what might happen to them if they abused their offices.

By David's time, Bruges was in serious decline, with a failing economy and struggles against the powerful Austrian Habsburg family. The Primitive style also was fading. Italian art was popular, so David tried to spice up his retro-Primitive work with pseudo-Renaissance knickknacks—*putti* (baby angels, over the judgment throne), Roman-style medallions, and garlands. But he couldn't quite master the Italian specialty of 3-D perspective. We view the flayed man at an angle from slightly above, but the table he lies on is shown more from the side.

• Head to Room 2 for...

Jan van Eyck (c. 1390-1441)—*Virgin and Child with Canon Joris van der Paele* (1436)

Jan van Eyck was the world's first and greatest oil painter, and this is his masterpiece—three debatable but defensible assertions.

Mary, in a magnificent red gown, sits playing with her little baby, Jesus. Jesus glances up as St. George, the dragon-slaying knight, enters the room, tips his cap, and says, "I'd like to introduce my namesake, George (Joris)." Mary glances down at the kneeling Joris, a church official dressed in white. Joris takes off his glasses and looks up from his prayer book to see a bishop in blue, St. Donatian, patron of the church he hopes to be buried in.

Canon Joris, who hired Van Eyck, is not a pretty sight. He's old and wrinkled, with a double chin, weird earlobes, and bloodshot eyes. But the portrait isn't unflattering; it just shows unvarnished reality with crystal clarity.

Van Eyck brings Mary and the saints down from heaven and into a typical (rich) Bruges home. He strips off their haloes, banishes all angels, and pulls the plug on heavenly radiance. If this is a religious painting, then where's God?

God's in the details. From the bishop's damask robe and Mary's wispy hair to the folds in Jesus' baby fat and the oriental carpet to "Adonai" (Lord) written on St. George's breastplate, the painting is as complex and beautiful as God's creation. The color scheme—red Mary, white canon, and blue-and-gold saints—are Bruges' city colors, from its coat of arms.

Mary, crowned with a jeweled "halo" and surrounded by beautiful things, makes an appearance in 1400s Bruges, where she can be adored in all her human beauty by Canon Joris...and by us, reflected in the mirror-like shield on St. George's back.

Jan van Eyck—*Portrait of Margareta van Eyck* (1439)

At 35, shortly after moving to Bruges, Jan van Eyck married 20-year-old Margareta. They had two kids, and after Jan died, Margareta took charge of his studio of assistants and kept it running until her death. This portrait (age 33), when paired with a matching self-portrait of Jan, was one of Europe's first husband-and-wife companion sets.

She sits half-turned, looking out of the frame. (Jan might have seen this

Flemish Primitives

Despite the "Primitive" label, the Low Countries of the 1400s (along with Venice and Florence) produced the most refined art in Europe. Here are some common features of Flemish Primitive art:

- **Primitive 3-D Perspective:** Expect unnaturally cramped-looking rooms; oddly slanted tables; and flat, cardboard-cutout people with stiff posture. Yes, these works are more primitive (hence the label) than those with the later Italian Renaissance perspective.

- **Realism:** Everyday bankers and clothmakers in their Sunday best are painted with clinical, warts-and-all precision. Even saints and heavenly visions are brought down to earth.

- **Details:** Like meticulous Bruges craftsmen, painters used fine-point brushes to capture almost microscopic details—flower petals, wrinkled foreheads, intricately patterned clothes, the sparkle in a ruby. The closer you get to a painting, the better it looks.

- **Oil Painted on Wood:** They were the pioneers of new-fangled oil-based paint (while Italy still used egg-yolk tempera), working on wood, before canvas became popular.

- **Portraits and Altarpieces:** Wealthy merchants and clergymen paid to have themselves painted either alone or mingling with saints.

- **Symbolism:** In earlier times, everyone understood that a dog symbolized fidelity, a lily meant chastity, and a rose was love.

- **Materialism:** Rich Flanders celebrated the beauty of luxury goods—the latest Italian dresses, jewels, carpets, oak tables—and the ordinary beauty that radiates from flesh-and-blood people.

"where-have-you-been?" expression in the window late one night.) She's dressed in a red, fur-lined coat, and we catch a glimpse of her wedding ring. Her hair is invisible—very fashionable at the time—pulled back tightly, bunched into horn-like hairnets, and draped with a headdress. Stray hairs along the perimeter were plucked to achieve the high forehead look.

This simple portrait is revolutionary—one of history's first individual portraits that wasn't of a saint, a king, a duke, or a pope, and wasn't part of a religious work. It signals the advent of humanism, celebrating the glory of ordinary people. Van Eyck proudly signed the work on the original frame, with his motto saying he painted it "*als ik kan*" *(ALC IXH KAN)*..."as good as I can."

Rogier van der Weyden (c. 1399-1464)—*St. Luke Drawing the Virgin's Portrait* (c. 1435)

Rogier van der Weyden, the other giant among the Flemish Primitives, adds the human touch to Van Eyck's rather detached precision.

As Mary prepares to nurse, baby Jesus can't contain his glee, wiggling his fingers and toes, anticipating lunch. Mary, dressed in

everyday clothes, doesn't try to hide her love as she tilts her head down with a proud smile. Meanwhile, St. Luke (the patron saint of painters, who was said to have experienced this vision) looks on intently with a sketch pad in his hand, trying to catch the scene. These small gestures, movements, and facial expressions add an element of human emotion that later artists would amplify.

The painting is neatly divided by a spacious view out the window, showing a river stretching off to a spacious horizon. Van der Weyden experimented with 3-D effects like this one (though ultimately it's just window-dressing).

Rogier van der Weyden—*Duke Philip the Good* (c. 1450)

Tall, lean, and elegant, this charismatic duke transformed Bruges from a commercial powerhouse to a cultural one. In 1425, Philip

moved his court to Bruges, making it the de facto capital of a Burgundian empire stretching from Amsterdam to Switzerland.

Philip wears a big hat to hide his hair, a fashion trend he himself began. He's also wearing the gold-chain necklace of the Order of the Golden Fleece, a distinguished knightly honor he gave himself. He inaugurated the Golden Fleece in a lavish ceremony at the Bruges City Hall, complete with parades, jousting, and festive pies that contained live people hiding inside to surprise his guests.

As a lover of painting, hunting, fine clothes, and many mistresses, Philip was a role model for Italian princes, such as Lorenzo the Magnificent—the *uomo universale,* the Renaissance Man.

Hugo van der Goes (c. 1430-c. 1482)— *Death of the Virgin* (c. 1470)

The long deathwatch is over—their beloved Mary has passed on,

Oil Paint

Take vegetable oil pressed from linseeds (flax), blend in dry powdered pigments, whip to a paste the consistency of room-temperature butter, then brush onto a panel of whitewashed oak—you're painting in oils. First popularized in the early 1400s, oil eventually overshadowed egg-yolk-based tempera. Though tempera was great for making fine lines shaded with simple blocks of color, oil could blend colors together seamlessly.

Watch a master create a single dog's hair: He paints a dark stroke of brown, then lets it dry. Then comes a second layer painted over it, of translucent orange. The brown shows through, blending with the orange to match the color of a collie. Finally, he applies a third, transparent layer (a "glaze"), giving the collie her healthy sheen.

Many great artists were not necessarily great painters (e.g., Michelangelo). Van Eyck, Rembrandt, Hals, Velázquez, and Rubens were master painters, meticulously building objects with successive layers of paint...but they're not everyone's favorite artists.

and the disciples are bleary-eyed and dazed with grief, as though hit with a spiritual two-by-four. Each etched face is a study in sadness, as they all have their own way of coping—lighting a candle, fidgeting, praying, or just staring off into space. Blues and reds dominate, and there's little eye-catching ornamentation, which lets the lined faces and expressive hand gestures do the talking.

Hugo van der Goes painted this, his last major work, the same year he attempted suicide. Hugo had built a successful career in Ghent, then abruptly dropped out to join a monastery. His paintings became increasingly emotionally charged, his personality more troubled.

Above the bed floats a heavenly vision, as Jesus and the angels prepare to receive Mary's soul. Their smooth skin and serene expressions contrast with the gritty, wrinkled death pallor of those on Earth. Caught up in their own grief, the disciples can't see the silver lining.

• *Head to Room 3 for the surreal scene that's...*

Attributed to Hieronymus Bosch (c. 1450-1516)—
***Last Judgment* (late 15th century)**
It's the end of the world, and Christ descends in a bubble to pass

judgment on puny humans. Little naked people dance and cavort in a theme park of medieval symbolism, desperately trying to squeeze in their last bit of fun. Meanwhile, some wicked souls are being punished, victims either of their own stupidity or of genetically engineered demons. The good are sent to the left panel to frolic in the innocence of paradise, while the rest are damned to hell (right panel) to be tortured under a burning sky. Bosch paints the scenes with a high horizon line, making it seem that the chaos extends forever.

The bizarre work of Bosch (who, by the way, was not from Bruges) is open to many interpretations, but some see it as a warning for the turbulent times. He painted during the dawn of a new age. Secular ideas and materialism were encroaching, and the pious, serene medieval world was shattering into chaos.

• *At the entrance to Room 4 is...*

Jan Provoost (c. 1465-1529)—*Death and the Miser*

A Bruges businessman in his office strikes a deal with Death. The grinning skeleton lays coins on the table and, in return, the man—looking unhealthy and with fear in his eyes—reaches across the divide in the panels to give Death a promissory note, then marks the transaction in his ledger book. He's trading away a few years of his life for a little more

money. The worried man on the right (the artist's self-portrait) says, "Don't do it."

Jan Provoost (also known as Provost) worked for businessmen like this. He knew their offices, full of moneybags, paperwork, and books. Bruges' materialistic capitalism was at odds with Christian poverty, and society was divided over whether to praise or condemn it. Ironically, this painting's flip side is a religious work bought and paid for by...rich merchants.

No Joke

An enthusiastic American teenager approaches the ticket seller at the Groeninge Museum:

"This is the Torture Museum, right?!"

"No," the ticket man replies, "it's art."

"Oh..." mumbles the kid, "art..."

And he walks away, not realizing that, for him, the Groeninge Museum would indeed be torture.

Petrus Christus (c. 1420-c. 1475)—
Annunciation and Nativity (1452)

Italian art was soon all the rage. Ships from Genoa and Venice would unload Renaissance paintings, wowing the Northerners with their window-on-the-world, 3-D realism. Petrus Christus, one of Jan van Eyck's students, studied the Italian style and set out to conquer space.

The focus of Christus' *Annunciation* panel is not the winged angel announcing Jesus' coming birth, nor is it the swooning, astonished Mary—it's the empty space between them. Your eye focuses back across the floor tiles and through the open doorway to gabled houses on a quiet canal in the far distance.

In the *Nativity* panel, the three angels hovering overhead really should be bigger, and the porch over the group looks a little rickety. Compared with the work of Florence's Renaissance painters, this is quite...primitive.

• *Fast-forward a few centuries (through Rooms 5-8), past paintings by no-name artists from Bruges' years of decline, to a couple of Belgium's 20th-century masters in Room 9.*

Paul Delvaux
(1897-1994)—*Serenity* (1970)

Perhaps there's some vague connection between Van Eyck's medieval symbols and the Surrealist images of Paul Delvaux. Delvaux gained fame for his nudes sleepwalking through moonlit, video-game landscapes.

René Magritte (1898-1967)—*The Assault* (c. 1932)

Magritte had his own private reserve of symbolic images. The cloudy sky, the female torso, windows, and a horsebell (the ball with the slit) appear in other works as well. They're arranged here side by side as if they should mean something, but they—as well as the title—only serve to short-circuit your thoughts when you try to make sense of them. Magritte paints real objects with photographic clarity, then jumbles them together in new and provocative ways.

Scenes of Bruges

Remember that Jan van Eyck, Petrus Christus, Hans Memling, Gerard David, Jan Provoost, and possibly Rogier van der Weyden (for a few years) all lived and worked in Bruges.

In addition, many other artists included scenes of the picturesque city in their art, proving that it looks today much as it did way back when. Enjoy the many painted scenes of old Bruges as a slice-of-life peek into the city and its people back in its glory days.

MEMLING
MUSEUM TOUR

*Memling in Sint-Jan
Hospitaalmuseum*

Located in the former hospital wards and church of St. John's Hospital, the Memling Museum offers you a glimpse into medieval medicine, displaying surgical instruments, documents, and visual aids as you work your way to the museum's climax: several of Hans Memling's glowing masterpieces.

Orientation

Cost: €8, includes good audioguide and free loaner folding chairs (if you'd like to sit and study the paintings).

Hours: Tue-Sun 9:30-17:00, closed Mon, last entry 30 minutes before closing.

Getting There: The museum is at Mariastraat 38, across the street from the Church of Our Lady.

Information: Bruges museums tel. 050-448-713, www.brugge.be.

Length of This Tour: Allow one hour.

Overview

Hans Memling's art was the culmination of Bruges' Flemish Primitive style. His serene, soft-focus, motionless scenes capture a medieval piety that was quickly fading. The popular style made Memling (c. 1430-1494) one of Bruges' wealthiest citizens, and his work was gobbled up by visiting Italian merchants, who took it home with them, cross-pollinating European art.

The displays on medieval medicine are all on one floor of the former church, with the Memlings in a chapel at the far end.

MEMLING MUSEUM

The Tour Begins

The Church as a Hospital

Some 500 years ago, the nave of this former church was lined with beds filled with the sick and dying. Nuns served as nurses. At the far end was the high altar, which once displayed Memling's *St. John Altarpiece* (which we'll see). Bedridden patients could gaze on this peaceful, colorful vision and gain a moment's comfort from their agonies.

As the museum displays make clear, medicine of the day was well-intentioned but very crude. In many ways, this was less a hos-

pital than a hospice, helping the down-and-out make the transition from this world to the next. Religious art (displayed further along in the museum) was therapeutic, addressing the patients' mental and spiritual health. The numerous Crucifixions reminded the sufferers that Christ could feel their pain, having lived it himself.

• *Continue through the displays of religious art—past paintings that make you thankful for modern medicine. Head through the wooden doorway to the black-and-white tiled room where Memling's paintings are displayed. A large triptych (three-paneled altarpiece) dominates the space.*

St. John Altarpiece (a.k.a. *The Mystical Marriage of St. Catherine,* 1474)

Sick and dying patients lay in their beds in the hospital and

looked at this colorful, three-part work, which sat atop the hospital/church's high altar. The piece was dedicated to the hospital's patron saints, John the Baptist and John the Evangelist (see the inscription along the bottom of the frame), but Memling broadened the focus to take in a vision of heaven and the end of the world.

Central Panel: Mary, with baby Jesus on her lap, sits in a canopied chair, crowned by hovering blue angels. It's an imaginary gathering of conversing saints *(Sacra Conversazione),* though nobody in this meditative group is saying a word or even exchanging meaningful eye contact.

Some Memling Trademarks

- Serene symmetry, with little motion or emotion
- Serious faces that are realistic but timeless, with blemishes airbrushed out
- Eye-catching details such as precious carpets, mirrors, and brocaded clothes
- Glowing colors, even lighting, no shadows
- Cityscape backgrounds

Mary is flanked by the two Johns—John the Baptist to the left, and John the Evangelist (in red) to the right. Everyone else

sits symmetrically around Mary. An organist angel to the left is matched by a book-holding acolyte to the right. St. Catherine (left, in white, red, and gold) balances St. Barbara, in green, who's absorbed in her book. Behind them, classical columns are also perfectly balanced left and right.

At the center of it all, baby Jesus tips the balance by leaning over to place a ring on Catherine's finger, sealing the "mystical marriage" between them.

St. Catherine of Alexandria, born rich, smart, and pagan to Roman parents, joined the outlawed Christian faith. She spoke out against pagan Rome, attracting the attention of the emperor, Maxentius, who sent 50 philosophers to talk some sense into her— but she countered every argument, even converting the emperor's own wife. Maxentius killed his wife, then asked Catherine to marry him. She refused, determined to remain true to the man she'd already "married" in a mystical vision—Christ.

Frustrated, Maxentius ordered Catherine to be stretched across a large, spiked wheel (the rather quaint-looking object at her feet), but the wheel flew apart, sparing her and killing many of her torturers. So they just cut her head off, which is why she has a sword, along with her "Catherine Wheel."

Looking through the columns, we see scenes of Bruges. Just to the right of the chair's canopy, the wooden contraption is a crane, used to hoist barrels from barges on Kraanplein.

Left Panel—The Beheading of John the Baptist: Even this gruesome scene, with blood still spurting from John's severed neck, becomes serene under Memling's gentle brush. Everyone is solemn, graceful, and emotionless—including both parts of the decapitated John. Memling depicts Salomé (in green) receiving the head on her silver platter with a humble servant's downcast eyes, as if accepting her role in God's wonderful, if sometimes painful, plan.

In the background, left, we can look into Herod's palace, where he sits at a banquet table with his wife while Salomé dances modestly in front of him. Herod's lust is only hinted at with the naked statues—a man between two women—that adorn the palace exterior.

Right Panel—John the Evangelist's Vision of the Apocalypse: John sits on a high, rocky bluff on the island of Patmos and sees the end of the world as we know it...and he feels fine.

Overhead, in a rainbow bubble, God appears on his throne, resting his hand on a sealed book. A lamb steps up to open the seals, unleashing the awful events at the end of time. Standing at the bottom of the rainbow, an angel in green gestures to John and says, "Write this down." John starts to dip his quill into the inkwell (his other hand holds the quill-sharpener), but he pauses, absolutely transfixed, experiencing the Apocalypse now.

He sees wars, fires, and plagues on the horizon, the Virgin in the sky rebuking a red dragon, and many other wonders. Fervent fundamentalists should bring their Bibles along, because there are many specific references brought to life in a literal way.

In the center ride the dreaded Four Horsemen, wreaking havoc on the cosmos (galloping over either islands or clouds). Horseman number four is a skeleton, followed by a human-eating monster head. Helpless mortals on the right seek shelter in the rocks, but find none.

Memling has been criticized for building a career by copying the formulas of his predecessors, but this panel is a complete original. Its theme had never been so fully expressed, and the bright, contrasting colors and vivid imagery are almost modern. In the *St. John Altarpiece*, Memling shows us the full range of his palette, from medieval grace to Renaissance symmetry, from the real to the surreal.

• *In a glass case, find the...*

MEMLING MUSEUM

St. Ursula Shrine (c. 1489)

On October 21, 1489, the mortal remains of St. Ursula were brought here to the church and placed in this gilded oak shrine, built spe-

cially for the occasion and decorated with paintings by Memling. Ursula, yet another Christian martyred by the ancient Romans, became a sensation in the Middle Ages when builders in Germany's Köln (Cologne) unearthed a huge pile of bones believed to belong to her and her 11,000 slaughtered cohorts.

The shrine, carved of wood and covered with gold, looks like a miniature Gothic church (similar to the hospital church). Memling was asked to fill in the "church's" stained-glass windows with six arch-shaped paintings describing Ursula's well-known legend.

• *Stand with your back to the wall, facing the shrine. "Read" the shrine's story from left to right, circling counterclockwise, but begin with the...*

Left Panel: Ursula—in white and blue—arrives by boat at the city of Köln and enters through the city gate. She's on a pilgrimage to Rome, accompanied by 11,000 (female) virgins. That night (look in the two windows of the house in the background, right), an angel appears and tells her this trip will mean her death, but she is undaunted.

Center Panel: Continuing up the Rhine, they arrive in Basel. (Memling knew the Rhine, having grown up near it.) Memling condenses the 11,000 virgins to a more manageable 11, making each one pure enough for a thousand. From Basel they set out on foot (in the background, right) over the snowy Alps.

Right Panel: They arrive in Rome—formally portrayed by a round Renaissance tower decorated with *putti* (little angels)— where Ursula falls to her knees before the pope at the church steps. Kneeling behind Ursula is her fiancé, Etherus, the pagan prince of England. She has agreed to marry him only if he becomes a Christian and refrains from the marriage bed long enough for her to make this three-year pilgrimage as a virgin (making, I guess, number 11,001). Inside the church, on the right side, he is baptized a Christian.

Opposite Side—Left Panel: They head back home. They're leaving Basel, boarding ships to go north on the Rhine. The pope was so inspired by these virgins that he joined them. These "crowd" scenes are hardly realistic—more like a collage of individual poses and faces. And Memling tells the story with extremely minimal acting. Perhaps his inspiration was the pomp and ceremony of

Bruges parades, which were introduced by the Burgundian dukes. He would have seen *tableaux vivants,* where Brugeois would pose in costume like human statues to enact an event from the Bible or from city history. (Today's "living Christmas crèches" carry on this medieval art form.)

Middle Panel: Back in Köln, a surprise awaits them—the city has been taken over by vicious Huns. They grab Etherus and stab him. He dies in Ursula's arms.

Right Panel: The Hun king (in red with turban and beard) woos Ursula, placing his hand over his heart, but she says, "No way." So a Hun soldier draws his arrow and prepares to shoot her dead. Even here, at the climax of the story, there are no histrionics. Even the dog just sits down, crosses his paws, and watches. The whole shrine cycle is as posed, motionless, and colorful as the *tableaux vivants* that may have inaugurated the shrine here in this church in 1489.

In the background, behind Ursula, a Bruges couple looks on sympathetically. This may be Memling himself (in red coat with fur lining) and his wife, Anna, who bore their three children. Behind them, Memling renders an accurate city skyline of Köln, including a side view of the Köln Cathedral (missing its still-unfinished tall spires).

• *In the small adjoining room, find more Memlings.*

Diptych of Martin van Nieuwenhove (1489)

Three-dimensional effects—borrowed from the Italian Renaissance style—enliven this traditional two-panel altarpiece. Both Mary and Child and the 23-year-old Martin, though in different panels, inhabit the same space within the painting.

Stand right in front of Mary, facing her directly. If you line up the paintings' horizons (seen in the distance, out the room's windows), you'll see that both panels depict the same room—with two windows at the back and two along the right wall.

Want proof? In the convex mirror on the back wall (just to the left of Mary), the scene is reflected back at us, showing Mary and Martin from behind, silhouetted in the two "windows" of the picture frames. Apparently, Mary makes house calls, appearing right in the living room of the young donor Martin, the wealthy, unique-looking heir to his father's business.

• *Before leaving this area, find, to your right, a...*

Portrait of a Young Woman (1480)

Memling's bread and butter was portraits created for families of wealthy merchants (especially visiting Italians and Portuguese). This portrait takes us right back to that time.

The young woman looks out of the frame as if she were look- ing out a window. Her hands rest on the "sill," with the fingertips sticking over. The frame is original, but the banner and Van Eyck-like lettering are not.

Her clothes look somewhat simple, but they were high-class in their day. A dark damask dress is brightened by a red sash and a detachable white collar. She's pulled her hair into a tight bun at the back, pinned there with a fez-like cap and draped with a transparent veil. She's shaved her hairline and plucked her brows to get that clean, high-forehead look. Her ensemble is animated by a well-placed necklace of small stones.

Memling accentuates her fashionably pale complexion and gives her a pensive, sober expression, portraying her like a medieval saint. Still, she keeps her personality, with distinct features like her broad nose, neck tendons, and realistic hands. She peers out from her subtly painted veil, which sweeps down over the side of her face. What's she thinking? (My guess: "It's time for a waffle.")

MEMLING MUSEUM

BRUGES SLEEPING, EATING, NIGHTLIFE & CONNECTIONS

Bruges is the most inviting town in Belgium for an overnight. This chapter describes the town's top accommodations, eateries, and nightlife options, as well as train connections to other cities.

Sleeping in Bruges

Bruges is a great place to sleep, with Gothic spires out your window, no traffic noise, and the cheerily out-of-tune carillon heralding each new day at 8:00 sharp. (Thankfully, the bell tower is silent from 22:00 to 8:00.) Most Bruges accommodations are located between the train station and the old center, with the most distant (and best) being a few blocks to the north and east of the Markt (Market Square).

B&Bs offer the best value (listed on page 394). All are on quiet streets and (with a few exceptions) keep the same prices throughout the year.

Bruges is most crowded Friday and Saturday evenings from Easter through October—July and August weekends are the worst. Many hotels charge a bit more on Friday and Saturday, and won't let you stay just one night if it's a Saturday.

Hotels

$$$ **Hotel Heritage** offers 24 rooms, with chandeliers that seem hung especially for you, in a solid and completely modernized old building with luxurious public spaces. Tastefully decorated and offering all the amenities, it's one of those places that does everything just right yet still feels warm and inviting—if you can afford it (Db-€170, superior Db-€218, deluxe Db-€270, extra bed-€60, wonderful buffet breakfast-€21/person, continental breakfast-€11/ person, air-con, elevator, free Internet access and Wi-Fi, sauna,

Sleep Code

(€1 = about $1.40, country code: 32)
S = Single, **D** = Double/Twin, **T** = Triple, **Q** = Quad, **b** = bathroom, **s** = shower only. Everyone speaks English. Unless otherwise noted, breakfast is included and credit cards are accepted.

To help you easily sort through these listings, I've divided the rooms into three categories, based on the price for a standard double room with bath:

$$$ Higher Priced—Most rooms €125 or more.
$$ Moderately Priced—Most rooms between €80-125.
$ Lower Priced—Most rooms €80 or less.

Prices can change without notice; verify the hotel's current rates online or by email. For other updates, see www.ricksteves.com/update.

tanning bed, fitness room, bike rental, free 2-hour guided city tour, parking-€22/day, Niklaas Desparsstraat 11, a block north of the Markt, tel. 050-444-444, fax 050-444-440, www.hotel-heritage.com, info@hotel-heritage.com). It's run by cheery and hardworking Johan and Isabelle Creytens.

$$$ Hotel Adornes is small and classy—a great value situated in the most charming part of town. This 17th-century canalside house has 20 rooms with full modern bathrooms, free parking (reserve in advance), free loaner bikes, and a cellar lounge with games and videos (small Db-€120, larger Db-€140-150, Tb-€175, Qb-€180, elevator, free Wi-Fi in lobby, some street noise, near Carmersstraat at St. Annarei 26, tel. 050-341-336, fax 050-342-085, www.adornes.be, info@adornes.be). Nathalie runs the family business.

$$ Hotel Patritius, family-run and centrally located, is a grand, circa-1830 Neoclassical mansion with hardwood oak floors in its 16 stately, high-ceilinged rooms. It features a plush lounge, a chandeliered breakfast room, and a courtyard garden. This is the best value in its price range (Db-€100-130, Tb-€140-155, Qb-€165-180, cheaper in off-season, rates depend on room size and demand—check site for best price, extra bed-€25, air-con, elevator, pay Internet access, free Wi-Fi on ground floor, coin-op laundry, parking-€8, garage parking-€14, Riddersstraat 11, tel. 050-338-454, fax 050-339-634, www.hotelpatritius.be, info@hotelpatritius.be, Garrett and Elvi Spaey).

$$ Hotel Egmond is a creaky mansion located in the middle of the quietly idyllic Minnewater. Its eight 18th-century rooms are plain, with small modern baths shoehorned in, and the guests-only

Bruges Accommodations near the Center

SLEEPING IN BRUGES

P PARKING
B BOAT TOURS

1 Hotels Heritage & Nicolas
2 Hotel Adornes
3 Hotel Patritius
4 Hotel Botaniek
5 Hotel ter Reien
6 Walwyck Cool Down Hotel
7 Hotel Cordoeanier
8 Hotel Cavalier
9 To Hotel de Pauw
10 Hotel Imperial & Passage Hostel

11 Hotel Notre Dame
12 Absoluut Verhulst B&B
13 Gastenhuis Sint-Andriescruyse
14 B&B Gheeraert
15 B&B Setola
16 Dieltiens B&B
17 To Debruyne B&B
18 't Geerwijn B&B
19 Royal Stewart B&B
20 Charlie Rockets Hostel
21 To Snuffel Backpacker Hostel

garden is just waiting for a tea party. This hotel is ideal for romantics who want a countryside setting—where you sleep surrounded by a park, not a city (Sb-€95, small twin Db-€105, larger Db-€115, Tb-€150, cheaper in winter, free Wi-Fi, parking-€10, Minnewater 15, for location see map on pages 344-345, tel. 050-341-445, fax 050-342-940, www.egmond.be, info@egmond.be, Steven).

$$ Hotel Botaniek, quietly located a block from Astrid Park, is a lovely pint-sized hotel with a comfy lounge, renting nine rooms—some of them quite big (Db-€95 weekday special for my readers, €99 Fri-Sat; Tb-€130 on weekdays, €140 Fri-Sat; Qb-€145, €149 Fri-Sat; less for longer and off-season stays, free museum-discount card, elevator, Waalsestraat 23, tel. 050-341-424, fax 050-345-939, www.botaniek.be, info@botaniek.be, Andy Bonheure).

$$ Hotel ter Reien is big and basic, with 26 rooms overlooking a canal in the town center (Db-€80-110, Tb-€110-130, Qb-€140-160, rates vary widely with demand—check their website for best prices; cheapest rates for weekdays, stays of at least 3 nights, rooms without canal views; extra bed-€24-29, pay Internet access and Wi-Fi, Langestraat 1, tel. 050-349-100, fax 050-340-048, www.hotelterreien.be, info@hotelter reien.be, owned by Diederik and Stephanie Pille-Maes).

$$ Walwyck Cool Down Hotel—a bit of modern comfort, chic design, and English verbiage in a medieval shell—is a nicely located hotel with 18 spacious rooms (small Db-€90, standard Db-€100, "superior" Db-€120, Tb-€135, family room-€155, "superior" family room-€180, Internet access, free Wi-Fi, Leeuwstraat 8, tel. 050-616-360, fax 050-616-560, www.walwyck .com, rooms@walwyck.com).

$$ Hotel Cordoeanier, a charming family-run hotel, rents 22 simple, fresh, hardwood-floor rooms on a quiet street two blocks off the Markt. It's one of the best deals in town (Sb-€70-95, Db-€75-100, twin Db-€85-100, Tb-€95-110, Qb-€125, Quint/b-€145, cheaper with cash if you show this book, breakfast buffet served in their pleasant Café Rose Red, no elevator, pay Internet access, free Wi-Fi, patio, Cordoeanierstraat 16-18, tel. 050-339-051, fax 050-346-111, www.cordoeanier.be, info@cordoeanier.be, Kris).

$ Hotel Cavalier, with more stairs than character, rents eight decent rooms and serves a hearty buffet breakfast in a once-royal setting (Sb-€55, Db-€70, Tb-€90 if you book direct, Qb-€100, 2 lofty en-suite "back-packers' doubles" on fourth floor-€45-50, book direct and mention this book for special Rick Steves price, pay Wi-Fi, Kuipersstraat 25, tel. 050-330-207, fax 050-347-199, www.hotelcavalier .be, info@hotelcavalier.be, run by friendly Viviane De Clerck).

$ Hotel de Pauw is tall, skinny, flower-bedecked, and family-run, with eight straightforward rooms on a quiet street next to a church (Sb-€65-75, Db-€70-85, no elevator, free and easy street parking, Sint Gilliskerkhof 8, tel. 050-337-118, fax 050-345-140, www.hoteldepauw.be, info@hoteldepauw.be, Philippe and Hilde).

$ Hotel 't Keizershof is a dollhouse of a hotel that lives by its motto, "Spend a night...not a fortune." (Its other motto: "When you're asleep, we look just like those big fancy hotels.") It's simple and tidy, with seven small, cheery, old-time rooms split between two floors, with a shower and toilet on each (S-€30-45, D-€45, T-€66, Q-€84, cash only, free Wi-Fi, free and easy parking, laundry service-€7.50, Oostmeers 126, a block in front of station, for location see map on pages 344-345, tel. 050-338-728, www.hotelkeizershof.be, info @hotelkeizershof.be). The hotel is run by Stefaan and Hilde, with decor by their children, Lorie and Fien; it's situated in a pleasant area near the train station and Minnewater, a 15 minute-walk from the Markt.

$ Hotel Nicolas feels like an old-time boarding house that missed Bruges' affluence bandwagon. Its 14 big, plain rooms are a good value, and the location is ideal—on a quiet street a block off the Markt (Sb-€55, Db-€63, Tb-€75, elevator, pay Wi-Fi, TV on request, closed in Jan, Niklaas Desparsstraat 9, tel. 050-335-502, fax 050-343-544, www.hotelnicolas.be, hotel.nicolas@telenet.be, Yi-Ling and Thomas).

$ Hotel Imperial is an old-school hotel with seven old-school rooms. It's simple and well-run in a charming building on a handy, quiet street (Db-€70-90, cash only, no elevator, pay Wi-Fi, Dweersstraat 24, tel. 050-339-014, www.hotelimperial.be, info @hotelimperial.be, Paul Bernolet and Hilde).

$ Hotel Notre Dame is a humble and blocky little budget option, renting 12 worn rooms in the busy thick of things (Db-€70-75, free Internet access and Wi-Fi, Mariastraat 3, tel. 050-333-193, fax 050-337-608, www.hotelnotredame.be, info@hotelnotre dame.be).

Bed-and-Breakfasts

These B&Bs, run by people who enjoy their work, offer a better value than hotels. Most families rent out their entire top floor—generally three rooms and a small sitting area. And most are mod and stylish—they're just in medieval shells. Each is central, with lots of stairs and €70 doubles you'd pay €100 for in a hotel. Most places charge €10 extra for one-night stays. It's possible to find parking on the street in the evening (pay 9:00-19:00, 2-hour maximum for metered parking during the day, free overnight).

$$ Absoluut Verhulst is a great, modern-feeling B&B with three rooms in a 400-year-old house, run by friendly Frieda and Benno (Db-€95; huge and lofty suite-€130 for 2, €160 for 3, €180 for 4; €10 more for one-night stays, cash only, non-smoking, free

Wi-Fi, 5-minute walk east of the Markt at Verbrand Nieuwland 1, tel. 050-334-515, www.b-bverhulst.com, b-b.verhulst@pandora.be).

$$ Gastenhuis Sint-Andriescruyse offers warmly decorated rooms with high ceilings in a spacious, cheerfully red canalside house a short walk from the Old Town action. Owners Luc and Christiane treat guests like long-lost family (S-€75, D/Db-€100, T-€125, Q-€150, family room for up to 5 comes with board games, cash only, free soft drinks, free Internet access, free pick-up at station, Verversdijk 15A, tel. 050-789-168, mobile 0477-973-933, www.gastenhuisst-andriescruyse.be, luc.cloet@telenet.be).

$$ B&B Gheeraert is a Neoclassical mansion where Inne rents three huge, bright, comfy rooms (Sb-€75, Db-€85, Tb-€95, two-night minimum stay required, cash only, personal check required for first-night's deposit, strictly non-smoking, fridges in rooms, free Internet access and Wi-Fi, Riddersstraat 9, 5-minute walk east of the Markt, tel. 050-335-627, fax 050-345-201, www .bb-bruges.be, bb-bruges@skynet.be).

$ B&B Setola, run by Lut and Bruno Setola, offers three expansive rooms and a spacious breakfast/living room on the top floor of their house. Wooden ceiling beams give the modern rooms a touch of Old World flair, and the family room has a fun loft (Sb-€60, Db-€70, €20 per extra person, €10 more for one-night stays, free Wi-Fi, 5-minute walk from the Markt, Sint Walburgastraat 12, tel. 050-334-977, fax 050-332-551, www.bedandbreakfast -bruges.com, setola@bedandbreakfast-bruges.com).

$ Koen and Annemie Dieltiens are a friendly couple who enjoy getting to know their guests while sharing a wealth of information on Bruges. You'll eat a hearty breakfast around a big table in their comfortable house (Sb-€60, Db-€70, Tb-€90, €10 more for one-night stays, cash only, free Internet access and Wi-Fi, Waalsestraat 40, three blocks southeast of Burg Square, tel. 050-334-294, www.bedandbreakfastbruges.be, dieltiens@bedand breakfastbruges.be).

$ Debruyne B&B, run by Marie-Rose and her architect husband, Ronny, offers three rooms with artsy, modern decor (check out the elephant-size white doors—Ronny's design) and genuine warmth (Sb-€60, Db-€65, Tb-€85, €10 more for one-night stays, cash only, Internet access, free Wi-Fi, 7-minute walk north of the Markt, 2 blocks from the little church at Lange Raamstraat 18, tel. 050-347-606, www.bedandbreakfastbruges.com, mietjedebruyne @yahoo.co.uk).

$ 't Geerwijn B&B, run by Chris de Loof, offers homey rooms in the old center. Check out the fun, lofty A-frame room upstairs (Ds/Db-€75-80 depending on season, Tb-€85-90, cash only, pleasant breakfast room and royal lounge, free Wi-Fi, Geerwijn straat 14, tel. 050-340-544, fax 050-343-721, www.geerwijn.be, info@geerwijn.be). Chris also rents an apartment that sleeps five.

$ Royal Stewart B&B, run by Scottish Maggie and her husband, Gilbert, has three thoughtfully decorated rooms in a quiet, almost cloistered 17th-century house that was inhabited by nuns until 1953 (S-€48, D/Db-€65, Tb-€85, cash only, pleasant breakfast room, Genthof 25-27, 5-minute walk from the Markt, tel. 050-337-918, fax 050-337-918, www.royalstewart.be, r.stewart @pandora.be).

$ Waterside B&B two fresh, Zen-like rooms, one floor above a peaceful canal south of the town center (D-€75, €5 more on Sat, continental breakfast, free Wi-Fi, 15-minute walk from Burg Square at Kazernevest 88, for location see map on pages 344-345, tel. & fax 050-616-686, mobile 0476-744-525, www.waterside.be, waterside@telenet.be, run by Mieke of recommended Pink Bear Bike Tours).

$ B&B AM/PM sports three ultra-modern rooms in a residential neighborhood just west of the old town (Db-€70, Tb-€90, €10 more for one-night stay, cash only, free Internet access—mornings only, free Wi-Fi, 5-minute walk from 't Zand at Singel 10, for location see map on pages 344-345, mobile 0485-071-003, www .bruges-bedandbreakfast.com, info@bruges-bedandbreakfast.com, artsy young couple Tiny and Kevin). From the train station, head left down busy Buiten Begijnevest to the roundabout. Stay to the left, take the pedestrian underpass, then follow the busy road (now on your left). Just before the next bridge, turn right onto the footpath called Buiten Boeverievest, then turn left onto Singel; the B&B is at #10.

Hostels

Bruges has several good hostels offering beds for around €15 in two- to eight-bed rooms. Breakfast is about €3 extra. The American-style **$ Charlie Rockets** hostel (and bar), a backpacker dive, is the liveliest and most central. The ground floor feels like a 19th-century sports bar, with a foosball-and-movie-posters party ambience. Upstairs is an industrial-strength pile of hostel dorms (90 beds, €18/bed with sheets, €20/bed with sheets and breakfast, 4-6 beds/room, D-€50 includes breakfast, lockers, pay Internet access, Hoogstraat 19, tel. 050-330-660, www.charlierockets.com). Other small and loose places are the minimal, funky, and central **$ Passage** (€15/bed with sheets, 4-7 beds/room, D-€50, Db-€65, Dweerstraat 26, tel. 050-340-232, www.passagebruges.com, info @passagebruges.com) and **$ Snuffel Backpacker Hostel,** which is less central and pretty grungy, but friendly and laid-back (60 beds, €15-19/bed includes sheets and breakfast, 4-14 beds/room, Ezelstraat 47, tel. 050-333-133, www.snuffel.be).

Eating in Bruges

Bruges' specialties include mussels cooked a variety of ways (one order can feed two), fish dishes, grilled meats, and french fries (for more on Belgian cuisine, see page 331).
The town's two indigenous beers are the prizewinning Brugse Zot (Bruges Fool), a golden ale, and Straffe Hendrik, a potent, bitter triple ale.

You'll find plenty of affordable, touristy restaurants on floodlit squares and along dreamy canals. Bruges feeds 3.5 million tourists a year, and most are seduced by a high-profile location. These can be great experiences for the magical setting and views, but the quality of food and service will likely be low. I wouldn't blame you for eating at one of these places, but I won't recommend any. I prefer the candle-cool bistros that flicker on back streets.

Restaurants

Rock Fort is a chic spot with a modern, fresh coziness and a high-powered respect for good food. Two young chefs, Peter Laloo and Hermes Vanliefde, give their French cuisine a creative, gourmet twist. At the bar they serve a separate tapas menu. Reservations are required for dinner and recommended for lunch. This place is a winner (€6-12 tapas, great pastas and salads, €15 Mon-Fri lunch special, beautifully presented €19-34 dinner plates, €40 five-tapas special, fancy €50 fixed-price four-course meal, open Mon-Fri 12:00-14:30 & 18:30-23:00, closed Sat-Sun, Langestraat 15, tel. 050-334-113).

Bistro de Bekoring, cute, candlelit, and Gothic, fills two almshouses and a delightful terrace with people thankful for good food. Rotund and friendly Chef Roland and his wife, Gerda, love to tempt the hungry—as the name of their bistro implies. They serve traditional Flemish food (especially eel and beer-soaked stew) from a small menu to people who like holding hands while they dine. Reservations are smart (€15 weekday lunch, €30 fixed-price dinners, €42 with wine, Wed-Sat 11:45-13:45 & 18:30-21:00, closed Sun evening and Mon-Tue; out past the Begijnhof at Arsenaalstraat 53, for location see map on pages 344-345, tel. 050-344-157).

Bistro in den Wittenkop, very Flemish, is a stylishly small, laid-back, old-time place specializing in the local favorites. It's a classy spot to enjoy hand-cut fries, which go particularly well with Straffe Hendrik beer (€37-40 three-course meal, €20-25 plates, Tue-Sat 18:00-21:30, closed Sun-Mon, reserve ahead, terrace in

Bruges Restaurants

EATING IN BRUGES

1. Rock Fort Restaurant
2. Bistro in den Wittenkop
3. Bistro den Amand & Medard Brasserie
4. The Flemish Pot
5. Lotus Vegetarian Restaurant
6. De Hobbit
7. Rest. de Koetse
8. Carlito's
9. Restaurant Sint-Barbe
10. Café-Brasserie Craenenburg
11. 't Brugs Beertje Pub
12. De Garre Pub
13. Café Terrastje
14. Herberg Vlissinghe Pub
15. L'Estaminet Restaurant
16. Pub 't Gezelleke
17. Frituur Stands
18. 't Brugsch Friethuys
19. Laurenzino Waffles
20. Gelateria Da Vinci & Grocery
21. Tom's Diner

P PARKING
B BOAT TOURS

back in summer, Sint Jakobsstraat 14, tel. 050-332-059).

Bistro den Amand, with a plain interior and a few outdoor tables, exudes unpretentious quality the moment you step in. In this mussels-free zone, Chef An is enthusiastic about vegetables, as her busy wok and fun salads prove. The creative dishes—some with a hint of Asian influence—are a welcome departure from Bruges' mostly predictable traditional restaurants. It's on a busy pedestrian lane a half-block off the Markt (€33-35 three-course meal, €20 plates; Mon-Tue and Thu-Sat 12:00-14:00 & 18:00-21:00, closed Wed and Sun; Sint-Amandstraat 4, tel. 050-340-122, An Vissers and Arnout Beyaert). Reservations are smart for dinner.

The Flemish Pot (a.k.a. The Little Pancake House) is a hard-working eatery serving up traditional peasant-style meals. They crank out pancakes (savory and sweet) and homemade *wafels* for lunch. Then, at 18:00, enthusiastic chefs Mario and Rik stow their waffle irons and pull out a traditional menu of vintage Flemish specialties served in little iron pots and skillets. Seating is tight and cluttered. You'll enjoy huge portions, refills from the hovering "fries angel," and a good selection of local beers (€26-30 three-course meals, €16-24 plates, Wed-Sun 12:00-22:00, closed Mon-Tue, reservations smart, family-friendly, just off Geldmuntstraat at Helmstraat 3, tel. 050-340-086).

Lotus Vegetarian Restaurant serves serious lunch plates (€10 *plat du jour* offered daily), salads, and homemade chocolate cake in a pleasantly small, bustling, and upscale setting. To keep carnivorous companions happy, they also serve several very good, organic meat dishes (Mon-Fri from 11:45, last orders at 14:00, closed Sat-Sun, cash only, just north of Burg Square at Wapenmakersstraat 5, tel. 050-331-078).

De Hobbit, featuring an entertaining menu, is always busy with happy eaters. For a swinging deal, try the all-you-can-eat spareribs with bread and salad for €18.50. It's nothing fancy, just good, basic food served in a fun, crowded, traditional grill house (daily 18:00-23:00, Fri-Sat until 23:30, family-friendly, Kemelstraat 8-10, reservations smart, tel. 050-335-520).

Tom's Diner is a trendy, cozy little candlelit bistro in a quiet, cobbled residential area a 10-minute walk from the center. Young chef Tom gives traditional dishes a delightful modern twist. If you want to flee the tourists and experience a popular neighborhood joint, this is it—the locals love it (€15-20 plates, Wed-Mon 18:00-24:00, closed Tue, north of the Markt near Sint-Gilliskerk at West-Gistelhof 23, tel. 050-333-382).

Restaurant de Koetse is a good spot for central, good-quality, local-style food. The feeling is traditional, a bit formal (stuffy even), and dressy, yet accessible. The cuisine is Belgian and French, with an emphasis on grilled meat, seafood, and mussels (€30 three-course meals, €20-30 plates include vegetables and a salad, Fri-Wed 12:00-14:30 & 18:00-22:00, closed Thu, non-smoking section, Oude Burg 31, tel. 050-337-680, Piet).

Carlito's is a good choice for basic Italian fare. Their informal space, with whitewashed walls and tea-light candles, is two blocks from Burg Square (€8-13 pizzas and pastas, daily 12:00-14:00 & 18:00-22:30, patio seating in back, Hoogstraat 21, tel. 050-490-075).

Restaurant Sint-Barbe, on the eastern edge of town, serves classy Flemish dishes made from local ingredients in a fresh, modern space on two floors. Their €12 soup-and-main lunch is a great deal (€14-25 main courses, Thu-Mon 11:30-14:30 & 18:00-22:00, closed Tue-Wed, food served until 21:00, St. Annaplein 29, tel. 050-330-999, Evi).

Restaurants on the Markt: Most tourists seem to be eating on the Markt with the bell tower high overhead and horse carriages clip-clopping by. The square is ringed by tourist traps with aggressive waiters expert at getting you to consume more than you intended. Still, if you order smartly, you can have a memorable meal or drink here on one of the finest squares in Europe at a reasonable price. Consider **Café-Brasserie Craenenburg,** with a straightforward menu, where you can get pasta and beer for €15 and spend all the time you want ogling the magic of Bruges (daily 7:30-23:00, Markt 16, tel. 050-333-402).

Cheap Eats: **Medard Brasserie,** just a block off the Markt, serves the cheapest hot meal in town—hearty meat spaghetti (big plate-€3, huge plate-€5.50, sit inside or out, Fri-Wed 11:00-20:30 except opens on Sun at 12:30, closed Thu, Sint Amandstraat 18, tel. 050-348-684).

Bars Offering Light Meals, Beer, and Ambience

My best budget-eating tip for Bruges: Stop into one of the city's bars for a simple meal and a couple of world-class beers with great Bruges ambience. For information on beer, see page 333. The last three pubs listed are in the wonderfully *gezellig* (cozy) quarter, northeast of the Markt.

The **'t Brugs Beertje** is young and convivial. Although any pub or restaurant carries the basic beers, you'll find a selection here of more than 300 types, including brews to suit any season. They serve light meals, including pâté, spaghetti, toasted sandwiches, and a traditional cheese plate. You're welcome to sit at the bar and talk with the staff (5 cheeses, bread, and salad for €11; Thu-Tue 16:00-24:00, closed Wed, Kemelstraat 5, tel. 050-339-616, run by fun-loving manager Daisy).

De Garre is another good place to gain an appreciation of the Belgian beer culture. Rather than a noisy pub scene, it has a dressy, sit-down-and-focus-on-your-friend-and-the-fine-beer vibe. It's mature and cozy with tables, light meals (cold cuts, pâtés, and toasted sandwiches), and a selection of 150 beers (daily 12:00-24:00, additional seating up tiny staircase, off Breidelstraat between Burg and Markt, on tiny Garre alley, tel. 050-341-029).

Café Terrastje is a cozy pub serving light meals. Experience the grown-up ambience inside, or relax on the front terrace overlooking the canal and heart of the *gezellig* district (€6-8 sandwiches, €10-18 dishes; food served Fri-Mon 12:00-21:00, open until 23:30; Tue 12:00-18:00; closed Wed-Thu; corner of Genthof and Langerei, tel. 050-330-919, Ian and Patricia).

Herberg Vlissinghe is the oldest pub in town (1515). Bruno keeps things simple and laid-back, serving simple plates (lasagna, grilled cheese sandwiches, and famous €8 angel-hair spaghetti) and great beer in the best old-time tavern atmosphere in town. This must have been the Dutch Masters' rec room. The garden outside comes with a *boules* court—free for guests to watch or play (Wed-Sat 11:00-24:00, Sun 11:00-19:00, closed Mon-Tue, Blekersstraat 2, tel. 050-343-737).

L'Estaminet is a youthful, jazz-filled eatery, similar to one of Amsterdam's brown cafés. Don't be intimidated by its lack of tourists. Local students flock here for the Tolkien-chic ambience, hearty €9 spaghetti, and big dinner salads. This is Belgium—it serves more beer than wine. For outdoor dining under an all-weather canopy, enjoy the relaxed patio facing peaceful Astrid Park (Fri-Wed 11:30-24:00, Thu 16:00-24:00, Park 5, tel. 050-330-916).

Pub 't Gezelleke lacks the mystique of the Vlissinghe, but it's a true neighborhood pub offering quality fare and a good chance to drink with locals. Its name is an appropriate play on the word for *cozy* and the name of a great local poet (Mon-Fri 11:00-24:00, closed Sat-Sun, Carmersstraat 15, tel. 050-338-381, Zena).

Fries, Fast Food, and Picnics

Local french fries *(frites)* are a treat. Proud and traditional *frituur*s serve tubs of fries and various local-style shish kebabs. Belgians dip their *frites* in mayonnaise, but ketchup is there for the Yankees (along with spicier sauces). For a quick, cheap, hot, and scenic snack, hit a *frituur* and sit on the steps or benches overlooking the Markt (convenience benches are about 50 yards past the post office).

Markt *Frituur*s: Twin take-away fry carts are on the Markt at the base of the bell tower (daily 10:00-24:00). Skip the ketchup and have a sauce adventure. I find the cart on the left more user-friendly.

't Brugsch Friethuys, a block off the Markt, is handy for fries you can sit down and enjoy. Its forte is greasy, fast, deep-fried Flemish fast food. The €11 "menu 1" comes with three traditional gut bombs: shrimp, *frikandel* minced-meat sausage, and "gypsy stick" sausage (daily 11:00-late, at the corner of Geldmuntstraat and Sint Jakobstraat).

Delhaize-Proxy Supermarket is ideal for picnics. Its push-button produce pricer lets you buy as little as one mushroom (Mon-Sat 9:00-19:00, closed Sun, 3 blocks off the Markt on Geldmuntstraat). For midnight snacks, you'll find Indian-run corner grocery stores scattered around town.

Belgian Waffles and Ice Cream

You'll see waffles sold at restaurants and take-away stands. **Laurenzino** is particularly good, and a favorite with Bruges' teens when they get the waffle munchies. Their classic waffle with chocolate costs €2.50 (daily in summer 10:00-22:00, until 23:00 Fri-Sat; winter 10:00-20:00, until 22:00 Fri-Sat; across from Gelateria Da Vinci at Noordzandstraat 1, tel. 050-333-213).

Gelateria Da Vinci, the local favorite for homemade ice cream, has creative flavors and a lively atmosphere. As you approach, you'll see a line of happy lickers. Before ordering, ask to sample the Ferrero Rocher (chocolate, nuts, and crunchy cookie) and plain yogurt (daily 10:00-22:00, until 24:00 April-Sept and in good-weather off-season, Geldmuntstraat 34, run by Sylvia from Austria).

Nightlife in Bruges

Herberg Vlissinghe (page 401) and **De Garre** (page 400), are great places to just nurse a beer and enjoy new friends.

Charlie Rockets is an American-style bar—lively and central—with foosball games, darts, and five pool tables (€9/hour) in the inviting back room. It also runs a youth hostel upstairs and therefore is filled with a young, international crowd (a block off the Markt at Hoogstraat 19). It's open nightly until 3:00 in the morning with nonstop rock 'n' roll.

Nighttime Bike Ride: Great as these pubs are, my favorite way to spend a late-summer evening in Bruges is in the twilight on a rental bike, savoring the cobbled wonders of its back streets, far from the touristic commotion.

Evening Carillon Concerts: The tiny courtyard behind the bell tower has a few benches where people can enjoy the free carillon concerts (generally Mon, Wed, and Sat at 21:00 in the summer; schedule posted on courtyard wall).

Bruges Connections

For information on rail deals in Belgium, see page 583.

From Bruges by Train to: Brussels (2/hour, usually at :31 and :58, 1 hour, €12.90), **Brussels Airport** (2/hour, 1.5 hours, transfer at Brussels Nord), **Ghent** (4/hour, 30 minutes), **Antwerp** (2/hour, 1.5 hours, half the trains change in Ghent), **Ypres/Ieper** (hourly, 2 hours, change in Kortrijk), **Ostende** (3/hour, 15 minutes), **Delft** (hourly, 3 hours, change in Ghent, Antwerp, and Rotterdam), **The Hague** (hourly, 3 hours, change in Antwerp), **Köln** (8/day, 3.25 hours, change to fast Thalys train at Brussels Midi), **Paris** (roughly hourly via Brussels, 2.5 hours on fast Thalys trains—it's best to book by 20:00 the day before), **Amsterdam** (hourly, 3.25-3.75 hours, transfer at Ghent and Antwerp Central or Brussels Midi; transfer can be tight—be alert and check with conductor; some trips via Thalys train, which requires supplement), **Amsterdam's Schiphol Airport** (hourly, 3.5 hours, change in Ghent and/or Antwerp; less frequent connections via Brussels with Thalys save 30 minutes), **Haarlem** (hourly, 3.5 hours, 2-3 changes—avoid Thalys if traveling with a railpass). Train info: tel. 050/302-424.

Trains from London: Bruges is an ideal "Welcome to Europe" stop after London. Take the Eurostar train from London to Brussels (10/day, 2.5 hours), then transfer, backtracking to Bruges (2/hour, 1 hour, entire trip just a few dollars more with Eurostar ticket; see Eurostar details on page 502).

BRUGES CONNECTIONS

FLANDERS FIELDS

These World War I battlefields, about 40 miles southwest of Bruges, remain infamous in military history. In Flanders Fields, the second decade of the 20th century saw the invention of modern warfare: Machine guns, trenches, poison gas, and a war of attrition. The most intense fighting occurred in the area called the Ypres Salient, a nondescript but hilly—and therefore terrifically strategic—bulge of land just east of the medieval trading town of Ypres (which the Flemish call "Ieper"). Over a period of three and a half years, it was here that hundreds of thousands of soldiers from fifty nations and five continents drew their last breath. Fields and forests were turned first to trenches and battlefields, and then to desolate wastelands with mud several feet deep, entirely devoid of life.

Poppies are the first flowers to bloom in a desolate battlefield once the dust (and mustard gas) clears. And today, this far-western corner of Belgium is blooming once more, having adopted that flower as its symbol. It represents sacrifice and renewal.

Today visitors can't drive through this part of Flanders without passing countless artillery craters, monuments and memorials, stones marking this advance or that conquest, and war cemeteries standing stoically between the cow-speckled pastures. Local farmers pull live shells and ammunition from the earth when they till their fields each spring and fall. (It's so commonplace, most don't even bother to call the bomb squad... they just throw it on a pile with the rest of the rusty ordnance.) Every local has his own garage collection of rusty "Great War" debris

he fished out of a field. Human remains are also regularly disin-
terred here, with every effort made to identify the fallen soldier
and notify any surviving family.

If you're interested in this chapter of history, you can visit several Flanders Fields sites in a one-day side-trip from Bruges (best
by car or guided tour). The most important and accessible sites are
the pleasant and completely rebuilt market town of Ypres, with its
impressive In Flanders Fields Museum (closed mid-Nov of 2011
until June of 2012); the town of Passchendaele (a.k.a. "Passiondale"),
with a nearby, more humble, but still interesting museum; and
Tyne Cot Cemetery, where thousands of enlisted men from the
British Commonwealth are buried and honored. Because most of
the fighting here involved British Commonwealth troops, the vast
majority of visitors are Brits, Canadians, Australians, and New
Zealanders, for whom the stories of Flanders Fields are etched,
like names on gravestones, into their national consciousness. You'll
notice on maps that many places have English names—often
anglicized approximations of the Flemish names (Passiondale
for Passchendaele), or more blunt new names for existing locales
(Mount Sorrow, Hellfire Corner).

The years 2014 through 2018 will be a banner time in this
area, as the centennial of various battles and other events are commemorated.

Between the sites, you'll drive through idyllic Belgian coun-

tryside, streaked with cornfields,
dotted with pudgy cows, and
punctuated by the occasional
artillery crater—now overgrown
with grass or trees, or serving
as a handy little pond. On your
Flanders Fields journey, be sure
to take time to slow down and
smell the cabbage.

Planning Your Time

By Tour: If you really want to delve into Flanders Fields, your
best bet is to take a **tour.** These come with a rolling history lec-
ture, and take you to off-the-beaten-path sites you'd likely not
find on your own. Several companies based in Ypres run tours of
the area (for information, check with the TI listed on page 412);
if you're coming from Bruges, it's more convenient to take either
Nathan's minibus tours or the Quasimodo big-bus tours (both
described on page 346).

By Car: Drivers can easily link the three main sites in a day.
Be aware that road signs use the Flemish "Ieper," not "Ypres." Shop
around locally for a good guidebook to point you to additional

In Flanders Fields

In Flanders fields the poppies blow
Between the crosses, row on row,
That mark our place; and in the sky
The larks, still bravely singing, fly
Scarce heard amid the guns below.

We are the Dead. Short days ago
We lived, felt dawn, saw sunset glow,
Loved and were loved, and now we lie,
In Flanders fields.

Take up our quarrel with the foe:
To you from failing hands we throw
The torch; be yours to hold it high.
If ye break faith with us who die
We shall not sleep, though poppies grow
In Flanders fields.

John McCrae

options. The local tourist board publishes a free guidebooklet called *The Flanders Fields Country & The Great War*, which is a good starting place.

Here's a one-day plan for seeing the sites listed in this chapter. There's much more to see; if you're a WWI battlefield buff, invest in a good local guidebook and map to hunt down the many sites.

From Bruges, head south on the A17 expressway. If you want to make a beeline to Ypres, take this all the way to A19, which you'll take east and follow *Ieper Centrum* signs. For a slower, much more scenic route that takes you to more sites, exit the A17 expressway at R32 and circle around the northern edge of Roeselare, then head west on N36, then south on N313. This takes you to Langemark and the German cemetery there. Then take Zonnebaekestraat southeast to the village of Zonnebaeke and the Passchendaele Museum. From there follow the Menin Road (N37) right on into Ypres, crossing under the Menin Gate as you enter town. After touring Ypres' excellent In Flanders Fields Museum, you can explore more countryside sites, or head directly back to Bruges (fastest route between Ypres and Bruges: A19 expressway east to the A17 interchange near Kortrijk, then zip north on A17).

By Public Transportation: Non-drivers will find it time-consuming to get from Bruges to Ypres (2 hours one-way with a transfer in Kortrijk; note that Ypres is "Ieper" on timetables). Once at Ypres, it's very difficult to see the scattered sites using

Flanders Fields

2 KM
2 MILES

GERMAN CEMETERY 🏳
LANGEMARK
N-313
→ TO BRUGES
VIA N-36, R-32 & A-17
POELKAPELLE

PASSCHEN-DAELE

● PILKEM

ST. JULIAAN

TYNE COT CEMETERY 🏳

N-303

YPRES CANAL

N-38
N-313
A-19
N-332

PASSCHENDAELE MUSEUM

BROODS-EINDE
ZONNEBEKE

N-8

IN FLANDERS FIELDS MUSEUM

YPRES

MENIN GATE

N-37
MENIN ROAD

HOOGE CRATER

A-19 FREEWAY

TO KORTRIJK & BRUGES VIA A-17

HOOGE

ZILLE-BEKE

N-8

GELUVELD

→ TO KORTRIJK, BRUSSELS & BRUGES

DCH

🏳 CEMETERY
■ MUSEUM
● TOWN

---

public transit. Taking a tour (from Ypres or Bruges) or renting a car is a must.

Background

Flanders Fields and the Ypres Salient

Because American forces played a relatively minor role in the fight-

ing at Flanders Fields, its history is obscure to many visitors from the US. If visiting the sites, it helps to get up to speed by doing a little homework to make it all more meaningful. This section will give you a good start.

From 1830, Belgium was established as an independent and neutral state—an essential buffer zone to protect European peace, surrounded as it was by four big powers: France, Prussia, the Netherlands, and Britain. After defeating France and unifying in 1870, Germany was on the rise—an upstart power-house hungry for overseas colonies to fuel its growing economy. Germany amassed an intimidating army, and the rest of Europe worriedly watched flickering newsreel footage of wave after wave of German soldiers, goose-stepping past the camera in perfect sync, followed by gleaming, state-of-the-art cannons. Some of Europe's nations scrambled to ally with their neighbors against potential German encroachment; others allied with Germany. Because many alliances were secret, and often conflicting, no one knew for sure exactly where anyone else stood. As H. G. Welles said, "Every intelligent person in the world knew that disaster was impending and knew no way to avoid it."

On June 28, 1914, while on a visit to Sarajevo, the heir to the Austro-Hungarian throne, Archduke Franz Ferdinand, and his wife were assassinated by a teenage terrorist working for Bosnian Serb separatists. The Austrians held Serbia responsible and declared war. Germany joined Austria, and Russia (allied with France) backed Serbia. Through an intricate web of alliances—which ironically had been created to prevent war—soon all of Europe was drawn in the conflict. On August 4, 1914, Germany sent some 800,000 troops across the border into neutral Belgium en route to France. By August 20, they had already taken Brussels, and four days later they were in western Flanders. The Germans expected to blow through the country quickly. Their ultimate goal: Paris to the south and, to the north, the French ports of Dunkerque and Calais. If they could control those, Germany would command the English Channel.

However, the small but determined Belgian army—less than a quarter the size of the German army—pushed back hard, as they waited for British reinforcements to come from across the Channel. In the **Battle of the IJzer River,** the Belgians opened a sea gate at a pivotal moment to flood a low-lying plain just before a German advance. This diverted the German effort slightly to the south, around the town of Ypres.

Ypres (Ieper in Flemish)—an important market center in the Middle Ages (similar to Bruges)—was just an ordinary town. But its location, surrounding terrain, and modern weaponry turned it into a perpetual battlefield. This conflict saw the advent of the machine gun—a new invention that, before the war, had been called "the peacekeeper," because it was assumed that no sane commander would ever send his boys into its fire. The extremely flat terrain of Flanders Fields, combined with these newly emerging battlefield techniques, made even the slightest gain in elevation strategically important. From any ridge, machine guns and artillery could be used to mow down enemy troops—advancing armies would be sitting ducks. (The names of some of the land features here—such as "Hill 60," as in 60 meters above sea level—indicate how the surrounding flatness emphasized even the most modest gain in elevation.) Consequently, the low-lying ridges just east of Ypres—which came to be known as the **Ypres Salient** (the French term for "bulge")—saw some of the fiercest, most devastating fighting of World War I.

The **First Battle of Ypres** began on October 20, 1914, when German troops attempted to invade the town. It became a priority of the Allies—Belgians, French, and British Commonwealth troops—to hold the Germans at bay. Both sides sustained huge losses, but the German troops—mostly inexperienced young conscripts who had underestimated the opposition—were devastated; to this day, Germans call the battle *Kindermord*, "Massacre of the Innocents." For a while, at least, the Allies succeeded in preventing Germany from pushing through. It was the last mobile combat of a conflict that would come to be known for its grueling trench warfare.

Both sides regrouped and prepared for a harsh winter. They dug trenches. Nobody planned it—it was simply human nature for soldiers ducking machine-gun bullets to burrow down. Separated by as little as 50 yards, enemy armies were close enough to offer each other a *Gesundheit!* after each sneeze. It was during this time that the famous "Christmas Truce" took place, in which the German soldiers erected little candlelit *Tanenbaum*s beside their trenches and even approached the English trenches with gifts, kind words, and a pick-up soccer game.

In the spring of 1915, the Germans tried again in the **Second Battle of Ypres.** During this battle, the Germans used poison gas for the first time on a large scale, catching the Allies off-guard. Chlorine gas (a.k.a. bertholite) reacts with moisture in the lungs to form hydrochloric acid—choking soldiers from the inside out. It was also one of the first times flamethrowers were used in battle. Despite these gruesome innovations, Germany was still unable to take the town. By May of 1915, the opposing forces were deadlocked near the town of Passchendaele, seven miles east of Ypres; for two years, little progress was made in either direction.

Although the Western Front appeared to be "all quiet," each side fortified its positions. The Germans in particular established an elaborate network of five successive trenches, connected to and supplied by one another with perpendicular "switches." They built stout fortresses with flat tops, designed to protect troops from British artillery while allowing them to quickly emerge to man nearby machine-gun nests. These flat-topped German fortresses—which you'll still see everywhere—were dubbed "pillboxes." The British opted for underground wooden tunnels called "dugouts," and reserved concrete bunkers for more specialized use, as command posts and shelters for the wounded. (Their rounded-top bunkers proved to be a more effective deterrent to artillery blasts than the Germans' flat-top design—leading the Germans to adopt the round British style in World War II.)

In the summer of 1917, the Allies attempted their own offensive against the newly strengthened German threat, the **Third Battle of Ypres** (a.k.a. the Battle of Passchendaele). After a sustained two-week artillery bombardment of German positions, some four million projectiles turned the countryside into a desolate wasteland. One solider said that "the earth had been churned and rechurned"; another termed it "as featureless as the Sahara."

Then British infantry took to the battlefield...going "over the top" (giving us that phrase), rather than staying in the trenches. They faced barbed wire, machine-gun fire, dangerously exposed high ground, and liquid mud. The utter devastation of the shelling, combined with historic rainfall (the most in the history of Flanders), turned the Ypres Salient into a sea of mud. The same flatness that made the high ground here so strategic turned the low ground into quicksand in heavy rain. Fields became flooded with stagnant water. Troops' boots and tank treads could barely move, causing the British to gain only two of the four miles they so desperately needed to conquer. This battle was also the first time the Germans used the notorious mustard gas, which causes exposed skin to blister agonizingly on contact.

As the summer of 1917 turned to fall, and the heavy rains continued to deluge the area, British soldiers made more and more inroads, bunker by bunker. Their goal was the destroyed village of **Passchendaele,** perched on a modest ridge with a strategic view over the flat lands below. The village's name literally meant "passing the valley," but the Brits dubbed it "Passiondale"...the valley of suffering. Menin Road, which connected Ypres to Passchendaele (now road N37), was the focus of much warfare—especially the notorious intersection dubbed "Hellfire Corner."

But British forces never succeeded in taking Passchendaele, and it became clear that this would be a **war of attrition.** Each side had lost about a quarter of a million men. And, as both sides poured troops and resources into the fighting, neither could actually break through; they simply wanted to be the last man standing.

Two pivotal events took place over the winter of 1917-1918: The United States entered the war on the side of the Allies; and Germany agreed to a separate peace with Russia, allowing it to steer more resources to the Ypres Salient. In spring of 1918, the **Fourth Battle of Ypres** (a.k.a. the Battle of the Lys) saw German forces trying to push through to the town of Ypres before US troops could arrive. They were emboldened by the collapse of Russia in the Bolshevik Revolution, which freed up more German troops and resources to direct at this front. Always innovative on the battlefield, the Germans introduced an elite squad of storm

Dulce et Decorum Est

Bent double, like old beggars under sacks,
Knock-kneed, coughing like hags, we cursed
    through sludge,
Till on the haunting flares we turned our backs
And towards our distant rest began to trudge.
Men marched asleep. Many had lost their boots
But limped on, blood-shod. All went lame; all
    blind;
Drunk with fatigue; deaf even to the hoots
Of tired, outstripped Five-Nines that dropped
    behind.

Gas! Gas! Quick, boys!—An ecstasy of fumbling,
Fitting the clumsy helmets just in time;
But someone still was yelling out and stumbling,
And floundʼring like a man in fire or lime...
Dim, through the misty panes and thick green
    light,
As under a green sea, I saw him drowning.

In all my dreams, before my helpless sight,
He plunges at me, guttering, choking, drowning.

If in some smothering dreams you too could
    pace
Behind the wagon that we flung him in,
And watch the white eyes writhing in his face,
His hanging face, like a devilʼs sick of sin;
If you could hear, at every jolt, the blood
Come gargling from the froth-corrupted lungs,
Obscene as cancer, bitter as the cud
Of vile, incurable sores on innocent tongues, —
My friend, you would not tell with such high zest
To children ardent for some desperate glory,
The old Lie: *Dulce et decorum est
Pro patria mori.*

Wilfred Owen

troopers (*Stosstruppen*, literally "shock troops")—lightly armed but well-trained and highly mobile special units tasked with breaking through enemy lines.

But by late April, the German advance stalled for lack of supplies; meanwhile, American troops had come to the rescue. By summer it was evident that Germany was losing the war of attrition, and in September and October of 1918, in the **Fifth Battle of Ypres,** Allied forces made huge gains. Less than a month later,

Armistice Day (Nov 11, 1918) brought an end to the war to end all wars...until the next war.

World War I claimed the lives of an estimated nine million people; about a million were killed, wounded, or declared missing in action here in the Ypres Salient. By war's end, the British Commonwealth forces had suffered 720,000 casualties, including (officially) 185,000 dead. In the century since, Flanders Fields has recovered, and has become a compelling tourist attraction for the descendants of the victims and survivors of the fighting here. As you tour the place, keep in mind that everything you see—every building, every tree—dates from after 1918.

Sites in Flanders Fields

Ypres (Ieper)

About 40 miles southwest of Bruges is the town most English-speakers call Ypres (EE-preh, though some pronounce it "Wipers"); its official Flemish name is Ieper (YEE-per). By the end of the war, Ypres was so devastated that Winston Churchill advocated keeping it in ruins as a monument to the travesty of warfare. But locals did rebuild, resurrecting its charming main market square (Grote Markt), watched

over by the grand and impressive Cloth Hall (which houses the In Flanders Fields Museum). Today's Ypres is a downright pleasant market town, with a steady stream of mostly British tourists interested in the WWI sites. The **TI,** downstairs in the Cloth Hall, has information on tours (below the museum; April-mid-Nov Mon-Sat 9:00-18:00, Sun 10:00-18:00; mid-Nov-March Mon-Sat 9:00-17:00, Sun 10:00-17:00; tel. 057-239-220, www.ieper.be). Saturday morning is **market** day.

Getting There: If you're based in Bruges without a car, take a tour (see recommended tours on page 346). Less than an hour away, Ypres is easy for drivers (see route tips under "Planning Your Time," earlier). There's parking right on the main market square, next to the giant Cloth Hall that houses the museum (€0.50/hour, 3-hour limit).

▲▲In Flanders Fields Museum—This excellent museum provides a moving look at the battles fought near Ypres. The focus is not on the strategy and the commanders, but on the ordinary people who fought and died here. The evocative descriptions personalize the miserable day-to-day existence in the trenches, and interactive computer displays trace the wartime lives of individual soldiers and citizens. Actual artifacts, engaging descriptions, and thoughtful presentations all bring the war-torn places to life.

The museum began an extensive renovation in 2011 (open during renovation until mid-Nov 2011, when it will close until June of 2012). When the museum reopens, it will expand its focus to the entire Belgian front, rather than just the Ypres Salient. They're planning a renewed focus on specific locations where wartime events took place (tying the museum's exhibits to the actual sites in the surrounding countryside) and a look at the century of remembrances that have passed since the war's end.

As a part of the renovation, they plan to open the Cloth Hall's **belfry** to visitors (200 steps to the top, likely €2 extra), offering a panoramic view of the surrounding countryside, which was so prized and so costly in human lives a century ago.

Cost and Hours: €8; April-mid-Nov daily 10:00-18:00; mid-Nov-March Tue-Sun 10:00-17:00, closed Mon and for three weeks in Jan; last entry one hour before closing; closed mid-Nov 2011 to June 2012; in Ypres' huge Cloth Hall at Grote Markt 34, tel. 057-239-220, www.inflandersfields.be.

▲**Menin Gate**—This impressive Victorian archway is an easy two-block walk from the museum (past the end of Grote Markt). Built

into the old town wall of Ypres, it's etched with the names of British Commonwealth victims of the fighting here. It marks the Menin Road, where many Brits, Canadians, Aussies, and Kiwis left this town for the grueling battlefields and trenches, never to return. The gate is formally a mausoleum for "the Missing," 54,896 troops who likely perished at Flanders Fields but whose remains were never found. To honor the hundreds of thousands of British subjects who gave their lives, every night under the arch at 20:00, a Belgian bugle corps plays the **"Last Post"** to honor the dead.

Other Sites

Most of the following sites are on or near the Menin Road between Ypres and Passchendaele (to the northeast), where the most famous battles took place. The German Cemetery is a bit to the north (but still within a few miles).

▲**Passchendaele Museum**—Although not as extensive or well-presented as the In Flanders Fields Museum, this good exhibit supplements it nicely, with a focus on the strategy and battles of the fighting here. Presented chronologically on the top floor of a chalet-like mansion, it details each advance and retreat from the first German boot on Belgian soil to Armistice Day. You'll see displays of uniforms, medical instruments, and objects illustrating day-to-day life at the front. One exhibit explains—and lets you sniff—the four basic types of poison gas used here. You'll exit through a simulation of the wooden underground "dugout" tunnels used by British forces as their headquarters, after the ground level was so scorched by artillery that nothing was left up above (€5, Feb-Nov daily 10:00-18:00, closed Dec-Jan, Ieperstraat 5, in Zonnebeke about 5 miles east of Ypres and 2 miles west of Passchendaele, tel. 051-770-441, www.passchendaele.be).

▲Tyne Cot Cemetery—This evocative site is the largest cemetery honoring soldiers of the British Commonwealth. It's the final resting place of 11,956 British, Canadian, Australian, New

Zealander, South African, and other British Commonwealth soldiers. Named for a blockhouse on this site that was taken by British forces, who nicknamed it "Tyne Cottage" after the river in North England, the cemetery grounds also hold three German pillbox bunkers. Between those are seemingly endless rows of white headstones, marked with the deceased soldier's name and the emblem from his unit (many of these are regional, such as the maple leaf of Canada). Many graves are marked simply "A soldier of the Great War, known to God." In the center of the cemetery, near the tallest cross (marking the location of Tyne Cottage), notice the higgledy-piggledy arrangement of graves. During the war, when this cottage was a makeshift medic station, this area became an impromptu burial ground. (In contrast, any cemetery that's neat and symmetrical—like the surrounding headstones—dates from after the war.) Running along the top of the cemetery is a wall inscribed with the names of 34,857 "officers and men to whom the fortune of war denied the known and honoured burial given to their comrades in death." Inside the visitors center, you'll see a few artifacts and exhibits about the fighting here (cemetery and visitors center free, open daily 10:00-18:00, closed Dec-Jan, just northeast of Zonnebeke, off of N37 toward Passchendaele, about 6.5 miles east of Ypres, www.cwgc.org).

Hooge Crater—This giant flooded crater, about three miles east of Ypres, was created when British forces detonated a vast store of artillery that destroyed the château they had been using as a headquarters. This desperate act was only partly successful, as the strategic high ground around the château (now a crater) switched hands repeatedly throughout the war. Today the Hooge Crater area has a large British Commonwealth **cemetery**, the **Hooge**

Crater Museum (a touristy exhibit with historic information about the fighting here, €4.50, Tue-Sun 10:00-18:00, closed Mon, www .hoogecrater.com), and—hiding out in the woods just down the road—a hotel/restaurant called **Kasteelhof 't Hooghe,** where you can pay €1 to stroll around the adjacent crater-pond and see some old bunkers and trenches (www.hotelkasteelhofthooghe.be).

German Military Cemetery (Deutscher Soldatenfriedhof) at Langemark—A relatively rare site dedicated to the invaders

of this region, this is the final resting place of 44,324 Central Powers soldiers (along with two Brits who were originally mis-identified). Compared with the gleaming British Commonwealth cemeteries nearby, it's dull and drab. That's because the Treaty of Versailles (which concluded World War I) forbade German WWI cemeteries from using white stones; instead, it uses basalt and even oak. As you wander the cemetery, you'll notice that many of these "German" troops have Slavic names, as they were imported here to fight from the far-eastern corners of the multiethnic Austro-Hungarian Empire. In the center is a mass grave with 25,000 soldiers (free, always open, on the northern outskirts of Langemark, about five miles north/northeast of Ypres).

Other Cemeteries, Memorials, and Craters—The sites listed above are just the beginning. You can't drive a mile or two without passing a monument or a memorial. Tranquil forests suddenly open into clearings with eerily rippled contours—overgrown trenches, pockmarks, and craters. Several nondescript ponds and lakes in the area are actually huge, flooded artillery craters. Joining a tour helps you find some of the more out-of-the-way remnants of the war, but if you're exploring on your own, be sure to get a good guidebook on the region (several are available at local bookstores and tourist offices—find one that suits your needs). If you have a special interest—for example, a nationality or a specific battle an ancestor participated in—just ask around, and you'll find it's easy to seek out related sites.

BRUSSELS
Bruxelles

ORIENTATION TO BRUSSELS

Six hundred years ago, Brussels was just a nice place to stop and buy a waffle on the way to Bruges. With no strategic importance, it was allowed to grow as a free trading town. Today it's a city of 1.8 million, the capital of Belgium, the headquarters of NATO, and the seat of the European Union.

The Bruxelloise are cultured and genteel—even a bit snobby compared to their more earthy Flemish cousins. And yet you may notice an impish sparkle and *joie de vivre,* as evidenced by their love of comic strips (giant comic-strip panels are painted on buildings all over town) and their civic symbol: a statue of a little boy peeing.

Many of the people you'll encounter here, however, aren't Bruxelloise, or even Belgian. As the unofficial capital of Europe, Brussels is multicultural, hosting politicians and businesspeople (not to mention immigrants) from around the globe, and featuring a world of ethnic restaurants.

Brussels enjoyed a Golden Age of peace and prosperity (1400-1550) while England and France were duking it out in the Hundred Years' War. It was then that many of the fine structures that distinguish the city today were built. In the late 1800s, Brussels had another growth spurt, fueled by industrialization, wealth taken from the Belgian Congo, and the exhilaration of the country's recent independence (1830). City expansion peaked at the end of the 19th century, when the "Builder King" Leopold II erected grand monuments and palaces.

Brussels speaks French. Bone up on *bonjour* and *s'il vous plaît* (see the French Survival Phrases in the appendix). Although it's entirely contained within the Flemish-speaking region of Flanders, 65 percent of Bruxelloise speak French as their first language, and only 5 percent speak Flemish. The remaining third are non-natives who speak their own languages (English is the common default). Traditionally, locals spoke a French-Flemish hybrid dialect...but, like French-Flemish unity, that's dying away. Language aside, the whole feel of the town is urban French, not rural Flemish.

Tourists zipping between Amsterdam and Bruges or Paris by train usually miss Brussels, but its rich, chocolaty mix of food and culture pleasantly surprises those who stop.

Planning Your Time

For a city of its size and prominence, Brussels is low on great sights, but high on ambience. On a quick trip, a day and a night are enough for a good first taste (but if you have more time, Brussels has enjoyable ways to fill it). Even better, if you're in a hurry, Brussels can be done as a day trip by train from Bruges, Ghent, or Antwerp (frequent trains, less than an hour from any of these) or a stopover on the Amsterdam-Paris or Amsterdam-Bruges ride (hourly trains). The main reason to visit Brussels—the Grand Place—takes only a few minutes to see. With very limited time, skip the indoor sights and just enjoy a coffee or a beer on the square.

Brussels in Three to Five Hours

Brussels makes a great stopover between trains. First toss your bag in a locker at Central Station and confirm your departure time and station (if you're catching a fast international train, factor in any necessary transit time to the Midi/Zuid/South Station—described on page 423). Then walk about five minutes into town and do this Brussels blitz:

Head directly for the Grand Place and take my Grand Place Walk. To streamline, skip the *Manneken-Pis* until later, and end the walk at the Bourse (stock-exchange building), where you can catch bus #95 to Place Royale/Koningsplein. Enjoy a handful of masterpieces at the Royal Museums of Fine Arts (twin museums—ancient and modern—covered by the same ticket) or the Magritte Museum (devoted entirely to this Belgian pioneer of Modernism). If you're rushing to get back to your train, make a beeline to the station; if you have another hour or two to kill, do my Upper Town Walk, which ends back at the *Manneken-Pis* and the Grand Place. Buy a box of chocolates and a bottle of Belgian beer, and pop the top as your train pulls out of the station. Ahhh!

Brussels in a Day or More

A full day (with one or two overnights) is about right to get a more complete taste of Brussels. With a second day, you can slow things down and really delve into the city. A side-trip to Bruges, Antwerp, or Ghent (each a short train-ride away) is more satisfying than a

BRUSSELS ORIENTATION

third day in Brussels.

Get your bearings in the morning with my Grand Place Walk, then tour the Royal Museums of Fine Arts of Belgium and the Magritte Museum (enjoyable to art-lovers and novices alike), and do the Upper Town Walk. With additional time, choose from a good selection of other sights. Very near the Royal Museums, historians enjoy the excellent story of Belgium at the BELvue Museum, and even the tone-deaf can appreciate the Musical Instruments Museum. In the Lower Town, aficionados of the funny pages head for the Belgian Comic Strip Center (a 15-minute walk from the Grand Place). And political-science majors visit the EU Parliament complex for a lesson in Euro-civics. In the evening, consider exploring the fun and colorful streets around Place St-Géry and Ste. Catherine, where you'll find plenty of good dinner options. With more time or a special interest, head out to the museums at the Park of the Cinquantenaire, visit the kitschy former fairgrounds at the giant Atomium, or venture to the adjacent town of Tervuren to tour the Royal Museum of the Belgian Congo and relax in a big park.

Brussels Overview

Central Brussels is surrounded by a ring of roads (which replaced the old city wall) called the Pentagon. (Romantics think it looks more like a heart.) All hotels and nearly all the sights I mention are within this ring. The epicenter holds the main square (the Grand Place), the TI, and Central Station (all within three blocks of one another).

What isn't so apparent from maps is that Brussels is a city divided by altitude. A ridgeline that runs north-south splits the town into the Upper Town (east half, elevation 200 feet) and Lower Town (west, at sea level), with Central Station in between. The Upper Town, traditionally the home of nobility and the rich, has big marble palaces, broad boulevards, and the major museums.

The Lower Town, with the Grand Place (grahn plahs; in Flemish: Grote Markt, HHHROH-teh markt), narrow streets, old buildings, modern shops, colorful eateries, and the famous *Manneken-Pis* peeing-boy statue, has more character. Running along the western edge of the touristic center is a bustling boulevard (Boulevard Anspach/Anspachlaan) that runs over the city's forgotten river. Just beyond that—past a block or two of high-rise ugliness—is the lively market square called Place St-Géry/Sint-Goriksplein, and a charming village-within-a-city huddled around the old fish market: the Ste. Catherine neighborhood, home to several recommended hotels and restaurants.

Brussels Overview

TO ATOMIUM

NORD/NOORD/NORTH STATION

TO AIRPORT & ANTWERP

M

PETIT RING

N

Rogier M

STE. CATHERINE

Ste. Cath. M

De Brouckère M

Belgian Comic Strip Center

TO ROYAL MUSEUM OF CENTRAL AFRICA →

L O W E R

PLACE ST-GERY

Bourse

M

GRAND PLACE & i

Madou M

RUE CROIX

St. MICHAEL

Arts-Loi

TO PARK OF THE CINQUANTE-NAIRE

T O W N

TUNNEL

CENTRAL STATION M

U P P E R

RUE DE LA LOI →

MANNEKEN-PIS

M Parc

MIDI/ZUID/SOUTH STATION

Lemonnier

ROYAL MUSEUMS OF FINE ARTS & MAGRITTE MUSEUM

ROYAL PALACE

T O W N

M Trone

RUE DU LUXEMBOURG

M

EU PARLIAMENT

M

AVE. FONSNY

PALAIS DE JUSTICE

PETIT RING

¼ MILE

.5 KM

TO GHENT & BRUGES

DCH

M SUBWAY STOP

Outside the pentagon-shaped center, sprawling suburbs and vast green zones contain more tourist attractions. To the east are the European Parliament and, beyond that, the Park of the Cinquantenaire (Royal Museum of the Army and Military History, Autoworld, and a lesser art museum). And far to the north is the 1958 World's Fair site, with the Atomium and Mini-Europe.

Because the city is officially bilingual, most of Brussels' street signs and maps are in both French and Flemish; I've tried to follow suit in this text, but due to space constraints, on my maps I've generally only given the French name. Because the languages are so different (French is a Romance language, Flemish is Germanic), many places have two names that barely resemble each other (for example, Marché-aux-Herbes/Grasmarkt, or Place Royale/Koningsplein). This can make navigating the city confusing. Use one of the good local maps (such as the TI's free map), which list both languages, so you'll know both street names to look for.

Tourist Information

Brussels has two competing TIs (indicative of Belgium's latent French-Flemish tension). The TI at Rue du Marché-aux-Herbes/Grasmarkt 63 covers **Brussels and Flanders,** with a good room-recommendation service (July-Aug daily 9:00-19:00; April-June and Sept Mon-Sat 9:00-18:00, Sun 10:00-17:00; Oct-March Mon-Sat 9:00-17:00, Sun 10:00-16:00; three blocks downhill from Central Station, tel. 02-504-0390, www.visitflanders.com, fun Europe store nearby). They offer free Wi-Fi and one Internet terminal where you can get online free for up to 15 minutes (and print a few pages—handy for checking in for a flight and printing boarding passes).

The other TI, which focuses on just the **city of Brussels** (no outlying towns), is inside the Town Hall on the Grand Place (Mon-Sat 9:00-18:00; Sun 9:00-18:00 April-Nov, 10:00-14:00 Dec, and closed Sun Jan-March; tel. 02-513-8940, www.brussels international.be).

Both TIs have countless fliers. Day-trippers should pick up a free city map and a public transit map. The €4 *Brussels Guide & Map* booklet is worthwhile if you want a better map (map also sold separately for €0.50), a more complete explanation of the city's many museums, and a series of neighborhood walks (including ones focusing on Art Nouveau, comic strips, and shopping). For current listings of concerts and other entertainment options, look for the free weekly magazines *Agenda* (in English, French, and Flemish) and *Brussels Unlimited* (only in English).

Sightseeing Deals: The **Brussels Card,** sold at the TIs, provides unlimited public transportation and free entrance to nearly all the major museums (€24/24 hours, €34/48 hours, €40/72 hours, also sold at museums, public transportation offices, and some hotels, www.brusselscard.be). If you're in town for less than a day, it's unlikely this pass will pay for itself; but with more time here, busy sightseers will get their money's worth. The TIs also offer a deal called **Must of Brussels**—you pay €18 for 10 vouchers that you can mix and match for discounted entries into top sights. Though complicated to figure out, it could save you a few euros (www.mustofbrussels.com).

Alternative Tourist Information: The excellent, welcoming **USE-IT** information office, which is geared toward youthful backpackers, offers free Internet access and Wi-Fi, free coffee and tea, and in-the-know advice about Brussels and other Belgian destinations, including Bruges, Antwerp, and Ghent (Mon-Sat 10:00-13:00 & 14:00-18:00, closed Sun, Quai à la Houille/Steenkoolkaai 9B, Metro: Ste. Catherine, www.use-it.be). They also publish free user-friendly maps of Brussels and several other Belgian cities; all of their maps are packed with homegrown insight.

Arrival in Brussels

By Train

Brussels has three different stations: Centraal/Central, Nord/Noord/North, and Midi/Zuid/South. Although none is officially the "main" train station, Central Station (a short walk from the Grand Place) is by far the easiest for arriving sightseers, whereas Midi/Zuid/South Station is the only one served by high-speed trains (with the fastest connections to Paris, Amsterdam, and Germany). If you're arriving on one of these fast trains, you'll enter the city through Midi/Zuid/South Station; all other trains stop at all three stations. No matter how you arrive, your goal is eventually to reach Central Station (pay close attention and ask your conductor for help to ensure you get off at the right stop).

Nord/Noord/North Station

Any train that goes through North Station (surrounded by a seedy red light district, far from any significant sightseeing) will also stop at the other two. Don't bother getting off at North Station—disembark at Central Station instead.

Midi/Zuid/South Station

About a mile and a half southwest of the city center, this station's various names mystify tourists (especially since *midi* is French for "middle," not "south"). But as Brussels' lone station for speedy, long-distance trains, it's considered the city's primary international hub. Fortunately, the station is a lot more user-friendly than its name.

South Station serves the fastest high-speed connections: Eurostar (to/from London); Thalys (to/from Amsterdam, Paris, Köln in Germany, and a few other destinations—such as Marseille, France, in the summer and the French Alps in the winter); TGV (to/from Paris' Charles de Gaulle Airport—but not central Paris, as Thalys has a monopoly there, and then on to destinations in southern France); and ICE (to/from Frankfurt). These special fast trains stop only at South Station, not at the other two Brussels stations. All other trains—including slower trains to many of these same destinations, and trains to anywhere in Belgium—stop at all three stations. Unless your train only stops here, get off at Central Station instead (explained later).

South Station's tracks are connected by a long, gloomy, gray-steel concourse with ample computer screens showing upcoming trains. High-speed trains use tracks 1-6 (1-2 for Eurostar and 3-6 for the others). The station has plenty of luggage lockers (€3-4, between tracks 6 and 7), as well as three separate Travel Centre ticket offices (for domestic, international, and international/immediate departures). The area around South Station is a rough-and-tumble immigrant neighborhood (marked by its towering Ferris wheel).

Getting from Midi/Zuid/South Station to Central Station: If you must disembark at South Station, your first step on arrival will be to make your way to Central Station. It's fast and easy by train, but also possible by taxi.

Trains zip under the city, connecting all three stations every few minutes or so. The €1.70 fare between the stations is covered by any train ticket into or out of Brussels (or an activated railpass). Scan the computer departure screens for trains leaving in the next few minutes. While these boards usually don't list Central Station as a destination, trains headed for any of the following places will stop there: the Airport, Alost/Aalst, Antwerpen, Leuven, Liège, Namur, and many others. If you see a train going to any of these places in the next few minutes, just head to that track. (But note that trains headed in the opposite direction—including those to Ghent and Bruges—do *not* stop at Central Station.)

Alternatively, you can take a **taxi** from South Station into the city center. It should cost you no more than €10; however, cabbies from this station are notorious for taking a roundabout route to overcharge arriving tourists. If you do opt for a taxi, insist on the meter, follow the route on a map, and if the total fare seems too high, enlist the help of your hotel receptionist.

Centraal/Central Station

This station, nearest to the sights and my recommended hotels, has handy services: a small grocery store, fast food, waiting rooms, and luggage lockers (€3-4, between tracks 3 and 4). Walking from Central Station to the Grand Place takes about five minutes: Exit the station from the top floor (to the left of the ticket windows), where you'll see Le Meridien Hôtel across the square. Pass through the arch of Le Meridien Hôtel, turn right, and walk one block downhill on l'Infante Isabelle street to a small square with a fountain (officially "Herb Market"—Rue du Marché-aux-Herbes/Grasmarkt—but nicknamed "Agora"). For the Grand Place, turn left at the far end of the little square. Or, to head directly to the TI, exit the small square at the far end and continue straight for one block, then look left.

Competitive hop-on, hop-off tourist buses depart from just in front of Central Station (you'll meet ticket hustlers as you leave). You could hop on one of these buses upon arrival to orient yourself from the top deck (see "Tours in Brussels," later).

By Plane

Brussels is served by two airports. Most flights use the primary

Brussels Airport, a.k.a. Zaventem; no-frills carriers use the Brussels South Charleroi Airport. For details on both, see "Brussels Connections" on page 503.

Helpful Hints

Theft Alert: Brussels is a huge, international, multiethnic city—the type of place that attracts diplomats, tourists...and thieves. As you would in any big city, keep your wits about you and wear a money belt. And though the tourist zone—the area within the pentagon-shaped ring road—is basically safe at any hour of day or night, muggings do occur in some rough-and-tumble areas farther afield. (Near the Midi/Zuid/South Station is a mostly Muslim immigrant neighborhood; near the North Station is a red-light district. Locals joke that as you walk from one end of town to the other, you go from seeing women entirely covered to women entirely uncovered.) If you're venturing beyond the city center, get local advice about safety—and, if you're outside of this area after midnight, when the Métro shuts down, consider taking a taxi back to your hotel.

Sightseeing Schedules: Brussels' most important museums are closed on Monday. Of course, the city's single best sight—the Grand Place—is always open. You can also enjoy a bus tour any day of the week, or visit the more far-flung sights (which *are* open on Monday), such as the Atomium/Mini-Europe and the European Parliament. Most importantly, this is a city to browse and wander.

Internet Access: The **USE-IT** information office (listed earlier) has four free Internet terminals and free Wi-Fi; the **Brussels and Flanders TI** on Rue du Marché-aux-Herbes/Grasmarkt has one Internet terminal and offers 15 minutes free (plus unlimited free Wi-Fi). There's also an **Internet café** in a dreary urban area between the Grand Place and Ste. Catherine (€1.50/hour, also cheap calls and printing, calling cabins downstairs, computer terminals upstairs, daily 9:30-23:15, 18 Rue Marché aux Poulets/Kiekenmarkt).

Laundry: Coin-op launderettes aren't too hard to find. There's one near the Grand Place at Rue du Midi/Zuidstraat 65 (daily 7:00-21:00, change machine) and another in Ste. Catherine, at Rue Flandres/Vlaamsesteenweg 51 (daily 7:00-22:00, no change machine).

Travel Bookstore: Anticyclone des Açores has a wide selection of maps and travel books, including many in English (Mon-Sat 11:00-18:00, closed Sun, Rue Fossé aux Loups/Wolvengracht 34, tel. 02-217-5246).

Getting Around Brussels

Most of central Brussels' sights can be reached on foot. But public transport is handy for connecting the train stations, climbing to the Upper Town (bus #95 from the Bourse), or visiting sights outside the central core. To reach these outlying sights, such as the European Parliament, take the Métro or jump on a hop-on, hop-off tour bus from Central Station (described under "Tours in Brussels," next page; check tour bus route map to make sure it covers the sights you want to see).

By Métro, Bus, Tram, and Train: A single €1.70 ticket is good for one hour on all public transportation—Métro, buses, trams, and even trains shuttling between Brussels' three train stations. Validate your ticket when you enter, feeding it into one of the breadbox-size orange machines. Notice the time when you first stamp it (you have an hour), and stamp your ticket again if you transfer lines. Transit info: tel. 02-515-2000, www.mivb.be.

A five-ride card costs €7.30 (€1.46/ride), and a 10-ride card is €12.50. An all-day pass is €4.50—cheaper than three single tickets—and on Sat-Sun and holidays, this pass covers two people. A 72-hour ticket costs €9.50. (Skip the Mobib, a prepaid card for public transit that's practical only for locals.)

Buy individual tickets at newsstands, in Métro stations (vending machines accept credit cards or coins), or (for €0.30 extra) from the bus driver. Get multiride cards and passes from the Brussels and Flanders TI or at Métro stations. The excellent, free *Métro Tram Bus Plan* is available at either TI or any Métro station.

Like the streets, Brussels' transit stops are labeled in both French and Flemish (unless the spelling is the same in both languages); I've followed suit in this book.

Brussels' Métro has four lines: Line 1 runs west-east (from Gare de l'Ouest/Weststation to Stockel/Stokkel); the circular line 2 starts and ends at Simonis; line 5 runs west-east from Erasme/Erasmus to Herrmann-Debroux; and line 6 starts at Roi Baudouin/Koning Boudewijn in the northwest, then ties into the circular line at Simonis. A series of tram lines run north-south through the city center, connecting the Métro lines and the North, Central, and Midi/Zuid/South train stations; two of these are considered part of the Métro (lines 3 and 4). Buses go where the Métro and trams don't (buses marked *Noctis* travel at night, after other transit stops running).

Near the Grand Place are two transportation hubs: Central Station and the Bourse. If you're staying at a hotel northwest of the Grand Place, you've got good access to the Métro system via the Ste. Catherine/Sint-Katelijne and De Brouckère stops.

By Taxi: Drivers in big-city Brussels are happy to take you for a ride; find out the approximate cost to your destination before you head out. Cabbies charge a €2.40 drop fee, as well as €1.50 per additional kilometer. After 22:00, they hit you with a €2 surcharge. You'll pay about €10 to ride from the center to the European Parliament. Convenient taxi stands are at the Bourse (near the Grand Place), at the "Agora" square near the Grand Place (Rue du Marché-aux-Herbes/Grasmarkt), and at Place du Grand Sablon (in the Upper Town). To call a cab, try **Taxi Bleu** (tel. 02-268-0000) or **Autolux** (tel. 02-512-3123).

By Bike: The city of Brussels subsidizes a network of cheap bikes designed to be borrowed for short rides within the city. The program, called **Villo,** has rental stations around town. After you register at the automated kiosk with your credit card (€1.50/day, €7/week), you can borrow bikes at will for short durations, then drop them off at any other station (free for up to 30 minutes, €0.50/30-60 minutes, €1/1-1.5 hours, €2/1.5-2 hours, www.villo.be). Stations with an automated kiosk also show you which nearby stations have bikes available, and how many. But bike stands at higher altitudes (in the Upper Town) are often empty, whereas they're full—surprise, surprise—at lower altitudes (in the Lower Town).

Tours in Brussels

Hop-On, Hop-Off Bus Tours—Various companies offer nearly identical introductory city tours. The 1.5-hour loop and recorded narration give you a once-over-lightly of the city from the top deck (open on sunny days) of a double-decker bus. You can hop on and off for 24 hours with one ticket, but schedules are sparse (figure €18-20 for each company, about 2/hour, times listed on each flier; all companies run roughly April-Oct daily 10:00-16:00, Sat until 17:00; Nov-March daily 10:00-15:00, Sat until 16:00). Except for the trip out to the European Parliament and Cinquantenaire Park (which hosts the military and auto museums), I'd just stay on to enjoy the views and the minimal commentary. The fiercely competitive companies often have hustlers at Central Station trying to get you on board (offering "student" discounts to customers of all ages). The handiest starting points are Central Station and the Bourse. The companies are **City Tours** (tel. 02-513-7744, www.brussels-city-tours.com), **CitySightseeing/Open Tours** (tel. 02-466-1111, www.citysightseeingbrussel.be), and **Golden Tours** (mobile 0486-053-981, www.goldentours.be).

Bus Tours—City Tours also offers a typical three-hour guided (in up to five languages) bus tour, providing you an easy way to get the grand perspective on Brussels. You start with a walk around the Grand Place, then jump on a tour bus (€27, year-round daily at 10:00 and 14:00, they'll pick you up at your hotel or depart from their office a block off Grand Place at Rue du Marché-aux-Herbes 82; you can buy tickets there, at TI, or in your hotel; tel. 02-513-7744, www.brussels-city-tours.com). You'll get off the bus at the Atomium for a quick photo stop.

Private Guide—Claude and Dominique Janssens are a father-and-son team who lead tours both in Brussels and to other Belgian cities, including Bruges, Ghent, and Antwerp (€110/3 hours, €230/full day plus €25 for lunch, Claude's mobile 0485-025-423, Dominique's mobile 0486-451-155, www.discover-b.be, claude @discover-b.be).

SIGHTS IN BRUSSELS

The Grand Place may be Brussels' top sight, but the city offers a variety of museums, big and small, to fill your time here. I've divided the sights between the Lower Town, the Upper Town, and the outskirts.

In the Lower Town

On the Grand Place

Brussels' Grand Place—as well as some of the sights fronting it, including the Town Hall, City Museum, and chocolate shops—are described in more detail in the ☉ Grand Place Walk chapter.

▲▲▲**Grand Place**—Brussels' main square, aptly called the Grand Place (grahn plahs; in Flemish: Grote Markt, HHHROH-teh markt), is the heart of the old town and Brussels' greatest sight. Any time of day, it's worth swinging by to see what's going on. Concerts, flower markets, sound-and-light shows, endless people-watching—it entertains (as do the streets around it). The museums on the square are well-advertised but dull.

Town Hall (Hôtel de Ville)—With the Grand Place's tallest spire, this is the square's centerpiece, but its interior is no big deal. Admission is only possible with a 45-minute English tour, which also covers city history and the building's tapestries and architecture (€3, Tue-Wed at 15:15, Sun at 10:45 and 12:15 except no Sun tours Oct-March). Only 25 people are allowed per tour; assure a spot by buying tickets from the guide exactly 40 minutes before the tour starts (in the courtyard behind the spire).

▲**City Museum (Musée de la Ville de Bruxelles)**—Inside the King's House (Maison du Roi) building, across the Grand Place from the Town Hall, is the one museum on the square that's actually worth visiting. The museum's top floor has a roomful of goofy

Brussels

TO NORD/NOORD/
NORTH
STATION

TO Ⓜ Rogier

R. DU GRAND

QUAI AU BOIS

QUAI AUX BRIQUES

R. DE FLANDRE

RUE DANSAERT

HOSPICE

PL. BEG.

Ste. Cath.

Ⓜ

FISH MKT.

De Brouckère

PL. S. CATH.

STE. CATH.

Ⓜ

STE. CATH. MARCHE

V. PRAET.

A. ORTS

ANSPACH

FRIPIERS

R. POULETS

R. DES BOUCHERS

ADOLPHE MAX

NEUVE

BLVD.

RUE

PL. MART.

PLACE DE LA MONNAIE

FRIPIERS

THEATRE ROYALE

R. DE LA BLANCH.

SABLES

R. MARAIS

COMEDIENS

BLVD. BERLAYMONT

BELGIAN
COMIC BOOK
CENTER

GALERIES ST. HUBERT

PL. ST-GERY

Ⓜ

BOURSE

Ⓜ

Ⓑ

MIDI

GRAND
PLACE

TOWN HALL

ⓘ

ⓘ

"AGORA" SQ.

MONT.

L'IMPERATRICE

MERC.

LOXUM

ST. MICHAEL'S

COLONIES

TO Parc Ⓜ

Ⓜ Gare Central

CENTRAL
STATION

R. ROYALE

BLVD. DE L'ETUVE

KOLENMARKT

RUE DE

MANNEKEN-PIS

ST. JEAN

LOMBARD

TOUR D'ANGLE

MAD.

Ⓑ

BLVD. DE L'EMPEREUR

MUSICAL
INSTRUMENTS
MUSEUM

BELVUE
MUSEUM

PLACE DES PALAIS

LOWER
TOWN

Anneessens

Ⓜ

ALEXIENS

R. CHENE

NOTRE

R. LEB.

ROLLE

ROYAL MUSEUMS
OF FINE
ARTS

PL. ROYALE

ROYAL PALACE

MAGRITTE
MUSEUM

UPPER

TOWN

TO
MIDI/ZUID/
SOUTH
STATION

R. BLAES

R. HAUTE

BODEN

SABLONS

R. REGENCE

NOTRE-DAME
DU SABLON

TO PALACE OF JUSTICE

Ⅲ STAIRS

Ⓜ SUBWAY STOP

Ⓑ TOUR BUS DEPARTURE POINTS (2)

→ 5 MIN. WALK - CENTRAL STATION
TO GRAND PLACE

200 YARDS

200 METERS

DCH

costumes the *Manneken* statue has pissed through (and an engrossing video of tourists' reactions to the statue), the middle floor features maps and models of old Brussels, and the bottom floor has some old artwork.

Cost and Hours: €3, borrow English descriptions in each room, Tue-Sun 10:00-17:00, closed Mon, Grand Place, tel. 02-279-4350. For local history, the best choice is not this museum, but the BELvue Museum (see page 441).

▲**Chocolate Shops on the Grand Place**—For many, the best thing about the Grand Place is the chocolate sold at the five venerable chocolate shops: Godiva, Neuhaus, Galler, Leonidas, and Corné Port-Royal (shops generally open Mon-Sat 9:00-22:00, Sun 10:00-22:00). Each has inviting displays and sells mixes of 100 grams (your choice of 6-8 pieces) or individual pieces for about €1.60. It takes a lot of sampling to judge. See the "choco-crawl" described in the Grand Place Walk chapter.

Brewery Museum—This little bar-like place has one room of old brewing paraphernalia and one room of new, plus a beer video in English. It's pretty lame...but a good excuse for a beer (€6 includes an unnamed local beer, daily 10:00-17:00, Dec-March Sat-Sun opens at 12:00, Grand Place 10, tel. 02-511-4987).

Museum of Cocoa and Chocolate—This touristy exhibit, to the right of Town Hall, is a delightful concept and tries hard, but it's overpriced at €5.50 for three floors of meager displays, a ho-hum video, a look at a "chocolate master" at work (live demos 2/hour), and a choco-sample (Tue-Sun 10:00-16:30, until 17:00 July-Aug, closed Mon, Rue de la Tête d'Or 9, tel. 02-514-2048, www.mucc.be).

Near the Grand Place

▲▲*Manneken-Pis*—Brussels is a great city with a cheesy mascot: a statue of a little boy urinating (apparently symbolizing the city's irreverence and love of the good life). Read up on his story at any postcard stand. He's three short blocks off the Grand Place, but, for exact directions, take my Grand Place Walk; look for small, white *Manneken-Pis* signs; or just ask a local, *"Où est le Manneken-Pis?"* (oo ay luh man-ay-kehn peese). The little squirt may be wearing some clever outfit, as costumes are sent to Brussels from around the world. Cases full of these are on display in the City Museum (described earlier).

For more details, ✪ see page 463 of the Grand Place Walk chapter.

Costume and Lace Museum—This is worthwhile only to those few who have devoted their lives to the making or wearing of lace (€3, Mon-Tue and Thu-Fri 10:00-12:30 & 13:30-17:00, Sat-Sun

14:00-17:00, closed Wed, Rue de la Violette 12, a block off the Grand Place, tel. 02-213-4450).

West of the Grand Place

These two fun-to-explore neighborhoods, just across the busy Boulevard Anspach from the Bourse, offer some of Brussels' most appealing restaurants (far less touristy than those near the Grand Place). Ste. Catherine is also a fine place to sleep. If you're look-ing for a bustling nighttime neighborhood full of inviting eateries and bars, you'll enjoy strolling these two areas and the five-minute walk between them. For details, see page 500.

Ste. Catherine and the Old Fish Market (Vieux Marché aux Poissons/Vismet)—Two blocks northwest of the Bourse is the ragtag Church of Ste. Catherine, which marks an inviting "village in the city" area with great eating options. The church itself is falling apart—during its construction, the architect got the commission for the Place of Justice in the Upper Town, and rushed to complete this church so he could begin the more lucrative new job as quickly as possible. In front of the church stretches the long, skinny former fish market, lined with a range of upscale fish restaurants. Alongside the church is Place Ste. Catherine/ Sint-Katelijneplein, with more restaurants, bars, and the city's best cheap-and-fast lunch options (including a charming little cheese shop and a pair of seafood bars).

Place St-Géry/Sint-Goriksplein—This square was actually once an island, and the market hall in the middle of the square evokes a time when goods—which were offloaded a few blocks away, at the old fish market (see above)—were brought here for sale. Today the hall houses a café and special exhibits. On Sunday mornings, the surrounding square is filled with a comics market. Across from the southwest corner of the hall, at #23 (next to the *Au Lion d'Or* information board), duck through the little gateway to find a relaxing courtyard. You might see businesspeople dozing on their lunch break here, in this oasis in the heart of the city. At the far end of the courtyard you'll see a small stretch of the river that used to be Brussels' trading lifeline, but was long ago covered over and forgotten.

North of Central Station

▲**St. Michael's Cathedral**—One of Europe's classic Gothic churches, built between roughly 1200 and 1500, Brussels' cathedral

is made from white stone and topped by twin towers. For nearly 1,000 years, it's been the most important church in this largely Catholic country. (Whereas the Netherlands went in a Protestant direction in the 1500s, Belgium remains 80 percent Catholic—although only about 20 percent attend Mass.)

The white-themed nave is bare but impressive, with a few nice stained-glass windows and a marvelous carved pulpit of Adam and Eve supporting the preacher. On top, St. Michael stabs Satan in serpent form.

This church is where royal weddings and funerals take place. Photographs (to the right of the entrance) show the funeral of the popular King Baudouin, who died in 1993. He was succeeded by his younger brother, Albert II (whose face is on Belgium's euro coins). Albert will be succeeded by his son, Prince Philippe. Traditionally, the ruler was always a male, but in 1992 the constitution was changed to allow the oldest child of either gender—boy or girl—to take the throne. In 1999, Prince Philippe and his bride, Mathilde—after a civil ceremony at the Town Hall—paraded up

Brussels at a Glance

▲▲▲Grand Place Main square and spirited heart of the Lower Town, surrounded by mediocre museums and delectable chocolate shops. **Hours:** Always open. See page 429.

▲▲▲Royal Museums of Fine Arts of Belgium Museums displaying ancient art (14th-18th centuries) and modern art (19th-20th centuries). **Hours:** Tue-Sun 10:00-17:00, closed Mon. See page 438.

▲▲*Manneken-Pis* World-famous statue of a leaky little boy. **Hours:** Always peeing. See page 431.

▲▲Magritte Museum Biographical collection of works by the prominent Belgian Surrealist painter René Magritte. **Hours:** Tue-Sun 10:00-17:00, Wed until 20:00, closed Mon. See page 440.

▲▲BELvue Museum Interesting Belgian history museum with a focus on the popular royal family. **Hours:** Tue-Fri 10:00-17:00, Sat-Sun 10:00-18:00, closed Mon. See page 441.

▲City Museum Costumes worn by the *Manneken-Pis* statue and models of Brussels' history. **Hours:** Tue-Sun 10:00-17:00, closed Mon. See page 429.

▲Chocolate on Grand Place Choco-crawl through Godiva, Neuhaus, Galler, Leonidas, and Corné Port-Royal. **Hours:** Generally Mon-Sat 9:00-22:00, Sun 10:00-22:00. See page 431.

▲St. Michael's Cathedral White-stone Gothic church where Belgian royals are married and buried. **Hours:** Mon-Fri 7:00-18:00, Sat-Sun 8:30-18:00, until 19:00 in summer. See page 433.

▲Belgian Comic Strip Center Homage to hometown heroes including the Smurfs, Tintin, and Lucky Luke. **Hours:** Tue-Sun 10:00-18:00, closed Mon. See page 436.

▲Musical Instruments Museum Exhibits with more than 1,500 instruments, complete with audio. **Hours:** Tue-Fri 9:30-16:45, Sat-Sun 10:00-16:45, closed Mon. See page 440.

▲European Parliament Soaring home of Europe's governing body. **Hours:** Mon-Thu 9:00-17:15, Fri 9:00-13:00, closed Sat-Sun; audioguide tours Mon-Thu at 10:00 and 15:00, additional tours

July-Aug—last departure at 16:00, Fri at 10:00 only. See page 443.

▲**Royal Army and Military History Museum** Vast collection of weaponry and uniforms. **Hours:** Tue-Sun 9:00-16:45, closed Mon. See page 447.

▲**Autoworld** Hundreds of historic vehicles, including Mr. Benz's 1886 motorized tricycle. **Hours:** Daily April-Sept 10:00-18:00, Oct-March 10:00-17:00. See page 447.

▲**Royal Museum of Central Africa** Excellent but far-flung exhibit about the former Belgian Congo, featuring ethnology, artifacts, and wildlife. **Hours:** Tue-Fri 10:00-17:00, Sat-Sun 10:00-18:00, closed Mon. See page 449.

Town Hall Focal point of the Grand Place, with arresting spire but boring interior. **Hours:** Tours depart Tue-Wed at 15:15, Sun at 10:45 and 12:15, no Sun tours Oct-March. See page 429.

Costume and Lace Museum World-famous Brussels lace, as well as outfits, embroideries, and accessories from the 17th-20th centuries. **Hours:** Mon-Tue and Thu-Fri 10:00-12:30 & 13:30-17:00, Sat-Sun 14:00-17:00, closed Wed. See page 431.

Ste. Catherine Neighborhood and Place St-Géry Pleasant areas with fun eateries west of the Grand Place. **Hours:** Always buzzing. See page 432-433.

Royal Belgian Institute of Natural Sciences Europe's largest dinosaur gallery. **Hours:** Tue-Fri 9:30-17:00, Sat-Sun 10:00-18:00, closed Mon. See page 446.

Royal Museum of Art and History Eclectic but unexciting art museum. **Hours:** Tue-Fri 9:30-17:00, Sat-Sun 10:00-17:00, closed Mon. See page 448.

Atomium Giant homage to the atomic age with fun exhibit and panorama deck. **Hours:** Daily 10:00-18:00, later in summer. See page 448.

Mini-Europe Models of 350 famous European landmarks. **Hours:** Easter-Sept daily 9:30-18:00, July-Aug until 20:00; Oct-Dec 10:00-18:00; closed Jan-Easter. See page 449.

Shopping in Brussels

The obvious temptations—available absolutely everywhere—are **chocolate** and **lace**. (For tips on specific shops for each one, see the Grand Place Walk chapter.) Other popular Brussels souvenirs include EU gear (flags, T-shirts, etc., with the gold circle of stars on a blue background) and miniature reproductions of the *Manneken-Pis*.

To get beyond the touristy city center, consider browsing along some of the following streets:

Rue Neuve/Nieuwstraat, a few blocks north of the Grand Place, is where you'll find big department stores and other international shops. The giant **City2** complex on this street is the downtown's primary modern shopping mall.

Antoine Dansaert street, directly across the boulevard from the Bourse, is lined with boutiques and galleries.

The somewhat seedy **Marolles neighborhood** is well-known for its secondhand shops. Rue Blaes/Blaesstraat and Rue Haute/Hoogstraat, which run southwest from near the old Tour d'Angle (described in the Upper Town Walk chapter) to the Midi/Zuid/South Train Station, are lined with several characteristic stores. There's a lively flea market each morning (7:00-14:00, best on weekends) on Place du Jeu de Balle/Vossenplein, just off of Rue Blaes/Blaesstraat.

here for a two-hour Catholic ceremony with all the trimmings. Their daughter Elisabeth, born in 2001, is in line to become Belgium's queen.

Before leaving, pause on the outer porch to enjoy the great view of the Town Hall spire with its gold statue of St. Michael.

Cost and Hours: Free, but small fees to visit the underwhelming crypt and treasury, Mon-Fri 7:00-18:00, Sat-Sun 8:30-18:00, until 19:00 in summer.

▲Belgian Comic Strip Center (Centre Belge de la Bande Dessinée)—Belgians are as proud of their comics as they are of their beer, lace, and chocolates. Something about the comic medium resonates with the wry and artistic-yet-unpretentious Belgian sensibility. Belgium has produced some of the world's most popular comic characters, including the Smurfs, Tintin, and Lucky Luke. You'll find these, and many less famous local comics, at the Comic Strip Center.

Even if you don't have time or interest to visit the museum's collection, pop in to the lobby to see the groundbreaking Art Nouveau building (a former department store designed in 1903 by Belgian architect Victor Horta), browse through comics in the bookshop, and snap a photo with a three-foot-tall Smurf. That's enough for many people. Kids might find the museum, like, totally boring, but those who appreciate art in general will enjoy this sometimes humorous, sometimes probing, often beautiful medium. The displays are mostly in French and Flemish, but there is some English. The free, essential English guidebooklet describes the comics-making process (comparing it to the filmmaking process) and has short bios of famous cartoonists.

The collection changes often, but no matter what's on you'll see how comics are made and watch early animated films. The heart of the collection is the golden age of comics in the 1950s and 60s. You'll likely see a sprawling exhibit on Tintin, the intrepid young reporter with the button eyes and wavy shock of hair, launched in 1929 by Hergé and much loved by older Europeans (see sidebar on next page). Brussels' own Peyo (a.k.a. Pierre Culliford, 1928-1992) invented the Smurfs—the little blue forest creatures that stand "three apples high." First popular across much Europe, especially in Belgium (where they're known as Les Schtroumpfs), the Smurfs became well-known to a generation of Americans after they starred in Hanna-Barbera's 1980s televised cartoons. The cowboy Lucky Luke (by Morris, a.k.a. Maurice De Bevere, 1923-2001) exemplifies Belgians' fascination for exotic locales, especially America's Wild West.

The top floor's temporary exhibits are often dedicated to "serious" comics, where more adult themes and high-quality drawing aspire to turn kids' stuff into that "Ninth Art." These works can be grimly realistic, openly erotic or graphic, or darker in tone, often featuring flawed antiheroes. The museum's bookstore is nearly as interesting, giving you the chance to page through reproductions of classic comics.

Cost and Hours: €7.50, Tue-Sun 10:00-18:00, closed Mon, 10-minute walk from the Grand Place to Rue des Sables 20, tel. 02-219-1980, www.comicscenter.net.

Getting There: From Central Station, walk north along the big boulevard, then turn left down the stairs at the giant comic character.

Nearby: The related **Marc Sleen Museum,** across the street, is dedicated to one Belgian cartoonist in particular. Sleen's big-nosed, caricatured drawings are recognizable even to many Americans, and is oh-so-typically Belgian. His *Adventures of Nero and Co.*, which he churned out in two strips a day for a staggering 55 years, holds the record for the longest-running comic by a single artist. Still, the collection is worth a visit only to his fans (€1 extra

Tintin 101

Although relatively unknown in the United States, the Belgian comic character Tintin is beloved to several generations of Europeans who have grown up reading of his adventures.

In 1929, a French-speaking Brussels comics artist named Georges Rémi (1907-1983) created a dedicated young reporter with a shock of blond hair who's constantly getting into and out of misadventures. The artist reversed his initials to create the pseudonym Hergé (the French pronunciation for "R.G."). A precise artist, Hergé used a simple, uncluttered style called *ligne claire* ("clear line").

Combining fantasy, mystery, and sci-fi, with a dash of humor, the Tintin stories quickly found an appreciative audience. *The Adventures of Tintin* spanned 47 years and 24 books (selling some 200 million copies—and counting—in 50 languages). Tintin's popularity continues even today, as nostalgic parents buy the comics they grew up on for their own kids.

Tintin (pronounced a nasal "tan-tan" in French) is the smart, upbeat, inquisitive, noble, brave-but-not-foolhardy young man whose adventures propel the plot. His newspaper sends him on assignments all over the world. **Snowy** (Milou in French), Tintin's loyal fox terrier, is his constant canine companion—and often saves the day. The grizzled, grouchy, heavy-drinking **Captain Haddock** is as cynical as Tintin is optimistic, with a penchant

with Comic Strip Center entry, or €2.50 alone, Tue-Sun 11:00-18:00, closed Mon, tel. 02-219-1980, www.marc-sleen.be).

In the Upper Town

Brussels' grandiose Upper Town, with its huge palace, is described in the ❂ Upper Town Walk chapter. Along that walk, you'll pass the following sights.

▲▲▲**Royal Museums of Fine Arts of Belgium (Musées Royaux des Beaux-Arts de Belgique)**—This sprawling complex is worth visiting for its twin museums that show off the country's best all-around art collection (as well as the Magritte Museum—described next—which is in the same complex). The **Museum of Ancient Art** and the **Museum of Modern Art** are covered by the same ticket (enter through the main foyer for both). The Museum of Ancient Art—featuring Flemish and Belgian art of the 14th-18th centuries—is packed with a dazzling collecfor colorful curses ("Blistering barnacles!"). **Professor Calculus** (a.k.a. Professeur Tournesol) is as brilliant as he is absentminded and hard of hearing, and comic relief is provided by the bumbling, nearly identical detectives called **Thomson and Thompson** (Dupont et Dupond).

Throughout his swashbuckling adventures, Tintin travels far and wide to many exotic destinations. Hergé has been acclaimed for his meticulous research—he studied up on the actual places he portrayed, and tried to avoid basing his stories on assumptions or stereotypes (though by today's standards, some of the comics still betray an ugly Eurocentrism—one of the earliest, *Tintin in the Congo*, Hergé himself later acknowledged was regretfully racist).

And though the supporting characters are dynamic and colorful, Tintin himself has a rather bland personality. His expressions are usually indistinct (Hergé wanted the young reader to project his or her own emotions onto Tintin's blank-canvas face). While presumably a teenager, Tintin's age is unclear—at times we imagine him to be a young boy, while others he's seen drinking a beer, piloting a plane, or living in his own apartment (we never meet his family, if he has one). All of this is intentional: Hergé's style subconsciously encourages each reader to put him- or herself in Tintin's everyman shoes.

While Tintin has found success in the United States elusive, things might be changing. Stephen Spielberg's film *The Adventures of Tintin: Secret of the Unicorn*—created in partnership with *Lord of the Rings* filmmaker Peter Jackson, and using the motion-capture animation technique made famous by those films and *Avatar*—is scheduled for release in 2011.

tion of masterpieces by Van der Weyden, Brueghel, Bosch, and Rubens. The Museum of Modern Art gives visitors an easy-to-enjoy walk through the art of the 19th and 20th centuries, from Neoclassical to Surrealism. Highlights here include works by Seurat, Gauguin, and Delvaux.

Cost and Hours: €8, €13 combo-ticket with Magritte Museum, free first Wed of month after 13:00; open Tue-Sun 10:00-17:00, closed Mon, last entry 30 minutes before closing; audioguide-€4, tour booklet-€2.50, pricey cafeteria with salad bar, Rue de la Régence 3, recorded info tel. 02-508-3211, www.fine-arts-museum.be.

✪ See the Royal Museums of Fine Arts and Magritte Museum Tour chapter.

▲▲**Magritte Museum (Musée Magritte)**—This exhibit, examining Surrealist painter René Magritte, is in the same museum complex as the Royal Museums of Fine Arts (above), and contains more than 150 works housed on three floors of a Neoclassical building. Although you won't see many of Magritte's most famous pieces, this lovingly presented museum offers an unusually intimate look at the life and work of one of Belgium's top artists.

Cost and Hours: €8, €13 combo-ticket with Royal Museums of Fine Arts, free first Wed of month after 13:00; open Tue-Sun 10:00-17:00, Wed until 20:00, closed Mon, last entry 30 minutes before closing; tel. 02-508-3333, www.musee-magritte-museum .be. Your ticket comes with an assigned entry time. It's possible to buy tickets in advance (and reserve an entry time) on the Magritte Museum's website, avoiding possible wait time at the museum.

✪ See the Royal Museums of Fine Arts and Magritte Museum Tour chapter.

▲**Musical Instruments Museum (Musée des Instruments de Musique)**—One of Europe's best music museums (nicknamed "MIM") is housed in one of Brussels' most impressive Art Nouveau buildings, the beautifully renovated Old England department store. Part of the Royal Museum of Art and History, this museum has more than 1,500 instruments—from Egyptian harps, to medieval lutes, to groundbreaking harpsichords, to the Brussels-built saxophone. Inside you'll be given a pair of headphones and set free to wander several levels: folk instruments from around the world on the ground floor, a history of Western musical instruments on the first, and an entire floor devoted to strings and pianos on the second. As you approach an instrument, you hear it playing on your headphones (which actually work...most of the time). On the fifth floor is an exhibit about the history of the building and Brussels Art Nouveau in general. The museum is skimpy on English information—except for a laminated sheet in each section that simply identifies instruments—but the music you'll hear is an international language.

Cost and Hours: €5, Tue-Fri 9:30-16:45, Sat-Sun 10:00-16:45, closed Mon, last entry 45 minutes before closing, Rue Montagne de la Cour 2, just downhill and toward the Grand Place from the Royal Museums of Fine Arts, tel. 02-545-0130, www.mim.be.

Cuisine Art and Views: The sixth floor has a restaurant, a terrace, and a great view of Brussels (€10-15 *plats du jour*, same hours as museum but also open until 23:00 Thu-Sat, pick up free access pass at museum entrance). The corner alcoves on each level (accessible as you tour the museum) have even better views.

▲▲**BELvue Museum**—In a remarkable feat of museum magic, this sight achieves the impossible: It makes Belgian history fas-

cinating. The exhibit—which fills two palatial floors with lots of real historical artifacts—illustrates the short sweep of this nation's story, from its 1830 inception to today. To make the most of your visit, follow along with the wonderful and extensive flier translating all of the descriptions. Skip the €2.50 audioguide, which simply repeats the information on the flier.

With rooms that proceed in chronological order, the museum explains Belgium's push for independence from the Netherlands, the roots of the ongoing friction between its Francophone-dominated ruling class and its generally Flemish peasant class, and how Belgium cleverly managed to assert itself as a fledgling nation in a changing world (for example, its new royalty agreed to not wear crowns or sit on a throne, in deference to its parliament).

The exhibit doesn't shy away from the controversial, such as the appalling story of the Belgian Congo, which King Leopold II acquired as his personal property in 1885 and proceeded to exploit mercilessly until a storm of public anger forced him to turn it over to the Belgian government in 1908. Leopold's wealth was poured into city development—including the stately Neoclassical buildings of the Upper Town, as well as some slinky Art Nouveau masterpieces—making the 1890s a belle époque for Belgium. But it was also a time of extreme social stratification, when only French aristocrats (about 2 percent of the population) had the power to elect the government. (One poster provocatively compares the disenfranchised Flemish to the oppressed Congolese.) The Belgian workers' movement, based in the socialist hotbed of Ghent, achieved universal male suffrage in 1893.

After outlining the devastation of the World Wars, the exhibit examines postwar Belgium's recovery, its successful implementation of one of Europe's most socialistic governments, and its gradual emergence as the capital of Europe. The conclusion explains how even today, the Flemish-Francophone conflict festers, while reforms implemented since 1970 aspire to prevent Belgium from splitting completely in half.

Outside in the hallway, biographical sketches and intimate family photos provide you a chance to get to know the (generally) much-loved royal family. Since these imported German monarchs arrived in 1830, each of the six "Kings of the Belgians" (as they're officially known) has had his own style and claim to fame—or infamy: visionary Leopold I; "Builder King" and Congo exploiter Leopold II; appreciated World War I leader Albert I (who won many fans for the monarchy); controversial World War II-era Leopold III (who abdicated in disgrace); well-respected Baudouin (r. 1950-1993); and his equally popular brother, current King Albert II.

Cost and Hours: €5, €8 combo-ticket includes Coudenberg Palace, Tue-Fri 10:00-17:00, Sat-Sun 10:00-18:00, closed Mon, to the right of the palace at place des Palais 7, tel. 070-220-492, www .belvue.be.

Cuisine Art: Healthy lunches are served in the cool "Green Kitchen" café in the lobby of this former princess' palace (€10-15 plates, same hours as museum).

Coudenberg Palace—The BELvue Museum stands atop the barren archaeological remains of a 12th-century Brussels palace. Though well-lit and well-described, these long, vaulted cellars require too much imagination to make them meaningful. A small museum explains artifacts from the palace. The best thing is the free orientation video you see before descending. If you do tour the palace ruins, do so after you're finished at the BELvue Museum, because you'll exit the Coudenberg downhill, near the Musical Instruments Museum.

Cost and Hours: €5, €8 combo-ticket includes BELvue Museum; €2.50 audioguide does not cover BELvue Museum, yet must be (inconveniently) returned to BELvue entrance; same hours as BELvue Museum.

Outer Brussels

East of Downtown

Several interesting sights lie just east of the city center: First, the European Parliament (just beyond the Pentagon ring road); beyond that, the museums at the Park of the Cinquantenaire. Because these are in the same direction and connected by a quick bus ride (explained next), they're easy to visit in one fell swoop.

Connecting the Sights: Handy public-transportation connections make it easy to see both the European Parliament and the Park of the Cinquantenaire. The Métro zips you from the center out to the Park of the Cinquantenaire in minutes (Métro stop: Merode). From the park, catch bus #27 (bus stop: Gaulois/Galliërs, direction: Gare du Midi/Zuidstation, 4-5/hour Mon-Fri, 2-3/hour Sat-Sun) to the Luxembourg stop (for the European Parliament) and on to the Royale/Koning stop (for the Royal Palace and great nearby museums). It's cheap and easy, plus you'll feel quite clever doing it.

▲European Parliament

Europe's governing body welcomes visitors with an information center and audioguide tours. This sprawling complex of glass skyscrapers is a cacophony of black-suited politicians speaking 23 different Euro-languages. It's exciting just to be here—a fly on the wall of a place that aspires to chart the future of Europe "with respect for all political thinking... consolidating democracy in the spirit of peace and solidarity." The 785 parliament members, representing 27 countries and more than 500 million citizens, shape Europe with an €130 billion budget.

Getting There: The European Parliament is next to Place du Luxembourg. From the Bourse in downtown Brussels, take bus #95; from the museums at the Park of the Cinquantenaire or the Royal Palace, take bus #27. Place du Luxembourg is also a seven-minute walk from the Trône/Troon Métro stop (straight ahead up Luxembourg street). To find the Info Point (described next) from Place du Luxembourg, go behind the old train station and beneath the semicircular glass walkway, and look for the *Info* sign.

Visitors Center: The **Info Point** is a welcoming place, with 28 flags (one for each member country, plus the EU's circle of gold stars on a blue field), videos promoting the concept and beauties of the European Union, and racks of entertaining freebies—including maps outlining the member states, the free *Troubled Waters* comic book that explains how the parliament works, and bins of miniature *My Fundamental Rights in the EU* booklets—everything in 23 different languages, of course (free entry, Mon-Thu 9:00-17:15, Fri 9:00-13:00, closed Sat-Sun, www.europarl.europa.eu). An adjacent bigger-and-even-better visitors center, planned for September 2011, may be open in time for your visit.

Audioguide Tours: The only way to get inside the European Parliament itself is to join a free 30-minute audioguide tour. These leave from the visitors entrance, down the stairs and across the street from the Info Point (around the left side of the round, glassy building; Mon-Thu at 10:00 and 15:00, additional tours in July-Aug—last one usually departs at 16:00; Fri only at 10:00; busiest on Mon, no visitors under 14 years old). It's smart and easy to call ahead to confirm the schedule and reserve a space (tel. 02-284-2111). If you're just showing up, try to arrive about 30 minutes early to secure a place on busy days. *Note:* On the two days each month that parliament is in session, visitors are allowed to watch the proceedings, but no tours are offered.

The European Union

Brussels is the capital of one of the biggest, most powerful, and most idealistic states in the world (and, arguably, in history): The European Union (EU). In just one genera-tion, more than two dozen European coun-tries have gone from being bitter rivals to compatriots. This union of such a diverse collection of separate nations—with dif-ferent languages, cultures, and soccer teams—is almost unprecedented. And it all started in the rubble of a devastating war.

World War II left 40 million dead and a continent in ruins, and it convinced Europeans that they had to work together to maintain peace. Poised between com-peting superpowers (the US and the USSR), they also needed to cooperate economically to survive in an increas-ingly globalized economy. Just after the war ended, visionary "Eurocrats" began the task of convincing reluctant European nations to relinquish elements of their sovereignty and merge into a united body.

The transition happened very gradually, in fits and starts. It began in 1948, when Belgium, the Netherlands, and Luxembourg—jointly called "BeNeLux"—established a free-trade zone. That evolved into an ever-broadening alliance of states (the European Coal and Steel Union, then the European Economic Community, or "Common Market"). In 1992, with the Treaty of Maastricht, the 12 member countries of the Common Market made a leap of faith: They created a "European Union" that would eventually allow for free movement of capital, goods, services, and labor.

In 2002, most EU members adopted a single currency (the euro), and for all practical purposes, economic unity was a reality. Ten additional member states joined in 2004 and two more in 2007, bringing the total to 27—encompassing the British Isles, nearly all of Western Europe, and much of Eastern Europe and Scandinavia. Almost all EU members have joined the open-borders Schengen Agreement, making passport checkpoints

When you check in, you'll be given an audioguide and sent through a security checkpoint. Head up the stairs and wait for your tour to begin in the atrium, with exhibits and a gift shop. At the appointed time, your escort leads you to various viewpoints in the complex where you'll be instructed to listen to the related audioguide commentary.

The slow-paced audioguide—with helpful video illustra-tions—dryly takes you through the history of the EU, as well as its obsolete. This makes the EU the world's seventh-largest "country" (1.7 million square miles), with the third-largest population (more than 500 million people), and an economy that beats the US's as the world's biggest ($16 trillion GDP).

The EU is governed from Brussels (though some EU institutions meet in Strasbourg, Frankfurt, Luxembourg, and other cities). While it has a parliament, the EU is primarily led by the European Commission (with commissioners appointed by individual member governments and approved by its parliament) and the Council of Ministers. Daily business is conducted by an army of bureaucrats and policy wonks.

Unlike America's federation of 50 states, Europe's member states retain the right to opt out of some EU policies. Britain, for example, belongs to the EU but chose not to adopt the euro as its currency. While the Lisbon Treaty (enacted in 2009) streamlines EU responses to conflicts and issues, there's no unified foreign or economic policy among the member countries. The EU also lacks a powerful chief executive—the president of the European Council, appointed for a two-and-a-half-year term, is much weaker than the US president, as EU laws require consensus on taxes, foreign policy, defense, and social programs.

The EU is currently financing an ambitious 21st-century infrastructure of roads, high-speed trains, high-tech industries, and communication networks. The goal is to create a competitive, sustainable, environmentally friendly economy that improves the quality of life for all Europeans.

Still, many "Euroskeptics" remain unconvinced that the EU is a good thing. Some chafe at the highly regulated business environment and high taxes. They complain about the bureaucracy and worry that their national cultures will be swallowed up and Euro-fied. The wealthier member countries (mostly in the north) are reluctant to bail out their economically unsound compatriots (mostly in the south) in order to prop up the euro, while the troubled countries resent the cuts demanded by the richer ones.

Despite the problems facing them, Europeans don't want to go back to the days of division and strife. Most recognize that a strong, unified Europe is necessary to keep the peace and compete in a global economy.

current structure and procedures. You'll learn how early visionary utopians (like Churchill, who in 1946 called for a "United States of Europe" to avoid future wars) led the way as Europe gradually evolved into the European Union (1992).

From the balcony overlooking the building's lobby, you can see the giant *Confluence* sculpture with moving metal-wire pieces—representing people coming together for a common purpose. The audioguide tells you all about the building itself: In line with EU idealism, it's functional, transparent, and very "green."

The grand finale is the vast "hemicycle," where the members of the European Parliament sit. Here you'll listen to a political-science lesson about the all-Europe system of governance. Parliamentarians representing 160 different national political parties, organized into seven different voting blocs based on political ideals (rather than nationality), hash out pan-European issues in this hall. It's the largest multilingual operation on the planet. Yet somehow things get done; recent pieces of legislation include a crackdown on mobile-phone roaming fees within EU member states and a cap on carbon dioxide emissions.

Near the European Parliament
Royal Belgian Institute of Natural Sciences (Institut Royal des Sciences Naturelles de Belgique)—Dinosaur enthusiasts come to this museum, practically next door to the European Parliament, for the world's largest collection of iguanodon skeletons (€7, Tue-Fri 9:30-17:00, Sat-Sun 10:00-18:00, closed Mon, last entry 30 minutes before closing, Rue Vautier 29; bus #95 from the Bourse to Luxembourg, plus a 10-minute walk; or bus #34 from the Porte de Namur/Naamsepoort or Trône/Troon Métro stops to Museum; tel. 02-627-4211, www.naturalsciences.be).

Park of the Cinquantenaire (Parc du Cinquantenaire)
Standing proudly in a big park in eastern Brussels is a trio of sprawling museums housed in cavernous halls: the Royal Army and Military History Museum, Autoworld, and the Royal Museum

of Art and History. These decent attractions thrill specialists but bore most others. The complex itself is interesting to see and has a grandiose history: The ambitious 19th-century Belgian King Leopold II wanted Brussels to rival Paris. In 1880 he celebrated the 50th anniversary *(cinquantenaire)* of Belgian independence by building a huge monumental arch flanked by massive exhibition halls, which today house the museums.

Getting There: The Merode Métro stop is 200 yards from the museums (exit the Métro station following signs to *Yser/IJzer*, then cross the street toward the big arch). All of these are also within steps of the Gaulois/Galliërs stop for bus #27 (with handy connections to the European Parliament, then the Royal Palace and Upper Town—see "Connecting the Sights" on page 442).

▲**Royal Army and Military History Museum (Musée Royal de l'Armée et d'Histoire Militaire)**—Wander through this enor-

mous collection of weaponry, uniforms, tanks, warplanes, and endless exhibits about military history, focusing on the 19th and 20th centuries. The museum—which is gradually getting a much-needed makeover—is filled with real, tangible history. This impressively complete museum made me want to watch my favorite war movies all over again. It's a nirvana for fans of military history and aviation, but skippable for those who think a "panzer" is a pretty flower. Current renovation work might mean that some sections are closed during your visit, and staff cuts may temporarily close some sections midday.

Exploring the whole place is exhausting, so be selective and use the floor plan and directional signs to navigate. Each item is labeled in French and Flemish, but some good English descriptions are available; to get the most out of your visit, pay €3 for the essential audioguide (available 9:00-11:30 & 13:00-16:30).

From the entrance, to the right is a hall with historic exhibits, then a large and very good section on World War I, with the best collection of WWI weaponry anywhere. Don't miss the primitive WWI tanks—able to break through the stalemated "Western Front," but so clumsy that they couldn't do anything in enemy territory. The grand finale of this wing is the vast (and I mean vast) hall filled with warplanes. To the left from the entrance are impressively displayed armor and weapons, and a huge hall with information on modern conflict (including World War II) and temporary exhibits. Upstairs is a rooftop terrace with "Napoleonic" views over the park complex and the Brussels skyline (open in summer only, find the elevator at the front of the armory section).

Cost and Hours: Free, Tue-Sun 9:00-16:45, closed Mon, Parc du Cinquantenaire 3, tel. 02-737-7811, www.klm-mra.be. Most of the museum (except for the aviation section) closes from 12:00 to 13:00.

▲**Autoworld**—Starting with Mr. Benz's motorized tricycle of 1886, stroll through a giant hall filled with 400 historic cars, each one labeled and briefly explained in four languages. Car buffs can ogle circa-1905 models from Peugeot, Renault, Oldsmobile, Cadillac, and Rolls-Royce. It's well-described in English (€6, daily April-Sept 10:00-18:00, Oct-March 10:00-17:00, in Palais Mondial, Parc du Cinquantenaire 11, tel. 02-736-4165, www.autoworld.be).

Royal Museum of Art and History—This varied, decent (but not spectacular) collection features both European and non-European items from prehistoric times to the present. As you wander the almost-empty halls, you'll see fine tapestries, exquisite altarpieces, an impressive Islamic collection, gorgeous Art Nouveau and Art Deco, and a "museum of the heart" (featuring various creative depictions of everyone's favorite organ, donated by a local heart doctor). The collection is arranged somewhat haphazardly; pick up the brochure at the entry to figure out which items you'd like to find, then follow the signposts. While it's sometimes called the "Belgian Louvre," that's an overstatement; this place pales in comparison to the excellent Royal Museums of Fine Art in the Upper Town.

Cost and Hours: €5, includes audioguide that covers only some of the museum, limited English information posted, Tue-Fri 9:30-17:00, Sat-Sun 10:00-17:00, closed Mon, hiding behind Autoworld at Jubelpark 10, Parc du Cinquantenaire, tel. 02-741-7211.

North of Downtown: The 1958 World's Fair Grounds

These sights are next to each other about four miles north of the Grand Place at Bruparck, a complex of tacky-but-fun attractions at the old 1958 World's Fair grounds.

Getting There: It's easy but fairly time-consuming to reach from the center. Ride the Métro to Heysel/Heizel and walk about five minutes toward the can't-miss-it Atomium. You'll come to a little pavilion with a walkway going over the train tracks; to reach Mini-Europe, take this walkway and enter "The Village," a corny food circus (with a giant cineplex and a water park) done up like a European village. Entering this area, turn left and head down the stairs to reach the Mini-Europe entrance. If you're only going to the Atomium, simply go straight through the pavilion and head for the big silver balls.

Atomium—This giant, silvery iron molecule, with escalators and stairs connecting the various "atoms" and a view from the top sphere, was the über-optimistic symbol of the 1958 World's Fair. It's Brussels' answer to Paris' Eiffel Tower, Seattle's Space Needle, and St. Louis' Gateway Arch. Recently reopened after an extensive renovation, the Atomium celebrates its kitschy past with fun space-age videos and displays. Your ticket includes an elevator ride to the panorama deck, with views over the fairgrounds and Mini-Europe (which looks *really* mini from up here)—but, disappointingly, you can't actually see the landmarks of downtown Brussels. Then meander on endless escalators and stairs through five of the nine balls on your way back down. The good €2 audioguide explains the building and the 1958 World Expo, including sound clips from people who actually attended the festivities. If you don't like heights or tight spaces, tell your friends you'll wave to them...from the ground.

Cost and Hours: €11, €22.50 combo-ticket with Mini-Europe, daily 10:00-18:00, later in summer, last entry 30 minutes before closing, overpriced restaurant inside, tel. 02-475-4777, www.atomium.be.

Mini-Europe—This kid-pleasing sight, sharing a park with the Atomium, has 1:25-scale models of 350 famous European landmarks, such as Big Ben, the Eiffel Tower, and Venice's canals. The "Spirit of Europe" section is an interactive educational exhibit about the European Union (€13, €22.50 combo-ticket with Atomium, Easter-Sept daily 9:30-18:00, July-Aug until 20:00, Oct-Dec 10:00-18:00, closed Jan-Easter, last entry one hour before closing, tel. 02-474-1313, www.minieurope.com).

In Tervuren, East of Brussels
▲Royal Museum of Central Africa (Musée Royal de l'Afrique Centrale)—Remember the Belgian Congo? About an hour by public transit from downtown Brussels, this worthwhile museum covers the Congo and much more of Africa, including ethnography, sculpture, jewelry, colonial history, flora, and fauna. It's a great place to learn about both the history of Belgian adventure in the Congo (when it was the king's private plantation) and the region's natural wonders. Unfortunately, there's barely a word of English. The museum, housed in an immense palace, is surrounded by a vast, well-kept park. A trip out here puts you in a lush, wooded oasis a world away from the big, noisy city.

Cost and Hours: €4, more for special exhibits, audioguide-€2, Tue-Fri 10:00-17:00, Sat-Sun 10:00-18:00, closed Mon, Leuvensesteenweg 13 in the town of Tervuren, tel. 02-769-5211, www.africamuseum.be.

Getting There: Take Métro line 1 (direction: Stockel/ Stokkel) to Montgomery, and then catch tram #44 and ride it about 20 minutes to its final stop, Tervuren. From there, walk 300 yards through the park to the palace. On summer weekend afternoons, a charming old-time trolley connects Tervuren to the Tram Museum at Brussels' Woluwe Park; on Sundays, it goes all the way to the Park of the Cinquantenaire (€8 one-way, April-Oct Sat-Sun only).

GRAND PLACE WALK

This walk takes in Brussels' delightful old center, starting at its spectacular main square. After exploring the Grand Place, we'll loop a couple blocks north, see the Bourse, and then end south of the Grand Place at the *Manneken-Pis*.

Orientation

Length of This Walk: Allow two hours.
Brewery Museum: €6, daily 10:00-17:00 except Dec-March opens Sat-Sun at 12:00, Grand Place 10, tel. 02-511-4987.
City Museum: €3, Tue-Sun 10:00-17:00, closed Mon, Grand Place, tel. 02-279-4350.
Chocolate Shops: Generally Mon-Sat 9:00-22:00, Sun 10:00-22:00, along the north side of the Grand Place.

The Walk Begins

The Grand Place

This colorful cobblestone square is the heart—historically and geographically—of heart-shaped Brussels. As the town's market square for 1,000 years, this was where farmers and merchants sold their wares in open-air stalls, enticing travelers from the main east-west highway across Belgium, which ran a block north of the square. Today, shops and cafés sell chocolates, *gaufres* (waffles), beer, mussels, fries, *dentelles* (lace), and flowers.

Brussels was born about 1,000 years ago around a now-long-gone castle built by Germans to fight off the French (long before either of those countries actually existed as nations). The villagers supplied the needs of the soldiers, and a city grew up on the banks of the Senne (not Seine) River, which today is completely bricked

GRAND PLACE WALK

Grand Place Walk

- **1** Town Hall
- **2** King's House & City Museum
- **3** Swan House & Brewery Museum
- **4** Godiva Chocolates
- **5** Neuhaus Chocolates
- **6** Galler & Corné Port-Royal Chocolates
- **7** Leonidas Chocolates
- **8** Galeries Royales St. Hubert
- **9** La Belgique Gourmande (history exhibit)
- **10** Rue des Bouchers
- **11** Church of St. Nicolas
- **12** The Bourse
- **13** Le Cirio Café & Ruins
- **14** Falstaff Café & Tour Bus Stop
- **15** Place de la Bourse
- **16** Bus #95 Stop
- **17** Brass Statue
- **18** N. Toebac Lace Shop
- **19** Textilux Center
- **20** Comic Strip Panel
- **21** Manneken-Pis Statue

over. The river crossed the main road from Köln to Bruges.

Pan the square to get oriented. Face the Town Hall, with your back to the King's House. You're facing roughly southwest. The TI is one block behind you, and "restaurant row" is another block beyond that. To your right, a block away, catch a glimpse of the Bourse building (with buses, taxis, and cafés). The Upper Town is to your left, rising up the hill beyond the Central Station. Over your left shoulder a few blocks away is St. Michael's Cathedral. And most important? The *Manneken-Pis* is three blocks ahead, down the street that runs along the left side of the Town Hall.

The **Town Hall** (Hôtel de Ville) dominates the square with its 300-foot-tall tower, topped by a golden statue of St. Michael slaying a devil (skippable interior; see page 429 for tour times if you're interested). This was where the city council met to rule this free trading town. Brussels proudly maintained its self-governing independence while dukes, kings, and clergymen ruled much of Europe. These days, the Town Hall hosts weddings—Crown Prince Philippe got married here in 1999. (The Belgian government demands that all marriages first be performed in simple civil ceremonies.)

Opposite the Town Hall is the impressive, gray **King's House** (Maison du Roi), used by the Habsburg kings not as a house, but as an administrative center. Rebuilt in the 1890s, it's a stately and prickly Neo-Gothic building. Inside is the mildly interesting City Museum (described later).

The fancy smaller buildings giving the square its uniquely grand medieval character are former **guild halls** (now mostly shops

and restaurants), their impressive gabled roofs topped with statues. Once the home offices for the town's different professions (brewers, bakers, and *Manneken-Pis*-corkscrew-makers), they all date from shortly after 1695—the year French king Louis XIV's troops surrounded the city, sighted their cannons on the Town Hall spire, and managed to level everything around it (4,000 wooden buildings) without ever hitting the spire itself. As a matter of pride, these Brussels businessmen rebuilt their offices better than ever, completing everything within seven years. They're in stone, taller, and with ornamented gables and classical statues.

The **Swan House** (#9, just to the left of the Town Hall) once housed a bar where Karl Marx and Friedrich Engels met in February of 1848 to write their *Communist Manifesto*. Later that year, when the treatise sparked socialist revolution around Europe,

Brussels exiled them. Today, the once-proletarian bar is one of the city's most expensive restaurants. Next door (#10) was and still is the brewers' guild, now housing the **Brewery Museum** (see page 431).

Each rooftop **statue** comes with its own uninteresting legend, but the Bruxelloise have an earthier explanation: "What's that smell?" say the statues on the roof of the Swan House. "Someone farted." "Yeah," says the golden man riding a horse atop the Brewery Museum next door, "it was that guy over there," and he points north across the square to another statue. "It wasn't me," says that statue, "it was him—way over there." Follow his gaze to the

middle of the northwest side of the square, where the statue of a saint with a shepherd's staff hangs his head in shame.

Imagine this already glorious square filled with a **carpet of flowers.** Every other year (next on the weekend of August 15, 2012; www.flowercarpet.be), florists create a colorful 19,000-square-foot pattern of tightly packed begonias—that's about three-quarters of a million individual flowers. Begun in 1971 by a begonia salesman as a way to promote his wares, this gorgeous display has become a biannual Brussels fixture that makes this grand space even grander.

• *Inside the King's House (Maison du Roi)—across the Grand Place from the Town Hall—is the only museum of any importance on the square, the...*

City Museum

This museum has three stories of exhibits: The top floor displays a chronological history of the city and an enjoyable room full of

costumes dampened by the *Manneken-Pis* statue (see page 463); the middle floor has a 20-minute film on city history and maps and models of 13th- and 17th-century Brussels; and the ground floor features tapestries and paintings. Borrow the English descriptions in each room.

Most visitors aim straight for the *Manneken-Pis* outfits, **upstairs.** It's a longstanding tradition for the statue to be outfitted in clothing—the little guy goes through several costume changes each week. Many of the costumes you'll see here were donated by other countries—you'll see everything from a Civil War Union soldier to an El Salvadorian farmer, from a Polish hussar to a Japanese samurai, from an Indian maharajah to a Spanish bullfighter, from a Russian cosmonaut to a Fiji islander...and much more. Once up here, sit down and enjoy the video showing visitors' reactions to the ridiculous little statue.

On the **middle floor,** be sure to find the model of the city in the 13th century. (To follow the directions in this description, uphill is east.) The largest structure is St. Michael's Cathedral (northeast). The Upper Town hasn't a hint of its monumental future. The Grand Place's embryonic beginning is roughly in the center of town, amid a cluster of houses.

The city was a port town—see the crane unloading barges—since it was at this point that the shallow Senne became navigable. Grain from the area was processed in the watermills, then shipped downstream to Antwerp and on to the North Sea.

By the 1200s, Brussels—though tiny by today's standards—was an important commercial center, and St. Michael's was the region's religious hub. Still, most of the area inside the 2.5-mile-long city wall was farmland, dotted with a few churches, towers, markets, and convents (such as the Carmelite convent hugging the south wall).

The model in the far end of the room shows the city a couple centuries later—much bigger, but still within the same wall. By this time, the Upper and Lower Towns are clearly defined. In the Upper Town, the huge palace of the dukes of Burgundy marks the site of today's Royal Palace (described on page 467).

On the **ground floor** you'll see the original statues that once adorned the Town Hall. The limestone is no match for the corrosive acidic air, so they were brought inside for protection. Also on this floor are a few old paintings, fine carved altarpieces, tapestries, sculpture, and porcelain.

Tasty Treats on the Grand Place

Cafés: Mussels in Brussels, Belgian-style french fries, yeasty local beers, waffles...if all you do here is plop down at a café on the square, try some of these specialties, and watch the world go by—hey, that's a great afternoon in Brussels.

The outdoor cafés are casual and come with fair prices (a good Belgian beer costs €3.50—with no cover or service charge). Have a seat, and a waiter will serve you. The half-dozen or so cafés are all roughly equal in price and quality for simple drinks and foods—check the posted menus.

Choco-Crawl: The best chocolate shops all lie along the north (uphill) side of the square, starting with Godiva at the high end

A Brief History of Chocolate

In 1519, Montezuma served Cortés a cup of hot cocoa *(xocoatl)* made from cocoa beans, which were native to the New World.

It ignited a food fad in Europe—by 1700, elegant "chocolate houses" in Europe's capitals served hot chocolate (with milk and sugar added) to wealthy aristocrats. By the 1850s, the process of making chocolate candies for eating was developed, and Brussels, with a long tradition of quality handmade luxuries, was at the forefront.

Cocoa beans are husked, fermented, and roasted, then ground into chocolate paste. (Chocolate straight from the bean is very bitter.) The vegetable fat is pressed out to make cocoa butter. Cocoa butter and chocolate paste are mixed together and sweetened with sugar to make chocolates. In 1876, a Swiss man named Henry Nestlé added concentrated milk, creating milk chocolate—a lighter, sweeter variation, with less pure chocolate.

(higher in both altitude and price). The cost goes down slightly as you descend to the other shops. Each shop has a mouth-watering display case of 20 or so chocolates and sells mixes of 100 grams—your choice of 6-8 pieces—for about €5, or individual pieces for about €1.60. Americans use the word "chocolates" indiscriminately to describe the different varieties you'd find in a box of chocolates, but the Belgians call them either "truffles" (soft, crumbly chocolate shells filled with buttercream) or "pralines" (made of a hard chocolate shell with a wide range of fillings—uniquely Belgian and totally different from the sugar-and-nuts French praline). Chocolate shops are generally open Monday to Saturday from 9:00 to 22:00 and Sunday from 10:00 to 22:00.

Godiva, with the top reputation internationally, is synonymous with fine Belgian chocolate. Now owned by a Turkish company, Godiva still has its management and the original factory (built in 1926) in Belgium. This store, at Grand Place 22, was Godiva's first (est. 1937). The almond and honey goes way beyond almond roca.

Neuhaus, a few doors down at #27, has been encouraging local chocoholics since 1857. Their main store is in the Galeries St. Hubert (described later). Neuhaus publishes a good little pamphlet explaining its products. The "caprice" (toffee with vanilla crème) tastes like Easter. Neuhaus claims to be the inventor of the praline.

Galler, just off the square at Rue au Beurre 44, is homier and less famous because it doesn't export. Still family-run (and the royal favorite), it proudly serves less sugary chocolate—dark. The new top-end choice, 85 percent pure chocolate, is called simply "Black 85"—and worth a sample if you like chocolate without the sweetness. Galler's products are well-described in English.

Leonidas, four doors down at Rue au Beurre 34, is where cost-conscious Bruxelloise get their fix, sacrificing 10 percent in quality to nearly triple their take (machine-made, only €1.60/100 grams). White chocolate is their specialty.

Corné Port-Royal outlets are sprouting up everywhere. It seems like the new kid on the block, but only the name is new—they've been making chocolates for 75 years.

If all the chocolate has made you thirsty, wash it down with **250 Beers,** next to Leonidas.

• *Exit the Grand Place next to Godiva (from the northeast, or uphill, corner of the square), and go north one block on Rue de la Colline (passing a popular Tintin shop at #13 and a Europe shop across the street) to Rue du Marché-aux-Herbes/Grasmarkt, which was once the main east-west highway through Belgium. The little park-like square just to your right—a modest gathering place with market stalls—is nicknamed "Agora" (after the marketplaces of ancient Greece).*

Looking to the right, notice that it's all uphill from here to the Upper Town, another four blocks (and 200-foot elevation gain) beyond. Straight ahead, you enter the arcaded shopping mall called...

Galeries Royales St. Hubert

Built in 1847, Europe's oldest still-operating shopping mall served as the glass-covered model that inspired many other shopping

galleries in Paris, London, and beyond. It celebrated the town's new modern attitude (having recently gained its independence from the Netherlands). Built in an age of expansion and industrialization, the mall demonstrated efficient modern living, with elegant apartments upstairs above trendy shops, theaters, and cafés.

Originally, you had to pay to get in to see its fancy shops, and that elite sensibility survives today. Even today, people live in the upstairs apartments.

Looking down the arcade, you'll notice that it bends halfway down, designed to lure shoppers farther. Its iron-and-glass look is still popular, but the decorative columns, cameos, and pastel colors evoke a more elegant time. It's Neo-Renaissance, like a pastel

Florentine palace.

There's no Gap (yet), no Foot Locker, no Karmelkorn. Instead, you'll find hat, cane, and, umbrella stores that sell...hats, canes, and umbrellas—that's it, all made on the premises. **Philippe** (halfway down the first section, on the left), carries shoes made especially for the curves of your feet, handcrafted by a family that's been doing it for generations. Since 1857, **Neuhaus** (near the end of the first section, on the right) has sold chocolates from here at its flagship store, where many Brussels natives buy their pralines. Across from Neuhaus, the **Taverne du Passage** restaurant serves the same local specialties that singer Jacques Brel used to come here for: *croquettes de crevettes* (shrimp croquettes), *tête de veau* (calf's head), *anguilles au vert* (eels with herb sauce), and *fondue au fromage* (cheese fondue; €10-20 meals, daily 12:00-24:00).

Inside **La Belgique Gourmande** chocolate shop (on the right, at #17) is a strange and sprawling exhibit about the history of Brussels. You enter through the back of the chocolate shop and descend into a huge underground exhibit that cleverly and artistically gives you the sweep of the city with fine English descriptions (€6, daily 10:00-17:00, tel. 02-512-5745).

• *Midway down the mall, where the two sections bend, turn left and exit the mall onto...*

Rue des Bouchers

Yikes! During meal times, this street is absolutely crawling with tourists browsing through wall-to-wall, midlevel-quality restaurants. Brussels is known worldwide for its food, serving all kinds of cuisine, but specializing in seafood (particularly mussels). You'll have plenty to choose from along this table-clogged "restaurant row." To get an idea of prices, compare their posted *menùs*—the fixed-price, several-course meal offered by most restaurants. But don't count on getting a good value—better restaurants are just a few steps away (for specifics, see page 492).

Many diners here are day-trippers. Colin from London, Marie from Paris, Martje from Holland, and Dietrich from Frankfurt could easily all "do lunch" together in Brussels—just three hours away.

The first intersection, with Petite Rue des Bouchers, is the heart of the restaurant quarter, which sprawls for several blocks around. The street names reveal what sorts of shops used to stand here—butchers *(bouchers)*, herbs, chickens, and cheese.

• *At this intersection, turn left onto Petite Rue des Bouchers and walk straight back to the Grand Place. (You'll see the Town Hall tower ahead.)*

At the Grand Place, turn right (west) on Rue du Beurre. Comparison-shop a little more at the Galler and Leonidas chocolate stores and pass by the little "Is it raining?" fountain. At the intersection with Rue du Midi is the...

Church of St. Nicolas

Since the 12th century, there's been a church here. Inside, along the left aisle, see rough stones in some of the arches from the early church. Outside, notice the barnacle-like shops, such as De Witte Jewelers, built right into the church. The church was rebuilt 300 years ago with money provided by the town's jewelers. As thanks, they were given these shops with apartments upstairs. Close to God, this was prime real estate. And jewelers are still here.

• *Just beyond the church, you run into the back entrance of a big Neoclassical building.*

The Bourse (Stock Exchange) and Art Nouveau Cafés

The stock exchange was built in the 1870s in the Historicist style—a mix-and-match, Neo-everything architectural movement. The **ruins** under glass on the right side of the Bourse are from a 13th-century convent; there's a small museum inside.

Several **historic cafés** huddle around the Bourse. To the right (next to the covered ruins) is the woody **Le Cirio,** with its delightful circa-1900 interior. Around the left side of the Bourse is the **Falstaff Café,** which is worth a peek inside. Some Brussels cafés, like the Falstaff, are still decorated in the early 20th-century style called Art Nouveau. Ironwork columns twist and bend like flower stems, and lots of Tiffany-style stained glass and mirrors make them light and spacious. Slender, elegant, willowy Gibson Girls decorate the wallpaper, while waiters in bowties glide by.

• *Circle around to the front of the Bourse, toward the busy Boulevard Anspach. Note that the street in front of the Falstaff Café is a convenient place to catch a hop-on, hop-off bus tour (see page 427).*

Place de la Bourse and Boulevard Anspach

Brussels is the political nerve center of Europe (only Washington, DC, has more lobbyists), and the city sees several hundred demonstrations a year. When the local team wins a soccer match or some political group wants to make a statement, this is where people flock to wave flags and honk horns.

It's also where the old town

meets the new. To the right along Boulevard Anspach are two shopping malls and several first-run movie theaters. Rue Neuve, which parallels Anspach, is a bustling pedestrian-only shopping street.

Boulevard Anspach covers the still-flowing Senne River (which was open until 1850). Remember that Brussels was once a port, with North Sea boats coming as far as this point to unload their goods. But with frequent cholera epidemics killing thousands of its citizens, the city decided to cover up its stinky river.

Beyond Boulevard Anspach—two blocks past the ugly skyscrapers—is the charming **Ste. Catherine** neighborhood, clustered around the former fish market and the Church of Ste. Catherine. This village-like zone is the easiest escape from the bustle of downtown Brussels, and features two ideal lunch stops: the Mer du Nord/Nordzee fish bar and the delightful Belgian cheese shop Cremerie de Linkebeek (both worth a detour and described on page 497).

• *For efficient sightseeing, consider catching bus #95 from alongside the Bourse (on Rue Henri Maus, in front of Falstaff Café) to the Place Royale, where you can follow my Upper Town Walk (see next chapter), also ending at the* Manneken-Pis. *But if you'd rather stay in the Lower Town, return to the Grand Place.*

From the Grand Place to the *Manneken-Pis*

• *Leave the square kitty-corner, heading south down the street running along the left side of the Town Hall, Rue Charles Buls (which soon changes its name to Stoofstraat). Just five yards off the square, under the arch, is a well-polished, well-loved brass statue.*

You'll see tourists and locals rubbing a **brass statue** of a reclining man. This was Mayor Evrard 't Serclaes, who in 1356 bravely refused to surrender the keys of the city to invaders, and so was tortured and killed. Touch him, and his misfortune becomes your good luck. Judging by the reverence with which locals treat this ritual, I figure there must be something to it.

A half-block farther (on the left), the **N. Toebac Lace Shop** is a welcoming place with fine lace, a knowledgeable staff, and an interesting three-minute

Lace

In the 1500s, lace collars, sleeves, headdresses, and veils were fashionable among rich men and women. For the next 200 years, the fashion raged (peaking in about 1700). All this lace had to be made by hand, and many women earned extra income from the demand. But the French Revolution of 1789 suddenly made lace for men undemocratic and unmanly. Then,

in about 1800, machines replaced human hands, and except for ornamental pieces, the fashion died out among women, too.

These days, handmade lace is usually also homemade—not produced in factories, but at home by dedicated, sharp-eyed hobbyists who love their work. Unlike knitting, it requires total concentration as the lacemaker follows intricate patterns. Lacemakers create their own patterns or trace tried-and-true designs. A piece of lace takes days, not hours, to make—which is why a handmade tablecloth can easily sell for €250.

There are two basic kinds of lace: bobbin lace (which originated in Bruges) and needle lace. To make bobbin lace, the lacemaker juggles many different strands tied to bobbins, "weaving" a design by overlapping the threads. Because of the difficulties, the resulting pattern is usually rather rough and simple compared with other techniques.

Needle lace is more like sewing—stitching pre-made bits onto a pattern. For example, the "Renaissance" design is made by sewing a pre-made ribbon onto a pattern in a fancy design. This is then attached as a fringe to a piece of linen—to make a fancy tablecloth, for instance.

In the "Princess" design, pre-made pieces are stitched onto a cotton net. This method is often used to make all sorts of pieces, from small doilies to full wedding veils.

"Rose point"—no longer practiced—used authentic bits of handmade antique lace as an ornament in a frame or to fill a pendant. Antique pieces can be very expensive.

video. Brussels is perhaps the best-known city for traditional lace-making, and this shop still sells handmade pieces in the old style: lace clothing, doilies, tablecloths, and ornamental pieces (daily 9:30-19:30, Rue Charles Buls 10). The shop gives travelers with this book a 15 percent discount. For more on lace, the Costume and Lace Museum is a block away and just around the corner (closed Wed, see page 431).

A block farther down the street on the left (at the little yellow

Tapestries

In 1500, tapestry workshops in Brussels were famous, cranking out high-quality tapestries for the walls of Europe's palaces. They were functional (as insulation and propaganda for a church, king, or nobleman) and beautiful—an intricate design formed by colored thread. Even great painters, such as Rubens and Raphael, designed tapestries, which rivaled Renaissance canvases.

To make a tapestry, neutral-colored threads are stretched vertically over a loom. (In Renaissance Belgium, the threads were made from imported English wool.) The design of the tapestry is created with the horizontal weave, from the colored threads that (mostly) overlay the vertical threads. Tapestry-making is much more difficult than basic weaving, as each horizontal thread is only as long as the detail it's meant to create. A single horizontal row can be made up of many individual pieces of thread. Before weaving begins, an artist designs a pattern for the larger picture, called a "cartoon," which weavers follow for guidance as they work.

Flanders and Paris (in the Gobelins workshop) were the two centers of tapestry-making until the art died out, mirroring the decline of Europe's noble class.

window before the busy street) is the always-popular **Waffle Factory,** where €2 gets you a freshly made take-away "Belgian" (Liège-style) waffle (up to €5 more if you opt for any of the fun toppings).

Across the busy street, step into the **Textilux Center** (Rue Lombard 41, on the left) for a good look at Belgian tapestries—both traditional wall-hangings and modern goods, such as tapestry purses and luggage in traditional designs.

High on the wall to the right, notice the delightful **comic strip panel** depicting that favorite of Belgian comic heroes, Tintin, climbing a fire escape. (For those unfamiliar with this character—beloved by virtually all Europeans—his dog is named Snowy, Captain Haddock keeps an eye out for him, and the trio are always getting into misadventures. For more details, see the sidebar on page 438.) Dozens of these building-sized comic-strip panels decorate Brussels (marked on the TI's €0.50 map), celebrating the Belgians' favorite medium. Just as Ireland has its writers, Italy its painters, and France its chefs, Belgium has a knack for turning out world-class comic artists.

• *Follow the crowds, noticing the excitement build, because in another block you reach the...*

Manneken-Pis

Even with low expectations, this bronze statue is smaller than you'd think—the little squirt's under two feet tall, practically the size of a newborn. Still, the little peeing boy is an appropriately low-key symbol for the unpretentious Bruxelloise. The statue was made in 1619 to provide drinking water for the neighborhood. Notice that the baby, sculpted in Renaissance style, actually has the musculature of a man instead of the pudgy limbs of a child. The statue was actually knighted by the occupying King

Louis XV—so French soldiers had to salute the eternally pissing lad when they passed. Sometimes, *Manneken-Pis* is dressed in one of the 700 different costumes that visiting VIPs have brought for him (including an Elvis Pissley outfit).

There are several different legends about the story behind *Manneken*—take your pick. He was a naughty boy who peed inside a witch's house, so she froze him. A rich man lost his son and declared, "Find my son, and we'll make a statue of him doing what he did when found." A bishop cured a nobleman's infertile wife, and when the baby was born, he immediately urinated on the bishop. Or—the locals' favorite version—the little tyke loved his beer, which came in handy when a fire threatened the wooden city: He bravely put it out. Want the truth? The city commissioned it to show the freedom and joie de vivre of living in Brussels—where happy people eat, drink...and drink...and then pee.

The gathering crowds make the scene more interesting. Hang out for a while and watch the commotion this little guy makes as tour groups come and go. When I was there, a Russian man marveled at the statue, shook his head, and said, "He never stop!"

UPPER TOWN WALK

The Upper Town has always had a more aristocratic feel than the medieval, commercial streets of the Lower Town. With broad boulevards, big marble buildings, palaces, museums, and so many things called "royal," it also seems much newer and a bit more sterile. But the Upper Town has a history that stretches back to Brussels' beginnings.

Use this walk to get acquainted with this less-touristed part of town, sample some world-class museums, see the palace, explore art galleries, and get the lay of the land from a panoramic viewpoint. The tour starts a half-block from the one essential art sight in town, the complex that holds the Royal Museums of Fine Arts of Belgium (museums of ancient and modern art) and the Magritte Museum. Consider a visit while you're here (see next chapter). The Musical Instruments Museum is also in the neighborhood (see page 440).

Orientation

Length of This Walk: Allow 1.5 hours.

Getting There: The walk begins at Place Royale/Koningsplein in the Upper Town. You have several ways to get there:

1. From the Grand Place, walk uphill for 15 minutes (follow your map).

2. From the Bourse, near Falstaff Café, take bus #95, which leaves every few minutes for Place Royale (bus signs call it *Royale/Koning*; buy ticket from driver, validate it in machine).

3. Catch a taxi (figure €6 from the Bourse).

4. Hop off here during a hop-on, hop-off bus tour (see page 427).

Upper Town Walk

GRAND PLACE

BELGIAN PARLIAMENT

CENTRAL STATION

END — MANNEKEN-PIS

PARC DE BRUXELLES

MUSICAL INSTRUMENTS MUSEUM

RENE MAGRITTE MUSEUM

BELVUE MUSEUM

ROYAL MUSEUMS OF FINE ARTS

PLACE ROYALE

START

ROYAL PALACE

MUSIC ACADEMY

SYNAGOGUE

PALAIS DE JUSTICE

DCH

200 YARDS
200 METERS

- **>i** View
- **||||** Stairs
- **Ⓜ** Subway Stop
- **→** Entry Point to Sights

1. Place Royale
2. Parc de Bruxelles
3. Royal Palace, BELvue Museum & Coudenberg Palace Ruins
4. Sculpture Garden
5. Mercedes House
6. Notre-Dame du Sablon Church
7. Place du Petit Sablon
8. Palace of Justice
9. Viewpoint from Place Poelaert
10. Place du Grand Sablon
11. Tour d'Angle

Route Overview: From Place Royale, walk south along the ridge. On the way, pop in to a stained-glass-filled Gothic church, then continue on to reach the towering Palace of Justice, which has the best view of the city. Backtrack a bit and descend through the well-worn tapestry of the Sablon Quarter's antiques stores, art galleries, and cafés, ending down to the *Manneken-Pis* at the foot of the hill.

Starring: Brussels' genteel Upper Town, with its best museums, top views, and a bit of personality poking out from behind its stuffy veneer.

The Walk Begins

❶ Place Royale (Koningsplein)

At the crest of the hill sits Place Royale, encircled by cars and trams and enclosed by white Neoclassical buildings forming a mirror image across a cobblestone square. A big, green statue of a horseman stands in the center.

The **statue** depicts Belgium-born Godfrey de Bouillon, who led the First Crusade (in 1096). He rides forward with his flag, gazing down on the Town Hall spire. If Godfrey turned and looked left down Rue de la Régence, he'd see the domed Palace of Justice at the end of the boulevard. Over his right shoulder, just outside the square, is the Royal Palace, the king's residence.

In the 1800s, as Belgium exerted itself to industrialize and modernize, this area was rebuilt as a sign that Brussels had arrived as a world capital. Broad vistas down wide boulevards end at gleaming white, Greek-columned monuments—this look was all the rage, seen in Paris, London, Washington, DC...and here.

The cupola of the **Church of St. Jacques sur Coudenberg**—the central portion of the square's ring of buildings—makes the church look more like a bank building. But St. Jacques' church goes back much farther than this building (from 1787); the original was built here in the 13th century near a 12th-century castle. Nobles chose to build their mansions in the neighborhood—and, later, so did the king.

The square has several worthwhile museums: the Royal Museums of Fine Arts of Belgium (main entrance a half-block to the right) and the associated Magritte Museum (facing the crusader statue; see tour chapter), and the Musical Instruments Museum, straight downhill from the square—if Godfrey spurred his horse straight ahead, he'd pass it on his right. It's housed in an early 20th-century iron-and-glass former department store. Its Art Nouveau facade was a deliberate attempt to get beyond the retro-looking Greek columns and domes of the Place Royale. Even if you don't visit the Musical Instruments Museum, you can ride the elevator up to the museum café for a superb Lower Town view.

• *Before heading south, exit Place Royale on the north side (to the left as you face Godfrey), which opens up to a large, tree-lined park.*

❷ Parc de Bruxelles

Copying Versailles, the Habsburg empress Maria Theresa of Austria (Marie-Antoinette's mom) had this symmetrical park laid out in 1776, when she ruled (but never visited) the city. This is just one of many large parks in Brussels, which expanded with an awareness of the importance of city planning.

At the far (north) end of the park (directly opposite the Royal Palace, no need to actually walk there) is the Parliament building. Which parliament? The city hosts several: the European Parliament, the Belgian Parliament, and several local, city-council-type parliaments. This is the Belgian Parliament, seen on nightly newscasts as a backdrop for talking heads and politicians.

In 1830, Belgian patriots rose up and converged on the park, where they attacked the troops of the Dutch king. This was the first blow in a short, almost bloodless revolution that drove out the foreign-born king and gave the Belgians independence...and a different foreign-born king.

• *The long building facing the park is the...*

❸ Royal Palace (Palais Royale)

Belgium struck out twice trying to convince someone to be their new king. Finally, Leopold I (r. 1831-1865), a nobleman from Germany, agreed to become "King of the Belgians." Leopold was a steadying influence as the country modernized. His son rebuilt this palace—near the site of earlier palaces, dating back to the 10th century—by linking a row of townhouse mansions with a unifying facade (around 1870).

Leopold's great-great-great-grandnephew, King Albert II, today uses the palace as an office. (His head is on Belgium's euro coins.) Albert and his wife, Queen Paola, live in a palace north of here (near the Atomium) and on the French Riviera. If the Belgian flag (black-yellow-red) is flying from the palace, the king is somewhere in Belgium.

Albert II (born 1932) is a figurehead king, as in many European democracies, but he serves an important function as a common bond between bickering Flemish and Walloon citizens. His son, Prince Philippe, is slated to succeed him, though Philippe—

awkward and standoffish—is not as popular as his wife, Mathilde, also a Belgian native. Their daughter, Elisabeth, born in 2001, will someday become the first Belgian queen.

The bulk of the palace is off-limits to tourists except from late July through early September (see www.opt.be for the latest schedule; gardens open April-May). The adjacent **BELvue Museum** has an impressive exhibit on Belgian history and the royal family, but I'd skip the ho-hum **Coudenberg Palace** ruins (same entry for both; see page 442).

• *Return to Place Royale, then continue south along Rue de la Régence, noticing the main entrance to the Royal Museums of Fine Arts of Belgium complex (see tour on page 475). Just past the museums, on the right, you'll see a...*

❹ Sculpture Garden (Jardin de Sculpture)

This pleasant public garden features a statue by Rodin's contemporary, Aristide Maillol, a master of the female form. In *The River* (1938-1943), the moving water is personified as a woman sprawled on her side (and looking terrified, or at least stressed—the statue

was originally conceived to represent a victim of war). The wave-like figure teeters on the edge of a pool of water, about to pour in. Or is she just washing her hair? Another copy of this bronze statue sprawls near a pool in the courtyard of New York's Museum of Modern Art.

The garden looks like a great way to descend into the Sablon Quarter, but the gates at the bottom are often locked.

• *About 75 yards farther along Rue de la Régence, on your right at the intersection, is the...*

❺ Mercedes House

This sleek, modern showroom is free to the public, hosting temporary exhibits on cars that change every six months. There's usually a bit of history for classic-car enthusiasts, plus a peek at the latest Mercedes models. The venue also hosts cultural events such as chamber music and jazz (Mon-Sat 10:00-20:00, Fri until 22:00, Sun 10:00-16:00, Rue Bodenbroek 22-24, tel. 02-400-4250, www.mercedeshouse.be). Its classy café/brasserie is open weekdays for lunch and until late on Fridays (closed Sat-Sun).

• *A few yards farther along, you reach the top of the Sablon neighborhood, dominated by the...*

❻ Notre-Dame du Sablon Church

The round, rose, stained-glass windows in the clerestory of this 14th-century Flamboyant Gothic church are nice by day, but are

thrilling at night, when the church is lit from inside and glows like a lantern, enjoyed by locals at the cafés in the surrounding square.

Step inside (enter at the far end, facing the Palace of Justice; free, open daily 8:00-18:00). An artistically carved pulpit stands midway up the nave. The stained-glass windows in the nave are notable for their symmetry—rows

of saints in Gothic niches topped by coats of arms. The glorious apse behind the altar—bathed in colorful light—is what Gothic is all about. The left transept has relics of Karl I, the last Habsburg emperor (1887-1922), who was deposed when Austria became a republic after World War I. Karl's Catholic devotion was legendary, and he was beatified in 2004. Many devoted people pray here, inspired by his patient suffering in exile.

Next to the altar, see a small wooden **statue of Mary** dressed in white with a lace veil. This is a copy, made after iconoclastic Protestant vandals destroyed the original. The original statue was thought to have had miraculous powers that saved the town from plagues. In 1348, when the statue was in Antwerp, it spoke to a godly woman named Beatrix, prompting her to snatch Mary,

board a boat, and steal the statue away from Antwerp. (That's why the church is decorated with several images of boats, including the small **wooden boat** high up in the right transept.) When the citizens of Antwerp tried to stop Beatrix, the Mary statue froze them in their tracks.

When Beatrix and the statue arrived here, the Bruxelloise welcomed Mary with a joyous parade. Not long after, this large church was erected in her honor. Every summer, in Brussels' famous Ommegang procession, locals in tights and flamboyant costumes re-create the joyous arrival with colorful banners and large puppets. Imagine the scene as they carry Mary from here through the city streets to the parade's climax on the Grand Place.

• *We'll return to the colorful Place du grand Sablon later in the walk.*

For now, head to the other side of Rue de la Régence from the church, where you'll find a leafy, fenced-off garden called the...

➐ Place du Petit Sablon

This is a pleasant refuge from the busy street, part of why this neighborhood is considered so livable. The 48 small statues atop the wrought-iron fence represent the craftsman guilds—weavers, brewers, and butchers—of medieval Brussels. Inside the garden, 10 large statues represent hometown thinkers of the 16th century— a time of great intellectual accomplishments in Brussels. Gerardus Mercator (1512-1594), the Belgian mapmaker who

devised a way to more accurately show the spherical Earth on a flat surface, holds a globe.

• *We'll visit the Sablon neighborhood below the church later, but before losing elevation, let's continue along Rue de la Régence, passing on the left the Music Academy and Brussels' main synagogue—its sidewalk fortified with concrete posts to keep car bombs at a distance—before reaching the long-scaffolded...*

➑ Palace of Justice (Palais de Justice)

This domed mountain of marble sits on the edge of the Upper Town ridge, dominating the Brussels skyline. Built in wedding-cake layers of Greek columns, it's topped with a dome taller than St. Peter's in Rome, rising 340 feet. Covering more than six acres, it's the size of a baseball stadium.

The palace was built in the time of King Leopold II (son of Leo I, r. 1865-1909) and epitomizes the brassy, showy grandeur of his reign. Leopold became obscenely wealthy by turning Africa's Congo region—80 times the size of Belgium—into his personal colony. Whip-wielding Belgian masters forced Congolese slaves to tend lucrative rubber plantations, exploiting the new craze for bicycle tires. Leopold spent much of this wealth expanding and beautifying the city of Brussels.

The building (which stands on the historic site of the town gallows) serves as a Hall of Justice, where major court cases are tried. If you pop in to the lobby, you may see lawyers in black robes buzzing about.

Notice the rack of city bikes. Like many other European cities, Brussels subsidizes a public-bike system. The program, called "Villo," lets locals use bikes scattered all over town (note the map here) for a token €1 per hour (see details on page 427). You can pick up a bike in one part of town and drop it off anywhere else. But the scheme doesn't always work as well as intended: These bike racks are often empty, since this is a popular place to grab a bike for the easy ride back down to the Lower Town.

• *One of the best views of Brussels is immediately to the right of the Palace of Justice.*

❾ Viewpoint from Place Poelaert

You're standing 200 feet above the former Senne River Valley. Gazing west over the Lower Town, pan the valley from right (north) to left:

Near you is the stubby **clock tower** of the Minimen Church (which hosts lunchtime concerts in the summer). To the left of that, in the distance past a tall square skyscraper, is the lacy, white Town Hall **spire** (marking the Grand Place).

In the far distance, six miles away, you can see one of the city's landmarks, the **Atomium.** (No doubt, someone atop it is looking back at you.) The Atomium's nine shiny steel balls form the shape of an iron molecule that's the size of the Palace of Justice behind you. Built for the 1958 World's Fair, it's now a middle-aged symbol of the dawn of the Atomic Era.

Next (closer to you) rises the **black clock tower** of the Notre-Dame de la Chapelle church, the city's oldest (from 1134, with a

tower that starts Gothic and ends Baroque). On the distant horizon, see **five boxy skyscrapers,** part of the residential sprawl of this city of 1.8 million, which now covers 62 square miles. Breaking the horizon to the left is a **green dome,** which belongs to the Basilica of Koekelberg (fourth biggest in the world). And finally (panning quickly to the left), you see a **black glass skyscraper** marking the Midi/Zuid/South train station, where you can catch special high-speed train lines, such as the Eurostar, to London.

UPPER TOWN WALK

At your feet lies the **Marolles neighborhood.** Once a funky, poor place where locals developed their own quirky dialogue, today it can be either seedy or colorful, depending on the time of day and your perception. The area is famous for its sprawling flea market (daily 7:00-14:00, best on weekends). Two of the streets just below you—Rue Haute/Hoogstraat and Rue Blaes/Blaesstraat—are lined with secondhand shops. An **elevator** (free, daily 6:00-23:00) connects Place Poelaert with the Marolles neighborhood, which is worth a 10-minute detour to descend to the café-lined square. People who brake for garage sales may want to cut out of this walk early and head to the Marolles from here.

Gazing off into the distance to the far left (south), you can't quite see the suburb of **Waterloo,** 10 miles away. But try to imagine it, because it was there that the tide of European history turned. On the morning of June 18, 1815, Napoleon waited two hours for the ground to dry before sending his troops into battle. That time lag may have cost him the battle. His 72,000 soldiers could have defeated Wellington's 68,000, but the two-hour delay was just enough time for Wellington's reinforcements to arrive—45,000 Prussian troops. Napoleon had to surrender, his rule of Europe ended, and Belgium was placed under a Dutch king—until the Belgians won their independence in the 1830 revolution.

Behind you, in Place Poelaert, is a memorial to the two World Wars, both of which slashed through Belgium with deadly force.

• *Backtrack east, descending to Place du Grand Sablon by walking down Rue Ernest Allard.*

❿ Place du Grand Sablon

The Sablon neighborhood features cafés and restaurants, antiques stores, and art galleries. Chocolatier Wittamer (on the far side of

the square, at #6) often has elaborate window displays. Every weekend, there's an antiques market on the square. On warm summer evenings, the square sparks magic, as sophisticated locals sip apéritifs at the café tables, admiring the church's glowing stained glass.

• *Sloping Place du Grand Sablon funnels downhill into the pedestrian-only street called Rue de Rollebeek, which leads you past fun shops to the busy Boulevard de l'Empereur. To the right on the boulevard, just past the bowling alley, is the...*

⓫ Tour d'Angle

The "Corner Tower" is a rare surviving section of Brussels' 13th-century city wall, and was one of 7 gates along the 2.5-mile-long wall that enclosed Brussels, one of Europe's great cities.

• *Central Station is two blocks directly ahead. To reach the Grand Place, continue downhill two long blocks on Rue des Alexiens (angling off ahead of the bowling alley), and when you hit level ground, turn right on Rue l'Etuve,* which leads you directly there. A block along, you'll run into our old friend *Manneken-Pis, eternally relieving himself (if you're urine-ing to learn more about this leaky little tyke, see page 463).*

ROYAL MUSEUMS OF FINE ARTS & MAGRITTE MUSEUM TOUR

Musées Royaux des Beaux-Arts de Belgique • Musée Magritte

This museum complex, spread throughout three large buildings, covers the entire history of Western painting. There are technically three museums here: The Museum of Ancient Art (pre-1800), the Museum of Modern Art (post-1800), and—covered by a separate ticket—the Magritte Museum, which celebrates the work of the popular Belgian Surrealist painter. The collections, while enjoyable, can be overwhelming, so this chapter gives you a tour highlighting the museums' strengths: Flemish and Belgian artists. But don't plan your visit around these works—let the museums surprise you.

Orientation

Cost: €8 for Ancient Art and Modern Art museums; €8 for Magritte Museum; €13 combo-ticket covers all three. All are free the first Wed of the month after 13:00. Temporary exhibits (optional) may have an additional charge.

Hours: Tue-Sun 10:00-17:00, closed Mon, last entry 30 minutes before closing. The Magritte Museum stays open Wed until 20:00.

Reservations for the Magritte Museum: A set number of visitors are allowed into the Magritte Museum each hour—you'll reserve an entrance time when you buy your ticket. You must enter the museum during the one-hour window printed on your ticket; the ticket is invalid outside that time. On busy weekends there can be up to a three-hour wait to get in.

If you buy your ticket in advance online (www.musee-magritte-museum.be, no refunds or exchanges), you can skip the wait and enter the Magritte Museum via its doorway on Place Royale/Koningsplein; otherwise, buy your ticket at the main complex entrance at Rue de la Régence 3.

Getting There: The main entrance, with access to all three museums, is at Rue de la Régence 3 in the Upper Town, just a five-minute walk uphill from Central Station (or take bus #38, #71, or #95; or tram #92 or #94). Bus #27 connects this area with the European Parliament and the Park of the Cinquantenaire. You'll also encounter these museums if you take my Upper Town Walk (see previous chapter).

Keep Your Magrittes Straight: Don't confuse this Magritte Museum with the much smaller René Magritte Museum, located in Magritte's former home on the outskirts of Brussels.

Information: Consider the €4 audioguide or the €2.50 tour booklet (*Twenty Masterpieces of the Art of Painting: A Brief Guided Tour,* sold in the museum shop). Ancient Art and Modern Art museums: Tel. 02-508-3211, www.fine-arts-museum.be. Magritte Museum: Tel. 02-508-3333, www.musee-magritte -museum.be.

Length of This Tour: Allow one hour for the ancient and modern art museums, and another hour for the Magritte Museum.

Cuisine Art: The Greshem, a restaurant and tea room, is nearby at Place Royale (daily 11:00-18:00). The museums also have a pricey café and a fancy brasserie on site.

The Tour Begins

Plan your visit to the ancient and modern art museums around your reserved entry time for the Magritte Museum. This tour

assumes you'll visit the ancient and modern art museums first, then the Magritte Museum.

Enter at Rue de la Régence 3 and buy your ticket (advance tickets available online for Magritte Museum—see above). Continue into the large entrance hall and get oriented. The Museum of Ancient Art is on the second floor (in the galleries above you), reached by the staircase directly ahead. The Museum of Modern Art is through the doorway to the right, down several levels. The Magritte Museum is also to the right, through a passageway.

Stop first at the information desk, which has the latest on renovations, room closings, and where paintings are currently located. This is also where you can rent an audioguide. Armed with the museum's free map, make your way through the maze, enjoying whatever you find. Along the way, look for these highlights.

Museum of Ancient Art

• *Go up to the second floor and start with the Flemish masters. Notice how the rooms on the second floor surround a central hall. The art is displayed in (roughly) chronological order, working counterclockwise around the central gallery. In the first room, look for...*

Rogier van der Weyden (c. 1399-1464)—*Portrait of Anthony of Burgundy (Portrait d' Antoine de Bourgogne)*

Anthony was known in his day as the Great Bastard, the bravest and most distinguished of the many bastards fathered by prolific

Duke Philip the Good (a Renaissance prince whose sense of style impressed Florence's young Lorenzo the Magnificent, patron of the arts).

Anthony, a member of the Archers Guild, fingers the arrow like a bowstring. From his gold necklace dangles a Golden Fleece, one of Europe's more prestigious knightly honors. Wearing a black cloak, a bowl-cut hairdo, and a dark-red cap, with his pale face and hand emerging from a dark background, the man who'd been called a bastard all his life gazes to the distance, his clear, sad eyes lit with a speckle of white paint.

Van der Weyden, Brussels' official portrait painter, faithfully rendered life-size, lifelike portraits of wealthy traders, bankers, and craftsmen. Here he captures the wrinkles in Anthony's neck and the faint shadow his chin casts on his Adam's apple. Van der Weyden had also painted Philip the Good (in Bruges' Groeninge Museum—see page 378), and young Anthony's long, elegant face and full lips are a mirror image—pretty convincing DNA evidence in a paternity suit.

Capitalist Flanders in the 1400s was one of the richest, most cultured, and progressive areas in Europe, rivaling Florence and Venice.

• *Continue counterclockwise around the central gallery. As you head up the right side (in the third section), find...*

Hans Memling (c. 1430-1494)—*Martyrdom of St. Sebastian (Volets d'un Triptyque)*

Serene Sebastian is filled with arrows by a serene firing squad in a serene landscape. Sebastian, a Roman captain who'd converted to Christianity, was ordered to be shot to death. (He miraculously survived, so they clubbed him to death.)

Ready, freeze! Like a *tableau vivant* (popular with Philip

the Good's crowd), the well-dressed archers and saint freeze this moment in the martyrdom so the crowd can applaud the colorful costumes and painted cityscape backdrop.

Hans Memling, along with his former employer, Rogier van der Weyden, are called Flemish Primitives. Why "Primitive"? The term comes from the lack of 3-D realism so admired in Italy at the time (for more on Flemish Primitives, see sidebar on page 377). Sebastian's arm is tied to a branch that's not arching overhead, as it should be, but instead is behind him. An archer aims slightly behind, not at, Sebastian. The other archer strings his bow in a stilted pose. But Memling is clearly a master of detail, and the faces, beautiful textiles, and hazy landscape combine to create a meditative mood appropriate to the church altar in Bruges where this painting was once placed.

• *Next, head for the far-right corner of Room 68, where paintings by Pieter Brueghel I often are displayed.*

Pieter Brueghel I, the Elder (c. 1527-1569)— *The Census at Bethlehem*

Perched at treetop level, you have a bird's-eye view over a snow-covered village near Brussels. The canals are frozen over, but life

goes on, with everyone doing something. Kids throw snowballs and sled across the ice. A crowd gathers at the inn (lower left), where a woman holds a pan to catch blood while a man slaughters a pig. Most everyone has his or her back to us or head covered, so the figures speak through poses and motions.

Into the scene rides a woman on a donkey led by a man—it's Mary and husband Joseph hoping to find a room at the inn (or at least a manger), because Mary's going into labor.

The year is 1566—the same year that Protestant extremists throughout the Low Countries vandalized Catholic churches, tearing down "idolatrous" statues and paintings of the Virgin Mary. Brueghel (more discreetly) brings Mary down to earth from her Triumphant Coronation in heaven, and places Jesus' birth in the humble here and now. The busy villagers put their heads down and work, oblivious to the future Mother of God and the wonderous birth about to take place.

Brueghel the Elder was famous for his landscapes filled with crowds of peasants in motion. His religious paintings place the miraculous in everyday settings.

In this room you'll see Brueghel's works, as well as those of his less famous sons. Pieter Brueghel II, the younger Pieter, copied his dad's style (and even some paintings, like the *Census at Bethlehem*—displayed to the left). Another son, Jan, was known as the "Velvet Brueghel" for his glossy still lifes of flower arrangements.

• *Circle counterclockwise through the rest of the Ancient Art collection, until you finally reach works by Rubens in Rooms 52 and 53, including the wall-sized...*

Peter Paul Rubens (1577-1640)—*The Ascent to Calvary* (*La Montée au Calvaire*)

Life-size figures scale this 18-foot-tall canvas on the way to Christ's Crucifixion. The scene ripples with motion, from the windblown clothes to steroid-enhanced muscles to billowing flags and a troubled sky. Christ stumbles—he might get trampled by the surging crowd. Veronica kneels to gently wipe his bloody head.

This 200-square-foot canvas was manufactured by Rubens at his studio in Antwerp. Hiring top-notch assistants, Rubens could

crank out large altarpieces for the area's Catholic churches. First, Rubens himself did a small-scale sketch in oil (like many of the studies in Room 52). He would then make other sketches, highlighting individual details. His assistants would reproduce them on the large canvas, and Rubens would then add the final touches.

This work is from late in Rubens' long and very successful career. He got a second wind in his 50s, when he married 16-year-old Hélène Fourment. She was the model for Veronica, who consoles the faltering Christ in this painting.

• *Exit the Rubens room to the left, go into the perpendicular Room 53, and look right to find...*

Jacques-Louis David (1748-1825)—*The Death of Marat* (1793)

In a scene ripped from the day's headlines, Jean-Paul Marat—a well-known crusading French journalist—has been stabbed to death in his bathtub by Charlotte Corday, a conservative fanatic. Marat's life drains out of him, turning the bathwater red. With his last strength, he pens a final, patriotic, *"Vive la Révolution"* message to his fellow patriots. Corday, a young noblewoman angered by Marat's campaign to behead the French king, was arrested and guillotined three days later.

Jacques-Louis David, one of Marat's fellow revolutionaries, set to work painting a tribute to his fallen comrade. (He signed the painting: *"À Marat"*—"To Marat.")

David makes it a secular *pietà*, with the brave writer portrayed as a martyred Christ in a classic dangling-arm pose. Still, the deathly pallor and harsh lighting pull no punches, creating in-your-face realism.

David, the official art director of the French Revolution, supervised propaganda and the costumes worn for patriotic parades. A year after finishing this painting, in 1794, his extreme brand of revolution (which included guillotining thousands of supposed enemies) was squelched by moderates, and David was jailed. He emerged later as Napoleon's court painter. When Napoleon was exiled in 1815, so was David, spending his last years in Brussels.

• *To get to the Museum of Modern Art wing, return to the ground floor and the large main entrance hall of the Museum of Ancient Art. From there a passageway leads you to the Modern Art and Magritte museums. You'll pass the entrance to the Magritte Museum, then continue down into the Modern Art wing (entering on Level -3).*

Museum of Modern Art

• *Follow the "Circuit," which leads you down, down, down through several levels on a chronological route through the artwork. Keep an eye out for the following paintings; enlist the help of nearby guards if you can't find a piece.*

Watch Romanticism turn to Impressionism turn to Post-Impressionism. Paul Gauguin and Georges Seurat emerged from Paris' Impressionist community to forge their own styles. Begin on Level -6 by visiting with...

James Ensor (1860-1949)—*Shocked Masks* (1883)

At 22, James Ensor, an acclaimed child prodigy, proudly presented his lively Impressionist-style works to the Brussels Salon for exhibition. They were flatly rejected.

The artist withdrew from public view and, in seclusion,

ROYAL MUSEUMS

painted *Shocked Masks*, a dark and murky scene set in a small room of an ordinary couple wearing grotesque masks. Once again, everyone disliked this disturbing canvas and heaped more criticism on him. For the next six decades, Ensor painted the world as he saw it—full of bizarre, carnival-masked, stupid-looking crowds of cruel strangers who mock the viewer.

• *Farther along on Level –6 is something a bit cheerier...*

Georges Seurat (1859-1891)—*The Seine at Grand-Jatte* (*La Seine à la Grande-Jatte*, 1888)

Seurat paints a Sunday-in-the-park view from his favorite island in the Seine. Taking Impressionism to its extreme, he builds the scene out of small points of primary colors that blend at a distance to form objects. The bright colors capture the dazzling, sunlit atmosphere of this hazy day.

• *Behind you is...*

Paul Gauguin (1848-1903)—*Breton Calvary* (*Calvaire Breton*, 1889; a.k.a. *The Green Christ/Le Christ Vert*)

Paul Gauguin returned to the bold, black, coloring-book outlines of more Primitive (pre-3-D) art. The Christian statue and countryside look less like Brittany and more like primitive Tahiti, where Gauguin would soon settle.

• *Level –8 features work by Salvador Dalí, Francis Bacon, and Belgium's own...*

Paul Delvaux (1897-1994)—*Spitzner Museum* (*Le Musée Spitzner*, 1943)

Delvaux, who studied, worked, and taught in Brussels, became famous for his surrealistic paintings of nude women, often wan-

dering through weirdly lit landscapes. They cast long shadows,
wandering bare-breasted among
classical ruins.

• *Belgium has a special affinity for*
Surrealist artists, represented in this
museum by the likes of Joan Miró,
Salvador Dalí, Max Ernst, Yves
Tanguy, and Roberto Matta. If you
want more, consider visiting the
Magritte Museum, described next.

Magritte Museum

Entry to the Magritte Museum is covered by a separate ticket,
which comes with a reserved entry time (see "Reservations for the
Magritte Museum" on page 474).

This museum takes you on a chronological route (spread over
several levels of the building) through René Magritte's life and
art. The museum divides his life into three sections, with one floor
devoted to each. At the start of each section is a detailed timeline,
followed by the artist's work. Fascinating quotes from Magritte are
posted around the museum, but only in the original French; pick
up the English translation as you enter.

Magritte's works are perhaps best described in his own words:
"My paintings are visible images which conceal nothing; they
evoke mystery and, indeed, when one sees one of my pictures,
one asks oneself this simple question, 'What does that mean'? It
does not mean anything, because mystery means nothing either,
it is unknowable." If that brain-teaser titillates you, you'll love this
museum; if it frustrates you, consider skipping it.

• *From the entrance, you'll board an elevator that takes you up to Level*
+3. (Notice the woman's body parts—slowly panning up from the feet to
head—in the window in the back of the elevator.)

1898-1929 (Level +3)

Born to a middle-class Belgian family, René moved to Brussels at
age 17 to study at the Academy, where he learned to draw meticulously and got a broad liberal-arts education. In the 1920s, he eked
out a living designing advertisements, posters, and sheet music,
and wrote for the avant-garde *7 Arts* magazine (you'll see samples
posted). Meanwhile, he dabbled in Post-Impressionism, Futurism,
and Cubism, in search of his own voice.

In 1922, he married his childhood sweetheart, Georgette,
who became his lifelong companion and muse. It's said that all
the women he would paint (and you'll see many of them in this

René Magritte
(1898-1967)

René Magritte trained and worked in Brussels. Though he's world-famous now, it took decades before his peculiar brand of Surrealism caught on. He painted real objects with photographic clarity, and then jumbled them together in new and provocative ways.

Magritte had his own private reserve of symbolic images. You'll see clouds, blue sky, windows, the female torso, men in bowler hats, rocks, pipes, sleigh bells, birds, turtles, and castles arranged side by side as if the arrangement meant something. He heightens the mystery by making objects unnaturally large or small. People morph into animals or inanimate objects. The juxtaposition short-circuits your brain only when you try to make sense of it. Magritte's works are at once playful and disorienting...and, at times, disturbing.

collection) were versions of Georgette.

Influenced by the Dada and Surrealist movements coming out of Paris (Salvador Dalí, Marcel Duchamp, Giorgio de Chirico), Magritte became intrigued with the idea of painting dreamscapes that capture an air of mystery. You'll see mysterious figures on beaches, inspired by de Chirico's similar canvases.

For Magritte, 1927 was a watershed year, when he painted his first truly Surrealist works. *The Man from the Sea* featured a man on a beach with a wood-block head, pulling a lever. At the far end of the next room, *The Secret Player* perplexed the public (then and now) with a man swinging a bat and missing a flying turtle. In this section, and throughout this floor, you can see Magritte toying with Surrealist thoughts and techniques.

Together, René and Georgette mingled in sophisticated, bohemian circles. Photos show that their creativity went beyond the canvas. Looking at Georgette pose for René's lens (as she often did for his paintbrush), it's touching to think that he had found a soulmate who seemed to truly understand and encourage his weirdness. In the same section, see the series of photos of René, Georgette, and their friends striking wacky tableaux that intentionally distort normal poses. Called *The Fidelity of the Image*, this series was knocking on the door of Magritte's next breakthrough.

He experimented with writing words on the paintings, culminating in *The Treachery of Images*. The original (from 1928-1929, in the Los Angeles County Museum of Art) is Magritte's most famous work—not for its physical appearance, but for the bold conceptual point that it made. It's a photorealistic painting of a pipe with the words (in French) "This is not a pipe." Of course it's not a pipe, Magritte always insisted—it's a *painting* of a pipe. Magritte's wordplay forces the viewer to ponder the relationship between the object and its name—between the "signified" and the "signifier," to quote the deconstructionist philosophy that Magritte's paradoxical paintings inspired. Some credit this work for planting the seeds of postmodernism. At the end of this section you'll see a later ink-and-paper version (1952) with the message (also in French): "This continues not to be a pipe."

• *Head downstairs to...*

1930-1950 (Level +2)

After a few years in Paris, Magritte survived the Depression in Brussels by doing ad work and painting portraits of friends. (You'll see several women on his trademark Surrealist beaches.)

By the late 1930s, he'd refined his signature style: combining two arresting images to disrupt rational thought and produce an emotion of mystery. The paintings' weird titles added another layer of disruption. These were intentional nonsequiturs, which he and his Surrealist friends concocted at Sunday-night naming soirees. Perusing the paintings in here, it's fun to wonder which titles were random...and which meant something. *Forbidden Literature... The Kiss... The Unexpected Answer... God Is No Saint...*

During the World War II years—spent under Nazi occupation—Magritte used birds as a metaphor for the longing to be free *(The Companions of Fear, Treasure Island)*.

In 1943, he had a brief Impressionistic period of bright colors and rough brushwork. His characteristic Georgette-inspired nude becomes Technicolor in *The Harvest*. He also took to painting tongue-in-cheek-serious "portraits" of animals *(Stroke of Luck)*. Soon after, his series called *Black Magic* continued to colorize women's bodies. But he also created plenty of his distinctive paintings where the background and foreground seem to shift, with plenty of familiar motifs such as clouds and bowler hats.

In the postwar years, Magritte went through a *vache* ("cow") period, where he painted a series of comic-book-inspired paintings (including the green man with rifle-barrel nose, called *The Ellipsis*). Almost childlike, these are a dramatic departure from his normally photorealistic style.

1951-1967 (Level +1)

This floor is divided into two sections (don't overlook the easy-to-miss second one), and feels like a valedictory lap for all of the symbols and styles we've seen so far. At the foot of the stairs, you're greeted by a sculpture of a sleigh bell, curtains, and a blue sky entitled *Mona Lisa*—you'll see more renditions of this in the collection.

Like Picasso (and many other artists) nearing the end of a life of impressive output and experimentation, Magritte had a quiver full of artistic arrows to shoot at the canvas. And yet something feels rote about his final years of work—he seemed to rehash familiar territory, expressing things he'd already mastered—rather than experiment with bold new directions.

The collection culminates at his *Empire of Lights*, which shows how even well-scrubbed suburbia can possess an ominous air of mystery. Magritte loved night-sky tones. He often created several versions of the same work (which explains why there are several *Empire of Lights* canvases in the world).

By the end of his life, Magritte was well-known, especially in America. His use of everyday objects and poster-art style inspired Pop Art.

• *Exit through Level -1, which has a book shop and an appropriately perplexing 50-minute film about Magritte. Descend to Level -2 to find the passageway back to the Royal Museums...and reality.*

BRUSSELS SLEEPING, EATING, NIGHTLIFE & CONNECTIONS

The capital of Belgium—and of the European Union—Brussels is a great place to spend some time. This chapter provides suggestions for the best places to sleep and eat; tips for after-hours fun; and a rundown of the complicated connections (from the city's three different train stations) to points throughout Belgium, the Netherlands, and beyond, as well as tips for getting to and from the city's two airports.

Sleeping in Brussels

Normal hotel prices are high in central Brussels. A popular business destination, it tends to be busiest, and most expensive, on weekdays. But if you arrive in July, August, or on a Friday or Saturday night, the city's fancy business-class hotels rent rooms for half-price, making them your best budget bet. (Conversely, Bruges—a pleasure destination—has higher demand on weekends. If your trip is flexible, consider arranging your overnights in these two towns with these deal-finding patterns in mind.)

April, May, September, and October are very crowded in Brussels, and finding a room without a reservation can be impossible. The busiest time of year is the European Seafood Exhibition (May 3-5 in 2011, www.euroseafood.com), when the city is awash in seafood-industry employees.

You do have budget options here. The modern hostels, which rent double rooms, are especially good.

Business Hotels with Summer Rates
Brussels' fancy hotels (Db-€150-200) survive because of the business and diplomatic trade. But they're desperately empty most of July and August (sometimes June, too) and on most weekends (Fri,

Sleep Code

(€1 = about $1.40, country code: 32)
S = Single, **D** = Double/Twin, **T** = Triple, **Q** = Quad, **b** = bathroom, **s** = shower only. Everyone speaks English and accepts credit cards. Unless otherwise noted, breakfast is included.

To help you easily sort through these listings, I've divided the rooms into three categories, based on the price for a standard double room with bath:

$$$ Higher Priced—Most rooms €100 or more.
 $$ Moderately Priced—Most rooms between €80-100.
  $ Lower Priced—Most rooms €80 or less.

Prices can change without notice; verify the hotel's current rates online or by email. For other updates, see www.ricksteves.com/update.

Sat, and, to a lesser extent, Sun nights). During these slow times, rates drop by a third to two-thirds. Three-star hotels in the center abound with amazing summer rates—you can rent a double room with enough comforts to keep a diplomat happy, including a fancy breakfast, for about €60.

There are two ways to get these great rates: You can go through a **booking website** (most Brussels hotels list their rooms through www.booking.com, but you might also find deals on other sites—check www.expedia.com, www.orbitz.com, or your favorite). Or you can book in person (or sometimes by phone or email) at one of Brussels' **TIs**. (Whereas TI booking services in many cities are a bad value, Brussels' is an exception—the TIs here can actually save you some money.) If you simply show up at the TI without a reservation during slow times, they can usually find you a great deal. Because some hotels hold out until the last minute to cut their rates, prices tend to plummet as the date approaches; booking a room a month ahead could cost you substantially more than booking a few days ahead.

Waiting does, however, pose some risks—for example, you might wind up in a less-than-ideal location farther from the action. If waiting seems too risky, do a little homework to gauge what the demand will be when you visit: Check rates online well before your trip. If rates are only slightly discounted, demand is probably pretty strong, so you should book sooner rather than later; if rates are already deeply discounted, consider holding off, to see if they go even lower.

Alternatively, you can contact the TI by email (info@visit flanders.us) or by phone (numbers listed on page 422; Town Hall

TI room-booking desk is 02-563-6104) and ask which business-class hotels will have special rates during your visit. Ask for the cheapest three-star place near the Grand Place. Historically, some business hotels have rented double rooms with bath and breakfast for €50 through the summer.

Note that many of the hotels I list below offer these deals. If you prefer to book direct with the hotel (rather than through the TI or a booking website), try this strategy: Check online booking sites to see what your hotel of choice is offering for the dates of your trip. Then contact the hotel directly to see if they'll honor that same price (or give you a better one).

These seasonal rates apply only to business-class hotels. Because of this, budget accommodations, which charge the same throughout the year, may go from being a good value one day (say, a Thursday in October) to a bad value the next (a Friday in October).

Hotels near the Grand Place

$$$ **Hotel Ibis off Grand Place,** well-situated halfway between Central Station and the Grand Place, is the best of six Ibis locations in or near Brussels. It's a sprawling, modern hotel offering 184 quiet, simple, industrial-strength-yet-comfy rooms (Sb/Db-€145-169 Mon-Thu, generally around €79 Fri-Sun and daily July-Aug, extra bed-€20, breakfast-€14, non-smoking, air-con, elevator, pay Internet access and Wi-Fi, Marché-aux-Herbes/Grasmarkt 100, tel. 02-514-4040, fax 02-514-5067, www.ibishotel.com, h1046@accor.com).

$$$ **Hotel Le Dixseptième,** a four-star luxury hotel ideally located a block below Central Station, is an expensive oasis in the heart of town. Prim, proper, and peaceful, with chandeliers and squeaky hardwood floors, its 24 rooms come with all the comforts. Each is decorated with a different theme (Db-€200, Db suites-€270, extra bed-€30, 25 percent off Fri-Sat, often Db-€100 with no breakfast in July-Aug, see their website for deals, air-con, elevator, pay Internet access and Wi-Fi, Rue de la Madeleine/Magdalenasteenweg 25, tel. 02-517-1717, fax 02-502-6424, www.ledixseptieme.be, info@ledixseptieme.be).

$$$ **Hotel La Madeleine,** on the small "Agora" square between Central Station and the Grand Place, rents 56 plain, dimly lit rooms. It has a great location and a friendly staff (S-€55; Ss-€78, Sb-€108, Db-€115; bigger "executive" rooms: Sb-€125, Db-€130, Tb-€138, family Qb-€180; 20 percent off Fri-Sat, 30 percent off July-Aug—see website for deals, book direct and mention Rick Steves to get the best rates; request a quieter back room when you reserve, non-smoking, elevator, pay Internet access and Wi-Fi, Rue de la Montagne/Bergstraat 22, tel. 02-513-2973,

Brussels Accommodations

SLEEPING IN BRUSSELS

Legend:

||| Stairs

Ⓜ Subway Stop

Ⓑ Tour Bus Departure Points (2)

200 YARDS
200 METERS

① Hotel Ibis off Grand Place
② Hotel Le Dixseptième
③ Hotel La Madeleine
④ Hotel Opéra
⑤ Hotel La Légende
⑥ Hotel Ibis Centre Ste. Catherine
⑦ Hotel the Moon
⑧ Hotel Welcome
⑨ Maison Noble B&B
⑩ Hotel Noga
⑪ Citadines Sainte-Catherine Apart'hotel
⑫ Bruegel Hostel
⑬ To Sleep Well Hostel
⑭ To Jacques Brel Hostel
⑮ Launderettes (2)

fax 02-502-1350, www.hotel-la-madeleine.be, info@hotel-la -madeleine.be, Philippe).

$$$ Hotel Opéra, on a people-filled street near the Grand Place, is professional but standardized, with lots of street noise and 49 well-worn rooms (Sb-€89, Db-€119 or €85 in July-Aug, Tb-€135, Qb-€150, 10 percent less with this book in 2011; request a quieter courtyard room, elevator, free Wi-Fi, Grétry street 53, tel. 02-219-4343, fax 02-219-1720, www.hotel-opera.be, reception @hotel-opera.be).

$$$ Hotel La Légende rents 26 small, straightforward rooms a block from the *Manneken-Pis* statue. Although it's on a busy road, it has a pleasant courtyard. The furnishings are basic, but the location and price are right and the rooms are comfortable enough (prices very flexible—generally Sb-€110, Db-€120, bigger Db-€5-40 extra, Tb-€145, Qb-€155, 30 percent off on weekends and July-Aug, request a quieter courtyard room, elevator, free Wi-Fi, Lombard street 35, tel. 02-512-8290, fax 02-512-3493, www.hotel lalegende.com, info@hotellalegende.com).

$$ Hotel Ibis Centre Ste. Catherine is a big, impersonal, perfectly comfortable place with 236 rooms in a great location that may offer very deep discounts during its slow times, ask at the TI, as discounts are only available if booked there, and not at the hotel itself (Db-€119 during the week, €79-85 on weekends, breakfast-€14, air-con, elevator, pay Wi-Fi, Joseph Plateau street 2 at Place Ste. Catherine/Sint-Katelijneplein, tel. 02-513-7620, fax 02-514-2214, www.ibishotel.com, h1454@accor.com).

$$ Hotel the Moon is a concrete and efficient last resort, with 17 bare-bones rooms and no public spaces. It has absolutely no character, the dust bunnies run rampant, and the thin walls and doors, along with noise from the square out front, can make for a very noisy night. But the location is super-convenient— just steps from the Grand Place—and it's the cheapest centrally located hotel this side of a youth hostel (Sb-€55-70, Db-€65-90, Tb-€81-110, lower prices are for slow times including July-Aug, 10 percent discount if you book direct with the latest edition of this book, ask for a quieter room in the back, stairs but no elevator, on the small "Agora" square at Rue de la Montagne/Bergstraat 4, tel. 02-508-1580, fax 02-508-1585, www.hotelthemoon.com, info@ hotelthemoon.com).

Hotels in Ste. Catherine, near the Old Fish Market

The next three listings are a 10-minute walk from the intensity of the old center, near the Ste. Catherine/Sint-Katelijne Métro stop. This charming neighborhood, called "the village in Brussels," faces the canalside fish market and has many of the town's best restaurants.

$$$ Hotel Welcome, owned by an energetic bundle of hospitality named Meester Smeesters, offers outrageously creative rooms, exuberantly decorated with artifacts he's picked up in his world travels. Each of the 16 rooms has a different geographic theme, from India to Japan to Bali: Take a virtual tour of the rooms on their website. Owners Sophie and Michel Smeesters (and their helpers, Vincent and

Anna) are the rare hoteliers who actually sleep in their rooms occasionally just to figure out how they can make their guests' experience even better (Sb-€120, standard Db-€125, deluxe Db-€140, large suite-€210, family room, cheaper on weekends, much lower rates in Aug, elevator, free Internet access and Wi-Fi, reasonably priced laundry service, parking-€13, free airport transfer—3 people max—if you book direct and show this book on arrival, 23 Quai au Bois à Brûler/Brandhoutkaai, tel. 02-219-9546, fax 02-217-1887, www.hotelwelcome.com, info@hotelwelcome.com).

$$$ Maison Noble is a charming boutique B&B run by Matthieu and Brendon. This gay-friendly place (the well-hung art gravitates toward male nudes) has three classy, mod rooms, a gorgeous Art Nouveau/Art Deco stained-glass window over the breakfast table, and a free steam room. It's on a dull street just a block off the old fish market (D-€129, big Db-€149, 1-night stay-€10 extra, €10 less for 4 nights or longer, €20 less mid-July-Aug, free Internet access and Wi-Fi, 10 Marcq street, tel. 02-219-2339, www.maison-noble.eu, info@maison-noble.eu).

$$$ Hotel Noga feels extremely homey, with 19 rooms, a welcoming game room, and old photos of Belgian royalty lining the hallways. It's carefully run by Frederich Faucher and his son, Mourad (Sb-€95, Db-€110, Tb-€135, Qb-€160, all rooms about 20 percent off Fri-Sat and in Aug, 5 percent discount if you pay in cash, very quiet, non-smoking, pay Internet access and Wi-Fi, garage-€15, Rue du Beguinage/Begijnhofstraat 38, tel. 02-218-6763, fax 02-218-1603, www.nogahotel.com, info@nogahotel.com).

$$$ Citadines Sainte-Catherine Apart'hotel, part of a Europe-wide chain, is a huge apartment-style hotel with modern, shipshape rooms. Choose from efficiency studios with fold-out double beds or two-room apartments with a bedroom and a fold-out couch in the living room. All 163 units come with a kitchen, stocked cupboards, a stereo, and everything you need to settle right in (official rates: one- or two-person studio-€135, apartment for up to four people-€170, but rates very flexible—check online, much less July-Aug, 15 percent cheaper by the week, breakfast-€13, free Internet access and Wi-Fi, parking-€17, 51 Quai au Bois à Brûler/ Brandhoutkaai, tel. 02-221-1411, fax 02-221-1599, www.citadines .com, stecatherine@citadines.com).

Hostels

Three classy and modern hostels—in buildings that could double as small, state-of-the-art, minimum-security prisons—are within a 10-minute walk of Central Station. Each accepts people of all ages, serves cheap and hot meals, takes credit cards, and charges about the same price. All rates include breakfast and showers down the hall.

$ **Bruegel Hostel,** a fortress of cleanliness, is handiest and most comfortable, with 135 beds. Of its many rooms, 22 are bunk-bed doubles (S-€32, D-€47, beds in quads or dorms-€20, nonmembers and guests over age 26 pay €3 extra/night, includes sheets and breakfast, open 7:00-10:00 & 14:00-1:00 in the morning, pay Internet access, midway between Midi/Zuid/South and Central stations, behind Chapelle church at Rue de St. Esprit/H. Geeststraat 2, tel. 02-511-0436, fax 02-512-0711, www.youth hostels.be, brussel@vjh.be).

$ **Sleep Well Hostel,** surrounded by high-rise parking structures, is also comfortable (S-€36, Sb-€46, D-€54, Db-€66, T-€71, Tb-€92, dorm beds-€20-22, includes sheets and breakfast, nonsmoking, Internet access and Wi-Fi, lockout 11:00-15:00, Rue de Damier 23, tel. 02-218-5050, fax 02-218-1313, www.sleepwell.be, info@sleepwell.be).

$ **Jacques Brel Hostel,** with 164 beds, is a little farther out, but it's still a reasonable walk from everything (S-€35, D-€48-52, dorm bed-€17-19, nonmembers and guests over age 26 pay €3 extra/night, includes sheets and breakfast, no curfew, non-smoking rooms, laundry, Rue de la Sablonnière/Zavelput 30, tel. 02-218-0187, fax 02-217-2005, www.laj.be, brussels.brel@laj.be).

Eating in Brussels

For many, the obvious eating tip in Brussels is simply to enjoy the Grand Place. My vote for northern Europe's grandest medieval square is lined with hardworking eateries that serve predictable dishes to tourist crowds. Of course, you won't get the best quality or prices—but, after all, it's the Grand Place. Locals advise eating well elsewhere and enjoying a Grand Place perch for dessert or a drink. While many tourists congregate at the Rue des Bouchers, "Restaurant Row," consider a wander through the new, emerging eating zone—gay, ethnic, and trendy—past the Bourse near Place St-Géry/Sint-Goriksplein. Compare the ambience, check posted menus, and choose your favorite.

Brussels is known for both its high-quality, French-style cuisine and for multicultural variety. Seafood—fish, eel, shrimp, and oysters—is especially well-prepared here. As in France, if you ask for the *menù* (muh-noo) at a restaurant, you won't get a list of dishes; you'll get a fixed-price meal. *Menùs,* which include three or four courses, are generally a good value if you're hungry. Ask for *la carte* (lah kart) if you want to see a printed menu and order à la carte, like the locals do. For more on Belgian cuisine, see page 331. To read local restaurant reviews, check out www.resto.be.

Mussels in Brussels

Mussels *(moules)* are available all over town. For an atmospheric cellar or a table right on the Grand Place, eat at **L'Estaminet du Kelderke.** Its one steamy vault under the square is always packed with both natives and tourists—a real Brussels fixture. It serves local specialties, including mussels (a splittable kilo bucket—just more than 2 pounds—for €20-22; daily 12:00-24:00, Thu-Sat until 2:00 in the morning, no reservations taken, Grand Place 15, tel. 02-513-7344). Also see Restaurant Chez Leon, next.

Rue des Bouchers ("Restaurant Row")

Brussels' restaurant streets, two blocks north of the Grand Place, are touristy and notorious for touts who aggressively suck you in and predatory servers who greedily rip you off. It's a little hard to justify dining here when far better options sit just a block or two away (see later listings). But the area is an exhilarating spectacle and is fun for at least a walk. If you are seduced into a meal here, order carefully, understand the prices thoroughly, and watch your wallet.

Restaurant Chez Leon is a touristy mussels factory, slamming out piles of good, cheap buckets since 1893. It's the original flagship branch of a chain that's now spreading throughout France. It's big and welcoming, with busy green-aproned waiters

Brussels Restaurants

EATING IN BRUSSELS

1. L'Estaminet du Kelderke
2. Rest. Chez Leon & Rest. Vincent
3. Aux Armes de Bruxelles
4. Restaurant de l'Ogenblik
5. Belga Queen Brasserie
6. Le Mokafé
7. La Maison des Crêpes
8. Osteria a l'Ombra
9. De Pistolei Sandwiches
10. "Pita Street"
11. AD Delhaize Grocery
12. Super GB Grocery
13. Bij den Boer
14. La Marie Joseph
15. Le Royal Rest.
16. La Villette Rest.
17. Rest. La Marée
18. Rest. Le Pré Salé
19. Mer du Nord/Nordzee
20. Cremerie de Linkebeek
21. Le Pain Quotidien
22. A la Mort Subite Bar
23. Le Cirio Café
24. A la Bécasse Café
25. Fin de Siècle & Le Greenwich Bars

offering a "Formula Leon" for €12.90—a light meal consisting of a small bucket of mussels, fries, and a beer. They also offer a €31.30 fixed-price meal that comes with a starter, a large bucket of mussels, fries, and beer (daily 12:00-23:00, kids under 12 eat free, Rue des Bouchers/Beenhouwers 18, tel. 02-511-1415). In the family portrait of Leon's brother Honoré (hanging in the corner), the wife actually looks like a mussel.

Aux Armes de Bruxelles is a venerable restaurant that has been serving reliably good food to locals in a dressy setting for generations. This is another food factory, with white-suited waiters serving an older clientele impressed by the restaurant's reputation. You'll pay a bit more for the formality (€8-18 starters, €16-32 main dishes, €20 fixed-price lunch, €35-46 fixed-price dinner, daily 12:00-23:00, indoor seating only, Rue des Bouchers/Beenhouwers 13, tel. 02-511-5550).

Restaurant Vincent has you enter through the kitchen to enjoy their 1905-era ambience. This place is better for meat dishes than for seafood. Enjoy the engaging old tile murals of the seaside and countryside (€12-19 starters, €20-32 main dishes, €37 fixed-price meal, Mon-Sat 12:00-14:30 & 18:30-23:00, Sun 12:00-15:00 & 18:30-22:30, Rue des Dominicains/Predikherenstraat 8-10, tel. 02-511-2607, Michel and Jacques).

Finer Dining near Rue des Bouchers

These options, though just steps away from those listed above, are more authentic and a better value.

Restaurant de l'Ogenblik, a remarkably peaceful eddy just off the raging restaurant row, fills an early 20th-century space in the corner of an arcade. The waiters serve well-presented, near-gourmet French cuisine. This mussels-free zone has a great, split-table rack of lamb with 10 vegetables (€23-28 plates, Mon-Sat 12:00-14:30 & 19:00-24:00, closed Sun, across from Restaurant Vincent—listed above—at Galerie des Princes 1, tel. 02-511-6151, Yves).

Belga Queen Brasserie bills itself as a "wonderfood place." A huge, trendy, dressy brasserie filling a palatial former bank building, it's *the* spot for Brussels' beautiful people and visiting European diplomats. Although a little more expensive than the alternatives, the "creative Belgian cuisine" is excellent, the service is sharp, and the experience is memorable—from the fries served in silver cones, to the double-decker platters of iced shellfish, to the transparent toilets stalls (which become opaque only after you nervously lock the door). The high-powered trendiness can make you feel a little gawky, but if you've got the money, this is a great splurge. Consider their €33 three-course, fixed-price meal with matching beers (€15-25 starters, €20-30 main dishes,

€30-47 fixed-price meals, daily 12:00-14:30 & 19:00-24:00, call to reserve, bar open all day, Rue Fosse-aux-Loups/Wolvengracht 32, tel. 02-217-2187). The vault downstairs is a plush cigar and cocktail lounge. For just a drink, grab a stool at the white-marble oyster bar.

More Eateries near the Grand Place

Le Mokafé is inexpensive but feels splurgy. They dish up light café fare at the quiet end of the elegant Galeries St. Hubert, with great people-watching outdoor tables (€3-6 sandwiches, €7-11 salads, €8-10 pastas, €9-12 main dishes, daily 8:00-24:00, Galerie du Roi 9, tel. 02-511-7870).

La Maison des Crêpes, a little eatery a half-block south of the Bourse, looks underwhelming but serves delicious €8-10 crêpes (both savory and sweet varieties) and salads. It has a brown café ambience, and even though it's just a few steps away from the tourist bustle, it feels laid-back and local (good beers, fresh mint tea, sidewalk seating, daily 12:00-23:00, Rue du Midi/Zuidstraat 13, mobile 0475-957-368).

Osteria a l'Ombra, a true Italian joint, is perfect for anyone needing a quality bowl of pasta with a glass of fine Italian wine. Across the lane from the TI and just a block off the Grand Place, it's pricey, but the woody bistro ambience and tasty food make it a good value. If you choose a main dish (€14-18), your choice of pasta or salad is included in the price (otherwise €9-13 pasta meals). The ground-floor seating on high stools is fine, but also consider sitting upstairs (Mon-Fri 12:00-15:00 & 18:30-23:30, Sat 18:30-23:30, closed Sun, Rue des Harengs/Haringstraat 2, tel. 02-511-6710).

Cheap Eats near the Grand Place: The super-central square dubbed the "Agora" (officially Marché-aux-Herbes/Grasmarkt, just between the Grand Place and Central Station) is lined with low-end eateries, and is especially fun on sunny days. Pick one of the chain restaurants, or head a few steps up Rue de la Madeleine (toward the train station) to **De Pistolei,** a family-run lunch counter serving tasty made-to-order sandwiches (€3, daily 7:00-20:00, Rue de la Madeleine/Magdalenasteenweg 5, tel. 02-502-9502). At the other end of the Grand Place, Rue du Marché-aux-Fromages/Kaasmarkt—nicknamed **"Pita Street"**—is lined with affordable Turkish and Greek eateries.

Groceries: Two supermarkets are located about a block from the Bourse and a few blocks from the Grand Place. **AD Delhaize** is at the intersection of Anspach and Marché-aux-Poulets/Kiekenmarkt (Mon-Sat 9:00-20:00, Fri until 21:00, Sun 9:00-18:00), and **Super GB** is half a block away at Halles and Marché-aux-Poulets/Kiekenmarkt (Mon-Sat 9:00-20:00, Fri until 21:00, closed Sun). Mini-markets dot the city. Often run by Pakistani

EATING IN BRUSSELS

and Indian immigrants, they're pricier than supermarkets but handy (open very late, drinks, groceries, phone cards).

In Ste. Catherine, near the Old Fish Market

A 10-minute walk from the old center puts you in "the village within the city" area of Ste. Catherine (Métro: Ste. Catherine/ Sint-Katelijne). The historic fish market here has spawned a tradition of fine restaurants specializing mostly in seafood. The old fish canal survives, and if you walk around it, you'll see plenty of enticing places to eat. Make the circuit, considering these very good, yet very different, options.

Bij den Boer, a fun, noisy eatery popular with locals and tourists, has inviting tables out on the park and feels like a traditional and very successful brasserie. Their specialty: fish (€12-16 starters, €20-30 main dishes, €28 four-course fixed-price meal, Mon-Sat 12:00-14:30 & 18:00-22:30, closed Sun, Quai aux Briques/ Baksteenkai 60, tel. 02-512-6122).

La Marie Joseph, stylish and modern—both the food and the clientele—serves fancy fish and fries, and earns raves from the natives (€16-22 starters, €23-32 plates, Tue-Sun 12:00-15:00 & 18:30-23:00, closed Mon, no reservations taken, Quai au Bois à Brûler/Brandhoutkaai 47, tel. 02-218-0596).

Le Royal is a youthful, rollicking brasserie serving good food. They offer both traditional (and well-executed) Belgian staples and modern fusion dishes—some with a hint of Asian influence. Sit in the high-energy interior, or choose a sidewalk table (€8-15 starters, €13-22 main dishes, €3 sides, daily 12:00-15:00 & 18:00-23:00, later on weekends, Rue de Flandre/Vlaamsesteenweg 103, tel. 02-217-8500).

La Villette Restaurant ("The Slaughterhouse") is a romantic, subdued, seafood-free alternative, serving traditional Belgian cuisine: heavy, meaty stews and dishes with beer. It has a charming red-and-white-tablecloth interior and good outdoor seating facing a small square (€14 two-course fixed-price lunch, €15-22 meals, Mon-Fri 12:00-14:30 & 18:30-22:30, Sat 18:30-22:30 only, closed Sun, Rue du Vieux Marché-aux-Grains/Oude Graanmarkt 3, tel. 02-512-7550, Agata).

Restaurant La Marée is a classic local scene a couple of blocks away from the trendy canalside places. A nontouristy, less trendy bistro with an older clientele, an open kitchen, and an inviting menu, it specializes in mussels and seafood (€19-26 meals, Tue-Sat 12:00-14:00 & 18:30-22:00, closed Sun-Mon, near Rue du Marché aux Porcs/Varkensmarkt at Rue de Flandre/Vlaamsesteenweg 99, tel. 02-511-0040).

Restaurant Le Pré Salé is noisy and family-friendly. A Brussels fixture for its traditional local cuisine, it fills a former butcher shop with happy eaters and a busy open kitchen. Although the service can be spotty, and the place has gone a bit downhill in recent years, it's still a reliable neighborhood choice (big, shareable €21 pots of mussels come with a salad, €13-19 meals, Wed-Sun 12:00-14:30 & 18:30-22:30, closed Mon-Tue, a block off the fish market at Rue de Flandre/Vlaamsesteenweg 20, tel. 02-513-6545).

Cheap, Fast, and Tasty Lunches in Ste. Catherine

Place Ste. Catherine/Sint-Katelijneplein, which branches off from the side of Ste. Catherine Church, is lined with enjoyable cafés with outdoor seating, La Villette (described earlier), and the following two excellent lunch options. (The third place listed below is about a block away, down Dansaert street.)

Mer du Nord/Nordzee is as delicious as it is inexpensive. This seafood bar—basically a grill attached to a fresh fish shop—grills up whatever it catches and serves it on small tapas-like plates with glasses of wine to a very appreciative local crowd. Just belly up to the counter and place your order, then eat it standing at the tables. The €7 *scampi à la plancha* (grilled shrimp) is exquisite (€4-7 small dishes, Tue-Thu 11:00-17:00, Fri-Sat 11:00-18:00, Sun 11:00-20:00, closed Mon, Rue Ste. Catherine/Sint-Katelijnestraat 45, at corner with Place Ste. Catherine, tel. 02-513-1192). The similar **Poissonerie/Vishandel ABC,** across the street, has a comparable operation (closed Sun).

Cremerie de Linkebeek, owned by Jordan (who's part American) and Laurence, is the best place in town to shop for local

Belgian cheeses—rubbed and flavored with beer rather than wine or alcohol. The English-speaking staff is happy to help you explore the options and choose the perfect cheese for your picnic (they also sell baguettes, wine, and crackers—you could assemble a light meal or a snack right here). At midday, they also sell delicious €4 baguette sandwiches to go—grab one before they sell out (Mon 9:00-15:00, Tue-Sat 9:00-18:00, closed Sun, 4 Rue du Vieux Marché aux Grains/Oude Graanmarkt, tel. 02-512-3510).

Le Pain Quotidien ("The Daily Bread") is a popular, upscale, artisan bakery chain selling good sandwiches and other dishes in a rustic yet dignified setting. There's a handy location just below Place Ste. Catherine (Mon-Sat 7:30-19:00, Sun 7:30-18:00, Dansaert street 16A, tel. 02-502-2361). Across the street is **Comocomo,** serving mediocre Basque-style tapas with an innovative twist: on a conveyor belt, sushi bar-style.

EATING IN BRUSSELS

Sampling Belgian Beer with Food and Ambience

Looking for a good spot to enjoy that famous Belgian beer? Brussels is full of atmospheric cafés to savor the local brew. The eateries lining the Grand Place are touristy, but the setting—plush, old medieval guild halls fronting all that cobbled wonder—is hard to beat. I've listed three places a few minutes' walk off the square, all with a magical, old-time feel. If you'd like something to wash down with your beer, you can generally get a cold-meat plate, an open-face sandwich, or a salad.

All varieties of Belgian beer are available, but Brussels' most distinctive beers are *lambic*-based. Look for *lambic doux, lambic blanche, gueuze* (pronounced "kurrs"), and *faro*, as well as fruit-flavored *lambics*, such as *kriek* (cherry) and *framboise* (raspberry—*frambozen* in Flemish). These beers look and taste more like a dry, somewhat bitter cider. The brewer doesn't add yeast—the beer ferments naturally from yeast found floating only in the marshy air around Brussels. For more on Belgian beer, see page 333.

A la Mort Subite, a few steps above the top end of the Galeries St. Hubert, is a classic old bar that has retained its 1928 decor...and many of its 1928 cus-tomers (Mon-Sat 11:00-24:00, Sun 12:00-23:00, Rue Montagne-aux-Herbes Potagères/Warmoesberg 7, tel. 02-513-1318). Named after the "sudden death" playoff that work-ingmen used to end their lunchtime dice games, it still has an unpreten-tious, working-class feel. The decor is simple, with wood tables, grimy yellow wallpaper, and some-other-era garland trim. Tiny metal plates on the walls mark spots where gas-powered flames once flickered—used by patrons to light their cigars. A typical lunch or snack here is a *tartine* (open-face sand-wich, €5) spread with *fromage blanc* (cream cheese) or pressed meat. Eat it with one of the home-brewed, *lambic*-based beers. This is a good place to try the *kriek* (cherry-flavored) beer. The Bruxelloise claim it goes well with sandwiches.

At **Le Cirio,** across from the Bourse, the dark tables bear the skid marks of over a century's worth of beer steins (daily 10:00-1:00 in the morning, Rue de la Bourse/Beursstraat 18-20, tel. 02-512-1395).

A la Bécasse is lower profile than Le Cirio, with a simple wood-panel and wood-table decor that appeals to both poor stu-dents and lunching businessmen. The *lambic doux* has been served in clay jars since 1825. This place is just around the corner from Le

Cirio, toward the Grand Place, hidden away at the end of a court-yard (€3-5 *tartine* sandwiches, €5-9 light meals, daily 11:00-24:00, Tabora street 11, tel. 02-511-0006).

Youthful Fun at Place St-Géry

The classics recommended above are famous among tourists, and understandably so. For a more local and youthful scene, head a few blocks west to Place St-Géry/Sint-Goriksplein. Here you'll find bar and restaurant hangouts that offer a more basic, neighborhood feel. The epicenter is at the northeast corner of the square (intersection of Pont de la Carpe/Karperbrug and Plétinckx street), where you'll find a high concentration of Asian eateries. Rather than recommend a particular place, I'd suggest exploring your options and choosing the menu and indoor ambience or outdoor views you like best.

Perhaps the best options are actually hiding a block away from this lively zone (head up Plétinckx street, turn right up St. Kristoffels street, go one block, then look left). Here you'll find two inviting options: **Fin de Siècle** is a youthful bohemian scene serving basic, unpretentious Belgian/French fare in a classic turn-of-the-century atmosphere (€11-17 meals, daily from 18:00, Rue des Chartreux/Katuizerstraat 9). The adjacent **Le Greenwich** is a chess bar with a rough, circa-1900 former elegance serving good beer and simpler plates (closed Sun, Rue des Chartreux/Katuizerstraat 7, tel. 02-511-4167).

Nightlife in Brussels

After dark, the **Grand Place** becomes even more magical—as day-tripping tourists are gone and the Town Hall spire is floodlit.

Pick up the free *Agenda* and *Brussels Unlimited* magazines from the TI, which list events including opera, symphony, and ballet.

At one time, Brussels had a wide range of characteristic little cinemas. These days, most Bruxelloise flock to the multiplexes; a handy one is the **UGC** cinema on De Brouckère square (look for *v.o.* for the original version; *v.f.* means it's dubbed in French). There's also a small art-house cinema in the Galeries St. Hubert; movies here play in their original language (generally not English, as these are typically international films), with Flemish and French subtitles.

The most interesting neighborhood to explore after-hours

(or any time of day) is just a few steps west of the Grand Place: **Rue du Marché-au-Charbon/ Kolenmarkt** is the center of Brussels' gay scene, with many lively cafés and restaurants with outdoor seating. The trendy eateries, shops, and businesses along here change so fast, the locals can't keep track.

Across the Boulevard Anspach is **Place St-Géry,** where you'll find a raucous collection of lively bars with rollicking interiors and

a sea of outdoor tables. Van Praet street, which stretches from here to the Bourse, is lined with mostly Asian eateries. A five-minute walk northeast is the pleasant **Ste. Catherine** district, with lively local restaurants and hotels huddled around the Church of

Ste. Catherine and the old fish market. You'll find more in-depth descriptions of both of these areas on page 432; restaurant suggestions on page 496; and hotels in the Ste. Catherine area on page 489.

Brussels Connections

By Train

Brussels has three train stations: Centraal/Central, Midi/Zuid/ South, and Nord/Noord/North. Most trains stop at all three stations, but high-speed international trains serve only the Midi/ Zuid/South Station. For more details on all three stations—and tips on connecting between them—see page 423. For information on rail deals in Belgium, see page 583.

At any station, as you wait on the platform for your train, watch the track notice board that tells you which train is approaching. Trains zip in and out constantly, so a train with an open door on your train's track—three minutes before your departure time— may well be the wrong train. Anxious travelers, who think their train has arrived early, often board the wrong train on the right track.

Regular Trains to Belgium and the Netherlands

From All Brussels Stations by Train to: Bruges (2/hour, 1 hour, catch InterCity train—direction: Ostende or Knokke-

Belgian Train Lines

Blankenberge, €12.90), **Antwerp** (5/hour, 40-50 minutes), **Ghent** (3/hour, 35 minutes), **Ypres/Ieper** (hourly, 1.75 hours, some change in Kortrijk), **Amsterdam** (stops at Amsterdam's Schiphol Airport en route, hourly, 2.75 hours), **Haarlem** (hourly, 2.75 hours, transfer in Rotterdam), **Delft** (hourly, 2 hours, change in Rotterdam), **The Hague** (hourly, 2 hours).

High-Speed International Trains
Catch the following special, high-speed train lines at Midi/Zuid/South Station, tracks 1-6 (described in detail on page 423). Note that these trains do not stop at the Central or North train stations. For schedules, see http://bahn.hafas.de/bin/query.exe/en.

From Brussels by Thalys Train: The Thalys company has a pricey monopoly on trains to **Paris** (2/hour, 1.5 hours), and runs trains to **Köln**, Germany (9/day, 1.75 hours). They also run special seasonal trains, such as to **Marseille**, France, in the summer and to the **French Alps** in the winter. From Brussels to Paris, a regular second-class Thalys ticket costs about €60-80 second class (compared to about €25 by bus; buy ticket the day before or earlier, as same-day fares are even higher). Railpass-holders need to buy a seat reservation for €26 in second class or €41-54 in first class (first class generally includes a meal). If your railpass covers only France but not BeNeLux, it'll cost you €44 in second class or €69 in first class. Railpasses without France are not accepted on Thalys trains. Train info: Tel. 02-528-2828 (long wait), www.thalys.com.

By TGV Train to France: French TGV trains connect to **Paris' Charles de Gaulle Airport** (7/day, 1.25-1.75 hours, www.tgv-europe.com) and then continue on to various destinations in southern France, including Marseille, Nice, and Bordeaux. Note that Thalys has exclusive rights for the Brussels-Paris route, TGV trains do not go to downtown Paris—to get there, you must transfer at the airport. All TGV seats are reserved, and railpass-holders pay €5 for a reservation (very limited availability).

By ICE Train to Germany: Germany's InterCity Express trains zip to **Köln** (3/day, 1.75 hours) and **Frankfurt** (3/day, 3 hours). Reservations are not required except for advance-ticket discounts.

To Other Places in Germany: The fastest way to most German destinations, as well as to Vienna, Austria, is to change in Köln (on the Thalys or ICE connection) or in Frankfurt (on the ICE connection).

By Eurostar to/from London: Brussels and London are 2.5 hours apart by Eurostar train (10/day). Trains to London leave from tracks 1 and 2 at Brussels' Midi/Zuid/South Station. Arrive 30 minutes early to get your ticket validated and your luggage and passport checked by British authorities (similar to airport check-in for an international flight).

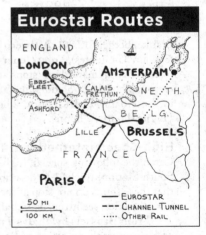

Fares are reasonable but complicated. Prices vary depending on how far ahead you reserve (up to six months out), whether you can live with restrictions, and whether you're eligible for any discounts (children, youths, seniors, and railpass-holders all qualify). Rates are lowest for round-trips. Fares can change without notice, but typically a **one-way, full-fare ticket** (with no restrictions on refundability) runs about $425 for first class and $310 for second class. Accepting more restrictions lowers the price substantially (figure $90-200 for second class, one-way), but these **cheaper rates** can sell out quickly. Railpasses qualify you for a discount on a Eurostar ticket. Those traveling with a railpass that covers Belgium, France, or Britain should look first at the **passholder** fare (about $90-160 for second-class, one-way Eurostar trips, sold through most agents but not through Eurostar website). See more general info at www .ricksteves.com/eurostar or buy most ticket types at www.eurostar .com (prices in pounds; Belgian tel. 02-528-2828).

More Discounts: A Thalys ticket between Brussels and Paris or a Eurostar ticket between Brussels and London can also cover a regional train connection to/from any Belgian station for a few dollars more, if you choose the "ABS option" at the time of purchase. Just show your ticket when boarding the connecting train(s) within 24 hours of the reserved Brussels arrival or departure (as long as the connecting train is not a Thalys).

All of these fast-train services offer significant price discounts, with restrictions, on tickets reserved in advance (most available 3 months ahead, Eurostar available 6 months ahead). Each company sells e-tickets through its website or through US agents such as www.raileurope.com (prices in dollars, US tel. 800-438-7245). In Europe, you can buy tickets at any major train station in any country or at any travel agency that handles train tickets (expect a booking fee).

By Bus

You can save money—but not time—by traveling by Eurolines bus from Brussels to Paris or London (Eurolines tel. 02-274-1350 in Brussels, www.eurolines.be).

From Brussels by Bus to: Paris (generally €22-26 one-way, €41-44 round-trip, about 4 hours), **London** (generally €35 one-way, €70 round-trip, about 6 hours).

By Plane

Brussels Airport

Brussels' big but well-organized main airport is nine miles north of downtown (many arriving flights pass over the giant, silver molecule-shaped Atomium). The airport is sometimes called "Zaventem," for the nearby town. Departures are at level 3, arrivals are at level 2, buses are at level 0, and the train station is in the basement at level -1. Airport info: Tel. 0900-70000, www .brusselsairport.be.

The clear winner for getting to and from the airport is the **shuttle train** that runs between the airport and all three Brussels train stations (€5, 4/hour, 25 minutes, daily 6:00-23:00). Note that because of a special airport train tax, even if you're using a railpass, you'll have to pay a €2.05 fee to take this train (buy from ticket window or pay conductor directly). If you're connecting the airport with Bruges, take this shuttle train and transfer at Brussels' North Station (about 1.5 hours total). For a **taxi,** figure on spending around €40 between downtown Brussels and the airport.

Thrifty Brussels Airlines flies between Brussels and several European cities, including Athens, Milan, Florence, Zürich, Nice, Lisbon, Barcelona, Madrid, and more (Belgian tel. 07-035-1111, www.brusselsairlines.com). Bmi british midland has inexpensive flights from Brussels to London and the British Isles (www.flybmi.com). Non-discount airlines, such as Lufthansa (www.lufthansa.com), Finnair (www.finnair.com), and Alitalia (www.alitalia.com), offer daily flights from Brussels Airport.

Brussels South Charleroi Airport

Discount airlines Ryanair (www.ryanair.com) and Wizz Air (www.wizzair.com) use this smaller airport, located about 30 miles from downtown Brussels in the town of Gosselies, on the outskirts of the city of Charleroi.

The easiest way to connect to downtown Brussels is to take the **shuttle bus** to Brussels' Midi/Zuid/South Station (2/hour, about 1 hour, runs 4:00-22:30, €13; stops right in front of airport terminal; if you're taking the bus from Brussels' South Station, look for it outside at the corner of Rue de France/Frankrijkstraat and Rue de l'Instruction/Onderwijsstraat, www.voyages-lelan.be). You can also take a **bus-plus-train** connection: Bus #A connects Charleroi Airport and Charleroi Station (2/hour, 18 minutes), where you can take the train to all three Brussels train stations (2/hour, 40 minutes). It's costly by taxi (figure around €85-90); depending on traffic, it can take between 45 minutes and 1.5 hours to drive between downtown Brussels and Charleroi Airport. Airport info: Tel. 07-125-1211, www.charleroi-airport.com.

ANTWERP

Antwerpen

Antwerp (Antwerpen in Flemish, Anvers in French) is one of Europe's great once-drab, now-reborn port cities—ranking right up there with Liverpool, Barcelona, and Gdańsk. It's the biggest city and de facto capital of Flanders, with an illustrious history, a collection of top-tier museums, and a unique urban grittiness (some might say seediness) mingling with avant-garde fashion and a youthful trendiness. Its big-city bustle is the yang to Bruges' cutesy-village yin. Once Europe's most important trading city, later the hometown of accomplished painter Peter Paul Rubens, destroyed by World War II and then reborn, and recently emerging as a European fashion capital, Antwerp is more than the sum of its parts.

In the late 15th century, as Bruges' harbor silted up, Antwerp became a major trading center and the Low Countries' top city of the Baroque period. As the Age of Exploration dawned, Portuguese and Spanish ships returning from the New World laden with exotic goods docked here in Antwerp. During Antwerp's 16th-century Golden Age, it became Europe's wealthiest city, with a population of about 100,000.

In the mid-16th century, Antwerp was pulled into the Eighty Years' War between the Dutch rebel Protestants and the ruling Spanish Catholics. In 1576, after growing impatient at not being paid by Habsburg King Philip II, Spanish troops relentlessly sacked Antwerp for three days—massacring thousands of its residents and destroying hundreds of homes. The outraged public response to this so-called "Spanish Fury" elevated Antwerp to the capital of the Dutch Revolt. (Meanwhile, the event irrevocably damaged Antwerp's trade ties with partners who wanted no business with a war zone.) But the crushing, Spanish-led Siege of Antwerp (July 1584 through August 1585) wore down the independence

Antwerp

TO
BREDA &
AMSTERDAM
(NETHERLANDS)

NOORDERLAAN

ITALIELIE

VONDELSTRAAT

OSYR STR.

DIAMOND
QUARTER

F.D.R.
PL.

GEMEENTE

DE KEYSERLEI

DIAMOND
MUSEUM

CARNOT-STRAAT

Opera

Diamant

ZOO
CENTRAL TRAIN
STATION

TO
EINDHOVEN
(NETHERLANDS)

LEI

QUINTEN MATSIJSLEI

PELIKAANSTR.

PLOEGSTR.

PARK

EYCKLEI

Plantin

1 Hotel Julien
2 Matelote Hotel
3 Le Patio B&B
4 Big Sleep B&B
5 Enich Anders B&B
6 Ibis Antwerpen Centrum Hotel
7 't Katshuis Hotel
8 Pelgrimsstraat Eateries
9 Hendrik Conscienceplein Eateries
10 Fresh 'n Fruity Sandwich Shop
11 Hungry Henrietta Restaurant
12 Horta Brasserie
13 Marnixplaats Eateries
14 Zuidcafé
15 Hippodroom

400 YARDS

400 METERS

M METRO STATION
T TRAM STOP

DCH

ANTWERP

movement, and the city fell under Spanish/Catholic control. More than half of the city's population fled to Amsterdam, where they restarted their businesses. Amsterdam's ensuing Golden Age was, in many ways, a direct result of talent and resources that Antwerp lost during this postwar "brain drain."

Seeking to rehabilitate its image in the aftermath of the bloody warfare, the Catholic Church invested mightily in building and decorating churches in Antwerp. A local artist named Peter Paul Rubens (1577-1640)—while arguably less talented than some of his contemporaries—found himself in the right place at the right time, and was a brilliant salesman who allied himself with the Church to win big commission after big commission. Rubens' style epitomized exactly what the Church was looking for: bold, bombastic images trumpeting the glory of God (and his Church on earth).

The treaty that ended the Eighty Years' War in 1648 imposed rigid regulations on shipping on the Scheldt River, restricting Antwerp's outlet to the North Sea. This caused the city to become more of a regional port than an international one. Antwerp's industry, led by an elite group of pro-Catholic traders, began to specialize in luxury goods—cabinets, paintings, tapestries, and so on. The city would languish as a Catholic backwater and second-rate shipping city for centuries, although its industry was kick-started by Napoleon, then by Belgian independence, in the early 1800s. By the 20th century, Antwerp ranked as Europe's second-busiest port (just after Dutch rival Rotterdam). Damaged in both World Wars, Antwerp has only recently begun to enjoy a new gentrification that's making it one of Europe's most exciting young cities.

Antwerpenaars (as locals are called) have a love of life. If funky urbanity is your thing, Antwerp is one of Europe's most intriguing cities. It's a great place for browsing without a sightseeing agenda. But its sights are easily on par with Brussels' and Bruges': Antwerp boasts a wide range of well-presented museums with exciting new exhibits opening all the time, interesting churches packed with great art, and fun-to-explore neighborhoods. And compared to stodgy, bureaucratic Brussels, Antwerp has a colorful personality that respects its storied past even as it embraces a bright future.

Planning Your Time

While Antwerp could easily fill a day or two, it's worth at least a few hours (as a side-trip from Brussels—less than an hour away by train—or on the way between Brussels and Amsterdam). Take my self-guided walk from the train station to the Old Town (by way of the Rubens House), tour the cathedral, ogle the Grote Markt, and pay a quick visit to other sights that intrigue you. (Historians enjoy the Museum Plantin-Moretus, art-lovers savor the Rockox House, fashionistas love the ModeMuseum and nearby window-shopping, and gem-and-jewelry fans covet the sparkle at the Diamond Museum.) Then zip back to the train station on the metro. If you have more time, Antwerp's diverse restaurant scene and lively nightlife make it worth considering for an overnight. With a different variety of quirky boutiques and cafés on each street, it's a delightful place to linger. As in most of Belgium, be aware that most Antwerp museums are closed on Mondays.

Orientation to Antwerp

Belgium's "second city" (with 460,000 people), Antwerp sits along the east bank of the Scheldt River (Schelde in Flemish). The main tourist area is fairly compact. On a quick trip, narrow your focus to these main zones: the **Old Town** along the river; the **train station area** and **Diamond Quarter** to the east, and the **Meir** shopping district between the Old Town and train station; the newly rejuvenated **Little Island** (Eilandje) zone and the red light district to the north; and, to the south, the **Sint-Andries** fashion district and, beyond that, the happening nightlife zone aptly called **'t Zuid** ("The South"). All of these areas are within about a 30-minute walk (or a quick tram or taxi ride) of one another.

Tourist Information

Antwerp's TI has two branches: in the train station (at the head of the tracks, on level 0), and right on the Grote Markt (both open Mon-Sat 9:00-17:45, Sun 9:00-16:45; tel. 03-232-0103, phone answered Mon-Sat 9:00-17:50, not on Sun; www.visitantwerp .be). Peruse their racks of fliers and pick up a free town map. The **Museum Card,** which covers public transportation and entry to most museums and churches (plus discounts on special exhibits), will easily save a busy sightseer some money (€20/48 hours, sold at TI or participating sights).

The Grote Markt TI also has a desk where you can get information and buy tickets for musical events (€1 service charge, Tue-Fri 10:00-16:50, Sat 12:00-17:00, closed Sun-Mon).

Arrival in Antwerp

By Train: Antwerp's Central Station (Antwerpen Centraal)—with a grand century-old shell recently refurbished and expanded with a modern underground zone—is one of Europe's most impressive. With tracks on three levels (connected by escalators and elevators), the station can be tricky to navigate—follow posted signs, or pick up a copy of the free station map. Tracks 1-6 are on level +1, above ground; tracks 11-14 are on level -1, below ground; and tracks 21-24 are on level -2, even deeper underground.

The ground floor's atrium (on level 0) is the hub of activity, where escalators funnel passengers from all three track levels. At the front of this area is the large TI, and behind that (through the passage, tucked under the stairs) are luggage lockers (€3-4). Continuing past the lockers, you emerge into the great hall, a gorgeously restored temple of travel. Here you'll find ticket windows. Exiting straight ahead out the front door puts you in the vast and somewhat seedy Koningin Astridplein, with the Diamond Museum and the city's zoo on your right.

To get to the Old Town and most sights, you have two basic options: You can walk (see my self-guided walk, facing page); or, if you're in a hurry (or the weather's bad) and you want to make a beeline to the Grote Markt, ride the **metro** (actually an underground tram line). From next to the TI, take the escalator marked *metro* to the underground tracks. Buy a ticket from the automated machines, and take tram #2 or #15 in the direction of *Linkeroever*; get off at the Groenplaats stop for the Grote Markt and the historical center. Note: The train station's metro stop is named Diamant (for the surrounding Diamond Quarter).

Getting Around Antwerp

Sprawling Antwerp is walkable, but using the city's good public-transit network saves time and sweat. For visitors, the handiest option is the misnamed "metro," which is actually a tram line running underground through the town center. The metro's tracks carry various numbered trams, including #2 and #15, which conveniently connect many of the city's most important sights. Stops on these lines include (from east to west) Diamant (train station), Opera (at east end of Meir shopping street), Meir (at west end of Meir shopping street, a block from the Rubens House), and Groenplaats (near the cathedral and Grote Markt). Other trams (such as #8, which runs between Groenplaats and the Museum stop in 't Zuid) and buses round out your options.

Tickets (€1.20) are easy to buy at automated machines at each stop, or you can pay €2 to buy one on board. If you'll be using public transit a lot, invest in a day pass (€6/1 day, €10/3 days) or a shareable 10-ride ticket (€8, just €0.80 per ride). Information: Toll tel. 070-220-200, €0.30/minute; www.delijn.be.

Tours in Antwerp

Walking Tours—The TI organizes a historical **walking tour** through town, in both English and French (€6 if you book at least a day in advance at the TI, €8 same-day ticket, July-Aug daily at 14:00, Sept-June Sat-Sun only, departs from TI on Grote Markt).

Local Guide—The TI can arrange a private guide for an afford-able city tour (€65/2 hours, tel. 03-338-9539, gidsenwerking @stad.antwerpen.be). One of their excellent guides, **Ariane Van Duytekom,** tells Antwerp's story well, with a knack for psycho-analyzing its complicated history. If Ariane isn't available, they can arrange another good guide for you.

Self-Guided Walk

▲From Antwerp's Train Station to the Old Town

You can zip from the train station to the historical center by metro, but it's a short (25-30 minute) and enjoyable stroll that takes you through an interesting and diverse stretch of Antwerp—and passes one of the city's top sights (the Rubens House).

The **train station** itself is a work of art. It was built around the turn of the 20th century, and was thoroughly renovated a few years

ago. If you didn't arrive by train—or haven't yet seen its remarkable main hall—step inside to take a look.

From inside the station, in the atrium at the head of the tracks, face the TI and exit the door to your left (marked *Keyserlei/ Meir/Centrum*). You'll walk basi-cally straight ahead on this street all the way to the Old Town.

The area around the train station is known as the **Diamond Quarter**—one of the world's top centers where diamonds are both sold and cleaved (split into smaller pieces to prepare them for cut-ting). Although the industry is highly secretive, experts guess that four out of every five of the world's rough diamonds pass through Antwerp at some point. The diamond industry is located in the train-station neighborhood for good reason: If you're carrying mil-lions of dollars worth of precious jewels in your briefcase through a strange city, you don't want to have to venture too far to reach a trader or diamond-cutter.

Beginning in the 16th century, the diamond industry in Antwerp was dominated by Sephardic Jews from Spain, but under Catholic rule, they fled to Amsterdam. Then, in the late 19th century, Hasidic Orthodox Jews fleeing the pogroms in Russia settled here and took up the industry. In the streets around the train station, you'll likely see men wearing tall hats, black coats, long beards, and curly locks at their temples, and women with long dresses and hair-covers. More recently, the diamond trade here is increasingly dominated by Indians. As it's a center for trade rather than tourism, there's little to actually see in this district, but if you want to learn more about the local diamond trade, visit the Diamond Museum (fronting the square in front of the train station, and described later, under "Sights in Antwerp").

Head three blocks up the bustling, tree-shaded boulevard called **De Keyserlei,** lined with chain restaurants and shops. You'll

run into the big boulevard called Frankrijklei, which marks the former course of the town wall. Continue straight across the street, then between the twin grand facades that exemplify the style called Historicism. All the rage in the late 19th century, this school of architectural thought borrowed the best, most bombastic bits and pieces from past styles to wow the viewer.

Passing between the facades, you enter a delightful pedestrians-only shopping zone. Bear left as the road curves at the statue of Anthony Van Dyck (1599-1641), a talented Antwerp artist who became the court painter for English King Charles I, and whose works now appear in many local museums. This puts you on

the Meir (pronounced "mare"), Antwerp's showcase shopping zone. (Meir is the name of both the street and the neighborhood.) A block later, on the left, notice the grand Stadsfeestzaal shopping mall (with the gold niche over the door). Venture inside for a look at its astonishing interior.

One block later, the big gap in the buildings on your left marks the square called Wapper; a half-block down this square on the left is one of the city's top sights, the **Rubens House** (described later). Just beyond the end of the square is a remarkable **Art Nouveau Hall** called Horta (for the renowned Belgian architect Victor Horta). Like Brussels, Antwerp has a proud Art Nouveau tradition, as the local shipping industry was spurring city growth just as that style was becoming popular in the early 20th century. Today the hall houses a recommended café with a pricey menu but an opportunity to enjoy a coffee or a meal immersed in slinky Art Nouveau. A block farther past the Art Nouveau Hall is Antwerp's new **City Theater** (Stadsschouwburg), with a gigantic rain-shield overhang that seems to cover the entire square.

Back on the Meir, the ornate building on the left-hand corner just after Wapper is the **Paleis op de Meir,** a gorgeous Rococo-style palace built in 1745 by a local aristocrat who died before he could actually move in. Later, Napoleon purchased the home and decorated the interior in Empire Style. With Belgium independence in 1830, this became an official residence of the King of the Belgians. Around 1900, the "builder king" Leopold II spiffed it up even more—you'll see his double-cursive-L monogram everywhere. Finally, in 1969, the royal family donated it to the government of Flanders, who recently refurbished it and opened it to the public. You can enjoy the gourmet chocolate shop and chandeliered tea room on the ground floor, or pay to go upstairs and tour the apartments (guided tours only, €8 to join a 1.5-hour Flemish-only tour, Sun-Fri at 15:00, Sat at 11:00, for English you must hire your own private guide for €145, Meir 50, tel. 03-206-2121, www .paleisopdemeir.be).

From here Rubens fans can detour a block north to **St. James' Church** (Sint-Jacobskerk) to see his tomb. Go up Lange Klarenstraat (across from the Paleis op de Meir), then turn right onto Lange Nieuwstraat to enter the church through its right transept. True to its name, this church was a stop for pilgrims on the Camino de Santiago, walking from here all the way to the shrine of St. James in northwest Spain. Rubens' tomb is in the chapel behind the high altar (€2, daily 14:00-17:00, Lange Nieuwstraat 73-75).

Continue along the Meir, passing the Meir metro stop. Then cross the tram tracks and continue straight, bearing right on Eiermarkt around the giant Art Deco, Gotham City-style **Farmers Tower** (Boerentoren, marked for its current occupant, KBC). Completed in 1932, this was considered the first American-style skyscraper in Europe, and held the title of Europe's tallest skyscraper for 20 years.

After two blocks on Eiermarkt, you come to the square called **Groenplaats,** with its statue of Rubens and the cathedral spire hovering just beyond. This square, the cathedral, the Grote Markt (main square), and other sights are described starting on page 518.

sights are described starting on page 518.

Sights in Antwerp

Antwerp offers visitors an eclectic array of sightseeing. If you have just one day (or less), you'll need to be selective: art, churches, history, fashion, and so on. I've listed these sights in the order you might encounter them, beginning at the train station.

Near the Train Station

▲**Diamond Museum (Diamantmuseum)**—This small museum offers you a good look at one of Antwerp's most famous and important industries. Each year, the city trades some $29 billion in diamonds—representing 8 percent of Belgium's entire export market. That's a lot of glittering stones. Because the museum sits on the big square directly in front of the train station, a visit here is easy—you could drop in before catching your train (lockers are provided at the entry). Ride the elevator up to the third floor, then wind your way down through the sleek, almost futuristic, but fairly dry exhibit (with English descriptions and an included audioguide).

The history of the diamond trade focuses on Africa, where diamond-seekers dug the world's biggest manmade hole, the Kimberley Crater in South Africa. (In some parts of Africa, the exploitative conditions for finding these gems haven't improved much since the early days of Belgian colonialism. A strict new diamond-certification process, introduced here in Antwerp in 2000, attempts to block the sale of so-called "blood diamonds"—sold by rebels fighting governments in war zones in central and western Africa.) Peruse the remarkable collection of diamond jewelry, but don't linger too long or take photos...these security guys are se-ri-ous. Watch an actual diamond-cutter shaping and polishing a stone. By the end, you'll find out where we get the "karat" measurement for diamonds, why diamond-cutters use strobe lights, and what the only material is that's hard enough to cut a diamond.

Cost and Hours: €6, includes audioguide, Thu-Tue 10:00-17:30, closed Wed, Koningin Astridplein 19-23, tel. 03-202-4890, www.diamantmuseum.be.

Between the Train Station and the Old Town

▲▲**Rubens House (Rubenshuis)**—The most popular sight in town, this former home of Peter Paul Rubens does a fine job of introducing visitors both to the artist's works (several of which are displayed here) and to his lifestyle. There are better places in Antwerp to see Rubens' paintings, but this exhibit offers you a unique opportunity to also learn about how he lived and the methods he employed—interesting even to people who think Peter Paul Rubens is the guy who plays Pee-Wee Herman.

Though the house looks untouched, after Rubens' death in 1640, his heirs sold it, and it was updated and remodeled over the years. In the 1940s, it was restored to its original condition. As you tour the place, keep in mind that it's basically a replica of where Rubens lived (for more authentic period houses, visit the home of Rubens' friend at the Rockox House Museum—see page 523, or the Museum Plantin-Moretus—see page 524).

Peter Paul Rubens
(1577-1640)

Born in Germany in 1577, Rubens moved with his family to Antwerp at age 12, where he was apprenticed to a local painter. Showing great promise, Rubens went to study in Italy

during his twenties. After eight years, in 1608, he returned to Antwerp to care for his dying mother. He married Flemish aristocrat Isabella Brant and settled down here, buying today's Rubens House in 1610, and living in it for the next 25 years. He added on to the house, turning it into a workshop that churned out painting after painting.

In Rubens' work, everything is on a larger-than-life scale. Many canvases almost fill entire walls—you can see the seams where the cloth pieces were stitched together. Rubens famously did not actually paint all of the approximately 2,500 canvases that bear his name. As was standard at the time, his assistants, students, and colleagues did much of the work, then Rubens would swoop in at the last minute, add a flourish or two, and sign it.

Rubens distinguished himself not necessarily with his technical ability, but as a smart businessman who knew how to provide wealthy benefactors (such as the Catholic Church) with exactly what they wanted. During those Counter-Reformation days, when the Church was eager to win back fans after their ruthlessness in the Eighty Years' War, Rubens' flashy and fleshy Baroque style was perfect. His fascination with plus-size models, and his skill at capturing their rippling folds of fat, introduced the term "Rubenesque" into the English language. These chubby damsels were inspired by Hélène Fourment, 37 years Rubens' junior, whom the artist married in 1630 after his first wife died. A true Renaissance man in the Baroque Age, Rubens was also an accomplished diplomat, who helped to negotiate peace between England and Spain (and was knighted by the kings of both countries in appreciation).

Cost and Hours: €6, includes essential audioguide, Tue-Sun 10:00-17:00, last entry 30 minutes before closing, closed Mon, Wapper 9-11, tel. 03-201-1555, www.rubenshuis.be. The house is between the train station and the Old Town—to walk here, follow my self-guided walk, described earlier. To get here quickly, you can ride the metro to the Meir stop, then walk one long block east (back toward the station).

⊙ Self-Guided Tour: Buy your ticket at the glass pavilion in the middle of the square in front of the house, then head inside. The excellent, included 1.5-hour audioguide explains all the details (or you can pick up a booklet with detailed descriptions). Here are the highlights:

In the **courtyard,** you can see the original 16th-century house (on the left), the studio that Rubens added on to the complex (on the right), and the elaborate Michelangelo-flavored portico that connects them. An architect as well as a painter, Rubens designed the additions himself. The influence of his time in Italy is evident: Notice the dramatic contrast between the traditional Flemish home and the flamboyant Italian palazzo-style studio.

Now go inside the **house** and follow the one-way route through the various rooms. Many of the paintings are not by Rubens, but by other artists he admired; in fact, his personal art collection was the biggest in the Low Countries. In the dining room (with leather-tooled walls) is a rare self-portrait of Rubens in his fifties—one of only four known Rubens self-portraits. Facing him from across the room is a portrait (not by Rubens) of his second wife, Hélène Fourment. After his first wife died, Rubens married the much younger Hélène for love instead of entering into a strategic marriage with a noblewoman. Upstairs in his bedroom is a short, carved-wood bed like the one Rubens likely used—people slept sitting up in those days. Nearby is Rubens' portrait of his top student, Anthony Van Dyck, a prodigiously talented painter whose skill eclipsed that of his teacher. Van Dyck's deservedly self-confident air, masterfully captured here, probably bugged Rubens even as it provoked his begrudging respect.

Continue into the **studio,** where Rubens and his students produced thousands of paintings. Lingering over the selection of canvases displayed here helps you understand their production process. In general, Rubens' paintings came about in one of three ways: For an important commission, he'd paint the entire thing himself. More often, he'd paint an original, then have his school make many copies of it for him to sell on a wide scale (each one would just get a few personal highlights from the master...only Rubens himself could create just the perfect twinkle in an eye, or glimmer of light on that cellulite). And other times, he would simply do a rough oil sketch of what he wanted, then enlist experts in certain areas (such as flowers or portraits) to fill in the blanks. Then he'd sweep through at the end to finalize the work.

In the main hall, peruse the paintings counterclockwise,

beginning with the canvases to the right as you enter. In the two early (pre-Italy) Rubens canvases of *St. Sebastian* and *Adam and Eve,* notice that the colors are subdued, and the bodies aren't as developed—lacking the rippling muscles and folds of fat that would later become Rubens' trademark.

The end of the room is flanked by twin portraits of the Spanish monarchs of the Netherlands, **Archduke Albert** and **Infanta Isabella.** Rubens was this couple's official court painter, and these original Rubens works were copied in large numbers by his assistants. The monarchs' time was valuable, so Rubens worked quickly. To pose for the painting of herself dressed in a nun's habit, Isabella reportedly came to Antwerp for only one night; Rubens sketched her face quickly, just enough to capture her likeness, then filed in the details later.

High on the wall between the Spanish rulers is *The Annunciation,* with an Italian-inspired dynamism typical of the master.

The unfinished **battle scene,** *Henry IV at the Battle of Ivry,* illustrates Rubens' collaborative process. Rubens never completed this oil sketch, but you can see—at the top of the canvas—where the battle specialist has already filled in his section.

The Feast of St. Martin was actually painted by a lesser-known artist, then purchased by Rubens, who added his own touches to make it his own. Rubens enjoyed doing this as a fun pastime, to get a painting just right for his own collection—not to sell.

Finally is **a portrait by Anthony Van Dyck.** While Rubens got the lion's share of the fame, some of his students were even more talented than he was—and Van Dyck was a verifiable genius, who prodded Rubens to become a better painter. And yet Van Dyck was just a painter...whereas Rubens was also an architect, an aristocrat, and a diplomat—a true jack of all trades.

In and near the Old Town

These sights are listed roughly in the order you'll reach them, whether you come from the train station on the metro (Groenplaats stop) or by foot (see my self-guided walk, earlier).

Groenplaats—This urban-feeling square, with a handy metro stop, is dominated by a larger-than-life sculpture of Antwerp's favorite son, Peter Paul Rubens. Bear left up "Little Italy Lane"—the narrow street at the top of the square (Jan Blomstraat), passing a row of Italian restaurants—until you pop out at Handschoenmarkt in front of the cathedral.

▲▲Cathedral of Our Lady (Onze-Lieve-Vrouwekathedraal)—Antwerp's biggest church has a

spire that shoots 400 feet up from the middle of the Old Town, like a Gothic rocket...the tallest church steeple in the Low Countries. Its cavernous interior is packed with fine artwork, including four paintings by Peter Paul Rubens. You'd normally only see copies of these pieces, but while the Museum of Fine Art is closed for renovation (through late 2017), you'll see the original canvases *in situ* (in the setting for which they were intended).

Cost and Hours: €5, Mon-Fri 10:00-17:00, Sat 10:00-15:00, Sun 13:00-16:00, free English tours daily at 11:00 and 14:15, €2 audioguide, Handschoenmarkt, tel. 03-213-9951, www .dekathedraal.be.

❷ Self-Guided Tour: Stepping inside, notice how remarkably wide the cathedral is, with seven aisles (three on either side of the nave). Looking up, you'll see that the Gothic design is also dramatically vertical—everything stretches upward, toward heaven. In the Middle Ages, the interior was filled with thousands of candles, and this was the only place to find bright light after dark. The stained-glass windows (some of them still original) colorized the light emanating from inside, drawing worshippers like moths to a flame.

The cathedral has a dynamic, troubled history—in fact, it's amazing the place has survived at all. Built over many generations in the Middle Ages (1352-1521), two tragedies befell it soon after completion: In 1533, it was scorched by fire; and in 1566, it was gutted by iconoclastic Protestants, who stripped it of its medieval decoration. (Though most of the interior was whitewashed, you can still see fragments of some very colorful murals on the underside of the vaults, where the iconoclasts couldn't reach.) After the Catholics came to power here, in 1585, they decorated the church in bubbly Baroque, including several pieces by Rubens. Each local guild had their own private altar area (at the base of each pillar), where they celebrated baptisms, weddings, and funerals—this was truly a community church.

When Napoleon's troops arrived in the late 18th century, they again emptied the church of its decorations, turned the building into a stable, and had plans to destroy it entirely before Napoleon was defeated. Once again needing to redecorate the place, church leaders bought a hodgepodge of ecclesiastical art from other churches and monasteries throughout the region, which Napoleon had also shut down.

In the left transept is Rubens' famous *Raising of the Cross* (1610-1611). Biblical bodybuilders strain to upright the cross,

which is heavy with the swooning body of Christ. The painting is emotive, sumptuous, and almost sensual, especially considering its painful theme. Having just returned from eight years in Italy—where he'd studied the works of Michelangelo and Caravaggio (both of whose influence is evident here)—Rubens was eager to show off his mastery of musculature and human skin. Notice how lifelike Jesus' skin appears—a Rubens forte. The bold diagonal composition, thickly muscled bodies in motion, bright (almost garish) colors, and illusion of movement are vintage Rubens. The painting is the inner panel of a hinged altarpiece; it was normally kept closed, and opened to reveal this scene only on special occasions—when its color and motion must have been even more striking to churchgoers unaccustomed to this sort of spectacle.

Duck in to the chapel behind this painting, where you'll see some of the church's oldest stained glass. Find the wood-carved **medieval altarpiece** (actually a replica—the original was destroyed by iconoclasts). Notice that it's drab and hard to see from far away, making it difficult to grasp and emotionally connect with the story it presents. If the purpose of church art is to excite the congregation, this is a failure—no wonder Rubens' bombastic approach was a perfect fit for the Counter-Reformation Catholics.

Continue farther into the church, and go into the choir area. Over the main altar is another Rubens painting, *The Assumption* (1626), showing the moment that the cathedral's namesake was brought up to heaven. Beneath Mary are the twelve apostles (after the Resurrection, the faithful disciple Matthias replaced Judas) and the three women who were present at her death. The role of Mary in church doctrine was one of the major dividing lines between Catholics and Protestants; whereas the Catholic Church considered her a saint to be venerated, the Protestants embraced the notion that she was an ordinary woman called to do God's work. The gauzy heroine-worship of this canvas makes it clear who finally controlled the turf here.

On the right side of the church, in a red chapel, is a less impressive Rubens painting, *The Resurrection of Christ* (unfortunately, it's likely covered by scaffolding).

Circle back up into the right transept to see another Rubens canvas, *Descent from the Cross* (1612-1614). Rubens' diagonal composition is the mirror image of the one we saw earlier, across the nave. It's a freeze-frame of an action-packed moment...just as workers strained to erect the cross with Christ's limp body, now they struggle to lower him from it. But at this somber moment, the subjects seem to be moving more slowly, methodically. Notice the pale pallor of Christ's dead skin—a strong contrast to the lifelike luster of the other painting. The details make the poignancy of this moment come to life: the man in the top-right corner who's holding onto the shroud with his teeth; Mary's outstretched

arm, in a tender matronly effort to comfort her son even in death; and, in the lower-right section, a blood-filled bronze basin holding the crown of thorns and the nails.

• *After visiting the cathedral, head straight out from the main entrance and squeeze out through the little gap at the far end of the square. Bearing right, you'll wind up in the...*

▲**Grote Markt**—Antwerp's main square is dominated by the looming tower of the cathedral at one end, and the stately Town Hall at the other. With a facade dating from Antwerp's Golden Age (16th century), the **Town Hall** (Stadhuis) is adorned with flags from many different countries—representing the importance of international trade to the city.

The other buildings fronting the square are **guild houses,** celebrating the trade associations of each of the city's industries. Each one is topped with a golden statue, which typically represents that guild's patron saint. The many ground-floor cafés are a good place for a drink with a view. Locals say that when the outdoor terraces open up, they know it's summertime in Antwerp.

The **fountain** in the middle of the square illustrates a gruesome story from Flemish folklore. Supposedly a giant named Druon Antigoon collected tolls along the Scheldt River. If someone was unable or unwilling to pay, the giant would sever their hand. His reign of terror was finally ended when a brave young Roman soldier named Silvius Brabo defeated Antigoon, then cut off the giant's own hand and threw it into the river. Here we see Brabo on the windup to toss Antigoon's hand, which spouts blood. Tour guides love to explain that *hand werpen* ("to throw a hand") evolved into "Antwerpen"...though scholars prefer less glamorous alternatives: *an 't werf,* "on the wharf"; or *ando verpis,* "where land is thrown up against land" (the river has long deposited sludge along the bank here).

• *From the Grote Markt, you can head toward the waterfront by going up the big street called Suikerrui.*

Waterfront—Though historically important, Antwerp's waterfront is now dingy and drab. From the Grote Markt, Suikerrui street leads you to the busy riverfront street and, beyond it, a long parking lot, a tiny park, and a forgotten castle. Cross the street and stand along the river.

This now-derelict waterfront, with its priceless access to where the Scheldt River spills into the North Sea, is where the shipping settlement of Antwerp began in the Middle Ages. All that's left from those glory days is the forlorn **castle** (to the right), which was once part of a city wall that fortified the heart of town. While this building once housed a museum, its collection has been folded into the new Museum aan de Stroom (MAS) at Little Island (described later)...so for now, it sits empty. This is representative of how Antwerp has turned its back on the river that once made it wealthy. When a train station opened across town in 1836, it pushed the city to the east. The shipping ports to the north are still busy, but most of the city is happy to ignore its river.

But the river doesn't always cooperate. Notice the orange **flood gates**—with long, heavy, waist-high steel doors that can roll open and closed on railroad tracks. Because the Scheldt is a tidal river, there's a huge risk of flooding—made more serious because of the town center's proximity to the river. Plans are afoot to replace the ugly portside wall with walkable dikes.

Gloomy as it seems, the broad **embankment** is a popular place for Antwerpenaars to walk, and young people enjoy hanging out along the river on warm summer evenings. Notice the 19th-century, Industrial-Age-style steel canopies that line the water-front. These formerly functioned as warehouses; now they're used for other purposes: as you face the river, the stretch to the left is covered parking; to the right is an impressive array of seafaring vessels that were once part of the Maritime Museum inside the castle. The fancy elevated terrace, across the little park from the castle, provides a view of the river (notice I didn't say "good" view), and has WCs below; this is also the cruise-ship terminal.

• *To reach the Old Meat Hall (described next), cross the busy street from the castle and head a few steps downriver (with the water on your left) to Repenstraat, which leads in two blocks up to the...*

Musical Instruments Museum at the Old Meat Hall (Museum Vleeshuis)—This recently restored brick palace, erected to house meat during Antwerp's glory days, now houses a fine collection of

musical instruments. The Klank van de Stad ("Sound of the City") exhibition presents two floors of instruments and old music manuscripts (don't miss the cellar). English information is limited (unless you buy a €3.50 booklet with descriptions), and even the included touchscreen audioguide is mostly in Flemish—but at least it lets you hear some of the instruments. And though the collection itself isn't too exciting, it's fun to see the impressive brick vaults inside; consider just ducking into the entry area for a peek (it's a fine place to use the bathroom, or to warm up on a cold day).

Cost and Hours: €5, Tue-Sun 10:00-17:00, closed Mon, last entry 30 minutes before closing, Vleeshouwersstraat 38-40, tel. 03-233-6404, www.museumvleeshuis.be. To get here from the Grote Markt, face the Town Hall and turn right up Braderijstraat, take the first left on Kuipersstraat, then look right.

Nearby: My self-guided stroll through the red light district, ending at the up-and-coming Little Island district, begins from right in front of this building—see page 523.

▲**Hendrik Conscienceplein**—Nicknamed "Antwerp's Piazza," this delightful square, tucked in an attractive maze of lanes in

the town center, dates from the Counter-Reformation period when the Catholic Church was keen to demonstrate its worthiness. Dominating the square is the very Italian-looking, early 16th-century, Jesuit **Church of Carolus Borromeus** (Carolus Borromeuskerk). Compared with

Antwerp's many grand Gothic churches, such as the big-and-bold cathedral, notice how this church is more horizontal than vertical—melting into its neighborhood. You don't even see it until you're right on top of it. After the ruthless, deadly "persuasion" of the Inquisition, the Catholic Church wanted to soften its image and entice worshippers without coming on too strong. While a Gothic steeple—reaching dramatically up toward heaven—is meant to intimidate, this Baroque church's delicate facade is designed to invite people in without overwhelming them. Once inside, its sumptuous interior seals the deal by re-creating heaven here on earth. Rubens himself designed many decorations for the original interior of the church—including 39 paintings—but these were completely destroyed in a 1718 fire (free entry, Mon-Sat 10:00-12:30 & 14:00-17:00, closed Sun). Near this square are some of the city's most appealing restaurants (see "Eating in Antwerp," later).

▲**Rockox House Museum (Museum Rockoxhuis)**—Nicolaas Rockox (1560-1640) was a mayor of Antwerp and a friend and sponsor of Peter Paul Rubens. Today his house—buried in a residential zone a 10-minute walk northeast of the cathedral and Grote Markt—is a lovely museum. Here you can get a truly authentic look at an aristocratic home from the period (unlike the Rubens House, which was rebuilt), while viewing impressive artwork. The house also has interesting themed exhibits (which highlight, for example, period food or clothing). Rounding out the experience is a fine furniture collection and a beautiful period garden/courtyard.

While the walls were originally covered from floor to ceiling with paintings, these days the curator is more selective; he regularly assembles good temporary exhibits that draw from Rockox's vast personal art collection. People decorated with art as a way of expressing themselves—their values, the people they knew, and so on—so viewing the collection lets you psychoanalyze Rockox. Highlights include an original Rubens canvas of Mary looking tenderly over Baby Jesus (modeled after Rubens' own first wife and son), and Van Dyck's study of two old men's heads. David Teniers the Younger's *Village Feast* evokes the action-packed canvases of the Brueghels (in fact, Teniers—a contemporary of Rubens—married into that prolific clan).

Though the collection is always good, it's particularly worth seeing while the Museum of Fine Arts is closed for restoration

(through late 2017); during this time, the Rockox House is displaying Rubens' *Doubting Thomas* triptych, the left panel of which features a portrait of Nicolaas Rockox (who commissioned the work for the chapel where he was ultimately entombed). It's clear that Rubens really knew this man, as the portrait truly captures his personality. Nearby are usually displayed two replicas, in which Rockox's gaze is less intense—clearly executed by a lesser artist.

Another highlight—and just plain fun to look at—is Peter Brueghel the Younger's *The Proverbs* (actually a copy of his father's earlier work), which strives to make literal more than a hundred Flemish sayings of the day. Try to find some of the examples: "armed to the teeth," "banging your head against the wall," "the die is cast," "going against the tide," "the blind leading the blind," and dozens of others that make no sense in English ("Who knows why the geese go barefoot?").

Cost and Hours: €2.50, Tue-Sun 10:00-17:00, closed Mon, Keizerstraat 10-12, tel. 03-201-9250, www.rockoxhuis.be.

▲▲**Museum Plantin-Moretus**—More interesting than it sounds, this museum about the history of the local printing industry offers an engaging look at Antwerp's 16th-century Golden Age. You'll find out how Antwerp became one of Europe's most important printing cities. Every Flemish kid comes here on a field trip to ogle the old printing presses, smartly decorated aristocratic rooms, and fine collection of antique manuscripts. The excellent, included audioguide tells the whole story. You'll need at least an hour or two to really see the place.

The museum is named for two influential Antwerp printers: Frenchman Christoffel Plantin, who began a printing business here in 1546; and his son-in-law Jan Moretus, who carried on the family business. Eventually their business became the official court printer for the Spanish monarchs of the Low Countries. This building was both the family's home and their workshop, and, since the family was wealthy enough to maintain the property, it's a remarkably well-preserved look at 16th- and 17th-century aristocratic life. The sprawling complex surrounds a pleasant garden, with wings dating from different periods. You'll follow the one-way, counterclockwise tour route through the ground floor, then head upstairs. Sprinkled throughout these rooms are ample samples of period manuscripts and maps, a Gutenberg Bible, and more.

The ground floor is devoted mostly to the printing shop, starting with the reception rooms. In the bookshop, look for the list of

books forbidden by the Catholic Church—the list was printed by, and includes books sold by, Christoffel Plantin. In the proofreaders' room, you can imagine diligent editors huddled around the shared oak desk, debating the 17th-century equivalent of whether "email" takes a hyphen.

The publisher's private leatherbound office is a class act. In the print shop you'll see some of the oldest printing presses in the world (c. 1600); neatly stacked in the back room are some 10 tons of lead letters.

Upstairs is the residence, showing off how the upper crust lived 300 years ago—tapestry wall hangings, high-beamed ceilings, leather-tooled walls, and so on. The 18th-century library displays a polyglot bible, with five languages on one page, printed by Christoffel Plantin. The Rubens Room is a reminder that the famous painter was an old family friend.

Cost and Hours: €6, includes audioguide, Tue-Sun 10:00-17:00, closed Mon; last entry 30 minutes before closing—but give yourself at least an hour; Vrijdagmarkt 22, tel. 03-221-1450, www.museumplantinmoretus.be.

Nearby: The museum is on a charming square called Vrijdagmarkt, where there really is a "Friday market" each week with an auction of secondhand stuff.

North of the Old Town

▲**"Little Island" (Eilandje) at the Old Dockyards**—Antwerp's formerly derelict and dangerous old port area, just a 15-minute walk from the Grote Markt, has been rejuvenated and redeveloped. Built by Napoleon in the early 1800s, and filled with brick warehouses around the turn of the 20th century, this part of town became deserted in the 1950s and 1960s, when the city's shipping industry relocated to the larger ports farther north. In the mid-1980s, city leaders decided it was time to reclaim this prime real estate, and invested heavily in a systematic gentrification program. Today it's a youthful Soho-type area, home to a tidy little yacht marina, a row of desirable condos, some trendy restaurants, and—soon—a pair of the city's top museums.

Perched on the Little Island in the middle of the harbor area is the area's main attraction: The new **Museum aan de Stroom** (Museum on the River), or **MAS** for short. It's housed in a purpose-built, 210-foot-tall blocky tower, encased in hand-cut red stone, and speckled with silver hands (the symbol of Antwerp). Designed to resemble the spiraling stacks of goods in an old maritime warehouse, the museum emphasizes the way that Antwerp's status as a shipping center has made it a crossroads for people from around the world. The collections of several smaller Antwerp museums—including the maritime, ethnographic, and folklore museums—have been brought together in this brand-new facility. Billed as a "museum of, for, and about the city and the world," MAS includes four semi-permanent exhibits (on the fourth through the eighth floors) that emphasize connections between people by juxtaposing old items in new ways, temporary exhibits, and a top-floor restaurant with panoramic views. The building's many windows also offer great views over Antwerp—and you're welcome to come inside even if you're not paying for the museum (€5 for permanent collection, €8 for temporary exhibits, €10 for both; Tue-Sun 10:00-17:00, closed Mon, Hanzestedenplaats 1, tel. 03-338-4434, www.mas.be).

A five-minute walk beyond the MAS (north, past the greenish skyscraper) is another promising, brand-new exhibit that's scheduled to open in 2012: the **Red Star Line Museum** (a.k.a. People on the Move), which promises to show the "other end" of the Ellis Island experience. During the great migration to the US and Canada between 1873 and 1935, the Red Star shipping line brought some two million emigrants to New York City, and those steamers began their journey here in Antwerp. In addition to "steerage-class" peasants, the line also transported luxury travelers and cargo. By the 1930s, many of the emigrants were Jews fleeing the Nazi regime in Germany. In these red-brick warehouses, emigrants were given humiliating health exams, had their clothes and luggage fumigated, and nervously waited while clerks processed their paperwork. Today, the same buildings are being turned into a museum documenting the experience of the people who said their final farewell to Europe right here. The exhibit traces the history of the Red Star Line and its passengers, displays actual artifacts from the emigrants, and shows off evocative artwork depicting emigrants poignantly waiting for a steam ship to whisk them off to the New World in pursuit of the American Dream (cost and hours not yet set, Rijnkaai 15, tel. 03-206-0350, www.redstarline.org).

Red Light District Walk—On your way to or from the Little Island area, you might want to pass through (or avoid) Belgium's biggest hub of legalized prostitution. This zone lacks the touristy patina of Amsterdam's...which makes it feel that much creepier. You'll see fewer rowdy "stag parties" making a racket, but lots of lonely men silently prowling the pedestrian zone. As with other red light districts, this area is not as dangerous as it might initially seem—the mayor actually encourages visitors to stroll here—but it's also not entirely safe. If you're curious to see it, wander here during the day (combined with a visit to the Little Island area described earlier). If you're wary, or if it's after dark, this neighborhood is best avoided.

Begin in the Old Town, in front of the Old Meat Hall (housing the Musical Instruments Museum, described on page 522). Head up the street called **Vleeshouwersstraat,** walking along the drab brick "projects"—subsidized housing built during the 1970s. These sterile rows of buildings replaced a very run-down, overpopulated, and lively old quarter that some residents miss—notice there are no pubs or shops along here.

Cut diagonally through the square and continue up Nosestraat, passing a church...and some sex-toys shops. You'll wind up at the square called **Sint-Paulusplein,** which used to be a medieval harbor, then a dangerous wasteland, and then a bustling sailors' quarter with red lights in the windows. While you'll still see sex workers, peep shows, and tattoo parlors, this area also has its share of trendy restaurants.

Head up Oudemanstraat, which becomes **Vingerlingstraat,** in the heart of the red light district. Here you'll really begin to see ladies shimmying in windows. In the 19th century, Antwerp's red light district was known (or notorious) the world over; these days, it's a much tamer place...but still provocative.

Bear right on Blauwbroekstraat/Schippersstraat. Halfway down the block on the right is **Villa Tinto,** a modern-looking mall, designed by prominent artist Arne Quinze, where you can window-shop for sex. It's considered one of Europe's most high-tech brothels, with a system of "panic buttons" for sex workers to call for help if necessary. Notice the police station right in the middle of the complex. In Belgium, as throughout the Low Countries, prostitution is pragmatically integrated into the larger society without blushing. City leaders firmly believe that concentrating prostitution in this small neighborhood makes things safer both for the sex workers and for city residents at large.

Pass all the way through Villa Tinto, then bear left (or, to skip the Villa Tinto experience, just continue on Schippersstraat). You'll pop out on a long, narrow square called **Falconplein.** This used to be dubbed "Red Square," for its Russian-dominated illegal activity (Russian mafia-style thugs selling designer knock-offs...and worse). Nervous about sketchy stuff just a few steps from its up-and-coming museum scene, spunky city leaders recently cracked down, evicted the worst offenders, and spiffed up the square.

Turn left and walk up Falconplein, then cross the big, tree-lined Brouwersvliet (which used to be a canal). This puts you right at the old docklands in the heart of the Little Island.

South of the Old Town
Sint-Andries Fashion District

Worth ▲▲▲ for lovers of couture, Antwerp's fashion district is fun for anybody to window-shop. It's mostly in the Sint-Andries

area, a few minutes' walk south of the Old Town, centered on the street called Nationalestraat. In the shops along the streets of Sint-Andries, you'll find everything from top-name international designers to funky hole-in-the-wall boutiques to vintage shops to jewelers. (For tips on shopping here, see "Shopping in Antwerp," facing page.) Antwerp's status as a fashion mecca is a relatively recent development. In 1988, six students from the Royal Academy of Fine Arts' Fashion Department (www.antwerp-fashion.be) traveled to a London show, where they got a lot of attention. Because their Flemish names were too challenging to pronounce, the English press simply dubbed them the "Antwerp Six." Each one opened a shop here in Sint-Andries, which at the time was a very poor neighborhood. They put this area on the map, other designers began to move in, and now it's one of Europe's top fashion zones. The academy is still up and running; it has a small enrollment and a strong focus on creativity.

▲**ModeMuseum ("MoMu")**—The collection here, like fashion itself, is always changing...but it's also always good. Housed in the modern ModeNatie facility in the heart of the Sint-Andries fashion zone, this museum presents good rotating exhibits about big-name designers, with a new exhibit every six months. The building is also home to the Antwerp Fashion Academy, a library with books about fashion, a good bookshop, and—on the ground floor near the ticket desk—a gallery of works by students. Everything is (no surprise) very stylishly presented.

Cost and Hours: €7, Tue-Sun 10:00-18:00, closed Mon, last entry 30 minutes before closing, a five-minute walk south of Groenplaats at Nationalestraat 28, tel. 03-470-2770, www.momu.be.

▲▲ 't Zuid

Literally "The South," 't Zuid (pronounced "tzowd") has emerged as Antwerp's trendiest zone. It's the best place to go for fun and funky boutiques, and a wide array of lively restaurants and bars. With the multiyear closure of the Royal Museum of Fine Arts, there's little sightseeing here, but it's the best place to head in the evenings to stroll and find an enticing place for a meal (for suggestions, see "Eating in Antwerp," later).

To get to 't Zuid from the Old Town, you can either hop on a tram (#8, from Groenplaats, to Museum stop in front of the Royal Museum of Fine Arts), or walk about 20-25 minutes. From the Grote Markt, head down Hoogstraat, which turns into Kloosterstraat, lined with lots of fun antiques stores, retro-style boutiques, and so on.

Royal Museum of Fine Arts of Antwerp (Koninklijk Museum voor Schone Kunsten Antwerpen, a.k.a. KMSKA)—Currently closed for an extensive renovation (through late 2017), this museum normally collects many of Antwerp's most exciting art treasures under one roof. While it's out of commission, many of its items are on display at other museums around town (Leopold De Waelplaats 2, tel. 03-238-7809, www.kmska.be).

Shopping in Antwerp

As a capital of both fashion and avant-garde culture, Antwerp is a shopper's delight, with a seemingly endless array of creative little corner boutiques selling unique items, as well as outlets for big-name international designers. The fanciest shops are on the boulevard called **the Meir,** between the train station and Old Town (see page 512). The **Sint-Andries** district, just to the west along Nationalestraat, is the center of the fashion scene (described earlier).

As you explore, you'll discover that each street has its own personality and specialties. For example, Schuttershofstraat and Hopland are where you'll find famous-label international couture, while Kammenstraat is better for young, trendy, retro-hipster fashions. For antiques, head to Kloosterstraat (to the west) and Leopoldstraat (to the east); for more antiques and home decor near Leopoldstraat, check out Sint-Jorispoort and Mechelsteenweg.

Sleeping in Antwerp

$$$ Hotel Julien, an extremely chic boutique hotel, is Antwerp's most enticing splurge. Located in a renovated 16th-century building on a drab street just outside the Old Town, its 22 rooms are a perfectly executed combination of old and new. The public areas, with high ceilings and lots of unfinished wood, feel like an art gallery (Db-€170-290 depending on size and amenities, air-con in most rooms, elevator, free Internet access and Wi-Fi, spa in basement, Korte Nieuwstraat 24, tel. 03-229-0600, www.hotel-julien .com, info@hotel-julien.com).

$$$ Matelote Hotel ("Fisherman") is a less pretentious boutique hotel, with a central location on a characteristic street deep in the Old Town. Its 10 rooms have artistic decor and some nice touches (small "cozy comfort" Db-€80-130—usually €90-100, deluxe Db-€100-150—usually €120, breakfast-€12.50, free Internet access and Wi-Fi, Haarstraat 11a, tel. 03-201-8800, www .hotel-matelote.be, info@matelote.be).

$$ Le Patio is the best B&B I found in Antwerp, with three comfortable, thoughtfully appointed ground-floor rooms around a little courtyard on the restaurant-lined Pelgrimstraat (Db-€95, Tb-€120, 20 percent less for 3 nights or more, free Wi-Fi, Pelgrimstraat 8, tel. 03-232-7661, www.lepatio.be, info@lepatio .be, Nicole and Roger).

$$ Big Sleep B&B, between the Old Town and 't Zuid, has two very mod rooms in an old warehouse, with lots of minimalist white and frosted glass—a little too transparent if privacy is a priority (Sb-€55, Db-€80, includes breakfast in your room, cash

---

Sleep Code

(€1 = about $1.40, country code: 32)
S = Single, **D** = Double/Twin, **T** = Triple, **Q** = Quad, **b** = bathroom, **s** = shower only. Everyone speaks English. Unless otherwise noted, breakfast is included and credit cards are accepted.

To help you easily sort through these listings, I've divided the rooms into three categories, based on the price for a standard double room with bath:

$$$ Higher Priced—Most rooms €100 or more.
$$ Moderately Priced—Most rooms between €60-100.
$ Lower Priced—Most rooms €60 or less.

Prices can change without notice; verify the hotel's current rates online or by email. For other updates, see www .ricksteves.com/update.

only, free Wi-Fi, Kromme-Elleboogstraat 4, mobile 0474-849-565, www.intro04.be/thebigsleep, els.hubert@skynet.be, Els Hubert).

$$ Enich Anders B&B is well-priced and nicely located above an art gallery around the corner from Vrijdagmarkt, in the heart of town (Sb-€66, Db-€72, Tb-€88, Qb-€104, €5 cheaper per night with two-night stay, includes breakfast served in your own kitchenette, cash only, free Wi-Fi, tight and steep stairs, Leeuwenstraat 12, mobile 0476-998-601, www.enich-anders.be, Ine and Jan).

$$ Ibis Antwerpen Centrum, the cookie-cutter standby, has 150 predictable rooms sharing the big Oudevaartplaats square with the modern City Theater, just south of the Meir and the Rubens House between the train station and Old Town (Sb/Db-€92-109 depending in demand, as low as €59 in slow times if you book online 3 weeks ahead, breakfast-€14/person, air-con, elevator, free Wi-Fi in lobby, pay Wi-Fi in rooms, Meistraat 39, tel. 03-231-8830, www.ibishotel.com, h1453@accor.com).

$ 't Katshuis is a very rough-around-the edges budget option, with nine sketchy but affordable rooms in two buildings right in the heart of town. Because central Antwerp doesn't yet have an official youth hostel (though one is planned soon), this last resort has the best-located cheap beds in town (Ss-€35, Ds-€50, Db-€55, includes coffee but not breakfast, cash only, Grote Pieter Potstraat 18 and 19—reception at #19, mobile 0476-206-947, www.katshuis.be, katshuis@gmail.com).

Eating in Antwerp

This trendy, youthful city is changing all the time, and the range of options is impressive. Because what's good one year is old news the next, it's risky to recommend any particular place. Instead, I suggest poking around the neighborhoods described next and choosing the menu and ambience that appeal to you the most. Exploring this evolving scene is actually enjoyable—a fun part of the Antwerp experience. Ask your hotelier for pointers.

If you're dining in the Old Town area, simply accept that anywhere you go will cater at least partly to tourists. But since Antwerp isn't overrun by visitors, these places also entertain their share of locals. For a more authentic Antwerp experience, head south to 't Zuid.

In the Old Town

Touristy restaurants with outdoor seating abound on the Grote Markt and Handschoenmarkt, the square in front of the cathedral. Choose your view and overpay for mediocre food. Better yet, venture a few blocks away to one of these neighborhoods.

Pelgrimsstraat: Just a block south of the cathedral, this delightful, cobbled, traffic-free lane is still a tourist zone—but a bit more respectable than the high-profile squares. You'll find a staggering variety along here: Italian and tapas, sushi and Thai, rustic taverns and chic bars. Keep an eye out for these (coming from the cathedral): **Pasta Hippo** has a reputation for good pasta (Mon-Sat for lunch and dinner, Sun only for dinner). On the right at #4, go through the doorway to discover a series of narrow alleyways (called **Vlaeykensngang**) that twist through the middle of the block, passing a trio of well-regarded restaurants en route. Back on the main drag, on the left is **Pelgrom,** a tavern in a cozy brick cellar that oozes atmosphere. Farther down on the right is **Lollapalooza,** with a fun, eclectic menu, a rocker-grrl pink-and-tattoos ambience, and a charming little brick grotto across the street. Two nearby streets (Grote Pieterpotstraat and Haarstraat) are similar, but less developed and more bar-oriented.

Near "Antwerp's Piazza": The streets branching off from Hendrik Conscienceplein (about a block northeast of the cathedral), with its very Italian-feeling Baroque Jesuit church, are a charming cobbles-and-red-brick maze of alleys with intriguing little eateries. Two good, upscale choices are kitty-corner in the heart of this neighborhood: **Aurelia** (French and Belgian, cozy, white-tablecloth but rustic, under low wooden beams, €13-18 starters, €25-30 main dishes, €55 fixed-price meals, Thu-Mon 18:00-22:30, closed Tue-Wed, Wijngaardstraat 22, tel. 03-233-6259) and **Neuze Neuze** (French, gastronomic, dressy, white stucco and old beams, €20-30 starters and mains, Mon-Sat 12:00-14:00 & 19:00-21:30, closed for lunch Wed and Sat and all day Sun, Wijngaardstraat 19-21, tel. 03-232-2797). This area is fun to stroll, whether or not you dine here.

Just South and East of the Old Town

In Sint-Andries: The area called Sint-Andries, the center of the fashion district, has its share of enjoyable bars and restaurants. For a quick lunch, try **Fresh 'n Fruity,** selling good €2-5 baguette sandwiches and fresh-squeezed fruit juice (closed Sun, Kammenstraat 19, tel. 03-231-1308). **Hungry Henrietta,** tucked away in a nondescript, businesslike neighborhood just south of Groenplaats, has mod black decor and good Belgian food (€9-15 starters, €20-26 main dishes, €15 daily specials, daily 12:00-14:00 & 18:00-21:00, Lombardenvest 19, tel. 03-232-2928).

In the Meir: **Horta** is a brasserie with a pricey menu located in a gorgeously restored Art Nouveau hall a few steps south of the Rubens House. Come here not for the food, but for the remarkable setting, with its glassy spaciousness and iron adornments (€10-15 light meals served until 17:00, €13-18 starters, €16-30 main dishes, daily 11:30-22:00, until 23:30 on weekends, Hopland 2, tel. 03-203-5660).

In 't Zuid

Literally "The South," this zone is emerging as Antwerp's top restaurant and nightlife zone (for tips on getting here, see page 529). Frequented mostly by urbanites, this is where you'll find most of the city's hot new restaurants. Options are scattered around a several-block area, with one or two tempting eateries on each block. The long parking lot that runs parallel to the river a block inland (between Waalsekaai and Vlaamsekaai) is lined with several options.

At **Marnixplaats,** the confluence of eight streets creates a circle of corner buildings made-to-order for restaurants with outdoor seating. **Fiskebar** is done up like a fish market (as its name implies), and lists a wide range of seafood specialties on its chalkboard menu high on the wall (€7-10 starters, €15-25 main dishes, €17-20 specials, open daily, Marnixplaats 12-13, tel. 03-257-1357). **Osteria Casa Zaga** dishes up Italian food in one long room that stretches along the open kitchen (€16-18 pastas and salads, €23 main dishes, open daily, Marnixplaats 10, tel. 03-216-4616).

Although the Royal Museum of Fine Arts is closed for renovation, the area in front of it is still lined with several good options. **Zuidcafé** is a lively, youthful spot with an eclectic menu (€10-12 pastas and salads, €13-15 main dishes, open daily, Volkstraat 69, tel. 03-248-8189). **Hippodroom** also has a varied menu, but feels a bit more upscale (€11-17 starters, €19-30 main dishes, closed Sun, Leopold De Waelplaats 10, tel. 03-248-5252).

Antwerp Connections

From Antwerp by Train to: Brussels (5/hour, 40-50 minutes), **Ghent** (3/hour, 50-55 minutes), **Bruges** (2/hour, 1.5 hours, half change in Ghent), **Ypres/Ieper** (hourly, 2.25 hours, change in Kortrijk), **Amsterdam** (about hourly on Thalys, 1.25 hours; also possible on slower but still direct IC, some with a transfer at Schiphol Airport—see next, 2 hours total), Amsterdam's **Schiphol Airport** (hourly on IC, 1.75 hours), **Delft** (hourly, 1.5 hours, change in Rotterdam), **Paris** (about hourly direct on Thalys, 2 hours; more possible with a transfer at Brussels Midi/Zuid/South to Thalys, 2.5 hours). In Belgium, dial 050-302-424 for train information—press 4 for English, www.b-rail.be.

GHENT

Gent

Made terrifically wealthy by the textile trade, medieval Ghent was a powerhouse—for a time, it was one of the biggest cities in Europe. It erected grand churches and ornate guild houses to celebrate its resident industry. But, like its rival Bruges, eventually Ghent's fortunes fell, leaving it with a well-preserved historic nucleus surrounded by a fairly drab modern shell.

Ghent doesn't ooze with cobbles and charm, as Bruges does; this is a living, thriving city—home to Belgium's biggest university. In contrast to the manicured-but-empty back lanes of Bruges, Ghent enjoys more urban grittiness and a thriving restaurant and nightlife scene. It's also a browser's delight, with a wide range of fun and characteristic little shops and boutiques that aren't aimed squarely at the tourist crowds. Simply put, Ghent feels more real than idyllic. Visitors enjoy exploring its historic quarter, ogling the breathtaking Van Eyck altarpiece in its massive cathedral, touring its impressive art and design museums, strolling its picturesque embankments, basking in its finely decorated historic gables, and prowling its newly revitalized Patershol restaurant quarter.

Planning Your Time

Ghent is ideally located, about halfway between Brussels and Bruges. It's easy to get the gist of the town in a few hours (either toss your bag in a locker at Ghent's train station on your way between those two cities, or side-trip here from either one). With limited time, focus on the historical center: Follow my self-guided walk, tour the cathedral, and dip into any museums that intrigue you. With more time or a strong interest in art, also visit the art museums closer to the train station. Be aware that nearly all museums in Ghent are closed on Mondays (though the cathedral and other churches remain open).

If you'd like to home-base in Belgium, Ghent couldn't be more handy—just a half-hour from either Brussels or Bruges and 50 minutes from Antwerp (though be aware that most Ghent hotels are a tram ride away from the train station).

Orientation to Ghent

Although it's a mid-sized city (pop. 240,000), the tourist's Ghent is appealingly compact—you can walk from one end of the central zone to the other in about 15 minutes. Its Flemish residents call it Gent (gutturally: hhhent), while its French name is Gand (sounds like "gone").

Tourist Information

Ghent's TI is in the process of moving; if it's not in its original home, on the ground floor of the Cloth Hall beneath the Belfry, you'll find it in the newly renovated Fish Market (Vismijn) building next to the Castle of the Counts (daily mid-March-mid-Oct 9:30-18:30, off-season 10:30-17:30, tel. 09-266-5232, www.visit gent.be). They also hope to open branches in the train station and the City Museum (STAM). At any TI, you can pick up a free town map and a pile of brochures (including a good self-guided walk; vegetarian info; and lists of hotels, B&Bs, bars, and restaurants).

The **Gent Museum Card,** which includes public transit and entrance to all the major museums and monuments in town, is worth the price if you'll be visiting four or more sights (€20/3 days, sold at TI, hotels, and museums).

Arrival in Ghent

By Train: Ghent's main train station, called Gent-Sint-Pieters, is about a mile and a half south of the city center. As the station is undergoing an extensive renovation (through 2020), you might find things different than described. The left-luggage desk (daily 6:15-21:30) is across the hall from the Travel Centre ticket office, and lockers are just down the same hall on the right (€3-4/day for either bag-storage option).

It's a dull 30-minute **walk** to the city center. Instead, take the **tram:** Buy a ticket from the Relay shop just inside the train station exit, then head outside to find the stop for tram #1 (likely out the front door and to the left; the location might change depending on the renovation—ask around or look for signs). Board tram #1 in the direction of Wondelgem/Evergem (departs about every 10 minutes, ride into town takes 10-15 minutes, €1.20 if you buy the ticket in advance at a shop or automated machine, €2 from the driver; you can also get a shareable 10-ride ticket for €8). Get off at the Veldstraat stop; continue two blocks straight ahead to Korenmarkt, where you can see most of the city's landmark towers (St. Michael's Bridge, where my self-guided walk begins, is just to the left). Figure €10 for a **taxi** into town.

To reach the art museums in Citadelpark, simply exit the station straight ahead, then bear right at the end of the square (onto Koningin Astridlaan); for more details, see page 552.

By Car: Exit the E40 expressway at the Gent Centrum exit, then follow the *P-route* (parking route) to various pay garages in town; the most central include P1 (Vrijdagmarkt) and P5 (Kouter).

Helpful Hints

Festivals: Ghent is proud of its Gentse Feesten (Ghent Festivities), which last for 10 days and begin around the city holiday of July 21. This open-air music festival, featuring different types of music in venues around town, books up hotels—reserve ahead. Other events include a jazz festival (the week before the big festival), and a film festival each mid-October.

Market Day: Sunday is the main market day in Ghent, with small markets filling squares around town: a flower market at Kouter, secondhand books along Ajuinlei, clothes and pets on Vrijdagmarkt, and more. There are also smaller markets on Fridays and Saturdays.

Laundry: A handy, unstaffed coin-op launderette is in the heart of the Patershol restaurant neighborhood...handy for multitaskers (daily 7:00-22:00, corner of Oudburg and Zwaanstraat, mobile 0475-274-686).

Tours in Ghent

Walking Tours—Guided two-hour tours of Ghent (in English and sometimes also other languages) depart daily from the TI (€7, May-Oct daily at 14:30, Sun only off-season, reserve at the TI or by calling 09-233-0772).

Local Guide—**Toon Van den Abeele** enthusiastically shares Ghent's charms (€65/2-hour tour, book through Gidsenbond Gent agency: tel. 09-233-0772, www.gidsenbond-gent.be, info @gidsenbond-gent.be).

Self-Guided Walk

Welcome to Ghent

This walk takes in the historic center of Ghent. Begin at the bridge in the heart of town, next to the bustling Korenmarkt square.

St. Michael's Bridge (Sint-Michielsbrug)

This viewpoint offers Ghent's best 360-degree panorama. The city was founded at the confluence (the origin of the word "Ghent")

of two rivers: the Lys (Leie in Flemish) and the Scheldt (Schelde in Flemish, Escaut in French). Ghent boomed in the Middle Ages, when the wool trade made it wealthy. By the 14th century, Ghent's population was around 65,000—positively massive in an age when most of

Europe was rural farmland. Two-thirds of the city's population were textile workers, making Ghent arguably Europe's first industrial city. The waterway in front of you—now plied by tourist-laden boats—was the city's busy harbor. Lining the embankment on the right are several ornately decorated guild houses—meeting halls for the town's industries (such as corn traders or seamen). Straight ahead is the newly renovated Fish Market (the new home of the TI, likely sometime in 2011), which marks the start of the seedy-chic Patershol zone (a residential district sprinkled with great restaurants); behind that is the imposing Castle of the Counts. (We'll circle through town and end near there.)

• *Turn to the right and walk to...*

Korenmarkt

This "Corn Market" is one of many small squares throughout the city. Whereas many Belgian cities (including Brussels, Bruges, and Antwerp) have a single "Great Market" (Grote Markt), Ghent was too big for just one such square. Instead it had a smattering of smaller squares that specialized in different areas of commerce. They retain these traditional names today.

The big building on the left is the former **post office** (now the Post Plaza mall). While it seems to match the classic medi-

eval style of old Ghent, it's much newer—Neo-Gothic, from the early 20th century. As throughout Europe, the late 1800s and early 1900s were a time of powerful nationalism, when smaller minority groups (such as the Flemish) rose up against the

more dominant groups (such as the French-speaking Belgians) to assert their worth. There was a flurry of Neo-Gothic construction, hearkening back to a time when the Flemish had more power.

GHENT

Ghent

1. St. Michael's Bridge
2. Korenmarkt
3. St. Nicholas' Church
4. Belfry
5. St. Bavo's Square
6. Cathedral of St. Bavo
7. Hoogpoort
8. Friday Market Square & Van Artevelde Statue
9. Patershol
10. Vegetable Market

T Tram #1
B Canal Cruises
← View

200 YARDS
200 METERS

DCH

Looking straight ahead, you can see the spires of Ghent's three main buildings (left to right): the Church of St. Nicholas, the Belfry, and St. Bavo's Cathedral.
As you tour Ghent, you can play amateur archaeologist to quickly deduce the age of various buildings. Before the year 1400, when Ghent was rolling in wool money, they built with valuable, imported gray limestone. Between 1400 and 1500, as the economy slowed,

they used yellow sandstone, which was quarried nearby. And after 1500—when competition from Brussels and England, combined with very conservative guild leadership that was slow to adapt to the changing markets, caused Ghent's economy to tank—they resorted to the cheapest material: locally produced red brick. Even in a single building—such as these old churches—you can spot several centuries of construction at a glance. (People from Ghent gleefully point out that their rival, Bruges, is built mostly of brick—indicating that city's lowlier economic status in medieval times.)

• *Turn your attention to the big church at the end of the square.*

St. Nicholas' Church (Sint-Niklaaskerk)

This stout church is made mostly of gray limestone, indicating that it dates from a boom time for Ghent. Before entering, look around the left (north) side of the church, where the facade appears more like cinderblock than the rough stonework of the rest of the building. Looking more closely, you'll see that it's covered with an inch-thick layer of plaster, and the "gaps" between the "blocks" are painted on. This was the fashion in the Middle Ages, when painted plaster facades were considered superior to naked stone... especially the asymmetrical stonework of this church.

Now go inside (free, daily 10:00-17:00). You can tell it was built from the back to the front, as the gray limestone transitions to the yellow sandstone. While the building itself is Gothic, the decorations inside—like most in Ghent—are much newer. As this region was at the forefront of the Protestant Reformation in the 16th century, the interior of Ghent's churches suffered at the hands of the iconoclasts—Protestants who stripped churches of all adornments to unclutter their communion with God. The church was later partly redecorated by Catholics, who installed the very Baroque altar, with modern stained glass above (representing the seven sacraments).

• *Exiting the church, look straight ahead and notice the stepped gable of the Masons' Guild House. This 15th-century facade was only revealed in the 1980s, when workers peeled back a more modern layer on top of it. They restored the building, added the decorations at the tops of the gables (bottom row: humans; middle row: devils; top row: angels), then added a very modern section behind it (notice the glass-and-steel structure down St.-Niklaasstraat).*

The square beyond St. Nicholas, **Emil-Braunplein,** *is in transition; they recently excavated the brick foundations of humble buildings that once stood here, and hope to build a grassy park and a new market hall; expect some construction work around here.*

The next tall building is the...

Belfry

Although most of this tower has stood here since the 14th century, the Neo-Gothic top spire (from the gargoyles up) was added when Ghent proudly hosted a World's Fair in 1913. The tower was originally built to house and protect the parchment record of Ghent's favored privileges, granted to the city by the Counts of Flanders in exchange for financial support. The dragon topping the spire symbolizes not the devil (as was typical in the Middle Ages), but a protector who never sleeps as it watches over the city's rights. It was also a fire watchtower, represented by the four sentries positioned at the corners. The carillon in the tower plays the Ghent town anthem each hour.

Visitors enjoy ascending the belfry for a view over town. It's just a couple of flights of stairs, then an elevator most of the way (€5, borrow English explanations as you enter, daily 10:00-18:00, last entry 30 minutes before closing, www.belfortgent.be). On the way, you'll pass a modest exhibit about the history of the building, including models of former spires that topped it.

The long building at the base of (and behind) the belfry is the **Cloth Hall,** which was important to this textile center. The TI is located here, unless it has already moved across town to the Fish Market.

• *The square beyond the Belfry is...*

St. Bavo's Square (Sint-Baafsplein)

This square became a symbolic battleground during the period of Flemish nationalism in the early 20th century. Previously, when Belgium gained its independence from the Netherlands in 1830, it was ruled by its Francophone (French-speaking) aristocracy, even though the Flemish-speakers were in the majority. Flemish people felt mistreated by their Francophone overlords. (It took a century after independence for Ghent's prestigious university to finally start offering classes in Dutch; to mark that day in 1930, the Francophone-aristocracy-owned electric company spitefully cut power to mourn the university's end of "enlightened" thinking.) For more on the Flemish-Francophone conflict, see "The Battle for Belgium: Flemish vs. French" on page 328.

The ornate building on the square is the **Dutch Theater** (Koninklijke Nederlandse Schouwburg, a.k.a. NT Gent), built in 1899 to provide the town's Flemish speakers a place to perform plays of their own. By embracing Dutch as a language worthy of theater, the spunky Flemish were asserting their cultural legitimacy. The golden mosaic depicts Apollo returning to Mount Parnassus, much as the Flemish felt they were coming home to their beloved language.

Circle around for a look at the far side of the **statue** in the middle of the square. The relief on the base (facing the theater) depicts Jan Frans Willems, one of the founders of the Flemish movement. The man and woman in the statue represent the resurrection of the Dutch (Flemish) language—notice the lion, a symbol of Flanders, on their flag.

As you face the theater, look to the left to see **Van Hoorebeke Chocolatier,** a producer of fine pralines. Peek in the window (or go in the shop and look through the glass floor) to see the chocolate-makers hard at work (€4/100 grams—about 7 pieces, daily 10:00-18:00, tel. 09-221-0381).

• *At the end of the square is Ghent's top sight...*

▲▲Cathedral of St. Bavo (Sint-Baafskathedraal)

The main church of Ghent, this also houses three of the city's art treasures: the exquisite *Adoration of the Mystic Lamb* altarpiece, by Jan Van Eyck and his brother, Hubert; an elaborately carved pulpit; and an altar painting by Rubens depicting the town's patron saint (and the church's namesake).

Cost and Hours: Free, Mon-Sat 9:30-16:45, Sun 13:00-16:30, later in summer. During busy times, volunteer guides can show you around.

◐ Self-Guided Tour: Step inside. This giant Gothic cathedral was built over many centuries—notice the telltale three materials: gray stone (choir), red brick (nave), and yellow stone (tower). As in St. Nicholas' Church, all of the decorations and stained glass date from the 19th century (following the iconoclasm of the 16th century).

Below, I've first described the great altarpiece, and then the rest of the church. Note that there are two opportunities to see the altarpiece: You can view a replica in the chapel that originally contained the piece (at the front-right corner of the church) for free. Or you can pay €4 to see the original, in a small room in the back-left corner of the church (€1 audioguide). The locations of both the original and the replica are explained under "The Rest of the Church," later.

The Adoration of the Mystic Lamb: The highlight of the church (and, for art-lovers, of all Ghent) is Jan and Hubert Van Eyck's *Adoration of the Mystic Lamb* altarpiece. Hubert Van Eyck (c. 1385-1426) began the painting, but after his death, his better-known younger brother, Jan (1395-1441), picked up the brush and completed Hubert's vision. Finished in 1432, this altarpiece represents a monumental stride in Northern European art from medieval stiffness to Renaissance humanism, with a closely observed attention to detail. The first work signed by Jan Van Eyck, it's also considered one of the first works of the Flemish Primitives (characterized by a precise dedication to detail, if an imperfect mastery of perspective).

During the wave of iconoclasm in the 16th century, the altar was hidden in the cathedral tower. And later, during World War II, the altar was on its way to safe storage at the Vatican when it was caught up in the fighting and squirreled away in the French Pyrenees, then swiped by Hitler and stored in a Bavarian castle, then a salt mine, before being returned here by US forces at war's end.

The altarpiece has a dozen separate paintings on each side (front and back). On weekdays, the altarpiece was closed to show only the outside panels; it was opened up on Sundays and holidays to reveal the scenes inside. (On the replica, you can actually open and close the panels; on the original, you'll have to circle around back to see them in their open state.)

First, look at the **outside panels,** showing the Annunciation—when the archangel Gabriel comes to Mary to tell her she will bear God's child. Gabriel, holding a lily (representing purity), says to Mary, "Hail Mary, full of grace." Mary (with the Holy Spirit above her) replies, "I am the servant of the Lord." Notice that Mary's words are upside-down—intended for God above. Through the windows, we get a glimpse of medieval Ghent, and in the niche is a medieval "bathroom" (with a pitcher and basin). Below are the kneeling couple who commissioned the work for their private chapel, and statues of St. John the Baptist (holding the lamb) and St. John the Evangelist (holding the cup of poison). Above are two sibyls (pagan prophets) flanked by the Old Testament prophets Zechariah (on the left) and Micah (on the right)—all of whom prophesied the coming of Christ.

Now get the full feast-day effect of the **inside panels.** The main scene, playing out at the bottom, depicts the adoration of the lamb (representing Jesus) at the Revelation. The scene is a big Christ-celebrating party, and everyone's here: angels, church teachers, holy virgins, Old Testament prophets (in the left-foreground), the 12 apostles (in the right-foreground), saints, popes, pagan writers, Jewish prophets, knights and judges (on the left panel) and pilgrims and hermits (on the right panel)... all coming to worship their savior. Notice the diversity of the people assembled, wearing all different styles of clothing and headwear—from Asia, India, and the entire known world at the time. Hovering overhead is a dove (the Holy Spirit), and in the foreground is the well of life, spewing water and jewels. As in Christian tradition, the lamb at the very center is a stand-in for Christ—but it also has a special meaning here in Ghent, whose wool trade put it on the map. It's too bad that the lamb itself—which scholars suspect was later retouched by a lesser artist—isn't particularly well-depicted. He looks more like a sheep...and is that an extra right ear I see?

Above this scene are (from left to right) Mary, the resurrected Christ (or is it God himself, wearing a triple-tiara to represent the Trinity?), and John the Baptist (wearing a garment of camel hair, per biblical descriptions). On the upper outside panels are angels playing music, and a pair of famous portraits of **Adam and Eve**—which scholars believe were the first Renaissance-era nudes painted north of the Alps. The tiny, wedge-shaped panels above them tell the story of Cain and Abel.

Take a moment to simply bask in the astonishing level of detail. You can see each hair on Adam's legs (and notice the not-quite-perfectly executed, Italian-inspired perspective—with Adam's toes breaking the plane as they seem to emerge from the panel). Hymnals of the time indicated which face a singer should make when singing a particular note; today's experts can guess which notes the angels are singing from their expressions. The countryside scenes are decorated with dozens of different, identifiable species of plants and flowers, and the angels around the lamb in the lower panel have feathers from a variety of actual birds (peacocks, pigeons, and swallows). And in the amulet around the neck of the angel by Adam, you can actually see a faint reflection of the stained-glass window that decorated the chapel where this altarpiece originally stood.

The Rest of the Church: Go for a counterclockwise spin around the cathedral's interior. Along the way, you'll have a chance to see both the replica and the original of the altarpiece described above.

Begin in the back-right corner of the church (to the right as you enter). Near the information desk, see the panels showing **Adam and Eve with clothes**—added to cover Van Eyck's nudes during the puritanical 19th century (1825-1896). Instead of discreetly covering their nudity, now they just look like they're scratching their privates through their clothes. Is this really an improvement?

Along the right wall of the church, near the shop, find the chapel with a statue of **Pater Damiaan** (Father Damien, 1840-1889), a Flemish missionary who went to Hawaii to care for lepers, but after 16 years died of leprosy himself. Canonized in 2009, he's a rare saint with a connection to the United States, and an important figure both to Belgians and to Hawaiians.

Inside the main nave, on the right-hand side, you can't miss the elaborately carved, remarkable Rococo **pulpit,** representing the tree of life and the tree of knowledge. Notice the golden serpent entwined around the top of the pulpit; follow its body to find the pudgy, winged baby (a sure sign of Rococo) prying the apple of sin from the snake's

mouth. The Carrara marble statues just beneath the pulpit drive home a Counter-Reformation message: The woman on the right (with the quill, representing faith) wakes up the winged old man on the left (representing time): It's time to wake up to the Catholic faith. The goody-two-shoes angels at the bases of the staircases offer a lesson in appropriate worship: The angel on the left watches the pulpit intently, and the one on the right points up to the pulpit while glancing scoldingly to the back of the church: Hey, you in the back row—pay attention!

Go up the right aisle toward the front of the church. Above the main altar is **St. Bavo,** the beloved local saint, on his way to heaven. This seventh-century saint was once a wealthy and rambunctious young soldier, but became a born-again Christian after the death of his wife. Bavo rejected his life of materialism and became a monk, living for a time in a hollow tree. He is also the patron saint of Haarlem, the Netherlands.

In the front-right part of the church (just to the right, as you face the main altar) is the Vijdt Chapel, housing the **replica of the Van Eyck altarpiece** (described earlier). Van Eyck painted the altarpiece specifically to be displayed in this room—in fact, the light and subtle reflections in his work are designed to complement this space.

Circling around the back of the church to the left transept, you'll find another great work of art, **Peter Paul Rubens'** *Entrance of St. Bavo into the Monastery of Ghent,* depicting the moment this local-boy-done-good started on his righteous course. Notice the parallel, diagonal composition: On the top, Bavo, in the red cloak (and with the face of the painter, Rubens—a rare self-portrait), kneels before the abbot. The lower group shows Bavo's estate manager distributing his belongings to the poor. The women on the left, representing Bavo's daughter and her servant, are modeled after Rubens' two wives— his older first wife, wearing the giant hat; and his much younger, more voluptuous second

wife, Hélène Fourment, in the red dress. (The Flemish like to say, with a wink, "An old billy goat loves a young leaf.") Compare the very static composition of Van Eyck's altarpiece (1432) with this dynamic canvas, pregnant with motion (1624)—illustrating the contrast between staid medieval and exuberant Baroque. For more about Rubens, see page 515.

Across from this canvas is the entrance to the **crypt,** where you can see some of the building's Romanesque foundations and various chapels decorated with ecclesiastical art both old and modern.

Circling back to the entrance, you reach the chapel with the **original Van Eyck painting.** If you want a closer look at this remarkable work in its original form, you can pay €4 to see it now.

• *Exiting the cathedral, turn right and head down the narrow, twisty*

Biezekapelstraat. You'll pass the turrets and other medieval-looking features of the back of the Achtersikkel mansion, the home of a powerful aristocratic family. The music you might hear is provided by students rehearsing at the nearby music college. Exiting this narrow street, turn left and head up...

Hoogpoort

This "High Gate" street connects Ghent's two rivers. As you walk, notice you're on a slight hill; Ghent was founded at a high point between two rivers, which people made ample use of for trade.

Crossing Belfortstraat, you'll see the giant, eclectic, slightly run-down **City Hall** on your left. Onto the ornate Gothic core of

the building, from the early 16th century, have been grafted many centuries of additions (for example, the blocky Renaissance-style section just down Belfortstraat). Continue along Hoogpoort, observing the many facets of this one building.

At the end of the City Hall, watch (on the right) for the narrow, covered lane called Werregarn Straat. Once used to drain water away from this high ground, today it has a different purpose and nickname: **Graffitistraat.** Walk down the lane, enjoying the artwork provided by the people

of Ghent. This is a typically pragmatic Belgian solution to a social problem: Rather than outlawing graffiti entirely, the police have designated this one street to give would-be artists a legal, controlled outlet for their impulses. Halfway down the

lane, notice the beautiful fenced-in garden on your right. This restful, picnic-perfect space is open to the public: When you emerge from Graffitistraat, turn right on Onderstraat; on the right, at #22, you can go through the giant green door (if it's open) into this city-owned garden courtyard.

• *Roughly across the street from #22—and just before the worth-a-peek* **Flamingo's Pub**, *with its avant-garde, funky-kitsch interior and Barbie chandelier—head down Serpentstraat, which is lined with some fun boutiques and colorful secondhand stores. When you pop out, turn left and you'll be in...*

Friday Market Square (Vrijdagmarkt)

While these days, the primary market day is Sunday, this square's name indicates its history. The church a block beyond the square is **St. Jacob's** (Sint-Jacobskerk), a pilgrimage stop for those walking from here to northwest Spain on the Camino de Santiago (the Camino's telltale scallop-shell symbol is at the church's entrance).

The statue in the square depicts a different Jacob: **Jakob Van Artevelde,** a clever businessman who saved the day in the 14th century, when the Hundred Years' War between France (which then controlled Ghent) and England (which provided Ghent with much-needed wool) threatened local industry. When the English king refused to export his wool to Ghent, Van Artevelde—not an aristocrat, but an ordinary citizen—boldly negotiated directly with the king to keep Ghent neutral in the conflict and keep the wool coming in. Largely forgotten by history, Van Artevelde's memory was resurrected during the nationalism of the late 19th century, as a symbol of the Flemish people of Ghent asserting their independence from the Francophones. Today he's still celebrated by the people of Ghent, who sometimes call their city "Artevelde-Stad."

Behind the statue is the eclectic **"House of the People"** (Ons Huis), the headquarters for the region's socialist movement. Not surprisingly for a city with a long industrial heritage, Ghent is a hotbed of left-leaning politics, and the birthplace of the Belgian Labor Party. Above the door on the right, notice the rooster—crowing to wake up the workers.

Farther to the right, peek up the street called **Baudelostraat** for some particularly beautiful gables.

• *Go down the narrow street that Van Artevelde is pointing down (Meerseniersstraat). In a block you reach a bridge. Notice the giant red cannon on the left. Several different tour-guide stories have circulated about this giant piece of artillery, but most are probably made up.*

Cross the bridge to enter the district called...

Patershol

Once a dingy and deserted danger zone, this neighborhood has turned into one of Ghent's trendiest. And though it's predominantly residential, Patershol is also a great place for restaurant-hunting (see "Eating in Ghent," later).

Looking straight ahead as you cross the bridge, you'll see two particularly fine (and symbolism-packed) gabled **facades.** The red one on the right features five panels showing the five senses, each one represented by an animal that exemplifies it (taste =

monkey; sight = eagle; hearing = deer; smell = dog; and touch = humans, since we have no hair on our hands). The building on the left has panels demonstrating six virtuous acts (the seventh—burying the dead—was deemed too gruesome to depict, so it's symbolized by the urn on top).

The ground floor of this building houses a favorite old-fashioned candy shop, **Temmerman,** with some unique Ghent treats, including Wippers—toffee with sugar coating; Lieve Vrouwkens—in the shape of the Virgin Mary; and the local favorite, raspberry-flavored Cuperdons (Wed-Sat 11:00-18:00, closed Sun-Tue, Kraanlei 79, tel. 09-224-0041).

• *Turn left and walk along Kraanlei, passing the Alijn House (with a tourable interior—see next page). Continue along the embankment, curving right with the road. Pause at the next intersection.*

At the corner on the right, notice the brasserie called 't Stopkje ("The Noose"). The people of Ghent are called **"noose-wearers"** *(Stopkens)*. This dates back to the time of King Charles V, who had been born here in Ghent but ruled from Spain. In 1540, he demanded a huge tribute from the people of Ghent. When they refused and revolted, he came here personally to enforce his authority. The leaders of Ghent had to beg on their knees with nooses around their necks for his forgiveness.

Across the street, the imposing **Castle of the Counts** is worth touring, if you have time (described later, under "Sights in Ghent").

Across the little square from the castle is the fancy arched facade of the **Old Fish Market** (Oude Vismijn). Deserted for years, this is now being renovated to house the TI, a conference center, and a café. Study the facade: That's Neptune on top; below him are Ghent's two rivers: Scheldt (male) and Lys (female). It's said that Ghent is the child of these two rivers.

• *Now cross the bridge to one final stop.*

Vegetable Market (Groentenmarkt)

The long, white **Meat Hall** (Groot Vleeshuis) looks like it's seen better days, but it's worth a peek inside to see its impressive wooden vault (built entirely without nails, and clearly employing ship-builders' expertise). You'll see local cured ham hanging from the rafters. The shop inside sells specialty products from East Flanders (Tue-Sun 10:00-18:00, closed Mon).

Back out on the square are more snacking opportunities. Across the square from the Meat Hall is a good traditional bakery (Himschoot); next to that, a café selling delicious take-away waffles; and to the right of that, the **Tierenteyn Verlent mustard shop.** Made in the cellar, then pumped into a barrel in the back of the shop, the mustard is some of the horseradish-hottest you'll ever sample. They use no preservatives, so you'll need to refrigerate it—or use it for today's picnic (Mon-Fri 8:30-18:00, Sat 9:00-18:00, closed Sun, Groentenmarkt 3, tel. 09-225-8336, www.tierenteyn -verlent.be).

• *Head to the far end of the Meat Hall, then the building beyond it. The bridge here affords another good view of Ghent's canals. Just across the bridge and to the right is the good* **Design Museum** *(described later). Near this bridge, various companies sell 40-minute* **cruises** *around the canals of Ghent (€6, includes commentary). Or you can backtrack (turn right along the river) to the* **Castle of the Counts** *or the* **House of Alijn.** *Most of what's worth seeing in Ghent is within a few steps of right here. Enjoy.*

Sights in Ghent

Most of Ghent's sights cluster in one of two areas: in the historic city center, or at a park two long blocks from the train station.

In the Historic Center
The House of Alijn (Huis van Alijn)

—This museum shows how everyday Belgian lifestyles evolved over the course of the 20th

century. It assembles an intriguing collection of bric-a-brac from various themes and walks of life (including an old pharmacy, grocery, and candy shop). However, the museum administration has chosen not to include much in the way of description, to encourage visitors to experience the place on their own—making the fine collection difficult to appreciate. And though this place could be fascinating with a good audioguide or regularly scheduled guided tour, neither is available; instead you'll borrow generalized explanations in each section. It's exhibited in several buildings around a tranquil courtyard, which used to be a refuge for poor elderly people (similar to a begijnhof). The courtyard

hosts an authentic Ghent pub where you can sample *jenever*, or gin
('t plumeetse).

Cost and Hours: €5, Tue-Sat 11:00-17:00, Sun 10:00-17:00,
closed Mon, Kraanlei 65, tel. 09-269-2350, www.huisvanalijn.be.

▲**Castle of the Counts (Gravensteen)**—Built in 1180 by Philip
of Alsace, this fortress was designed not to protect the people of

Ghent, but to intimidate the city's
independence-minded citizens.
Built outside the city walls, it's
morphed over the centuries, and
was partly destroyed by an acci-
dental explosion (when it served as
a textile factory), then restored. It's
impressive from the outside, but
explanations and exhibits inside
are pretty modest. Still, it's a fun
opportunity to twist through tow-
ers and ramble over ramparts. You'll see a sparse armory collection, a better torture museum, paintings and photos that explain
the history of the place, an 18-foot-deep dungeon, and great views
from the tops of the towers (be prepared for lots of climbing up
claustrophobic stairs). Although good explanations would help
bring this mostly empty shell to life, instead you get a few perfunc-
tory words. Admission includes a pointless, portable "movieguide,"
with corny dramatizations of actual historic events in each room
(45 minutes; you watch clips as you walk through the grounds).

Cost and Hours: €8, dry €1.50 guidebook tells the history of
the place, daily May-Sept 9:00-18:00, Oct-April 9:00-17:00, last
entry one hour before closing, tel. 09-225-9306.

▲**Design Museum**—Worth ▲▲▲ for those interested in decorative arts and design, and enjoyable to anybody, this collection cel-

ebrates the Belgian knack
for design. It combines a
classic old building with a
creaky wood interior, with a
bright-white, spacious, and
glassy new hall in the center.
You'll cross back and forth
between these sections, seeing both old-timey rooms
and exquisite pieces of Art Nouveau, Art Deco, and contemporary
design. Just explore: Everything is clearly explained in English
and easy to appreciate. The temporary exhibits are well-presented
and interesting. Don't miss the 18th-century dining room, with a
remarkable wood-carved chandelier. If you visit the bathroom—in
a courtyard around back—walk around a bit to discover that the

little building is in the shape of a giant roll of toilet paper.

Cost and Hours: €5, Tue-Sun 10:00-18:00, closed Mon, Jan Breydelstraat 5, tel. 09-267-9999, www.designmuseumgent.be.

Near the Train Station

These museums cluster closer to the train station than to the historical center—making them ideal to visit on your way into or out of Ghent (lockers are at the station).

Getting There: To reach the two art museums from the train station (about a 10-minute walk), exit straight ahead to the modern sculpture in the middle of the plaza. Turn right and walk up the tree- and bike-lined Koningin Astridstraat about five minutes, then cross the road and enter Citadel Park. Walk straight ahead, then curl around the left side of the big, modern building at the center of the park; as you round the far side, the Neoclassical entrance to the Fine Arts Museum is across the small street, and the SMAK is on your right.

▲Fine Arts Museum (Museum voor Schone Kunsten)—This museum offers a good, representative look at Northern European art. It's one of the most user-friendly collections of Low Countries art you'll find in Belgium, with lesser-known yet fun works by artists such as Bosch, Rubens, Van Dyck, and Magritte. As you enter, to the right (in numbered rooms) are older works, and to the left (in lettered rooms) are 19th- and 20th-century works and temporary exhibits. The €2.50 audioguide is both essential and excellent.

Cost and Hours: €5, Tue-Sun 10:00-18:00, closed Mon, in Citadelpark along Fernand Scribedreef street, tel. 09-240-0700, www.mskgent.be.

Highlights: Turn right from the entrance, and take a counterclockwise, chronological spin though the collection, keeping an eye out for these fine pieces.

In room 2, **Hieronymus Bosch's** jarring *Christ Carrying the Cross* (1515-1516) features a severe-looking Jesus surrounded by

grotesque faces. Typical of the Middle Ages, Bosch believed that evil was ugly—and all but three faces on this canvas (forming a diagonal, from lower-left to upper-right) are hideous. The serene woman to the left of Christ is Veronica, who has just wiped his face. In the upper-right, with an ashen complexion, is the stoic good thief, flanked by a doctor and a taunting monk. Meanwhile, in the lower-right, the orange-tinged unrepentant thief sneers back at his hecklers. Nearby, Bosch's portrait of St. Jerome

(c. 1505)—who was his personal patron saint—shows the holy hermit having discarded his clothes. Just above his legs, notice the owl (representing evil) sinisterly eyeing a titmouse (good). Also in this room, in **Rogier Van der Weyden**'s *The Virgin with a Carnation* (1480), the Baby Jesus makes a benediction gesture with his little hand. This painting was designed as a focal point for meditation.

Room 5 displays **Peter Paul Rubens'** altarpiece painting of *St. Francis of Assisi Receiving the Stigmata*, with Francis' brother Leo staring in amazement from below. According to Church accounts, an angel appeared to Francis in the form of a six-winged seraphim.

In Room 7, Rubens' student **Anthony Van Dyck** depicts the mythological story of *Jupiter and Antiope*—a horned-and-horny god about to inseminate a sleeping woman.

Room 8 features **Pieter Brueghel the Younger**'s copy of his more famous father, Pieter Brueghel the Elder's, much-loved

Peasant Wedding in a Barn. The elder painter trained his kids to carry on the family business. But Brueghel the Younger was a talented painter in his own right: In his *Village Lawyer*, we see the attorney behind a desk piled with papers, as peasants bring items to barter for his services.

Circle into the modern (lettered) wing. Near the front of this section, in Room B's *Portrait of Physician Ludwig Adler*, Viennese Secessionist painter **Oskar Kokoschka** uses dynamic, expressionistic brushstrokes to capture the personality, rather than a precise reproduction, of his subject.

In Room F you'll find works by homegrown Belgian modernist **René Magritte**. His clever *Perspective II*—part of a larger series—wryly replaces the four subjects on Edouard Manet's famous *Balcony* with coffins.

Stedelijk Contemporary Art Museum (Stedelijk Museum voor Actuele Kunst, a.k.a. SMAK)—This art gallery is constantly changing, both the "permanent" collection and many temporary exhibits. It's worth a visit only for art-lovers, and is conveniently located just across the street from the Fine Arts Museum (€6, more for special exhibits, Tue-Sun 10:00-18:00, closed Mon, tel. 09-240-7601, www.smak.be).

Ghent City Museum (Stadsmuseum Gent, a.k.a. STAM)—This new facility, which opened in October of 2010, explains the history of Ghent. It's housed in a beautiful 14th-century Gothic abbey complex called Bijloke and in a modern annex. The permanent exhibit traces the city's history with high-tech exhibits (€6, Tue-Sun 10:00-18:00, closed Mon, Godshuizenlaan 2, tel. 09-267-1400, www.stamgent.be). In addition to the exhibit, officials plan to eventually have a TI desk here, provide bike rentals, and offer boat trips up the canal and into the town center.

From the train station, it's about a 15-20-minute walk: Exit straight ahead, then angle left up the busy tram-tracks-lined Koningin Maria Hendrikaplein. After the bridge, turn right on Godshuizenlaan. Or, from the station, you could ride tram #1, #4, #21, or #22 to the STAM stop.

Sleeping in Ghent

A convention town, Ghent is busiest in spring (April-June) and fall (Sept-mid-Dec); things are quieter (and prices lower) in July and August, and even more so in the winter.

$$$ Chambre Plus is a three-room B&B run with an impeccable French flair for design by Mia (a cook) and Hendrik (a chocolatier, who makes chocolates in the basement). They say the "Plus" is for the personal touch they put into their B&B. This place, with a cozy lounge and an inviting garden, oozes class with a contemporary touch (rooms are €95 or €115; cottage out back is €165; air-con, free Internet access and cable Internet in rooms, Hoogpoort 31, tel. 09-225-3775, www.chambreplus.be, chambre plus@telenet.be).

$$$ Hotel Harmony is a pricey, classy, four-star, family-run boutique hotel with modern style and 25 rooms ideally located on the embankment in the town center (Db-€150-225 depending on size and amenities, Sb for €15 less, air-con, elevator, pay Internet access and Wi-Fi, very medieval breakfast room and music room/parlor, heated outdoor pool in summer, Kraanlei 37, tel. 09-324-2680, fax 09-324-2688, www.hotel-harmony.be, info@hotel-harmony.be).

$$ B&B King, hiding in a nondescript residential area a 10-minute walk from the main tourist zone, is a find. Charmingly run by Sarah and Dominiek, this mod B&B has two rooms and artistic flair, with modern art exhibited in the halls (Sb-€75, Db-€80, free Wi-Fi, Brouwersstraat 22, mobile 0489-572-909, www.bbking.be, info@bbking.be). From Drabstraat/Poelstraat, swing right onto the big street, then turn immediately right again on Ramen, then left on Brouwersstraat; it's the last house on the right.

$$ Erasmus Hotel, well-run by Peter, has 12 well-maintained rooms around a creaky wooden staircase in a classic 400-year-old building. It's on a boring street, just a short walk from the embank-

Sleep Code

(€1 = about $1.40, country code: 32)
S = Single, **D** = Double/Twin, **T** = Triple, **Q** = Quad, **b** = bathroom, **s** = shower only. Everyone speaks English. Unless otherwise noted, breakfast is included and credit cards are accepted.

To help you easily sort through these listings, I've divided the rooms into three categories, based on the price for a standard double room with bath:

$$$ Higher Priced—Most rooms €100 or more.
$$ Moderately Priced—Most rooms between €50-100.
$ Lower Priced—Most rooms €50 or less.

Prices can change without notice; verify the hotel's current rates online or by email. For other updates, see www.ricksteves.com/update.

ment (Sb-€79, Db-€99, large Db-€120, prices can flex depending on demand, no elevator, pay Wi-Fi, Poel 25, tel. 09-224-2195, fax 09-233-4241, www.erasmushotel.be, info@erasmushotel.be)

$$ Ibis Gent Centrum St-Baafs Kathedraal is a good branch of the Europe-wide chain, offering affordable, predictable cookie-cutter comfort in 120 rooms right next door to the cathedral (Db-€79-109—generally €82 in summer, €99 in high season, and €109 for special events; breakfast-€14, elevator, free Internet access, pay Wi-Fi, Limburgstraat 2, tel. 09-233-0000, www.ibishotel.com, h1455-re@accor.com).

$$ _Other B&Bs:_ Other good rooms in the town center include **In's Inn** (1 room, in Patershol, Db-€85, Corduwaniersstraat 11, tel. 09-225-1705, mobile 0494-361-861, insinn@telenet.be), **Simon Says** (2 rooms over a colorful café at the far end of Patershol, Db-€95, Sluizeken 8, tel. 09-233-0343, www.simon-says.be, info@simon-says.be), and **Brooderie** (3 rustic, woody rooms sharing a single bathroom over a café along the embankment in the heart of town, D-€70-75, Jan Breydelstraat 8, tel. 09-225-0623, www.brooderie.be, brooderie@pandora.be).

$ De Draecke, Ghent's very institutional HI youth hostel, has 106 beds—including some private rooms—in a residential zone a short walk from the castle (all rooms have private bathrooms inside, €18 for a dorm bed, Sb-€32, Db-€45, €3 extra for nonmembers, about €2-3 extra for guests older than 26, includes breakfast and sheets, towel rental extra, pay Internet access and Wi-Fi, Sint-Widostraat 11, tel. 09-233-7050, www.vjh.be, gent@vjh.be).

Ghent Accommodations and

GHENT

Restaurants

1. Chambre Plus B&B
2. Hotel Harmony
3. B&B King
4. Erasmus Hotel
5. Ibis Gent Centrum St-Baafs Kathedraal
6. In's Inn
7. Simon Says Rooms
8. Brooderie Rooms
9. De Draecke Hostel
10. Pakhuis Restaurant
11. Belga Queen
12. Marco Polo Trattoria
13. Bij den Wijzen en den Zot Restaurant
14. Valentijn Restaurant
15. Avalon Restaurant
16. 't Stropke Brasserie
17. Souplounge
18. Tasty World
19. De Dulle Griet Bar
20. 't Dreupelhof Bar

T TRAM #1
B CANAL CRUISES
↙ VIEW

200 YARDS
200 METERS

DCH

Eating in Ghent

All of my listings are in the city center. Ghent prides itself on being a particularly vegetarian-friendly city. Especially on Thursdays, most restaurants offer a veggie option.

Pakhuis is a gorgeously restored, late 19th-century warehouse now filled with a classy, lively brasserie and bar. In this light, airy, two-story, glassed-in birdhouse of a restaurant, they serve up good traditional Belgian food with an emphasis on locally sourced and organic ingredients. It's tucked down a nondescript brick alley, but it's worth going a few steps out of your way for (€12 weekday two-course lunch menu is a great deal, otherwise €9-14 starters, €14-30 main dishes, €25-42 fixed-price meals, Mon-Sat 12:00-23:00, closed Sun, Schuurkenstraat 4, tel. 09-223-5555).

Belga Queen, an outpost of a similarly popular eatery in Brussels (see page 494), is the most enticing of the restaurants with seating sprawling along the embankment in the picturesque core of Ghent. The food is "Belgian-inspired international," and the interior is extremely trendy and minimalist/industrialist (with three floors of seating, plus a top-floor lounge). While pricey, the place is packed with locals and visitors (€16 lunches, €15-22 starters, €21-35 main dishes, €33-42 fixed-price dinners, daily 12:00-14:30 & 19:00-22:30, Graslei 10, tel. 09-280-0100).

Marco Polo Trattoria is a good choice for Italian-style "slow food" (specializing in fish) at reasonable prices. It fills one long, cozy, tight room with warm, mellow music and tables crowded by locals celebrating special occasions. Reservations are smart (€9-14 antipasti, €14-19 pastas, €10-15 pizzas, Tue-Sun 18:00-22:00, Fri also 12:00-15:00, closed Mon, Serpentstraat 11, tel. 09-225-0420).

In Patershol

For decades this former sailors' quarter was a derelict and dangerous no-man's land, where only fools and thieves dared to tread. But a generation ago, restaurateurs began to reclaim the area, and today it's one of Ghent's most inviting and happening neighborhoods for dining. Stroll the streets and simply drop in on any place that looks good. Continue north beyond the end of Oudburg to find Sleepstraat, which is lined with cheap Turkish eateries (locals recommend Gok Palace).

It's hard to go wrong in Patershol, but here are some particularly well-regarded favorites:

Bij den Wijzen en den Zot ("By the Wise One and the Crazy One") was the first restaurant that opened in Patershol, back when people figured you were either a genius or a madman to open up shop in such a sketchy area (traditional Belgian with some French, €11-15 starters, €20-30 main dishes, Tue-Sat 12:00-14:00 & 18:30-

22:00, closed Sun-Mon, Hertogstraat 42, tel. 09-223-4230).

Valentijn, in the heart of the district, has a romantic, dressy interior and a no-fuss menu of classics (€20-25 main dishes, €33 meals, Mon-Wed and Fri-Sat from 18:30, closed Thu, Sun open for lunch only, Rodekoningstraat 1, tel. 09-225-0429).

Avalon, across the street from the castle, offers tasty vegetarian fare (€11-13 main dishes, €16-19 specials, daily 11:30-14:30, lunch only, Geldmuntstraat 32, tel. 09-244-3724).

't Stropke ("The Noose"), down the street from Avalon, is a brasserie with bright, woody, rustic ambience and a treehouse floor plan. They serve Belgian and French food, with Ghent specialties, such as the creamy soup called *waterzooi* (€8 sandwiches served until 18:00, €10-14 starters, €16-20 main dishes, Fri-Wed 9:00-22:00, closed Thu, Kraanlei 1, tel. 09-329-8335).

Fast and Cheap

These centrally located options are suitable for a quick lunch.

Souplounge is basic, but cheap and good. They offer four daily soups, along with salads; a bowl of soup, two rolls, and a piece of fruit runs just €3.50. Eat in the mod interior, or at the outdoor tables overlooking one of Ghent's most scenic stretches of canal (also €5 salads, daily 10:00-19:00, Zuivelbrugstraat 6, tel. 09-223-6203).

Tasty World serves up decent €5 veggie burgers with various toppings, plus a wide range of fresh fruit juices and salads (Mon-Sat 11:00-20:00, closed Sun, Hoogpoort 1, tel. 09-225-7407).

Bar Scene

Two touristy bars in the center are worth considering if you want to sample a wide range of Belgian favorites: beer or gin.

De Dulle Griet, on Vrijdagmarkt, serves up 249 types of beer in a cozy, sprawling bar with beer glasses hanging from the ceiling. The local beer, Gruut, is made with no hops; instead, it's flavored with a medieval (pre-hops) mix of herbs that brewers call *gruit* (Tue-Sat 12:00-1:00 in the morning, Sun 12:00-19:00, Mon 16:30-1:00 in the morning, Vrijdagmarkt 50, tel. 09-244-2455).

't Dreupelhof is a cozy little bar along the river, helmed by chain-smoking Pol, who offers a lukewarm welcome and 100 different types of Dutch and Flemish gin, or *jenever* (€2-5 shots, daily from 16:00, or from 18:00 in July-Aug, open until late, Groentenmarkt 12, tel. 09-224-2120).

Ghent Connections

From Ghent by Train to: Brussels (3/hour, 35 minutes), **Bruges** (4/hour, 30 minutes), **Antwerp** (3/hour, 50-55 minutes), **Ypres/ Ieper** (hourly, 1.25 hours, transfer in Kortrijk), **Paris** (2/hour,

2-2.5 hours, change at Brussels Midi/Zuid/South to Thalys train), **Amsterdam** (hourly, 2.25 hours, transfer in Antwerp), **Delft** (2/hour, 2-2.5 hours, transfer in Antwerp and Rotterdam). In Belgium, dial 050-302-424 for train information—press 4 for English, www.b-rail.be.

HISTORY

Twenty Centuries in Six Pages

A.D. 1-1300—Romans and Invasions

When Rome falls (c. 400), the Low Countries shatter into a patch-work of local dukedoms that are ravaged by Viking raids. Out of this poor, agricultural, and feudal landscape emerge three self-governing urban centers—Amsterdam, Bruges, and Brussels—each in a prime location for trade. Amsterdam and Bruges sit where rivers flow into the North Sea, while Brussels hugs a main trading highway.

Sights

- Amsterdam's Dam Square
- Exhibits in Amsterdam Museum
- Haarlem's Grote Markt
- The Hague's Ridderzaal and Binnenhof
- Bruges' original fort and church ruins
- Bruges' Basilica of the Holy Blood (1150)
- Brussels' St. Michael's Cathedral, model in the City Museum, and Tour d'Angle (tower) from city wall
- Ghent's Castle of the Counts

1300-1500—Booming Trade Towns

Bruges, the midway port between North Sea and Mediterranean trade routes, becomes one of Europe's busiest and richest cities.

When Bruges' harbor silts up in the late 15th century, trade shifts to the bustling port city of Antwerp. Amsterdam augments its beer and herring trade with budding capitalism: banking, loans, and speculation in stock and futures. Brussels sells waffles and beer to passing travelers. Politically, the Low Countries are united through marriage with the cultured empire of the Dukes of Burgundy.

Sights

- Churches: Amsterdam's Old Church (Oude Kerk) and New Church (Nieuwe Kerk), Delft's New Church (Nieuwe Kerk), Haarlem's Grote Kerk, Antwerp's Cathedral of Our Lady, and Ghent's Cathedral of St. Bavo
- Amsterdam's Waag (in the Red Light District), the Mint Tower from the original city wall, and the wooden house at Begijnhof 34

- Bruges' bell tower, the Gothic Room in the City Hall, and the Church of Our Lady
- Flemish Primitive art (Van Eyck, Memling, Van der Weyden) in Bruges' Groeninge and Memling museums, and in Brussels' Royal Museums of Fine Arts of Belgium, as well as Van Eyck's *The Adoration of the Mystic Lamb* altarpiece in Ghent's cathedral
- Brussels' Grand Place, medieval street Rue des Bouchers (Restaurant Row), and Notre-Dame du Sablon Church
- Antwerp's riverfront and Old Town

1500s—Protestants vs. Catholics, Freedom-Fighters vs. Spanish Rulers

Protestantism spreads through the Low Countries, particularly in Holland (while Belgium remains more Catholic). Thanks to other

royal marriages, the Low Countries are ruled from afar by the very Catholic Habsburg family in Spain. In 1566, angry Protestants rise up against Spain and Catholicism, vandalizing Catholic churches ("iconoclasm") and deposing Spanish governors. King Philip II of Spain sends troops to restore order and brutally punish the rebel-heretics, beginning the Eighty Years' War, also known as the Dutch War of Independence (1568-1648).

Sights
- Amsterdam's whitewashed, simply decorated, post-iconoclasm churches
- Civic Guard portraits in Amsterdam Museum
- Mementos of the Siege of Haarlem in Haarlem's Grote Kerk
- Brussels' tapestry designs

1600s—Holland's Golden Age

Holland gains its independence from the Habsburgs (officially in 1648), while Belgium languishes under Spanish rule. Amsterdam invents the global economy, as its hardy sailors ply the open seas, trading in Indonesian spices and South American sugar. Establishing colonies all over the world, they also conceive the African slave trade. Their nautical and capitalist skills combine to make Amsterdam the world's wealthiest city.

Sights
- Amsterdam's Rijksmuseum and Haarlem's Frans Hals Museum—paintings by Rembrandt, Hals, Vermeer, and Steen
- Old townhouses and gables in Amsterdam's Jordaan neighborhood and Red Light District
- Amsterdam's Begijnhof, Royal Palace, Westerkerk, and Rembrandt's House
- Delftware porcelain
- The Hague's Mauritshuis Royal Picture Gallery—paintings by Vermeer, Rembrandt, and Rubens
- Edam's Grote Kerk
- Brussels' *Manneken-Pis*
- Lace (popularity peaks c. 1700)
- Antwerp's Rubens House, Rockox House, and Museum Plantin-Moretus

1700s—Elegant Decline

Holland and Belgium are both surpassed by the rise of superpowers France and England. Wars with those powers drain their economies and scuttle Holland's fleet. Still, they survive as bankers, small manufacturers, and craftsmen in luxury goods—but on a small scale fitting their geographical size. They hit rock-bottom in 1795, when French troops occupy the Low Countries (1795-1815), and Europe's powers subsequently saddle them with a monarchy.

HISTORY

Islam and the Netherlands Today

The hottest hot-button issue in the Netherlands today is the culture clash between secular, multicultural Netherlands and its recent Muslim immigrants. Many Muslims arrived in the last half of the 20th century after Indonesia (a Dutch colony) gained independence. Guest workers from Turkey and Morocco—drawn by economic incentives—swelled the ranks. Today, one in ten Amsterdammers is Muslim. The Muslim cultures have not meshed seamlessly with the Netherlands' Western, secular, and liberal culture.

The Dutch are still haunted by a shameful episode concerning Muslims during the Bosnian War. In 1995, Dutch soldiers were stationed in Bosnia, charged by the UN with keeping peace during that region's troubled civil war. In July, the Dutch-protected town of Srebrenica was overrun by Bosnian Serbs. The 400 Dutch troops were outnumbered, and the UN gave them no logistical support. While Dutch soldiers huddled helplessly in their compound, the Serbs rounded up 8,000 Muslim men and boys and massacred them. In hindsight, there was little the soldiers could have done to prevent the atrocity, but it remains disturbing to the Dutch psyche. Discussions of current events still tend to mention this episode.

In spring of 2002, a charismatic Dutch politician named Pim Fortuyn campaigned for Parliament on a strong anti-immigration platform. Like many Dutch, he was socially liberal (including being openly gay, pro-feminist, pro-drug, and pro-euthanasia) but was concerned that Islam posed a threat to Dutch tolerance. On May 6, Fortuyn was gunned down in a parking lot by a mentally troubled man who disagreed with his politics (though the assassin's full motives remain unclear). Dutch people were

Sights
- Amsterdam's Amstelkring Museum (hidden church), Willet-Holthuysen Museum (Herengracht Canal Mansion), and Jewish Historical Museum synagogue
- Brussels' Grand Place guildhalls
- Antwerp's Paleis op de Meir (Napoleon's palace)

1800s—Dutch Revival and Belgian Independence

Though slow to join the Industrial Revolution, Holland picks up speed by century's end. A canal to the North Sea rejuvenates Amsterdam's port, railroads lace cities together, and Amsterdam stunned by the violence, the kind of thing they thought happened only in America. Fortuyn's controversial legacy seems to be that his outspokenness broke taboos of political correctness and opened the floodgates of debate about these touchy issues.

On the morning of November 2, 2004, the great-great-nephew of Vincent van Gogh was bicycling past Amsterdam's Oosterpark on his way to work. Theo van Gogh was a well-known filmmaker who'd recently released a controversial film about women and Islam. A Muslim Dutch citizen of Moroccan descent shot Van Gogh, then stabbed a letter into his dead body threatening to harm the film's female screenwriter as well.

The screenwriter, Ayaan Hirsi Ali, has become a lightning rod for Western/Muslim controversy. Born a Muslim in Somalia, she emigrated to the Netherlands, where she became a member of Parliament and an outspoken critic of Islam and its treatment of women. (She also gained notoriety for gaining her citizenship under false pretenses.) Hirsi Ali, who is under a 24-hour security watch, currently lives in the US and is a fellow at the American Enterprise Institute in Washington, DC.

Lately, Dutch politician Geert Wilders has taken up the mantle of Fortuyn, advocating the banning of the Quran and the end to Muslim immigration (he's proposed that current immigrants be paid to leave). His party won 15 percent of the votes in the 2010 elections and is now the third largest in the Dutch parliament.

Whatever happened to peaceful, tolerant, quaint old Holland? That's what the Dutch want to know. The Muslim immigration issue has forced the Dutch to confront a difficult paradox—how to be tolerant of what they perceive to be an intolerant culture.

hosts a World Exhibition. Meanwhile, Belgium—having been placed under a Dutch king—revolts, gains its independence (1830), and picks its own king, a German this time (Leopold I). King Leopold II claims Africa's Congo as his own private colony (1885), exploiting both its natural resources (ivory, rubber) and its people to finance massive building projects in his capital, Brussels—earning him the nickname "The Builder King."

Sights
- Amsterdam's Central Station, Rijksmuseum, Stadsschouwburg theater, Concertgebouw music hall, and Magna Plaza
- Van Gogh paintings at the Van Gogh Museum

- Indonesian foods from the colonial era
- Brussels' Upper Town buildings and boulevards
- Brussels' Galeries Royales St. Hubert and BELvue Museum
- Ghent's Dutch Theater
- Chocolate

1900s-2000s—Invasions by Germans, Hippies, and Immigrants

The century starts off badly, as Belgium is a major battleground in World War I, particularly in Flanders. In the 1930s, the Netherlands gets significantly bigger when it dikes off huge areas of its inland sea to create more farmland. Holland, neutral in World War I, joins Belgium in suffering a brutal occupation by the Nazis during World War II (Rotterdam is utterly destroyed). After the war, Brussels becomes the center of the budding movement toward European economic unity. In Amsterdam, postwar prosperity and a tolerant atmosphere in the 1960s and 1970s make it a global magnet for hippies...and your co-authors. In the 1970s and 1980s, Amsterdam

ANNE FRANK
TAGEBUCH

and Brussels are flooded with immigrants from their former colonies, causing friction and bringing a degree of ethnic diversity to the population. Beginning in the 1990s, as Europe's nations unite to form the European Union, Brussels gradually becomes the de facto capital of this "United States of Europe." Facing an uncertain future today, the "Low Countries"—with much of their territory below sea level—keep a close watch on global warming with its associated bigger storms and rising seas.

Sights
- Amsterdam's Beurs, Tuschinski Theater, and National Monument on Dam Square
- Belgium's Flanders Fields
- Enkhuizen's Zuiderzee Museum
- Amsterdam's Anne Frank House and Dutch Resistance Museum
- Amsterdam's Heineken Brewery, rock-and-roll clubs Paradiso and Melkweg, and the new "Stopera" opera house
- Haarlem's Corrie ten Boom House
- Paintings by René Magritte in Bruges' Groeninge Museum and in Brussels' Magritte Museum
- Brussels' Atomium and European Parliament quarter
- Antwerp's Sint-Andries fashion district, ModeMuseum, "Little Island" area, and 't Zuid district
- Ghent's Design Museum

HISTORY

The Netherlands and Belgium— A Timeline

57 B.C. Julius Caesar invades the Low Countries, conquering local Batavian, Frisian, and Belgae tribes, beginning four centuries of Roman rule.

A.D. 406 Frankish tribes from Germany drive out the last Roman legions as Rome's Europe-wide empire collapses. Christian missionaries work to prevent the area from reverting to paganism.

c. 800 Charlemagne, born in Belgium, rules the Low Countries as part of a large northern European empire. After his death, his grandsons divide the kingdom and bicker among themselves.

c. 880-1000 Vikings rape and pillage during two centuries of raids in the Low Countries.

c. 900 The Low Countries are a patchwork of small dukedoms ruled by bishops and local counts (of Holland, Flanders, Brabant, and so on), who owe allegiance to greater kings in France, Germany, and England.

c. 1250 In Amsterdam, fishermen build a dike (dam) where the Amstel River flows into the North Sea, creating a prime trading port. Soon the town gains independence and trading privileges from the local count and bishop. Meanwhile, Bruges becomes a major weaver of textiles, and Brussels becomes a minor trading town along the Germany-Bruges highway.

c. 1300 Italian and Portuguese sailors forge a coast-hugging trade route from the Mediterranean to the North Sea, with Bruges as the final stop.

1302 In Bruges, Flemish rebels drive out French rulers at the Battle of the Golden Spurs.

1345 Amsterdam experiences the Miracle of the Host, when a flame-resistant communion wafer causes miracles and attracts pilgrims.

1384 The discovery of a process to cure herring with salt makes Amsterdam a major fish exporter (to augment its thriving beer trade).

1384 Mary of Flanders marries Duke Philip the Bold of Burgundy, turning Holland and Belgium into part of a Burgundian empire that eventually stretches from Amsterdam to Switzerland.

c. 1400 Bruges is Europe's greatest trade city, the middleman between North and South.

1432 Painter Jan Van Eyck completes *The Adoration of the Mystic Lamb* altarpiece (in Ghent's cathedral)—considered the first work of the Flemish Primitives, known for their painstakingly detailed style.

1433 Burgundy's empire peaks when Duke Philip the Good takes over the titles of the local counts. His cultured court makes the Low Countries a center of art, literature, ideas, and pageantry.

1482 Mary of Burgundy, the last heir to the Burgundian throne, falls from a horse and dies. Her possessions (including Holland and Belgium) pass to her Austrian Habsburg husband, Maximilian, and get swallowed up in his family's large Holy Roman Empire, ruled from Austria and later Spain.

1492 Columbus' voyage demonstrates the potential wealth of New World trade.

c. 1510 Bruges' harbor silts up, and business migrates to the port city of Antwerp, which becomes northern Europe's greatest trading city.

1517 The German Martin Luther's 95 theses inspire Protestantism, which becomes popular in the Low Countries (especially Holland). Later, refugees of religious persecution, including Calvinists and Anabaptists (such as the Amish and Mennonites), find a home in tolerant Amsterdam.

1519 King Charles V (1500-1558), the grandson of Mary of Burgundy and Maximilian, inherits all of his family's combined possessions. Charles rules Holland and Belgium, as well as Austria, Spain, Germany, Spain's New World colonies, and much more. A staunch Catholic, Charles battles rebellious Protestant princes.

1535 On Amsterdam's Dam Square, Anabaptist rebels are hanged, drawn, and quartered.

1540 Emperor Charles' son, Philip of Spain, invites the Inquisition to Spain.

1556 Philip II, based in Spain, succeeds his father as ruler of the Netherlands and intensifies the wars on Protestants (especially Calvinists).

1566 The "Dutch Revolt" begins when, in a wave of anti-Catholic and anti-Spanish fury, extreme Protestants storm Catholic churches, vandalizing religious objects and converting the churches to Protestant ("iconoclasm"). Philip II sends soldiers to the Low Countries to establish order and punish rebels and heretics.

1568 Holland's Protestant counts rally around William "The Silent" of Orange, demanding freedom from Spanish Habsburg rule (the Beggars' Revolt). This begins 80 years of on-again-off-again war with Spain, called...the Eighty Years' War.

1572-1573 The Spanish conquer Haarlem after a long siege, but Haarlem's brave stand inspires other towns to carry on the fight.

1576 In the "Spanish Fury," Antwerp is sacked by Spanish troops impatient at not being paid by King Philip II. This devastates the city, causes irreparable damage to its trade ties, and turns public opinion in the Low Countries against the Habsburgs. Antwerp becomes the hot spot of the Dutch revolt.

1578 Amsterdam switches sides (the Alteration), joining the Protestant independence movement. Extreme Calvinists control the city for several decades, officially outlawing Catholic services. Within a few years, Spanish troops are driven south out of Holland, and future battles take place mostly on Belgian soil.

1580 Holland and Belgium go separate ways in the war. Holland's towns and nobles form a Protestant military alliance (the United Provinces) against Catholic Spain, while Belgium remains Catholic, with Brussels as the capital of Spanish Habsburg rule.

1585 After a brutal siege, Protestant-holdout Antwerp falls to Spanish troops. In the chaos, half the population flees, leaving Antwerp a largely forgotten Catholic backwater. Many Antwerp businessmen restart their businesses in industrious Amsterdam, which gradually steps up to fill the vacuum of trade.

1588 Elizabeth I of England defeats the Spanish Armada (navy), breaking Spain's monopoly on overseas trade.

1602 The Dutch East India Company (VOC), a government-subsidized trading company, is formed, soon followed by the West India Company (1622). Together, they make Amsterdam (pop. 100,000) the center of a global trading empire, spawning the Dutch Golden Age (c. 1600-1650).

1608 Peter Paul Rubens returns to Antwerp after eight years studying painting in Italy. His brush becomes the ambassador of the Counter-Reformation aesthetic, with bombastic biblical scenes extolling the glory of God (and his Church on earth).

1609 Henry Hudson's *Half Moon*, sailing for the Dutch East India Company, departs Amsterdam in search of a western passage to the Orient. Instead, Hudson finds the island of Manhattan, which soon becomes New Amsterdam (New York, 1625).

1616 Frans Hals paints the *St. George Civic Guards* (Frans Hals Museum, Haarlem).

1620 Pilgrims from England stop in Holland on their way to America.

1631 Rembrandt moves to Amsterdam, a wealthy city of 120,000 people, including René Descartes, plus many different religious sects and a thriving Jewish Quarter.

1637 After several years of insanely lucrative trade in tulip bulbs ("tulip mania"), the market crashes.

1648 The Treaty of Munster (and the Treaty of Westphalia) officially ends the Eighty Years' War with Spain. The United Provinces (today's Netherlands) are now an independent nation.

1652-1654 Holland battles England over control of the seas. This is the first of three wars with England (also in 1665 and 1672) that sap Holland's wealth.

1672-1678 Louis XIV of France invades Holland and gets to within 15 miles of Amsterdam, but is finally stopped when the citizens open the Amstel locks and flood the city. After another draining war with France (1701-1713), England and France overtake Holland in overseas trade.

1689 Holland's William of Orange is invited by England's Parliament to replace the despot they'd deposed. He, ruling with wife Mary, becomes King William III of England.

1695 Louis XIV of France bombs and incinerates Brussels during the Nine Years' War, punishing William III for allying against him.

1776 The American Revolution inspires European democrats and worries nobles.

1787 Holland's budding democratic movement, the Patriots, is suppressed and exiled when Prussian troops invade Holland.

1789 The French Revolution begins.

1795 France, battling Europe's monarchs to keep their Revolution alive, invades and occupies Holland (establishing the "Batavian Republic," 1795-1806) and Belgium.

1806 Napoleon Bonaparte, who turned France's Revolution into a dictatorship, proclaims his brother, Louis Napoleon, to be King of Holland (1806-1810).

1815 After Napoleon's defeat at Waterloo (near Brussels), Europe's nobles decide that the Low Countries should be a monarchy, ruled jointly by a Dutch prince, who becomes King William I. (Today's Queen Beatrix is descended from him.)

1830 Belgium rebels against the Dutch-born king, becoming an independent constitutional monarchy under the German-born Leopold I, King of the Belgians. French-speaking aristocrats control the government, while the lower class consists mainly of Dutch-speaking Flemish peasants.

1860 The novel *Max Havelaar,* by the Dutch writer Multatuli, exposes the dark side of Holland's repressive colonial rule in Indonesia.

1876 The North Sea Canal opens after 52 years of building, revitalizing Amsterdam's port. In the next decade, the city builds the Central Station, Rijksmuseum, and Concertgebouw, and hosts a World Exhibition (1883) that attracts three million visitors.

1885 King Leopold II of Belgium acquires Africa's Congo region as his personal realm, robbing its resources to rebuild Brussels with broad boulevards and big marble buildings (Neoclassical style).

1908 After three decades of exploiting the Congo for his personal financial gain, growing public outcry convinces King Leopold II to turn it over to the government of Belgium.

1914 In World War I, Holland remains neutral, while Belgium becomes a horrific battleground where Germany dukes it out with England and France; some of the worst fighting takes place at Flanders Fields near Ypres (Ieper).

1929 Belgian cartoonist Hergé publishes the first of nearly 50 years' worth of comics about an adventurous young reporter named Tintin, who will become beloved by all Europeans.

1932 The Dutch Zuiderzee dike is completed, turning the former arm of the North Sea into a freshwater lake (the IJsselmeer) and creating many square miles of reclaimed land.

1940-1945 Nazi Germany bombs Holland's Rotterdam and easily occupies the Netherlands and Belgium (1940). Belgium's king officially surrenders, and Holland's Queen Wilhelmina (1880-1962) flees to England. In Amsterdam, Anne Frank and her Jewish family go into hiding in an attempt to avoid arrest by the Nazis (1942-1944). Late in the war, Belgium is the site of Germany's last-gasp offensive, the Battle of the Bulge—Hitler's attempt to divide the Allied armies and capture Antwerp (1944-1945).

1945 Holland and Belgium are liberated by Allied troops.

1949 Indonesia gains its independence from Holland.

1953 Major floods in Holland kill almost 2,000 people, prompting more dams and storm barriers (the Delta Project, 1958-1997).

1957 Belgium and the Netherlands join the EEC (Common Market)—the forerunner of today's European Union—with headquarters in Brussels.

1960 The BeNeLux economic union between Belgium, the Netherlands, and Luxembourg—first proposed in 1944—becomes fully operational. After years of protests in the Belgian Congo, Belgium grants independence to the African nation.

1967 Amsterdam is Europe's center for hippies and the youth movement.

1970 Belgium passes reforms designed to ease long-standing tensions between its Flemish and French factions; the nation is divided into three semi-autonomous regions: Flanders (Flemish), Wallonia (French), and Brussels (bicultural).

1975 Suriname (Dutch Guyana) gains its independence from Holland, and many emigrants flock to Holland.

1980 Queen Beatrix (b. 1938) becomes ruler of Holland.

1992 Belgium and the Netherlands sign the Treaty of Maastricht, which creates the European Union (EU).

1993 King Albert II (b. 1934) becomes King of the Belgians.

1995 Floods in the Netherlands cause a billion dollars in damage.

2005 Dutch voters reject the adoption of a European Constitution in the first national referendum in more than 200 years.

2010 In the Belgian general election, the nationalistic Nieuw-Vlaamse Alliantie (N-VA) party—which promotes Flemish independence from Belgium—wins more votes than any other party.

Today You arrive in Amsterdam, Bruges, and Brussels and make your own history.

APPENDIX

Contents

Tourist Information

National tourist offices **in the US** can be a wealth of information. Before your trip, request or download any specific information you may want (such as city maps and schedules of upcoming festivals).

For the Netherlands, call 212/370-7360, visit www.holland .com, or email information@holland.com. They no longer distribute printed material; all information is now available only on the Internet. Another useful website is www.iamsterdam.com (Amsterdam Tourism Board).

For Belgium, call 212/758-8130 or go to www.visitbelgium .com. Over the phone or filling out the online form, you can request hotel and city guides; brochures for ABC lovers—antiques, beer, and chocolates; a map of Brussels; information on WWI and WWII battlefields; and a list of Jewish sights.

In the **Netherlands** or **Belgium,** the tourist information office (abbreviated **TI** in this book) is generally your best first stop in any new town (although Amsterdam's TIs are so crowded that you're better off visiting the airport TI or the TI in Haarlem). Try to arrive, or at least telephone, before it closes. Have a list of questions ready, and pick up maps, brochures, and walking-tour information.

Most TIs offer English-speaking staff; a free map of the town; biking maps; listings of events, activities, and accommodations; bus and train schedules; and Internet access. Note that in the Netherlands, TIs tend to be privately run, which can color their advice; however, in Belgium, they are state-run, so they're not tainted by a drive for profits. Steer clear of the room-finding services at for-profit TIs, especially in the Netherlands (bloated prices, booking fees, and they take a sizeable cut from your host). In Belgium (especially Brussels), however, TI room-finding services can have a line on the best deals in town.

Communicating

Telephones
Smart travelers use the telephone to reserve or reconfirm rooms, get tourist information, reserve restaurants, confirm tour times, or phone home. This section covers dialing instructions, phone cards, and types of phones (for more in-depth information, see www .ricksteves.com/phoning).

How to Dial
Calling from the US to Europe, or vice versa, is simple—once you break the code. The European calling chart in this chapter will walk you through it.

Dialing Domestically Within the Low Countries
The Netherlands, like much of the US, uses an area-code dialing system. If you're dialing within an area code, you just dial the local number to be connected; but if you're calling outside your area code, you have to dial both the area code (which starts with a 0) and the local number. For example, the number of a recommended hotel in Haarlem is 023/532-4530. To call it within Haarlem, dial 532-4530. To call it from Amsterdam, dial 023/532-4530.

Belgium uses a direct-dial system (no area codes). To call anywhere within Belgium, you always dial a nine-digit number.

Dialing Internationally to or from the Low Countries
To make an international call, follow these steps:
• Dial the international access code (00 if you're calling from Europe, 011 from the US or Canada).

What Language Barrier?

People speak Dutch in Amsterdam, Flemish (nearly identical to Dutch) in Bruges, and French in Brussels. But you'll find almost no language barrier in the Netherlands, as all well-educated folks, nearly all young people, and almost everyone in the tourist trade speak English. (When asked if they speak English, the Dutch reply, *"Natuurlijk"*—"naturally.") In tourist-friendly Bruges, you also won't encounter any difficulties with English. You will meet French-only speakers in Brussels, but it's generally a minor language barrier. Regardless, it's polite to use some Dutch, Flemish, or French pleasantries (see pages 599, 601, and 603).

• Dial the country code of the country you're calling (31 for the Netherlands, 32 for Belgium, or 1 for the US or Canada).

• Dial the area code (without its initial 0) and the local number.

Calling from the US to the Low Countries: To call a Haarlem hotel from the US, dial 011 (the US international access code), 31 (the Netherlands' country code), 23 (Haarlem's area code without the initial 0), and then the hotel's phone number (e.g., 532-4530). To call a hotel in Bruges from the US, dial 011 (the US international access code), 32 (Belgium's country code), and then the hotel's number without its initial zero (e.g., 50-444-444).

Calling from any European Country to the US: To call my office in Edmonds, Washington, from the Netherlands or from Belgium, I dial 00 (Europe's international access code), 1 (the US country code), 425 (Edmonds' area code), and 771-8303.

Note: You might see a + in front of a European number. When dialing the number, replace the + with the international access code of the country you're calling from (00 from Europe, 011 from the US or Canada).

Public Phones and Hotel-Room Phones

To make calls from public phones in the Low Countries, you'll need a prepaid phone card. There are two different kinds of phone cards: insertable and international. If you have a still-lively card at the end of your trip, give it to another traveler to use.

Insertable Phone Cards: These cards are a convenient way to make a call from public pay phones. Buy these cards at TIs, newsstands, post offices, and train stations. They are sold in several denominations starting at about €5. To use the card, physically insert it into a slot in the pay phone. While you can use these cards to call anywhere in the world, they're only a good deal for making quick local calls from a phone booth. Each European country has

European Calling Chart

Just smile and dial, using this key:
AC = Area Code, LN = Local Number.

European Country	Calling long distance within ...	Calling from the US or Canada to ...	Calling from a European country to ...
Austria	AC + LN	011 + 43 + AC (without the initial zero) + LN	00 + 43 + AC (without the initial zero) + LN
Belgium	LN	011 + 32 + LN (without initial zero)	00 + 32 + LN (without initial zero)
Bosnia-Herzegovina	AC + LN	011 + 387 + AC (without initial zero) + LN	00 + 387 + AC (without initial zero) + LN
Britain	AC + LN	011 + 44 + AC (without initial zero) + LN	00 + 44 + AC (without initial zero) + LN
Croatia	AC + LN	011 + 385 + AC (without initial zero) + LN	00 + 385 + AC (without initial zero) + LN
Czech Republic	LN	011 + 420 + LN	00 + 420 + LN
Denmark	LN	011 + 45 + LN	00 + 45 + LN
Estonia	LN	011 + 372 + LN	00 + 372 + LN
Finland	AC + LN	011 + 358 + AC (without initial zero) + LN	999 (or other 900 number) + 358 + AC (without initial zero) + LN
France	LN	011 + 33 + LN (without initial zero)	00 + 33 + LN (without initial zero)
Germany	AC + LN	011 + 49 + AC (without initial zero) + LN	00 + 49 + AC (without initial zero) + LN
Gibraltar	LN	011 + 350 + LN	00 + 350 + LN
Greece	LN	011 + 30 + LN	00 + 30 + LN
Hungary	06 + AC + LN	011 + 36 + AC + LN	00 + 36 + AC + LN
Ireland	AC + LN	011 + 353 + AC (without initial zero) + LN	00 + 353 + AC (without initial zero) + LN

European Country	Calling long distance within ...	Calling from the US or Canada to ...	Calling from a European country to ...
Italy	LN	011 + 39 + LN	00 + 39 + LN
Montenegro	AC + LN	011 + 382 + AC (without initial zero) + LN	00 + 382 + AC (without initial zero) + LN
Morocco	LN	011 + 212 + LN (without initial zero)	00 + 212 + LN (without initial zero)
Netherlands	AC + LN	011 + 31 + AC (without initial zero) + LN	00 + 31 + AC (without initial zero) + LN
Norway	LN	011 + 47 + LN	00 + 47 + LN
Poland	LN	011 + 48 + LN (without initial zero)	00 + 48 + LN (without initial zero)
Portugal	LN	011 + 351 + LN	00 + 351 + LN
Slovakia	AC + LN	011 + 421 + AC (without initial zero) + LN	00 + 421 + AC (without initial zero) + LN
Slovenia	AC + LN	011 + 386 + AC (without initial zero) + LN	00 + 386 + AC (without initial zero) + LN
Spain	LN	011 + 34 + LN	00 + 34 + LN
Sweden	AC + LN	011 + 46 + AC (without initial zero) + LN	00 + 46 + AC (without initial zero) + LN
Switzerland	LN	011 + 41 + LN (without initial zero)	00 + 41 + LN (without initial zero)
Turkey	AC (if there's no initial zero, add one) + LN	011 + 90 + AC (without initial zero) + LN	00 + 90 + AC (without initial zero) + LN

- The instructions above apply whether you're calling a land line or mobile phone.
- The international access codes (the first numbers you dial when making an international call) are 011 if you're calling from the US or Canada, or 00 if you're calling from virtually anywhere in Europe (except Finland, where it's 999 or another 900 number, depending on the phone service you're using).
- To call the US or Canada from Europe, dial 00, then 1 (the country code for the US and Canada), then the area code and number. In short, 00 + 1 + AC + LN = Hi, Mom!

its own insertable phone card—so your Dutch card won't work in a Belgian phone. Be aware that with the prevalence of mobile phones, public phones are becoming harder to find.

International Phone Cards: These are the cheapest way to make international calls from the Netherlands or Belgium (generally around 25-50 cents per minute; they also work for local calls). You can use international phone cards from most phones, including the phone in your hotel room (but ask first at the front desk if there are any fees for using the phone to make toll-free calls). Some international phone cards may not work if you're calling from a pay phone.

These cards are sold at small newsstand kiosks, electronics stores, and hole-in-the-wall Internet shops. Ask the clerk which brands have the best rates for calls to America. Before buying a card, make sure the access number you'll dial is toll-free, not a local number (or else you'll be paying for a local call *and* deducting time from your calling card). Because cards are occasionally duds, avoid the more expensive denominations. Some international phone cards work in multiple countries—if traveling to both the Netherlands and Belgium, try to buy a card that will work in both places.

To use a card, scratch off the back to reveal your PIN code, dial the access number, and follow the prompts. If the prompts are in Dutch or French, wait to see if the announcement also follows in English. If not, experiment: Dial your code, followed by the pound sign (#), then the number, then the pound sign again, and so on, until it works.

Remember that you don't need the actual card to use a card account. You can write down the access number and code in your notebook and share it with friends.

Hotel-Room Phones: Calling from the phone in your room can be cheap for local calls (ask for rates at the front desk first), but is often a rip-off for long-distance calls, unless you use an international phone card. Incoming calls are free, making this an inexpensive way for friends and family to stay in touch (provided they have a good long-distance plan for calls to Europe—and a list of your hotels' phone numbers).

US Calling Cards: These cards, such as the ones offered by AT&T, Verizon, or Sprint, are the worst option. You'll nearly always save a lot of money by using a locally purchased phone card instead.

Mobile Phones

Many travelers enjoy the convenience of using a mobile phone to make calls.

Using Your Mobile Phone: Your US mobile phone works in Europe if it's GSM-enabled, tri-band or quad-band, and on a calling plan that includes international calls. Phones from T-Mobile and AT&T, which use the same GSM technology that Europe does, are more likely to work overseas than Verizon or Sprint phones (if you're not sure, ask your service provider). Most US providers charge $1.29 per minute while roaming internationally to make or receive calls, and 20-50 cents to send or receive text messages. Contact your provider before you leave to be sure international roaming is allowed and to ask them about rates.

You'll pay cheaper rates if your phone is electronically "unlocked" (ask your provider about this); then, in Europe, you can simply buy a tiny **SIM card,** which gives you a European phone number. SIM cards start at around €15 and are available at mobile-phone stores, most newsstand kiosks, and most GWK Travelex counters. On my last trip, I spent €25 for a Dutch SIM card and about 90 minutes of call time, which was plenty for a two-week trip.

When you buy a SIM card, you may need to show ID, such as your passport. Insert the SIM card in your phone (sometimes in a slot behind the battery), and it'll work like a European mobile phone. When buying a SIM card and time, always ask about fees for domestic and international calls, roaming charges, and how to check your credit balance and buy more time.

Many **smartphones,** such as the iPhone, BlackBerry, or Android-based phones, work in Europe—but beware of sky-high fees, especially for data downloading (checking email, browsing the Internet, watching streaming videos, and so on). Ask your provider in advance how to avoid unwittingly roaming your way to a huge bill. Some applications allow for cheap or free smartphone calls over a Wi-Fi connection (see "Calling over the Internet," below).

Using a European Mobile Phone: In the Netherlands and Belgium, mobile phones are affordable and come without contracts. These phones are loaded with prepaid calling time that you can recharge. As long as you're not roaming outside the phone's home country, incoming calls are free. If you're traveling to multiple countries within Europe, make sure the phone is "unlocked," so that you can swap out its SIM card for a new one in other countries.

Calling over the Internet

Some things that seem too good to be true...actually are true. If you're traveling with a laptop, you can make calls using VoIP (Voice over Internet Protocol). With VoIP, two computers act as the phones, and the Internet-based calls are free (or you can pay a few cents to call from your computer to a telephone). If both computers have webcams, you can even see each other while you chat. The major providers are Skype (www.skype.com), followed by Google Talk (www.google.com/talk). It's not essential to have a laptop to use VoIP; some smartphones allow you to make VoIP calls over a Wi-Fi connection.

Useful Phone Numbers
Emergency Needs
Police, Ambulance, or Fire (Netherlands): 112
Police (Belgium): 101 or 112
Ambulance or Fire (Belgium): 100 or 112

Embassies/Consulates in the Netherlands
US Embassies and Consulates: Amsterdam—tel. 020/575-5309 during office hours, otherwise in case of emergency call after-duty officer at tel. 070/310-2209 (Museumplein 19, http://amsterdam .usconsulate.gov). Consulate open for general services Mon-Fri 8:30-11:30, afternoons for immigrant visas only, closed Sat-Sun.
The Hague—tel. 070/310-2209, visits by appointment only (Lange Voorhout 102, http://netherlands.usembassy.gov).
Canadian Embassy: The Hague—tel. 070/311-1600 (Sophialaan 7, Mon-Thu 8:30-12:30 & 13:15-17:30, Fri 8:30-13:00, closed Sat-Sun; consular services Mon-Thu 10:00-12:30 & 14:00-16:30, Fri 9:30-12:30, closed Sat-Sun; www.canada.nl).

Embassies/Consulates in Belgium
US Embassies and Consulates: Brussels—tel. 02-508-2111 (Boulevard du Régent 27, Mon-Fri 9:00-18:00, closed Sat-Sun, for after-hours emergencies, call and ask to be connected to the duty officer, http://belgium.usembassy.gov). Consulate is next door to embassy (Boulevard du Régent 25, passport services Mon-Thu 13:30-15:30, Fri 9:00-11:00, closed Sat-Sun).
Canadian Embassy: Brussels—tel. 02-741-0611 (Avenue de Tervueren 2, Mon-Fri 9:00-12:30 & 13:30-17:00, closed Sat-Sun; consulate open Mon-Fri 9:00-12:00, afternoon by appointment only, www.ambassade-canada.be).

Travel Advisories
US Department of State: US tel. 202/647-5225 (www.travel.state .gov)
Canadian Department of Foreign Affairs: Canadian tel. 800-267-6788 (www.dfait-maeci.gc.ca)
US Centers for Disease Control and Prevention: US tel. 800-CDC-INFO (800-232-4636, www.cdc.gov/travel)

Internet Access and Wi-Fi
It's useful to get online periodically while you travel—to confirm trip plans, check train or bus schedules, get weather forecasts,

catch up on email, blog or post photos from your trip, or call folks back home (explained earlier, under "Calling over the Internet").

Some hotels offer a dedicated computer in the lobby with Internet access for guests. If you ask politely, smaller places may sometimes let you sit at their desk for a few minutes just to check your email.

If you have a laptop, netbook, or other Wi-Fi-enabled device, it's easy to get online at hotels that have Wi-Fi (wireless Internet access, sometimes called "WLAN" in Europe). When you check in, ask them for the network name and password. Other hotels have a port in your room for connecting your laptop with a cable (if you don't carry a cable, ask to borrow one from the front desk). Some hotels offer Wi-Fi or cable Internet access for free; others charge by the minute or hour. A cellular modem—which lets your laptop access the Internet over a mobile phone network—provides more extensive coverage, but is much more expensive than Wi-Fi.

If your hotel doesn't have access, your hotelier can direct you to the nearest place to get online. You'll find plenty of cafés that offer Wi-Fi to customers.

Mail

Recently, the Netherlands began closing down its post offices in all but the biggest cities. You can buy stamps at any newsstand with an orange *TNT* logo. To send a package in a smaller town, ask your hotelier for assistance. You can arrange for mail delivery to your hotel (allow 10 days for a letter to arrive), but phoning and emailing are so easy that I've dispensed with mail stops altogether.

Transportation

By Car or Train?

Because of the short distances and excellent public transportation systems in the Low Countries, and the fact that this book covers three big cities, I recommend connecting Amsterdam, Bruges, and Brussels by train, not by car. You absolutely do not want or need a car in any of these cities.

Hourly trains connect each of these towns faster and easier than you could by driving. Just buy tickets as you go. You don't need advance reservations to ride a train between these cities, unless you take the pricey Amsterdam-Brussels Thalys train (it's avoidable; plenty of regular trains make this run).

Trains

The easiest way to reach nearly any Dutch or Belgian destination is by train. Connections are fast and frequent. InterCity (IC) and Fyra trains are speedy for connecting big cities, and the high-speed

Thalys is the fastest (the speed comes at a price; see "Reservations for Railpass Holders," later). InterRegio (IR) and *sneltreins* connect smaller towns; *stoptreins* are pokey milk-run trains that stop at every station; and the Netherlands' misnamed "Sprinter" trains are actually slow *stoptreins*. Throughout the Netherlands and Belgium, smoking is prohibited in trains and train stations.

Schedules

To get train schedules in advance, use the German Rail (Deutsche Bahn) website, which has comprehensive schedules for almost anywhere in Europe (http://bahn.hafas.de/bin/query.exe/en). Or try the Dutch Rail site (www.ns.nl for domestic trains, www.ns internationaal.nl for trains to Belgium and beyond) and the Belgian rail site (www.b-rail.be).

In the Netherlands dial 0900-9292 for information on local trains (€0.70/minute) or 0900-9296 for international trains (€0.35/minute, Mon-Fri 8:00-21:00, Sat-Sun 10:00-18:00, wait through recording and hold...hold...hold...). These numbers are frustrating phone trees in Dutch and—if you wait—maybe in English. In Belgium, dial 050/302-424 for any train information (press 4 for English).

To find schedules at train stations, check the yellow schedule posters, or look for TV screens listing upcoming departures. If you can't find your train, or are unclear on departure details, visit an information booth or enlist the help of any official-looking employee (many wear portable computers with timetables).

Buying Tickets in the Netherlands

Although getting train tickets in Belgium is straightforward, Dutch stations are often understaffed (meaning ticket-window lines are long), or not staffed at all (where ticket machines are your only option).

Your best option for avoiding the stress of hitting a long ticket-buying line (or a frantic search for a machine that takes cash) is to buy tickets a day or two in advance. You can buy tickets from a station ticket window (€0.50 extra, more for international trips, worth it if the lines are short, long hours, credit cards accepted), or at a yellow-and-blue machine. Nearly all machines have instructions in English (press the British flag). And though the machines levy no additional fees, most don't take US credit or debit cards (despite having a "pay with debit card" option); this means you'll probably need to pay with cash—which not every machine accepts—or buy a special "chip-and-PIN card" from a GWK Travelex counter that will work in the machines (see page 11). Most machines have icons at the top next to the word "Tickets," showing what kind of

Train Lines in the Low Countries

✈ AIRPORT

50 MILES
100 KM

See Day Trips Detail Map

NORTH SEA

GRONINGEN
LEEUW.
MEPPEL

NETHERLANDS

HAARLEM
THE HAGUE
DELFT
ROTTERDAM

AMSTERDAM

DEVENTER
HENGELO

UTRECHT
GOUDA
ARNHEM
GERMANY

RHINE

Roos.
EINDHOVEN

BRUGES
OSTENDE
BUS

FLANDERS
ANTWERP
MAAS-TRICHT
KÖLN

YPRES
GHENT
Kortrijk
BRUSSELS

EUROSTAR
TO LONDON
LILLE

BELGIUM
AACHEN
LIEGE
RHINE

MONS
NAMUR
WALLONIE
KOBLENZ

N

BASTOGNE

LUX.
TRIER

TO PARIS
FRANCE
DCH
LUXEMBOURG CITY

payment you can use (some don't take cash at all, some take only euro coins, others take only euro bills). Forms of payment are also shown on the upper-right corner of the screen (items with an "X" through them are not accepted).

Types of Tickets: For one-way trips, same-day and "open date" tickets cost the same. Same-day tickets come prestamped with today's date, but to use an open-date ticket you have to validate it before boarding the train in one of the yellow stamping posts in the station (ka-chunk!). Round-trip tickets are always a bit cheaper than two one-way tickets, but are only issued for same-day travel (it's a small country). If you're going somewhere and back on different days, you'll need two one-way tickets. The exception: weekend return tickets, which give you the round-trip discount, but can be used on different days (valid from 19:00 Fri to 4:00 in

Railpasses

Prices listed are for 2012 and are subject to change. For the latest prices, details, and train schedules (and easy online ordering), see my comprehensive *Guide to Eurail Passes* at www.ricksteves.com/rail.

Benelux = Belgium, Netherlands and Luxembourg. "Saver" prices are per person for two or more people traveling together. "Youth" means under age 26. The fare for children 4–11 is half the adult individual fare or Saver fare. Kids under age 4 travel free.

BENELUX PASS

	Indiv. 1st Cl.	Indiv. 2nd Cl.	Youth 2nd Cl.
5 days in 1 month	$424	$273	$180
Saverpass, 5 days in 1 month	$362	$232	N/A

Valid on Thalys trains within Benelux (with paid seat reservation), but not to/from Paris.

BENELUX–FRANCE PASS

	Individual 1st Class	Individual 2nd Class	Saver 1st Class	Saver 2nd Class	Youth 2nd Class
5 days in 2 months	$477	$411	$398	$351	$304
6 days in 2 months	$522	$457	$439	$398	$338
8 days in 2 months	$604	$538	$517	$463	$400
10 days in 2 months	$682	$615	$582	$525	$460

BENELUX–GERMANY PASS

	Individual 1st Class	Individual 2nd Class	Saver 1st Class	Saver 2nd Class	Youth 2nd Class
5 days in 2 months	$457	$344	$344	$279	$279
6 days in 2 months	$506	$382	$382	$305	$305
8 days in 2 months	$597	$449	$449	$459	$459
10 days in 2 months	$695	$522	$522	$418	$418

SELECTPASS

This pass covers travel in three adjacent countries. Please visit **www.ricksteves.com/rail** for four- and five-country options.

	Individual 1st Class	Saver 1st Class	Youth 2nd Class
5 days in 2 months	$486	$413	$317
6 days in 2 months	$536	$456	$350
8 days in 2 months	$633	$539	$413
10 days in 2 months	$734	$624	$478

the morning on Mon, each leg of the trip has to be taken within one day; if Fri or Mon is a holiday, validity is extended to 4:00 in the morning on Tue).

Ticket Deals

If you're not traveling with a railpass, consider the region's money-saving deals.

For €55 and a photo, the Netherlands Off-Peak Discount Card (sold at stations) saves 40 percent on most tickets and can be shared by up to four people (valid all day on weekends, and weekdays only after 9:00; works all day all week in July-Aug). Also, keep in mind that same-day round-trip tickets will save you money over two one-way tickets (explained earlier).

In Belgium, youths under age 26 can get a Go Pass (€50 for 10 rides anywhere in Belgium, €6.50 for a single ride). A similar deal is available for anyone over 26 for €74. Seniors (age 65-plus) can get a same-day round-trip ticket to anywhere in Belgium for €5.20 (weekdays: after 9:00; weekends: no restrictions mid-Sept-April, not valid July-Aug). There are also weekend discounts for round-trips (50 percent off, valid Fri after 19:00). For more information, visit www.b-rail.be.

Bikes on Trains

If you're traveling with a bike, you'll pay extra to bring it on the train. In the Netherlands, bikes are only allowed during off-peak hours (all day on weekends, and weekdays only after 9:00) and require a "Bicycle Day Travel Card" (€6, no matter the destination). In Belgium, bikes cost €5 extra for a one-way trip, and €8 round-trip.

Railpasses

Most visits to the Netherlands and Belgium don't cover enough miles to justify a railpass, but if you're traveling beyond these countries, a railpass could save you money. For instance, good railpass options exist for those traveling between BeNeLux (Belgium, the Netherlands, and Luxembourg) and either France or Germany; Eurail Select Passes (or a Global Pass) make sense if you're touring the Netherlands and Belgium as part of a larger trip (see sidebar).

Reservations for Railpass Holders: Regional and InterCity trains do not require reservations, allowing you plenty of flexibility as you explore BeNeLux. Between Amsterdam-Brussels or Brussels-Köln, fast Thalys trains cost more (for point-to-point tickets) or require expensive reservations with a railpass, so I'd choose regular, nonreserved trains on those routes. The only direct service from Amsterdam, Brussels, or Köln to Paris is by Thalys, with reservations costing €25-60 in addition to a pass that covers BeNeLux and France. To avoid Thalys fees when heading from Bruges or Brussels to Paris, you can take a little more time and connect in Lille to a TGV with cheaper (but limited) €3-5 reservations. Note that you can buy a Thalys ticket if you don't have a railpass; you'll simply pay more for it.

Eurostar: Any pass that covers Belgium allows you a discounted ticket price on the Eurostar to/from London. (For information on the Eurostar train, see page 502.)

Buses

While you'll mostly use trains to travel in this region, a few destinations (for example, the tulip gardens of Keukenhof and the flower auction in Aalsmeer) are reachable only by bus.

Confusingly, there's no unified national bus company for the Netherlands or Belgium—various destinations are served by different companies. Arriva (www.arriva.nl) and Connexxion (www.connexxion.nl) are the main companies serving the Netherlands, which offers an all-inclusive public transit website with schedules for most buses (www.9292ov.nl). In Belgium, Flanders is served largely by De Lijn (www.delijn.be), while French-speaking areas have TEC (www.infotec.be).

Cheap Flights

If you're visiting other countries in Europe, consider intra-European airlines. Whereas trains are usually the best way to connect places that are close together, a flight can save both time and money on longer journeys.

One of the best websites for comparing inexpensive flights is www.skyscanner.com. Other comparison search engines include www.wegolo.com and www.whichbudget.com. Well-known cheapo airlines in Europe include easyJet (www.easyjet.com) and Ryanair (www.ryanair.com), along with Amsterdam-based Transavia (www.transavia.com) and Brussels Airlines (www.brusselsairlines.com).

Buy tickets in advance. Although you can usually book right up until the flight departs, the cheap seats will often have sold out long before, leaving the most expensive seats for latecomers.

Be aware of the potential drawbacks of flying on the cheap: nonrefundable and nonchangeable tickets, minimal or nonexistent customer service, additional charges for everything, treks to airports far outside town, and pricey baggage fees. Read the small print—especially baggage policies—before you book.

Resources

Resources from Rick Steves

Rick Steves' Amsterdam, Bruges & Brussels is one of many books in my series on European travel, which includes country guidebooks, city and regional guidebooks, Snapshot guides (excerpted chapters from my country guides), Pocket guides (full-color little books on big cities), and my budget-travel skills handbook, *Rick Steves' Europe Through the Back Door*. My phrase books—for German, French, Italian, Spanish, and Portuguese—are practical and budget-oriented. My other books include *Europe 101* (a crash course on art and history, now expanded and in full color) and *Travel as a Political Act* (a travelogue sprinkled with tips for bringing home a global perspective). For a complete list of my books, see the inside of the last page of this book.

Video: My TV series, *Rick Steves' Europe,* covers European destinations in 100 shows, with two shows on the Low Countries. To watch episodes, visit www.hulu.com/rick-steves-europe; for scripts and other details, see www.ricksteves.com/tv.

Audio: My weekly public radio show, *Travel with Rick Steves,* features interviews with travel experts from around the world. This audio content is available for free at Rick Steves Audio Europe, an extensive online library organized by destination. Choose whatever interests you, and download it for free to your iPod, smartphone, or computer at www.ricksteves.com/audioeurope or iTunes. Rick Steves Audio Europe is also available as a free app for your iPhone, BlackBerry, or Android.

Maps

The black-and-white maps in this book, drawn by Dave Hoerlein, are concise and simple. Dave, who is well-traveled in the Low Countries, has designed the maps to help you quickly orient yourself and painlessly get to where you want to go. For more detail, consider buying a city map at any of the cities' TIs for a euro or two. Before you buy a map, look at it to make sure it has the level of detail you want. For most Belgian cities, look for Use It tourist maps, designed by locals and geared for backpackers, but loaded with insight and informative for anyone.

Begin Your Trip at www.ricksteves.com

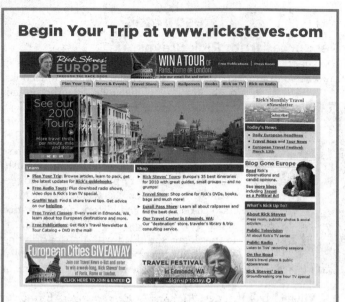

At our travel website, you'll find a wealth of free information on European destinations, including fresh monthly news and helpful tips from thousands of fellow travelers. You'll also find my latest guidebook updates (www.ricksteves.com/update) and my travel blog.

Our **online Travel Store** offers travel bags and accessories specially designed to help you travel smarter and lighter. These include my popular carry-on bags (roll-aboard and rucksack versions), money belts, totes, toiletries kits, adapters, other accessories, and a wide selection of guidebooks, journals, planning maps, and DVDs.

Choosing the right **railpass** for your trip—amidst hundreds of options—can drive you nutty. We'll help you choose the best pass for your needs, plus give you a bunch of free extras.

Rick Steves' Europe Through the Back Door travel company offers **tours** with more than three dozen itineraries and 400 departures reaching the best destinations in this book... and beyond. We offer an 11-day Heart of Belgium and Holland tour and a 21-day tour of Europe that includes Amsterdam and Haarlem. You'll enjoy great guides, a fun bunch of travel partners (with small groups of generally around 24-28), and plenty of room to spread out in a big, comfy bus. You'll find European adventures to fit every vacation length. For all the details, and to get our Tour Catalog and a free Rick Steves Tour Experience DVD (filmed on location during an actual tour), visit www.ricksteves.com or call our Tour Department at 425/608-4217.

APPENDIX

Other Guidebooks

Especially if you'll be traveling beyond my recommended destinations, $40 for extra maps and books is money well-spent.

The following books are worthwhile, though most are not updated annually; check the publication date before you buy. Historians like the green Michelin guides and the Cadogan series; both have individual books on all three cities—Amsterdam, Bruges, and Brussels. Others go for the well-illustrated Eyewitness guides (titles include *Amsterdam; Holland;* and *Brussels/Bruges/Ghent/Antwerp*). The Lonely Planet series (which has books on Amsterdam, the Netherlands, and Belgium & Luxembourg) is well researched and geared for a mature audience. Students and vagabonds enjoy *Let's Go: Amsterdam* (updated annually) for its coverage of hosteling, nightlife, and the student scene.

Recommended Books and Movies

To learn more about the Netherlands and Belgium past and present, check out some of these books and films.

Nonfiction

If you're interested in the WWII years in the Netherlands, read *The Diary of a Young Girl* (Anne Frank), *The Hiding Place* (Corrie ten Boom), and *A Bridge Too Far* (the story of the battle of Arnhem, by Cornelius Ryan).

Amsterdam (Mak) is an academic but engaging look at centuries of the city's history. Equally comprehensive is Simon Schama's *The Embarrassment of Riches: An Interpretation of Dutch Culture in the Golden Age.* Covering a similar timeframe, *Daily Life in Rembrandt's Holland* (Zumthor) focuses more on the everyday concerns of Dutch society in the 17th century.

Tulipmania (Dash) is about the Golden Age financial craze. Holland was at the center of the spice trade back when a pinch of cinnamon was worth its weight in gold. For engaging histories of these times, try *Spice: The History of a Temptation* (Turner) and *Nathaniel's Nutmeg: Or the True and Incredible Adventures of the Spice Trader Who Changed the Course of History* (Milton).

The Undutchables: An Observation of the Netherlands, Its Culture and Its Inhabitants (White and Boucke) is an irreverent guide to modern Dutch culture. *My 'Dam Life: Three Years in Holland* (Condon) is a humorous account of adventures in a low country.

Fans of Vincent may want to consider *Dear Theo: The Autobiography of Vincent van Gogh,* edited by Irving Stone. (Stone also wrote the fictional book about Van Gogh, *Lust for Life.*)

If you're visiting Belgium and have an interest in World War I, read Barbara Tuchman's Pulitzer Prize–winning book, *The Guns of*

August. For a look at contemporary Belgium, try *A Tall Man in a Low Land* (Pearson).

Fiction
Set in 17th-century Holland, Alexandre Dumas' *The Black Tulip* tells a swashbuckling story of fortunes held in the balance. *Max Havelaar: Or the Coffee Auctions of the Dutch Trading Company* is another literary classic, in which the author, Multatuli, writes of the injustices of the Dutch colonial system in Indonesia.

For more modern reads, best sellers set in Holland include *Girl in Hyacinth Blue* (Vreeland), *Girl with a Pearl Earring* (Chevalier), *Tulip Fever* (Moggach), and *Confessions of an Ugly Stepsister* (Maguire). For Belgium, consider *Resistance* (Shreve) and *The Adventures of Tintin* (featuring the famous Belgian comic-book character, by Hergé).

Films
Vincent and Theo (1990) captures the relationship between the great artist and his brother. *Girl with a Pearl Earring* (2003) shows a fictionalized Vermeer in love with his servant in Delft.

The Diary of Anne Frank (1959) is a good version of Anne's story, which has been translated into film and theater many times. Paul Verhoeven's *Soldier of Orange* (1977) delves into the bleak WWII years (it's also a fine book). In *Black Book* (2006)—another Verhoeven film, which was filmed in Holland—a sexy blonde bombshell fights for the Dutch Resistance.

Set partially in the modern era, *Antonia's Line* (1995) tells the story of five generations of Dutch women. *Ocean's Twelve* (2004) has many scenes set in Amsterdam's Jordaan neighborhood. The dark and violent comedy *In Bruges* (2008) was filmed just where you'd think.

Holidays and Festivals

This list includes many—but not all—big festivals in major cities, plus national holidays. Before planning a trip around a festival, make sure you verify its dates by checking the festival's website or the national TI websites: www.holland.com and www.visit belgium.com.

Here are some major holidays:

Jan 1	New Year's Day
Feb	Carnival (Mardi Gras)
March-May	Keukenhof flower show, Lisse, Netherlands (www.keukenhof.nl)
Easter Weekend	Good Friday through Easter Monday (April 22-24 in 2011, April 6-8 in 2012)

April	Flower Parade (April 16 in 2011, April 21 in 2012, www.bloemencorso-bollenstreek.nl), Noordwijk to Haarlem, Netherlands
April 30	Queen's Day (Koninginnedag), birthday of the late Queen Mother Juliana, party in the streets of Amsterdam
May 1	Labor Day (some closures in Belgium)
May 4	Remembrance of WWII Dead (Dodenherdenking), Netherlands
May 5	Liberation Day (Bevrijdingsdag), Netherlands
May	Art Amsterdam—contemporary-art exhibition (May 11-15 in 2011, www.kunstrai.nl), Amsterdam
May or June	Ascension (June 2 in 2011, May 17 in 2012); Procession of the Holy Blood (takes place on Ascension day), Bruges
May or June	Pentecost (June 12 in 2011, May 27 in 2012)
Mid-June	Grachtenloop (June 17 in 2011; run around canals, www.grachtenloop.nl), Haarlem
June	Holland Arts Festival (concerts, theater, etc., www.hollandfestival.nl), Amsterdam
June	Amsterdam Roots Festival—Oosterpark (ethnic food, music, world culture; www.amsterdamroots.nl)
June	The Hague Festivals—three weeks of music festivals: Festival Classique, Parkpop, and The Hague jazz (www.thehaguefestivals.com)
Late June/early July	Ommegang Pageant—historic costumed parade to Grand Place (www.ommegang.be), Brussels
Mid-July	North Sea Jazz Festival (July 8-10 in 2011, www.northseajazz.nl), The Hague
July 21	Belgian Independence Day (parades, fireworks)
Early Aug (first weekend)	Gay Pride (Aug 5-7 in 2011, Aug 3-5 in 2012), Amsterdam
Early-mid-Aug	Pluk de Nacht—outdoor film festival on the site of an old harbor (www.plukdenacht.nl), Amsterdam
Aug 15	Assumption Day, Procession in Bruges

Mid-Aug	Prinsengracht canal concert on barges—music and other festivities (August 12-21 in 2011, www.grachtenfestival.nl), Amsterdam
Aug	Carpet of Flowers (celebrated only in even years, Aug 15 in 2012, www.flowercarpet.be), Brussels
Aug	Open-air spectacle staged on the canals, held every three years, next in 2011 (Reiefeesten, www.reiefeest.be), Bruges
Late Aug	Haarlem Jazz—free jazz festival held on Grote Markt (third weekend of August, www.haarlemjazzstad.nl)
Sept (first week)	Flower parade on canals, Aalsmeer to Amsterdam
Mid-Sept	Jordaan Festival—neighborhood street party (www.jordaanfestival.nl), Amsterdam
Sept or Oct	Yom Kippur (Oct 8 in 2011, Sept 26 in 2012, Jewish holiday, some closures, including Anne Frank House and Jewish Historical Museum in Amsterdam)
Nov 1	All Saints' Day, Belgium
Nov 11	Armistice Day (banks closed), Belgium
Mid-Nov	Sinterklaas ("Santa Claus") procession, Amsterdam
Dec	"Winter Wonders" European Christmas Market (www.plaisirsdhiver.be), Brussels
Dec 5	St. Nicholas' Eve (Sinterklaasavond, when Sinterklaas and Zwarte Piet arrive), procession and presents
Dec 25	Christmas
Dec 26	"Second Day" of Christmas (Tweede Kerstdag), Netherlands

Conversions and Climate

Numbers and Stumblers

- Europeans write a few of their numbers differently than we do. 1 = 1, 4 = 4, 7 = 7.
- In Europe, dates appear as day/month/year, so Christmas is 25/12/12.
- Commas are decimal points and decimals commas. A dollar and a half is 1,50, and there are 5.280 feet in a mile.
- When counting with fingers, start with your thumb. If you hold up your first finger to request one item, you'll probably get two.
- What Americans call the second floor of a building is the first floor in Europe.
- On escalators and moving sidewalks, Europeans keep the left "lane" open for passing. Keep to the right.

Metric Conversions (approximate)

A kilogram is 2.2 pounds, and 1 liter is about a quart, or almost four to a gallon. A kilometer is six-tenths of a mile. I figure kilometers to miles by cutting them in half and adding back 10 percent of the original (120 km: 60 + 12 = 72 miles, 300 km: 150 + 30 = 180 miles).

1 foot = 0.3 meter	1 square yard = 0.8 square meter
1 yard = 0.9 meter	1 square mile = 2.6 square kilometers
1 mile = 1.6 kilometers	1 ounce = 28 grams
1 centimeter = 0.4 inch	1 quart = 0.95 liter
1 meter = 39.4 inches	1 kilogram = 2.2 pounds
1 kilometer = 0.62 mile	32°F = 0°C

Clothing Sizes

When shopping for clothing, use these US-to-European comparisons as general guidelines (but note that no conversion is perfect).

- Women's dresses and blouses: Add 30
  (US size 10 = European size 40)
- Men's suits and jackets: Add 10
  (US size 40 regular = European size 50)
- Men's shirts: Multiply by 2 and add about 8
  (US size 15 collar = European size 38)
- Women's shoes: Add about 30
  (US size 8 = European size 38-39)
- Men's shoes: Add 32-34
  (US size 9 = European size 41; US size 11 = European size 45)

Climate

The first line is the average daily temperature; the second line, the average daily low; the third line, average days without rain. For more detailed weather statistics for destinations throughout the Low Countries (as well as the rest of the world), check www .worldclimate.com.

	J	F	M	A	M	J	J	A	S	O	N	D
Amsterdam												
	41°	42°	49°	55°	64°	70°	72°	71°	66°	56°	48°	41°
	30°	31°	35°	40°	45°	52°	55°	55°	51°	43°	37°	33°
	8	9	16	14	16	16	14	12	11	11	10	9
Brussels												
	41°	44°	51°	58°	65°	71°	73°	72°	69°	60°	48°	42°
	30°	32°	34°	40°	45°	53°	55°	55°	52°	45°	38°	32°
	9	11	14	12	15	15	13	12	15	13	10	11

Temperature Conversion: Fahrenheit and Celsius

Europe takes its temperature using the Celsius scale, while we opt for Fahrenheit. For a rough conversion from Celsius to Fahrenheit, double the number and add 30. For weather, remember that 28°C is 82°F—perfect. For health, 37°C is just right.

APPENDIX

Essential Packing Checklist

Whether you're traveling for five days or five weeks, here's what you'll need to bring. Remember to pack light to enjoy the sweet freedom of true mobility. Happy travels!

- ❏ 5 shirts
- ❏ 1 sweater or lightweight fleece jacket
- ❏ 2 pairs pants
- ❏ 1 pair shorts
- ❏ 1 swimsuit (women only—men can use shorts)
- ❏ 5 pairs underwear and socks
- ❏ 1 pair shoes
- ❏ 1 rainproof jacket
- ❏ Tie or scarf
- ❏ Money belt
- ❏ Money—your mix of:
  - ❏ Debit card for ATM withdrawals
  - ❏ Credit card
  - ❏ Hard cash in US dollars (in easy-to-exchange $20 bills)
- ❏ Documents (and back-up photocopies):
  - ❏ Passport
  - ❏ Printout of airline e-ticket
  - ❏ Driver's license
  - ❏ Student ID and hostel card
  - ❏ Railpass/car rental voucher
  - ❏ Insurance details
- ❏ Daypack
- ❏ Sealable plastic baggies
- ❏ Camera and related gear
- ❏ Empty water bottle
- ❏ Wristwatch and alarm clock
- ❏ Earplugs
- ❏ First-aid kit
- ❏ Medicine (labeled)
- ❏ Extra glasses/contacts and prescriptions
- ❏ Sunscreen and sunglasses
- ❏ Toiletries kit
- ❏ Soap
- ❏ Laundry soap (if liquid and carry-on, limit to 3 oz.)
- ❏ Clothesline
- ❏ Small towel
- ❏ Sewing kit
- ❏ Travel information
- ❏ Necessary map(s)
- ❏ Address list (email and mailing addresses)
- ❏ Postcards and photos from home
- ❏ Notepad and pen
- ❏ Journal

If you plan to carry on your luggage, note that all liquids must be in three-ounce or smaller containers and fit within a single quart-size baggie. For details, see www.tsa.gov/travelers.

Hotel Reservation

To: _____   _____
            hotel   **email or fax**

From: _____   _____
              name   **email or fax**

Today's date: _____ / _____ / _____
                      day   **month**   **year**

Dear Hotel _____ ,
Please make this reservation for me:

Name: _____

Total # of people: _____   # of rooms: _____   # of nights: _____

Arriving: _____ / _____ / _____   My time of arrival (24-hr clock): _____
              day **month** **year**   (I will telephone if I will be late)

Departing: ____ / ____ / _____
                 day **month** **year**

Room(s): Single____   Double ____   Twin ____   Triple ____   Quad____

With: Toilet ____   Shower____   Bath ____   Sink only____

Special needs: View____   Quiet____   Cheapest____   Ground Floor____

Please email or fax confirmation of my reservation, along with the type of
room reserved and the price. Please also inform me of your cancellation
policy. After I hear from you, I will quickly send my credit-card information
as a deposit to hold the room. Thank you.

_____
Name

_____
Address

_____
City   *State*   *Zip Code*   *Country*

*Before hoteliers can make your reservation, they want to know the informa-
tion listed above. You can use this form as the basis for your email, or you can
photocopy this page, fill in the information, and send it as a fax (also available
online at www.ricksteves.com/reservation).*

Dutch Survival Phrases

You won't need to learn Dutch, but knowing a few phrases can help if you're traveling off the beaten path. Taking a few moments to learn the pleasantries (such as please and thank you) will improve your connections with locals even in the bigger cities.

To pronounce the difficult Dutch "g" (indicated in phonetics by hhh) make a hard, guttural, clear-your-throat sound, similar to the "ch" in the Scottish word "loch."

Hello.	Hallo.	hol-LOH
Good day.	Dag.	dahhh
Good morning.	Goeiemorgen.	hhhoy-ah MOR-hhhen
Good afternoon.	Goeiemiddag.	hhhoy-ah MIT-tahk
Ma'am	Mevrouw	meh-frow
Sir	Meneer	men-ear
Yes	Ja	yah
No	Nee	nay
Please	Alstublieft	AHL-stoo-bleeft
Thank you.	Dank u wel.	dahnk yoo vehl
You're welcome.	Graag gedaan.	hhhrahhk hhkeh-dahn
Excuse me.	Pardon.	par-DOHN
Do you speak English?	Spreekt u Engels?	spraykt oo ENG-els
Okay.	Oké.	"okay"
Goodbye.	Tot ziens.	toht zeens
one / two	een / twee	ayn / t'vay
three / four	drie / vier	dree / feer
five / six	vijf / zes	fife / ses
seven / eight	zeven / acht	say-fen / ahkht
nine / ten	negen / tien	nay-hhhen / teen
What does it cost?	Wat kost?	vaht kost
I would like...	Ik wil graag...	ik vil hhhrahhhk
...a room.	...een kamer.	un kah-mer
...a ticket.	...een kaart.	un kart
...a bike.	...een fiets.	un feets
Where is...?	Waar is...?	vahr is
...the station	...het station	het sta-tsee-on
...the tourist info office	...de VVV	duh vay vay vay
left / right	links / rechts	links / rechts
open / closed	open / gesloten	"open" / hhhe-sloh-ten

In the Restaurant

The Dutch have an all-purpose word, alstublieft (AHL-stoo-bleeft), that means: "Please," or "Here you are," (if handing you something), or "Thanks," (if taking payment from you), or "You're welcome" (when handing you change). Here are other words that might come in handy at restaurants, particularly if you're day-tripping to small towns:

I would like...	Ik wil graag…	ik vil hhhrahhk
…a cup of coffee.	…kopje koffee.	kop-yeh "coffee"
non-smoking	niet-roken	neet roh-ken
smoking	roken	roh-ken
with / without	met / buiten	met / bow-ten
and / or	en / of	en / of
bread	brood	broht
salad	sla	slah
cheese	kaas	kahs
meat	vlees	flays
chicken	kip	kip
fish	vis	fis
egg	ei	eye
fruit	vrucht	frucht
pastries	gebak	hhhe-bak
I am vegetarian.	Ik ben vegetarish.	ik ben vay-hhhe-tah-rish
Tasty.	Lekker.	lek-ker
Enjoy!	Smakelijk!	smak-kuh-luk
Cheers!	Proost!	prohst

Flemish Survival Phrases

Northern Belgium speaks Flemish—closely related to Dutch. You won't need to learn Flemish, but knowing a few phrases can help. Taking a few moments to learn the pleasantries (such as please and thank you) will improve your connections with locals.

To pronounce the difficult Flemish "g" (indicated in phonetics by hhh), make a hard, guttural, clear-your-throat sound, similar to the "ch" in the Scottish word "loch."

Hello.	**Hallo.**	hol-LOH
Good day.	**Dag.**	dahhh
Good morning.	**Goeiemorgen.**	hhhoy-ah-MOR-hhhen
Good afternoon.	**Goeiemiddag.**	hhhoy-ah-MIT-tahk
Ma'am	**Mevrouw**	meh-frow
Sir	**Meneer**	men-ear
Yes	**Ja**	yah
No	**Nee**	nay
Please	**Alstublieft**	AHL-stoo-bleeft
Thank you.	**Dank u wel.**	dahnk yoo vehl
You're welcome.	**Graag gedaan.**	hhhrahhk hhkeh-dahn
Excuse me.	**Pardon.**	par-DOHN
Do you speak English?	**Spreekt u Engels?**	spraykt oo ENG-els
Okay.	**Oké.**	"okay"
Goodbye.	**Tot ziens.**	toht zeens
one / two	**een / twee**	ayn / t'vay
three / four	**drie / vier**	dree / feer
five / six	**vijf / zes**	fife / ses
seven / eight	**zeven / acht**	say-fen / ahkht
nine / ten	**negen / tien**	nay-hhhen / teen
What does it cost?	**Wat kost?**	vaht kost
I would like...	**Ik wil graag...**	ik vil hhhrahhhk
...a room.	**...een kamer.**	un kah-mer
...a ticket.	**...een kaart.**	un kart
...a bike.	**...een fiets.**	un feets
Where is...?	**Waar is...?**	vahr is
...the station	**...het station**	het sta-tsee-on
...the tourist info office	**...de VVV**	duh vay vay vay
left / right	**links / rechts**	links / rechts
open / closed	**open / gesloten**	"open" / hhhe-sloh-ten

In the Restaurant

The Belgians have an all-purpose word, *alstublieft* (AHL-stoo-bleeft), that means: "Please" or "Here you are" (if handing you something), or "Thanks" (if taking payment from you), or "You're welcome" (when handing you change). Here are other words that might come in handy at restaurants:

I would like...	**Ik wil graag...**	ik vil hhhrahhk
...a cup of coffee.	**...kopje koffee.**	kop-yeh "coffee"
non-smoking	**niet-roken**	neet roh-ken
smoking	**roken**	roh-ken
with / without	**met / buiten**	met / bow-ten
and / or	**en / of**	en / of
bread	**brood**	broht
salad	**sla**	slah
cheese	**kaas**	kahs
meat	**vlees**	flays
chicken	**kip**	kip
fish	**vis**	fis
egg	**ei**	eye
fruit	**vrucht**	frucht
pastries	**gebak**	hhhe-bak
I am vegetarian.	**Ik ben vegetarish.**	ik ben vay-hhhe-tah-rish
Tasty.	**•Lekker.**	lek-ker
Enjoy!	**Smakelijk!**	smak-kuh-luk
Cheers!	**Proost!**	prohst

French Survival Phrases

When using the phonetics, try to nasalize the <u>n</u> sound.

Good day.	**Bonjour.**	boh<u>n</u>-zhoor
Mrs. / Mr.	**Madame / Monsieur**	mah-dahm / muhs-yur
Do you speak English?	**Parlez-vous anglais?**	par-lay-voo ah<u>n</u>-glay
Yes. / No.	**Oui. / Non.**	wee / noh<u>n</u>
I understand.	**Je comprends.**	zhuh koh<u>n</u>-prah<u>n</u>
I don't understand.	**Je ne comprends pas.**	zhuh nuh koh<u>n</u>-prah<u>n</u> pah
Please.	**S'il vous plaît.**	see voo play
Thank you.	**Merci.**	mehr-see
I'm sorry.	**Désolé.**	day-zoh-lay
Excuse me.	**Pardon.**	par-doh<u>n</u>
(No) problem.	**(Pas de) problème.**	(pah duh) proh-blehm
It's good.	**C'est bon.**	say boh<u>n</u>
Goodbye.	**Au revoir.**	oh vwahr
one / two	**un / deux**	uh<u>n</u> / duh
three / four	**trois / quatre**	twah / kah-truh
five / six	**cinq / six**	sa<u>n</u>k / sees
seven / eight	**sept / huit**	seht / weet
nine / ten	**neuf / dix**	nuhf / dees
How much is it?	**Combien?**	koh<u>n</u>-bee-a<u>n</u>
Write it?	**Ecrivez?**	ay-kree-vay
Is it free?	**C'est gratuit?**	say grah-twee
Included?	**Inclus?**	a<u>n</u>-klew
Where can I buy / find...?	**Où puis-je acheter / trouver...?**	oo pwee-zhuh ah-shuh-tay / troo-vay
I'd like / We'd like...	**Je voudrais / Nous voudrions...**	zhuh voo-dray / noo voo-dree-oh<u>n</u>
...a room.	**...une chambre.**	ewn shah<u>n</u>-bruh
...a ticket to ___.	**...un billet pour ___.**	uh<u>n</u> bee-yay poor
Is it possible?	**C'est possible?**	say poh-see-bluh
Where is...?	**Où est...?**	oo ay
...the train station	**...la gare**	lah gar
...the bus station	**...la gare routière**	lah gar root-yehr
...tourist information	**...l'office du tourisme**	loh-fees dew too-reez-muh
Where are the toilets?	**Où sont les toilettes?**	oo soh<u>n</u> lay twah-leht
men	**hommes**	ohm
women	**dames**	dahm
left / right	**à gauche / à droite**	ah gohsh / ah dwaht
straight	**tout droit**	too dwah
When does this open / close?	**Ça ouvre / ferme à quelle heure?**	sah oo-vruh / fehrm ah kehl ur
At what time?	**À quelle heure?**	ah kehl ur
Just a moment.	**Un moment.**	uh<u>n</u> moh-mah<u>n</u>
now / soon / later	**maintenant / bientôt / plus tard**	ma<u>n</u>-tuh-nah<u>n</u> / bee-a<u>n</u>-toh / plew tar
today / tomorrow	**aujourd'hui / demain**	oh-zhoor-dwee / duh-ma<u>n</u>

In the Restaurant

I'd like / We'd like...	Je voudrais / Nous voudrions...	zhuh voo-dray / noo voo-dree-ohn
...to reserve...	...réserver...	ray-zehr-vay
...a table for one / two.	...une table pour un / deux.	ewn tah-bluh poor uhn / duh
Non-smoking.	Non fumeur.	nohn few-mur
Is this seat free?	C'est libre?	say lee-bruh
The menu (in English), please.	La carte (en anglais), s'il vous plaît.	lah kart (ahn ahn-glay) see voo play
service (not) included	service (non) compris	sehr-vees (nohn) kohn-pree
to go	à emporter	ah ahn-por-tay
with / without	avec / sans	ah-vehk / sahn
and / or	et / ou	ay / oo
special of the day	plat du jour	plah dew zhoor
specialty of the house	spécialité de la maison	spay-see-ah-lee-tay duh lah may-zohn
appetizers	hors-d'oeuvre	or-duh-vruh
first course (soup, salad)	entrée	ahn-tray
main course (meat, fish)	plat principal	plah pran-see-pahl
bread	pain	pan
cheese	fromage	froh-mahzh
sandwich	sandwich	sahnd-weech
soup	soupe	soop
salad	salade	sah-lahd
meat	viande	vee-ahnd
chicken	poulet	poo-lay
fish	poisson	pwah-sohn
seafood	fruits de mer	frwee duh mehr
fruit	fruit	frwee
vegetables	légumes	lay-gewm
dessert	dessert	duh-sehr
mineral water	eau minérale	oh mee-nay-rahl
tap water	l'eau du robinet	loh dew roh-bee-nay
milk	lait	lay
(orange) juice	jus (d'orange)	zhew (doh-rahnzh)
coffee	café	kah-fay
tea	thé	tay
wine	vin	van
red / white	rouge / blanc	roozh / blahn
glass / bottle	verre / bouteille	vehr / boo-teh-ee
beer	bière	bee-ehr
Cheers!	Santé!	sahn-tay
More. / Another.	Plus. / Un autre.	plew / uhn oh-truh
The same.	La même chose.	lah mehm shohz
The bill, please.	L'addition, s'il vous plaît.	lah-dee-see-ohn see voo play
tip	pourboire	poor-bwar
Delicious!	Délicieux!	day-lee-see-uh

For more user-friendly French phrases, check out *Rick Steves' French Phrase Book and Dictionary* or *Rick Steves' French, Italian & German Phrase Book*.

APPENDIX

INDEX

INDEX

INDEX

MAP INDEX

Audio Europe

RICK STEVES AUDIO EUROPE

Rick's free app and podcasts

The FREE **Rick Steves Audio Europe**™ app for iPhone, iPad and iPod Touch gives you 29 self-guided audio tours of Europe's top museums, sights and historic walks—plus more than 200 tracks filled with cultural insights and sightseeing tips from Rick's radio interviews—all organized into geographic-specific playlists.

Let **Rick Steves Audio Europe**™ amplify your guidebook.

With Rick whispering in your ear, Europe gets even better.

Thanks Facebook fans for submitting photos while on location! From top: John Kuijper in Florence, Brenda Mamer with her mother in Rome, Angel Capobianco in London, and Alyssa Passey with her friend in Paris.

Find out more at ricksteves.com

▶ Plan Your Trip

Browse thousands of articles and a wealth of money-saving tips for planning your dream trip. You'll find up-to-date information on Europe's best destinations, packing smart, getting around, finding rooms, staying healthy, avoiding scams and more.

▶ Eurail Passes

Find out, step-by-step, if a railpass makes sense for your trip—and how to avoid buying more than you need. Get free shipping on online orders

▶ Graffiti Wall & Travelers Helpline

Learn, ask, share—our online community of savvy travelers is a great resource for first-time travelers to Europe, as well as seasoned pros.

Rick Steves' Europe Through the Back Door, Inc.

Rick Steves

EUROPE GUIDES

Best of Europe
Eastern Europe
Europe Through the Back Door
Mediterranean Cruise Ports

COUNTRY GUIDES

Croatia & Slovenia
England
France
Germany
Great Britain
Ireland
Italy
Portugal
Scandinavia
Spain
Switzerland

CITY & REGIONAL GUIDES

Amsterdam, Bruges & Brussels
Budapest
Florence & Tuscany
Greece: Athens & the Peloponnese
Istanbul
London
Paris
Prague & the Czech Republic
Provence & the French Riviera
Rome
Venice
Vienna, Salzburg & Tirol

SNAPSHOT GUIDES

Barcelona
Berlin
Bruges & Brussels
Copenhagen & the Best of
   Denmark
Dublin
Dubrovnik
Hill Towns of Central Italy
Italy's Cinque Terre
Krakow, Warsaw & Gdansk
Lisbon
Madrid & Toledo
Munich, Bavaria & Salzburg
Naples & the Amalfi Coast
Northern Ireland
Norway
Scotland
Sevilla, Granada & Southern Spain
Stockholm

POCKET GUIDES

London
Paris
Rome

TRAVEL CULTURE

Europe 101
European Christmas
Postcards from Europe
Travel as a Political Act

Rick Steves guidebooks are published by Avalon Travel,
a member of the Perseus Books Group.

NOW AVAILABLE:
eBOOKS, APPS & BLU-RAY

eBOOKS

Most guides are available as eBooks from Amazon, Barnes & Noble, Borders, Apple, and Sony. Free apps for eBook reading are available in the Apple App Store and Android Market, and eBook readers such as Kindle, Nook, and Kobo all have free apps that work on smartphones.

RICK STEVES' EUROPE DVDs

10 New Shows 2011–2012
Austria & the Alps
Eastern Europe
England & Wales
European Christmas
European Travel Skills & Specials
France
Germany, BeNeLux & More
Greece & Turkey
Iran
Ireland & Scotland
Italy's Cities
Italy's Countryside
Scandinavia
Spain
Travel Extras

BLU-RAY

Celtic Charms
Eastern Europe Favorites
European Christmas
Italy Through the Back Door
Mediterranean Mosaic
Surprising Cities of Europe

PHRASE BOOKS & DICTIONARIES

French
French, Italian & German
German
Italian
Portuguese
Spanish

JOURNALS

Rick Steves' Pocket Travel Journal
Rick Steves' Travel Journal

APPS

Select Rick Steves guides are available as apps in the Apple App Store.

PLANNING MAPS

Britain, Ireland & London
Europe
France & Paris
Germany, Austria & Switzerland
Ireland
Italy
Spain & Portugal

Credits

For help with this edition, Rick and Gene relied on...

Cameron Hewitt, Writer and Researcher

Cameron writes and edits guidebooks for Rick Steves. For this book, Cameron delved into Belgium—rattling his *fiets* over cobbles, ogling great artwork from Van Eyck to Van Dyck to Tintin, and writing new chapters on Antwerp, Ghent, and Flanders Fields. When he's not sampling fresh Flemish pralines, he lives in Seattle with his wife Shawna.

Gretchen Strauch, Researcher

Before Gretchen became a guidebook editor for Rick Steves, she lived in Europe for four years: studying in Scotland, teaching in Germany, and traveling constantly. She gladly attempts Dutch pronunciation in return for tulips, pancakes, and canals, and she'd do just about anything for a fresh Liège waffle.

Images

Location	Photographer
Netherlands full-page: Edam	Jennifer Hauseman
Amsterdam full-page: Amsterdam Canal	
Haarlem full-page: Haarlem Hofje	Cameron Hewitt
Belgium full-page: Belgium Canal	Rick Steves
Bruges full-page: Belgium Canal	Dominic Bonuccelli
Brussels full-page: Brussels	Dominic Bonuccelli
	Rick Steves

Rick Steves' Guidebook Series

Country Guides

Rick Steves' Best of Europe
Rick Steves' Croatia &
  Slovenia
Rick Steves' Eastern Europe
Rick Steves' England
Rick Steves' France
Rick Steves' Germany

Rick Steves' Great Britain
Rick Steves' Ireland
Rick Steves' Italy
Rick Steves' Portugal
Rick Steves' Scandinavia
Rick Steves' Spain
Rick Steves' Switzerland

City and Regional Guides

Rick Steves' Amsterdam,
  Bruges & Brussels
Rick Steves' Budapest
Rick Steves' Florence &
  Tuscany
Rick Steves' Greece:
  Athens & the Peloponnese
Rick Steves' Istanbul
Rick Steves' London

Rick Steves' Paris
Rick Steves' Prague &
  the Czech Republic
Rick Steves' Provence &
  the French Riviera
Rick Steves' Rome
Rick Steves' Venice
Rick Steves' Vienna,
  Salzburg & Tirol

Rick Steves' Phrase Books

French
French/Italian/German
German
Italian
Portuguese
Spanish

Snapshot Guides

Excerpted chapters from country guides, such as *Rick Steves'
Snapshot Barcelona, Rick Steves' Snapshot Scotland,* and
Rick Steves' Snapshot Hill Towns of Central Italy.

Pocket Guides (new in 2011)

Condensed, pocket-size, full-color guides to Europe's top
cities: Rome, Paris, and London.

Other Books

Rick Steves' Europe 101: History and Art for the Traveler
Rick Steves' Europe Through the Back Door
Rick Steves' European Christmas
Rick Steves' Postcards from Europe
Rick Steves' Travel as a Political Act

Avalon Travel
a member of the Perseus Books Group
1700 Fourth Street
Berkeley, CA 94710, USA

Printed in Canada by Friesens
Second printing June 2012

ISBN 978-1-59880-768-4
ISSN 1543-012X

For the latest on Rick's lectures, books, tours, public radio show, and public television series, contact Europe Through the Back Door, Box 2009, Edmonds, WA 98020, tel. 425/771-8303, fax 425/771-0833, www.ricksteves.com, rick@ricksteves.com.

Europe Through the Back Door Reviewing Editors: Jennifer Madison Davis, Cathy McDonald
ETBD Editors: Tom Griffin, Gretchen Strauch, Cathy Lu
ETBD Managing Editor: Risa Laib
Avalon Travel Senior Editor & Series Manager: Madhu Prasher
Avalon Travel Project Editor: Kelly Lydick
Research Assistance: Cameron Hewitt, Gretchen Strauch, Elizabeth Wang
Copy Editor: Jennifer Malnick
Proofreader: Janet Walden
Indexer: Stephen Callahan
Production & Typesetting: McGuire Barber Design
Cover Design: Kimberly Glyder Design
Graphic Content Director: Laura VanDeventer
Maps and Graphics: David C. Hoerlein, Laura VanDeventer, Lauren Mills, Pat O'Connor, Barb Geisler, Mike Morgenfeld
Photography: Rick Steves, Dominic Bonuccelli, Gene Openshaw, Cameron Hewitt, Jennifer Hauseman, Gretchen Strauch, Laura VanDeventer, Bruce VanDeventer
Front matter color photos: p. i, Amsterdam at night, © Rick Steves; p. viii, Amsterdam © Rick Steves
Cover Photo: Amsterdam canal © Rick Steves